Operation Barbarossa: the Complete Organisational and Statistical Analysis, and Military Simulation

Volume IIB

Nigel Askey

Published in the United States by
Nigel Askey, 2018

Hardback and colour edition

Cover images of German AFVs © 2014 Laurent Lecocq - at www.profils.tk.
Cover images of aircraft © 2014 William Dady - at www.clavework-graphics.co.uk.

Further information on the author and the forthcoming volumes in this series can be found at
operationbarbarossa.net

DEDICATION

This book is affectionately dedicated to my son, Edward.

Operation Barbarossa: the Complete Organisational and Statistical Analysis, and Military Simulation
Volume IIB
The German Armed Forces (Wehrmacht), Mobilisation and War Economy from June to December 1941
Table of Contents

List of Abbreviations ix

Introduction 1

1. **The Order of Battle (OOB) of German Land Combat Units from 22nd June to 4th July 1941** 5

   1) The German Deployment Matrix 5

2. **German Land Combat Unit Reinforcements on the East Front from 5th July to 31st December 1941** 65

3. **The Total Personnel and Equipment in a Deployed (D) State in the Reich from 22nd June to 4th July 1941** 73

   1) The Total Personnel and Equipment Allocated to Combat Units and in a Deployed (D) state in the German Army, Waffen SS, Luftwaffe Ground Forces and Naval Coastal Artillery from 22nd June to 4th July 1941 73

      a. The German Army, Waffen SS, Luftwaffe Ground Forces and Naval Coastal Artillery Deployed (D) in Support of Operation Barbarossa from 22nd June to 4th July 1941 78

         i. Army Group North 78
         ii. Army Group Centre 78
         iii. Army Group South 79
         iv. Norway Army, *Befehlsstelle Finnland* (East Front Only) 79
         v. OKH Reserves 80
         vi. Total, East Front 80

      b. The German Army, Waffen SS, Luftwaffe Ground Forces and Naval Coastal Artillery, Deployed (D) in the Western Fronts and the Replacement Army from 22nd June to 4th July 1941 86

         i. Norway Army (Norway Occupation Duties) 86
         ii. Army Group D (France-Low Countries) 86
         iii. 12th Army (Yugoslavia-Serbia-Greece-Crete) 86
         iv. Deutsches Afrikakorps (D.A.K) (North Africa) 87
         v. Germany and the Remainder of Occupied Europe, and the Replacement Army 87

      c. The Total German Army, Waffen SS, Luftwaffe Ground Forces and Naval Coastal Artillery Deployed (D) in the Reich from 22nd June to 4th July 1941 89

      d. Rear Area Transport Available for Supply Distribution from 22nd June to 4th July 1941 92

   2) The Total Available Personnel and Equipment in the Reich on 1st June 1941 95

      a. Review of Available Small Arms and Other Infantry Weapons 100
      b. Review of Available Anti-Tank Weapons 101
      c. Review of Available Artillery Pieces 102
      d. Review of Available Anti-Aircraft Weapons 105
      e. Review of Available Tanks and other AFVs 108
      f. Review of Available Motor Vehicles and Other Transport Types 110
      g. Review of Available Wehrmacht and Waffen SS Personnel 116

   3) The Proportion of Total Available Resources which were in a Deployed (D) State in the Reich from 22nd June to 4th July 1941 122

4. German Mobilisation after 22nd June 1941: the Actual Strength of German Land Combat Units Mobilised from 22nd June to 31st December 1941.............129

1) Definition of Deployed (D), Mobilised and Deployed (MD), and Mobilised and Not Deployed (MND) in the German FILARM Model...............129

2) German Land Combat Units Mobilised from 22nd June to 31st December 1941...............130
   a. The German Tank MD and MND Matrix 135

3) The Total Resources Allocated to Newly Mobilised Combat Units from 22nd June to 31st December 1941...............138
   a. Rear Area Transport Available for Supply Distribution from 22nd June to 31st December 1941...............139

4) The Total Resources in the Reich that were Available for Use by Newly Mobilised Units from 22nd June to 31st December 1941 144
   a. Total Available Resources in the Reich Unallocated to Deployed (D) Units from 22nd June to 4th July 1941 144
   b. New Resources Produced and Received in the Reich from June to 31st December 1941 144
      i. Small Arms and Other Infantry Weapons...............144
      ii. Anti-Tank Weapons...............145
      iii. Artillery Pieces...............146
      iv. Anti-Aircraft Weapons 147
      v. Tanks and other AFVs...............148
      vi. Motor Vehicles and Other Transport Types...............150
      vii. Newly Conscripted Wehrmacht and Waffen SS Personnel 152

5) Resources Unallocated to any Deployed (D), MD or MND Units in 1941 153

6) The Proportion of Total Available Resources Allocated to Deployed (D) and Newly Mobilised Units in 1941...............155
   a. A Comparison of the Percentages of German and Soviet Resources which were allocated to D, MD and MND Combat Units During 1941 155

7) The Resource Replacements (R) Available to the German Army, Waffen SS, Luftwaffe Ground Forces and Naval Coastal Artillery, from 22nd June to 31st December 1941 159
   a. The German Replacement Army (*Ersatzheer*) and the Military-Districts (*Wehrkreise*) System 159
      i. German Armed-Forces Auxiliary (*Wehrmachtsgefolge*) Organizations 166
   b. Replacements (R) available to the Wehrmacht from June to December 1941 171
   c. Replacements (R) Actually Issued to the German Ground Forces on the East Front During 1941 176
      i. German Personnel Losses (Casualties) and Replacements 176
      ii. German Tank and Assault Gun Losses and Replacements 182
   d. Small Arms Used by all Ground Combat Units in the Reich in 1941, including Replacements (R)...............190
   e. Personnel Used by all Types of Replacements (R) 191

5. The Luftwaffe in 1941...............193

1) The Structure of the Luftwaffe: June to December 1941 193
   a. The *Geschwader* and *Gruppe*...............193
   b. The *Staffel*...............196
   c. Luftwaffe Higher-Level Command Structure 199

2) The Order of Battle and Actual Strength of all Luftwaffe Air Combat Units in a Deployed (D) State on 21st June 1941 202
   a. Luftwaffe Higher Level Organisation and Deployment on 21st June 1941 202
   b. Luftflotte 1 206
   c. Luftflotte 2 211
   d. Luftflotte 4 216
   e. Luftflotte 5 224
   f. Luftflotte 3 232

    g.   X. Fliegerkorps 243

    h.   Luftwaffenbefehlshaber Mitte 249

    i.   Luftflotte ObdL...253

    j.   Luftwaffe Seeluftstreitkrafte and Küstenfliegergruppen 255

3)   Luftwaffe Strengths on 21st June 1941 257

    a.   Luftwaffe Strength Available to Support Operation Barbarossa on 21st June 1941 257

    b.   A Comparison of Luftwaffe Forces Supporting Operation Barbarossa and VVS Strengths in the Western Special Military Districts on 22nd June 1941 259

    c.   An Assessment of the Actual Luftwaffe Forces Available to Support German Ground Operations during Operation Barbarossa..262

    d.   Overall Luftwaffe Strength on 21st June 1941 265

4)   Luftwaffe Air Combat Unit Reinforcements: June to December 1941 267

    a.   The Transfer of Deployed (D) and Newly Mobilised Air Combat Units to the Eastern Front: June to December 1941..267

    b.   The Transfer of Deployed (D) Air Combat Units from the Eastern Front to the West: June to December 1941..271

    c.   Newly Mobilised Luftwaffe Air Combat Units: June to December 1941 275

5)   Overall Luftwaffe Combat Aircraft Usage, Production and Replacements (R): 22nd June to 31st December 1941... 277

    a.   German Aircraft Production and Replacements (R) in 1941 280

    b.   Review of the Luftwaffe Aircraft Losses and Casualties in 1941.....................283

6.   The Supply Distribution Efficiency (SDE) for the Wehrmacht on the East Front from 22nd June to 31st December 1941...............................**291**

1)   The SDE for all Deployed (D) Land Combat Units on the East Front from 22nd June to 4th July 1941 298

2)   The SDE for all Reinforcement (R) Land Combat Units on the East Front from 5th July to 31st December 1941 298

3)   The SDE for all Deployed (D) and Reinforcement (R) Land Combat Units on the East Front from 22nd June to 31st December 1941 299

4)   Inclusion of the Luftwaffe's Air Combat Units in the SDE Calculation............ 300

5)   Parameters Relating Specifically to the Calculation of the Wehrmacht SDE in 1941 302

    a.   Specific Weapon System or Squad Supply Demand Factors (SDFs) 302

    b.   Proportion of Available Rear Area Trucks, Tractors (Prime Movers) and Light Transports Allocated to Rear Area SDE functions 302

        i.   Proportion Available on 22nd June 1941 302

        ii.   Proportion Available from 22nd June to 31st December 1941...................... 303

    c.   Average Lift Capacity of the Wehrmacht's Motorised Vehicles and Horse Teams: Measured in Metric Ton Kilometres per Day 304

        i.   Average Transport Load Capacity (L) 304

        ii.   Average Distance Moved Per Day (D) 308

        iii.   Comparison of the Average Soviet and German Lift Capacity (L*D) 312

6)   Conclusions Relating to the Wehrmacht 's SDE during 1941 313

7.   German Naval Forces on the East Front; June to December 1941......................**317**

1)   Kriegsmarine High Level Operational Commands: June 1941............................ 318

2)   Orders and Objectives of the German Naval forces in the Baltic in 1941 319

3)   The Actual Strength of German Naval Units in the Baltic during 1941 321

4)   A History of German Naval Operations in the Baltic: June to December 1941................. 327

8.   Wehrmacht and Waffen SS Casualties from June 1941 to February 1942.........**333**

Appendix A..**355**

    Overall Status of Selected Weapons within the Army on 1st April 1941 355

Manufacture of Small Arms and Selected Artillery Types for the Wehrmacht during 1941 356

Approximate Overall Status for Selected Weapons within the Wehrmacht:
1st October 1939 to 1st January 1942 357

German Tank and Assault Gun Losses, Production, Rebuilt and Inventory:
June to December 1941 359

Production of Military Standard Motor Vehicles for the Army and Luftwaffe,
August 1939 to December 1941 361

Appendix B **363**

Table of Contents, Volume I Part I: The Concepts and General Structure of the
Integrated Land and Air Resource Model 363

Table of Contents, Volume I Part II: The Methodology Used for Analysing Weapon System
Effectiveness, and the Structure of the 1941 Soviet and Axis Resource Database 364

Appendix C **367**

Table of Contents, Volume IIA: The German Armed Forces (Wehrmacht), Mobilisation
and War Economy from June to December 1941 367

Appendix D **375**

Table of Contents, Volume IIIA: The Soviet Armed Forces, Mobilisation and
War Economy from June to December 1941 375

Appendix E **381**

Table of Contents, Volume IIIB: The Soviet Armed Forces, Mobilisation and
War Economy from June to December 1941 381

Selected Bibliography **387**

List of Abbreviations

A	Accuracy	DUR	Aircraft Durability Factor
A Cars	Armoured Cars	EnB	Engineering Battalion
AA	Anti-Aircraft and	EnC	Engineering Company
	Relative Anti-Aircraft Value	Eng	Engineering
AAB	Anti-Aircraft Battalion	EnP	Engineering Platoon
AAC	Anti-Aircraft Company	EnR	Engineering Regiment
AAG	Anti-Aircraft Gun	FCE	Fire Control Effect
AAMG	Anti-Aircraft Machine Gun	FDE	Relative Fortification Destruction Effect
AAP	Anti-Aircraft Platoon	FILARM	Fully Integrated Land and Air Resource Model
AAS	Relative Assault Attack Strength	GPMG	General Purpose Machine Gum
AcCo	Armoured Car Company	Gun/Can	Gun/Cannon
ADS	Relative Assault Defence Strength	HAR	Heavy Artillery Regiment
AE	Aircraft Mounted Weapon Effect	HCavS	Heavy Cavalry Squadron
AFV	Armoured Fighting Vehicle	HIC	Heavy Infantry Company
AP	Armour Piercing	HMG	Heavy Machine Gun
APC	Armour Piercing Capped	How	Howitzer
APC	Armoured Personnel Carrier	HQ	Headquarter
APCBC	Armour Piercing Capped Ballistic Capped	HR Sqd	Heavy Rifle (or Infantry) Squad
APer	Relative Anti-Personnel Value	HRC	Heavy Rifle Company
ArB	Artillery Battalion		(w HMGs &/or mortars)
ARM	Relative Armour Defence Strength	I Bat	Infantry Battalion
ArP	Artillery Platoon (or Battery)	I Div	Infantry Division
ArR	Artillery Regiment	I Reg	Infantry Regiment
ASE	Ammunition Supply Effect	ICo	Infantry Company
ASig Pl	Armoured Signal Platoon	ILARM	Integrated Land and Air Resource Model
AT	Anti-Tank and Relative Anti-Armour Value	InG Co	Infantry Gun Company
ATB	Anti-Tank Battalion	InG P	Infantry Gun Platoon (or Battery)
ATC	Anti-Tank Company	IPl	Infantry Platoon
ATG	Anti Tank Gun	LAR	Light Artillery Regiment
ATP	Anti-Tank Platoon (or Battery)	LMG	Light Machine Gun
ATT	Relative Overall Attack Factor	LR Sqd	Light Rifle Squad
B Sup	Battalion Support	LS	*Landesschutzen*, (Local Defence Unit)
BicBat	Bicycle Battalion	LS Reg	*Landesschutzen* Regiment
Br	Bridging	MAR	Medium Artillery Regiment
BrB	Bridging Battalion (pontoon)	MBE	Multi Barrelled Weapon Effect
BrC	Bridging Company (pontoon) or	MD	Mobilised and Deployed
	Bridging Column (pontoon)	MDS	Minimum Divisional Size
BrCB	Bridge Construction Battalion	MFM	Motorised Mobile Fighting Machine
Bri Sup	Brigade Support	MG Bat	Machine Gun Battalion
BrP	Bridging Platoon (pontoon)	MG/Art Bat	Machine Gun and Artillery Battalion
Cav	Cavalry	MgCo	Machine Gun Company
Cav B	Cavalry Battalion	MgPl	Machine Gun Platoon
Cav Brig	Cavalry Brigade	MGS	Machine Gun Squadron
Cav Reg	Cavalry Regiment	MGT	Machine Gun Troop
CavP	Cavalry Platoon	MMG	Medium Machine Gun
CavS	Cavalry Squadron	MND	Mobilised and Not Deployed
CavSC	Cavalry Support Company	MoB	Mortar Battalion
CavT	Cavalry Troop	MOB	Relative Overall Mobility
CL	Aircraft Ceiling Effect Factor	MoC	Mortar Company
Cons Bat	Construction Battalion	MoCyBat	Motor Cycle Battalion
CPF	Concealment and Protection Factor	MoCyCo	Motor Cycle Company
D	Deployed	MoCyPl	Motor Cycle Platoon
D Sup	Divisional Support	MOF	Battlefield Mobility Factor (for land units
DDF	Defensive Dispersion Factor		and aircraft)
DEF	Relative Overall Defence Factor	MoP	Mortar Platoon (or Battery)

Mor	Mortar
MP	Military Police
MPBat	Military Police Battalion
NerW Bat	*Nerbelwerfer* Battalion
OCPC	Overall Combat Power Coefficient
OOB	Order of Battle
OPQ	Main-gun Optics Quality
OTF	Open Top Factor
PiC	Pionier Company
PILARM	Partially Integrated Land and Air Resource Model
PR	Protection Factor
PTS	Number of Potential Targets per Strike
Pz	Panzer
QJM	Quantified Judgement Model
R	Effective Combat Ranges or (Aircraft) Combat Radius, and Replacements
R Bat	Rifle Battalion
R Div	Rifle Division
R Reg	Rifle Regiment
R Sqd	Rifle (or Infantry) Squad
R Sup	Regimental Support
RA	Range of Action for land units, or Radius of Action for aircraft
RArB	Rocket Artillery Battalion
RArP	Rocket Artillery Platoon (or Battery)
RCo	Rifle Company
ReB	Reconnaissance Battalion
ReC	Reconnaissance Company
ReP	Reconnaissance Platoon
RF	Rate of Fire
RFE	Rapidity of Fire Effect
RIE	Relative Incapacitating Effect
RL	Reliability Factor
RN	Range Factors
ROCP	Relative Overall Combat Proficiency
RPl	Rifle Platoon
SaB	Sapper/Pionier Battalion
SaC	Sapper Company

SaP	Sapper/Pionier Platoon
SapS	Sapper Squadron
SchBat	*Schnell* Battalion (Fast Battalion)
SDE	Supply Distribution Efficiency
SDF	Supply Demand Factor
Sig B	Signal Battalion
Sig C	Signal Company
Sig Pl	Signal Platoon
SMG	Sub Machine Gun
SMGC	Sub Machine Gun Company
SPA	Self-Propelled Artillery Factor
SpMvr	Aircraft Maximum Speed and Manoeuvrability Factor
Sqd	Squad
SSF	Shape and Size Factor (for land units and aircraft)
StuGC	StuG Company (German assault gun co)
StuGP	StuG Platoon (German assault gun platoon)
TankB	Tank Battalion (or Panzer Battalion)
TankC	Tank Company (or Panzer Company)
TankP	Tank Platoon (or Panzer Platoon)
TankR	Tank Regiment (or Panzer Regiment)
TankS	Tank Squadron
TBE	Turret Basket Effect
TCE	Turret Crew Efficiency
TDi	Typical Target Dispersion Factor
TDR	Rotating Turret y/n, and Turret Drive Reliability
TID	Target observation and Indicator Devices
TNDM	Tactical Numerical Deterministic Model
TOE	Tables of Organisation and Equipment (Soviet - Shtaty and German - KStN)
Tra	Transport Infrastructure
TRF	Tactical Responsiveness Factor
W	*Wach* (Watch)
W Bat	*Wach* Battalion
WCPC	Weapon Combat Power Coefficient
WHT	Half Track/Wheeled Effect

Introduction

On 22nd June 1941 the Wehrmacht launched the largest invasion in recorded history, under the code name Operation Barbarossa. Operation Barbarossa needs no introduction to students of the Second World War, as it is unrivalled in military history for size, speed of operations, and the magnitude of its geographic objectives. The Wehrmacht's objective was no less than the complete defeat of the USSR, a nation possessing by far the largest army and air force in the world at that time. This study focuses on the period from 22nd June to 31st December 1941: the period when the Soviet Union came closest to defeat, and arguably the only period when Germany could still win WWII outright. Since the end of WWII, debate has raged about the key operational and strategic decisions made by the German and Soviet high commands, especially during the critical period from July to September 1941.

Operation Barbarossa: the Complete Organisational and Statistical Analysis, and Military Simulation is essentially the history of the Axis invasion of the USSR during 1941, expressed in the form of a detailed statistical analysis and an accompanying military simulation methodology. The objective of this work is to create the most historically accurate, advanced and comprehensive quantitative model yet, of the first six months of the largest and costliest military campaign in history (encompassing Operation Barbarossa and Operation Typhoon). The work includes full analyses of the belligerents' military, economic and logistical structure and capabilities, as related to their war effort on the East Front during 1941. This includes extensive data on: the structure of the relevant military and security organisations (land, sea and air), the available equipment and personnel, analyses of the weapons used, transport, logistics, economic production of war materials, mobilisation, and the replacements available and used during the campaign.

In addition, this enormous amount of historical data is organised and presented in such a way as to be 'ready' for incorporation into a comprehensive computer based military simulation of Operation Barbarossa. The work therefore includes an analytical and quantitative based methodology for creating a mathematical model of a country's armed forces and its overall war effort. This is the bulk of the content of Volume I. The methodologies defined in this work are designed to be generic, in that they can be employed to create a military simulation of a campaign other than Operation Barbarossa. One of the distinguishing features of this work is that it formalises and documents a military simulation methodology extending from the tactical to the strategic level. This includes a formal methodology to calculate and assess an armed force's Relative Overall Combat Proficiency (ROCP), detailed in Volume V and applied to the forces involved on the East Front during 1941.

However, the user is not obliged to follow or even understand the details of the quantitative methodology used if they so choose. *Operation Barbarossa: the Complete Organisational and Statistical Analysis, and Military Simulation* is structured so that the user does not need to be familiar with military simulation technology or terminology: the historical data is presented and referenced for the user to conduct their own research or analyses, or extract specific historical data regarding the campaign. The analytical methodology employed is mostly transparent to the user in subsequent volumes (see below), and they may not even be aware that it is being employed. Nevertheless, the analytical discipline enforced by the methodology is present at each stage, and all the belligerent nations and their armed forces undergo the equivalent detailed scrutiny.

The work spans the disciplines of military history, operational research, applied physics and mathematics, statistical analysis, and analytical methodology (usually relating to modern military simulations or war gaming). *Operation Barbarossa: the Complete Organisational and Statistical Analysis, and Military Simulation* does not assume the reader has detailed knowledge of the history of the East Front in WWII or extensive knowledge of the disciplines mentioned.

The key rationales behind this work are:

- To bring together an immense amount of information from many disparate sources, and present it in the form of a large 'data-warehouse' in a single work. The professional researcher or amateur scholar of WWII is provided with a comprehensive data source, containing the details of all the armed forces involved on the East Front from 22nd June to 31st December 1941. Currently there is no single source detailing the actual land, air and naval forces involved in Operation Barbarossa and Operation Typhoon.

- To fully analyse the belligerents' economic and logistical capabilities, as related to the East Front in 1941 and in the strategic context of their overall war effort.

- To bring in-depth quantitative analyses to bear on the most probable outcomes resulting from different (historical) operational and strategic decisions, by the German and Soviet high commands during 1941. It presents the advanced student of this campaign with a mechanism to quantitatively analyse in-depth, the actual forces involved, and much more significantly, to examine the probable outcome of various 'what if' scenarios. In so doing, many of the historically accepted myths surrounding Operation Barbarossa are exposed, while other less appreciated historical factors are shown to have been far more significant than commonly perceived.

- To provide the user with a generic methodology for researching, cataloguing and building the elements needed to create a realistic simulation of a historical military event.

- To demonstrate the application of quantitative analysis to military history (as opposed to largely qualitative analyses), and to demonstrate the potential power of modern military simulations in the study of military history. Selecting the largest land campaign in history as the historical case study, demonstrates the scalability of the methodology employed. In addition, incorporating the multitude of interrelated factors and circumstances faced by each of the belligerents on the East front during 1941, makes it evident how sophisticated and historically accurate operational-strategic military simulations provide a most powerful method of studying military history available today. In so doing, *Operation Barbarossa: the Complete Organisational and Statistical Analysis, and Military Simulation* produces a new perspective on a very famous, immensely important and tragic historical event.

***

Operation Barbarossa: the Complete Organisational and Statistical Analysis, and Military Simulation is separated into six volumes as follows:

1. Volume I - The Concepts and General Structure of the Integrated Land and Air Resource Model (Part I), and The Methodology Used for Analysing Weapon System Effectiveness, and the Structure of the 1941 Soviet and Axis Resource Database (Part II).

   The table of contents for Volume I is shown in Appendix B.

2. Volume IIA and IIB - The German Armed Forces (Wehrmacht), Mobilisation and War Economy from June to December 1941.

   The size of Volume II dictates it is published in two parts. The table of contents for Volume IIA (the precursor to this volume) is shown in Appendix C.

3. Volume IIIA and IIIB - The Soviet Armed Forces, Mobilisation and War Economy from June to December 1941.

   The size of Volume III dictates it is published in two parts. The table of contents for Volume IIIA is shown in Appendix D, and the table of contents for Volume IIIB is shown in Appendix E.

4. Volume IV - The Finnish, Rumanian, Hungarian, Slovakian and Italian Armed Forces Involved on the East Front in 1941.

5. Volume V - Relative Overall Combat Proficiency (ROCP): the ROCP of Soviet and Axis Forces on the East Front during WWII.

6. Volume VI – The Science of War Gaming, and Operation Barbarossa, the Complete Operational - Strategic Level Simulation from 22nd June to 31st December 1941.

Volume VI, the final part of the work, will include the actual Operation Barbarossa simulation.[1] This uses the methodologies and most of the historical data presented in the preceding volumes. Using the work and data in the simulation as a historical reference, the user is able to wander through this momentous historical event, changing variables if desired, and still be in context. This allows close examination and analysis of almost all the military aspects associated with Operation Barbarossa.

Further detailed information on Operation Barbarossa, changes of publishing schedule for impending volumes, and ongoing content updates, can be obtained from the website operationbarbarossa.net.

---

[1] At this time it is envisaged that it will employ The Operational Art of War (TOAW, currently version III) system, originally developed by Talonsoft, and currently being further developed and marketed by Matrix Games. If a superior system becomes available, especially one where the space and time scales can (also) be altered, then this will be reviewed. The necessary 'scale', to do justice to *Operation Barbarossa: Complete Organisational and Statistical Analysis, and Military Simulation*, is a minimum of 5km per hex and one day (24 hour) turns. The reasons for this, and the many pitfalls of inappropriate space-time scales in military simulations, are also reviewed in Volume VI. As of July 2013, a huge map of the Western USSR is being built and scaled at 2.5km per hex. It is being constructed by Jack Bechtold using the 1:250,000 scale topographic maps located at Texas University. The maps were compiled from German and Allied sources dating between 1930 and 1946 by the Army Map Service in the mid-1950s. The map sections were pieced together using Jasc Paintshop Pro 8 and Corel Paint Shop Pro 6X. The hex grid was applied using Opart Design and Debug 4.0 by Curt Chambers.

Volume IIB is the second volume relating to (and completing) the German forces, mobilisation and war economy from June to December 1941. It should be used in conjunction with Volume IIA. This is because Volume IIA contains the details of the actual organisation and equipment in all the Wehrmacht ground units used at the start of the campaign in the East (i.e. on 22nd June 1941), as well as those deployed on this date in other areas of the Reich. The data in the organisation and equipment tables for each unit is incorporated into the relevant tables in Volume IIB. In this way the German Resource Database (i.e. the weapon systems and squads) and the data relating to each ground-unit in Volume IIA is fully integrated into Volume IIB. Together, these two volumes then constitute the German FILARM model.[2]

Volume IIB is organised into eight chapters as follows:

- Chapter 1 covers the OOB (Orders of Battle) of all the German land combat units, in all areas of the Reich, between 22nd June and 4th July 1941. The many tables showing this detail are, together, known as the 'German Deployment Matrix' in the German FILARM model. At time of publication, the German Deployment Matrix represents the most detailed OOB ever published of the Wehrmacht ground forces fielded during the initial phase of Operation Barbarossa. Each German Army HQ (and army reserve) is presented separately, with all divisional and separate units shown. The latter includes even very small units such as: anti-aircraft companies, artillery HQs, artillery observation battalions, bridge construction battalions, *Landesschützen* battalions and traffic control battalions.

- Chapter 2 contains information on the German land combat units that were sent as reinforcements to the East Front from 5th July to 31st December 1941. The format used is the same as used for the German OOBs in chapter 1.

- Chapter 3 examines the overall status of the Wehrmacht forces across the Reich during the first thirteen days of Operation Barbarossa. It scrutinises the personnel and equipment allocated to combat units in each army-group and reserve force assigned to support Operation Barbarossa. The same process is then carried out for all the other commands across the Reich at this time. The total available resources in the Reich are then examined in order to understand how 'stretched' the German economy and populace was whilst supporting the first phase of Operation Barbarossa.

- Chapter 4 studies the new German units mobilised between 22nd June and 31st December 1941, as well as the overall mobilisation and replacement process. Particular attention is paid to AFVs at various points in this chapter. The total German resources (personnel and equipment) used in newly mobilised units is examined, and the total available resources in the Reich are then surveyed. The German Replacement Army is examined, and the German personnel and equipment replacements sent to the East Front during 1941 are scrutinised. This data is then used to analyse how strained the German economy and populace was in supporting their mobilisation and replacement process during the second half of 1941.

- Chapter 5 is concerned exclusively with the Luftwaffe. This large chapter includes: the structure of the Luftwaffe (including the command structure), a detailed OOB of all the German air units deployed across the Reich on 21st June 1941 (except training units), details on aircraft types and strengths in each air unit on 21st June 1941, details on aircraft strengths and readiness in each major Luftwaffe command area (including the air-fleets supporting Operation Barbarossa), and the movement of air units around the Reich in the second half of 1941 (comprising reinforcements to, and withdrawals from, the East Front). The Luftwaffe's OOB is treated with similar thoroughness as that for the ground forces: all *Luftflotte* and *Fliegerkorps* are shown separately, and the detail includes such small units as *Kurierstaffel*, *Verbindungsstaffel* and even *Sanitätsflugbereitschaft* (ambulance flights). The final section in chapter 5 reviews overall aircraft usage, production and replacements during the second half of 1941.

- Chapter 6 assesses the overall logistical supply of the Wehrmacht during 1941. Collectively, this comes under the general term Supply Distribution Efficiency (SDE). The SDE for German land units during the initial phase of Operation Barbarossa is analysed, as well as over the extended period from July to December 1941. Supply of the Luftwaffe's air units is also considered, i.e. the Luftwaffe forces are integrated into the German FILARM model. The various parameters relating to SDE are scrutinised at various points in this chapter. These include: the equipment and personnel supply demand, the proportion of available motorised vehicles available to support SDE functions, and the average lift capacity of the Wehrmacht's motorised vehicles and horse-drawn transport.

---

[2] FILARM (Fully Integrated Land and Air Resource Model). Refer Volume I Part I - 'The Concepts and General Structure of the Integrated Land and Air Resource Model'.

- Chapter 7 focuses on the German naval forces that supported operations on the East Front during 1941. It includes a description of the Kriegsmarine commands involved and their objectives in the East, a detailed OOB of the named vessels, and a brief history of German naval operations in the Baltic during 1941.

- Chapter 8 investigates the Wehrmacht and Waffen SS casualties from 22nd June to 28th February 1942. It includes historical data from multiple sources relating to killed, wounded, missing/POW, and sick and unfit casualties. Medical records are also used to examine the numbers of wounded and unfit casualties that were recuperated to active service (in 1941), and the overall change in strength of the Wehrmacht forces on the East Front from June to December 1941.

***

Finally, it is worth stating that *Operation Barbarossa: the Complete Organisational and Statistical Analysis, and Military Simulation* is a massive project, and one which is likely to be ongoing, reviewed and updated for many years to come. Research for this project goes as far back as the 1980s, with the 1990s and the opening of many of the Russian (ex-Soviet) archives as an enabling milestone. However, there are still many areas of contention and missing detail (especially Russian and ex-Soviet areas), and in this regard the details of the work may never be 'complete'. Nevertheless, these updates and changes will now be relatively minor, and although they may be pleasing to include for the military history purist, they would not have significantly affected the outcome of Operation Barbarossa at the macroscopic operational-strategic level.

Is all this research and work worth the effort for one campaign during WWII? Consider that the Axis invasion of the USSR in 1941 was by far the largest land invasion in recorded history, and one which ultimately led to the greatest loss of human life ever experienced in a single campaign. In addition, this campaign was by far the most decisive of WWII, and the one in which the Axis powers came closest to outright victory. Ultimately, over 70% of the German Army's WWII casualties were sustained on the East Front, while Soviet military casualties suffered while fighting the Axis powers in the western USSR amounted to a staggering 29,593,000 persons. Notwithstanding the huge Western Allied war effort, there can be no doubt where the centre of gravity of the fighting during most of WWII was, and where the outcome of WWII mostly hinged.

***

1. The Order of Battle (OOB) of German Land Combat Units from 22nd June to 4th July 1941

1) The German Deployment Matrix

The Orders of Battle (OOB) of the German Army, Waffen SS and Luftwaffe flak combat units, in all areas of the Reich between 22nd June and 4th July 1941, are shown in the series of tables with the common title <u>German Deployment Matrix</u> (shown on pages 10 to 63).

Together, these tables will henceforth be referred to as the 'German Deployment Matrix', and <u>all</u> combat units in the 'German Deployment Matrix' are classified as being in a Deployed (D) state in the German FILARM model.

For the purposes of this work (i.e. the German FILARM model and the German Deployment Matrix), the terms **'the East Front'** (or the Eastern Front or the East), **'the Western Fronts'** (or the West), and **'the Replacement Army'** are used. These are defined as:

- **The East Front**: includes Army Group North, Army Group Centre, Army Group South, the Norway Army - *Befehlsstelle Finnland* (East Front only) and OKH Reserves.

- **The Western Fronts**: includes Army Group D (also the *Oberbefehlshaber West*), the Norway Army (Norway occupation duties), the 12th Army (Yugoslavia-Serbia-Greece-Crete) and the German Africa Corps (*Deutsches Afrika Korps* - D.A.K).

- **The Replacement Army**: includes all forces under the *Chef Heeresrustung und Befehlshaber der Erstazarmee* (Chef H.Rust. u. B.d.E. or Commander of the Replacement Army).[3] The Commander of the Replacement Army controlled the German troops in Denmark (the *Befehlshaber der deutschen Truppen in Danemark)* and the Replacement Army troops (*Erstazarmee Truppen)* in the various military districts in Germany, Austria, and the protectorate of Bohemia and Moravia (the *Wehrkreise*).

In addition, for the German FILARM model, the 'Replacement Army' includes the administration and security forces under *Militärbefehlshaber* (MB) *Belgien & Nordfrankreich*, MB *Frankreich*, MB *Serbien* and MB *im General-Gouvernement* (Poland), and any additional forces in Germany, Austria and Czechoslovakia (e.g. the Luftwaffe Flak forces).[4]

***

All the combat units that existed between 22nd June and 4th July 1941, and that are identified in Volume IIA 3. (The Tables of Organisation and Equipment (TOE) for German Land Combat Units), are listed in the left hand column of the Deployment Matrix pages.

The German Deployment Matrix lists each army group, separate army, separate corps (the DAK), OKH reserves, and major rear area commands in the *Reich* on 22nd June 1941. Within each army group the subordinate armies, panzer groups and army group reserves are shown as columns. In addition, within each army, panzer group and army group reserve, the subordinate corps, army reserves, panzer group reserves and rear-area commands are shown in further columns. The individual combat units assigned to each corps, army reserve, panzer group reserve, or rear-area command, are then listed. Relevant notes at the bottom of each column provide additional information on the combat units listed. Importantly, these notes also provide information on when units transferred from the Western Fronts or the Replacement Army, to the East Front during 1941 (also, refer to chapter Volume IIB 2. on German reinforcements to the East Front).

The German Deployment Matrix indicates that on 22nd June 1941 there were 4 army groups, 4 panzer groups and 13 armies in the *Reich*. They controlled 34 infantry corps, 12 reduced strength special corps, 12 motorised (panzer) corps and 2 flak corps. The divisional forces in the German armed forces, including the Waffen SS, contained 208 ground divisions. These comprised 152 infantry divisions, 4 light infantry divisions, 1 SS police infantry division, 20 panzer divisions, 11 motorised divisions (including the 5th Light Division in Africa), 3 Waffen SS motorised divisions, 1 cavalry division, 6 mountain divisions, 1 parachute division and 9 security divisions.[5]

---

[3] The commander of the Replacement Army was Colonel General Friedrick 'Fritz' Fromm until 20th July 1944.

[4] MB *Belgien & Nordfrankreich* (Military Commander Belgium and North France), and MB *Frankreich* (Military Commander France), also reported to the *Oberbefehlshaber West*. The MD *Serbien* (Military Commander Serbia) also came under the 12th Army. These were primarily administration (non-combat) HQs which controlled the district's military security forces as well as local recruitment and initial indoctrination.

[5] The 5th Light Division (in the DAK in North Africa) was still classified as a motorised division in June 1941. It is therefore counted as motorised division in the Deployment Matrix despite having a panzer regiment attached.

The forces outside of the divisions included the following:

- Signals (communication) forces with 12 army/army group signal regiments, 11 army/army group signal battalions and 4 panzer group signal regiments.

- Motorised infantry forces with 5 motorised infantry brigades (including 4 Waffen SS brigades), 3 motorised infantry regiments and 3 motorised infantry battalions.

- Mixed transport infantry forces with 5 infantry regiments and 9.33 infantry battalions (separate companies are each counted as one third of a battalion). The latter comprised 4 infantry battalions, 3 bicycle infantry battalions, 1 infantry battalion for special purpose (zbv), 1 naval infantry battalion and 1 separate mountain company.

- Armoured forces with 2 tank brigades, 2 panzer battalions, 2 panzer companies, 18 assault gun (*Sturmgeschütz*) battalions, 5 independent assault gun batteries and 3 flame tank battalions.[6]

- Mixed transport security and army-militia forces (excluding military-police and order-police units) with 4 (*Ersatz*) security brigades, 45.33 Guard (*Wach*) battalions and 542 Army Militia (*Landesschützen*) Battalions (separate companies are each counted as one third of a battalion). Of this force, the *Ersatz* brigades, 2.33 *Wach* battalions and 361 *Landesschützen* Battalions, were in the Replacement Army (*Ersatzarmee*).

- Artillery forces with 2 *Harko* HQs, 59 *Arko* HQs, 40 special artillery regiment HQs (including 1 horse-drawn and 3 railroad artillery HQs), 36 artillery observation battalions (with 6 balloon artillery observation batteries attached), 129 artillery battalions, 7 separate artillery batteries, 171 coastal artillery batteries and 22 railroad artillery batteries.[7]

- Rocket artillery forces with 4 special rocket launcher regiment HQs, 5 *Nebelwerfer* regiments, 7 *Nebelwerfer* battalions, 1 *Nebelwerfer* battery and 8 decontamination battalions (*Entgiftungs-Abteilung*).[8]

- Army flak forces with 10 anti-aircraft battalions, 14 light anti-aircraft battalions and 51 light anti-aircraft companies.[9] 21 of these self-propelled light AA companies were attached to panzer and motorised divisions, and 2 self-propelled light AA companies were attached to infantry divisions.[10]

- Luftwaffe flak forces with 59 Luftwaffe flak regiment HQs, 308 Luftwaffe mixed flak battalions and 46 Luftwaffe light flak battalions.

- Anti-tank forces with 6 motorised anti-tank battalions, 10 self-propelled anti-tank battalions and 1 self-propelled heavy anti-tank company.[11]

- Machine gun forces with 6 motorised MG battalions and 2 semi-motorised MG battalions.[12]

- Cavalry forces with 2 SS cavalry regiments.

- Combat engineer (*Pionier*) and engineer construction forces with 29 special engineer regiment HQs, 23 motorised combat engineer battalions, 31 semi-motorised combat engineer battalions, 6 assault boat companies, 1 armoured mine-clearing battalion, 29 bridge construction battalions (including 2 motorised), 1 bridge construction company and 11 bridge guard-engineer battalions.[13]

- Bridging forces with 120 motorised type B bridge columns, 49 type A-T bridge columns (including all heavy bridges) and 1 motorised heavy bridge transport battalion (the 800th). This does not include 59 type B bridge columns in panzer divisions (19), motorised divisions (10), motorised *pionier* battalions (25), Waffen SS motorised divisions (3), the LSSAH motorised brigade (1) and the 900th Lehr Brigade (1). Also, it does not include 23 type T columns in the infantry divisions: 16 in 2nd wave infantry divisions, 1 in the 72nd Infantry

---

[6] The panzer companies are each counted as one third of a panzer battalion, and the assault gun batteries are each counted as one third of an assault gun battalion, in the Deployment Matrix.

[7] The separate artillery batteries are each counted as one third of an artillery battalion in the Deployment Matrix. The coastal artillery batteries are each counted as one third of a coastal artillery battalion in the Deployment Matrix.

[8] The 8./222nd Nebelwerfer Battery in Norway/Finland is counted as one third of a Nebelwerfer battalion in the Deployment Matrix. Includes 3 Road Decontamination Battalions.

[9] Does not include the 606th AA Battalion in the 5th Light Division, or the new 616th AA Battalion which was still forming.

[10] These AA companies were attached to the panzer and motorised divisions on a semi-permanent basis, but they were still corps units and were not part of these division's TOEs.

[11] Excludes the 605th Self-Propelled Anti-Tank Battalion which was permanently attached to the 5th Light Division (DAK).

[12] Excluding the 2nd and 8th MG Battalions in the 5th Light Division (DAK).

[13] The 4./17 *Ersatz* Bridge Construction Company (11th Army Reserve) is counted as one quarter of a bridge construction battalion in the Deployment Matrix.

Division, 1 in the 262nd Infantry Division, and 5 in the 5th wave infantry divisions.[14] In addition, it does <u>not</u> include 1 motorised type K bridge column attached to the 62nd Motorised Combat Engineer Battalion.

- Army construction forces with 47 construction HQs and 147 construction battalions. This does <u>not</u> include any battalions from the Todt Organisation (*Organisation Todt* – OT) or the Reich Labour Service (*Reichsarbeitsdienst* – RAD). The construction HQs comprised 10 main construction HQs (*Oberbaustab*), 31 commander of construction troops HQs (*Kommandeur Der Bautruppen*), 4 fortress engineering construction HQs, 1 special purpose construction HQ (in the 4th Army) and 1 special snow clearing HQ in Norway. The construction battalions comprised 101 construction battalions, 23 road construction battalions (including 2 motorised), 7 bicycle road construction battalions, 1 marine construction battalion and 15 fortress construction battalions.

- Railroad engineering and construction forces with 8 railroad engineering (*Eisenbahn-pionier*) regiment HQs, 8 railroad engineering battalion HQs, 53 railroad *pionier* companies, 13 railroad switching companies, 10 railroad engineer construction battalions and 27 railroad engineer construction companies.

- Motorised *Ordnungspolizei* (order-police) forces with 12 motorised police regiment HQs and 41 police rifle battalions. The latter were motorised for the most part, particularly those deployed in the East.

- Motorised *Feldgendarmerie des Heeres* (military field-police of the army) forces with 21 motorised military police battalions and 11 motorised traffic control battalions.

- 16 armoured trains.

***

From the German Deployment Matrix we can ascertain the German Army, Waffen SS and Luftwaffe flak combat units committed to support Operation Barbarossa (in the East) from 22nd June to 4th July 1941. These forces included those in Army Group North, Army Group Centre, Army Group South, the Norway Army - *Befehlsstelle Finnland* (East Front only) and OKH Reserves. The invasion forces used up to 4th July 1941 were as follows (refer to pages 52-53):

- High level HQs consisting of 3 army-group HQs, 4 panzer group HQs and 8 army HQs.

- Corps level HQs consisting of 31 infantry corps HQs, 3 reduced strength special corps HQs, 10 motorised (panzer) corps HQs, 3 army group rear-area HQs (RHG) and 2 flak corps HQs.

- Divisional forces with 138 ground divisions. These consisted of 90 infantry divisions, 4 light infantry divisions, 1 SS police infantry division, 17 panzer divisions, 9 motorised divisions, 3 Waffen SS motorised divisions, 1 cavalry division, 4 mountain divisions and 9 small security divisions. All the forces listed below were <u>outside</u> of these divisions (note, they are not included in the TOE of these divisions, as shown in Volume IIA 3.)

- Signals (communication) forces with 11 army/army group signal regiments, 6 army/army group signal battalions and 4 panzer group signal regiments.

- Motorised infantry forces with 5 motorised infantry brigades (including 4 Waffen SS brigades), and one and a half motorised infantry regiments.[15]

- Mixed transport infantry forces with 3 security regiments, 2 bicycle infantry battalions, 1 infantry battalion for special purpose (zbv), 1 naval infantry battalion and 1 separate mountain (separate companies are each counted as one third of a battalion).

- Armoured forces with 2 panzer battalions (deployed in Finland), 11 assault gun (*Sturmgeschütz*) battalions, 5 independent assault gun batteries and 3 flame tank battalions.

- Mixed transport security and army-militia forces (excluding military-police and order-police units) with 37 Guard (*Wach*) battalions and 42 Army Militia (*Landesschützen*) Battalions.

- Artillery forces with 2 *Harko* HQs, 54 *Arko* HQs, 36 special artillery regiment HQs (including 1 horse-drawn artillery HQ), 35 artillery observation battalions (with 6 balloon artillery observation batteries attached),

---

[14] 17 of these were motorised. The type T bridge column in the 78th Infantry Division and the 5 type T bridge columns in the 5th wave infantry divisions were horse-drawn.
[15] The LSSAH Brigade's 4th battalion remained in Germany as Hitler's bodyguard unit. This brigade therefore counts as 7/8 brigade in the Deployment Matrix. In addition, only half of the Lehr Regiment Brandenburg (800 zbV) was initially committed to Operation Barbarossa. The companies from this 'Special Forces' unit were distributed amongst the various army groups, and each company of the 800zbV is counted as one sixteenth of the regiment in the Deployment Matrix.

122 artillery battalions, 7 separate artillery batteries, 13 coastal artillery battalions and 11 railroad artillery batteries.

- Rocket artillery forces with 4 special rocket launcher regiment HQs, 5 *Nebelwerfer* regiments, 7 *Nebelwerfer* battalions, 1 *Nebelwerfer* battery and 8 decontamination battalions (*Entgiftungs-Abteilung*).

- Army flak forces with 10 anti-aircraft battalions, 10 light anti-aircraft battalions and 47 light anti-aircraft companies.

- Luftwaffe flak forces with 13 Luftwaffe flak regiment HQs, 41 Luftwaffe mixed flak battalions and 17 Luftwaffe light flak battalions.

- Anti-tank forces with 6 motorised anti-tank battalions, 9 self-propelled anti-tank battalions and 1 self-propelled heavy anti-tank company.

- Machine gun forces with 3 motorised MG battalions.

- Cavalry forces with 2 SS cavalry regiments.

- Combat engineer (*Pionier*) and engineer construction forces with 28 special engineer regiment HQs, 21 motorised combat engineer battalions, 30 semi-motorised combat engineer battalions, 5 assault boat companies, 1 armoured mine-clearing battalion, 27 bridge construction battalions (including 2 motorised) and 1 bridge construction company.

- Bridging forces with 119 motorised type B bridge columns, 45 type A-T bridge columns (including all heavy bridges) and 1 motorised heavy bridge transport battalion (the 800th).[16]

- Army construction forces with 41 construction HQs and 126 construction battalions (excluding any battalions from the Todt Organisation (*Organisation Todt* – OT) or the Reich Labour Service (*Reichsarbeitsdienst* – RAD). The construction HQs comprised 7 main construction HQs (*Oberbaustab*), 31 commander of construction troops HQs (*Kommandeur Der Bautruppen*), 2 fortress engineering construction HQs and 1 special purpose construction HQ (in the 4th Army). The construction battalions comprised 94 construction battalions, 23 road construction battalions (including 2 motorised), 7 bicycle road construction battalions and 2 fortress construction battalions.

- Railroad engineering and construction forces with 5 railroad engineering (*Eisenbahn-pionier*) regiment HQs, 7 railroad engineering battalion HQs, 47 railroad *pionier* companies, 10 railroad switching companies, 6 railroad engineer construction battalions and 16 railroad engineer construction companies.

- Motorised *Ordnungspolizei* (order-police) forces with 3 motorised police regiment HQs and 22 motorised police rifle battalions.

- Motorised *Feldgendarmerie des Heeres* (military field-police of the army) forces with 20 motorised military police battalions and 11 motorised traffic control battalions.

- 12 armoured trains.

***

---

[16] Includes le.Z. (*Leicht Zerlegbar*) heavy combat bridge columns, H. (*Herbert*) heavy combat bridge columns, and s.S. (*schwere Schiffsbrucke*) heavy bridge columns.

The German Deployment Matrix: Abbreviations Used and Additional Notes

Arm - Armoured

Art - Artillery

Batts - Battalions

Cols - Columns

Comp's - Companies

Const - Construction

Eng - Engineer

Fr - Fortress

G - *Wach* : Guard Units

Grp - Group

How - Howitzer

Hvy - Heavy

LS - *Landesschutzen* : Local Defence Units (Militia)

Luft - Luftwaffe

Mot - Motorised

Ob - *Oberbaustab* HQ

R - Road

Regs - Regiments

Sep - Separate

SP - Self Propelled

Spec P - Special Purpose

'Construction Reg HQs' and **'Construction Battalions'**: <u>Excludes</u> Reich Labour Service (RAD) Battalions, and Organisation Todt (OT) Labour Force Battalions.

'Sep Bridge Cols, Type (A-T)'* (refer text for detailed descriptions)

A - Type A Combat Bridge

B - Type B Medium Combat Bridge

C - Type C Light Combat Bridge

D - Light Reconnaissance Bridge on Trucks.

FR - Captured French Br Equipment

G - Mountain Bridging Device

H - Herbert, Heavy Box Girder Floating Bridge

K - Medium Bridge: Box Materials, Pontoons and Trestles

le.Z. - Heavy Combat Bridge

s.S. - Heavy Railroad Combat Bridge or Heavy Ships Bridge (Railway)

T - Former Czech Combat Bridge

* <u>Only</u> separate Bridge Columns are shown. Bridge Columns semi-permanently attached to Divisions or Motorised *Pionier* Battalions are not shown as separate Corps Units: these are included in the TOE of these units from 22nd June to 4th July 1941.

***

Table German Deployment Matrix

Deployment and Composition of the German Army, Waffen SS and Luftwaffe Flak Units, 22nd June 1941

Army Group North

18th Army

	XXVI Corps Description	No	I Corps Description	No	XXXVIII Corps Description	No	Army Reserve Description	No
Army & Panzer Group HQs								
Army HQs							18	1
Corps HQs	26	1	1	1	38	1		
Panzer Corps HQs								
Army Group Rear Area HQs								
Army & Army Grp Signal Regs							520	1
Army & Army Grp Signal Batts								
Panzer Group Signal Regs								
Infantry Divisions	61, 217	2	1, 11, 21	3	58	1	291	1
Panzer Divisions								
Motorised Divisions								
SS Motorised Divisions								
Cavalry Divisions								
Mountain Divisions								
Light Divisions								
Fleiger Divisions								
Motorised Infantry Brigades								
Motorised Infantry Regiments							7.IL/800zbV^^*	1/16
Motorised Infantry Battalions								
(Mixed) Infantry Regiments								
(Mixed) Infantry Battalions	402*, MAA^	2					403*^	1
Tank Brigades								
Tank Battalions								
Cavalry Regiments								
Security Divisions or Brigades					2	1	(571, 531)**^	2
Guard (*Wach*) Battalions			696*	1				
Landesschutzen Battalions								
Artillery HQs, *Harko & Arko*	113	1	123	1				
Art Observation Battalions	12	1	4, 26^	2				
Artillery Reg HQs (Spec P)	818	1	110, 609	2				
Mixed Artillery Battalions			IL/37, IL/58, 536	3				
150mm How Battalions	436, 633	2	511	1				
105mm Gun Battalions		2						
150mm Gun Battalions			2.3,/637	2/3				
210mm How Battalions (1)							1,/637	1/3
210mm How Battalions (2)								
210mm Gun Battalions								
Hvy 240mm How Battalions								
Hvy 240mm Gun Battalions								
Super Hvy How Battalions								
Coastal Artillery Battalions							(531, 910, 914J)^^^	3
Railroad Artillery Batteries							690	1
Anti-Air Battalions							273	1
Light Anti-Air Battalions							604	
SP Light AA Companies	6,/52	1					1/31*, 1/55	2

Unit Type	Grp 1 Des	No	Grp 2 Des	No	Grp 3 Des	No
Nebelwerfer Regiment HQs						
Nebelwerfer Regiments						
Nebelwerfer Battalions						
Entgiftungs Battalions					131 R***	1
Machine Gun Battalions	563	1			10^	1
Anti-Tank Battalions						
SP Anti-Tank Battalions						
SP Hvy Anti-Tank Companies						
Assault Gun Battalions			185	1		
Flame Tank Battalions						
Mot Eng Reg HQs (Spec P)	677	1	519	1		
Mot *Pionier* Battalions	660	1				
(Mixed) *Pionier* Battalions			676	1		
Bridge Const Battalions	2./683, 3./683	1/2	4./683	1/4	1./683	1/4
Assault Boat Companies						
Mot Sep Bridge Cols B	161, 401	2	1, 11, 21, 636	4	2xA, 2xle.Z	4
Sep Bridge Cols, Type (A-T)	1xA	1	1xA	1		
Arm Mine Clearing Battalions						
Luft Flak Corps HQs						
Luft Flak Reg HQs					164	1
Luft Mixed Flak Battalions					I./36, I./51, I./111	3
Luft Light Flak Battalions						
Construction Reg HQs	108	1	31	1	32	1
Construction Battalions	95, 100	2	124, 257, 679R	3	127^*, 141, 562R, 591R	4
Railroad Eng Reg HQs					II./3	1
Railroad *Pionier* Bat HQs						
Railroad *Pionier* Companies					8./3, 1./2, 2./6, 5./6, 305	5
Railroad Switching Comp's					172	1
Railroad Eng Const Comp's					106, 125	2
Railroad Eng Const Batts					512	1
Mot Police Regiment HQ						
Police Rifle Battalions						
Mot Military Police Battalions					689*^^	1
Mot Traffic Control Battalions					753*^^	1
Armoured Trains					6	1

* 402nd Bicycle Infantry Battalion.
^ MSK and MST Naval Infantry Battalion equivalent; stationed in Memel.

* 696th Railroad Battery had 2x280mm *kurz Bruno* Rail Guns
^ I Corps also had the 4./4 Motorised Balloon Battery attached.

* 1./31st Lt AA Co was attached to 291st Inf Div.
^ 10th MG Battalion was attached to the 291st Inf Division
*^ 403rd Bicycle Infantry Battalion attached to the 291st Infantry Division
^^ 127th Construction Battalion was assigned to the 29th Infantry Division. *** Road (Str.) Battalion.
*** Guard-Watch (Wach) and Landesschutzen (Local Defence) units, reporting to Korück 583.
*^^ Motorised units reporting to Korück 583. Note, Korück is abbreviation for *Kommandant des rückwärtigen Armeegebietes*: (Commandant of Rear Army Area)
^^^ Mobile units. ^^* Lehr Reg Brandenburg 800 zbV; (Special Forces), 7th Company.

Table German Deployment Matrix — Deployment and Composition of the German Army, Waffen SS and Luftwaffe Flak Units, 22nd June 1941

Army Group North

4th Panzer Group (4th Panzer Army from 1st January 1942)

Deployment Matrix	XXXXI Corps (Mot) Description	No	LVI Corps (Mot) Description	No	Pz Group Reserve Description	No
Army & Panzer Group HQs					4Pz Grp HQ	1
Army HQs						
Corps HQs						
Panzer Corps HQs	41	1	56	1		
Army Group Rear Area HQs						
Army & Army Grp Signal Regs						
Army & Army Grp Signal Batts						
Panzer Group Signal Regs					4.PzGr	1
Infantry Divisions	269	1	290	1		
Panzer Divisions	1, 6	2	8	1		
Motorised Divisions	36	1	3	1		
SS Motorised Divisions					SS T Division	1
Cavalry Divisions						
Mountain Divisions						
Light Divisions						
Fleiger Divisions						
Motorised Infantry Brigades						
Motorised Infantry Regiments					8.II./800zbV & Bat HQ^*	1/16
Motorised Infantry Battalions						
(Mixed) Infantry Regiments						
(Mixed) Infantry Battalions						
Tank Brigades						
Tank Battalions						
Cavalry Regiments						
Security Divisions or Brigades					326*^	1
Guard (*Wach*) Battalions						
Landesschutzen Battalions						
Artillery HQs, *Harko* & *Arko*	30	1	125	1		
Art Observation Battalions	2	1				
Artillery Reg HQs (Spec P)	618	1				
Mixed Artillery Battalions	II./59, II./67	2	II./61	1		
150mm How Battalions	611	1				
105mm Gun Battalions						
150mm Gun Battalions						
210mm How Battalions (1)	615	1				
210mm How Battalions (2)						
210mm Gun Battalions						
Hvy 240mm How Battalions						
Hvy 240mm Gun Battalions						
Super Hvy How Battalions						
Coastal Artillery Battalions						
Railroad Artillery Batteries						

Unit Type	Unit	No.	Unit	No.	Unit	No.
Anti-Air Battalions	601	1				
Light Anti-Air Battalions	3,/46*, 2,/59^	2	4,/48*	1		
SP Light AA Companies	52	1				
Nebelwerfer Regiment HQs						
Nebelwerfer Regiments						
Nebelwerfer Battalions						
Entgiftungs Battalions						
Machine Gun Battalions						
Anti-Tank Battalions			559	1		
SP Anti-Tank Battalions					616	1
SP Hvy Anti-Tank Companies						
Assault Gun Battalions						
Flame Tank Battalions						
Mot Eng Reg HQs (Spec P)	628	1	678	1		
Mot Pionier Battalions	52	1	48	1	62*	1
(Mixed) Pionier Battalions						
Bridge Const Battalions	26	1				
Assault Boat Companies					906	1
Mot Sep Bridge Cols B	1,/430, 661, 2,/406, 2,/411	4	2,/412, 2,/505, 649	3		
Sep Bridge Cols, Type (A-T)						
Arm Mine Clearing Battalions						
Luft Flak Corps HQs					133	1
Luft Flak Reg HQs	L/3	1	II,/23	1		
Luft Mixed Flak Battalions	83, II,/411	2	92	1		
Luft Light Flak Battalions						
Construction Reg HQs	71	1	4	1	32 Ob^	1
Construction Battalions	62, 254	2	44, 55, 87	3	507RBi**, 508RBi**	2
Railroad Eng Reg HQs					II,/6	1
Railroad Pionier Bat HQs						
Railroad Pionier Companies					1,/4, 3,/4, 6,/4, 7,/6, 7,/3	5
Railroad Switching Comp's					177	1
Railroad Eng Const Comp's					106, 125	2
Railroad Eng Const Batts					106	1
Mot Police Regiment HQ						
Police Rifle Battalions						
Mot Military Police Battalions					521	1
Mot Traffic Control Battalions						
Armoured Trains						

* 3,/46 Lt AA Co was attached to 6th Pz Div.
^ 2,/59th Lt AA Co was attached to 1st Pz Div.

* 4,/48 Lt AA Co was attached to 8th Pz Div.

* The 62nd Mot Mot Pionier Battalion had 3 Type B Bridge Columns (1-3,/62), and 1 Type K Bridge Column (62). It was attached directly to the 4th Panzer Group HQ.
^ Oberbaustab 32, (Brigade level HQ).
** Road Construction Bicycle Battalions.
*^ Bicycle mounted with mot support columns.
^^ Lehr Reg Brandenburg 800 zbV; Special Forces. 8th Company & II Battalion HQ.

Table German — Deployment and Composition of the German Army, Waffen SS and Luftwaffe Flak Units, 22nd June 1941

Deployment Matrix — Army Group North — 16th Army

	X Corps Description	No	XXVIII Corps Description	No	II Corps Description	No	Army Reserve Description	No
Army & Panzer Group HQs								
Army HQs							16	1
Corps HQs	10	1	28	1	2	1		
Panzer Corps HQs								
Army Group Rear Area HQs							501	1
Army & Army Grp Signal Regs								
Army & Army Grp Signal Batts								
Panzer Group Signal Regs								
Infantry Divisions	30, 126	2	122, 123	2	12, 32, 121	3	253	1
Panzer Divisions								
Motorised Divisions								
SS Motorised Divisions								
Cavalry Divisions								
Mountain Divisions								
Light Divisions								
Fleiger Divisions								
Motorised Infantry Brigades								
Motorised Infantry Regiments								
Motorised Infantry Battalions								
(Mixed) Infantry Regiments								
(Mixed) Infantry Battalions								
Tank Brigades								
Tank Battalions								
Cavalry Regiments								
Security Divisions or Brigades							(562, 615)**	2
Guard (*Wach*) Battalions								
Landesschutzen Battalions								
Artillery HQs, *Harko & Arko*	24, 135	2	19, 130	2	105, 111	2		
Art Observation Battalions	38	1	19	1	5, 14^	2		
Artillery Reg HQs (Spec P)	785	1	610	1	603, 782, 803	3		
Mixed Artillery Battalions					I./106	1		
150mm How Battalions	846, 850	2	II./47, 843	2	506, 526	2		
105mm Gun Battalions	I./818	1	153	1	II./72	1		
150mm Gun Battalions								
210mm How Battalions (1)					636, 809	2	625	1
210mm How Battalions (2)								
210mm Gun Battalions								
Hvy 240mm How Battalions								
Hvy 240mm Gun Battalions							II./84	1
Super Hvy How Battalions								
Coastal Artillery Battalions								

Unit Type	Col 1 (№)	Col 2 (№)	Col 3 (№)	Col 4 (№)
Railroad Artillery Batteries				
Anti-Air Battalions				280 (1)
Light Anti-Air Battalions				
SP Light AA Companies				3./52*, 4./55, 4./59 (3)
Nebelwerfer Regiment HQs			3 (1)	
Nebelwerfer Regiments				
Nebelwerfer Battalions			2, 9 (2)	
Entgiftungs Battalions			101 (1)	
Machine Gun Battalions				
Anti-Tank Battalions				
SP Anti-Tank Battalions				
SP Hvy Anti-Tank Companies		665*, 667* (2/3)	659*, 660*, 666* (1)	
Assault Gun Battalions				
Flame Tank Battalions				
Mot Eng Reg HQs (Spec P)		514 (1)	541 (1)	
Mot Pionier Battalions			44, 505 (2)	680 (1)
(Mixed) Pionier Battalions		655, 657, 662 (3)	656, 671 (2)	
Bridge Const Battalions			674 (1)	
Assault Boat Companies	2./566 (1/3)	1./566 (1/3)		3./566 (1/3)
Mot Sep Bridge Cols B	122, 123 (2)	30, 126 (2)	2, 12, 121, 652, 656, 663, 671 (7)	1./406, 658 (2)
Sep Bridge Cols, Type (A-T)		5xA (5)		1xH, 1xIe.Z (2)
Arm Mine Clearing Battalions				
Luft Flak Corps HQs				
Luft Flak Reg HQs				151 (1)
Luft Mixed Flak Battalions				
Luft Light Flak Battalions				I/13, I/291, I/411 (3)
Construction Reg HQs	35 (1)	7 (1)	16 (1)	I (Fr Ob)^ (1)
Construction Battalions	78, 132 (2)	98, 108 (2)	25, 121 (2)	101, 120, 306, 510R, 677R, 680R (6)
Railroad Eng Reg HQs				4 (1)
Railroad Pionier Bat HQs				I./4 (1)
Railroad Pionier Companies				4./3, 1./7, 7./3, 3./5, 7./5, 3./6, 306, 397 (8)
Railroad Switching Comp's				182, 183 (2)
Railroad Eng Const Comp's				114, 122 (2)
Railroad Eng Const Batts				15 (1)
Mot Police Regiment HQ				
Police Rifle Battalions				
Mot Military Police Battalions				561*^ (1)
Mot Traffic Control Battalions				751*^ (1)
Armoured Trains				26, 30 (2)

Notes:

* 665, 667 Assault Gun Batteries were independent Batteries.

* 659, 660 and 666 Assault Gun Batteries were independent Batteries which were attached to the 600th Assault Artillery Battalion HQ (600 Abt zbV).

^ II corps also had the 4./5 mot Balloon Battery attached.

* 3./52nd Lt AA Co was attached to 253rd Inf Div.

^ Stab Fest.Pi.Kdr. I (Fortress Eng Construction Brigade 1 HQ), Redesignated 'Oberbaustab 21' on 1st Nov 41.

** Guard (Wach) and Landesschützen units, reporting to Korück 584.

*^ Motorised units reporting to Korück 584.

© Nigel Askey, 2018

Table German Deployment Matrix — Deployment and Composition of the German Army, Waffen SS and Luftwaffe Flak Units, 22nd June 1941

Description	Army Group North — XXIII Corps Description	No	RHG 101 Description	No	Army Group North Reserve — Reserves Description	No	AG NORTH TOTAL No
Army & Panzer Group HQs					AGN HQ	1	2
Army HQs							2
Corps HQs	23	1					7
Panzer Corps HQs							2
Army Group Rear Area HQs			RHG 101	1			1
Army & Army Grp Signal Regs					639	1	3
Army & Army Grp Signal Batts			207	1			1
Panzer Group Signal Regs							1
Infantry Divisions	206, 251, 254	3					20
Panzer Divisions							3
Motorised Divisions							2
SS Motorised Divisions							1
Cavalry Divisions							
Mountain Divisions							
Light Divisions							
Fleiger Divisions							
Motorised Infantry Brigades							
Motorised Infantry Regiments							
Motorised Infantry Battalions							1/8
(Mixed) Infantry Regiments			Sich.Rgt 3*	1			1
(Mixed) Infantry Battalions							3
Tank Brigades							
Tank Battalions							
Cavalry Regiments							
Security Divisions or Brigades			207, 281, 285	3			3
Guard (Wach) Battalions			609, 706*^, 707^	3	47, 117	2	10
Landesschutzen Battalions			(306, 636, 859, 860)*^, (564, 638, 853, 972)^^, (865, 868, 869, 960)^	12	974	1	13
Artillery HQs, Harko & Arko	122	1					12
Art Observation Battalions	24	1					9
Artillery Reg HQs (Spec P)							9
Mixed Artillery Battalions							2
150mm How Battalions							11
105mm Gun Battalions							6
150mm Gun Battalions							2
210mm How Battalions (1)							4
210mm How Battalions (2)							
210mm Gun Battalions							
Hvy 240mm How Battalions							1
Hvy 240mm Gun Battalions							
Super Hvy How Battalions							

Unit Type	Qty				
Coastal Artillery Battalions	4			143*	1
Railroad Artillery Batteries	2				
Anti-Air Battalions	2				
Light Anti-Air Battalions	2				
SP Light AA Companies	10	1	5,/31		
Nebelwerfer Regiment HQs	1				
Nebelwerfer Regiments	1				
Nebelwerfer Battalions	2				
Entgiftungs Battalions	2				
Machine Gun Battalions	1				
Anti-Tank Battalions	1				
SP Anti-Tank Battalions	2				
SP Hvy Anti-Tank Companies					
Assault Gun Battalions	2 2/3				
Flame Tank Battalions					
Mot Eng Reg HQs (Spec P)	7				
Mot Pionier Battalions	5				
(Mixed) Pionier Battalions	8	1		207	
Bridge Const Battalions	5		3		
Assault Boat Companies					
Mot Sep Bridge Cols B	26				
Sep Bridge Cols, Type (A-T)	14	1	1xH		
Arm Mine Clearing Battalions					
Luft Flak Corps HQs					
Luft Flak Reg HQs	3				
Luft Mixed Flak Battalions	8				
Luft Light Flak Battalions	3				
Construction Reg HQs	10				
Construction Battalions	29	1	128		
Railroad Eng Reg HQs	2	1	3		
Railroad Pionier Bat HQs	3				
Railroad Pionier Companies	18				
Railroad Switching Comp's	4				
Railroad Eng Const Comp's	7	1	201		
Railroad Eng Const Batts	3				
Mot Police Regiment HQ	1			Pol.Rgt Nord (& SS)**	1
Police Rifle Battalions	6			(53, 319, 321)^^, 105*^, 2^, 65^^	6
Mot Military Police Battalions	4			691	1
Mot Traffic Control Battalions	3	1	758		
Armoured Trains	3				

* Includes bicycle mounted 619th and 620th *Wach* battalions.

** Attached to 207th Security Division.

^ Attached to 281st Security Division.

^^ Attached to 285th Security Division.

** Police (& SS) Regiment Nord (refer text).   ^^ Attached to Pol.Rgt Nord.

* 143rd Coastal Artillery Battalion, arriving 29th June 1941 (mobile unit).

© Nigel Askey, 2018

Table German Deployment Matrix — Deployment and Composition of the German Army, Waffen SS and Luftwaffe Flak Units, 22nd June 1941

Army Group Centre

3rd Panzer Group (3rd Panzer Army from 1st January 1942)

	XXXIX Corps (Mot)		LVII Corps (Mot)		Pz Group Reserve	
	Description	No	Description	No	Description	No
Army & Panzer Group HQs					3Pz Grp HQ	1
Army HQs						
Corps HQs	39	1				
Panzer Corps HQs			57	1		
Army Group Rear Area HQs						
Army & Army Grp Signal Regs						
Army & Army Grp Signal Batts						
Panzer Group Signal Regs					3.PzGr	1
Infantry Divisions						
Panzer Divisions	7, 20	2	12, 19	2		
Motorised Divisions	14, 20	2	18	1		
SS Motorised Divisions						
Cavalry Divisions						
Mountain Divisions						
Light Divisions						
Fleiger Divisions						
Motorised Infantry Brigades						
Motorised Infantry Regiments						
Motorised Infantry Battalions						
(Mixed) Infantry Regiments						
(Mixed) Infantry Battalions						
Tank Brigades						
Tank Battalions						
Cavalry Regiments						
Security Divisions or Brigades						
Guard (*Wach*) Battalions					50*	1
Landesschutzen Battalions						
Artillery HQs, *Harko & Arko*	35	1	121	1		
Art Observation Battalions	30	1				
Artillery Reg HQs (Spec P)	69	1				
Mixed Artillery Battalions	II./70	1				
150mm How Battalions			II./55	1		
105mm Gun Battalions			427	1		
150mm Gun Battalions	620	1				
210mm How Battalions (1)	733	1	816	1		
210mm How Battalions (2)						
210mm Gun Battalions						
Hvy 240mm How Battalions						
Hvy 240mm Gun Battalions						

Unit		#		#		#
Super Hvy How Battalions						
Coastal Artillery Battalions						
Railroad Artillery Batteries						
Anti-Air Battalions						
Light Anti-Air Battalions	605	1				
SP Light AA Companies	1,/52*, 3,/59^	2	4,/52*	1		
Nebelwerfer Regiment HQs	51	1				
Nebelwerfer Regiments						
Nebelwerfer Battalions						
Entgiftungs Battalions						
Machine Gun Battalions						
Anti-Tank Battalions						
SP Anti-Tank Battalions	643	1				
SP Hvy Anti-Tank Companies	1,/8	1				
Assault Gun Battalions						
Flame Tank Battalions	101	1				
Mot Eng Reg HQs (Spec P)	614	1	504	1		
Mot Pionier Battalions	Lehr	1	47	1		
(Mixed) Pionier Battalions						
Bridge Const Battalions	210 (mot)	1	548	1		
Assault Boat Companies					905	1
Mot Sep Bridge Cols B	129, 1,/411, 2,/422, 626, 644, 653, 657	7	33, 1,/412, 537, 539	4		
Sep Bridge Cols, Type (A-T)						
Arm Mine Clearing Battalions						
Luft Flak Corps HQs						
Luft Flak Reg HQs	I,/36**	1	I,/29	1	149	1
Luft Mixed Flak Battalions	74, 84	2	73, 75	2		
Luft Light Flak Battalions						
Construction Reg HQs						
Construction Battalions	502RBi*^	1	506RBi^	1		
Railroad Eng Reg HQs						
Railroad Eng Reg HQs						
Railroad Pionier Bat HQs						
Railroad Pionier Companies						
Railroad Switching Comp's						
Railroad Eng Const Comp's						
Railroad Eng Const Batts						
Mot Police Regiment HQ						
Police Rifle Battalions						
Mot Military Police Battalions					551, 694	2
Mot Traffic Control Battalions						
Armoured Trains						

* 1,/52nd Lt AA Co was attached to 20th Mot Div.
^ 3,/59th Lt AA Co was attached to 7th Pz Div.
** One Battery detached to Pz Group Reserves.
*^ 502nd Road Construction Bicycle Battalion.

* 4,/52nd Lt AA Co was attached to 12th Pz Div.
^ 506th Road Construction Bicycle Battalion.

* Bicycle mounted with motorised support columns.

© Nigel Askey, 2018

Table German Deployment Matrix — Deployment and Composition of the German Army, Waffen SS and Luftwaffe Flak Units, 22nd June 1941

Army Group Centre — 9th Army

	V Corps Description	No	VI Corps Description	No	VIII Corps Description	No	XX Corps Description	No	XXXXII Corps* Description	No	Army Reserve Description	No
Army & Panzer Group HQs												
Army HQs											9	1
Corps HQs	5	1	6	1	8	1	20	1	42	1		
Panzer Corps HQs												
Army Group Rear Area HQs												
Army & Army Grp Signal Regs											511	1
Army & Army Grp Signal Batts												
Panzer Group Signal Regs												
Infantry Divisions	5, 35	2	6, 26	2	8, 28, 161	3	162, 256	2	87, 102, 129	3	110*, 106^	2
Panzer Divisions												
Motorised Divisions												
SS Motorised Divisions												
Cavalry Divisions												
Mountain Divisions												
Light Divisions												
Fleiger Divisions												
Motorised Infantry Brigades									1st SS Brig RF^	1	2nd Brig RFSS**, 900th Lehr*^	2
Motorised Infantry Regiments												
Motorised Infantry Battalions												
(Mixed) Infantry Regiments												
(Mixed) Infantry Battalions												
Tank Brigades												
Tank Battalions												
Cavalry Regiments												
Security Divisions or Brigades											403	1
Guard (*Wach*) Battalions											(508, 720, 721)^**, 705^^^	4
Landesschutzen Battalions											(591, 663, 989)^^^	3
Artillery HQs, *Harko & Arko*	22	1	126	1	131, 136, 145	3	18, 103, 107	3	114	1		
Art Observation Battalions	15	1	6	1	22, 25*	2	9, 11, 35	3				
Artillery Reg HQs (Spec P)					627, 677, 783, 801, 802	5	70, 606, 613	3				
Mixed Artillery Battalions			II./57	1	IV./109	1	II./51	1				
150mm How Battalions	847	1	848	1	II./44, III./111, 646	3	II./38, II./39	2				
105mm Gun Battalions	842	1			445, 634	2	II./62, 151	2				
150mm Gun Battalions					680	1						
210mm How Battalions (1)					808	1	635	1				
210mm How Battalions (2)					860, 861, 862	3						
210mm Gun Battalions												
Hvy 240mm How Battalions					I./84	1						
Hvy 240mm Gun Battalions					641, 815	2						
Super Hvy How Battalions							624	1				
Coastal Artillery Battalions												
Railroad Artillery Batteries												
Anti-Air Battalions			1./46, 6./47	2	607	1					271, 272	2
Light Anti-Air Battalions					5./48, 3./66	2						
SP Light AA Companies												

Unit Type	units	#	units	#	units	#	units	#	units	#
Nebelwerfer Regiment HQs						1				
Nebelwerfer Regiments					3, 5	2				
Nebelwerfer Battalions					103	1				
Entgiftungs Battalions										
Machine Gun Battalions										
Anti-Tank Battalions										
SP Anti-Tank Battalions										
SP Hvy Anti-Tank Companies										
Assault Gun Battalions					184	1	210	1	561	1
Flame Tank Battalions										
Mot Eng Reg Reg HQs (Spec P)					517	1	512	1		
Mot *Pionier* Battalions					43	1			630	1
(Mixed) *Pionier* Battalions	745	1	742, 743, 754	3	746, 753	2	632	1		
Bridge Const Battalions	145	1	84	1	54	1	7	1		
Assault Boat Companies										
Mot Sep Bridge Cols B	5, 35	2	6, 26, 534, 535	4	8, 28, 442	3	2./404, 612, 664	3		
Sep Bridge Cols, Type (A-T)										
Arm Mine Clearing Battalions									1**	1
Luft Flak Corps HQs										
Luft Flak Reg HQs									125	1
Luft Mixed Flak Battalions			II./491	1	L./Lehr	1	II./4	1	L./52, L/401, L/701	3
Luft Light Flak Battalions										
Construction Reg HQs	104	1	10	1	34, 39	2	42	1	17 Ob^^	1
Construction Battalions	154, 218	2	22, 80, 320, 321	4	57, 79, 91, 137, 208	5	18, 123	2	135, 214, 408, 532R, 580R	5
Railroad Eng Reg HQs									7	1
Railroad Pionier Bat HQs									L/2	1
Railroad Pionier Companies									8./1, 3./2, 4./2, 5./5, 1./6, 302(F)*^^	6
Railroad Switching Comp's									173	1
Railroad Eng Const Comp's									107, 121	2
Railroad Eng Const Batts									139	1
Mot Police Regiment HQ										
Police Rifle Battalions									131^^^	1
Mot Military Police Battalions									531***	1
Mot Traffic Control Battalions									752***	1
Armoured Trains							1, 3	2		

* VIII Corps also had the 4./6 Motorised Balloon Battery attached

* The XXXII Corps was held in OKH Reserves just prior to being assigned to 9th Army. It was assigned to 18th Army by August 1941.

^ 1st SS Brigade Reichsfuhrer (Mot). Arriving 23rd June to 29th June 1941.

* 110th arriving (from Wehrkreis X (B.d.E.)) 21st to 26th June 1941, (ass XXXII Corps).

^ 106th arriving (from Wehrkreis VI (B.d.E.)) 25th June to 1st July 1941, (ass XXXII Corps).

** 2nd (Mot) Brigade Reichsfuhrer SS, arriving 25th June to 3rd July 1941.

*^ 900th Lehr Brig (Mot), arriving 22nd June to 23rd June 1941 (ass XXXII Corps).

^^ Oberbaustab 17, (Brigade level HQ).

^ Guard (Wach) and Landesschutzen units, reporting to Korück 582.

*** Motorised units reporting to Korück 582.

**^ Redesignated the 300 Panzer-Abteilung zbV on 15th September 1941.

*^^ (F) Field Railroad Pionier Company.

^^^ Attached to 403rd Security Division.

Table German Deployment and Composition of the German Army, Waffen SS and Luftwaffe Flak Units, 22nd June 1941

Deployment Matrix — Army Group Centre — 4th Army

	XIII Corps Description	No	VII Corps Description	No	IX Corps Description	No	XXXXIII Corps Description	No	Army Reserve Description	No
Army & Panzer Group HQs										
Army HQs									4	1
Corps HQs	13	1	7	1	9	1	43	1		
Panzer Corps HQs										
Army Group Rear Area HQs										
Army & Army Grp Signal Regs									589	1
Army & Army Grp Signal Batts										
Panzer Group Signal Regs										
Infantry Divisions	17, 78	2	7, 23, 258, 268	4	137, 263, 292	3	131, 134, 252	3		3
Panzer Divisions										
Motorised Divisions										
SS Motorised Divisions										
Cavalry Divisions										
Mountain Divisions										
Light Divisions										
Fleiger Divisions										
Motorised Infantry Brigades										
Motorised Infantry Regiments										
Motorised Infantry Battalions										
(Mixed) Infantry Regiments										
(Mixed) Infantry Battalions										
Tank Brigades										
Tank Battalions										
Cavalry Regiments										
Security Divisions or Brigades			221	1					286	1
Guard (*Wach*) Battalions			701*	1					(551, 581, 582)***, 704^^^^	4
Landesschutzen Battalions			(230, 257, 302, 352)*	4					(285, 578)^^^^	2
Artillery HQs, *Harko* & *Arko*	17	1	7, 147	2	44	1	133, 139	2		
Art Observation Battalions			7	1	28	1	1, 36	2		
Artillery Reg HQs (Spec P)			41	1	622	1	697, 786	2		
Mixed Artillery Battalions					I./108	1				
150mm How Battalions			II./43, III./818	2	841	1	101	1		
105mm Gun Battalions			II./41	1	I./109	1	II./68, 711	2		
150mm Gun Battalions										
210mm How Battalions (1)			736	1	856	1	III./109	1	768	1
210mm How Battalions (2)			859	1						
210mm Gun Battalions										
Hvy 240mm How Battalions										
Hvy 240mm Gun Battalions										
Super Hvy How Battalions									2./833*	1/2
Coastal Artillery Battalions			710	1						
Railroad Artillery Batteries									701, 712^, (713, 765)**	4
Anti-Air Battalions									274, 276	2
Light Anti-Air Battalions			6/46, 6,/55	2			611	1		
SP Light AA Companies							4./46	1		

Unit Type	Col 1	Col 2	Col 3	Col 4	Col 5
Nebelwerfer Regiment HQs					
Nebelwerfer Regiments					
Nebelwerfer Battalions					
Entgiftungs Battalions					
Machine Gun Battalions					
Anti-Tank Battalions					
SP Anti-Tank Battalions					
SP Hvy Anti-Tank Companies			1		
Assault Gun Battalions		529 (1)	226 (1)	518 (1)	41 (1)
Flame Tank Battalions					
Mot Eng Reg HQs (Spec P)		674* (1)	516 (1)		
Mot Pionier Battalions		635 (1)	752 (1)	751 (1)	
(Mixed) Pionier Battalions		221 (1)	42 (1)	577 (1)	
Bridge Const Battalions		203 (1)	221 (1)		
Assault Boat Companies					
Mot Sep Bridge Cols B			7, 23, 137, 2./41, 1./402, 2./407 (6)	134 (1)	1./404, 606 (2)
Sep Bridge Cols, Type (A-T)				73B*, (2,9)C^, (45,178,183,187)T** (7)	
Arm Mine Clearing Battalions					
Luft Flak Corps HQs					
Luft Flak Reg HQs					153 (1)
Luft Mixed Flak Battalions		II,/14 (1)			
Luft Light Flak Battalions			L./24 (1)	L./231 (1)	
Construction Reg HQs		40 (1)	106 (1)	6 (1)	33, HQ W zbV*^, 10 Ob^^ (3)
Construction Battalions	9, 134 (2)	17, 129, 217, 571R (4)	63, 222, 410 (3)	24, 125, 213 (3)	97, 248, 544R, 576R, 584R, 676R, 133*^^ (7)
Railroad Eng Reg HQs					5 (1)
Railroad Pionier Bat HQs					II./2 (1)
Railroad Pionier Companies					1./1,2,/1,5,-/1,8,/4, 2,/5, 6,/5, 303(F),308(F)^* (8)
Railroad Switching Comp's					178, 179 (2)
Railroad Eng Const Comp's					109, 119 (2)
Railroad Eng Const Batts					83 (1)
Mot Police Regiment HQ					
Police Rifle Battalions		309* (1)			317^^^ (1)
Mot Military Police Battalions					581***^ (1)
Mot Traffic Control Battalions					747, 757**^ (2)
Armoured Trains	2 (1)			29 (1)	

Notes:

* Also had the 435th Engineer Supply Company attached.
* Attached to 221st Security Division.

* 73rd Type B Bridge Column, Equipment only (no motorised transport).
^ 2nd and 9th Type C Motorised Bridge Columns.
** 45th, 178th, 183rd and 187th Type T Motorised Bridge Columns.

* 2,/833rd Battery was equipped with 2 x 60cm Morser 'Karl' (Great 040), called "Odin" and "Thor".
^ 712th Railroad Artillery Battery reported to the 702nd Railroad Artillery Battalion HQ (not shown).
** 713th and 765th Railroad Artillery Batteries reported to the 679th Railroad Art Battalion HQ (not shown).
*^ Engineer Command HQ 'Weichsel' (special purpose), (Pion.Kdo.zbV Weichsel).
^^ Oberbaustab 10 (Brigade level HQ).
^ (F) Field Railroad Pionier Company.
*** Guard (Wach) units, reporting to Korück 580.
***^ Motorised units reporting to Korück 580.
*^^ The 133rd Construction Battalion reported directly to Korück 580.
^^^ Attached to 286th Security Division.

Table German Deployment Matrix

Deployment and Composition of the German Army, Waffen SS and Luftwaffe Flak Units, 22nd June 1941

Army Group Centre

2nd Panzer Group (2nd Panzer Army from 5th October 1941)

	XXXXVI Corps (Mot)		XXXXVII Corps (Mot)		XII Corps		XXIV Corps (Mot)		Pz Group Reserve		1st Flak Corps*	
	Description	No	Description	No	Description	No	Description	No	Description	No	Description	No
Army & Panzer Group HQs									2. Pz Grp HQ	1		
Army HQs												
Corps HQs					12	1						
Panzer Corps HQs	46	1	47	1			24	1				
Army Group Rear Area HQs												
Army & Army Grp Signal Regs												
Army & Army Grp Signal Batts												
Panzer Group Signal Regs									2. Pz Grp	1		
Infantry Divisions			167	1	31, 34, 45	3	267	1	255	1		
Panzer Divisions	10	1	17, 18	2			3, 4	2				
Motorised Divisions			29	1			10	1				
SS Motorised Divisions	SS Das R Division	1										
Cavalry Divisions							1*	1				
Mountain Divisions												
Light Divisions												
Fleiger Divisions												
Motorised Infantry Brigades												
Motorised Infantry Regiments	GD Inf Reg (Mot)	1										
Motorised Infantry Battalions												
(Mixed) Infantry Regiments												
(Mixed) Infantry Battalions												
Tank Brigades												
Tank Battalions												
Cavalry Regiments												
Security Divisions or Brigades									143**	1		
Guard (*Wach*) Battalions												
Landesschutzen Battalions												
Artillery HQs, *Harko & Arko*	101	1	146	1	112, 148	2	143	1	302 (Harko)*	1		
Art Observation Battalions			20	1	8, 17*	2						
Artillery Reg HQs (Spec P)			792	1	617, 788	2	623	1				
Mixed Artillery Battalions			II./71	1								
150mm How Battalions			422	1	II./66, 845	2	II./42	1				
105mm Gun Battalions			631	1	430, 709	2	II./69	1				
150mm Gun Battalions									740	1		
210mm How Battalions (1)			604	1	II./109, (682, 683, 684 Batter's)^	2	616	1	817	1		
210mm How Battalions (2)					854	1						
210mm Gun Battalions												
Hvy 240mm How Battalions												
Hvy 240mm Gun Battalions												
Super Hvy How Battalions												
Coastal Artillery Battalions												
Railroad Artillery Batteries												
Anti-Air Battalions					610	1		1	602	1		1
Light Anti-Air Battalions												

SP Light AA Companies	3./55*	1	1./59*, 1./66^, 631**	3	3./31	1	6./59^, 5./66**	2				
Nebelwerfer Regiment HQs					4	1						
Nebelwerfer Regiments			53*^	1								
Nebelwerfer Battalions					6, 8	2						
Entgiftungs Battalions					105	1						
Machine Gun Battalions									5	1		
Anti-Tank Battalions					654	1						
SP Anti-Tank Battalions			611	1			521*^, 543	2				
SP Hvy Anti-Tank Companies												
Assault Gun Battalions					192, 201	2						
Flame Tank Battalions			100	1								
Mot Eng Reg HQs (Spec P)	513	1	413	1	507	1	515	1				
Mot *Pionier* Battalions	85	1	42	1			45	1				
(Mixed) *Pionier* Battalions					215, 750	2			654^	1		
Bridge Const Battalions					4, 593	2	21	1	159 (mot)	1		
Assault Boat Companies									902	1		
Mot Sep Bridge Cols B	22	1	1./422	1	17, 31, 34, 81, 131, 2./409	6	2./403, 2./408	2	2./402	1		
Sep Bridge Cols, Type (A-T)							(74B, 75B)^^	2				
Arm Mine Clearing Battalions												
Luft Flak Corps HQs											1*	1
Luft Flak Reg HQs											101, 104	2
Luft Mixed Flak Battalions					I./26, I./704	2					I./12, I./22, I./11, II./11	4
Luft Light Flak Battalions									94	1	77, 91	2
Construction Reg HQs					24	1						
Construction Battalions			504RBi^^	1	11, 46, 402	3	103, 136, 503RBi^*	3				
Railroad Eng Reg HQs												
Railroad Pionier Bat HQs												
Railroad Pionier Companies												
Railroad Switching Comp's												
Railroad Eng Const Comp's												
Railroad Eng Const Batts												
Mot Police Regiment HQ												
Police Rifle Battalions												
Mot Military Police Battalions									591	1		
Mot Traffic Control Battalions									755*^	1		
Armoured Trains					27, 28**	2						
	* 3/55th Lt AA Co was attached to 10th Pz Div.		* 1./59th Lt AA Co was attached to 29th Mot Div. ^ 1./66th Lt AA Co was attached to 17th Pz Div. ** 631st Lt AA Co was attached to 18th Pz Div. *^ I./53 Battalion was attached to XXIV Corps. ^^ Road Construction Bicycle Battalion		* XII corps also had the 100 and 101 Motorised Balloon Batteries attached ^ Independent Artillery Batteries 682, 683 and 684 with 3 21cm Morser 18s in each fully motorised Battery. ** 28th Armoured Train was initially assigned to AG South. It was supposed to advance on Kovel, but remained with PZ 27 before Brest-Litovsk and remained in AG Centre.		* Includes the Lehr Recon Battalion ^ 6./59th Lt AA Co was attached to 3rd Pz Div. ** 5./66th Lt AA Co was attached to 4th Pz Div. *^ 521st SP AT Battalion also had 2x 10cm K 18 auf Pz-Sfl IVa att, in a separate Plat. ^^ 74th and 75th Bridge Columns, equipment only: missing mot transport. ^* Road Construction Bicycle Battalion		* HQ Higher Artillery Command (Division-level echelon artillery headquarters) Harko. ^ Attached to 255th Infantry Division ** Bicycle mounted with mot sup column. *^ AGC Reserve, assigned Pz Grp on 6th July.		* Attached from the Luftwaffe, Luftflotte 2 (2nd Air Fleet). The 101st Flak Regiment was assigned the 77th, I./12th and I./22th Flak Battalions. The 104th Flak Regiment was assigned the 91st, I./11th and II./11th Flak Battalions.	

Table German Deployment Matrix — Deployment and Composition of the German Army, Waffen SS and Luftwaffe Flak Units, 22nd June 1941

Deployment Matrix	Army Group Centre Reserve						AG CENTRE TOTAL
	LIII Corps		RHG 102		Reserve		
	Description	No	Description	No	Description	No	No
Army & Panzer Group HQs					AGC HQ	1	3
Army HQs							2
Corps HQs	53	1					11
Panzer Corps HQs			RHG 102	1			5
Army Group Rear Area HQs							1
Army & Army Grp Signal Regs					537	1	3
Army & Army Grp Signal Batts			213	1			1
Panzer Group Signal Regs							2
Infantry Divisions	293	1					33
Panzer Divisions							9
Motorised Divisions							5
SS Motorised Divisions							1
Cavalry Divisions							1
Mountain Divisions							
Light Divisions							
Fleiger Divisions							
Motorised Infantry Brigades							3
Motorised Infantry Regiments					10. & 12.III./800 zbV & Bat HQ**	1/8	1 1/8
Motorised Infantry Battalions							
(Mixed) Infantry Regiments			Sich.Rgt 2	1			1
(Mixed) Infantry Battalions							
Tank Brigades							
Tank Battalions							
Cavalry Regiments					SS Kav 1*^, SS Kav 2*^	2	2
Security Divisions or Brigades			(3 Sec Divs detached)				3
Guard (*Wach*) Battalions					58, 99. 122, 561	4	16
Landesschutzen Battalions			502	1			9
Artillery HQs, *Harko & Arko*	27	1					24
Art Observation Battalions							15
Artillery Reg HQs (Spec P)							17
Mixed Artillery Battalions							5
150mm How Battalions							16
105mm Gun Battalions							15
150mm Gun Battalions							3
210mm How Battalions (1)							11
210mm How Battalions (2)							6
210mm Gun Battalions							1
Hvy 240mm How Battalions							
Hvy 240mm Gun Battalions							1
Super Hvy How Battalions							
Coastal Artillery Battalions							3 1/2
Railroad Artillery Batteries							5

Unit Type	Count					
Anti-Air Battalions	4					
Light Anti-Air Battalions	5					
SP Light AA Companies	18	1				5./55
Nebelwerfer Regiment HQs	2					
Nebelwerfer Regiments	2					
Nebelwerfer Battalions	4					
Entgiftungs Battalions	3		132 R*	1		
Machine Gun Battalions	1					
Anti-Tank Battalions	1					
SP Anti-Tank Battalions	6					
SP Hvy Anti-Tank Companies	1					
Assault Gun Battalions	6					
Flame Tank Battalions	2					
Mot Eng Reg HQs (Spec P)	11					
Mot Pionier Battalions	9					
(Mixed) Pionier Battalions	13					
Bridge Const Battalions	12					
Assault Boat Companies	2					
Mot Sep Bridge Cols B	43					
Sep Bridge Cols, Type (A-T)	14	5				5xle.Z^, 800 Bri Trans Bat*
Arm Mine Clearing Battalions	1					
Luft Flak Corps HQs	1					
Luft Flak Reg HQs	5					
Luft Mixed Flak Battalions	17					
Luft Light Flak Battalions	7					
Construction Reg HQs	15				2	9, 15
Construction Battalions	46					
Railroad Eng Reg HQs	2					
Railroad Pionier Bat HQs	2					
Railroad Pionier Companies	14					
Railroad Switching Comp's	3					
Railroad Eng Const Comp's	4					
Railroad Eng Const Batts	2					
Mot Police Regiment HQ	1				1	Pol.Rgt Mitte (& SS)^
Police Rifle Battalions	6				3	(307, 316, 322)**
Mot Military Police Battalions	6	1				690
Mot Traffic Control Battalions	5					754
Armoured Trains	6					

* Road (Stra.) Battalion

* Attached to AGC HQ
^ Police (& SS) Regiment Mitte (refer text).
** Attached to Pol.Rgt Mitte.

* The 800th motorised Heavy Bridge Transport Battalion for transporting 5x Type le.Z. (Leicht Zerlegbar) Heavy Combat Bridges.

^ Equipment only, no motorisation.

** Lehr Reg Brandenburg 800 zbV: Special Forces. 10th & 12th Company, & III Battalion HQ. The 9th Company arrived on the East Front in September 1941.

*^ SS-Kavallerie-Regiments 1 and 2, attached to the HQ staff 'Reichsfuhrer SS' on 21st June 41. Formed into the SS Cavalry Brigade on 30th August 1941.

Table German Deployment Matrix

Deployment and Composition of the German Army, Waffen SS and Luftwaffe Flak Units, 22nd June 1941

Army Group South

6th Army

Deployment Matrix	XVII Corps Description	No	XXXXIV Corps Description	No	LV Corps* Description	No	Army Reserve Description	No
Army & Panzer Group HQs								
Army HQs							6	1
Corps HQs	17	1	44	1	55	1		
Panzer Corps HQs								
Army Group Rear Area HQs								
Army & Army Grp Signal Regs							549	1
Army & Army Grp Signal Batts								
Panzer Group Signal Regs								
Infantry Divisions	56, 62	2	9, 297	2	168	1		
Panzer Divisions								
Motorised Divisions								
SS Motorised Divisions								
Cavalry Divisions								
Mountain Divisions								
Light Divisions								
Fleiger Divisions								
Motorised Infantry Brigades								
Motorised Infantry Regiments								
Motorised Infantry Battalions								
(Mixed) Infantry Regiments								
(Mixed) Infantry Battalions								
Tank Brigades								
Tank Battalions								
Cavalry Regiments								
Security Divisions or Brigades							213*^^	1
Guard (Wach) Battalions							(522, 541, 542)*^, 703***^	4
Landesschutzen Battalions							(380, 552, 582, 637)**^	4
Artillery HQs, Harko & Arko	137	1	15	1				
Art Observation Battalions	16	1	32	1				
Artillery Reg HQs (Spec P)								
Mixed Artillery Battalions	II./40	1	II./65	1				
150mm How Battalions			II./46	1				
105mm Gun Battalions								
150mm Gun Battalions	3./800	1/3						
210mm How Battalions (1)								
210mm How Battalions (2)			867	1			767	1
210mm Gun Battalions								
Hvy 240mm How Battalions								
Hvy 240mm Gun Battalions								
Super Hvy How Battalions								
Coastal Artillery Battalions								
Railroad Artillery Batteries								
Anti-Air Battalions							278, 279	2

Unit Type	Units	No.	Units	No.	Units	No.	Units	No.
Light Anti-Air Battalions								
SP Light AA Companies	4./47	1	3./48	1			2./52	1
Nebelwerfer Regiment HQs								
Nebelwerfer Regiments								
Nebelwerfer Battalions								
Entgiftungs Battalions							133 R*	1
Machine Gun Battalions					673	1		
Anti-Tank Battalions								
SP Anti-Tank Battalions								
SP Hvy Anti-Tank Companies								
Assault Gun Battalions								
Flame Tank Battalions								
Mot Eng Reg HQs (Spec P)	604	1					50	1
Mot Pionier Battalions	652	1						
(Mixed) Pionier Battalions	255	1						
Bridge Const Battalions								
Assault Boat Companies							560	1
Mot Sep Bridge Cols B	9, 2./413	2	297, 676	2			99, 125	2
Sep Bridge Cols, Type (A-T)	1xFR*	1	1xB*	1	1xFR^	1	1xFR^	1
Arm Mine Clearing Battalions								
Luft Flak Corps HQs								
Luft Flak Reg HQs							91	1
Luft Mixed Flak Battalions							I./8, I./9, II./241	3
Luft Light Flak Battalions								
Construction Reg HQs	23	1					26, 36, 37, II Fr Ob**	4
Construction Battalions	1, 146, 153	3	107, 216	2			64,130,155,161,407, 521R, 523Rmot***, 538Rmot***, 540R	9
Railroad Eng Reg HQs							6	1
Railroad Pionier Bat HQs							II./4	1
Railroad Pionier Companies							6./3, 2./7, 7./2, 7./4, 6./6, 8./6, 304(F)^	7
Railroad Switching Comp's							176, 180	2
Railroad Eng Const Comp's							110, 113	2
Railroad Eng Const Batts							513	1
Mot Police Regiment HQ							318**^	1
Police Rifle Battalions							541^^, 571	2
Mot Military Police Battalions							759^^	1
Mot Traffic Control Battalions								
Armoured Trains							4, 7	2

* Equipment only, no motorisation.

* Equipment only, no motorisation.

* LV Corps was in 6th Army Reserve.
^ Equipment only, no motorisation.

* Road (Stra.) Battalion.
^ Equipment only, no motorisation.
** Stab Fest.Pi.Kdr. II (Fortress Eng Construction Brig 2 HQ) Redesignated Oberbaustab 22 on 1st Nov 41.
*^ The 522nd, 541st, 542nd (Wach) Guard Infantry Battalions reported to Korück 585.
^^ Motorised units reporting to Korück 585.
^^ (F) Field Railroad Pionier Company.
*** Motorised road construction battalions
**^ Attached to 213th Security Division.
*^^ The 213th Security Div was detached from RHG 103 (Army GS).

© Nigel Askey, 2018

Table German Deployment Matrix — Deployment and Composition of the German Army, Waffen SS and Luftwaffe Flak Units, 22nd June 1941

Army Group South

1st Panzer Group (1st Panzer Army from 25th October 1941)

	III Corps (Mot) Description	No	XXIX Corps Description	No	XXXXVIII Corps (Mot) Description	No	XIV Corps (Mot) Description	No	Pz Group Reserve Description	No	2nd Flak Corps Description	No
Army & Panzer Group HQs									1Pz. Grp HQ	1		
Army HQs												
Corps HQs			29	1								
Panzer Corps HQs	3	1			48	1	14	1				
Army Group Rear Area HQs												
Army & Army Grp Signal Regs												
Army & Army Grp Signal Batts												
Panzer Group Signal Regs									1.PzGr	1		
Infantry Divisions	44, 298	2	111, 299	2	57, 75	2	9, 16	2				
Panzer Divisions	14	1			11	1			13^^	1		
Motorised Divisions									16^*, 25^^	2		
SS Motorised Divisions							SS W Division	1				
Cavalry Divisions												
Mountain Divisions												
Light Divisions												
Fleiger Divisions												
Motorised Infantry Brigades									LSSAH Mot Brigade***	7/8		
Motorised Infantry Regiments									3.I./800zbV**	1/16		
Motorised Infantry Battalions												
(Mixed) Infantry Regiments												
(Mixed) Infantry Battalions												
Tank Brigades												
Tank Battalions												
Cavalry Regiments												
Security Divisions or Brigades												
Guard (*Wach*) Battalions									45***^	1		
Landesschutzen Battalions												
Artillery HQs, *Harko & Arko*	3, 127	2	102	1	108, 124, 134	3			301 (Harko), 129	2		
Art Observation Battalions	13	1	44	1	3*	1						
Artillery Reg HQs (Spec P)	511, 704	2	614	1	612, 619	2			602	1		
Mixed Artillery Battalions												
150mm How Battalions	II./63	1			844	1						
105mm Gun Battalions	II./60	1	849	1	II./64, 852	2						
150mm Gun Battalions	731, I./2,/800	1 2/3										
210mm How Battalions (1)	607, 735	2			732, 777	2						
210mm How Battalions (2)	857	1	858	1								
210mm Gun Battalions												
Hvy 240mm How Battalions	I./814	1			II./814	1						
Hvy 240mm Gun Battalions												
Super Hvy How Battalions												
Coastal Artillery Battalions												
Railroad Artillery Batteries												
Anti-Air Battalions												
Light Anti-Air Battalions												
SP Light AA Companies	2,/608*	1	2,/48	1	5,/46, 1,/608^	2	3,/47*, 6,/66^	2	4,/31, 6,/31*, 5,/59, 4,/66^	4		
Nebelwerfer Regiment HQs						2						

Unit	Desig	#	Desig	#	Desig	#	Desig	#	Desig	#	Desig	#
Nebelwerfer Regiments	54	1										
Nebelwerfer Battalions					Nebel-Lehr-Reg 4**	1						
Entgiftungs Battalions					104	1						
Machine Gun Battalions	652	1										
Anti-Tank Battalions												
SP Anti-Tank Battalions												
SP Hvy Anti-Tank Companies	191	1			197	1			670	1		
Assault Gun Battalions												
Flame Tank Battalions					520	1			700	1		
Mot Eng Reg HQs (Spec P)	511	1										
Mot Pionier Battalions	627	1	667	1	51, 651	2						
(Mixed) Pionier Battalions	260	1	213	1	672	1						
Bridge Const Battalions			37	1	699	1						
Assault Boat Companies												
Mot Sep Bridge Cols B	298, 1./427, 602, 616	4	111, 610	2	80, 94, 672	3			901	1		
Sep Bridge Cols, Type (A-T)	1xFR^, 1xB^	2			1xFR*^	1			112, 615	2		
Arm Mine Clearing Battalions							60**	1				
Luft Flak Corps HQs											2*	1
Luft Flak Reg HQs											6, Gen Goring (GG)	2
Luft Mixed Flak Battalions											I./7,I./24,II./26,I./GG,II./43	5
Luft Light Flak Battalions					71	1	86	1			93, IV./GG, 74, 83, 84	5
Construction Reg HQs					45	1						
Construction Battalions	110, 119, 501RBi**	3	115, 244	2	52, 112	2						
Railroad Eng Reg HQs												
Railroad Pionier Bat HQs												
Railroad Pionier Companies												
Railroad Switching Comp's												
Railroad Eng Const Comp's												
Railroad Eng Const Batts												
Mot Police Regiment HQ												
Police Rifle Battalions												
Mot Military Police Battalions												
Mot Traffic Control Battalions							8./3	1				
Armoured Trains									682, 685	2		

Notes:

* 2./608th Lt AA Co was attached to 14th Pz. Div.
^ Equipment only, no motorisation.
** Road Construction Bicycle Battalion.

* XXXXVIII Corps also had the 4./1 Motorised Balloon Battery attached.
^ 1./608th Lt AA Co was attached to 11th Pz Div.
** 3./4 Battery was attached to XXXXIV Corps, 6th Army.
*^ Equipment only, no motorisation.

* 3./47th Lt AA Co was attached to 9th Pz. Div.
^ 6./66 Lt AA Co was attached to 16th Pz. Div.
** The 60th Mot Pionier Battalion had 2 Type B Bridge Columns(1-2./60). It was attached directly to the XIV Corps (Mot) HQ.

* 6./31st Lt AA Co was attached to 16th Mot Div.
^ 4./66th Lt AA Co was attached to 13th Pz Div.
** Lehr Reg Brandenburg 800 zbV; Special Forces, 3rd Company / 1 Battalion
^^ Assigned to III Corps (Mot) on 23rd June 1941.
^^ Assigned to XXXXVIII Corps (Mot) by 24th June 1941
^^^ Assigned to III Corps (Mot) by 30th June 1941. The LSSAH's 4th Battalion remained in the West as Hitler's bodyguard unit.
*^^ Bicycle mounted with mot sup columns.

* The 6th Flak Regiment was assigned the 93rd, I./7th I./24th and II./26th Flak Battalions.
The GG Flak Regiment was assigned the IV./GG, 74th, 83rd, 84th, I./GG and II./43rd Flak Battalions.

Table German Deployment Matrix — Deployment and Composition of the German Army, Waffen SS and Luftwaffe Flak Units, 22nd June 1941

Army Group South

17th Army

	IV Corps Description	IV Corps No	XXXXIX Mtn Corps Description	XXXXIX Mtn Corps No	LII Corps* Description	LII Corps* No	Army Reserve* Description	Army Reserve* No
Army & Panzer Group HQs								
Army HQs							17*	1
Corps HQs	4	1	49	1	52	1		
Panzer Corps HQs								
Army Group Rear Area HQs								
Army & Army Grp Signal Regs							596	1
Army & Army Grp Signal Batts								
Panzer Group Signal Regs								
Infantry Divisions	24, 71, 262, 295, 296	5	68, 257	2				
Panzer Divisions								
Motorised Divisions								
SS Motorised Divisions								
Cavalry Divisions								
Mountain Divisions			1st Mtn	1				
Light Divisions					101	1	97, 100	2
Fleiger Divisions								
Motorised Infantry Brigades								
Motorised Infantry Regiments								
Motorised Infantry Battalions							2.I./800zbV, 4.I./800 zbV & Bat HQ^^	1/8
(Mixed) Infantry Regiments								
(Mixed) Infantry Battalions			372 Mtn*	1/3	500 zbV^	1		
Tank Brigades								
Tank Battalions								
Cavalry Regiments								
Security Divisions or Brigades					(444, 454)**	2	(602, 617)**	2
Guard (*Wach*) Battalions					708*^	1		
Landesschutzen Battalions					(231, 258, 264, 901)*^, (416, 566, 987, 988)^^	8		
Artillery HQs, *Harko* & *Arko*	140, 144	2	132	1				
Art Observation Battalions	21, 23	2	27	1				
Artillery Reg HQs (Spec P)	213**	1	501	1				
Mixed Artillery Battalions	II./52	1						
150mm How Battalions	851, IV./207*^, IV./213*^	3	IV./221^	1				
105mm Gun Battalions			II./53	1			863	1
150mm Gun Battalions								
210mm How Battalions (1)								
210mm How Battalions (2)	855	1						
210mm Gun Battalions								
Hvy 240mm How Battalions								
Hvy 240mm Gun Battalions								
Super Hvy How Battalions	1./833*	1/2						
Coastal Artillery Battalions								
Railroad Artillery Batteries	(1./725, 2./725)^*	2					275, 277	2
Anti-Air Battalions							22	1
Light Anti-Air Battalions							2/66	1
SP Light AA Companies	1./48	1	6/48	1				

Unit Type	#	Unit(s)	#	Unit(s)	#	Unit(s)	#	Unit(s)
Nebelwerfer Regiment HQs								
Nebelwerfer Regiments								
Nebelwerfer Battalions								
Entgiftungs Battalions							1	102
Machine Gun Battalions			1	525				
Anti-Tank Battalions								
SP Anti-Tank Battalions								
SP Hvy Anti-Tank Companies								
Assault Gun Battalions	1	243						
Flame Tank Battalions	1	102^						
Mot Eng Reg HQs (Spec P)	1	601						
Mot Pionier Battalions			1	620				
(Mixed) Pionier Battalions	1	74	2	73, 658			1	531
Bridge Const Battalions					1	101		
Assault Boat Companies								
Mot Sep Bridge Cols B			2	54, 639			4	97, 100, 2./410, 667
Sep Bridge Cols, Type (A-T)	1	24						
Arm Mine Clearing Battalions								
Luft Flak Corps HQs								
Luft Flak Reg HQs							1	42
Luft Mixed Flak Battalions							3	II./24, L/37, L/61
Luft Light Flak Battalions							4	1, 18, 107, 7 Ob^
Construction Reg HQs					1	8		
Construction Battalions	1	94	1	105	1	403	12	2, 51, 96, 109, 131, 144, 156, 305, 404, 551R, 559R, 563R
Railroad Eng Reg HQs								
Railroad Pionier Bat HQs								
Railroad Pionier Companies								
Railroad Switching Comp's								
Railroad Eng Const Comp's								
Railroad Eng Const Batts								
Mot Police Regiment HQ								
Police Rifle Battalions					2	82^^, 311*^	1	693*^
Mot Military Police Battalions							1	760*^
Mot Traffic Control Battalions					1	31		
Armoured Trains								

* 1./833rd Battery was equipped with 2 x 60cm Morser 'Karl' (Gerat 040), called 'Adam' and 'Eva'. The 833rd Battalion HQ was also present in IV Corps.
^ 102nd Flame Tank Battalion had Pz-Char B Flamm(f) tanks. Assigned to the 24th Infantry Division on 24th June.
** Mixed Transport Artillery Reg HQ
*^ Horse Drawn Artillery Battalions IV./207 and IV./213.
^* The 725th Railroad Artillery Battalion HQ was also present.

* 372nd Mountain Infantry Company (bicycle mounted).
^ Horse Drawn Artillery Battalion IV./221.

* Also controlled the Slovak 'Mobile Group', otherwise known as the Pilfousek Fast Brigade.
^ 500th Infantry Battalion for special purpose. Note, as far as is known, 500 zbV was a penal unit (possibly bicycle mounted).
** Detached from RHG 103 - AG South.
*^ Attached to 444th Security Division.
^^ Attached to 454th Security Division.

* The 17th Army also controlled the Slovakian 1st Field Corps with the 1st and 2nd Slovak Infantry Divisions.
^ Oberbaustab 7 (Brigade level HQ)
** The 602nd and 617th Guard-Watch (Wach) Infantry Battalions reported to Korück 550.
*^ Motorised units reporting to Korück 550.
^^ Lehr Reg Brandenburg 800 zbV; Special Forces. 2nd and 4th Company, and 1 Battalion HQ.

© Nigel Askey, 2018

Table German Deployment Matrix — Deployment and Composition of the German Army, Waffen SS and Luftwaffe Flak Units, 22nd June 1941

Army Group South

11th Army**

Deployment Matrix	XI Corps* Description	No	XXX Corps* Description	No	LIV Corps* Description	No	Army Reserve* Description	No
Army & Panzer Group HQs								
Army HQs							11	1
Corps HQs	11	1	30	1	54	1		
Panzer Corps HQs								
Army Group Rear Area HQs							558	1
Army & Army Grp Signal Regs								
Army & Army Grp Signal Batts								
Panzer Group Signal Regs								
Infantry Divisions	76, 239	2	198	2	50, 170	2	22^, 72**	2
Panzer Divisions								
Motorised Divisions								
SS Motorised Divisions								
Cavalry Divisions								
Mountain Divisions								
Light Divisions								
Fleiger Divisions								
Motorised Infantry Brigades								
Motorised Infantry Regiments							6.II./800zbV^^^	1/16
Motorised Infantry Battalions								
(Mixed) Infantry Regiments								
(Mixed) Infantry Battalions								
Tank Brigades								
Tank Battalions								
Cavalry Regiments								
Security Divisions or Brigades								
Guard (*Wach*) Battalions							(49, 552)**^	2
Landesschutzen Battalions							(349, 514, 563, 885)*^, 836**^	5
Artillery HQs, *Harko & Arko*	6, 138	2	110	1	20	1		
Art Observation Battalions	34	1	31	1	29	1		
Artillery Reg HQs (Spec P)	787	1	49	1				
Mixed Artillery Battalions			II./54	1				
150mm How Battalions	154^	1	I./77^	1	737^	1		
105mm Gun Battalions	II./818	1						
150mm Gun Battalions								
210mm How Battalions (1)								
210mm How Battalions (2)								
210mm Gun Battalions								
Hvy 240mm How Battalions								
Hvy 240mm Gun Battalions								
Super Hvy How Battalions								
Coastal Artillery Battalions					901, 903, 906	3	789, 'Breslau' Battery, 'Tirpitz' Battery^^^	2
Railroad Artillery Batteries							688^^^	1
Anti-Air Battalions								
Light Anti-Air Battalions								
SP Light AA Companies							1/47	1

Unit Type				Units	No.
Nebelwerfer Regiment HQs					
Nebelwerfer Regiments					
Nebelwerfer Battalions					
Entgiftungs Battalions					
Machine Gun Battalions	560	1			
Anti-Tank Battalions	1/190	1/3			2/3
SP Anti-Tank Battalions					
SP Hvy Anti-Tank Companies					
Assault Gun Battalions				2./190, 3./190	2/3
Flame Tank Battalions					
Mot Eng Reg HQs (Spec P)				617, 690	2
Mot *Pionier* Battalions	46	1		70	1
(Mixed) *Pionier* Battalions				741, 744	2
Bridge Const Battalions				521, 552, 624, 646, 4./17(Ersatz Co)	4 1/4
Assault Boat Companies				903	1
Mot Sep Bridge Cols B	620	1	2./405, 668	2	88, 1./410, 2./427, 2./430, 533, 536, 624	7
Sep Bridge Cols, Type (A-T)				2x s.S.***	2
Arm Mine Clearing Battalions					
Luft Flak Corps HQs					
Luft Flak Reg HQs				18	1
Luft Mixed Flak Battalions				I./14, L/43, L/64	3
Luft Light Flak Battalions					
Construction Reg HQs				14 Ob^^, 19 Ob^^	2
Construction Battalions				86, 505R, 597R, 678R, 61Fr, 40Fr^^	6
Railroad Eng Reg HQs					
Railroad Pionier Bat HQs				II./1	1
Railroad Pionier Companies				2./2, 5./4, 3./7, 5/7	4
Railroad Switching Comp's				175	1
Railroad Eng Const Comp's				113, 126, 143	3
Railroad Eng Const Batts					
Mot Police Regiment HQ					
Police Rifle Battalions					
Mot Military Police Battalions				683*^^	1
Mot Traffic Control Battalions				756	1
Armoured Trains					

* Also contained the 6th Rumanian Cavalry Brigade, and main elements of the 1st Rumanian Armoured Division (refer Rumanian Deployment Matrix).
^ 154th How Battalion equipped with Czech sFH 35 (t) Howitzers.
** The German 11th Army supposedly came under Army Group Antonescu control, but in practice it reported directly to AGS.

* Also contained the 8th, 13th and 14th Rumanian Infantry Divisions (refer Rumanian Deployment Matrix).
^ I./77th How Battalion equipped with Czech sFH 35 (t) Howitzers

* The 5th Rumanian Infantry Division was attached to the German LIV Corps on 27th June 1941 (refer Rumanian Deployment Matrix).
^ 737th How Battalion equipped with Czech sFH 35 (t) Howitzers.

* 11th Army also controlled the Rumanian Mountain Corps and Rumanian Cavalry Corps in late June-July 1941 (Refer Rumanian Deployment Matrix - Volume IV).
^ "The 22nd was an "Air Landing", Infantry Division.
** Assigned to *Deutsche Heeresmission Rumanien*.
*^ The 349th, 514th, 563rd and 885th, were *Landesschutzen* (Mobilised Militia) Battalions used for security duties under the LS-Rgt 108 zbV HQ. They were all assigned to *Deutsche Heeresmission Rumanien*.
^^ Oberbaustab 14 and 19 (Brigade level HQs).
^* Only the 1./40 was available. Companies 2./40 and 3./40 arriving from the West.
*** Equipment only, no motorised transport.
^ Guard (*Wach*) Battalions, reporting to Korück 553.
*^^ Motorised unit reporting to Korück 553.
^^^ German Coastal Artillery Group, attached to the Rumanian coast defence forces defending Constanta harbour.
^^^ Lehr Reg Brandenburg 800 zbV; Special Forces. 6th Company / II Battalion.

Table German Deployment Matrix — Deployment and Composition of the German Army, Waffen SS and Luftwaffe Flak Units, 22nd June 1941

Army Group South

Unit	Army Group South Reserve* — Reserve Description	Reserve No	RHG 103 Description	RHG 103 No	AG SOUTH TOTAL No
Army & Panzer Group HQs	AGS HQ	1			2
Army HQs					3
Corps HQs					10
Panzer Corps HQs			RHG 103	1	3
Army Group Rear Area HQs					1
Army & Army Grp Signal Regs	570^	1			4
Army & Army Grp Signal Batts			221	1	1
Panzer Group Signal Regs					1
Infantry Divisions					25
Panzer Divisions					5
Motorised Divisions					2
SS Motorised Divisions					1
Cavalry Divisions					
Mountain Divisions					1
Light Divisions	99	1			4
Fleiger Divisions					
Motorised Infantry Brigades					7/8
Motorised Infantry Regiments					1/4
Motorised Infantry Battalions					
(Mixed) Infantry Regiments			Sich.Rgt 4**	1	1
(Mixed) Infantry Battalions					1 1/3
Tank Brigades					
Tank Battalions					
Cavalry Regiments					
Security Divisions or Brigades					3
Guard (*Wach*) Battalions	126	1			11
Landesschutzen Battalions	382	1	286	1	19
Artillery HQs, *Harko & Arko*					17
Art Observation Battalions					11
Artillery Reg HQs (Spec P)					9
Mixed Artillery Battalions					5
150mm How Battalions					10
105mm Gun Battalions					7
150mm Gun Battalions					2
210mm How Battalions (1)					4
210mm How Battalions (2)					4
210mm Gun Battalions					1
Hvy 240mm How Battalions					2
Hvy 240mm Gun Battalions					
Super Hvy How Battalions					1/2

Unit Type	Identifiers / Notes	Sub-count	Total
Coastal Artillery Battalions			5
Railroad Artillery Batteries			3
Anti-Air Battalions			4
Light Anti-Air Battalions			1
SP Light AA Companies	2./46	1	18
Nebelwerfer Regiment HQs			1
Nebelwerfer Regiments			2
Nebelwerfer Battalions			1
Entgiftungs Battalions			3
Machine Gun Battalions	9	1	1
Anti-Tank Battalions			3
SP Anti-Tank Battalions			1
SP Hvy Anti-Tank Companies			
Assault Gun Battalions			4
Flame Tank Battalions			1
Mot Eng Reg HQs (Spec P)			10
Mot Pionier Battalions			7
(Mixed) Pionier Battalions	41	1	9
Bridge Const Battalions			10 1/4
Assault Boat Companies			2
Mot Sep Bridge Cols B	102, 106, 110, 113	4	39
Sep Bridge Cols, Type (A-T)	3x s.S.**	3	12
Arm Mine Clearing Battalions			
Luft Flak Corps HQs			1
Luft Flak Reg HQs			5
Luft Mixed Flak Battalions			14
Luft Light Flak Battalions			7
Construction Reg HQs	103	1	14
Construction Battalions	16, 219, 221, 246	4	46
Railroad Eng Reg HQs			1
Railroad Pionier Bat HQs			2
Railroad Pionier Companies			12
Railroad Switching Comp's			3
Railroad Eng Const Comp's			5
Railroad Eng Const Batts			1
Mot Police Regiment HQ			1
Police Rifle Battalions	Pol.Rgt Sud (& SS)*	1	6
	(45, 303, 314)^	3	
	692	1	
Mot Military Police Battalions			7
Mot Traffic Control Battalions			3
Armoured Trains			3

* AG South also had control of Army Group Antonescu (Refer Rumanian Deployment Matrix).

^ Attached to AGS HQ.

** Equipment only, no motorised transport.

* Police (& SS) Regiment Sud (refer text).

^ Attached to Pol.Rgt Sud.

** Includes bicycle mounted 613rd and 614th Wach battalions.

© Nigel Askey, 2018

Table German Deployment Matrix — Deployment and Composition of the German Army, Waffen SS and Luftwaffe Flak Units, 22nd June 1941.

Norway Army — *Befehlsstelle Finnland* (East Front Only)

Deployment Matrix	Norway Mtn Corps Description	No	HoH. Kdo XXXVI*** Description	No	Bef. Finn. Reserve* Description	No	Bef Finn TOTAL No
Army & Panzer Group HQs							
Army HQs							
Corps HQs	Norwegen Mtn	1	36***	1	(3rd Finnish Corps)*	1	2
Panzer Corps HQs							
Army Group Rear Area HQs							
Army & Army Grp Signal Regs							
Army & Army Grp Signal Batts	463	1			(644zbV, 695zbV)**	2	3
Panzer Group Signal Regs							
Infantry Divisions			169	1	163^, (+ 3rd, 6th Fin)*	1	2
Panzer Divisions							
Motorised Divisions							
SS Motorised Divisions							
Cavalry Divisions							
Mountain Divisions	2nd Mtn*^, 3rd Mtn	2					2
Light Divisions							
Fleiger Divisions							
Motorised Infantry Brigades			SS Kampfgruppe Nord**	1			1
Motorised Infantry Regiments							
Motorised Infantry Battalions							
(Mixed) Infantry Regiments							
(Mixed) Infantry Battalions							
Tank Brigades							
Tank Battalions			211^, 40 zbV*	2			2
Cavalry Regiments							
Security Divisions or Brigades							
Guard (*Wach*) Battalions							
Landesschutzen Battalions							
Artillery HQs, *Harko & Arko*							
Art Observation Battalions							
Artillery Reg HQs (Spec P)							
Mixed Artillery Battalions	1./477*	1/3					1/3
150mm How Battalions							
105mm How Battalions	1./, 2./, 3./730^	1					1
150mm Gun Battalions							
210mm How Battalions (1)							
210mm How Battalions (2)							
210mm Gun Battalions							
Hvy 240mm How Battalions							
Hvy 240mm Gun Battalions							
Super Hvy How Battalions							
Coastal Artillery Battalions	(498, 504)**	2	496^^, 520^*	2			4
Railroad Artillery Batteries					655	1	1
Anti-Air Battalions							
Light Anti-Air Battalions							

Unit Type						Unit Type	
SP Light AA Companies						SP Light AA Companies	
Nebelwerfer Regiment HQs						Nebelwerfer Regiment HQs	
Nebelwerfer Regiments						Nebelwerfer Regiments	
Nebelwerfer Battalions			8./222	1/3	1/3	Nebelwerfer Battalions	
Entgiftungs Battalions						Entgiftungs Battalions	
Machine Gun Battalions						Machine Gun Battalions	
Anti-Tank Battalions	1	463			1	Anti-Tank Battalions	
SP Anti-Tank Battalions						SP Anti-Tank Battalions	
SP Hvy Anti-Tank Companies						SP Hvy Anti-Tank Companies	
Assault Gun Battalions						Assault Gun Battalions	
Flame Tank Battalions						Flame Tank Battalions	
Mot Eng Reg HQs (Spec P)						Mot Eng Reg HQs (Spec P)	
Mot Pionier Battalions						Mot Pionier Battalions	
(Mixed) Pionier Battalions						(Mixed) Pionier Battalions	
Bridge Const Battalions						Bridge Const Battalions	
Assault Boat Companies						Assault Boat Companies	
Mot Sep Bridge Cols B						Mot Sep Bridge Cols B	
Sep Bridge Cols, Type (A-T)			(206A, 207A, 213A, 221A, 239A)*^			Sep Bridge Cols, Type (A-T)	
Arm Mine Clearing Battalions			5	5	5	Arm Mine Clearing Battalions	
Luft Flak Corps HQs						Luft Flak Corps HQs	
Luft Flak Reg HQs	1/5					Luft Flak Reg HQs	
Luft Mixed Flak Battalions	1		1	467*^	2	Luft Mixed Flak Battalions	
Luft Light Flak Battalions						Luft Light Flak Battalions	
Construction Reg HQs		405	43	1	1	Construction Reg HQs	
Construction Battalions	1		406, 409	2	3	Construction Battalions	
Railroad Eng Reg HQs						Railroad Eng Reg HQs	
Railroad Pionier Bat HQs						Railroad Pionier Bat HQs	
Railroad Pionier Companies						Railroad Pionier Companies	
Railroad Switching Comp's						Railroad Switching Comp's	
Railroad Eng Const Comp's						Railroad Eng Const Comp's	
Railroad Eng Const Batts			5./2, 8./2, 4./4	3	3	Railroad Eng Const Batts	
Mot Police Regiment HQ						Mot Police Regiment HQ	
Police Rifle Battalions						Police Rifle Battalions	
Mot Military Police Battalions						Mot Military Police Battalions	
Mot Traffic Control Battalions						Mot Traffic Control Battalions	
Armoured Trains						Armoured Trains	

Left notes:

* 1./477th Artillery Battery was semi-motorised and equipped with 12cm Ex Norwegian Howitzers.

^ 730th Artillery Battalion was equipped with 3 Batteries of 10.5cm K35 (t) Czech guns. All Batteries were semi-motorised only. The HQ was not reformed until November 1941.

** Total of 7 Coastal Artillery Batteries.

*^ The 9the SS Motorised Infantry Regiment was attached SS Kampfgruppe Nord.

Middle notes:

* 40th Tank Battalion for Special Purposes. Moving from Denmark. The 3./40 Company was detached to the III Finnish Corps prior to the attack.

^ Equipped with captured French Tanks.

** Also called SS-Brigade Nord. One Regiment, the 9 SS, was attached to the 2nd Mtn Division.

*^ Equipment only, no transport. All assigned to the 169th Infantry Division.

^^ 2 Coastal Artillery Batteries only.

*^ 2 Light Artillery Batteries and 1 Hvy Artillery Battery (all motorised).

*** The HoH. Kdo XXXVI was redesignated XXXVI Gebirgskorps (Mtn Corps) on 18th Nov 1941.

Right notes:

* Befehlsstelle Finnland also controlled the III Finnish Corps with the 3rd and 6th Finnish Infantry Divisions, (refer Finnish Deployment Matrix; Volume IV).

^ 163rd was in the Finnish Karelian Army under Finnish control. It also reported to the German Special Corps Command LXX on 22nd June 41.

** Grouped under 550 zbV Signal Regiment HQ. 550 zbV also controlled the 467 Corps Signal Battalion, seconded from the Norwegen Mountain Corps. The 467th Corps Signal Battalion is included in the TOE for the Norwegen Mtn Corps HQ.

*^ 2./467 and 4./467 were detached to XXXVI Corps.

Table German Deployment Matrix

Deployment and Composition of the German Army, Waffen SS and Luftwaffe Flak Units, 22nd June 1941

| | OKH Reserves* | | | | | | | | | | | | OKH Res TOTAL |
| | 2nd Army* | | L Corps* | | HoH. Kdo. XXXV* | | HoH. Kdo. XXXIV* | | LI Corps* | | Unassigned | | |
	Description	No	Description	No	Description	No	Description	No	Description	No	Description	No	No
Army & Panzer Group HQs													
Army HQs	2	1											1
Corps HQs			50	1	35	1	34	1	51	1			4
Panzer Corps HQs													
Army Group Rear Area HQs													
Army & Army Grp Signal Regs	563	1									HQs for (597zbV, 598zbV, 604zbV)*		1
Army & Army Grp Signal Batts													
Panzer Group Signal Regs													
Infantry Divisions			86^, Police Div**	2	15^, 52**, 112*^, 197^^	4	113^, 125, 132**	3	79^, 95**	2			11
Panzer Divisions													
Motorised Divisions													
SS Motorised Divisions													
Cavalry Divisions													
Mountain Divisions							4th Mtn	1					1
Light Divisions													
Fleiger Divisions													
Motorised Infantry Brigades													
Motorised Infantry Regiments													
Motorised Infantry Battalions													
(Mixed) Infantry Regiments													
(Mixed) Infantry Battalions													
Tank Brigades													
Tank Battalions													
Cavalry Regiments													
Security Divisions or Brigades													
Guard (Wach) Battalions													
Landesschutzen Battalions											235	1	1
Artillery HQs, Harko & Arko	149	1	31	1					106	1			3
Art Observation Battalions													
Artillery Reg HQs (Spec P)	109	1											1
Mixed Artillery Battalions													
150mm How Battalions													
105mm Gun Battalions													
150mm Gun Battalions													
210mm How Battalions (1)													
210mm How Battalions (2)													
210mm Gun Battalions													
Hvy 240mm How Battalions													
Hvy 240mm Gun Battalions													
Super Hvy How Battalions													
Coastal Artillery Battalions													
Railroad Artillery Batteries													
Anti-Air Battalions													
Light Anti-Air Battalions											603, 614	2	2
SP Light AA Companies											5./47	1	1

Unit Type	Values
Nebelwerfer Regiment HQs	
Nebelwerfer Regiments	
Nebelwerfer Battalions	
Entgiftungs Battalions	
Machine Gun Battalions	
Anti-Tank Battalions	
SP Anti-Tank Battalions	
SP Hvy Anti-Tank Companies	
Assault Gun Battalions	
Flame Tank Battalions	
Mot Eng Reg HQs (Spec P)	
Mot Pionier Battalions	
(Mixed) Pionier Battalions	
Bridge Const Battalions	
Assault Boat Companies	
Mot Sep Bridge Cols B	10 / 11 — Refer to notes below **
Sep Bridge Cols, Type (A-T)	
Arm Mine Clearing Battalions	
Luft Flak Corps HQs	
Luft Flak Reg HQs	
Luft Mixed Flak Battalions	
Luft Light Flak Battalions	
Construction Reg HQs	18 Ob^ ; 15 ; 1
Construction Battalions	81, 401 ; 1 / 2 ; 2
Railroad Eng Reg HQs	1
Railroad Pionier Bat HQs	
Railroad Pionier Companies	
Railroad Switching Comp's	
Railroad Eng Const Comp's	
Railroad Eng Const Batts	
Mot Police Regiment HQ	
Police Rifle Battalions	1
Mot Military Police Battalions	254, 304, 315, 320 (695, 696, 697)^ ; 4 / 3
Mot Traffic Control Battalions	4 / 3
Armoured Trains	

Notes:

* Reserves behind Army Group Centre. 2nd Army was assigned to AGC on 2nd July 1941. 2nd Army's rear area was controlled by Korück 559.
^ Oberbaustab 18 (Brigade level HQ).

* From Wehrkreis III (B.d.E). Reserves behind Army Group North. The Corps was assigned to AG Centre, 9th Army.
^ 86th Division arriving 19th June to 26th June 1941.
** Polizei Division arriving 24th June to 1st July 1941.

* Reserves behind AGC. The Corps was assigned to 4th Army. The Corps HQ had the 435th AT Co and 435th Armoured Car Platoon assigned.
^ 15th Division arriving 26th June to 3rd July 1941.
** 52nd Division arriving 20th June to 26th June 1941.
*^ 112th Division arriving from Wehrkreis XII 25th June to 1st July 1941.
^^ 197th Division arriving from Wehrkreis XII 20th June to 26th June 1941.

* Reserves behind Army Group South. It was assigned to AG South Reserves.
^ 113th Division arriving from Wehrkreis XIII 23rd June to 29th June 1941
** 132nd Division arriving 28th June to 4th July 1941

* Reserves in 12th Army. Transferred East in June and assigned to AG South, 6th Army.
^ 79th Division arriving from Wehrkreis XVIII 22nd June to 27th June 1941.
** 95th Division arriving 27th June to 3rd July 1941.

* OKH Reserves included the HQs for the 597zbV, 598zbV and 604zbV Signal Regiments: zbV (zur besonderer Verwendung) for special purposes.
^ Motorised MP Battalions, in OKG Reserve but provisionally assigned to 4th Army.
** 160, 222, 1./408, 1./409, 1./413, 1./415, 2./415, 603, 609, 619

© Nigel Askey, 2018

Total German Army, Waffen SS and Luftwaffe Flak Units, on the East Front, from 22nd June to 4th July 1941.	
Table German Deployment Matrix	**Total E Front, to 4th July 1941 TOTAL No**
Army & Panzer Group HQs	7
Army HQs	8
Corps HQs	34
Panzer Corps HQs	10
Army Group Rear Area HQs	3
Army & Army Grp Signal Regs	11
Army & Army Grp Signal Batts	6
Panzer Group Signal Regs	4
Infantry Divisions	91
Panzer Divisions	17
Motorised Divisions	9
SS Motorised Divisions	3
Cavalry Divisions	1
Mountain Divisions	4
Light Divisions	4
Fleiger Divisions	
Motorised Infantry Brigades	4 7/8
Motorised Infantry Regiments	1 1/2
Motorised Infantry Battalions	
(Mixed) Infantry Regiments	3
(Mixed) Infantry Battalions	4 1/3
Tank Brigades	
Tank Battalions	2
Cavalry Regiments	2
Security Divisions or Brigades	9
Guard (*Wach*) Battalions	37
Landesschutzen Battalions	42
Artillery HQs, *Harko* & *Arko*	56
Art Observation Battalions	35
Artillery Reg HQs (Spec P)	36
Mixed Artillery Battalions	12 1/3
150mm How Battalions	37
105mm Gun Battalions	29
150mm Gun Battalions	7
210mm How Battalions (1)	19
210mm How Battalions (2)	10
210mm Gun Battalions	2
Hvy 240mm How Battalions	2
Hvy 240mm Gun Battalions	2
Super Hvy How Battalions	4
Coastal Artillery Battalions	13
Railroad Artillery Batteries	11
Anti-Air Battalions	10
Light Anti-Air Battalions	10
SP Light AA Companies	47

Total German Army, Waffen SS and Luftwaffe Flak Units, on the East Front, from 22nd June to 4th July 1941.	
Table German Deployment Matrix	**Total E Front, to 4th July 1941 TOTAL No**
Nebelwerfer Regiment HQs	4
Nebelwerfer Regiments	5
Nebelwerfer Battalions	7 1/3
Entgiftungs Battalions	8
Machine Gun Battalions	3
Anti-Tank Battalions	6
SP Anti-Tank Battalions	9
SP Hvy Anti-Tank Companies	1
Assault Gun Battalions	12 2/3
Flame Tank Battalions	3
Mot Eng Reg HQs (Spec P)	28
Mot *Pionier* Battalions	21
(Mixed) *Pionier* Battalions	30
Bridge Const Battalions	27 1/4
Assault Boat Companies	5
Mot Sep Bridge Cols B**	119
Sep Bridge Cols, Type (A-T)	45
Arm Mine Clearing Battalions	1
Luft Flak Corps HQs	2
Luft Flak Reg HQs	13
Luft Mixed Flak Battalions	41
Luft Light Flak Battalions	17
Construction Reg HQs	41
Construction Battalions	126
Railroad Eng Reg HQs	5
Railroad Pionier Bat HQs	7
Railroad Pionier Companies	47
Railroad Switching Comp's	10
Railroad Eng Const Comp's	16
Railroad Eng Const Batts	6
Mot Police Regiment HQ	3
Police Rifle Battalions	22
Mot Military Police Battalions	20
Mot Traffic Control Battalions	11
Armoured Trains	12

© Nigel Askey, 2018

Table German

Deployment and Composition of the German Army, Waffen SS and Luftwaffe Flak Units, 22nd June 1941

Deployment Matrix

Armed Forces Command Norway (*Wehrmachtsbefehlshaber Norwegen*)

Norway Army (Norway Occupation Duties)

	Norway Mtn Corps		HoH. Kdo. XXXIII		HoH. Kdo. LXX		Army Reserve	
	Description	No	Description	No	Description	No	Description	No
Army & Panzer Group HQs							Norway Army HQ	1
Army HQs	(HQ On East Front)*^							
Corps HQs			33	1	70	1		
Panzer Corps HQs								
Army Group Rear Area HQs								
Army & Army Grp Signal Regs								
Army & Army Grp Signal Batts							635	1
Panzer Group Signal Regs							710	1
Infantry Divisions	199, 702	2	181, 196	2	69^, 214**	2		
Panzer Divisions								
Motorised Divisions								
SS Motorised Divisions								
Cavalry Divisions								
Mountain Divisions								
Light Divisions								
Fleiger Divisions								
Motorised Infantry Brigades								
Motorised Infantry Regiments								
Motorised Infantry Battalions								
(Mixed) Infantry Regiments								
(Mixed) Infantry Battalions	233**	1						
Tank Brigades								
Tank Battalions								
Cavalry Regiments								
Security Divisions or Brigades								
Guard (*Wach*) Battalions								
Landesschutzen Battalions							366, 372, 809***	3
Artillery HQs, *Harko & Arko*								
Art Observation Battalions								
Artillery Reg HQs (Spec P)								
Mixed Artillery Battalions								
150mm How Battalions								
105mm Gun Battalions								
150mm Gun Battalions								
210mm How Battalions (1)								
210mm How Battalions (2)								
210mm Gun Battalions								
Hvy 240mm How Battalions								
Hvy 240mm Gun Battalions								
Super Hvy How Battalions								
Coastal Artillery Battalions	12 Battalions*	12	8 Battalions*	8	12 Battalions*	12		
Railroad Artillery Batteries							840 Reg HQ^^	12
Anti-Air Battalions								
Light Anti-Air Battalions								
SP Light AA Companies								

Unit Type	Norway Army^**
Nebelwerfer Regiment HQs	
Nebelwerfer Regiments	
Nebelwerfer Battalions	
Entgiftungs Battalions	
Machine Gun Battalions	3 (4, 13, 14)
Anti-Tank Battalions	
SP Anti-Tank Battalions	
SP Hvy Anti-Tank Companies	
Assault Gun Battalions	
Flame Tank Battalions	
Mot Eng Reg HQs (Spec P)	
Mot Pionier Battalions	
(Mixed) Pionier Battalions	
Bridge Const Battalions	
Assault Boat Companies	
Mot Sep Bridge Cols B	
Sep Bridge Cols, Type (A-T)	
Arm Mine Clearing Battalions	
Luft Flak Corps HQs	
Luft Flak Reg HQs	
Luft Mixed Flak Battalions	
Luft Light Flak Battalions	
Construction Reg HQs	2 (18Fr, HSC^)
Construction Battalions	60Fr, 20Fr, 160Fr
Railroad Eng Reg HQs	1 (19Fr)
Railroad Pionier Bat HQs	1 (1./6)
Railroad Pionier Companies	2 (206, 601)
Railroad Switching Comp's	
Railroad Eng Const Comp's	
Railroad Eng Const Batts	
Mot Police Regiment HQ	2 (Nordnorwegen*, Sudnorwegen^)
Police Rifle Battalions	7 ((255, 256, 302, 312)**, (251, 252, 253)*^)
Mot Military Police Battalions	
Mot Traffic Control Battalions	
Armoured Trains	

Notes:

* SK Kirkenes (Reg HQ) with 478, 479 and 513 (Marine) Battalions. SK Tromso (Reg HQ) with 480, 481, 484 and 512 (Marine) Battalions. SK Narvik (Reg HQ) with 482, 483, 499, 500 and 511 (Marine) Battalions. Included the 825th and 837th Coastal Artillery Regiment HQs (Total 73 Coastal Artillery Batteries).
^ Hesse Snow Clearing HQ, controlling 8 Snow Clearing Detachments.
** 233rd Bicycle Infantry Battalion.
*^ Had ad hoc Signals made up from the 2./635, 9./645 and 463 Signal Companies; seconded from the Infantry Divisions and other HQ units in Norway.

* SK Sandnesjoen (Reg HQ) with 487, 488 and 510 (Marine) Battalions. SK Drontheim (Reg HQ) with 485, 489 and 506 (Marine) Battalions. SK Molde (Reg HQ) with 486 and 505 (Marine) Battalions. Included the 839th and 853rd Coastal Artillery Regiment HQs. (Total 51 Coastal Artillery Batteries).

* SK Bergen (Reg HQ) with 491, 495, 505 and 504 (Marine) Battalions. SK Stavanger (Reg HQ) with 490, 492 and 503 (Marine) Battalions. SK Kristiansand (Reg HQ) with 493, 497 and 502 (Marine) Battalions. SK Horten (Reg HQ) with 494 and 501 (Marine) Battalions. Included the 824th and 836th Coastal Artillery Regiment HQs. (Total 71 Coastal Artillery Batteries).
^ The 69th Division's 193rd Inf Regiment transferred to Nth Norway/Finland in Oct 1941.
** The 214th Division's 388th Inf Regiment, I./214th Art Battalion and 2nd Co/214th Pionier Battalion transferred to Northern Norway/Finland in August 1941.

* Police (& SS) Nordnorwegen (North Norway) Regiment.
^ Police (& SS) Sudnorwegen (South Norway) Regiment. Both Police Regiments reported to a SS Police Brigade HQ in Oslo.
** Attached to Pol.Rgt Nordnorwegen. Also the 256th was mountain trained and equipped.
*^ Attached to Pol.Rgt Sudnorwegen.
^^ Included the 840th Coastal Artillery Regiment HQ (for Special Purpose).
^* Included the Norway Army Engineering Brigade HQ (mixed transport).
*** The 3rd and 4th Companies (809) were in Denmark.

© Nigel Askey, 2018

Table German Deployment Matrix

Deployment and Composition of the German Army, Waffen SS and Luftwaffe Flak Units, 22nd June 1941

Army Group D (Oberbefehlshaber West)

7th Army (Brittany-Atlantic Coast)

	HoH. Kdo. XXXI Description	No	HoH. Kdo. LIX Description	No	XXV Corps Description	No	Army Reserve Description	No
Army & Panzer Group HQs								
Army HQs							7	1
Corps HQs	31	1	59	1	25	1		
Panzer Corps HQs								
Army Group Rear Area HQs								
Army & Army Grp Signal Regs								
Army & Army Grp Signal Batts							531	1
Panzer Group Signal Regs								
Infantry Divisions	88**, 212^, 223*, 333, 708	5	81*, 246^, 305, 715	4	205, 211*, 709, 712	4		
Panzer Divisions								
Motorised Divisions								
SS Motorised Divisions								
Cavalry Divisions								
Mountain Divisions								
Light Divisions								
Fleiger Divisions								
Motorised Infantry Brigades								
Motorised Infantry Regiments								
Motorised Infantry Battalions								
(Mixed) Infantry Regiments								
(Mixed) Infantry Battalions								
Tank Brigades								
Tank Battalions								
Cavalry Regiments								
Security Divisions or Brigades								
Guard (Wach) Battalions								
Landesschutzen Battalions								
Artillery HQs, Harko & Arko	780zbV RR Art Bat HQ							
Art Observation Battalions								
Artillery Reg HQs (Spec P)								
Mixed Artillery Battalions								
150mm How Battalions								
105mm Gun Battalions								
150mm Gun Battalions								
210mm How Battalions (1)								
210mm How Battalions (2)								
210mm Gun Battalions								
Hvy 240mm How Battalions								
Hvy 240mm Gun Battalions								
Super Hvy How Battalions								
Coastal Artillery Battalions							2 Battalions	2
Railroad Artillery Batteries								

Unit Type		
Anti-Air Battalions		
Light Anti-Air Battalions		
SP Light AA Companies		
Nebelwerfer Regiment HQs		
Nebelwerfer Regiments		
Nebelwerfer Battalions		
Entgiftungs Battalions		
Machine Gun Battalions		
Anti-Tank Battalions		
SP Anti-Tank Battalions		
SP Hvy Anti-Tank Companies		
Assault Gun Battalions		
Flame Tank Battalions		
Mot Eng Reg HQs (Spec P)		
Mot *Pionier* Battalions		
(Mixed) *Pionier* Battalions		
Bridge Const Battalions		
Assault Boat Companies		
Mot Sep Bridge Cols B		
Sep Bridge Cols, Type (A-T)		
Arm Mine Clearing Battalions		
Luft Flak Corps HQs		
Luft Flak Reg HQs	I/49	
Luft Mixed Flak Battalions	1	
Luft Light Flak Battalions	4	
Construction Reg HQs		
Construction Battalions		
Railroad Eng Reg HQs		
Railroad Pionier Bat HQs		
Railroad Pionier Companies	103, 105, 117, 127	
Railroad Switching Comp's		
Railroad Eng Const Comp's		
Railroad Eng Const Batts		
Mot Police Regiment HQ		
Police Rifle Battalions		
Mot Military Police Battalions		
Mot Traffic Control Battalions		
Armoured Trains		

* 223rd Infantry Division was transferred to the East Front on 30th November 1941.
^ 212 Infantry Division was transferred to the East Front in late October 1941.
** 88th Infantry Division was transferred to the East Front in January-February 1942,

* 81st Infantry Division was transferred to the East Front in December 1941.
^ 246th Infantry Division was transferred to the East Front in January 1942, (sent on 31st December 1941).

* 211th Infantry Division was transferred to the East Front in January 1942.

© Nigel Askey, 2018

Table German Deployment Matrix — Deployment and Composition of the German Army, Waffen SS and Luftwaffe Flak Units, 22nd June 1941

Army Group D (Oberbefehlshaber West)

1st Army (Eastern France-Demarcation Line)

	HoH. Kdo. XXXXV Description	No	XXVII Corps Description	No	Army Reserve Description	No
Army & Panzer Group HQs					1	1
Army HQs	45	1				
Corps HQs			27**	1		
Panzer Corps HQs						
Army Group Rear Area HQs						
Army & Army Grp Signal Regs						
Army & Army Grp Signal Batts						
Panzer Group Signal Regs					512	1
Infantry Divisions	215**, 260*, 339^, 342*^	4	94*, 98^, 327, 335, 337	5		
Panzer Divisions						
Motorised Divisions						
SS Motorised Divisions						
Cavalry Divisions						
Mountain Divisions						
Light Divisions						
Fleiger Divisions						
Motorised Infantry Brigades						
Motorised Infantry Regiments						
Motorised Infantry Battalions						
(Mixed) Infantry Regiments						
(Mixed) Infantry Battalions						
Tank Brigades					100^, 101*	2
Tank Battalions					Panzer-Kompanie Paris**	1/3
Cavalry Regiments						
Security Divisions or Brigades						
Guard (*Wach*) Battalions					604, 702	2
Landesschutzen Battalions					109	1
Artillery HQs, *Harko & Arko*						
Art Observation Battalions						
Artillery Reg HQs (Spec P)						
Mixed Artillery Battalions						
150mm How Battalions						
105mm Gun Battalions						
150mm Gun Battalions						
210mm How Battalions (1)						
210mm How Battalions (2)						
210mm Gun Battalions						
Hvy 240mm How Battalions						
Hvy 240mm Gun Battalions						
Super Hvy How Battalions						
Coastal Artillery Battalions						
Railroad Artillery Batteries						

Anti-Air Battalions
Light Anti-Air Battalions
SP Light AA Companies
Nebelwerfer Regiment HQs
Nebelwerfer Regiments
Nebelwerfer Battalions
Entgiftungs Battalions
Machine Gun Battalions
Anti-Tank Battalions
SP Anti-Tank Battalions
SP Hvy Anti-Tank Companies
Assault Gun Battalions
Flame Tank Battalions
Mot Eng Reg HQs (Spec P)
Mot Pionier Battalions
(Mixed) Pionier Battalions
Bridge Const Battalions
Assault Boat Companies
Mot Sep Bridge Cols B
Sep Bridge Cols, Type (A-T)
Arm Mine Clearing Battalions
Luft Flak Corps HQs
Luft Flak Reg HQs
Luft Mixed Flak Battalions
Luft Light Flak Battalions
Construction Reg HQs
Construction Battalions
Railroad Eng Reg HQs
Railroad Pionier Bat HQs
Railroad Pionier Companies
Railroad Switching Comp's
Railroad Eng Const Comp's
Railroad Eng Const Batts
Mot Police Regiment HQ
Police Rifle Battalions
Mot Military Police Battalions
Mot Traffic Control Battalions
Armoured Trains   21   1

© Nigel Askey, 2018

* 260th Infantry Division was transferred to the East Front by 11th July 1941.
^ 339th Infantry Division was transferred to the East Front by 30th August 1941. It was assigned to security duties for Army Group Centre.
** 215th Infantry Division was transferred to the East Front by late November 1941.
*^ 342nd Infantry Division was sent to Yugoslavia in October 1941.

* 94th Infantry Division was transferred to the East Front by 9th July 1941. It was assigned to Army Group South.
^ 98th Infantry Division was transferred to the East Front by 21st July 1941. It was assigned to Army Group South.
** The XXVII Corps transferred to the East Front in October 1941. It was attached to 9th Army, Army Group Centre.

* 101st Panzer Brigade's Panzer Regiment was still forming. It had only one Panzer Company in each Regiment. Officially raised 5th July 1941.
^ Also administered the Panzer-Kompanie Paris (5 Platoons with Renault 35 tanks). Used for security duties.
** Controlled-supported by the 100th Panzer Brigade.

Table German Deployment Matrix — Deployment and Composition of the German Army, Waffen SS and Luftwaffe Flak Units, 22nd June 1941

Army Group D (*Oberbefehlshaber West*)

15th Army (English Channel Coast-The Netherlands)

	HoH. Kdo. LX		HoH. Kdo. XXXII Corps		HoH. Kdo. XXXVII		Army Reserve	
	Description	No	Description	No	Description	No	Description	No
Army & Panzer Group HQs								
Army HQs							15	1
Corps HQs	60	1	32	1	37	1		
Panzer Corps HQs								
Army Group Rear Area HQs								
Army & Army Grp Signal Regs							509	1
Army & Army Grp Signal Batts								
Panzer Group Signal Regs								
Infantry Divisions	83*, 216^, 319, 323	4	96*, 225^, 302, 332, 336, 716	6	208*, 227^, 304, 306, 320, 321, 340	7	93*, 711	2
Panzer Divisions								
Motorised Divisions								
SS Motorised Divisions								
Cavalry Divisions								
Mountain Divisions								
Light Divisions								
Fleiger Divisions								
Motorised Infantry Brigades								
Motorised Infantry Regiments								
Motorised Infantry Battalions								
(Mixed) Infantry Regiments								
(Mixed) Infantry Battalions								
Tank Brigades								
Tank Battalions								
Cavalry Regiments								
Security Divisions or Brigades								
Guard (*Wach*) Battalions								
Landesschutzen Battalions								
Artillery HQs, *Harko & Arko*								
Art Observation Battalions								
Artillery Reg HQs (Spec P)								
Mixed Artillery Battalions								
150mm How Battalions								
105mm Gun Battalions								
150mm Gun Battalions								
210mm How Battalions (1)								
210mm How Battalions (2)								
210mm Gun Battalions								
Hvy 240mm How Battalions								
Hvy 240mm Gun Battalions								
Super Hvy How Battalions								
Coastal Artillery Battalions							6 Battalions	6
Railroad Artillery Batteries								

Unit			
Anti-Air Battalions			
Light Anti-Air Battalions			
SP Light AA Companies			
Nebelwerfer Regiment HQs			
Nebelwerfer Regiments			
Nebelwerfer Battalions			
Entgiftungs Battalions		1	
Machine Gun Battalions	16**		17**
Anti-Tank Battalions			1
SP Anti-Tank Battalions			
SP Hvy Anti-Tank Companies			
Assault Gun Battalions			
Flame Tank Battalions			
Mot Eng Reg HQs (Spec P)			
Mot *Pionier* Battalions			
(Mixed) *Pionier* Battalions			
Bridge Const Battalions			
Assault Boat Companies			
Mot Sep Bridge Cols B		904	
Sep Bridge Cols, Type (A-T)			
Arm Mine Clearing Battalions			
Luft Flak Corps HQs			
Luft Flak Reg HQs			
Luft Mixed Flak Battalions			
Luft Light Flak Battalions			
Construction Reg HQs			
Construction Battalions			
Railroad Eng Reg HQs			
Railroad Pionier Bat HQs			
Railroad Pionier Companies			
Railroad Switching Comp's			
Railroad Eng Const Comp's			
Railroad Eng Const Batts			
Mot Police Regiment HQ			
Police Rifle Battalions			
Mot Military Police Battalions			
Mot Traffic Control Battalions			
Armoured Trains			

* 83rd Infantry Division was transferred to the East Front in late December 1941/Jan42.
^ 216th Infantry Division was transferred to the East Front in December 1941.
** 16th non-motorised MG Battalion, on the Channel Islands.

* 96th Infantry Division was transferred to the East Front by 20th July 1941. Assigned to Army Group North.
^ 225th Infantry Division was transferred to the East Front in January 1942.

* 208th Infantry Division was transferred to the East Front in January 1942.
^ 227th Infantry Division was transferred to the East Front in late September 1941.
** 17th non-motorised MG Battalion.

* 93rd Infantry Division was transferred to the East Front 29th June to 5th July 1941. Assigned to Army Group North.

© Nigel Askey, 2018

Table German Deployment Matrix — Deployment and Composition of the German Army, Waffen SS and Luftwaffe Flak Units, 22nd June 1941

Army Group D (Oberbefehlshaber West)

	Army Group D Reserve		Army Norway & AGD	
	Description	No	TOTAL	No
Army & Panzer Group HQs		1		1
Army HQs	AGD HQ			4
Corps HQs				10
Panzer Corps HQs				
Army Group Rear Area HQs				
Army & Army Grp Signal Regs	603*	1		5
Army & Army Grp Signal Batts				
Panzer Group Signal Regs				
Infantry Divisions	82^, 719^	2		50
Panzer Divisions				
Motorised Divisions				
SS Motorised Divisions				
Cavalry Divisions				
Mountain Divisions				
Light Divisions				
Fleiger Divisions				
Motorised Infantry Brigades				
Motorised Infantry Regiments				
Motorised Infantry Battalions	100 zbV**	1		1
(Mixed) Infantry Regiments				
(Mixed) Infantry Battalions				1
Tank Brigades				
Tank Battalions				2
Cavalry Regiments				1/3
Security Divisions or Brigades				
Guard (*Wach*) Battalions				2
Landesschutzen Battalions	702	1		4
Artillery HQs, *Harko & Arko*				1
Art Observation Battalions		3		3
Artillery Reg HQs (Spec P)	(720, 766**, 781^^ RR Art Reg HQs)*^	1		1
Mixed Artillery Battalions	510**^			
150mm How Battalions				
105mm Gun Battalions				
150mm Gun Battalions				
210mm How Battalions (1)				
210mm How Battalions (2)				
210mm Gun Battalions				
Hvy 240mm How Battalions				
Hvy 240mm Gun Battalions				
Super Hvy How Battalions				
Coastal Artillery Battalions				
Railroad Artillery Batteries	717, 718, 694, 674^^, 722^^, 689***, 695^^, 721^^	8		40
Anti-Air Battalions				8
Light Anti-Air Battalions				1
SP Light AA Companies	5./52^^	1		1

Nebelwerfer Regiment HQs
Nebelwerfer Regiments
Nebelwerfer Battalions
Entgiftungs Battalions
Machine Gun Battalions
Anti-Tank Battalions
SP Anti-Tank Battalions
SP Hvy Anti-Tank Companies
Assault Gun Battalions
Flame Tank Battalions
Mot Eng Reg HQs (Spec P)
Mot Pionier Battalions
(Mixed) Pionier Battalions
Bridge Const Battalions
Assault Boat Companies
Mot Sep Bridge Cols B
Sep Bridge Cols, Type (A-T)
Arm Mine Clearing Battalions
Luft Flak Corps HQs
Luft Flak Reg HQs
Luft Mixed Flak Battalions
Luft Light Flak Battalions
Construction Reg HQs
Construction Battalions
Railroad Eng Reg HQs
Railroad Pionier Bat HQs
Railroad Pionier Companies
Railroad Switching Comp's
Railroad Eng Const Comp's
Railroad Eng Const Batts
Mot Police Regiment HQ
Police Rifle Battalions
Mot Military Police Battalions
Mot Traffic Control Battalions
Armoured Trains

Unit			Designations
Nebelwerfer Regiment HQs			
Nebelwerfer Regiments			
Nebelwerfer Battalions			
Entgiftungs Battalions		5	
Machine Gun Battalions			
Anti-Tank Battalions			
SP Anti-Tank Battalions	1	1	625^^
SP Hvy Anti-Tank Companies			
Assault Gun Battalions			
Flame Tank Battalions			
Mot Eng Reg HQs (Spec P)			
Mot Pionier Battalions			
(Mixed) Pionier Battalions			
Bridge Const Battalions			
Assault Boat Companies			
Mot Sep Bridge Cols B			
Sep Bridge Cols, Type (A-T)		1	
Arm Mine Clearing Battalions			
Luft Flak Corps HQs			
Luft Flak Reg HQs			
Luft Mixed Flak Battalions		1	
Luft Light Flak Battalions			
Construction Reg HQs	2	5	11 Ob, 15 Ob
Construction Battalions	14	17	8, 59, 158, 211, 245, 360Mar*~, ((28*^^, 77, 82, 88, 89, 149, 152, 157)Fr)^^^
Railroad Eng Reg HQs	3	3	'Unknown Des'
Railroad Pionier Bat HQs		1	
Railroad Pionier Companies		6	
Railroad Switching Comp's			
Railroad Eng Const Comp's			
Railroad Eng Const Batts	3	3	111, 511, 514
Mot Police Regiment HQ	1	3	SS Pol. Rgt Nordwest***
Police Rifle Battalions	3	10	(67, 68, 203)^^*
Mot Military Police Battalions			
Mot Traffic Control Battalions			
Armoured Trains	1	2	22

* Attached to AGD HQ (Also HQ of the C in C West).

^ Stationed in Holland. 82nd transferred to Army Grp South in May 1942.

** 100th Motorised Infantry Battalion for Special Purpose.
  Became part of the 22nd Panzer Division on 30th September 1941.

*^ All Railroad Artillery Regimental HQs.

^^ Transferred to the East Front in July 1941.

^* Transferred to the East Front in September 1941.

*** Transferred to the East Front in August 1941.

**^ 510th Heavy Artillery Battalion, was redesignated an Army Coastal
  Artillery Battalion in August 1941 (Mixed Transport Battalion, 10cm guns).

*^^ Originally 220th Battalion; redesignated Festungs-Bau-Bataillon 28 on 30 June 1940.

^^^ Fortress Construction Battalions (Fr) (Festungs-Bau-Bataillon).

*~ Kriegsmarine Marine-Bau-Bataillon 360, deployed in Marseilles.

^** SS-Oberabschnitt Nordwest, stationed in The Hague.

^^* Attached to SS Pol. Rgt Nordwest.

Table German

Deployment Matrix

Deployment and Composition of the German Army, Waffen SS and Luftwaffe Flak Units, 22nd June 1941

Armed Forces Command Southeast (*Wehrmachtsbefehlshaber Sudost*)

12th Army (Yugoslavia-Serbia-Greece-Crete)

	HoH. Kdo. LXV		XVIII Mtn Corps		XI. Fliegerkorps**		Army (& WB) Reserve	
	Description	No	Description	No	Description	No	Description	No
Army & Panzer Group HQs								
Army HQs	65	1					12	1
Corps HQs			18	1				
Panzer Corps HQs								
Army Group Rear Area HQs								
Army & Army Grp Signal Regs							521	1
Army & Army Grp Signal Batts								
Panzer Group Signal Regs								
Infantry Divisions	704, 714, 717, 718*	4					46*, 73^, 183**, 294*^, 164^^	5
Panzer Divisions								
Motorised Divisions								
SS Motorised Divisions								
Cavalry Divisions								
Mountain Divisions			5th Mtn*, 6th Mtn^	2				
Light Divisions								
Fleiger Divisions					7*	1		
Motorised Infantry Brigades								
Motorised Infantry Regiments					1st Luftlande Sturm^	1		
Motorised Infantry Battalions								
(Mixed) Infantry Regiments							125	1
(Mixed) Infantry Battalions								
Tank Brigades								
Tank Battalions							5./Pz Reg 31/5th Pz Div^^	1/3
Cavalry Regiments								
Security Divisions or Brigades								
Guard (*Wach*) Battalions								
Landesschutzen Battalions							386, 562, 576, 592, 920	5
Artillery HQs, *Harko & Arko*							141, 142	2
Art Observation Battalions							33	1
Artillery Reg HQs (Spec P)								
Mixed Artillery Battalions			I./231**	1				
150mm How Battalions								
105mm Gun Battalions			716	1				
150mm Gun Battalions								
210mm How Battalions (1)								
210mm How Battalions (2)								
210mm Gun Battalions								
Hvy 240mm How Battalions								
Hvy 240mm Gun Battalions								
Super Hvy How Battalions								
Coastal Artillery Battalions								
Railroad Artillery Batteries							644	1
Anti-Air Battalions								
Light Anti-Air Battalions							609^^	1
SP Light AA Companies								

Unit Type	Qty	Designations	Qty	Designations
Nebelwerfer Regiment HQs				
Nebelwerfer Regiments				
Nebelwerfer Battalions				
Entgiftungs Battalions				
Machine Gun Battalions				
Anti-Tank Battalions				
SP Anti-Tank Battalions				
SP Hvy Anti-Tank Companies				
Assault Gun Battalions				
Flame Tank Battalions				
Mot Eng Reg HQs (Spec P)			1	685^*
Mot Pionier Battalions			1	666^*
(Mixed) Pionier Battalions	1	659*^	2	522, 655
Bridge Const Battalions				
Assault Boat Companies				
Mot Sep Bridge Cols B			1	132^^
Sep Bridge Cols, Type (A-T)			4	"Unknown Des"
Arm Mine Clearing Battalions				
Luft Flak Corps HQs				
Luft Flak Reg HQs				
Luft Mixed Flak Battalions				
Luft Light Flak Battalions				
Construction Reg HQs				
Construction Battalions				
Railroad Eng Reg HQs				
Railroad Pionier Bat HQs				
Railroad Pionier Companies				
Railroad Switching Comp's				
Railroad Eng Const Comp's				
Railroad Eng Const Batts				
Mot Police Regiment HQ				
Police Rifle Battalions	1	501		
Mot Military Police Battalions				
Mot Traffic Control Battalions			1	64
Armoured Trains			2	23, 24

* The 718th Infantry Division was scheduled to transfer to the East Front after 4th July 1941. However, it remained in Yugoslavia until April 1943.

* 5th Mountain Division was transferred back to Bavaria and Austria in October 1941. It was transferred to AGN in January 1942. The 5th Mtn Div's 95th Bicycle Battalion & 95th PzJag Battalion were transferred to Finland (East Front) in November 1941.
^ 6th Mountain Division was transferred to Finland (East Front) in September 1941.
** Horse drawn, unknown equip.
*^ 659th Pionier Battalion transferred to East Front July 1941; assigned to 17th Army.

* The 7th Flieger (Para) Division was rebuilding after operation Mercury. It transferred to AG North with its 1st and 3rd Parachute Regiments in early Sep 1941.
^ 1st Luftlande Sturm Regiment; a separate elite unit which operated as Glider Borne Infantry with 7th Flieger Division or with XI. Fliegerkorps. It transferred to AG North in September 1941.
** Luftwaffe Air Corps: included an Aviation Group which had Transport Groups, a Glider Group and Reconnaissance Squadrons. Formed I Parachute Corps (1. Fallschirmkorps) in January 1944. Still in the Balkans because of Operation Mercury.

* 46th Infantry Division transferred to the East Front by 5th July 1941, assigned to AG South.
^ 73rd Infantry Division transferred to the East Front by 13th July 1941, assigned to AG South.
** 183rd Infantry Division transferred to the East Front by Aug 1941 (Poland by July 1941).
*^ The 294th Infantry Division was transferred to the East Front by 29th July 1941, assigned to Army Group South.
^^ Defending Crete. The forces on Crete (mainly the 164th and 713th Divisions) formed 'Fortress Division Crete' in January 1942.
^^ 685th Eng Reg HQ, 666th Motorised Pionier Battalion, and the 132nd Motorised Type B Bridge Column, transferred to the East Front in late August 1941.

© Nigel Askey, 2018

Table German Deployment Matrix	Deployment and Composition of the German Army, Waffen SS and Luftwaffe Flak Units, 22nd June 1941	
	Deutsches Afrikakorps (D.A.K)	
	Description	No
Army & Panzer Group HQs		
Army HQs		
Corps HQs		
Panzer Corps HQs	DAK	1
Army Group Rear Area HQs		
Army & Army Grp Signal Regs		
Army & Army Grp Signal Batts		
Panzer Group Signal Regs		
Infantry Divisions		
Panzer Divisions	15	1
Motorised Divisions	5 Lt*	1
SS Motorised Divisions		
Cavalry Divisions		
Mountain Divisions		
Light Divisions	Divisions-Kommando z.b.V. Afrika, HQ*^^	
Fleiger Divisions		
Motorised Infantry Brigades		
Motorised Infantry Regiments		
Motorised Infantry Battalions	300 zbV^	1
(Mixed) Infantry Regiments	361**	1
(Mixed) Infantry Battalions	(III./241, III./255, III./258, III./347)*^	4
Tank Brigades		
Tank Battalions		
Cavalry Regiments		
Security Divisions or Brigades		
Guard (*Wach*) Battalions		
Landesschutzen Battalions	1./278**^	1/4
Artillery HQs, *Harko* & *Arko*	104	1
Art Observation Battalions		
Artillery Reg HQs (Spec P)	221	1
Mixed Artillery Battalions	(III./155)^^	
150mm How Battalions		
105mm Gun Battalions	408	1
150mm Gun Battalions		
210mm How Battalions (1)	II./115	1
210mm How Battalions (2)		
210mm Gun Battalions		
Hvy 240mm How Battalions		
Hvy 240mm Gun Battalions		
Super Hvy How Battalions		
Coastal Artillery Battalions	523, 528, 529, 533	4
Railroad Artillery Batteries		
Anti-Air Battalions		
Light Anti-Air Battalions	612, (606)^*	1
SP Light AA Companies		
Nebelwerfer Regiment HQs		
Nebelwerfer Regiments		
Nebelwerfer Battalions		
Entgiftungs Battalions		
Machine Gun Battalions	(2, 8)^*	
Anti-Tank Battalions		
SP Anti-Tank Battalions	(605)^*	
SP Hvy Anti-Tank Companies		
Assault Gun Battalions		
Flame Tank Battalions		
Mot Eng Reg HQs (Spec P)		
Mot *Pionier* Battalions	900	1
(Mixed) *Pionier* Battalions		

Table German Deployment Matrix	Deployment and Composition of the German Army, Waffen SS and Luftwaffe Flak Units, 22nd June 1941	
	Deutsches Afrika Korps (D.A.K)	
	Description	No
Bridge Const Battalions		
Assault Boat Companies		
Mot Sep Bridge Cols B		
Sep Bridge Cols, Type (A-T)		
Arm Mine Clearing Battalions		
Luft Flak Corps HQs		
Luft Flak Reg HQs		
Luft Mixed Flak Battalions	I./18, I./33	2
Luft Light Flak Battalions		
Construction Reg HQs		
Construction Battalions	85***	1
Railroad Eng Reg HQs		
Railroad Pionier Bat HQs		
Railroad Pionier Companies		
Railroad Switching Comp's		
Railroad Eng Const Comp's		
Railroad Eng Const Batts		
Mot Police Regiment HQ		
Police Rifle Battalions		
Mot Military Police Battalions		
Mot Traffic Control Battalions		
Armoured Trains		

* Officially listed as the 5th Light Division (mot) until 1st August 1941. However, its organisation was much closer to a Panzer Division than a Light Division: by 31st March 1941 it already had 2x Panzer Battalions with 168 tanks in its 5th Panzer Regiment.

^ 300th zbV was probably a Motorised Reconnaissance Battalion, (also used in special operations).

** The 361st Infantry Regiment had only 2x Infantry Battalions, but was reinforced with an Artillery Battery, an AA Battery and a Transport Column.

*^ The III./241, III./255, III./258 and III./347 Infantry Battalions were despatched from the 106th, 110th, 112th and 197th Infantry Divisions, respectively, in 1941. Only 8x Infantry battalions are included in the TOE of these Divisions. For operations in North Africa their supply and combat trains were motorised. The III./268 Infantry Battalion (from the 113th Infantry Division) arrived in May 1942.

^^ The I./155 (Light) and III./155 (Heavy Mixed) Artillery Battalions were still DAK (Corps) units and were officially part of the 5th Light Division on 1st August 1941. However, they are treated as part of the TOE for the 5th Light Division here (not Corps units) because this was already their operational role by June 1941.

^* Included in the TOE of the 5th Light Division.

*** Equipped with Siebel ferries and barges.

**^ LS Company reporting to DAK's Koruck 556 (rear area security).

*^^ An ah hoc HQ formed from Staff/155 *Schutzen Regiment*. Controlled the 361 Regiment and the III./241, III./255, III./258 and III./347 Battalions. Later formed the Division a.b.V. Afrika (and later the 90th Light Afrika Division)

© Nigel Askey, 2018

***

Table German Deployment Matrix	Deployment and Composition of the German Army, Waffen SS and Luftwaffe Flak Units, 22nd June 1941			
	Other Military Commands (*Militarbefehlshaber - XX*)*		Replacement Army (*Ersatzarmee*)^^* Chef H.Rust. u. B.d.E.	
	Description	No	Description	No
Army & Panzer Group HQs				
Army HQs				
Corps HQs				
Panzer Corps HQs			40*	1
Army Group Rear Area HQs				
Army & Army Grp Signal Regs				
Army & Army Grp Signal Batts				
Panzer Group Signal Regs				
Infantry Divisions			707***, 713**^, 218^* (+ 31 *Ersatz* Divisions & 19 Div HQ z.b.V.)^^*	3
Panzer Divisions			2*^, 5^^	2
Motorised Divisions			60**	1
SS Motorised Divisions				
Cavalry Divisions				
Mountain Divisions				
Light Divisions				
Fleiger Divisions				
Motorised Infantry Brigades				
Motorised Infantry Regiments				
Motorised Infantry Battalions				
(Mixed) Infantry Regiments				
(Mixed) Infantry Battalions				
Tank Brigades				
Tank Battalions				
Cavalry Regiments				
Security Divisions or Brigades			(201, 202, 203, 204 (Ersatz) Security Brigades)*^^	4
Guard (*Wach*) Battalions	48^^, 150, 591	3	603^**, 722, (*Wach. Kp* 709)	2 1/3
Landesschutzen Battalions	(128 Battalions, refer notes)^	124 3/4	361 LS Battalions in the Replacement Army ^^*	361
Artillery HQs, *Harko* & *Arko*			128^	1
Art Observation Battalions				
Artillery Reg HQs (Spec P)				
Mixed Artillery Battalions				
150mm How Battalions				
105mm Gun Battalions				
150mm Gun Battalions				
210mm How Battalions (1)				
210mm How Battalions (2)				
210mm Gun Battalions				
Hvy 240mm How Battalions				
Hvy 240mm Gun Battalions				
Super Hvy How Battalions				
Coastal Artillery Battalions				
Railroad Artillery Batteries	'Hel Peninsula'*^	2		
Anti-Air Battalions				
Light Anti-Air Battalions				
SP Light AA Companies			2./47~, 2./55*~, 3./608**~	3
Nebelwerfer Regiment HQs				
Nebelwerfer Regiments				
Nebelwerfer Battalions				
Entgiftungs Battalions				
Machine Gun Battalions				
Anti-Tank Battalions				
SP Anti-Tank Battalions				
SP Hvy Anti-Tank Companies				
Assault Gun Battalions				
Flame Tank Battalions				
Mot Eng Reg HQs (Spec P)				
Mot *Pionier* Battalions				
(Mixed) *Pionier* Battalions				
Bridge Const Battalions			Bridge Guard-Engineer	11
Assault Boat Companies				
Mot Sep Bridge Cols B				
Sep Bridge Cols, Type (A-T)				
Arm Mine Clearing Battalions				

Table German Deployment Matrix	Deployment and Composition of the German Army, Waffen SS and Luftwaffe Flak Units, 22nd June 1941			
	Other Military Commands (*Militarbefehlshaber - XX*)*		Replacement Army (*Ersatzarmee*)^^* Chef H.Rust. u. B.d.E.	
	Description	No	Description	No
Luft Flak Corps HQs				
Luft Flak Reg HQs				
Luft Mixed Flak Battalions				
Luft Light Flak Battalions			76^	1
Construction Reg HQs				
Construction Battalions				
Railroad Eng Reg HQs				
Railroad Pionier Bat HQs				
Railroad Pionier Companies				
Railroad Switching Comp's				
Railroad Eng Const Comp's				
Railroad Eng Const Batts				
Mot Police Regiment HQ	Warschau, Radom, Krakau & Lublin	4		
Police Rifle Battalions	301, 305, 306, 308, 310, 313	6		
Mot Military Police Battalions			(+ approximately 34 Motorised MP Sections)*~~	
Mot Traffic Control Battalions				
Armoured Trains				

* In the Field Army, includes: MB *Frankreich* (Military Governor in France), MB *Belgien und Nordfrankreich* (Military Governor in Belgium and Northern France), WB *Niederlande* (Armed Forces Command Netherlands), MB *im General-Gouvernement* (Occupied Poland, also abbreviated MiG). ^ Includes *Landesschutzen* Battalions: 221, 222, 266, 277, 2/3/4/278, 279 327, 328, 329, 330, 331, 340, 341 378, 385, 387, 388, 389, 390, 391, 414, 415, 418, 420, 421, 425 451, 452, 453, 454, 455, 457, 458, 459, 467, 480, 481, 482, 483, 484 485, 525, 526, 527, 528, 540, 541 575, 577, 579, 580, 581, 583 605, 625, 626, 627, 628, 629 630, 640, 641, 651, 654, 656, 657 658, 677, 678, 690, 691, 703, 722 735, 736, 737, 738, 745, 746, 751 753, 756, 758, 760, 761, 762, 763 764, 768, 769, 770, 771, 772, 773 774, 817, 835, 837, 838, 839, 845 846, 863, 886, 887, 888, 889, 903 904, 906, 907, 908, 951, 961, 971, 973, 990, 991, 992, 993, 994, 995, 996, 997, 998. *^ Railroad-Coastal Artillery Batteries; with 2x 38cm Siegfried K(E) railway guns. Used for coast defence of the Hel Peninsula in Poland. ^^ Bicycle mounted. Transferred to the East Front by 8th July 1941.	* 40th Pz Corps was attached to Wehrkreis XVII (B.d.E.) in June 1941. Along with the 60th Mot Division and other units, it was transferred to the East Front in July 1941. ^ Attached to 40th Pz Corps. ** 60th Motorised Division (in Wehrkreis XVII) was transferred to the East Front by 5th July 1941, assigned to Army Group South. *^ 2nd Panzer Div was attached to Wehrkreis VII (B.d.E.) in June 1941. It was transferred to the East Front in September 1941. ^^ 5th Panzer Div was attached to Wehrkreis III (B.d.E.) in June 1941. It was transferred to the East Front in September 1941. ^* Stationed in Denmark until January 1942. Possibly reported to 'Corps "Kaupisch"' (Befehlshaber der deutschen Truppen in Danemark). *** 707th (occupation) Infantry Div was attached to Wehrkreis VII in June 1941. It was transferred to the East Front by 16th August 1941 and assigned to security duties behind Army Group Centre. ***^ 713th (occupation) Infantry Div was attached to Wehrkreis XIII in OKH reserves in June 1941. It was scheduled to arrive on the East Front in July 1941 but was sent to Crete instead (became *Kreta* Fortress Division). *^^ The 201, 202, 203, 204 Ersatz Brigades were newly formed for occupation duties. They served as Replacement and Security Units. The 201st and 203rd Brigades formed the 201st and 203rd Security Divisions in June 1942. They dispatched 7x Battalions between them to the East Front in 1941. ~ 2./47th Lt AA Co was attached to 2nd Pz Div. *~ 2./55th Lt AA Co was attached to 5th Pz Div. **~ 3./608th Lt AA Co was attached to 60th Mot Div. *~~ Small units authorised only 43 men in the TOE. ^** Assigned to WK XX. ^^* Refer B.d.E Matrix (Table Rep Army) for details.

© Nigel Askey, 2018

***

Table German Deployment Matrix	Deployment and Composition of the German Army, Waffen SS and Luftwaffe Flak Units, 22nd June 1941		12th Army, DAK, B.d.E & Add Forces, Total No
	Additional Forces		
	Description	No	
Army & Panzer Group HQs			
Army HQs			1
Corps HQs	Special Staff 'F'*		2
Panzer Corps HQs			2
Army Group Rear Area HQs			
Army & Army Grp Signal Regs			1
Army & Army Grp Signal Batts			
Panzer Group Signal Regs			
Infantry Divisions			12
Panzer Divisions			3
Motorised Divisions			2
SS Motorised Divisions			
Cavalry Divisions			
Mountain Divisions			2
Light Divisions			
Fleiger Divisions			1
Motorised Infantry Brigades	IV./LSSAH Mot Brigade*^^	1/8	1/8
Motorised Infantry Regiments	1., 5., 9., 11., 13., 14., 16., 17./800zbV**^	1/2	1 1/2
Motorised Infantry Battalions	Fuhrer Escort Battalion (FBB)^	1	2
(Mixed) Infantry Regiments			2
(Mixed) Infantry Battalions			4
Tank Brigades			
Tank Battalions			1/3
Cavalry Regiments			
Security Divisions or Brigades			4
Guard (*Wach*) Battalions	43	1	6 1/3
Landesschutzen Battalions	318^^^, 335^**, 569^^*, 615^^~, 623	5	496
Artillery HQs, *Harko* & *Arko*			4
Art Observation Battalions			1
Artillery Reg HQs (Spec P)			1
Mixed Artillery Battalions	(865, 866)**	2	3
150mm How Battalions			
105mm Gun Battalions			2
150mm Gun Battalions			
210mm How Battalions (1)			1
210mm How Battalions (2)			
210mm Gun Battalions			
Hvy 240mm How Battalions			
Hvy 240mm Gun Battalions			
Super Hvy How Battalions			
Coastal Artillery Battalions			4
Railroad Artillery Batteries			3
Anti-Air Battalions			
Light Anti-Air Battalions	(613, 615)*^	2	4
SP Light AA Companies			3
Nebelwerfer Regiment HQs			
Nebelwerfer Regiments			
Nebelwerfer Battalions			
Entgiftungs Battalions			
Machine Gun Battalions			
Anti-Tank Battalions			
SP Anti-Tank Battalions			
SP Hvy Anti-Tank Companies			
Assault Gun Battalions	(177, 189, 202, 209, 244, 245, 249)^^	7	7
Flame Tank Battalions			
Mot Eng Reg HQs (Spec P)			1
Mot *Pionier* Battalions			2
(Mixed) *Pionier* Battalions			1
Bridge Const Battalions			13

Table German Deployment Matrix	Deployment and Composition of the German Army, Waffen SS and Luftwaffe Flak Units, 22nd June 1941		12th Army, DAK, B.d.E &
	Additional Forces		Add Forces,
	Description	No	Total No
Assault Boat Companies			
Mot Sep Bridge Cols B			1
Sep Bridge Cols, Type (A-T)			4
Arm Mine Clearing Battalions			
Luft Flak Corps HQs			
Luft Flak Reg HQs	Additional Luftwaffe FlaK Units	46	46
Luft Mixed Flak Battalions	(defending Germany and Occupied Europe)	264	266
Luft Light Flak Battalions		28	29
Construction Reg HQs	12 Ob	1	1
Construction Battalions	411***, 242Fr, 314Fr	3	4
Railroad Eng Reg HQs			
Railroad Pionier Bat HQs			
Railroad Pionier Companies			
Railroad Switching Comp's	'Unknown Des'	3	3
Railroad Eng Const Comp's	'Unknown Des'	11	11
Railroad Eng Const Batts	515	1	1
Mot Police Regiment HQ	Pol. Rgt Bohmen, Pol.Rgt Mahren	2	6
Police Rifle Battalions	32, 84	2	9
Mot Military Police Battalions			1
Mot Traffic Control Battalions			
Armoured Trains			2

* *Sonderstab* 'F' was the German 'military mission'
  formed for operations in Iraq and possibly Persia (Iran).
  Iraq was invaded in May 1941 and had capitulated
  by 30th May 1941. Iran was invaded (by the Allies)
  on 25th August 1941.
^ Fuhrer-Begleit-Bataillon (FBB), an elite unit which
  transferred to the East Front in September 1941
  (known as Kampfgruppe Nehring).
  Assigned to *Fuhrerhauptquartier* (*Wolfschanze*)
  East Prussia on 22nd June 1941.
** Forming in Wehrkreis XIII. Mixed Transport,
  disbanded in November 1941.
*^ The 613th and 615th Light AA Battalions were
  still forming in Wehrkreis VI and VII respectively.
  Transferred to the East Front in August 1941.
^^ In the Process of formation and training, partially
  equipped. Not immediately available as replacements.
  244th, 245th AG Battalions were transferred
  to the East Front in July 1941. 189th AG Battalion
  was transferred to the East Front in August 1941.
  177th and 202nd AG Battalions were transferred
  to the East Front in September 1941.
  209th AG Battalion was transferred
  to the East Front in January 1942.
*** Officially formed on 27th June 1941.
**^ Lehr Reg Brandenburg 800 zbV; Special Forces.
  1, 5, 9, 11, 13, 14, 16 and 17 Companies and Reg HQ
  The 9th and 16th Companies transferred to the East
  Front in September 1941.
*^^ Remained in Germany as Hitler's bodyguard unit
^^^ Att OKH, stationed in Berlin in WK III
^** Stationed in WK XVII
^^* Stationed in WK VIII
^^~ Slovakian Troops & in Slovakia.

© Nigel Askey, 2018

***

Table German Deployment Matrix	Total German Army, Waffen SS and Luftwaffe Flak Units, on all Fronts, 22nd June 1941	
	Total, All Fronts, 22-Jun-41 No	Additional Notes for Clarification
Army & Panzer Group HQs	8	Comprises 4 Army Group HQs and 4 Panzer Group HQs.
Army HQs	13	
Corps HQs	46	34 Infantry Corps and 12 Reduced Strength Corps (excludes 'Special Staff').
Panzer Corps HQs	12	
Army Group Rear Area HQs	3	Comprises RHG 101, RHG 102 and RHG 103.
Army & Army Grp Signal Regs	12	9 Army and 3 Army Group (AGD and Norway Army had 5 Signal Battalions only).
Army & Army Grp Signal Batts	11	5 in AGD & Norway Army, 3 in AGN,C,S RHG rear areas, 3 in Bef Finland.
Panzer Group Signal Regs	4	1 Pz Group Signal Regiment in each Panzer Group.
Infantry Divisions	153	Inc Police Div. Does not incl 250th (Span Blue Div) raised after 22nd June 1941.
Panzer Divisions	20	
Motorised Divisions	11	Includes 5th Light Div in Africa (became 21st Pz Div on 1st August 1941).
SS Motorised Divisions	3	
Cavalry Divisions	1	
Mountain Divisions	6	
Light Divisions	4	
Fleiger Divisions	1	
Motorised Infantry Brigades	5	Comprises 900th Lehr, 1st SS Brig RF, 2nd Brig RFSS, SS Brigade Nord, LSSAH.
Motorised Infantry Regiments	3	Comprises GD Inf Reg, 800zbV, 1st Luftlande Sturm Reg.
Motorised Infantry Battalions	3	Comprises 100zbV, FBB, 300zbV (in DAK - *Deutsches Afrika Korps*).
(Mixed) Infantry Regiments	5	Comprises 125th, 361 in DAK, and 2nd, 3rd and 4th Security Regs (*Sich.Rgt*).
(Mixed) Infantry Battalions	9 1/3	Comprises 8 Army & 1 Naval Security Battalion, and 1 Mountain Company.
Tank Brigades	2	
Tank Battalions	2 2/3	Includes 5./Pz Reg 31/5th Pz Div on Crete, and the Panzer-Kompanie Paris.
Cavalry Regiments	2	Comprises SS-*Kavallerie-Regiments* 1 and 2.
Security Divisions or Brigades	13	Includes 201, 202, 203, 204 (*Ersatz*) Security Brigades.
Guard (*Wach*) Battalions	45 1/3	Excludes 619, 620, 613 and 614 Battalions assigned to *Sich.Rgt* 3 and 4.
Landesschutzen Battalions	542	Comprises 181 in the Field Army and 361 in the Replacement Army.
Artillery HQs, *Harko* & *Arko*	61	Comprises 2 *Harko* HQs and 59 *Arko* HQs.
Art Observation Battalions	36	Excludes 6 Balloon Artillery Observation Batteries, which were attached.
Artillery Reg HQs (Spec P)	40	36 Mot Art Reg HQs, 213th Horse Drawn HQ, & 720, 766 and 781 Railroad HQs.
Mixed Artillery Battalions	16 1/3	Incs 1./477th Battery (No Mtn Cps), I./231 (12A), 510 (AGD), 865, 866 (R Army).
150mm How Battalions	37	Includes 3 Horse-Drawn Battalions in 17th Army.
105mm Gun Battalions	31	Includes 1./, 2./, 3./730 Horse-Drawn Batteries (without a HQ) in Bef Norway.
150mm Gun Battalions	7	
210mm How Battalions (1)	20	Inc 682, 683, 684 Independent Batteries (1 Bat Equiv) in XII Corps, 2nd Pz Grp.
210mm How Battalions (2)	10	
210mm Gun Battalions	2	
Hvy 240mm How Battalions	2	
Hvy 240mm Gun Battalions	2	
Super Hvy How Battalions	4	
Coastal Artillery Battalions	57	171 Coastal Artillery Batteries (57 Battalions).
Railroad Artillery Batteries	22	Includes 2 Batteries on the Hel (German *Hela*) Peninsula in Poland.
Anti-Air Battalions	10	
Light Anti-Air Battalions	14	Excludes the 606th in 5th Lt Div (DAK), and the 616th, which was forming.
SP Light AA Companies	51	Inc 21 SP Lt AA Companies attached to Pz & Mot Divs, and 2 attached to Inf Divs.
Nebelwerfer Regiment HQs	4	
Nebelwerfer Regiments	5	
Nebelwerfer Battalions	7 1/3	Includes 8./222nd Separate Battery in Norway/Finland (Bef Norway).
Entgiftungs Battalions	8	Includes 3 Motorised Road Decontamination Battalions

Table German Deployment Matrix	Total German Army, Waffen SS and Luftwaffe Flak Units, on all Fronts, 22nd June 1941	
	Total, All Fronts, 22-Jun-41 No	Additional Notes for Clarification
Machine Gun Battalions	8	Excludes 2nd & 8th in 5th Lt Div (DAK). Incs 16th & 17th non-mot Batts (AGD).
Anti-Tank Battalions	6	
SP Anti-Tank Battalions	10	Excludes the 605th, which is included in the TOE of 5th Light Division (DAK).
SP Hvy Anti-Tank Companies	1	
Assault Gun Battalions	19 2/3	Incs 600 Abt zbV HQ with 3 sep batteries, 2 indep batteries & 7 new battalions.
Flame Tank Battalions	3	
Mot Eng Reg HQs (Spec P)	29	
Mot *Pionier* Battalions	23	
(Mixed) *Pionier* Battalions	31	
Bridge Const Battalions	40 1/4	Includes the 4./17 *Ersatz* Company (11A) & 11 Bridge Guard-Eng Batts (BdE).
Assault Boat Companies	6	901st to 906th Motorised Assault Boat Companies (*Sturmboot Kdo*)
Mot Sep Bridge Cols B**	120	Refer Additional Notes Below *.
Sep Bridge Cols, Type (A-T)	49	Refer Additional Notes Below ^.
Arm Mine Clearing Battalions	1	
Luft Flak Corps HQs	2	
Luft Flak Reg HQs	59	
Luft Mixed Flak Battalions	308	
Luft Light Flak Battalions	46	
Construction Reg HQs	47	Refer Additional Notes Below **.
Construction Battalions	147	Refer Additional Notes Below *^.
Railroad Eng Reg HQs	8	
Railroad Pionier Bat HQs	8	
Railroad Pionier Companies	53	
Railroad Switching Comp's	13	
Railroad Eng Const Comp's	27	
Railroad Eng Const Batts	10	
Mot Police Regiment HQ	12	
Police Rifle Battalions	41	
Mot Military Police Battalions	21	
Mot Traffic Control Battalions	11	
Armoured Trains	16	

* Excludes 59 Columns assigned to combat units. These comprised 19 in Panzer Divisions, 10 in Motorised Divisions, 25 in Motorised Pionier Battalions, 3 in SS Motorised Divisions, 1 in the LSSAH Brigade and 1 in the 900th Lehr Brigade. These 59 Motorised Bridge Column Type Bs are included in the TOE of these units.

^ Excludes 24 Columns assigned to combat units. These comprised 23 Type T Columns in Infantry Divisions (16 in 2nd Wave Divisions, 1 in the 72nd Division, 1 in the 262nd Division, and 5 in 5th Wave Divisions), and 1 motorised Type K Bridge column assigned to the 62nd Motorised Combat Engineer Battalion. 18 Columns were motorised and 6 were horse-drawn (in 78th Div and all 5th Wave Divisions). These 24 Columns are included in the TOE of the relevant units. Also excluded is the 800th Motorised Heavy Bridge Transport Battalion for moving heavy bridges.

** Comprises 10 Main Construction HQs (*Oberbaustab*), 31 Commander of Construction Troops HQs (*Kdr. d. Bautruppen*), 4 Fortress Construction HQs, 1 Special HQ in 4th Army, and 1 Special Snow Clearing HQ in Norway.

*^ Comprises 101 Construction, 23 Road (2 motorised), 7 Bicycle Road, 1 Marine and 15 Fortress. Does not include any Battalions from the Organisation Todt (OT), or the Reich Labour Service (RAD, *Reichsarbeitsdienst*).

© Nigel Askey, 2018

***

2. German Land Combat Unit Reinforcements on the East Front from 5th July to 31st December 1941

Table German Reinforcement Matrix shows the German Army, Waffen SS and Luftwaffe Flak reinforcements to the East Front from 5th July to 31st December 1941. This table includes land combat units transferred to the East Front from the Western Fronts or the Replacement Army, and land combat units which were mobilised after 4th July 1941 and then deployed to the East Front before the end of the year (i.e. Mobilised and Deployed (MD) combat units). The '**East Front**' includes forces assigned to Army Group North, Army Group Centre, Army Group South, the Norway Army - *Befehlsstelle Finnland* (East Front only) and OKH Reserves. Relevant notes at the bottom of each column provide additional information on the combat units listed, including their initial assignment on the East Front (if known).

From this table we can see that a total of 24 divisions arrived as reinforcements from 4th July to the end of December 1941. This included 19 infantry divisions, the 2nd and 5th Panzer Divisions, the 60th Motorised Division, the 6th Mountain Division and the 7th Flieger Division. Of these divisions, only the 250th Infantry Division (the Spanish Blue Division) was mobilised after 4th July 1941 and quickly sent to the East Front. Most of the divisions arrived in July (nine divisions including one motorised division) and September (six divisions including two panzer divisions).

This means that of the 208 divisions that existed in the German Army and Waffen SS on 22nd June 1941, a total of 161 divisions (77%) were committed to the East Front in the second half of 1941. It should be noted, however, that considerably more than three quarters of the German Army's total combat capable strength was committed in the East in 1941. This was because 30 of the 47 divisions that remained in the Western Fronts or the Replacement Army were 13th, 14th and 15th wave infantry divisions: apart from the security divisions these were the smallest, weakest and least mobile divisions in the army. On the other side of the coin, the Replacement Army fielded an additional 31 replacement divisions, which were sizeable formations and are not included in the German Deployment Matrix as they are not considered combat-units in the German FILARM model.

Non-divisional forces (i.e. forces outside of the divisions), which arrived as reinforcements on the East Front from 4th July to 31st December 1941, included the following.

- The XXVII Corps and the XXXX Motorised Corps HQs.

- **Motorised infantry forces,** with 1 motorised infantry regiment (the 1st *Luftlande Sturm Regiment*), three companies from *the Lehr Regiment Brandenburg* (800 zbV), 1 motorised infantry battalion (the *Führer-Begleit Bataillon* - FBB) and 1 Waffen SS motorised infantry battalion (the SS *Freiwilligen Legion Flandern*).

  The 15./800zbV *Brandenburgers* Company (special forces) and the SS *Freiwilligen Legion Flandern* were mobilised after 4th July 1941, and are therefore Mobilised and Deployed (MD) combat units in the German FILARM model.

- **Mixed transport infantry forces,** with 4 infantry regiments and 14 infantry battalions. The regiments included the 193rd Infantry Regiment detached from the 69th Infantry Division, the 388th Infantry Regiment detached from the 214th Infantry Division, the 369th Reinforced (Croat) Infantry Regiment and the 638th Separate (French) Infantry Regiment.

  The 369th and 638th Infantry Regiments were mobilised after 4th July 1941 and are MD combat units in the German FILARM model.

  The mixed transport infantry battalions included the 373rd 'Wallonian' Infantry Battalion, 7 *Ersatz* Infantry Battalions (from the 201st, 202nd and 204th *Ersatz* Security Brigades in the Replacement Army), the 95th *Gebirgsjäger* Reconnaissance and 95th *Gebirgsjäger* Anti-Tank Battalions (detached from the 5th Mountain Division), and 4 *Skijäger* Battalions.

  The 373rd 'Wallonian' Infantry Battalion was mobilised after 4th July 1941 and is a MD combat units in the German FILARM model.[17]

- **Mixed transport security and army-militia forces,** with 35 battalions. These comprised the 48th Guard (*Wach*) Battalion, 27 *Landesschützen* battalions, 2 Ukrainian nationalist militia battalions, and 5 Estonian (ERNA) nationalist militia battalions.

---

[17] The 2nd, 3rd, 8th and 9th *Skijäger* Battalions were formed from existing *Gebirgsjäger* or *Jäger* Battalions on the East Front. In the German FILARM model they are therefore not MD units, but are D units (i.e. they were Deployed (D) on 22nd June 1941) and which were renamed as *Skijäger* Battalions and issued skies.

The *Landesschützen* and nationalist militia battalions were mobilised after 4th July 1941 and are MD combat units in the German FILARM model.

- **Armoured forces,** with the 203rd Panzer Regiment and 5 assault gun (*Sturmgeschütz*) battalions.

The 203rd Panzer Regiment was mobilised after 4th July 1941 and is a MD combat units in the German FILARM model.[18]

- **Artillery forces,** with 1 *Arko* HQ, 2 railroad artillery HQs, 1 artillery battalion, 1 separate artillery battery, and 7 railroad artillery batteries.

The II Artillery Battalion /Lehr-Rgt.2, 999th Artillery Battery, 459th Railroad Artillery Battery and 693rd Railroad Artillery Battery, were mobilised after 4th July 1941 and are MD combat units in the German FILARM model.

- **Army flak forces,** with 3 light anti-aircraft battalions and 4 light anti-aircraft companies.

The 616th Army Light Flak Battalion was mobilised after 4th July 1941 and is a MD combat units in the German FILARM model.

- **Luftwaffe flak forces,** with 5 Luftwaffe flak regiment HQs, 16 Luftwaffe mixed flak battalions and 5 Luftwaffe light flak battalions.

All the Luftwaffe flak units (above) were was mobilised after 4th July 1941 and are considered to be MD combat units in the German FILARM model.

- **Anti-tank forces,** with the 625th self-propelled anti-tank battalion.

- **Combat engineer (*Pionier*) and engineer construction forces,** with 3 special engineer regiment HQs, 1 motorised combat engineer battalion and 1 semi-motorised combat engineer battalion.

The 605th and 623rd Motorised Special Engineer Regiment HQs were mobilised after 4th July 1941 and are MD combat units in the German FILARM model.

- **Bridging forces,** with 1 motorised type B bridge column and 1 semi-motorised type A bridge column.

- **Army construction forces,** with 1 army construction battalion. Note this excludes any additional battalions from the Todt Organisation (*Organisation Todt* – OT) or the Reich Labour Service (*Reichsarbeitsdienst* – RAD)).

- **Snow clearing forces**, with 78 motorised snow clearing sections. These small units were usually attached to road construction companies.

All the snow clearing sections were mobilised in or after October 1941, and are considered to be MD units in the German FILARM model.

***

---

[18] Note, the assault-gun (*Sturmgeschütz*) battalions were in the process of completing their formation and training on 22nd June 1941 and were partially equipped. They are considered Deployed (D) combat units in the FILARM model, which were brought to full strength prior to being transferred to the East. They used some of the assault guns which were available between July and December 1941 (i.e. they used a proportion of the assault-gun Replacements (R)).
Refer Volume IIB 4. 2) a - 'The German Tank MD and MND Matrix' for details on German fully tracked AFV allocations from June to December 1941.

German Reinforcement Matrix — German Army, Waffen SS and Luftwaffe Flak Reinforcements to the East Front, 5th July 1941 - 31st December 1941

Month	July 1941		August 1914		September 1941	
	count	units	count	units	count	units
Army & Panzer Group HQs						
Army HQs						
Corps HQs						
Panzer Corps HQs	1	40				
Army Group Rear Area HQs						
Army & Army Grp Signal Regs						
Army & Army Grp Signal Batts						
Panzer Group Signal Regs						
Infantry Divisions	8	260*, 94^, 98**, 96*^, 93^^, 46*^, 73*~, 294~~	3	339*, 183^, 707**	2	227^, 250**
Panzer Divisions					2	2*,5*
Motorised Divisions	1	60~*				
SS Motorised Divisions						
Cavalry Divisions						
Mountain Divisions					1	6*^
Light Divisions						
Fleiger Divisions					2/3	7^^
Motorised Infantry Brigades						
Motorised Infantry Regiments					1 1/8	1st Luftlande Sturm^*, 9 & 16,/800zbV*~~
Motorised Infantry Battalions					1	Fuhrer Escort Battalion (FBB)*~
(Mixed) Infantry Regiments			2	388*^, 369^^		
(Mixed) Infantry Battalions	2	2xUKR Mil Bats*^^	5	5xEst Mil Bats (ERNA)^*		
Tank Brigades						
Tank Battalions						
Cavalry Regiments						
Security Divisions or Brigades						
Guard (*Wach*) Battalions	1	48				
Landesschutzen Battalions	2	2x LS Bats	2	2x LS Bats		
Artillery HQs, *Harko & Arko*	1	128				
Art Observation Battalions	1	781zbV^^^			1	766zbV~~
Artillery Reg HQs (Spec P)						
Mixed Artillery Battalions						
150mm How Battalions					1/3	999th Artillery Battery~*
105mm Gun Battalions					1	II,/Lehr-Rgt.2***
150mm Gun Battalions						
210mm How Battalions (1)						
210mm How Battalions (2)						
210mm Gun Battalions						
Hvy 240mm How Battalions						
Hvy 240mm Gun Battalions						
Super Hvy How Battalions						
Coastal Artillery Battalions						
Railroad Artillery Batteries	3	(674, 722, 721)***	1	689	2	(693, 695)**^
Anti-Air Battalions						
Light Anti-Air Battalions	2	5,/52, 3,/608^^*	3	613, 615, 616		
SP Light AA Companies					2	2,/47*^^, 2,/55^^^
Nebelwerfer Regiment HQs						
Nebelwerfer Regiments						
Nebelwerfer Battalions						
Entgiftungs Battalions						
Machine Gun Battalions						
Anti-Tank Battalions						
SP Anti-Tank Battalions	1	625				
SP Hvy Anti-Tank Companies						

	Units	No.	Units	No.	Units	No.
Assault Gun Battalions	244**~, 245*~~	2	189*~	1	177^~, 202^^*	2
Flame Tank Battalions						
Mot Eng Reg HQs (Spec P)			685	1		
Mot Pionier Battalions			666~~	1		
(Mixed) Pionier Battalions	659~~~	1				
Bridge Const Battalions						
Assault Boat Companies						
Mot Sep Bridge Cols B			132	1		
Sep Bridge Cols, Type (A-T)			660	1		
Arm Mine Clearing Battalions						
Luft Flak Corps HQs						
Luft Flak Reg HQs	21, 37, 136	3				
Luft Mixed Flak Battalions	9x Battalions	9			L/38	1
Luft Light Flak Battalions	76, 2x Battalions	3			245	1
Construction Reg HQs						
Construction Battalions						
Railroad Eng Reg HQs						
Railroad Pionier Bat HQs						
Railroad Pionier Companies						
Railroad Switching Comp's						
Railroad Eng Const Comp's						
Railroad Eng Const Batts						
Mot Police Regiment HQ						
Police Rifle Battalions						
Mot Military Police Battalions						
Mot Traffic Control Battalions						
Armoured Trains						

Notes/Location Codes:

AGN Army Group North
AGC Army Group Centre
AGS Army Group South
FIN/NOR Finland, Norway
OKH Reserve

* 260th Infantry Division was transferred to the East Front by 11th July 1941, AGC.

^ 94th Infantry Division was transferred to the East Front by 9th July 1941, AGS.

** 98th Infantry Division was transferred to the East Front by 21st July 1941, AGS.

*^ 96th Infantry Division was transferred to the East Front by 20th July 1941, AGN.

^^ 93rd Infantry Division was transferred to the East Front 29th June to 5th July 1941, AGN.

^* 46th Infantry Division transferred to the East Front by 5th July 1941, AGS.

*~ 73rd Infantry Division transferred to the East Front by 13th July 1941, AGS.

~~ 294th Infantry Division was transferred to the East Front by 29th July 1941, AGS.

~* 60th Motorised Division was transferred to the East Front by 5th July 1941, AGS.

*^^ 2x Ukrainian Nationalist Militia, remained in Ukraine.

^^^ 781st HQ was a Railroad Artillery HQ.

^** Controlled by the 676th, 681st and 780th Railroad Artillery Battalion HQs.

^^* 3,/608 was attached to 60th Motorised Division.

**~ Sturmgeschutz-Abteilung 244 arrived on 8th July 1941, assigned to 6th Army (AGS).

*~~ Sturmgeschutz-Abteilung 245 had arrived by 15th July. Assigned to the 100th Light Inf Div, 17th Army (AGS).

~~~ Assigned to 17th Army, AGS.

* 339th Infantry Division was transferred to the East Front by 30th August 1941, Security AGC.

^ 183rd Infantry Division transferred to the East Front by mid August 1941 (Poland by July 1941), AGN.

** 707th Infantry Division was transferred to the East Front by 16th August 1941, assigned to security duties behind Army Group Centre.

*^ 388th Infantry Regiment, FIN/NOR. Includes I,/214th Artillery Battalion and 2nd Company/214th Pionier Battalion. All detached from the 214th Infantry Division (which remained in Norway).

^^ 369th Reinforced (Croat) Infantry Regiment, AGS, attached to 100th Light Division.

^* 5 ERNA Militia Battalions, remained in Estonia. They include the Hirvel, Talpek, Kurg, Kant and Leith Battalions.

*~ Sturmgeschutz-Abteilung 189 arrived 5th-10th August 1941, assigned to 9th Army (AGC).

~~ Assigned to 4th Rumanian Army by September 41.

* 2nd and 5th Panzer Divisions were transferred to the East Front in early September 1941 after refitting their 3rd and 31st Panzer Regiments, respectively, OKH.

^ 227th Infantry Division was transferred to the East Front in late September 1941, AGN.

** Newly mobilised 250th Spanish 'Blue' Division, AGN.

*^ 6th Mountain Division was transferred to the East Front in September 1941, FIN/NOR (North Finland).

^^ The 7th Flieger (Para) Division, with its 1st and 3rd Fallschirmjäger Regiments only, AGN.

^* 1st Luftlande Sturm Regiment, AGN.

*~ Fuhrer-Begleit-Bataillon (FBB), OKH.

~ 766th Rail Art Reg HQ. Sent to 11th Army (Coastal Defence).

~* 999th Artillery Battery only. Horse-drawn & equipped with 15cm K(f) Hows. Assigned Mtn Corps, NOR/FIN.

*** II,/Lehr-Rgt 2 had 15cm K18s and was assigned to 11th Army AGS, by 15th September 1941.

*** Assigned to AGN.

*^ 2,/47th attached to 2nd Panzer Division.

^^ 2,/55th attached to 5th Panzer Division.

*** Sturmgeschutz-Abteilung 177 arrived at Smolensk on 10th September 1941, assigned to 4th Army (AGC).

^^ Sturmgeschutz-Abteilung 202 arrived 15th September 1941, assigned to 2nd Panzer Group (AGC).

**~ Assigned to 11th Army (AGS) by 15th September 1941.

*~~ Lehr Reg Brandenburg 800 zbV; Special Forces. 9th Company assigned to AGC. 16th Company assigned AGN and used to invade Osel Island.

German Reinforcement Matrix	German Army, Waffen SS and Luftwaffe Flak Reinforcements to the East Front, 5th July 1941 - 31st December 1941		
Month	**October 1941**	**November 1941**	**December 1941**
Army & Panzer Group HQs			
Army HQs	1 — 27*		
Corps HQs		1	
Panzer Corps HQs			
Army Group Rear Area HQs			
Army & Army Grp Signal Regs			
Army & Army Grp Signal Batts			
Panzer Group Signal Regs			
Infantry Divisions	1 — 212^	2 — 215*, 223^	3 — 81*, 83^, 216**
Panzer Divisions			
Motorised Divisions			
SS Motorised Divisions			
Cavalry Divisions			
Mountain Divisions			
Light Divisions			
Fleiger Divisions		1/3 — 2/7 Fj Reg**	1/16
Motorised Infantry Brigades			
Motorised Infantry Regiments	2 — 638*^, 193^^	1 — SS Freiwilligen Legion Flandern*^	15,/800zbV~*
Motorised Infantry Battalions			
(Mixed) Infantry Regiments			
(Mixed) Infantry Battalions	2 — 1/602**, 373***	2 — 95th Geb Rec Bat, 95th Geb Geb PzJag Bat***	10 — (1/601, 1/609, 1/611, 1/607, 2/605, 2/606)*^, (2, 3, 8, 9)Ski^^
Tank Brigades			
Tank Battalions			1 — 203rd Panzer Regiment^^
Cavalry Regiments			
Security Divisions or Brigades			
Guard (*Wach*) Battalions			
Landesschutzen Battalions	5 — 5 x LS Bats	13 — 13x LS Bats	5 — 5x LS Bats
Artillery HQs, *Harko & Arko*			
Art Observation Battalions			
Artillery Reg HQs (Spec P)			
Mixed Artillery Battalions			
150mm How Battalions			
105mm Gun Battalions			
150mm Gun Battalions			
210mm How Battalions (1)			
210mm How Battalions (2)			
210mm Gun Battalions			
Hvy 240mm How Battalions			
Hvy 240mm Gun Battalions			
Super Hvy How Battalions			
Coastal Artillery Battalions			
Railroad Artillery Batteries			1 — 459*~
Anti-Air Battalions			
Light Anti-Air Battalions			
SP Light AA Companies			
Nebelwerfer Regiment HQs			
Nebelwerfer Regiments			
Nebelwerfer Battalions			

Unit			
Entgiftungs Battalions		(103, 104, 105, 131, 132, 133)^^	
Machine Gun Battalions			
Anti-Tank Battalions			
SP Anti-Tank Battalions			
SP Hvy Anti-Tank Companies			
Assault Gun Battalions			
Flame Tank Battalions		1	1
Mot Eng Reg HQs (Spec P)		623^^	605~~
Mot Pionier Battalions			
(Mixed) Pionier Battalions			
Bridge Const Battalions			
Assault Boat Companies			
Mot Sep Bridge Cols B			
Sep Bridge Cols, Type (A-T)	1		1
Arm Mine Clearing Battalions	3		3
Luft Flak Corps HQs	1		1
Luft Flak Reg HQs	17		35
Luft Mixed Flak Battalions	3x Battalions		3x Battalions
Luft Light Flak Battalions	1x Battalion		1x Battalion
Construction Reg HQs			
Construction Battalions	Snow Clearing Sections	Snow Clearing Sections	Snow Clearing Sections (78 in total)
Railroad Eng Reg HQs			
Railroad Pionier Bat HQs			
Railroad Pionier Companies			
Railroad Switching Comp's			
Railroad Eng Const Comp's			
Railroad Eng Const Batts			
Mot Police Regiment HQ			
Police Rifle Battalions			
Mot Military Police Battalions			
Mot Traffic Control Battalions			
Armoured Trains			

Notes/Location Codes:

AGN Army Group North
AGC Army Group Centre
AGS Army Group South
FIN/NOR Finland, Norway
OKH Reserve

* Attached to 9th Army, AGC.

^ 212 Infantry Division was transferred to the East Front in late October 1941, AGN.

*^ 638th Separate (French) Infantry Regiment. Used French volunteer personnel (LVF) and German officers. Attached to 7th Infantry Division, AGC.

^^ 193 Infantry Regiment, FIN/NOR. Detached from the 69th Infantry Division (which remained in Norway).

*^ 1./602 Ersatz Infantry Battalion from the 202nd Ersatz Brigade, AGN

*** 373rd 'Wallonian' Infantry Battalion, AGS. Attached to 101st Light Division.

* 215 Infantry Division was transferred to the East Front in November 1941, AGN.

^ 223rd Infantry Division was transferred to the East Front on 30th November 1941, AGN.

** 2nd Fallschirmjager Regiment, AGN

*^ SS Freiwilligen Legion Flandern, OKH. Assigned to the 2nd SS RFB.

^^ All Entgiftungs Battalions upgraded with all Batteries having the 28/32cm Rocket systems. 131, 132 and 133 were redesignated as schw. Werfer Abteilung (Heavy Rocket Battalions). 101 and 102 were upgraded in January 1942.

^* Assigned 9th Army, AGC.

*** The 5th Mtn Division's 95th Bicycle Rec and 95th PzJag Battalions. Assigned FIN/NOR, 6th Mtn Division.

* 81st Infantry Division was transferred to the East Front in December 1941, AGC/AGN.

^ 83rd Infantry Division was transferred to the East Front in late December 1941, OKH/AGC

** 216th Infantry Division was transferred to the East Front in December 1941, AGC.

*^ All Ersatz Infantry Battalions from the 201st and 204th Ersatz Brigades, AGN.

^^ 2, 3, 8, 9 Skijager Battalions. These units were formed from existing Gebirgsjager or Jager Battalions on the East Front.

^* The 203rd Panzer Regiment was a separate unit. It was not a 'Tank Brigade' as such: it contained 2x Panzer Battalions without additional infantry or artillery units.

*~ Went to the Crimea in 1941/42

~~ Assigned to 4th Panzer Group, AGC.

~* Lehr Reg Brandenburg 800 zbV; Special Forces. 15th Company assigned to Norway Mountain Corps, Nth Finland.

© Nigel Askey, 2018

3. The Total Personnel and Equipment in a Deployed (D) State in the Reich from 22nd June to 4th July 1941

1) The Total Personnel and Equipment Allocated to Combat Units and in a Deployed (D) state in the German Army, Waffen SS, Luftwaffe Ground Forces and Naval Coastal Artillery from 22nd June to 4th July 1941

Drawing on the relevant information presented in Volume IIA 3. (The Tables of Organisation and Equipment for German Land Combat Units from 22nd June to 31st December 1941, and The Unit's Actual Organisation and Equipment in 1941), and Volume IIB 1. (The Order of Battle (OOB) of German Land Combat Units from 22nd June to 4th July 1941), we can ascertain the total personnel and equipment allocated to combat units in a Deployed (D) state in the Reich from 22nd June to 4th July 1941.

The results of this laborious and exhaustive process are shown in tables Ger Total Deployed (D) 1 (pp. 74-77) and Ger Total Deployed (D) 2 (pp 82-85).[19] Note, the information shown in these tables is based on the combat units' **actual strengths** wherever possible and **not simply on the units' TOEs**. As noted in the relevant sections, the actual strengths of individual combat units on 22nd June are (where possible) based directly on the unit's history (i.e. based on the heterogeneous or non-homogeneous model).[20] If specific unit strength data is unavailable, which is the case for most of the smaller than division combat units, then actual strengths are based on other methods (i.e. qualitative information, checksum reconciliation processes and use of a homogeneous model). All these combat units were available for ground combat if they came into contact with enemy forces. They all suffered losses and gained replacements as long as they survived as cohesive units in the Wehrmacht OOB and weren't literally wiped out.

Tables Ger Total Deployed (D) 1 and Ger Total Deployed (D) 2 focus specifically on any personnel and equipment, in any branch of the Wehrmacht and Waffen SS, likely to contribute in any significant way to direct combat in a ground battle. Many of the combat units involved (refer to the German Deployment Matrix) would be very weak in direct combat because their primary function was never to fight directly with enemy troops. Examples include the various army group, army and corps HQs, the high level signal regiments and battalions, the various types of construction regiments and battalions, and the separate bridging columns. Nevertheless, all these units contained armed troops and a Table of Organisation and Equipment (German KStN), and would fight if direct contact with the enemy was unavoidable. Note, the enemy would likely attempt to seek out and destroy (or at least disrupt) these 'weaker' combat units because their real value obviously lay in establishing critical support functions, and command and control. This was one of the principal aims of the Soviet 'deep operations' theories (what the Soviet's termed 'operational shock') and the German deep penetration panzer thrusts in WWII. Any realistic military simulation at the operational-strategic level must simulate these 'operational shock' effects in detail. In addition, any serious analysis or discussion of a particular military campaign should include how these 'support units' were affected historically, because their severe disruption almost invariably led to catastrophic collapse of the front in question. E.g., how disrupted were these units in determining the ability of a side to launch counter-offensive operations or even cohesive defensive operations? [21]

The key points for the reader to understand here are that if a unit is not shown in the German Deployment Matrix then: it **is not** considered a combat unit, personnel and equipment **is not** allocated to it in tables Ger Total Deployed (D) 1 and Ger Total Deployed (D) 2, and it **is not** considered to be in a Deployed (D) state. It still existed as a 'rear area' unit and it may have had an important support function, but its direct combat value was negligible. Examples were ground personnel and units supporting air-units (on airfields), naval personnel crewing or supporting ships (in ports), and 'battalions' from the *Organisation Todt* (OT) and the *Reichsarbeitsdienst* (RAD). These units (which are not classified as combat units and do not appear in the Deployment Matrix) still influenced combat operations, but they did so indirectly via air and naval operations, and building support infrastructures. In cases where personnel from these branches were armed and organised as infantry, they appear as combat units.

---

[19] Also refer to Volume I 3. 3) – 'Resource Allocation States inside the FILARM Model' for definitions of Deployed (D), Mobilised and Deployed (MD), and Mobilised and Not Deployed (MND) units. All the personnel and equipment (or resources) in tables Ger Total Deployed (D) 1 and Ger Total Deployed (D) 2 are classified as being in a Deployed (D) 'resource allocation state' in the German FILARM model.

[20] Refer Volume I 7. – 'The Heterogeneous vs. the Homogeneous Model'.

[21] I am still amazed at the fact that many current military-history commentators still demonstrate no grasp of the concepts behind 'deep operations' and 'operational shock', or the consequences of this happening. E.g., In Operation Barbarossa and Germany's Defeat in the East, David Stahel makes no mention of this vital effect on Soviet military operations in the Western or Reserve Fronts in July and August 1941 (it is as though this effect never existed, and panzer and motorised divisions were the only significant units fielded). Stahel. D., Cambridge University Press, New York, 2011.

Table Ger Total Deployed (D) 1

Total Personnel & Equipment Allocated to Combat Units in a Deployed (D) State in the German Army, Waffen SS, Luftwaffe Ground Forces and Naval Coastal Artillery; 22nd June to 4th July 1941

Resources/Equip.	Army Group North					Army Group Centre						Army Group South						Nor A (Bef Fin)	OKH Res	Total East Front*
	18th A	4th PzG	16th A	AGN Re	Total AGN	3rd PzG	9th A	4th A	2nd PzG	AGC Re	Total AGC	6th A	1st PzG	17th A	11th A	AGS Re	Total AGS			
Total Manpower	184776	200213	223066	103734	711788	172747	397516	326909	369527	41081	1307779	163565	357940	270596	180702	40608	1013411	87626	238740	3359345
Manpwr in (D) Units	148918	152326	176279	84579	562101	126265	316777	265195	282447	31405	1022089	130463	270237	224571	146675	31717	803662	77789	199829	2665470
Heavy Rifle Sqd	2268	1728	2520	1296	7812	1080	5058	4104	3348	324	13914	1728	3354	3360	2268	216	10926	1350	3708	37710
Light Rifle Sqd	317	135	282	312	1046	127	444	451	254	312	1588	299	241	307	256	143	1246	104	136	4120
Motor Cycle Sqd	849	2017	979	421	4266	2152	1945	1381	3434	258	9170	648	3188	1181	805	202	6024	559	1027	21046
Bicycle Sqd	186	152	150	370	858	116	294	357	260	141	1168	145	172	410	185	140	1052	117	235	3430
Cavalry Sqd	114	18	144	18	294	0	219	141	339	72	771	51	93	123	69	0	336	9	189	1599
Eng Sqd	321	482	513	144	1460	414	819	610	871	45	2759	261	871	501	381	33	2047	204	462	6932
Light Eng Sqd	916	603	1232	166	2917	153	1903	1873	748	37	4714	1367	725	1492	745	409	4738	285	278	12932
Ferry Bridging Sqd	142	227	362	174	905	246	192	189	319	75	1021	135	376	111	607	666	1895	35	135	3991
Military Police Sqd	62	39	62	480	643	60	148	229	69	264	770	155	74	206	62	241	738	14	379	2544
Irregular Sqd	0	0	0	416	416	0	96	192	0	0	288	128	0	256	160	64	608	0	32	1344
Rail Repair Sqd	308	292	407	31	1038	16	401	463	56	0	936	405	74	120	202	32	833	78	16	2901
HMG	880	764	930	581	3155	582	1833	1513	1578	246	5752	673	1424	1154	827	160	4238	500	1336	14981
LMG	805	1511	854	1241	4411	1602	1683	1629	2824	532	8270	752	2450	1460	925	326	5913	406	984	19984
AT Rifle	657	180	756	306	1899	0	1314	1208	597	96	3215	472	573	1061	648	72	2826	306	1041	9287
50mm Mor	567	516	645	309	2037	390	1332	1086	1035	111	3954	456	1008	897	591	87	3039	382	969	10381
81mm Mor	384	342	430	216	1372	246	846	684	676	62	2514	288	642	558	396	42	1926	264	624	6700
Horse Team	9022	2668	9563	5823	27076	56	18009	15404	8214	1469	43152	7190	7806	13224	9310	1221	38751	3949	14041	126969
Unit Trucks	6422	13159	8411	3536	31528	13814	14542	10754	22650	1854	63614	5442	21731	8688	5941	1522	43324	4310	7312	150088
Light Transport	3668	7503	4533	1813	17517	7841	8519	5809	12998	1120	36287	2901	12913	4802	3387	974	24977	2572	3527	84880
Light Halftrack	174	640	250	22	1086	717	320	224	1063	79	2403	95	961	274	81	24	1435	115	120	5159
Medium Halftrack	211	368	345	16	940	375	511	350	574	4	1814	200	587	288	254	36	1365	54	151	4324
Heavy Halftrack	76	66	91	0	233	127	206	110	240	0	683	32	242	33	38	0	345	4	0	1265

37mm ATG	466	409	505	235	1615	303	1050	763	870	90	3076	338	819	719	446	75	2397	258	772	8118
50mm ATG	45	72	66	6	189	81	50	54	144	6	335	6	114	43	45	0	208	37	43	812
47mm ATG	6	0	6	6	24	9	21	60	12	4	102	12	6	6	0	0	24	12	15	177
28mm sPzb 41	4	0	0	0	4	0	0	4	12	4	20	0	4	8	4	0	16	0	0	40
75mm InfG	136	150	166	82	534	128	312	250	306	32	1028	102	272	200	138	14	726	70	226	2584
150mm InfG	42	38	48	12	140	28	94	72	74	6	274	30	74	46	36	0	186	6	66	672
75mm Gun	2	0	0	0	2	0	4	2	36	8	50	4	0	28	6	8	40	68	0	160
105mm How	252	228	270	144	894	168	536	456	432	36	1628	192	432	368	243	20	1255	92	424	4293
105mm IG40	0	0	0	0	0	0	0	0	4	0	4	0	0	0	0	0	0	0	0	4
150mm How	108	125	170	36	439	100	274	200	216	12	802	88	196	164	116	8	572	19	140	1972
105mm Gun	24	16	40	0	80	20	80	52	64	0	216	8	64	28	16	0	116	16	0	428
150mm Gun	9	0	8	0	17	9	9	0	9	0	27	3	15	0	0	0	18	0	0	62
210mm How	9	9	18	0	36	18	54	42	57	0	171	12	60	12	0	0	84	0	0	291
210mm Gun	0	0	0	0	0	0	0	6	0	0	6	6	0	0	0	0	6	0	0	12
240mm How	0	0	0	0	0	0	0	0	0	0	0	0	8	0	0	0	8	0	0	8
240mm Gun	0	0	6	0	6	0	6	0	0	0	6	0	0	0	0	0	0	0	0	12
305mm How	0	0	0	0	0	0	16	0	0	0	16	0	0	0	0	0	0	0	0	16
355mm How	0	0	0	0	0	0	1	0	0	0	1	0	0	0	0	0	0	0	0	1
600mm How	0	0	0	0	0	0	0	2	0	0	2	0	0	2	0	0	2	0	0	4
150-200mm Rail G	0	0	0	0	0	0	0	0	0	0	0	0	0	0	0	0	0	3	0	3
210-280mm Rail G	4	0	0	0	4	0	0	10	0	0	10	0	0	4	3	0	7	0	0	21
380+mm Rail Gn/M	0	0	0	0	0	0	0	0	0	0	0	0	0	0	0	0	0	0	0	0
100-280mm Coast G	48	0	0	24	72	0	0	0	0	0	0	0	0	0	66	0	66	39	0	177
Nebelwerfer 35	0	0	24	0	24	0	18	0	24	0	42	0	0	0	0	0	0	6	0	72
Nebelwerfer 40	0	0	12	0	12	0	18	0	12	0	30	0	30	0	0	0	30	0	0	72
Nebelwerfer 41	0	54	0	0	54	54	0	0	54	0	108	0	48	0	0	0	48	0	0	210
28/32cm Rckt Syst	120	0	120	0	240	0	120	0	120	120	360	120	120	120	0	0	360	0	0	960
Sd Kfz 250 APC	0	20	0	0	20	0	0	0	19	0	19	0	0	0	0	0	0	0	0	39
Sd Kfz 251 APC	0	239	0	0	239	77	0	0	202	0	279	0	73	0	0	0	73	0	0	591
Sd Kfz 254 AOP	0	20	0	0	20	26	0	0	35	0	61	0	20	0	0	0	20	0	0	101

Notes: * Comprised approximately 3 138 600 Field Army and Waffen SS troops, and 220 700 Luftwaffe personnel in Luftwaffe Ground Forces (Refer text). Excludes approximately 146 300 Luftwaffe personnel in aircrew and directly supporting flight operations by air combat units. Luftwaffe personnel in, or supporting, flight operations (by air combat units), are not considered as "Luftwaffe Ground Forces" capable of any significant ground combat. (Also refer table 'Ger Total Deployed (D) 2').

© Nigel Askey, 2018

Table Ger Total Deployed (D) 1 (cont.)

Total Personnel & Equipment Allocated to Combat Units in a Deployed (D) State in the German Army, Waffen SS, Luftwaffe Ground Forces and Naval Coastal Artillery; 22nd June to 4th July 1941

Resources/Equip.	Army Group North					Army Group Centre						Army Group South						Nor A (Bef Fin)	OKH Res	Total East Front*
	18th A	4th PzG	16th A	AGN Re	Total AGN	3rd PzG	9th A	4th A	2nd PzG	AGC Re	Total AGC	6th A	1st PzG	17th A	11th A	AGS Re	Total AGS			
Sd Kfz 221 A Cars	8	40	2	0	50	32	12	4	69	18	135	2	74	6	4	0	86	0	6	277
Sd Kfz 222 A Cars	0	44	0	0	44	48	8	0	92	0	148	0	68	0	0	0	68	0	0	260
Sd Kfz 260/261 A Cars	0	16	0	0	16	18	0	0	53	0	71	0	12	0	0	0	12	0	0	99
Sd Kfz 223 A Cars	0	46	0	0	46	34	3	0	93	0	130	0	80	0	0	0	80	0	0	256
Sd Kfz 231/232 A Cars	0	30	0	0	30	30	0	0	54	0	84	0	48	0	0	0	48	0	0	162
Sd Kfz 263 A Cars	0	27	0	0	27	20	0	0	42	0	62	0	25	0	0	0	25	0	0	114
Sd Kfz 247 A Cars	0	0	0	0	0	0	0	0	9	0	9	0	0	0	0	0	0	0	0	9
Panhard 178	0	0	0	0	0	190	0	0	0	0	190	0	0	0	0	0	0	0	0	190
Pz Kpfw I	0	3	0	0	3	160	3	0	43	0	206	0	52	0	0	0	52	48	0	309
Kleine Pz Bef I ^	0	20	0	0	20	12	23	4	34	0	73	0	18	0	0	0	18	8	0	119
Pz Kpfw II	0	139	0	0	139	180	0	0	278	0	458	0	211	0	0	0	211	9	0	817
Pz Kpfw III (37mm)	0	0	0	0	0	0	0	0	159	0	159	0	100	0	0	0	100	15	0	274
Pz Kpfw III (50mm)	0	71	0	0	71	5	0	0	386	0	391	0	255	0	0	0	255	0	0	717
Pz Bef III (Gross)	0	11	0	0	11	1	0	0	58	0	59	0	52	0	0	0	52	0	0	122
Pz Kpfw IV	0	80	0	0	80	121	0	0	138	0	259	0	100	0	0	0	100	0	0	439
Pz Kpfw 38(t)	0	118	0	0	118	507	0	0	0	0	507	0	0	0	0	0	0	0	0	625
Pz Bef 38(t)	0	7	0	0	7	28	0	0	0	0	28	0	0	0	0	0	0	0	0	35
Pz Kpfw 35(t)	0	155	0	0	155	0	0	0	0	0	0	0	0	0	0	0	0	0	0	155
Pz Bef 35(t)	0	5	0	0	5	0	0	0	0	0	0	0	0	0	0	0	0	0	0	5
StuG III Assault Gun	21	7	35	0	63	0	49	42	56	0	147	0	49	21	21	0	91	0	0	301
Sd Kfz 252	9	3	15	0	27	0	21	18	24	0	63	0	21	9	9	0	39	0	0	129
Sd Kfz 253	0	38	0	0	38	50	0	0	69	0	119	0	38	0	0	0	38	0	0	195
15cm sIG33 SP G	0	6	0	0	6	6	0	0	6	0	12	0	6	0	0	0	6	0	0	24

Pz Jager I (47mm)	0	21	0	0	21	21	9	21	48	0	99	0	30	0	0	0	30	0	0	150
47mm, Pz Kpfw 35R(f)	0	27	0	0	27	0	27	0	27	0	54	0	0	0	0	0	0	0	0	81
Pz Kpfw 35R(f) (Bef)	0	4	0	0	4	0	4	0	4	0	8	0	0	0	0	0	0	0	0	12
SP 88 mm AAG	0	0	0	6	6	0	0	0	0	0	0	0	0	0	0	0	0	0	0	6
105mm K18 Pz Sfl IVa	0	0	0	0	0	0	0	0	2	0	2	0	0	0	0	0	0	0	0	2
Pz Kpfw II (F)	0	42	0	0	42	0	0	0	42	0	42	0	0	0	0	0	0	0	0	84
Pz Kpfw B2	0	0	0	0	0	0	0	0	0	0	0	0	0	6	0	0	6	0	0	6
Pz Kpfw B2 (F)	0	0	0	0	0	0	0	0	0	0	0	0	0	24	0	0	24	0	0	24
Pz Kpfw 35-S	0	0	6	0	6	0	0	0	9	0	9	0	3	0	0	0	3	10	0	28
Pz Kpfw 38H	0	0	0	0	0	0	0	0	0	0	0	0	0	0	0	0	0	24	0	24
Pz Kpfw I (Pio)	30	0	0	0	30	10	0	0	30	0	40	0	10	0	0	0	10	0	0	80
Sd Kfz 300	0	0	0	0	0	0	54	0	0	0	54	0	0	0	0	0	0	0	0	54
Pz IV Bridge Layer	4	0	0	0	4	0	0	0	0	0	0	0	0	0	0	0	0	0	0	4
Pz IV Ammo Carrier	0	0	0	0	0	0	0	4	0	0	4	0	4	0	0	0	4	0	0	8
Armoured Train	1	2	0	0	3	0	2	2	2	0	6	2	0	1	0	0	3	0	0	12
20 mm AAG	132	150	132	12	426	176	275	172	350	4	977	153	426	149	102	12	842	78	48	2371
20mm Quad AAG	4	0	0	0	4	0	10	0	0	0	10	0	4	4	0	0	8	0	0	22
37 mm AAG	4	24	0	0	28	32	0	10	24	0	66	0	56	0	2	0	58	0	0	152
88-105mm AAG	44	28	44	0	116	24	92	60	76	0	252	56	72	56	36	0	220	28	0	616
Truck 20mm AAG	12	12	0	0	24	12	12	0	12	0	36	0	0	0	0	0	0	0	0	60
Sd Kfz 10/4	40	56	12	0	108	32	32	8	92	8	172	0	40	40	0	0	80	0	24	384
Sd Kfz 6/2	0	21	0	0	21	12	3	0	18	0	33	0	51	0	0	0	51	9	0	114
Sd Kfz 7/1	0	6	2	0	8	4	0	8	0	0	12	0	10	8	0	0	18	0	6	44
AA Searchlights	24	60	24	0	108	64	56	24	92	0	236	24	144	24	24	0	216	24	0	584
Rear Area SDE Trucks	15499	20698	20223	8279	64699	20091	34897	26675	37638	4182	123483	14307	37908	19893	14708	3843	90659	3950	17120	299912
Rear Area SDE Lt Trpts	2187	2921	2854	1168	9131	2836	4925	3765	5312	590	17428	2019	5350	2808	2076	542	12795	652	2322	42328

^ Includes a small number of Pz-I (Sd Kfz 101) chassis and hull without turret, used in Self Propelled Anti-Tank Battalions (Panzer-Jager-Abteilung (motorisierter Selbstfahrlafette)). Similar function and capability as the Kleine Panzerbefehlswagen (Sd Kfz 265) (command tank).

a. The German Army, Waffen SS, Luftwaffe Ground Forces and Naval Coastal Artillery Deployed (D) in Support of Operation Barbarossa from 22nd June to 4th July 1941

From table <u>Ger Total Deployed (D) 1</u> and the German Deployment Matrix, we can summarise the German ground forces which supported Operation Barbarossa from 22nd June to 4th July 1941 as follows.

i. Army Group North

- 18th Army, 4th Panzer Group and 16th Army (deployed from north to south), with 29 divisions and approximately 712,000 personnel (total in the German Army, Waffen SS, Luftwaffe ground forces, naval ground forces in coastal artillery, and railroad troops). Approximately 562,000 personnel were allocated to Deployed (D) combat units (i.e. those units displayed in the German Deployment Matrix for Army Group North).

- 7 infantry corps HQs, 2 panzer (motorised) corps HQs, 1 army group rear area HQ, 20 infantry divisions, 3 panzer divisions, 2 motorised divisions, 1 Waffen SS motorised division and 3 (small) security divisions.

- 770 fully tracked AFVs (Armoured Fighting Vehicles) of all types. This included 619 tanks, command tanks and flame tanks. However only 214 tanks and assault guns had 50-75mm calibre guns, and only 274 AFVs had guns with a calibre greater than 45mm.

- 213 armoured cars of all types (including armoured radio cars), and 344 semi-tracked AFVs (including APCs and armoured observation vehicles).[22]

- 3,980 (28-600mm) artillery pieces (including anti-tank guns, and excluding coastal and rail guns, and rocket systems), 735 (20-105mm) AA guns (including all SP AA guns), and 3,409 (50-81mm) mortars.

- Approximately 122,900 motor vehicles (excluding halftracks, armoured cars and motorcycles), and 2,259 halftrack prime movers (excluding halftracks used as self-propelled guns).[23]

- Commander: *Generalfeldmarschall* Ritter von Leeb.

ii. Army Group Centre

- 3rd Panzer Group, 9th Army, 4th Army and 2nd Panzer Group (deployed from north to south), with 52 divisions and approximately 1,308,000 personnel (total in the German Army, Waffen SS, Luftwaffe ground forces, naval ground forces in coastal artillery, and railroad troops). Approximately 1,022,000 personnel were allocated to Deployed (D) combat units.

- 11 infantry corps HQs, 5 panzer (motorised) corps HQs, 1 army group rear area HQ, 33 infantry divisions, 9 panzer divisions, 5 motorised divisions, 1 Waffen SS motorised division, 1 cavalry division and 3 (small) security divisions.

- 2,599 fully tracked AFVs of all types. This included 2,241 tanks, command tanks and flame tanks. However only 797 tanks and assault guns had 50-75mm calibre guns, and only 973 AFVs had guns with a calibre greater than 45mm.

- 829 armoured cars of all types (including armoured radio cars), and 541 semi-tracked AFVs (including APCs and armoured observation vehicles).

- 7,764 (28-600mm) artillery pieces (including anti-tank guns, and excluding coastal and rail guns, and rocket systems), 1,564 (20-105mm) AA guns (including all SP AA guns), and 6,468 (50-81mm) mortars.

- Approximately 240,800 motor vehicles (excluding halftracks, armoured cars and motorcycles), and 4,900 halftrack prime movers (excluding halftracks used as self-propelled guns).

- Commander: *Generalfeldmarschall* Fedor von Bock.

***

---

[22] Includes the Sd KFz 254 wheel-cum-track medium armoured observation vehicle. This relatively rare vehicle had four wheels and a track system which was lowered below the wheels for cross-country use.

[23] The total number of motor vehicles used was slightly higher than this because a small proportion of 'rear-area' vehicles in non-Deployed (D) units are not shown in the tables. Refer Volume IIB 3. 1) d. - 'The Rear Area Transport Available for Supply Distribution from 22nd June to 4th July 1941'. Also, refer Volume IIB 6. 5) b. – 'Parameters Relating Specifically to The Calculation of the Wehrmacht SDE in 1941 - The Proportion of Available Rear Area Trucks, Tractors and Light Transport Allocated to Rear Area SDE Functions'.

iii. Army Group South

- 6th Army, 1st Panzer Group and 17th Army (deployed from north to south in southern Poland), and 11th Army in Rumania, with 41 divisions and approximately 1,013,000 personnel (total in the German Army, Waffen SS, Luftwaffe ground forces, naval ground forces in coastal artillery, and railroad troops). Approximately 804,000 personnel were allocated to Deployed (D) combat units.

- 10 infantry corps HQs, 3 panzer (motorised) corps HQs, 1 army group rear area HQ, 25 infantry divisions, 5 panzer divisions, 2 motorised divisions, 1 Waffen SS motorised division, 1 mountain division, 4 light infantry divisions and 3 (small) security divisions.

- 962 fully tracked AFVs of all types. This included 821 tanks, command tanks and flame tanks. However only 446 tanks and assault guns had 50-75mm calibre guns, and only 491 AFVs had guns with a calibre greater than 45mm.

- 319 armoured cars of all types (including armoured radio cars), and 170 semi-tracked AFVs (including APCs and armoured observation vehicles).

- 5,658 (28-600mm) artillery pieces (including anti-tank guns, and excluding coastal and rail guns, and rocket systems), 1,277 (20-105mm) AA guns (including all SP AA guns), and 4,965 (50-81mm) mortars.

- Approximately 171,800 motor vehicles (excluding halftracks, armoured cars and motorcycles), and 3,145 halftrack prime movers (excluding halftracks used as self-propelled guns).

- Commander: *Generalfeldmarschall* Gerd von Rundstedt.

As and aside, it is particularly noteworthy here that on 22nd June 1941 Army Group South possessed a massive a **1 to 5.8 numerical inferiority** in fully tracked AFVs compared to the opposing Soviet forces. On this date the Kiev Special Military District (Army Group South's immediate opponent) had a total of 5,465 tanks including 774 T-34 and KV tanks.[24] Army Group South (excluding the 11th Army which attacked Southern Front further south) had 577 Pz IIIs, IVs and StuGs of all types out of a total of 941 fully tracked AFVs. Of these only 425 were Pz IIIs, IVs and StuGs with 50-75mm guns. Therefore not only did the Southwestern Front (formed from the Kiev Special Military District) have a gigantic initial tank numerical superiority of around 5.8 to 1, but they also **had over 1.8 times as many T-34s and KVs as Army Group South's best main battle tanks**.

On top of all this, on 22nd June 1941, the Soviets had an additional 1,070 tanks in the 5th Mechanised Corps south of Kiev (in the Reserves of the STAVKA GK), and the Odessa Military District (which formed the basis of the Southern Front) had another 1,011 tanks. The latter faced only one assault gun battalion in 11th Army with 21 assault guns, and a handful of light and obsolescent Rumanian tanks. In late June and July 1941, the majority of these tanks moved north and east, and ended up also opposing Army Group South in the North Ukraine area. According to these numbers it's remarkable that Army Group South was the attacking force at all: on paper it should have been overwhelmed by the Soviet forces in the Ukraine; (arguably) even given the much lower readiness state of the Red Army's armoured and mechanised forces.

iv. Norway Army, *Befehlsstelle Finnland* (East Front Only)

- Part of the Norway Mountain Corps, and 36th Corps (a Reduced Strength Special Corps Command - HoH. Kdo.), (deployed from north to south), with 4 divisions and approximately 88,000 personnel (total in the German Army, Waffen SS, Luftwaffe ground forces, naval ground forces in coastal artillery, and railroad troops). Approximately 78,000 personnel were allocated to Deployed (D) combat units.

- 2 infantry corps HQs, 2 infantry divisions, 2 mountain divisions and 1 Waffen SS motorised brigade.

- 114 fully tracked AFVs of all types. This included 114 tanks, command tanks and flame tanks. However none of the tanks had 50-75mm calibre guns, and only 10 tanks had guns with a calibre greater than 45mm.

- 578 (28-600mm) artillery pieces (including anti-tank guns, and excluding coastal and rail guns, and rocket systems), 115 (20-105mm) AA guns (including all SP AA guns), and 646 (50-81mm) mortars.

- Approximately 11,500 motor vehicles (excluding halftracks, armoured cars and motorcycles), and 173 halftrack prime movers (excluding halftracks used as self-propelled guns).

- Commander Norway Army: *Generaloberst* von Falkenhorst.

---

[24] Refer to Volume IIIB 1. 12) 'The Soviet Tank Deployment Matrix' for a fully detailed breakdown of the Soviet tank deployments on 22nd June 1941 (shown by front, corps and division, as well as smaller separate units).

v. OKH Reserves

- 2nd Army (deployed behind Army Group Centre), 12 divisions and 239,000 personnel (total in the German Army, Waffen SS, Luftwaffe ground forces, naval ground forces in coastal artillery, and railroad troops). Approximately 200,000 personnel were allocated to Deployed (D) combat units.

- 4 infantry corps HQs, 11 infantry divisions (including the SS Police Division) and 1 mountain division.

- 6 armoured cars of all types (including armoured radio cars).

- 1,686 (28-600mm) artillery pieces (including anti-tank guns, and excluding coastal and rail guns, and rocket systems), 78 (20-105mm) AA guns (including all SP AA guns), and 1,593 (50-81mm) mortars.

- Approximately 30,300 motor vehicles (excluding halftracks, armoured cars and motorcycles), and 271 halftrack prime movers (excluding halftracks used as self-propelled guns).

vi. Total, East Front

- 3 Army Group HQs, 4 Panzer Group HQs, 8 army HQs, 34 infantry and mountain corps HQs, and 10 motorised (panzer) corps HQs, with 3,359,000 personnel (total in the German Army, Waffen SS, Luftwaffe ground forces, naval ground forces in coastal artillery, and railroad troops). Approximately 2,665,000 personnel were allocated to Deployed (D) combat units.

- 138 divisions made up of 91 infantry divisions (including the SS Police Division), 17 panzer divisions, 9 motorised divisions, 3 Waffen SS motorised divisions, 1 cavalry division, 4 mountain divisions, 4 light infantry divisions and 9 (small) security divisions.

- 4,445 fully tracked AFVs of all types. These comprised 3,795 tanks, command tanks and flame tanks, 301 assault guns, 257 light tank destroyers and SP guns, and 92 pionier (combat engineer) and ammunition transport vehicles. However, it should be noted that only 1,457 fully tracked AFVs (33%) were tanks or assault guns with 50-75mm calibre guns (i.e. were Pz IIIs (50mm), Pz IVs or StuG IIIs), and only 1,748 AFVs (39%) had guns with a calibre greater than 45mm. In addition, 642 fully tracked AFV (14%) had only MG armament or no mounted armament at all, while another 817 AFVs (18%) were light Pz IIs with only 20mm cannon armament.

- 1,367 armoured cars of all types (including armoured radio cars), and 1,055 semi-tracked AFVs (including APCs and armoured observation vehicles).

- 19,666 (28-600mm) artillery pieces (including anti-tank guns, and excluding coastal and rail guns, and rocket systems), 3,769 (20-105mm) AA guns (including all SP AA guns and 622 8.8cm Flak guns), and 17,081 (50-81mm) mortars.

- At least 577,200 motor vehicles (excluding halftracks, armoured cars and motorcycles), and 10,748 halftrack prime movers (excluding halftracks used as self-propelled guns).

***

At this point it is worth examining the distribution of personnel within the Wehrmacht forces that invaded the USSR on 22nd June 1941. As already noted, there were approximately 3,359,000 personnel in the German Army, Waffen SS, Luftwaffe ground forces, naval ground forces (in coastal artillery) and railroad troops, supporting Operation Barbarossa from 22nd June to 4th July 1941. This force comprised approximately 3,138,600 German Army, Waffen SS, naval coastal artillery and railroad personnel, and 220,700 Luftwaffe ground forces personnel. The Luftwaffe ground forces personnel was made up of 54,800 in Luftwaffe flak units, 20,500 in Luftwaffe-Army liaison units (these units were embedded in the field army), and 145,400 in Luftwaffe supply units.

Excluded from table Ger Total Deployed (D) 1 is approximately 146,300 Luftwaffe flight and flight support personnel, and all personnel from the Todt Organisation (*Organisation Todt* – OT) and the Reich Labour Service (*Reichsarbeitsdienst* – RAD)). The OT and RAD did not maintain ground combat units and were not part of the Wehrmacht. The total Luftwaffe personnel on the East Front from 22nd June to 4th July 1941 was therefore approximately 367,000. The 146,300 Luftwaffe flight (air crews) and flight support personnel were supporting 3,914 aircraft (of all types), which equates to around 37 personnel per aircraft.[25]

***

---

[25] Refer Volume IIB 5. - 'The Luftwaffe in 1941'. This was typical of a WWII era Western air force (the Soviet VVS in 1941 had considerably fewer support personnel per aircraft). Obviously bomber units and larger aircraft tended to have more supporting personnel. The flight support personnel includes those in aircraft ground crews, aircraft maintenance and repair units, aircraft refuelling and rearming units, air intelligence and weather units, and air-traffic control: generally all the personnel needed to support an operational airfield. The flight support personnel did not include those in 'Luftwaffe supply units'. The latter mostly operated 'off-airfield', and were responsible for moving the fuel, ordnance and aircraft spare parts from supply depots to the operational airfields.

Table Ger Total Deployed (D) 2

Total Personnel & Equipment Allocated to Combat Units in a Deployed (D) State in the German Army, Waffen SS, Luftwaffe Ground Forces and Naval Coastal Artillery; 22nd June to 4th July 1941

Resources/Equip.	Norway Army (Occupation)	Army Group D				12th A	Afrika Corps (DAK)	Commander-Replacement Army (plus other forces)*	Total Western Fronts & Replacement Army	Total German Army, Waffen SS and Luftwaffe Ground Forces^
		7th A	1st A	15th A	AGD Re					
Total Manpower	123,558	141,318	106,423	205,779	55,188	169,452	82,696	1,076,340	1,960,754	5,320,098
Manpwr in (D) units	103,436	122,888	87,576	178,309	47,394	138,558	44,750	851,954	1,574,865	4,240,335
Heavy Rifle Sqd	2,088	4,068	2,916	6,084	648	3,564	360	2,523	22,251	59,961
Light Rifle Sqd	76	84	135	103	106	154	19	418	1,095	5,215
Motor Cycle Sqd	538	542	507	805	137	778	554	3,119	6,980	28,026
Bicycle Sqd	190	203	192	364	20	149	0	109	1,227	4,657
Cavalry Sqd	0	0	9	9	0	69	3	0	90	1,689
Eng Sqd	204	372	327	639	49	408	110	208	2,317	9,249
Light Eng Sqd	330	81	85	153	1,301	123	91	742	2,906	15,838
Ferry Bridging Sqd	9	0	18	27	0	79	0	181	314	4,305
Military Police Sqd	446	25	14	25	216	35	3	719	1,483	4,027
Irregular Sqd	144	0	0	0	48	240	12	23,556	24,000	25,344
Rail Repair Sqd	64	72	0	0	373	0	8	382	899	3,800
HMG	736	934	1,007	1,880	168	1,010	252	536	6,523	21,504
LMG	940	474	511	776	166	916	424	13,024	17,231	37,215
AT Rifle	594	1,098	807	1,692	162	903	54	522	5,832	15,119
50mm Mor	480	639	471	810	114	636	132	402	3,684	14,065
81mm Mor	213	261	171	345	60	366	84	162	1,662	8,362
Horse Team	6,840	11,877	9,565	19,182	2,184	9,869	524	6,808	66,849	193,818
Unit Trucks	3,666	3,345	3,442	5,038	1,434	5,621	3,483	34,467	60,496	210,584
Light Transport	1,880	1,811	1,703	2,332	629	2,940	2,116	28,115	41,526	126,406
Light Halftrack	35	0	25	0	16	110	208	236	630	5,789
Medium Halftrack	16	25	11	25	2	72	77	1,665	1,893	6,217
Heavy Halftrack	0	0	26	0	0	0	44	44	114	1,379
37mm ATG	264	393	352	591	60	414	81	221	2,376	10,494
50mm ATG	10	0	0	0	0	42	38	30	120	932
47mm ATG	0	0	6	0	0	0	0	0	6	183
28mm sPzb 41	0	0	0	0	0	32	9	0	41	81

75mm Inf G	102	80	108	20	146	26	64	620	3,204
150mm Inf G	0	6	12	0	20	4	12	72	744
75mm Gun	60	0	3	3	34	0	0	100	260
105mm How	124	348	516	50	296	52	132	1,772	6,065
105mm IG40	0	0	0	0	0	0	0	0	4
150mm How	4	48	74	12	76	20	40	310	2,282
105mm Gun	0	0	0	12	24	16	32	84	512
150mm Gun	0	0	0	0	0	0	0	0	62
210mm How	0	0	0	0	0	0	0	9	300
210mm Gun	0	0	0	0	0	9	0	0	12
240mm How	0	0	0	0	0	0	0	0	8
240mm Gun	0	0	0	0	0	0	0	0	12
305mm How	0	0	0	0	0	0	0	0	16
355mm How	0	0	0	0	0	0	0	0	1
600mm How	0	0	0	0	0	0	0	0	4
150-200mm Rail G	0	0	0	6	0	0	0	6	9
210-280mm Rail G	0	0	0	12	2	0	0	14	35
380+mm Rail Gn/M	0	0	0	0	0	4	4	4	4
100-280mm Coast G	780	32	96	0	0	72	0	980	1,157
Nebelwerfer 35	6	0	0	0	0	0	0	6	78
Nebelwerfer 40	0	0	0	0	0	0	0	0	72
Nebelwerfer 41	0	0	0	0	0	0	0	0	210
28/32cm Rckt Syst	0	0	0	0	0	0	0	0	960
Sd Kfz 250 APC	0	0	0	0	0	0	0	0	39
Sd Kfz 251 APC	0	0	0	0	0	39	53	92	683
Sd Kfz 254 AOP	0	0	0	0	0	15	7	22	123

* Excluded in 'Manpower in the Replacement Army are 915,000 personnel in non-Deployed (D) Replacement Army units, (refer table 'Distribution of Strength within the Replacement Army, June 1941').

* Included in 'Total Manpower' in the Replacement Army plus other forces, are approximately: 210,000 in LS (Landesschutzen) Battalions (Army-Militia) or Guard (Wach) units, 115,000 Field Army (temporarily under the Commander Replacement Army), 143 000 army and Waffen SS personnel in security, administration, occupation and other 'support' functions (SDE), and 608,000 Luftwaffe ground force personnel (total 1,076,000, rounded). The latter were primarily in flak units, searchlight units or other air-defence units deployed for the strategic air-defence of the Reich.

^ Excluded in 'Total Manpower' are approx.: 721,000 Luftwaffe personnel in aircrew, air troops supporting flight operations, air-signals troops (except around 30,000 in the army liaison role and usually attached to Army units), Luftwaffe construction units, Home Defence units and other Luftwaffe auxiliary organisations. These Luftwaffe forces are not considered to be ground-combat capable.

Also excluded are approximately 353,000 Kriegsmarine personnel used for shipboard crew, supply, dockyard facilities and security, operations support and training. Refer table 'Wehrmacht & Waffen SS personnel distribution on 15th June 1941, and personnel included in the German FILARM model'. ^ Included in 'Total Manpower' are approx. 51,000 Kriegsmarine personnel in coastal artillery units.

Table Ger Total Deployed (D) 2 (cont.)

Total Personnel & Equipment Allocated to Combat Units in a Deployed (D) State in the German Army, Waffen SS, Luftwaffe Ground Forces and Naval Coastal Artillery; 22nd June to 4th July 1941

Resources/Equip.	Norway Army (Occupation)	Army Group D					Afrika Corps (DAK)	Commander-Replacement Army (plus other forces)	Total Western Fronts & Replacement Army	Total German Army, Waffen SS and Luftwaffe Ground Forces
		7th A	1st A	15th A	AGD Re	12th A				
Sd Kfz 221 A Cars	0	0	0	2	0	2	16	16	36	313
Sd Kfz 222 A Cars	0	0	0	2	0	0	16	20	36	296
Sd Kfz 260/261 A Cars	0	0	0	0	0	0	0	2	2	101
Sd Kfz 223 A Cars	0	0	0	0	0	0	22	11	33	289
Sd Kfz 231/232 A Cars	0	0	0	0	0	0	12	12	24	186
Sd Kfz 263 A Cars	0	0	0	0	0	0	4	2	6	120
Sd Kfz 247 A Cars	0	0	0	0	0	0	0	0	0	9
Panhard 178	0	0	0	0	0	0	0	0	0	190
Pz Kpfw I	0	0	0	0	0	0	26	10	36	345
Kleine Pz Bef I ^	0	0	0	0	4	0	7	0	11	130
Pz Kpfw II	0	0	0	0	0	5	91	64	160	977
Pz Kpfw III (37mm)	0	0	0	0	0	17	0	14	31	305
Pz Kpfw III (50mm)	0	0	0	0	0	0	142	38	180	897
Pz Bef III (*Gross*)	0	0	0	0	0	0	14	11	25	147
Pz Kpfw IV	0	0	0	0	0	0	40	16	56	495
Pz Kpfw 38(t)	0	0	0	0	0	0	0	17	17	642
Pz Bef 38(t)	0	0	0	0	0	0	0	0	0	35
Pz Kpfw 35(t)	0	0	0	0	0	0	0	0	0	155
Pz Bef 35(t)	0	0	0	0	0	0	0	0	0	5
StuG III Assault Gun	0	0	0	6	0	0	0	49	55	356
Sd Kfz 252	0	0	0	3	0	0	0	63	66	195
Sd Kfz 253	0	0	0	4	0	0	29	15	48	243
15cm sIG33 SP G	0	0	0	0	0	0	0	12	12	36

Pz Jager I (47mm)	0	0	0	21	0	0	27	0	48	198
47mm, Pz Kpfw 35R(f)	0	0	0	0	0	0	0	0	0	81
Pz Kpfw 35R(f) (Bef)	0	0	0	0	0	0	0	0	0	12
SP 88 mm AAG	0	0	0	0	0	0	0	0	0	6
105mm K18 Pz Sfl IVa	0	0	0	0	0	0	0	0	0	2
Pz Kpfw II (F)	0	0	0	0	0	0	0	0	0	84
Pz Kpfw B2	0	0	0	0	0	0	0	0	0	6
Pz Kpfw B2 (F)	0	0	0	0	0	0	0	0	0	24
Pz Kpfw 35-S	0	0	104	0	0	0	0	0	104	132
Pz Kpfw 38H	0	0	222	0	0	0	0	0	222	246
Pz Kpfw (Pio)	0	0	0	0	0	0	10	20	30	110
Sd Kfz 300	0	0	0	0	0	0	0	0	0	54
Pz IV Bridge Layer	0	0	0	0	0	0	0	0	0	4
Pz IV Ammo Carrier	0	0	0	0	0	0	0	0	0	8
Armoured Train	0	0	1	1	0	2	0	0	4	16
20 mm AAG	0	30	0	4	0	12	64	8,708	8,818	11,189
20mm Quad AAG	0	0	0	12	0	2	0	4	18	40
37 mm AAG	0	0	0	16	0	2	0	348	366	518
88-105mm AAG	0	12	0	0	0	0	24	3,168	3,204	3,820
Truck 20mm AAG	0	0	0	0	0	12	24	0	36	96
Sd Kfz 10/4	0	0	0	8	0	24	60	12	104	488
Sd Kfz 6/2	0	0	0	0	0	0	0	3	3	117
Sd Kfz 7/1	0	0	0	0	0	0	0	4	4	48
AA Searchlights	0	8	0	0	0	0	16	2,460	2,484	3,068
Rear Area SDE Trucks	7,326	6,684	6,878	10,067	2,865	11,232	13,920	68,873	127,845	427,757
Rear Area SDE Lt Trpts	938	903	849	1,163	314	1,466	1,583	14,020	21,236	63,564

© Nigel Askey, 2018

b. The German Army, Waffen SS, Luftwaffe Ground Forces and Naval Coastal Artillery, Deployed (D) in the Western Fronts and the Replacement Army from 22nd June to 4th July 1941

i. Norway Army (Norway Occupation Duties)

- Norway Army with 7 divisions and 124,000 personnel (total in the German Army, Waffen SS, Luftwaffe ground forces, naval ground forces in coastal artillery, and railroad troops). Approximately 103,000 personnel were allocated to Deployed (D) combat units.

- 2 infantry corps HQs, part of the Norway Mountain Corps, and 7 infantry divisions.

- 564 (28-600mm) artillery pieces (including anti-tank guns, and excluding coastal and rail guns, and rocket systems), approximately 780 (100-280mm) coastal guns, and 693 (50-81mm) mortars.[26]

- Approximately 13,800 motor vehicles (excluding halftracks, armoured cars and motorcycles), and 51 halftrack prime movers (excluding halftracks used as self-propelled guns).

- Commander: *Generaloberst* von Falkenhorst.

ii. Army Group D (France-Low Countries)

- 7th Army, 1st Army and 15th Army, with 43 divisions and 509,000 personnel (total in the German Army, Waffen SS, Luftwaffe ground forces, naval ground forces in coastal artillery, and railroad troops). Approximately 436,000 personnel were allocated to Deployed (D) combat units.

- 8 infantry corps HQs, 43 infantry divisions and 2 panzer brigades.

- 357 fully tracked AFVs of all types. This included 330 tanks, command tanks and flame tanks. However only 6 tanks and assault guns had 50-75mm calibre guns, and only 131 AFVs had guns with a calibre greater than 45mm.

- 2 (army) armoured cars and 7 semi-tracked AFVs (including APCs and armoured observation vehicles).[27]

- 3,076 (28-600mm) artillery pieces (including anti-tank guns, and excluding coastal and rail guns, and rocket systems), 82 (20-105mm) Army AA guns (including all SP AA guns), and 2,871 (50-81mm) mortars.[28]

- Approximately 49,500 motor vehicles (excluding halftracks, armoured cars and motorcycles), 130 halftrack prime movers (excluding halftracks used as self-propelled guns).

- Commander: *Generalfeldmarschall* von Witzleben, who also acted as the *Oberbefehlshaber West* (OB West - Commander in Chief, West).[29]

iii. 12th Army (Yugoslavia-Serbia-Greece-Crete)

- 12th Army with 12 divisions and 169,000 personnel (total in the German Army, Waffen SS, Luftwaffe ground forces including airborne forces, naval ground forces in coastal artillery, and railroad troops). Approximately 139,000 personnel were allocated to Deployed (D) combat units.[30]

- 2 infantry corps HQs, 9 infantry divisions, 2 mountain divisions, 1 Air Corps HQ (*Luftwaffe* organisation) and 1 Parachute Division (with an additional glider borne infantry regiment).

- 22 fully tracked AFVs of all types. This included 22 tanks, command tanks and flame tanks. However none of the AFVs had guns with a calibre greater than 45mm.

- 2 (army) armoured cars of all types (including armoured radio cars).[31]

---

[26] Excludes Luftwaffe flak guns (included in 'Germany and the Remainder of Occupied Europe, and the Replacement Army' below).

[27] These were in the 271st Infantry Division, which had the 227th Schnelle Battalion and an assault gun battery. Excludes a handful of obsolete armoured cars, such as the Kfz 13, issued to order-police units, and some captured French vehicles issued to security/occupation units. The precise number is unknown.

[28] Excludes Luftwaffe flak guns, Ibid note 26.

[29] *Oberbefehlshaber West* (OB West) was the German Army Command in the West, and had overall command of the German Army on the Western Front during most of World War II (the *Westheer*). It was directly subordinate to the German Armed Forces High Command (OKW). The area under the command of the OB West varied as the war progressed, and in 1941 it extended as far west as the French Atlantic coast. Note, at this time *Luftflotte* 3 (in France) reported directly to the *Oberkommando der Luftwaffe* (OKL), which in turn reported to OKW.

[30] Includes *Militärbefehlshaber* (MB) *Serbien* (Military Governor in Serbia).

[31] These were in the 46th Infantry Division, which had transferred to the East Front by 5th July 1941. Excludes a handful of obsolete armoured cars issued to security/occupation units. The precise number is unknown.

- 1,084 (28-600mm) artillery pieces (including anti-tank guns, and excluding coastal and rail guns, and rocket systems), 52 (20-105mm) Army AA guns (including all SP AA guns), and 1,002 (50-81mm) mortars.[32]

- Approximately 21,300 motor vehicles (excluding halftracks, armoured cars and motorcycles), and 182 halftrack prime movers (excluding halftracks used as self-propelled guns).

- Commander: *Generalfeldmarschall* List.

iv. Deutsches Afrikakorps (D.A.K) (North Africa)

- *Deutsches Afrikakorps* (D.A.K) with 2 divisions and 83,000 personnel (total in the German Army, Waffen SS, Luftwaffe ground forces, naval ground forces in coastal artillery, and railroad troops). Approximately 45,000 personnel were allocated to Deployed (D) combat units.

- 1 panzer (motorised) corps HQ, 1 panzer division and 1 motorised division (with a full panzer regiment attached).[33]

- 357 fully tracked AFVs of all types. This included 320 tanks, command tanks and flame tanks. However, only 182 tanks and assault guns had 50-75mm calibre guns, and only 209 AFVs had guns with a calibre greater than 45mm.

- 70 armoured cars of all types (including armoured radio cars), and 83 semi-tracked AFVs (including APCs and armoured observation vehicles).

- 255 (28-600mm) artillery pieces (including anti-tank guns, and excluding coastal and rail guns, and rocket systems), 172 (20-88mm) AA guns (including all SP AA guns), and 216 (50-81mm) mortars.

- Approximately 21,100 motor vehicles (excluding halftracks, armoured cars and motorcycles), and 329 halftrack prime movers (excluding halftracks used as self-propelled guns).

- Commander: *Generalleutnant* Rommel.

***

v. Germany and the Remainder of Occupied Europe, and the Replacement Army

Includes the following military and military-government administrative 'commands':

o *Militärbefehlshaber* (MB) *Belgien und Nordfrankreich*: Military Commander (also sometimes called Military Governor) in Belgium and Northern France.[34]

o *Militärbefehlshaber* (MB) *Frankreich*: Military Commander in France.

o *Wehrmachtsbefehlshaber* (WB) *Niederlande*: Armed Forces Commander Netherlands.

o *Militärbefehlshaber* (MB) *im General-Gouvernement* (Military Commander in Occupied Poland - also abbreviated MiG). [35]

o Luftwaffe ground forces in the West.

o *Ersatzarmee* (Replacement/Training Army); with 6 army divisions and 31 replacement divisions and 4 (*Ersatz*) security brigades. Includes the *Befehlshaber Deutsch Truppen Danemark* (Commander of German Troops in Denmark) and the Commander of the Replacement Army in Bohemia and Moravia.[36]

Note, most *Ersatzarmee* units, including the 31 replacement divisions, were not 'combat units', and the personnel and equipment in these divisions are therefore not considered to be Deployed (D) in the German FILARM model. Consequently, they are also not included in the German Deployment Matrix. However the *Ersatzarmee* also often had temporary control of various regular Wehrmacht combat units (e.g. the refitting army divisions in June 1941), which were combat units and are considered to be Deployed (D) in the German FILARM model. Consequently these units are included in the German Deployment Matrix.

---

[32] Excludes Luftwaffe flak guns, Ibid note 26.

[33] Note, the 5th Light Division's organisation was closer to a panzer division than a light motorised division. It was redesignated the 21st Panzer Division on 1st August 1941.

[34] Strictly translated, *Militärbefehlshaber* is military commander; but this position was also called 'Military Governor', which was more in line with the military government's administrative and security role.

[35] *Generalgouvernement* was a military government which refers to *Generalgouvernement für die besetzten polnischen Gebiete* (General Governorate for the Occupied Polish Territories). In October 1939 Hans Frank was appointed the 'Governor General', and in August 1941 Eastern Galicia (previously occupied by the Soviets) was included in this territory.

[36] The Bohemia and Moravia protectorate (*Protektorat*): the German occupied part of Czechoslovakia.

- Total personnel amounted to approximately 1,076,000 in the German Army, Waffen SS, Luftwaffe ground forces, naval ground forces in coastal artillery, railroad troops, *Landesschützen* (army-militia) units, *Wach* (Guard) units, and a few *Ersatz* (replacement) units deployed as combat capable. Approximately 852,000 of these personnel were allocated to Deployed (D) combat units (shown in the German Deployment Matrix).

    Excluded (in Total Manpower in the Replacement Army in table <u>Ger Total Deployed (D) 2</u>) are approximately 915,000 personnel in Replacement Army units, which are **not** considered Deployed (D) combat units. These forces included 31 replacement divisions and a great many smaller units involved in tasks such as rear-area administration, training, instruction, medical, POW infrastructure, transport and rear-area support. If these units were included, the total personnel would be 1,991,000. The total number of personnel reporting to the Commander Replacement Army (i.e. the *Chef Heeresrustung und Befehlshaber der Ersatzarmee*) was approximately 1,240,000.[37]

    Included (in Total Manpower in the Replacement Army plus other forces) are: approximately 210,000 in *Landesschützen* (army-militia) and *Wach* (Guard) battalions, 115,000 Field Army troops temporarily under the Commander Replacement Army, 143,000 army and SS personnel in security, administration, occupation and support functions (i.e. SDE functions), and 608,000 Luftwaffe ground force personnel. The large majority of the Luftwaffe personnel were in flak units and supporting infrastructure, deployed for the strategic air-defence of 'Greater Germany' (see below). Note, these Luftwaffe units did not report to the commander of the Replacement Army, and were under OKL and OKW control.

- 1 panzer (motorised) corps HQ, 3 infantry divisions, 2 panzer divisions, 1 motorised division, 31 replacement divisions (not Deployed (D)), and 18 Replacement Army command area HQs (*Wehrkreis*) including the 'protectorate' Bohemia and Moravia.[38]

    Excluding the non-Deployed (D) Replacement Army elements, the equipment comprised:

- 251 fully tracked AFVs of all types, of which 170 were tanks, command tanks and flame tanks. However only 103 tanks and assault guns had 50-75mm calibre guns, and only 115 AFVs had guns with a calibre greater than 45mm.

- 63 armoured cars of all types (including armoured radio cars), and 138 semi-tracked AFVs (including APCs and armoured observation vehicles).

- 531 (28-600mm) artillery pieces (including anti-tank guns, and excluding coastal and rail guns, and rocket systems), 12,247 (20-105mm) AA guns (including all SP AA guns), and 564 (50-81mm) mortars.

- Approximately 145,500 motor vehicles (excluding halftracks, armoured cars and motorcycles), 1,945 halftrack prime movers (excluding halftracks used as self-propelled guns).

- Commander Replacement Army (*Chef Heeresrustung und Befehlshaber der Erstazarmee*): *Generaloberst* Fromm.

***

---

[37] Refer Volume IIB 4. 7) a. - 'The German Replacement Army *Wehrkreise* System' and for more detail on the units in the Replacement Army in June 1941. Also, table 'Distribution of Personnel Strength within the Replacement Army, June 1941' shows more detail of the personnel functions within the Replacement Army. In addition, the next section shows a breakdown of personnel included in the German FILARM model, which includes some elements of the Replacement Army.

[38] Refer Volume IIB 4. 7) a. - 'The German Replacement Army *Wehrkreise* System'.

c. The Total German Army, Waffen SS, Luftwaffe Ground Forces and Naval Coastal Artillery Deployed (D) in the Reich from 22nd June to 4th July 1941

Excluding:

- **non-Deployed (D)** elements of the Replacement/Training Army (*Ersatzarmee*) (see above),

- non-coastal artillery elements of the German Navy (*Kriegsmarine*),

- Luftwaffe aircrew,

- Luftwaffe flight operations support and airfield support troops,

- Luftwaffe air-signals troops involved in radar, communication HQs and other strategic air-defence ground forces,

- Luftwaffe construction units, home defence units and other auxiliary organisations,

the Wehrmacht had the following personnel and equipment Deployed (D) during the early stages of Operation Barbarossa.[39]

- 4 Army Group HQs, 4 Panzer Group HQs, 13 army HQs, 34 Infantry and Mountain Corps HQs, 12 Reduced Strength Corps Command HQs and 12 motorised (panzer) corps HQs.

- Approximately 5,320,000 personnel (total in the German Army, Waffen SS, Luftwaffe ground forces, security/militia forces, naval ground forces in coastal artillery, and railroad troops).[40] Approximately 4,240,000 personnel were allocated to Deployed (D) combat units (i.e. those units displayed in the German Deployment Matrix).

- 208 divisions made up of 153 infantry divisions (including the SS Police Infantry Division), 20 panzer divisions, 11 motorised divisions (including the 5th Light Mechanised Division in Africa), 3 Waffen SS motorised divisions, 1 cavalry division, 6 mountain divisions, 4 light infantry divisions, 1 parachute division and 9 (small) security divisions.

- 5,432 fully tracked AFVs of all types. These comprised 4,637 tanks, command tanks and flame tanks, 356 assault guns, 317 light tank destroyers and SP guns, and 122 pionier (combat engineer) and ammunition transport vehicles. However it should be noted that only 1,748 fully tracked AFVs (32%) were tanks or assault guns with 50-75mm calibre guns (i.e. were Pz IIIs (50mm), Pz IVs or StuG IIIs), and only 2,203 AFVs (41%) had guns with a calibre greater than 45mm. In addition, 744 fully tracked AFVs (14%) had only MG armament or no mounted armament at all, while another 977 AFVs (18%) were light Pz IIs with only 20mm cannon armament.

- 1,504 armoured cars of all types (including armoured radio cars), and 1,283 semi-tracked AFVs (including APCs and armoured observation vehicles).

- 25,176 (28-600mm) artillery pieces (including anti-tank guns, and excluding coastal and rail guns, and rocket systems), 16,322 (20-105mm) AA guns (including all SP AA guns), and 22,427 (50-81mm) mortars.

- Approximately 828,300 motor vehicles (excluding halftracks, armoured cars and motorcycles), and 13,385 halftrack prime movers (excluding halftracks used as self-propelled guns).

***

At this point it is necessary to review the overall distribution of personnel within the Wehrmacht from 22nd June to 4th July 1941. As noted above, there were approximately 5,320,000 personnel in the German Army, Waffen SS, Luftwaffe ground forces, security/militia forces, naval ground forces in coastal artillery, and railroad troops from 22nd June to 4th July 1941. This force comprised approximately 4,521,000 personnel in the German Army, Waffen SS, Luftwaffe airborne forces, security/militia forces, naval ground forces in coastal artillery, and railroad troops; and around 799,000 Luftwaffe ground forces personnel (excluding airborne forces). The Luftwaffe ground forces personnel were made up of 502,000 in Luftwaffe flak units, 30,000 in Luftwaffe-Army liaison units (these units were mostly embedded in the Field Army), and 267,000 in Luftwaffe supply and support units.[41]

---

[39] See table - 'Wehrmacht & Waffen SS personnel distribution on 15th June 1941, and personnel included in the German FILARM model' below.

[40] Ibid.

[41] This correlates closely with E.B. Westermann, Flak-German Anti-Aircraft Defences 1941-1945, University Press of Kansas, Lawrence, Kansas, 2001, p. 272.

The following personnel are **excluded** from the 5,320,000 personnel figure (above), and in tables Ger Total Deployed (D) 2 and Ger Total Deployed (D) 1.

- Approximately 915,000 personnel in the Replacement Army, which were <u>not</u> Deployed (D) and are not shown in the German Deployment Matrix.

- Approximately 353,000 personnel in the *Kriegsmarine* (the German Navy) which were <u>not</u> part of the coastal artillery forces.

- Approximately 721,000 Luftwaffe personnel in: aircrew, flight operations support and airfield support, air-signals (except those Deployed (D) in the army liaison role with the Army and Waffen SS), construction units, home defence units and other auxiliary organisations. Note, the 262,000 personnel in aircrew, flight operations support and airfield support were supporting approximately 8,880 aircraft (including around 3,000 training aircraft), which equates to around 29 personnel per aircraft. This figure is comparable to most of the Western Allied air-forces at this time. All these Luftwaffe forces are not considered Luftwaffe ground forces capable of any significant ground combat. Thus the total Luftwaffe personnel fielded from 22nd June to 4th July 1941 amounted to around 1,520,000 (excluding around 25,000 in the airborne forces).[42]

- All personnel from the Todt Organisation (*Organisation Todt* – OT) and the Reich Labour Service (*Reichsarbeitsdienst* – RAD)). The OT and RAD did not maintain ground combat units and were not part of the German Army.

***

The following personnel are **included** in the 5,320,000 personnel figure (above), and in tables Ger Total Deployed (D) 2 and Ger Total Deployed (D) 1).

- 3,896,000 personnel in the Field Army (including military police and Deployed (D) order-police units).

- 160,000 personnel in the Waffen SS.

- 115,000 personnel in the Field Army and Waffen SS, which were Deployed (D) and temporarily under the Commander of the Replacement Army. These personnel were mainly from the 6 army divisions (including 2 panzer divisions) which were refitting in the Replacement Army on 22nd June 1941.

- 210,000 personnel in *Landesschützen* and *Wach* battalions, which are considered Deployed (D) units and which were under the control of the Commander of the Replacement Army. These units were mostly fulfilling rear-area security, POW guard and line-of-communication functions.

- 64,000 Army Railroad troops (including personnel seconded from the *Deutsche Reichsbahn*). Note, these individual units are in the German Deployment Matrix, and are considered Deployed (D) units.

- 25,000 Luftwaffe airborne forces in Deployed (D) combat units.

- 502,000 Flak troops which are considered Deployed (D). Note, the associated Flak units, and their Flak guns and other equipment, are considered Deployed (D) and are in the FILARM model. The large majority of these Flak troops were employed in the strategic air-defence of Germany.

- 30,000 Air Signals Troops used in the army liaison role. These small units were usually embedded in Field Army units, and included local liason HQs.

- 267,000 Luftwaffe personnel in Luftwaffe supply units. The latter were motorised units responsible for the maintenance of fuel, ammunition and spare-parts to forward airfields (i.e. SDE functions).

- 51,000 Kriegsmarine personnel in coastal artillery units which are considered Deployed (D).

***

A summary of the distribution of personnel within the Wehrmacht and Waffen SS from 22nd June to 4th July 1941, and which personnel are included in the German FILARM model, is shown in the table below.

---

[42] This correlates with: Germany and the Second World War; Volume I, Organisation and Mobilisation of the German Sphere of Power, Part 1, Wartime Administration, Economy and Manpower Resources 1939-1941, Kroener, B. R., et al, (German Research Institute for Military History at Potsdam), Clarendon Press (Oxford University Press Inc) New York, 2000, Diagram III.V.13, p. 751.

Wehrmacht & Waffen SS personnel distribution on 15th June 1941, and personnel included in the German FILARM model

Service Branch	Service elements and comments	Included in the FILARM Model
Army (Heer) and Waffen SS		
3,896,000	Field Army (including military police and Deployed (D) order-police units).	yes
64,000	Army Rail-road troops (including personnel seconded from the Deutsche Reichsbahn).	yes
115,000	Field Army temporarily under command of the Replacement Army.*	yes
210,000	LS & Guard Battalions under command of the Replacement Army.*	yes
915,000	All other Replacement Army units (including 31 Replacement Divisions).*	no
160,000	Waffen SS.^	yes
5,360,000	**Total, Army (Heer) and Waffen SS.**	
Luftwaffe		
33,000	Aircrew, including those in Luftwaffe training and replacement agencies.	no
229,000	Air Troops: flight operations support and airfield support personnel (e.g, ground-crews).	no
267,000	Air Troops: Motorised Supply Units (inc supply to air units and forward airfields, i.e. SDE functions).	yes
214,000	Air Signals Troops: radar, communication HQs and other strategic air-defence ground forces.	no
30,000	Air Signals Troops: in army liaison role (usually embedded in Field Army units, incl local liason HQs).	yes
502,000	Flak Troops (excluding Searchlight Batteries).	yes
245,000	Luftwaffe Construction Units, Home Defence units and other Auxiliary Organisations.**	no
25,000	Airborne Forces (part of the Luftwaffe, but mostly under Army operational control).	yes
1,545,000	**Total, Luftwaffe.**	
Kriegsmarine		
353,000	Shipboard, supply, dockyard facilities & security, operations support, training, etc.	no
51,000	Coastal artillery (ground forces).	yes
404,000	**Total, Kriegsmarine.**	
7,309,000	**Total Wehrmacht and Waffen SS.**	
5,320,000	**Total personnel included in the German FILARM Model.**	

* In the Replacement Army, which had around 1,240,000 personnel in total in June 1941 (shown in dark grey, refer table showing the 'Distribution of Personnel Strength within the Replacement Army, June 1941' for a more detailed breakdown.

^ Includes IV./LSSAH Batt which remained in Germany as Hitler's bodyguard unit. It did not report to the Chef H.Rust u. B.d.E.

** Auxiliary organisations such as the Reich Air Protection League, Technical Emergency Aid and Auxiliary Security Service.

© Nigel Askey, 2018

d. Rear Area Transport Available for Supply Distribution from 22nd June to 4th July 1941

One of the main objectives of the Fully Integrated Land and Air Resource Model (FILARM) is to enable an accurate calculation of the maximum efficiency of any supporting infrastructure to the armed forces in the field. In the FILARM model the relative Supply Distribution Efficiency (SDE) is a measure of the ability of support infrastructures to supply and support a specific number and type of combat units, over a fixed distance and terrain, during combat operations.[43] The support infrastructures include divisional and smaller unit internal support organisations, as well as all corps, army and front level support units. Although not stated in the title, SDE includes the ability of these same support infrastructures to maintain equipment in an operational condition. This includes maintenance, repair and recovery of equipment.[44]

As part of the first step in calculating the German SDE in June 1941, we need to know the amount of available motor transport in each army, army group reserve, separate corps (the DAK), OKH reserves, and major rear area commands in the *Reich*, which was not allocated directly to Deployed (D) combat units. This information has been separately ascertained for each of the 'commands' (above) in late June 1941. This calculation is essentially the difference between the total available transport in the command, and the sum of all the transport in all the Deployed (D) combat units under that command. The latter is determined from the German Deployment Matrix and the information presented in Volume IIA 3., which details each unit's actual organisation and equipment.

Where information on available transport in a particular command is scarce or unreliable, factors have been used which take into account the total personnel in the command and the total personnel in all the Deployed (D) combat units under that command.[45] This difference in personnel numbers is then indicative of the size of the supporting infrastructure for that command. In addition, the Supply Demand Factors (SDF) for each piece of equipment in that command are taken into account; thus most motorised corps (with tanks, etc) required a higher number of motor vehicles for SDE functions.[46] Note, a very important point (and a basic axiom of the FILARM model) is that at no point does the 'sum of the total available transports in each command' exceed 'the total transport in the next higher command level'. For example, the sum of the motorised transport in 18th Army, 16th Army, 4th Panzer Group, RHG 101 and AGN Reserves, must equal (or never exceed) the total motorised transport that was available to Army Group North. This applies to both motorised and horse-drawn transport (and for that matter to personnel and all types of equipment).[47]

***

To ascertain the SDE we are interested in the available rear-area transport (i.e. transport unallocated to Deployed (D) combat units) that was **also available** to support a SDE related function. This is determined using the following.

- 100% of trucks which were unallocated to Deployed (D) combat units. 'Trucks' are any motor vehicles with Kfz number from 23 to 100 (inclusive).

- 0% of halftracks which were unallocated to Deployed (D) combat units.

- 65% of light transports which were unallocated to Deployed (D) combat units. 'Light transports' are any motor vehicles with Kfz number from 1 to 21 (inclusive).

The results of this process are displayed in the bottom two rows of tables Ger Total Deployed (D) 1 and Ger Total Deployed (D) 2.

***

---

[43] Refer Volume I Part I 8. - 'The General Structure of the Integrated Land and Air Resource Model - Supply Distribution Efficiency (SDE)' for a description of the SDE concepts, and the full equations to calculate 'SDE', 'Supply Lift' and 'Supply Demand'.

[44] Ibid, on what measurable parameters most represent these abilities.

[45] This is again determined from the German Deployment Matrix and the information presented in Volume IIA 3.

[46] Refer Volume I Part II 3. 10) - 'Methodology for Calculating a Weapon System's or Database Unit's Specific Combat Attributes - Supply Demand Factor (SDF)'.

[47] As an aside, and purely as information for the benefit (and possible amusement) of the reader, all the FILARM models have taken several years to develop and exist as a series of very large interconnected excel spreadsheets. For the German FILARM model they start as TOE and actual equipment for each combat unit (as shown in Volume IIA). These then feed into spreadsheets for each command (built using the German Deployment Matrix as the template), and then into the overall FILARM model spreadsheets. At critical junctures there are 'alarms' which appear if any of the FILARM model's axioms (detailed in Volume I Part I) are not adhered to, due to adjustment of a particular parameter. Thus, in this respect, the Fully Integrated Land and Air Resource Model (FILARM) model is a truly 'integrated' model.

The percentages used above are the same as those used in the Soviet FILARM model, except for halftracks (German) and 'tractors' (Soviet). In the German FILARM model, 0% of halftracks which were unallocated to Deployed (D) combat units are used for SDE functions, while in the Soviet FILARM model 40% of tractors which were unallocated to Deployed (D) combat units are used to assist in SDE functions.[48] From June to December 1941, the Soviet Red Army possessed or commandeered (from the civilian economy) a lot more 'tractors' than the Wehrmacht had halftracks. However, apart from some excellent tracked vehicles built for the military, most of them were agricultural in design and/or origin.[49] Many had no tracks at all and were literally agricultural tractors. Many of these vehicles were unable to tow heavy guns, were unsuitable for tank recovery operations, etc. and were used for moving supplies up to the front (not least, because of chronic truck shortages). The Germans on the other hand would rarely put several hundred kilometers of wear and tear on their valuable halftracks simply to move supplies from a railhead to frontline units. The large majority of these vehicles were allocated to combat units anyway (usually as prime movers), and most of the ones that weren't were used for specialised work such as tank recovery, construction of mobile (pontoon) bridges, or similar army-pionier functions.

All the 'rear area' transport thus indicated in tables Ger Total Deployed (D) 1 and Ger Total Deployed (D) 2, as well as a proportion of the transport allocated to combat units (e.g. transport in divisional and smaller unit internal support organisations), will be used in calculating the German SDE for their forces on the East Front during 1941. This process is completed for June to December 1941 in chapter Volume IIB 6.[50]

As an aside to the above, it is worth examining briefly the total number of motor vehicles committed by the Wehrmacht and Waffen SS to support Operation Barbarossa from 22nd June to 4th July 1941. From the tables above we can see that approximately 150,100 trucks and 84,900 light transports were allocated to Deployed (D) combat units in the East. At the same time another 299,900 trucks and 42,300 light transports were also allocated in the East to a plethora of rear area supply and support units (directly affecting the SDE). Around another 22,800 light transports were also in the East, which were involved in non-SDE related functions such as additional signals support and additional HQ support. Therefore, in total, the Germans initially committed approximately 600,000 motor vehicles (excluding halftracks, armoured cars and motorcycles) in support of Operation Barbarossa.[51] The Wehrmacht and Waffen SS also committed approximately 10,750 halftracks and over 168,000 motorcycles to the East front from 22nd June to 4th July 1941, and these vehicles are not included in the German SDE calculations.[52]

In addition, the Germans had also committed around 625,000 horses to support their forces in the East by 20th June 1941.[53] The vast majority of these were allocated to the TOE of Deployed (D) combat units. This was because horse drawn columns were not effective at moving large volumes of ammunition, fuel and supplies the relatively long distances from the advancing railheads to the 'mobile' divisional and corps supply depots. If we assume around 50,000 horses were used for cavalry squads and other cavalry type units, then the large majority of the remaining 575,000 horses in the East were assigned to the 127,000 'horse-teams' (in Deployed (D) combat units) shown in table Ger Total Deployed (D) 1. From 22nd June to 4th July 1941, the German horse-teams therefore had an average of around 4.5 horses per team.

***

[48] Refer Volume IIIB 4. 6) c. – 'The Supply Distribution Efficiency (SDE) for the Soviet Armed Forces from 22nd June to 31st December 1941 - Parameters Relating Specifically to the Calculation of Soviet SDE in 1941 - Proportion of Available Rear Area Trucks, Tractors and Light Transports Allocated to Rear Area SDE functions'. Includes some discussion on percentages of transport types utilized for SDE functions.

[49] Refer Volume IIIA 2. 9) d. - 'The Soviet Personnel and Equipment Resource Database - Transport and Prime Movers - Tractors (Prime Movers)' for a full description of each of the Soviet 'tractor' types used during 1941.

[50] Refer Volume IIB 6. - 'The Supply Distribution Efficiency (SDE) for the Wehrmacht on the East Front from 22nd June to 31st December 1941'.

[51] This correlates with the figure of approximately 600,000 motor vehicles, stated by H. Boog et al, German Research Institute for Military History at Potsdam, Germany and the Second World War-Volume IV, The Attack on the Soviet Union, Oxford University Press, New York, 1996, p. 318.

[52] There is a strong case that the German Motorcycles should be included in the SDE calculation. Many of these motorcycles were not assigned to combat units (in the Deployment Matrix), and many of them were large machines with sidecars, which were often used to ferry supplies. For example, the BMW R75 and Zündapp KS 750 weighed around 400kg empty, had 25- 26bhp engines (at 4400rpm), and could carry three men and their full combat equipment (along with a mounted LMG) across quite poor terrain. This is not dissimilar to the capabilities of the famous Kübelwagen military car (with a 24bhp engine). The Red Army in 1941 had very few motorcycles in comparison, and no equivalent capability.

[53] H. Boog et al, German Research Institute for Military History at Potsdam, Germany and the Second World War-Volume IV, The Attack on the Soviet Union, Oxford University Press, New York, 1996, p. 318.

2) The Total Available Personnel and Equipment in the Reich on 1st June 1941

In order to assess how 'hard-pressed' or 'stretched' Germany and the Wehrmacht were while launching Operation Barbarossa, we need to examine what proportion of total available personnel and equipment (resources) were in a Deployed (D) state in the Reich in June 1941. We have already established the total personnel and equipment allocated to Deployed (D) combat units from 22nd June to 4th July 1941 in the previous section, so we now need to ascertain the total available personnel and equipment in the Reich around this time.

The results of this research are displayed in the fourth column of table % of Ger Resources Deployed (D) (pages 96-99). The information displayed shows the available inventory of personnel and equipment in the Reich on 1st June 1941. This date has been selected because most of the historical inventory returns are dated for the first of the month, and information related to war production is most commonly stated as output by month. In addition, the Wehrmacht launched no major military operations between 1st and 22nd June 1941 which might have significantly reduced the overall inventory immediately prior to Operation Barbarossa. This also means that in most cases war production that was released to the Wehrmacht from 1st and 22nd June 1941 is ignored. Consequently, the actual inventory available on 22nd June 1941 was (in most cases) slightly higher than that shown in table % of Ger Resources Deployed (D).

One of the primary sources of information for German equipment strengths in June 1941 is the 'Germany and the Second World War' series published in ten volumes from the German Research Institute for Military History at Potsdam. The approximately 12,000 pages of this work represents the current definitive and official German work on the subject of the political, economic and social aspects of the war from the German perspective.[54] The two volumes most related to Operation Barbarossa in 1941 are: Volume IV, The Attack on the Soviet Union; and Volume I, Organisation and Mobilisation of the German Sphere of Power, Part 1, Wartime Administration, Economy and Manpower Resources 1939-1941.[55]

Important information relating to this section has been compiled from the sources (above), and is shown in three tables shown in Appendix A. These are titled:

Appendix A, Table I - Overall Status for Selected Weapons within the Wehrmacht on 1st April 1941.

Appendix A, Table II - Manufacture of Small-Arms and Selected Artillery Types for the Wehrmacht during 1941.

Appendix A, Table III - Approximate Overall Status for Selected Weapons within the Wehrmacht: 1st October 1939 to 1st January 1942.

The figures in the various sources (above) appear as overall figures within the Reich, and therefore it is assumed they include the Waffen SS. However, the reader should note that inclusion of the Waffen SS is not specifically stated, and normally the term *Wehrmacht* only refers to the German Army, Navy and Air Force. Thus the actual figures for 1st June 1941 could be slightly higher than shown in these tables.

***

---

[54] The work was originally titled *Das Deutsche Reich und der Zweite Weltkreig* (The German Reich and the Second World War) from the Military History Research Institute of the Bundeswehr (MGFA), and published between 1979 and 2008. It was translated into English and republished in the 1990s by the Oxford University Press. Although the work has many insights, from a purely military perspective, this series is not recommended if the reader requires a clear and detailed account of military operations at the tactical, operational or strategic level.

[55] Germany and the Second World War, Volume IV: The Attack on the Soviet Union, Boog, H., et al. (German Research Institute for Military History at Potsdam), Clarendon Press (Oxford University Press Inc), New York, 1996. Also, Germany and the Second World War; Volume I, Organisation and Mobilisation of the German Sphere of Power, Part 1, Wartime Administration, Economy and Manpower Resources 1939-1941, Kroener, B. R., et al, (German Research Institute for Military History at Potsdam), Clarendon Press (Oxford University Press Inc), New York, 2000.

Table % of Ger Resources Deployed (D)

The Proportion of Total Available Personnel and Equipment (Resources) which were in a Deployed (D) State in the (German) Reich from 22nd June to 4th July 1941

Database unit	Total resources allocated to Deployed (D) combat units	Pi	Ri	SMG	LMG	Total equipment allocated to Deployed (D) combat units: grouped by equipment type (i.e. with weapon sub groupings)		Total available resources in the Reich on 1st June 1941*	Percentage of total available resources allocated to Deployed (D) combat units, on 22nd June 1941
Allocated Manpower	4,240,335							7,309,000	58%
Heavy Rifle Sqd	59,961	2	7	1	1	Total small arms used by all units			
Light Rifle Sqd	5,215	2	9	1		Pistols and Revolvers (Pi)	721,476	793,222	91%
Motor Cycle Sqd	28,026	2	7	1		Rifles and Carbines (Ri)	4,113,570	5,742,670	72%
Bicycle Sqd	4,657	2	9	1		Sub Machine Guns (SMG)	192,450	193,410	99.5%
Cavalry Sqd	1,689	2	9	1					
Eng Sqd	9,249	2	8	4	1	MGs (incl AFV mounted)	138,496	210,141	66%
Light Eng Sqd	15,838	2	12	2					
Ferry Bridging Sqd	4,305	1	5			Motorcycles (including those with	224,208	337000 ^	67%
Military Police Sqd	4,027	2	3	2		sidecars and Sd.Kfz.2s)^			
Irregular Sqd	25,344	1	10						
Rail Repair Sqd	3,800	1	5						
HMG	21,504	2	2		1				
LMG	37,215	2	2		1				
AT Rifle	15,119	1	1			AT Rifle	15,119	25,298	60%
50mm Mor	14,065	1	2			50mm Mor	14,065	16,126	87%
81mm Mor	8,362	1	3			81mm Mor	8,362	11,762	71%
Horse Team	193,818		3			Horse Team	193,818	286,000	68%
Unit Trucks	210,584		3			Unit and rear area trucks	638,341	1,132,000	56%
Light Transport	126,406	1	2			Unit and rear area light transports	189,970	2,208,000	9%
Light Halftrack	5,789	1	2			Light Halftrack (incl SP AA)	6,277	7,500	84%
Medium Halftrack	6,217	1	4			Medium Halftrack (incl SP AA)	6,382	6,430	99%
Heavy Halftrack	1,379	1	6			Heavy Halftrack	1,379	1,810	76%
37mm ATG	10,494	2	4			37mm ATG	10,494	15,515	68%
50mm ATG	932	2	5			50mm ATG	932	1,047	89%
47mm ATG	183	2	4			47mm ATG (PaK(t) only)	183	785	23%
28mm sPzb 41	81	2	2			28mm sPzb 41	81	183	44%

Weapon				Weapon			
75mm Inf G	3,204	2	4	75mm Inf G	3,204	4,175	77%
150mm Inf G	744	2	6	150mm Inf G	744	902	82%
75mm Gun	260	2	6	75mm Gun	260	451 **	60%
105mm How	6,065	2	6	105mm How	6,065	7,076	86%
105mm IG40	4	2	6	105mm IG40	4	77	5%
150mm How	2,282	2	8	150mm How	2,282	2,867	80%
105mm Gun	512	2	8	105mm Gun	512	760	67%
150mm Gun	62	2	14	150mm Gun	62	89	70%
210mm How	300	2	14	210mm How	300	388	77%
210mm Gun	12	2	16	210mm Gun	12	12	100%
240mm How	8	2	16	240mm How	8	10	80%
240mm Gun	12	2	22	240mm Gun	12	12	100%
305mm How	16	2	26	305mm How	16	23	70%
355mm How	1	2	26	355mm How	1	1	100%
600mm How	4	4	32	600mm How	4	4	100%
150-200 mm Rail Guns	9	4	14	150-200 mm Rail Guns	9	32	28%
210-280 mm Rail Guns	35	6	28	210-280 mm Rail Guns	35	38	92%
380+mm Rail Gun/Mor	4	8	32	380+mm Rail Gun/Mor	4	5	80%
100-280mm Coastal Guns	1,157	2	8	100-280mm Coastal Guns	1,157	1,157	
Nebelwerfer 35	78	1	4	Nebelwerfer 35 and 40	150	577	26%
Nebelwerfer 40	72	1	4	→			
Nebelwerfer 41	210	2	6	Nebelwerfer 41	210	556	38%
28/32cm Rocket Systems	960	1	2	28/32cm Rocket systems	960	c 72200 *^	

* Comprised approximately 5,360,000 personnel in the Field Army, Waffen SS and Replacement Army, 1,545,000 in the Luftwaffe (inc. 25,000 airborne troops), and 404,000 in the Navy (including 51,000 coastal artillery troops).

^ 247,000 Motorcycles, of which 86,000 were equipped with sidecars. Also includes 4,000 motorcycle halftracks (Sd.Kfz.2 kleines Kettenkraftrad). Excludes all pre-1939 motorcycle production.

** Comprises 136 7.5cm le FK18 (field cannon), 16 7.5cm Geb K 15 (mountain guns), 106 7.5cm Geb G 36 (mountain guns) and 193 7.5cm LG 40 (also called LG 1, recoilless artillery weapons). Excludes all old 7.5cm FK 16nA (revamped WWI field cannon).

*^ The approximate number of 28cm Wurfkorper Spreng (High Explosive Mortar) and 32cm Wurfkorper Flamm (Flame) rockets available. 'Rocket systems' normally only includes 'frame launchers', but these rockets could be fired individually from their carrying cases.

Table % of Ger Resources Deployed (D) (cont.)

The Proportion of Total Available Personnel and Equipment (Resources) which were in a Deployed (D) State in the (German) Reich from 22nd June to 4th July 1941

Database unit	Small arms distribution (usage) by database units				Total resources allocated to Deployed (D) combat units	Total equipment allocated to Deployed (D) combat units: grouped by equipment type (i.e. with weapon sub groupings)		Total available resources in the Reich on 1st June 1941*	Percentage of total available resources allocated to Deployed (D) combat units, on 22nd June 1941
	Pi	Ri	SMG	LMG					
Sd Kfz 250 APC	1		1	1	39	Sd Kfz 250 APC	39	39	100%
Sd Kfz 251 APC	1		2	1	683	Sd Kfz 251 APC	683	758	90%
Sd Kfz 254 AOP	2	2	3	1	123	Sd Kfz 254 AOP	123	128	96%
Sd Kfz 221 A Cars	1		2	1	313	Sd Kfz 221 A Cars	313	319	98%
Sd Kfz 222 A Cars	1		2	1	296	Sd Kfz 222 A Cars	296	339	87%
Sd Kfz 260/261 A Cars	2		3		101	Sd Kfz 260/261 A Cars	101	104	97%
Sd Kfz 223 A Cars	1		2	1	289	Sd Kfz 223 A Cars	289	294	98%
Sd Kfz 231/232 A Cars	2	1	3	1	186	Sd Kfz 231/232 A Cars	186	186	100%
Sd Kfz 263 A Cars	2	1	3	1	120	Sd Kfz 263 A Cars	120	120	100%
Sd Kfz 247 A Cars	2	1	3		9	Sd Kfz 247 A Cars	9	10	90%
Panhard 178	1	1	2	1	190	Panhard 178	190	190	100%
Pz Kpfw I	1		1	2	345	Pz Kpfw I and Pz Kpfw I (Pio)	455	877	52%
Kleine Pz Bef I	1		2	1	130	Kleine Pz Bef I	130	160	81%
Pz Kpfw II	1		2	1	977	Pz Kpfw II	977	1,074	91%
Pz Kpfw III (37mm)	2	1	2	2	305	Pz Kpfw III (37mm)	305	350	87%
Pz Kpfw III (50mm)	2	1	2	2	897	Pz Kpfw III (50mm)	897	1,090	82%
Pz Bef III (*Gross*)	2	1	3	1	147	Pz Bef III (*Gross*)	147	170	86%
Pz Kpfw IV	2	1	2	2	495	Pz Kpfw IV	495	517	96%
Pz Kpfw 38(t)	2		2	2	642	Pz Kpfw 38(t) and Pz Bef 38(t) →	677	746	91%
Pz Bef 38(t)	2		2	1	35				
Pz Kpfw 35(t)	2		2	2	155	Pz Kpfw 35(t) and PzBef 35(t) →	160	170	94%
Pz Bef 35(t)	2		2	1	5				

Item				Total		Item			%
StuG III Assault Gun	2	2	1	356		StuG III Assault Gun	356	377	94%
Sd Kfz 252	1	1		195		Sd Kfz 252	195	253	77%
Sd Kfz 253	2	2	1	243		Sd Kfz 253	243	249	98%
15cm sIG33 SP Guns	2	4	2	36		15cm sIG33 SP Guns	36	36	100%
Pz Jager I (47mm)	1	2		198		Pz Jager I (47mm)	198	202	98%
47mm, Pz Kpfw 35R(f)	1	2		81		47mm, Pz Kpfw 35R(f)	81	81	100%
Pz Kpfw 35R(f) (Bef only)	1	2	2	1	12	Pz Kpfw 35R(f) (Bef only)	12	26	46%
SP 88 mm AAG	2	6	2	6		SP 88 mm AAG	6	20	30%
105mm K18 Pz Sfl IVa	2	1	2	1	2	105mm K18 Pz Sfl IVa	2	2	100%
Pz Kpfw II (F)	1	2	1	84		Pz Kpfw II (F)	84	90	93%
Pz Kpfw B2	2	2	1	6		Pz Kpfw B2	6	unknown	
Pz Kpfw B2 (F)	2	2	1	24		Pz Kpfw B2 (F)	24	24	100%
Pz Kpfw 35-S	1	2	1	132		Pz Kpfw 35-S	132	unknown	
Pz Kpfw 38H	1	1	1	246		Pz Kpfw 38H	246	unknown	
Pz Kpfw I (Pio)	1	1	2	110		(Inc in Pz Kpfw I Figures)			
Sd Kfz 300				54		Sd Kfz 300 (type B II)	54	103	52%
Pz IV Bridge Layer	1	2		4		Pz IV Bridge Layer	4	5	80%
Pz IV Ammo Carrier	1	2		8		Pz IV Ammo Carrier	8	14	57%
Armoured Train	10	40	12	16		Armoured Train	16	16	100%
20 mm AAG	1	2		11,189		20 mm AAG (all types incl SP)	11,773	13,964	84%
20mm Quad AAG	1	4		40		20mm Quad AAG (all types incl SP)	88	494	18%
37 mm AAG	1	4		518		37 mm AAG (all types incl SP)	635	1,238	51%
88-105mm AAG	1	6		3,820		88-105mm AAG (all types incl SP)	3,826	4,409	87%
Truck 20mm AAG	1	4		96		Truck 20mm AAG	96		
Sd Kfz 10/4	2	5		488		Sd Kfz 10/4	488	494	99%
Sd Kfz 6/2	2	5		117		Sd Kfz 6/2	117	136	86%
Sd Kfz 7/1	2	8		48		Sd Kfz 7/1	48	51	94%
AA Searchlights	1	6		3,068					
Rear Area SDE Trucks	0.1	2		427,757					
Rear Area SDE Lt Lt Trpts	0.1	2		63,564					

a. Review of Available Small Arms and Other Infantry Weapons

According to the aforementioned works, the Wehrmacht and Waffen SS had the following small arms and other infantry weapons available in the period April to June 1941.[56]

	Total available in the Reich on 1st April 1941	Monthly production			Total available by 1st June 1941
		April 1941	May 1941	June 1941	
Pistols	716,300	37,347	39,575	32,466	**793,222**
Rifles and Carbines*	5,498,800	118,907	124,963	123,959	**5,742,670**
Sub Machine Guns^	144,460	23,050	19,000	17,250	**186,510**
MGs	192,600	10,167	7,374	6,620	**210,141**
50mm Mortars**	14,913	611	603	751	**16,126**
81mm Mortars	10,549	611	603	322	**11,762**
7.5cm Infantry Guns*^	3,951	108	116	117	**4,175**
15cm Infantry Guns	797	51	54	46	**902**

* Includes 4,198,800 Karabiner 98K rifles on 1st April. Also includes around a 1,300,000 other types still in service. These included the *Gewehr* 98 series (going back to WWI), *Karabiner* 98a and 98b, *Gewehr* 98/40, *Gewehr* 33/40, and the new Gewehr 41 semi-automatic (self-loading) rifle.
^ In the FILARM model, SMGs available on 22nd June include 40% of June 1941 production.
** 50mm mortars represented approximately 50% of April- June 1941 mortar production.
*^ 7.5cm infantry guns represented approximately 68% of 1941 infantry gun production.

Note, the total available equipment in the German FILARM model **excludes** June 1941 production: it is assumed that by 22nd June the bulk of this production was **not** yet released to the Wehrmacht (from factories), was in testing, etc. The only exception is SMGs where 40% of June 1941 production is assumed to have been released to the Wehrmacht and security forces by 22nd June. This was due to shortages of these weapons and the demand for them in almost all areas of the Wehrmacht. In addition, the small number of losses due to military operations in the months of April and May 1941 is ignored; and was (anyway) probably fewer than the number released from the factories between 1st and 22nd June 1941.

Overall, the figures also compare closely with other sources. From Appendix A, Table III we can see there were at least 6,564,200 pistols, SMGs and rifles in the Army (*Heer*) and Air Force (*Luftwaffe*) on 1st June 1941, which is approximately 158,000 fewer than in the table above. This is the approximate number of small arms used by the 404,000 Navy (*Kriegsmarine*) personnel at this time (mostly in coastal artillery and naval security forces). Similarly, we find Appendix A, Table III indicates 203,250 MGs in the Army and Air Force on 1st June 1941, which is approximately 6,900 fewer than in the table above. This is the approximate number of MGs used by *Kriegsmarine* personnel in coastal artillery and naval security forces. It is worth noting that the Army and Waffen SS had priority for delivery of the outstanding MG 34 GPMG, while the other armed services and security forces had to largely make do with older MGs. These included the leMG 08/15, leMG 13, MG 30, MG 15, leMG 26(t) and leMG 30(t).

The figures for light and medium mortars, and light and heavy infantry guns, from the various sources are very similar (to within a handful of units). In these cases, very few of these types of weapons were used by *Kriegsmarine* personnel during 1941.

***

---

[56] The inventory on 1st April 1941 is derived from Appendix A, Table I. The monthly production data is derived from Appendix A, Table II. Also note the proviso on the Waffen SS.

b. Review of Available Anti-Tank Weapons

The Wehrmacht had the following, German manufactured, anti-tank weapons available in the period early April to June 1941.[57]

	Total available in the Reich on 1st April 1941	Monthly production			Total available by 1st June 1941
		April 1941	May 1941	June 1941	
AT Rifle, PzB 38/39	18,101	3,625	3,811	2,780	**25,537**
2.8cm sPzb 41	130	n/a	n/a	n/a	**c 130**
3.7cm Pak 36	14,838	195	109	183	**15,142**
5cm Pak 38	719	154	177	163	**1,050**

Alternative sources state the following anti-tank weapons were available by 1st June 1941.[58]

	Total available in the Reich on 1st June 1941	Total available in the Reich on 1st June 1941
AT Rifle, PzB 38/39	25,481	**25,298**
2.8cm sPzb 41		**183**
3.7cm Pak 36	15,522	**15, 515 ***
4.7cm Pak 36(t)	785	
5cm Pak 38	1,047	**1,047**
* Figure for 22nd June 1941		

The figures in the second column (above) are used in the German FILARM model as these are more precise. Most importantly, however, is that we can see that there is a close correlation between the different sources.

It is worth digressing here to briefly discuss two significant foreign manufactured anti-tank guns in German service. The first was a very good Czech gun called the Skoda 47mm *kanon* P.U.V. vz.36, and which the Germans designated the 4.7cm *Panzerabwehrkanone* 36(t) (or often just 4.7cm PaK(t)).[59] From August 1939 to May 1941 (inclusive), a total of 566 4.7cm PaK(t) were produced under German supervision along with suitable ammunition.[60] It is unknown how many guns were produced in Czechoslovakia from 1936 to March 1939, but it was likely around 300-350. As this gun was considerably better than the German's own Pak 36, the Wehrmacht commandeered most of these weapons for their infantry divisions, while the Slovakian forces were forced to use the lighter 3.7cm Pak 37(t). Thus the figure of 785 4.7cm PaK(t) available on 1st June 1941 (in the above table) seems very reasonable.

The second significant foreign anti-tank gun was the excellent (for its day) French *Canon de 47mle* 1937 and *mle* 1939. These weapons were designated 4.7cm *Panzerabwehrkanone* 181*(f)* and 183*(f)*, respectively (or often just the 4.7cm PaK(f)).[61] It is unclear how many of these guns were available in June 1941 (or how much ammunition

---

[57] The inventory on 1st April 1941 is derived from Appendix A, Table I. The monthly production data is derived from Appendix A, Table II. Note, these figures only include man-portable or towed anti-tank weapons. They exclude vehicle mounted anti-tank weapons such as tank guns and self-propelled anti-tank guns.

[58] Appendix A, Table III. The second column: Buchner. A., The German Infantry Handbook 1939-1945, Schiffer Military History, Atglen, PA, 1991, pp. 40, 79 and 81. On 1st September 1939, the Army had 11,250 3.7cm *Pak* 35/36 AT guns. On 1st April 1940 the Army had only 2 5cm *Pak* 38 AT guns.

[59] There was also the 3.7cm *Panzerabwehrkanone* 37*(t)* (Skoda 37mm *kanon* P.U.V. vz. 37). There were 513 of these weapons produced in 1939 and 1940, and they were sometimes issued to second line or security divisions. They were used by Slovakian forces in 1941, and it is unclear how many entered German service.

[60] 441 in 1940 and 125 from Jan.-May 1941. Germany and the Second World War; Volume I, Organisation and Mobilisation of the German Sphere of Power, Part 1, Wartime Administration, Economy and Manpower Resources 1939-1941 Kroener, B. R., et al, Clarendon Press (Oxford University Press Inc), New York, 2000, Table II.VII.3.

[61] Full French designation was *Canon de* 47 *antichar* SA *mle* 1937 (German 4.7cm PaK 181(f)) and *Canon de* 47 *antichar* SA *mle* 1939 (German 4.7cm PaK 183(f)).

was available), but one source shows the German Army received 614 anti-tank guns as 'booty' from the French campaign from 10th May to 10th July 1940.[62] Unfortunately, ammunition shortages, as well as difficulties with logistics and supply for these weapons, meant that most of them were not used on the East Front. They were largely stockpiled in 1941-42, and were later issued to occupation troops in France or emplaced as light coastal artillery. For this reason the available 4.7cm PaK(f)s are not included in the German FILARM model for 1941.

***

c. Review of Available Artillery Pieces

The Wehrmacht had the following, German manufactured, artillery weapons (including rocket artillery) available in the period April to June 1941.[63]

	Total available in the Reich on 1st April 1941	Monthly production			Total available by 1st June 1941
		April 1941	May 1941	June 1941	
7.5cm Mtn Gun 15 and 36*	112	0	10	9	**122**
7.5cm leFK 18	106	0	30	24	**136**
10.5cm le FH	6,854	140	132	89	**7,126**
15cm s FH 18	2,750	46	53	38	**2,849**
10.5cm K 18	730	10	10	5	**750**
21cm Mrs 18	346	22	20	20	**388**
Nebelwerfer 35 and 40	459	61	57	34	**577**
Nebelwerfer 41^	411	75	70	42	**556**
* Includes 16 7.5cm Geb K 15 and 96 7.5cm Geb G 36s mountain guns on 1st April 1941. ^ Nebelwerfer 41 launchers represented approximately 55% of 1941 rocket artillery launcher production.					

Alternative sources state the following artillery weapons were available by 1st June 1941.[64]

	Total available in the Reich on 1st June 1941	Total available in the Reich on 1st June 1941
7.5cm Mtn 36	108	
7.5cm leFK 18	104	
10.5cm le FH	7,076	**7,076**
15cm s FH 18	2,867	**2,867**
10.5cm K 18	760	**760**
21cm Mrs 18		**388**
Nebelwerfer 35 and 40	567	
Nebelwerfer 41	545	

It is apparent that the figures in the table above for 7.5cm weapons are incorrect: they show fewer weapons available on 1st June 1941 than were available on 1st April 1941. In addition, a detailed examination of the German units with mountain guns in June 1941 indicates that there were at least 16 7.5cm old Geb K 15 guns in service, and

[62] Germany and the Second World War; Volume I, Organisation and Mobilisation of the German Sphere of Power, Part 1, Wartime Administration, Economy and Manpower Resources 1939-1941, Kroener, B. R., et al, Clarendon Press (Oxford University Press Inc), New York, 2000, Table II.VII.4 - "The Army's Booty and Losses of Weapons and Equipment, 1939-1941". Their ref: 10 day reports of the Quartermaster General, BA-MA RW 19/1379 ff.
[63] The inventory on 1st April 1941 is derived from Appendix A, Table I. The monthly production data is derived from Appendix A, Table II.
[64] Appendix A, Table III. The second column: Engelmann, German Artillery in WWII 1939-1945, Schiffer Military/Aviation History, Atglen, PA, 1995, pp. 109 and 110. Reference: Wa I Ru. WaStabSt/No 600/45 g/Kdos. Note, leFH figures include significant numbers of old leFH 16s as well as newer leFH 18s.

it is unclear if these are included. Therefore, for the German FILARM model, the more precise figures in the second column (in the above table) are used for 10.5cm to 21cm weapons. For the remaining weapon types, the figures in the first table are used as they appear to be more accurate. Most important, however, is that overall we can see a very close correlation between the different sources.

***

Although the above were by far the most important types of German artillery fielded during 1941, there were also numerous other types produced and fielded in relatively small numbers, as shown in the following table.[65] With the exception of the light and new recoilless LG weapons, all the weapons in the table below can be classified as 'heavy' or 'super-heavy' artillery.

	Annual production			Total available in the Reich on 1st June 1941
	1939	1940	1941	
7.5cm LG 40*		184	9	193
10.5cm LG 40*			184	77
15cm K 18		28	48	43
15cm K 39^	15	18	27	38
15cm SK C/28M		8		8
21cm K 39**		12	22	12
24cm H 39	1	9		10
24cm K (t)*^	6 (pre 1939)			6
24cm K L/46	2 (pre 1939)			2
24cm K 3		3	1	4
30.5cm Mrs (t)^^	17		6	23
35.5cm H M1	1			1
60cm Gerat		2	4	4

* Recoilless Artillery. The 7.5cm LG 40 entered service in 1940, and 450 were produced in total. 10.5cm LG 40 entered service in late 1941.

^ At least two guns were exported to Turkey prior to Sep. 1939.

** Also sometimes designated 21cm K 52, K 39/40 and K 39/41.

*^ Purchased from Czechoslovakia.

^^ 17 were seized from Czechoslovakia in 1939 and 6 from Yugoslavia in 1941.

Note, the 7.5cm LG 40 (7.5cm *Leicht Geschütz* 40) recoilless field gun is included in the figures for '75mm guns' in table % of Ger Resources Deployed (D). In addition, those weapons with a K (*Kanone*) designation are included as 'guns', while those weapons with a H (*Haubitze*), Mrs or M (*Mörser*) designation are included as 'howitzers', in table % of Ger Resources Deployed (D). The 60cm *Gerät* is included under the category '600mm howitzer'.

***

---

[65] Data compiled from: Appendix A, Tables II and III; T. Gander, Heavy Artillery of WWII, Airlife Publishing Ltd, Ramsbury, UK, 2004, p. 17; F. Haun, *Waffen und Geheimwaffen des deutschen Herres* (Weapons and secret Weapons of the German Army) 1933-1945, Bernard & Graefe Verlag GmbH, Monch 1998; I.V. Hogg, German Artillery of WWII, Greenhill Books, London, 1997, p. 108; P. Chamberlain, H. Doyle, T. L. Jentz, Encyclopedia pf German Tanks of WWII, Arms and Armour Press, London, 1993, p. 158; T. Gander, P. Chamberlain, Weapons of the Third Reich; an Encyclopedic Survey of all Small Arms, Artillery and Special Weapons of the German Land Forces 1939-1945, Doubleday and Company Inc, New York, 1979.

In addition to field and rocket artillery, the Germans produced and deployed significant numbers of heavy rail-artillery pieces during WWII. Those produced (by Germany) and in service by June 1941 were as follows.[66]

	Annual production				Total available in the Reich on 1st June 1941
	up to 1938	1939	1940	1941	
15cm K (E)	18				**18**
17cm K (E)	6				**6**
20cm K (E)			8		**8**
21cm K 12 (E)		1	1		**2**
24cm Th Br K (E)	4	2			**6**
24cm Theodor K (E)	3				**3**
28cm Kz Br K (E)	8				**8**
28cm lg Br K (E)	3				**3**
28cm s Br K (E)	2				**2**
28cm Br N K (E)			1	1	**2**
28cm K 5 (E)	1	3	4	7	**12**
38cm Siegfried K (E)			4		**4**
40.6cm Adolf K (E)*				1	
42cm Gamma H^	1				**1**
80cm K (E)*				1	
* Entered service in 1942.					
^ Fixed emplacement weapon, only moved on rail cars.				© Nigel Askey, 2018	

The above table excludes a number of good French rail-road artillery pieces which were pressed into German Service after 1940. These weapons ranged in size from the 65,000kg 19.4cm *Kanone* (*Eisenbahn*) 486(f) or 93(f), to the 260,000kg 52cm *Haubitze* (*Eisenbahn*) 871(f). The large majority of these guns were used for coastal defence in France; either left on their carriages or moved into fixed coastal-defence emplacements. A handful of the heaviest 40-52cm calibre weapons were used on the East Front as 'siege artillery' later in the war.

***

Finally, in addition to rocket artillery employing only frame-launchers (the *Nebelwerfer*), by late 1940 the Germans had developed two 'stand-alone' bombardment rockets designated the 28cm *Wurfkörper Spreng* (HE Mortar) and 32cm *Wurfkörper Flamm* (Flame Mortar). These weapons could also be fired from a simple fixed frame launcher which could fire up to four 28cm or 32cm rockets. In this form it was designated the *schweres Wurfgerät* 40 (s WG 40).[67] In addition, in mid-1941 the Germans introduced the 28/32cm *Nebelwerfer* 41, which was a towed launcher capable of launching up to six 28cm or 32cm rockets.

In 1940, approximately 10,000 *Wurfkörper Spreng* and 12,000 *Wurfkörper Flamm* rockets were produced, and in 1941 77,150 *Wurfkörper Spreng* and 62,550 *Wurfkörper Flamm* rockets were produced.[68] Assuming a linear rate of rocket production through 1941, excluding production in June 1941, and around 10% of all rockets having been expended, then the Germans had approximately 72,200 *Wurfkörper Spreng* and *Wurfkörper Flamm* rockets available on the eve of Operation Barbarossa.

---

[66] Compiled from: I.V. Hogg, German Artillery of WWII, Greenhill Books, London 1997, pp. 114 – 140. T. Gander, P. Chamberlain, Weapons of the Third Reich; an Encyclopedic Survey of all Small Arms, Artillery and Special Weapons of the German Land Forces 1939-1945, Doubleday and Company Inc, New York, 1979, pp. 231-242. Note, in the second work there are a few errors relating to total production numbers, and when some of these weapons were produced.

[67] This was a simple wooden frame on which the rockets (still in their carrying cases) were placed. The rockets were still fired from their carrying cases. T. Gander, P. Chamberlain, Weapons of the Third Reich; an Encyclopedic Survey of all Small Arms, Artillery and Special Weapons of the German Land Forces 1939-1945, Doubleday and Company Inc, New York, 1979, pp. 336 - 337.

[68] Germany and the Second World War; Volume I, Organisation and Mobilisation of the German Sphere of Power, Part 1, Wartime Administration, Economy and Manpower Resources 1939-1941, Kroener, B. R., et al, (German Research Institute for Military History at Potsdam), Clarendon Press (Oxford University Press Inc), New York, 2000. Table II.V.7. Also, F. Haun, *Waffen und Geheimwaffen des deutschen Herres* (Weapons and secret Weapons of the German Army) 1933-1945, Bernard & Graefe Verlag GmbH, Monch, 1998.

d. Review of Available Anti-Aircraft Weapons

Of the various weapon systems fielded by the Wehrmacht during WWII, accurate estimates of the numbers of available anti-aircraft guns (at various points in the war) have proved to be one of the most difficult to ascertain. At first this may appear somewhat surprising. However the problems appear to stem from the fact that, unlike many weapon types, anti-aircraft guns were extensively used by all branches of the armed services. In Germany's case the Luftwaffe was by far the largest user as it was responsible for the strategic air-defence forces across the Reich. However, the German Army progressively increased its share of available light and heavy anti-aircraft weapons, and during WWII the German Army and Luftwaffe flak troops developed the use of anti-aircraft weapons against ground targets to the point where it was the tactical norm. They were in fact the only major ground forces to consistently maintain this position for the duration of the war (with the arguable exception of the Red Army in 1941-42). In addition, the Kriegsmarine employed anti-aircraft guns on even their smallest vessels (including submarines) as well as in numerous coastal defence batteries.

The problem is that most inventory reports only indicate the weapons in a particular branch of service at a particular point in time, group weapons together so that multiple weapons are in one category (e.g. light antiaircraft guns are often shown as all weapons of calibre 20-37mm), and differentiate differently between the 'total number of gun barrels' and the 'total number of mountings'. In the latter case a particular anti-aircraft gun system could have multiple gun barrels on one mounting and still count as a single anti-aircraft gun. By example, some of these problems can be clearly seen in the tables shown in Appendix A. Table I only shows the 2cm flak guns in the Army on 1st April 1941, while Table III only shows the number of 2cm flak guns in the army (with no information on the other calibres) and for the Luftwaffe it groups all the flak guns into only two categories (20-37mm and 88-105mm). This is simply insufficient detail for the FILARM model, which models the availability of each major weapon system separately, and on its own this data is unverifiable.

In order to gain a more accurate and detailed picture of the available anti-aircraft weapons in the Reich in June 1941, we are forced to use the monthly production data for each major type of weapon, and then make a number of reasonable assumptions. As a start we can use Westermann's figures for flak forces at the start of WWII.[69] On 1st September 1939 the Wehrmacht had around 6,300 2cm flak guns, 300 37cm flak guns, 2,628 8.8-10.5cm flak guns, 1,692 50cm searchlights and 2,052 60cm searchlights.[70] The German flak guns produced from August 1939 to May 1941 (inclusive) and the approximate number in service by early June 1941, were therefore as follows (also see assumptions below).[71]

	German Anti-Aircraft Gun Production			Total available in the
	Aug-Dec. 1939	1940	Jan-May. 1941	Reich on 1st June 1941
2cm Flak 30 & 38*	1821	5026	2369	13964
3.7cm Flak 18 & 36^	225	489	281	1238
2cm Flakvierling 38**		222	282	494
8.8cm Flak 18, 36 & 37*^	207	1057	607	4148
10.5cm Flak 38 & 39^	47	129	88	261
12.8cm Flak 40^^	4	na	na	0
Sd Kfz 10/4		164	402	494
Sd Kfz 6/2			187	136
Sd Kfz 7/1			83	51

* 95, 863 and 873 2cm Flak were supplied to the Army in 1939, 1940 and 1941, respectively.
^ Supplied to the Luftwaffe and select Waffen SS units.
** Comprises 4 barrels per 'gun'. The Navy was a big user initially (1940/41), followed by the Army.
*^ 126 8.8cm Flak were supplied to the Army in 1941.
^^ Prototypes, etc, 128cm Flak 40 not yet in service by 1941.   © Nigel Askey, 2018

[69] E. B. Westermann, German Anti-Aircraft Defences 1914-1945, University Press of Kansas, Lawrence, Kansas, 2001. This highly recommended work is probably the most definitive published work on German flak forces during WWII.
[70] Ibid. p. 83. 657 heavy flak batteries, 560 light flak batteries and 188 searchlight batteries. Also I.V. Hogg, German Artillery of WWII, Greenhill Books, London, 1997, p. 142, gives the Germans 8,950 flak guns at the outbreak of war, of which 6,500 had a calibre less than 5cm.
[71] Production data from: Kroener, B. R., et al, Germany and the Second World War; Volume I, Organisation and Mobilisation of the German Sphere of Power, Part 1, Clarendon Press (Oxford University Press), Oxford, 2000, Table II.VII.3. Their ref: Reports on overall state of armaments, BA-MA RH 8/v. IO35ff. Also, P. Chamberlain, H. Doyle, T. L. Jentz, Encyclopedia of German Tanks of WWII, Arms and Armour Press, London, 1993, Appendix VII, p. 262, for add SP flak gun data.

In addition, we know that the total losses of flak guns by the Luftwaffe in the period 10th May 1940 to 31st December 1941 were as follows.[72]

Total Losses of AA guns by the Luftwaffe 10th May 1940 - 31st Dec. 1941		
	10th May 1940 to 20th June 1941	22nd June 1941 to 31st Dec. 1941
10.5cm guns	4	1
8.8cm guns	70	250
3.7cm guns	37	144
2cm guns	116	251

For the German FILARM model, the number of **towed** flak guns available on 1st June 1941 (i.e. used in table % of Ger Resources Deployed (D)) uses the following reasonable assumptions.

- Production in August 1939 is not included in the inventory on 1st September 1939 as it is assumed that the bulk of this production was not yet released to the Wehrmacht from factories, testing, etc.

- Production in June 1941 is ignored, as it is assumed that the bulk of this production was not yet released to the Wehrmacht from factories, testing, etc, by 22nd June 1941.

- Around 90% of all 2cm Flak 30/38 in service on 1st September 1939, and produced to the end of May 1941, were in service in June 1941. This includes losses from military campaigns from September 1939 to May 1941, and normal attrition losses from wear and tear, training accidents, etc. The 2cm Flak 30/38 was commonly used in ground combat when the opportunity arose, even early in the war, so its combat losses were consequently higher than most other towed flak gun types. However, these estimated total losses are still conservative and are considerably higher than shown in the 'loss table' above. It is therefore probable that the number of 2cm guns in service was slightly higher than 13,964.[73]

- Around 96% of all 3.7cm Flak 18/36 in service on 1st September 1939, and produced to the end of May 1941, were in service in June 1941. This was a much newer, heavier and more powerful weapon than the 2cm Flak 38. In 1940-41 it was almost exclusively issued to Luftwaffe flak units (and a few select Waffen SS units) and saw little significant ground combat in the 1939-1940 campaigns. Again, the estimated total losses are conservative and it is likely that the number of 3.7cm guns in service was slightly higher than 1,238. [74]

- Around 98% of all 2cm *Flakvierling* 38 produced were in service in June 1941. This was a new weapon which had only been introduced into service in 1940. A naval version was developed early on, and significant numbers were used on Kriegsmarine warships from 1940 onwards. In late 1940 and early 1941, land-based versions were largely issued to mobile Army flak units for low level air-defence.[75]

- Around 92% of all 8.8cm Flak 18/36/37 and 99% of 10.5cm Flak 38/39 in service on 1st September 1939, and produced to the end of May 1941, were in service in June 1941. As before, the estimated total losses are conservative and it is likely that the number of 8.8cm guns in service was slightly higher than 4,148.[76] The use of the 8.8cm Flak in ground combat during WWII is well known, and it was used in this role early in the war. However, the large majority of 8.8cm flak guns produced during the war were issued to Luftwaffe flak units defending Germany and parts of occupied Europe from strategic air attack, and after 1941 the proportion of medium to heavy flak guns deployed in this role progressively increased. In June 1941 all the available 10.5cm flak guns were already being used in this role and there were no 10.5cm flak guns used in the East in support of Operation Barbarossa.

---

[72] Germany and the Second World War; Volume I, Organisation and Mobilisation of the German Sphere of Power, Part 1, Kroener, B. R., et al, Clarendon Press (Oxford University Press), Oxford, 2000, Table II.VII.6. Their ref: Ten-day reports of the quartermaster-general, BA-MA RW 19/1385, 1392.

[73] This concurs with other data. E.g. in September 1942 the Luftwaffe had 14 434 2cm Flak 30 and 38 guns in service. This is the number we would expect after losses and production from June 1941 to August 1942. T. Gander, P. Chamberlain, Weapons of the Third Reich; an Encyclopedic Survey of all Small Arms, Artillery and Special Weapons of the German Land Forces 1939-1945, Doubleday and Company Inc, New York, 1979, p. 131.

[74] By September 1942 there were 1760 3.7cm Flak 18 and 36 guns in service. Ibid.

[75] By September 1942 there were 693 2cm *Flakvierling* guns in service. Ibid.

[76] By September 1942 there were 5184 8.8cm Flak 18/36/37 guns and 500 10.5cm Flak 38/39 guns in service. Ibid, p.152.

- Around 95% of all Sd Kfz 10/4 self-propelled flak guns produced were in service in June 1941. Only small numbers of the Sd Kfz 10/4 were produced from 1940 onwards, and very few (if any) were available for the French campaign. Similarly, the Sd Kfz 6/2 and 7/1 were produced in even smaller numbers with most Sd Kfz 6/2s being issued to Luftwaffe flak units (until 1942 at least, the Luftwaffe took priority for weapon systems using the 3.7cm Flak 18/36). Operation Barbarossa was the first major commitment of the Sd Kfz 10/4, 6/2 and 7/1 self-propelled flak guns. The large majority were destined to equip German Army and Luftwaffe flak units supporting the ground troops near (or at) the front lines.[77]

***

Finally, it is worth briefly mentioning captured anti-aircraft weapons used by the Wehrmacht during WWII. These weapons are excluded from the German FILARM model. These weapons were significant if we are considering the overall anti-aircraft defences across the Reich: but, mainly for logistical reasons, very few were deployed on the East Front in 1941-42. Most of these guns were deployed in Germany or the occupied territories in rear areas for the duration of WWII. Nevertheless, there was a considerable number of them and they represented a considerable threat to Allied aircraft. As shown in the table below, by August 1943 this force comprised at least 2,159 light to medium (2-4cm) flak guns and 1 124 heavy (7.5-9.4cm) flak guns.[78] With the exception of the guns captured in the USSR, all the guns shown in this table were available in June 1941 and most were already in service.

Foreign Anti-Aircraft guns in Wehrmacht Service in August 1943					
	2cm Flak 28/29	2.5cm Flak 38/39	3.7cm Flak M39a(r)	4cm Flak 28	7.5cm Flak*
Make	Oerlikon	Hotchkiss	Sov state arsenals	Bofors	Various
Number in Service	836	488	531	304	570
Captured from	Various	France	USSR	Various	France
	7.62/8.8cm Flak^	8.35cm Flak M 22(t)	9cm Flak M 39(f)	9cm Flak M12(t)	9.4cm Flak M 39(e)
Make	Sov state arsenals	Skoda	DCA	Skoda	Vickers
Number in Service	357	107	16	12	62
Captured from	USSR	Czech. & Yugoslavia	France	Various	UK
* Includes, 7.5cm FK 97(f), Flak M 17/34(f), Flak M 30(f), Flak M 33(f) and Flak M 36(f).					
^ Many of the captured Soviet 7.62cm and 8.5cm guns were rebored to take German 8.8cm ammunition.					
Includes 7.62cm M 38(r), 7.62/8.8cm Flak M 38(r) and 7.62/8.8cm Flak M 31(r).					

***

---

[77] The Sd Kfz 6/2 was mostly issued to Luftwaffe flak units as opposed to German Army flak units, so it was less commonly used in the ground combat role. However Luftwaffe flak units at the front came under the army's operational control and they didn't hesitate to use the Sd Kfz 6/2 in the ground combat role if required. Sd Kfz 6/2s were also issued to Waffen SS combat units and elite units like the GD Infantry Regiment in 1941.

[78] Data compiled from: T. Gander, P. Chamberlain, Weapons of the Third Reich; an Encyclopedic Survey of all Small Arms, Artillery and Special Weapons of the German Land Forces 1939-1945, Doubleday and Company Inc, New York, 1979, pp. 131, 152 and 153.

e. Review of Available Tanks and other AFVs

In terms of the strategic success or failure of Operation Barbarossa, the most important weapon systems fielded by the Germans were their AFVs (Armoured Fighting Vehicles). Of these, the tanks and assault guns were the most vital. It is therefore critical to the German FILARM model that the availability of AFVs to the Wehrmacht in 1941 is accurately analysed. Fortunately the importance of German tanks to their war effort during WWII is reflected in the historical record: the numbers of German tanks and assault guns manufactured, and their availability and serviceability, is better documented than any other weapon type fielded during the war.

An excellent and (arguably) definitive study of the state of the German *Panzerwaffe* (tank arm) during WWII, is T. Jentz's *Panzer Truppen*, Volume 1 and Volume 2.[79] Included in Jentz's work are details of tanks produced during each month, new and rebuilt tanks ready for issue during each month, tank losses during each month, and tank inventories on the 1st of each month.[80] Along with some additional data on assault guns, flame-thrower (*Flamm*) tanks and command tanks, the basic information contained in this work relating to the period June to December 1941 (inclusive) is shown in Appendix A Table IV and below.[81]

Equally authoritative figures on German tank numbers in June 1941 have been supplied by the German Research Institute for Military History at Potsdam. These figures have been published in their excellent works Volume I Part I and Volume IV.[82] The relevant data from these sources has been complied for comparison purposes, and we find that the Wehrmacht had the following tank numbers in service on 1st June 1941.

German Tank and Assault Gun Inventory, 1st June 1941			
Source	Jentz, T., (+ others)	Kroener, B. R., et al.	Boog, H., et al.
Pz Kpfw I *	877	966	877
Pz Kpfw II	1,074	1,159	1,157
Pz Kpfw II (F) *Flamm* (Flame Thrower Tanks)	90		
Pz Kpfw III (37mm)	350	1,440	1,440
Pz Kpfw III (50mm)	1,090		
Pz Kpfw IV	517	572	572
Pz Kpfw 38(t)^	746	754	754
Pz Kpfw 35(t)^	170	187	187
Pz Kpfw B2 (F) *Flamm* (Flame Thrower Tanks)	24	c 24	c 24
Sturmgeschutz (StuG) III (Assault Gun)	c 377	377	c 377
(Pz I) *Kleine* Pz Bef (Sd Kfz 265)**	160	c 330	330
(Pz III) *Gross* Pz Bef (Sd Kfz 266 - 268)**	170		
Totals	**5,645**	**5,809**	**5,718**
* Includes Pz I *pionier* vehicles and ammunition carriers (i.e. all types except command tanks).			
^ Includes all Pz 38(t) and Pz 35(t) used as command tanks.			
** MG armed command tanks based on Pz Kpfw I and Pz Kpfw III.			
c - circa, and indicates data was omitted from the original source figures.			© Nigel Askey, 2018

---

[79] T. L. Jentz, *Panzer Truppen* volume 1: The Complete Guide to the Creation and Combat Deployment of Germany's Tank Force – 1933-1942, Schiffer Military History, Atglen, PA, 1996. Also, T. L. Jentz, *Panzer Truppen* volume 2: The Complete Guide to the Creation and Combat Deployment of Germany's Tank Force – 1943-1945, Schiffer Military History, Atglen, PA, 1996.
[80] Ibid, Volume I, Appendices A1 to A9, pp. 254-271, for the period 1939 to December 1942.
[81] Additional data on flame-thrower and command tanks from: T. Jentz, H. Doyle, P. Sarson, *Flammpanzer*: German Flamethrowers 1941-1945, Osprey Military, Reed International Books Ltd, London, 1995, pp. 7, 13 and 16. P. Chamberlain, H. Doyle, T. L. Jentz, Encyclopedia of German Tanks of WWII, Arms and Armour Press, London, 1993, pp. 22, 34, 71, 72, 214.
[82] H. Boog, et al, Germany and the Second World War-Volume IV, The Attack on the Soviet Union, Clarendon Press (Oxford University Press), New York, 1996, Table I.III.4. Their ref: Muller-Hillerbrand, *Heer*, annexe 22. Kroener, B. R., et al, Germany and the Second World War; Volume I, Organisation and Mobilisation of the German Sphere of Power, Part 1, Wartime Administration, Economy and Manpower Resources 1939-1941, Clarendon Press (Oxford University Press), Oxford, 2000, Table II.V.7. Refer Appendix A Table III for their reference. The data also agrees with German 1941 AFV production data from: P. Chamberlain, H. Doyle, T. L. Jentz, Encyclopedia of German Tanks of WWII, Arms and Armour Press, London, 1993, Appendix VII, German AFV Production, pp. 261-263.

Significantly, the figures show a marked degree of consistency: a variation of only 73-164 AFVs from Jentz's (slightly modified) figures, or an overall variation of 1-3% from Jentz's figures. The largest discrepancy is in the number of available Pz Kpfw I (89 tanks), and this could be attributable to 'Kroener' adding additional vehicles as command tanks (as they are not shown separately). The second highest discrepancy is in Pz Kpfw IVs (55 tanks). For the purposes of the FILARM model, the slightly lower but more complete figures from Jentz have been used. The most noticeable thing about the above numbers is how few tanks the Germans actually had: a total of only 5,645 tanks, command tanks and assault guns. This is especially striking when one considers that the Wehrmacht was about to attack the USSR, with the largest army in the world and almost 23,300 tanks on strength, while simultaneously having to conduct a military campaign against the Commonwealth forces in North Africa.[83]

In addition to tanks and assault guns, the Germans also manufactured a wide range of specialised armoured fighting vehicles. Apart from the Sd Kfz 251 (armoured personnel carrier) however, these were all produced in relatively small numbers. The Wehrmacht had the following specialised AFVs in service in early June 1941.[84]

	Annual production up to 1938	1939	1940	1941	Total available by 1st June 1941
Armoured semi-tracks					
Sd Kfz 250 APC*				389	**39**
Sd Kfz 251 APC		232	337	424	**758**
Sd Kfz 254 AOP			121	7	**128**
Sd Kfz 252^			54	359	**253**
Sd Kfz 253**			85	200	**249**
Armoured cars					
Sd Kfz 221 A Cars	189	126	24		**319**
Sd Kfz 222 A Cars	144	64	52	179	**339**
Sd Kfz 260/261 A Cars			10	171	**104**
Sd Kfz 223 A Cars	117	59	71	112	**294**
Sd Kfz 231/232 A Cars	56	55	32	94	**186**
Sd Kfz 263 A Cars*^	92	20		8	**120**
Sd Kfz 247 A Cars	10			54	**10**
Panhard 178 A Cars***			233		**190**
Armoured self-propelled guns					
15cm sIG33 SP Guns			38		**36**
PzJager I (47mm)			171	31	**202**
47mm, Pz.Kpfw 35R(f) **^				174	**81**
Pz.Kpfw 35R(f) (Bef only)*^^				26	**26**
SP 88 mm AAG		10	15		**20**
105mm K18 Pz Sfl IVa				2	**2**
Armoured pionier vehicles					
Sd Kfz 300 (expendable AFVs)			100	53	**103**
Pz IV Bridge Layer			20		**5**
Pz IV Ammo Carrier	1			17	**14**
* Series production commenced in June 1941.				**Total**	**3,375**
^ Production ended in September 1941.				**Excluding Sd Kfz 300s**	

* Series production commenced in June 1941.
^ Production ended in September 1941.
** Production ended in June 1941.
*^ Includes 28 old Sd.Kfz 263 (6-Rad). These were retained as signal vehicles (*Panzerfunkwagen*).
*** Captured French vehicles. 43 were converted to run on rail lines as railway protection vehicles.
**^ Production ended in October 1941
*^^ Command vehicles for units equipped with the 47mm, Pz.Kpfw 35R(f)   © Nigel Askey, 2018

[83] Refer Volume IIIB 1. 12) – 'The Actual Strength of all Soviet land Combat Units in a Deployed (D) State on 22nd June 1941 - The Soviet Tank Deployment Matrix' for full details on Soviet tank numbers and deployments on 22nd June 1941.
[84] Main sources: P. Chamberlain, H. Doyle, T. L. Jentz, Encyclopedia of German Tanks of WWII, Arms and Armour Press, London, 1993, pp. 24, 25, 106, 114, 115, 117, 150, 162, 168, 169-178, 179, 186, 191, 192, 194, 196, 198, 201, 205, 213, 214, 220, 226, 261-263. L.W.G. Niehorster, German WWII Organisational Series, Volume 3/II, Higher Headquarters-Mechanized GHQ Units (22.06.1941), 2nd Revised Edition, The Military Press, Milton Keynes, UK, 2005, p. 64.
Dr. F. M., von Senger und Etterlin, German Tanks of WWII, Galahad Books, New York, 1969, Appendix 2, p. 193 and Appendix 4, pp. 211 and 212.

In addition, the Germans pressed several types of captured French tanks into service during 1940-41, without adapting their chassis for more specialised roles (such as the 47mm Pz.Kpfw 35R(f) and Pz.Kpfw B2 (F) in the table above). These were French Char B-1bis, Hotchkiss H-35/38 and Somua S-35 tanks. It is not known exactly how many of these were available in early June 1941, but it is known that at least 6 Char B-1bis (designated Pz.Kpfw B2), 246 Hotchkiss H-35/38 (designated Pz.Kpfw 38H) and 132 Somua S-35 (designated Pz.Kpfw 35-S) tanks were Deployed (D) with combat units. Apart from 34 tanks in Finland-Northern Norway, almost all these captured tanks remained in occupation and training units in France.

***

f. Review of Available Motor Vehicles and Other Transport Types

The table below shows the overall 'state of motorisation' within various countries during 1939 and early 1940. [85]

Total Number of Motor vehicles in Various Countries in 1939					
Country	Date	Cars, Vans Buses**	Trucks	Vehicles Total	Motor Vehicles per 1000 Inhabitants
Germany*	1st July 1939	1,535,481	450,641	1,986,122	25
USSR	(production 1928 -39)			1,002,600	5
USA	1st Jan. 1939	25,283,313	4,202,367	29,485,680	227
Britain	1st Jan. 1939	1,932,619	490,359	2,422,978	51
Italy	1st Jan. 1939	355,058	114,593	469,651	11
Japan	1st Jan. 1939	135,800	45,100	180,900	3
France	1st Jan. 1939	1,783,500	467,800	2,251,300	54
Belgium	1st Jan. 1939	155,930	77,852	233,782	28
Denmark	30th Sept. 1939	118,957	43,540	162,497	43
Luxemburg	1st Jan. 1940	7,246	3,434	10,680	35
Norway	1st Jan. 1940	62,980	36,397	99,377	34
Netherlands	1st Jan. 1940	c 110,000	c 50,000	c 160,000	18
Poland^	1st Jan. 1939	c 90,000	c 45,000	c 135,000	6
* Includes Austria, the Sudetenland and Memelland.					
^ Only includes the territory occupied by German forces after September 1939; population 21,500,000.					
** Includes all types of automobiles, light vans to heavy commercial full-size vans, and all types of bus.					

There are some very interesting observations (although not necessarily conclusions) which can be made from this data:

- We can see that, overall, Germany was only moderately motorised compared to the other major European powers. However, this is hardly surprising considering their economy was still emerging from the economic era imposed by the Treaty of Versailles, and the benefits of the Schell Vehicle Program were only just becoming apparent.[86]

- Even before 1941, and without the motorisation benefits from the occupied territories, the German economy was considerably more motorised than that of the USSR. The USSR's motor industry was however in a state

---

[85] Data compiled from: Kroener, B. R., et al, Germany and the Second World War; Volume I, Organisation and Mobilisation of the German Sphere of Power, Part 1, Clarendon Press (Oxford University Press), Oxford, 2000, Table II.VII.11. Ref: *Statisches Jahrbuch* 1941/42, 109. Data for the USSR is calculated from the figures in Harrison, Soviet Planning, 253, annexe 2, with a total USSR population of 183 million. Data for the Netherlands and Poland are estimates based on economic and population data from: The Oxford Companion to WWII, Dear, I. C. B., et al. (ed.), Oxford University Press, New York, 2001, p. 609-612 and 695-699.
[86] Refer Volume IIB, 2. 15) b. - 'Motor Vehicle Nomenclature and Development History', for more information on the Einheits and Schell Vehicle programs, and the types of German motor vehicles produced.

of rapid expansion, largely as a result of direct technical and manufacturing support from the US auto industry (which was paid for by the Soviets).[87]

- The US was by far the most motorised country on earth. Despite some economic problems, the achievements of US mass-production manufacturing are astonishing. Significantly, however, the large majority of these vehicles were not trucks: only 14% of the vehicles in the US were trucks. In Europe this figure varied from 20% in Britain, 21% in France, 23% in Germany and up to 37% in Norway. It is also worth noting the majority of vehicles in the USSR were trucks. Ultimately, the powerhouse US auto-industry would supply the large majority of vehicles used by the Western Allies and the USSR during WWII. Well over half the Red Army's WWII motorised transport would come from the US, and considerably more if considering the total motorised 'lift capacity'.

- The lack of motorisation in the other major Axis powers is stark. Italy could only supply its military with very limited numbers of motor vehicles, and then not without impacting its economy (which it did in 1940-41). At the same time Japan had about the same degree of absolute motorisation as Denmark, and actually had fewer vehicles than Belgium! This was presumably a result of an agrarian focused economy with very limited supplies of fossil fuels. When one considers the militaristic nature of Japan at this time, that Japan was maintaining a large army in Manchukuo (Manchuria) and was at war with China (the Second Sino-Japanese War), and that Japan would soon attack a nation with the most powerful economy on earth, these figures are even more astonishing.[88]

- The total number of vehicles in France, Belgium, Denmark, Luxembourg, Norway, the Netherlands and the Polish territory which was later occupied by German forces in 1939, amounted to some 3,053,000 vehicles, of which 724,000 were trucks. With the exception of the territory which became Vichy France, all these countries were conquered and occupied by German forces by the late summer of 1940. Subsequently many of the motor vehicles in these countries were captured intact or in repairable condition, along with most of the associated auto-industry (see below).

***

During the period 1940 to 1942, local German truck production actually declined slightly. However this was largely offset by production from the auto-industries in the occupied territories, as shown in the table below.[89] Also shown are the trucks exported to other Axis powers; most notably Italy and Rumania.

German Truck Production and Exports, 1940-1942									
	1940			1941			1942		
	No.	Payload, tonnes	Ave. Truck Payload	No.	Payload, tonnes	Ave. Truck Payload	No.	Payload, tonnes	Ave. Truck Payload
Delivered in the Reich for the Wehrmacht and Economy.	87,245	210,098	2.4	84,727	215,788	2.5	83,822	226,653	2.7
Exports*	-13,126	-34,419	2.6	-13,262	-37,564	2.8	-5,721	-16,339	2.9
Deliveries in the Occupied Territories	15,531	40,973	2.6	39,574	103,622	2.6	37,163	95,163	2.6
Total Avail.	89,650	216,652	2.4	111,039	281,846	2.5	115,264	305,477	2.7
* Exported to other Axis forces, and not considered to be available to the Wehrmacht, Waffen SS or German economy.									

---

[87] Refer Volume IIIA 2. 9) Sections b. c. and d., for a full description of the Soviet pre-war auto-industry, the types of vehicles produced (including tractors), and the input from the US auto-industry.

[88] It is unclear if the figure of 180 900 vehicles only includes vehicles in Japan itself, and not in Manchuria and China. However it is unlikely this would alter the 'vehicles per 1000 inhabitants' figure significantly.

[89] Kroener, B. R., et al, Germany and the Second World War; Volume I, Organisation and Mobilisation of the German Sphere of Power, Part 1, Wartime Administration, Economy and Manpower Resources 1939-1941, Clarendon Press (Oxford University Press), Oxford, 2000, Table II.VII.7. Ref: Central Committee for Motor Vehicles, Comparison of payload total of trucks 1940-43, BA R 3/518.

Significantly, the average payload per new truck is high; around 2.6 tonnes per truck. This compares well against Soviet trucks fielded in 1941, which had an average lift capacity of around 1.99 tonnes.[90] This indicates a high proportion of the new German trucks were 4-5 tonne capacity heavy trucks, which the Army preferred for its support and logistical functions.

The above table indicates total truck production, but a large proportion of the trucks produced in Germany were better quality military-vehicles, manufactured to meet the rigors of military use. Many of these vehicles had 4x4 or 6x4 drive configurations.[91] Appendix A Table V details the German production (each month) of military-standard motor vehicles for the Army and Luftwaffe from August 1939 to December 1941. We can see from this table that from August 1939 to May 1941, the Germans produced at least 128,628 motor vehicles (excluding semi-tracks and motorcycles). These comprised 41,176 light-transports, 13,752 light trucks, 53,965 medium trucks, 5,672 heavy trucks (73,389 trucks), and 14,063 specialised vehicles.[92] As these vehicles were manufactured for use by the armed forces, it is likely most found their way into the better Army and Luftwaffe motorised units and Waffen SS units.

From September 1939 to 1st June 1941, the Wehrmacht and Waffen SS lost approximately 95,000 motor vehicles, of which around a half were trucks (including specialised trucks and other vehicles).[93] This includes combat and attrition losses in the Polish, Norwegian, Western (French), Balkans and North African campaigns. By June 1941, the status of the truck inventory available to the Wehrmacht and Reich economy was as follows.[94]

Motor Vehicles Available to the Wehrmacht, SS and Reich Economy in June 1941		
	Trucks, Buses, Spec. Trucks *	Light Transports, Cars, ^
Available in July 1939	604,000	1,382,000
Net production: 1st July 1939 - 31st May 1941	181,000	c 110,000
Commandeered from the conquered and occupied territories (refer text)	395,000	763,000
Total Losses	-48,000	-47,000
Total	**1,132,000**	**2,208,000**
* Includes all types of trucks, specialised trucks, heavy or full-size vans, and buses. Wehrmacht designations: Kfz 22 to Kfz 100.		
^ Wehrmacht designations: Kfz 1 to Kfz 21.		© Nigel Askey, 2018

***

---

[90] Refer Volume IIIA 2. 9) b. and Volume IIIB 4. 6) d. - 'Average Lift Capacity of Soviet Motorised Vehicles and Horse Teams'. The large majority of Soviet trucks in 1941 were also commercial two-axle vehicles with rear axle drive only (i.e. 4x2).

[91] Refer Volume IIB, Appendix A Table V.

[92] This excludes specialised trucks produced from August 1939 to July 1940.

[93] Data compiled from: Kroener, B. R., et al, Germany and the Second World War; Volume I, Organisation and Mobilisation of the German Sphere of Power, Part 1, Clarendon Press (Oxford University Press), Oxford, 2000, Table II.VII.4, The Army's Booty and Losses of Weapons and Equipment 1939-1941. Ref: Ten-day reports of the quartermaster-general, BA-MA RW19/1379ff.

[94] 1. Approximately 10% of 'Cars, Vans and Buses' available in 1939 are assumed to be a 'supply or transport motor vehicle with a lift capacity greater than 1080kg' i.e. the definition of 'truck' used in the German FILARM model. This is a very conservative estimate and it could easily have been around 20%, especially if full-size vans and buses are included. Refer Volume IIA 2. 15) c. and d. for details, and for the Wehrmacht vehicular designations for Kfz 1 to Kfz 100.

2. 'Net production' only includes trucks available after export to other Axis powers, and 45,000 trucks produced from 1st July 1939 to 31st December 1939 (approximately 90,000 in 1939). Some sources place this figure at around 105,000.

3. 'Vehicles from the occupied territories' use the following: 30% of pre-war French trucks and 40% of pre-war French light transports remained in Vichy France under Vichy French control (i.e. were unavailable to the Germans and are excluded). 55% of the vehicles in France (excluding Vichy France), Belgium and Denmark, and 40% of the vehicles in Luxembourg, Norway, the Netherlands and Poland, were commandeered by German forces or used directly for benefit of the Reich economy. Any vehicles that were commandeered from the Balkans, Greece or any other occupied territory, are excluded.

By mid-1941 there around 828,000 motor vehicles in the Wehrmacht (including the Replacement Army - *Ersatzarmee*) and the various German paramilitary services; ranging from heavy 9-ton Büssing-NAG military trucks to light commercial staff-cars. By June 1941 these vehicles had mainly come from the following sources.

- German pre-war production under the *Kraftfahrrustungsprogramm* (motorisation program) initiated in 1927/28 by the German General Staff. The program was finalised in 1929 and formalised the nomenclature, standard specifications and requirements for military transport.

- German pre-war production under the *Einheits* vehicle program, which was initiated in 1934 after Hitler had come to power.[95] This was an attempt to produce a series of standardised vehicles suitable for the military and was part of the Wehrmacht's rearmament program. Although the *Einheits* vehicles were good military vehicles with a cross-county performance superior to most contemporaries, their complexity and quality resulted in relatively slow manufacture.

- German pre-war production under the *Schell* Vehicle Program, which was initiated in 1938 when it was apparent that the *Einheits* Program was not going to meet the future motorisation needs of the German Army. It was named after General Schell, Director of Motorisation for the Wehrmacht. It successfully resulted in the streamlining of production, reduction of the plethora of both commercial and military model types being produced, and a reduction in the number of spare parts requiring manufacture. On the down side the more abundant *Schell* Program semi-commercial vehicles did not usually have the durability or cross-country performance of the earlier *Einheits* Program vehicles.

- Military and commercial trucks from Austria and the German occupied part of Czechoslovakia (what the Germans called the Sudetenland) when those countries were annexed. In addition, many of the relevant factories in these countries maintained their pre-war vehicle production which went into the German war effort, or were re-tooled to produce German military vehicles. For example, Saurer and Steyr manufactured trucks in Austria for the German Army, as did Praga, Tatra and Skoda in Czechoslovakia.

- Commercial trucks and cars in Germany and Austria which were commandeered by the Wehrmacht, mainly upon the latter's mobilisation in August-September 1939.

- Commercial trucks and military-trucks manufactured in Germany, and from factories in the occupied territories, during the war years. Refer table 'German Truck Production and Exports, 1940-1942' above, and Appendix A Table V for military-trucks. Other sources give similar figures.[96] The largest producer of trucks outside of Germany was France. For example, from 1939 to 1944 Peugeot manufactured 48,813 trucks from 1.2 ton to 6 ton capacity, of which 90% were used by Germany.[97] A similar number were also supplied by Renault.

- Vehicles captured from the Polish, Norwegian, Danish, French, Belgium, Dutch and British armed forces (and to a lesser extent the Yugoslavian and Greek forces), and commandeered vehicles from the occupied territories. The majority of captured military-trucks came from the French forces, and, overall, the majority of foreign vehicles came from France (first) and then Belgium, the Netherlands and Denmark.

By June 1941, the overall number of motor-vehicles in the Wehrmacht and Waffen SS had more or less doubled from when it was mobilised in September 1939. Credit for this was largely claimed by Colonel Adolf von Schell (of the *Schell* Vehicle Program fame). He claimed his (organisation) efforts had resulted in 558,800 new 'fighting vehicles' for the forces between 1st September 1939 and 1st September 1941 (with around 100,000 from foreign sources), and made 273,526 vehicles available for newly established units from 1st October 1940 to 22nd June 1941.[98] Of the over one million motor vehicles available to the Wehrmacht and SS in June 1941, around 75% could be classified as trucks in the German FILARM model. In the Wehrmacht these vehicles had designations Kfz (*Kraftfahrzeug*) numbers from 23 to 100. The remaining vehicles could be classified as light transports in the

---

[95] Refer Volume IIA 2. 15) b., c. and d. for more details on German pre-war and wartime vehicle production.

[96] E.g. J. Ellis, WWII a Statistical Survey, Facts on File Inc, New York, 1993, table 91 p. 278, states Germany produced 32 558 military-trucks September-December 1939, 53 348 in 1940, and 51 085 in 1941, and 345 914 military-trucks during WWII. Note, the same source shows that the USSR's war time production was only 197 100 trucks, and they were significantly lighter and of lower quality. From 1943 onwards, most of the Red Army's transport and logistical supply needs met by Western Allied (mainly US) lend-lease vehicles (approximately 454 600 vehicles).

[97] R. Michulec, Wehrmacht Support Vehicles, Concord Publications Co, Hong Kong, 1999, p. 3. A fact not highlighted by the French post-war (unsurprisingly). The fact is that the benefits the Germans received from the tens of thousands of trucks produced by French companies for the Wehrmacht during WWII, alone, totally dwarfs any damage inflicted on the German war effort due to the activities of the French resistance.

[98] Memo for report by Schell on motorisation in the war, 1 Nov.1941, BA-MA Wi/I F 5.122, pt. 2; conference Col. Max Thoenissen (chief of Staff of the General Plenipotentiary for Motor Transport) with departmental head, ibid. 633 (2 Dec.1941), BA-MA RW 19/166.

German FILARM model. These vehicles in the Wehrmacht had designations Kfz (*Kraftfahrzeug*) numbers ranging from 1 to 21.[99]

To finish off this review of German motor vehicles in June 1941, it is worth pointing out that the German ground forces that invaded the USSR in June 1941 had almost twice as many motor-vehicles (and overall lift capacity) as the forces that invaded France in May 1940. As a WWII commentator, I find it fascinating to observe that many WWII books carefully highlight the fact that the Germans fielded similar numbers of tanks at the start of these respective campaigns, but then totally ignore (or are simply oblivious of) the overall motorisation change. This is often a prelude to claiming that the overall strength of the German Army in June 1941 was similar to its strength in France in 1940. Invariably, these same authors usually point out that many of the trucks used by the Germans came from France in order to highlight the logistical problems this entailed (i.e. more and different spares, etc), but then totally fail to actually discuss the numerical increase in available trucks or the degree of increase in overall motorisation of the army. These misinformed works often then compound the error in their already flawed 'analyses' by also failing to review the increase in average tank quality and power, the increase in numbers of halftrack prime-movers (see below) and motorised artillery forces, the very large relative increase in available assault-guns (StuGs) and armoured personnel carriers (APCs), and the increase in the number of motorised rear-area supply and support units.

***

During WWII, and especially during the first years of war, motorcycles represented an important (and most often underestimated) part of the German Army's overall transport and communication network.[100] The exact number produced pre-war is unknown, but production figures during the war years (shown below) reveal the importance of motorcycles to the German war effort.[101]

German Motorcycle Production, 1939-1943					
	1939	**1940**	**1941**	**1942**	**1943**
Motorcycles Produced*	c 100,000	116,081	74,167	53,083	33,733
* Approx. 35% were 750cc (+) machines, produced with sidecars and 3x2 drive.					

If we only include production from 1st January 1939 to 31st May 1941 (and ignore pre 1939 production), then the Germans had at least 247,000 German produced motorcycles available in June 1941. Many of these motorcycles were heavy 750cc machines with a shaft-drive to a side-car wheel (i.e. 3x2 drive). By June 1941 approximately 35% of the motorcycles being fielded by the Wehrmacht were equipped with sidecars. Undoubtedly, large numbers of motorcycles were also captured and commandeered from the occupied territories during 1939-40. However the German Army generally preferred to use German machines like the BMW R75 and Zündapp KS750, which were generally heavier, more robust and more suited to the rigours of military operations. For the above reason, and because the number of foreign motorcycles commandeered is unknown, only German motorcycles produced from 1939 to 1941 are included in the German FILARM model.

Apparent from the figures in the above table is the progressive decline in importance of motorcycles to the German Army after 1941: by 1943 production had dropped to around 33,700 machines. The motorcycle infantry's rapid-deployment and reconnaissance duties were progressively taken over by motorised infantry in light armoured half-tracks (like the Sd Kfz 250) and by armoured cars.

Another important motorcycle-like vehicle, included here for completeness, is the well-known Sd Kfz 2 *Kleines Kettenkraftrad* or *Kettenkrad* for short. The Sd Kfz 2 was built by NSU and was a half-tracked motorcycle which was officially classed as a light tractor. This was an extremely advanced and useful vehicle for its day, with some 8,345 being manufactured during WWII.[102] Of these around half, or 4,200, were in service by June 1941.

---

[99] Refer Volume IIA 2. 15) b. and c. for details on the German *Kraftfahrzeug* (Kfz) nomenclature used.

[100] Refer to Volume IIA 2. 15) e. for details on the importance of motorcycles to the German Army, and details of the types used.

[101] R. Michulec, Wehrmacht Support Vehicles, Concord Publications Co, Hong Kong, 1999, p. 4. Also, Kroener, B. R., et al, Germany and the Second World War; Volume I, Organisation and Mobilisation of the German Sphere of Power, Part 1, Wartime Administration, Economy and Manpower Resources 1939-1941, Clarendon Press (Oxford University Press), Oxford, 2000, Table II.VII.2. Ref: Overy, '*Mobilisierung*', 289.

[102] R. Michulec, Wehrmacht Support Vehicles, Concord Publications Co, Hong Kong, 1999, p. 8. Also, R. Frank, German Light Half-Tracked Prime Movers 1934-1945, Schiffer Military History, Atglen, PA, 1997, p. 46.

The above means that, even ignoring pre-1939 production and commandeered foreign motorcycles, the Wehrmacht had around 251,000 motorcycles or 'motorcycle-halftracks' available in June 1941. If we include sidecars and only one person per Sd Kfz 2, then the Germans could transport at least 337,000 troops on these machines. In fact the Wehrmacht had around 224,000 troops Deployed (D) on motorcycle equivalents across the Reich in the summer of 1941; possibly the largest military force ever transported on motorcycles alone.

***

In the area of prime movers the Germans fielded their well known range of light, medium and heavy half-tracks. The German half-tracks produced to December1941, and the approximate number in service by early June 1941, were as follows.[103]

| Half-Track | German Towing Half-Track Production up to Dec. 1941. | | | | | Appr. no avail. | Total |
	To July 1939	Aug.-Dec. 1939	1940	Jan.-May. 1941	June-Dec. 1941	1st June 1941	Produced
Sd Kfz 10 (1t)*	c 500	734	2,721	1,146	1,552	**5,100**	14,700
Sd Kfz 11 (3t)^	c 400	275	1,079	648	909	**2,400**	8,800
Sd Kfz 6 (5t)**	c 1000	113	346	171	199	**1,630**	3,500
Sd Kfz 7 (8t)*^	c 3,000	228	996	572	752	**4,800**	12,000
Sd Kfz 8 (12t)^*	c 400	23	513	360	460	**1,300**	4,000
Sd Kfz 9 (18t)^^	c 100	50	240	123	171	**510**	2,500

* Production of the definitive D 7 version commenced in 1938. Also provided the basis for the Sd Kfz 250 APC
^ Production of the definitive H kl 6 version commenced in 1938. Also provided the basis for the Sd Kfz 251 APC
** First models produced 1934. Production of the definitive BN 9 version commenced in 1939.
*^ First models produced 1935. Production of the definitive KM m11 version commenced in 1937.
^* First models produced 1934. Production of the definitive DB 10 version commenced in 1939.
^^ First models produced 1938. Production of the definitive F 3 version commenced in 1939.
© Nigel Askey, 2018

All the German half-tracks listed above were outstanding military vehicles. In terms of cross-country performance, durability, reliability and sophistication of design, they were un-matched by any equivalent competitor during WWII.[104] However, these is a strong case that they were somewhat over engineered because we can see from the table above that they were never produced in anything like enough numbers: total per-war and wartime production amounted to around 45,500 vehicles, and only approximately 15,740 were available by mid-1941. Generally speaking, they were unsuited to mass production, were very expensive, and their complexity made maintenance and repair more difficult in the field. For example, according to 'classified data sheets', one Sd Kfz 8 (12t) half-track cost 46,000 Reichsmark and took 15 months to produce.[105] Although production times were vastly reduced from this figure later in the war, these vehicles always remained difficult and time consuming to produce.

***

The last critical mode of transport to be considered here is horse drawn transport. It is well known that the German Army's infantry divisions relied heavily on horse-drawn transport throughout WWII. In all, there were around three million horses and mules that saw service with the Wehrmacht from 1939 to 1945.[106] In September 1939 the number of horses and mules in the German Army was 573,000 and by 1940 this figure had increased to 771,000.[107] By June 1941 there were almost one million horses available in the Wehrmacht, of which around 625,000 were committed to support Operation Barbarossa in the East by 20th June 1941.[108] The large majority of these horses

---

[103] Data compiled from: Appendix A, Table V. R. Frank, German Light Half-Tracked Prime Movers 1934-1945, Schiffer Military History, Atglen, PA, 1997, pp. 3 and 23. R. Frank, German Medium Half-Tracked Prime Movers 1934-1945, Schiffer Military History, Atglen, PA, 1997, pp. 4 and 23. R. Frank, German Heavy Half-Tracked Prime Movers 1934-1945, Schiffer Military/Aviation History, Atglen, PA, 1996, pp. 3 and 31.

[104] Refer Volume IIA 2. 15) f., g., and h. for a detailed description and history of the German WWII halftracks.

[105] R. Frank, German Heavy Half-Tracked Prime Movers 1934-1945, Schiffer Military/Aviation History, Atglen, PA, 1996, p. 3.

[106] A. Buchner, The German Infantry Handbook 1939-1945, Schiffer Military History, Atglen, PA, 1991, pp. 125. Buchner also states around 1.7 million horses were lost. W. S. Dunn, The Soviet Economy and the Red Army 1930-1945, Praeger Press, Westport CT, 1995, p. 225, states 2.75 million horses and mules served in the German Army during WWII.

[107] A. Buchner, The German Infantry Handbook 1939-1945, Schiffer Military History, Atglen, PA, 1991, p.124.

[108] H. Boog, et al (German Research Institute for Military history at Potsdam), Germany and the Second World War-Volume IV, The Attack on the Soviet Union, Clarendon Press (Oxford University Press), New York, 1996, p. 318. Also, A. Buchner, The German Infantry Handbook 1939-1945, Schiffer Military History, Atglen, PA, 1991, pp. 125.

were assigned to the 109 'partially motorised' infantry, mountain, cavalry, light-infantry and security divisions committed to support Operation Barbarossa from 22nd June to 4th July 1941. Almost all of these divisions were close to, or over, their authorised 'horse-strength' TOE on 22nd June 1941.[109]

g. Review of Available Wehrmacht and Waffen SS Personnel

The most conclusive available information on Wehrmacht and Waffen SS personnel strengths during 1941 shows the following.[110]

Development of the Wehrmacht and Waffen SS Services during 1941 and January 1942					
	15 Jan. 1941	15 Feb. 1941	15 Mar. 1941	14 Apr. 1941	15 May. 1941
Army*	4,855,000	5,086,000	5,059,000	5,174,000	5,200,000
Luftwaffe	1,361,000	1,448,000	1,444,000	1,452,000	1,537,000
Navy	299,000	300,000	321,000	341,000	372,000
Waffen SS	121,000	130,000	130,000	140,000	150,000
Total	6,636,000	6,964,000	6,954,000	7,107,000	7,259,000
	15th June 1941	4th Aug. 1941	4th Oct. 1941	4th Jan. 1942	27th Jan. 1942
Army*	5,200,000	5,200,000	5,129,000	5,428,000	5,353,000
Luftwaffe	1,545,000	1,570,000	1,800,000	1,600,000	1,700,000
Navy	404,000	421,000	435,000	450,000	490,000
Waffen SS	160,000	140,000	171,000	170,000	170,000
Total	7,309,000	7,331,000	7,535,000	7,648,000	7,713,000
* Includes the Field Army (*Feldheer*) and the Replacement/Training Army (*Ersatzarmee*). The Replacement Army had around 1 240 000 personel in June 1941. © Nigel Askey, 2018					

Although the figures above exhibit anomalies when comparing relative monthly strengths for some of the services, the 15th June 1941 figures compare well with other sources.[111] For example, all the figures (above) for 15th June 1941 are confirmed by other high level accounts of Wehrmacht manpower strengths in 1941.[112] The 5,200,000 figure for the Army can be broken down further into the Field Army (*Feldheer*) and the Replacement/Training Army (*Ersatzarmee*). In June 1941 the Replacement Army Commander had a total of 1,240,000 personnel under his command.[113]

Other works confirm these overall figures. For example, the well-known work *Das Heer* 1933-1945 (B. Mueller-Hillebrand) states that the German armed forces strength on 22nd June 1941 was approximately 7,234,000 men.[114] This number supposedly breaks down into 3,800,000 in the Field Army, 150,000 in the Waffen SS, 1,200,000 in the Replacement Army, 1,680,000 in the Luftwaffe, and 404,000 in the Navy (*Kriegsmarine*).

---

[109] This is demonstrated by the fact that a 1st wave infantry division's TOE called for over 1,740 saddle horses and 3,630 draft horses (5,370 horses). 625,000 horses divided amongst 109 divisions averages out to around 5,700 horses per division. Note, not all horses were allocated to divisions, but the large majority were.

[110] Kroener, B. R., et al (German Research Institute for Military history at Potsdam), Germany and the Second World War; Volume I, Organisation and Mobilisation of the German Sphere of Power, Part 1, Clarendon Press (Oxford University Press), Oxford, 2000, Diagram III.V.23. The data presented is compiled from various sources and covers the period Sept. 1939 to July 1942. For 1939- Jan. 42 ref: 1st Sept. 1939-4th Sept. 1941: Memorandum of Capt. Trahndorff, WiRuAmt, BA-MA Wi/I F 5.3358; 4 Sept. 1941: AHA/Ag/E, 31 Oct. 1941, BA-MA RH 2/v. 2410; 4 Oct. 1941 (also 1 Jan. 1942): OKH/OrgAbt, Ist-Starken der Wehrmacht, BA-MA RH 2/v. 1341; 1 Jan 1942: PA, Handakten Etzdorf, 26; 27 Jan. 1941: Deputy Chief WFSt No. 00296/42 g.Kdos. WFSt/Org/Qu, 27 Jan.1942, PA Handakten Ritter, No. 56. *For the Navy*: AMA/MWehr I a No. 1889/40 g.Kdos., 25 Nov. 1940, BA-MA RM 7/1206 (to 1 Nov. 1940) and M 282 (e), 25 May 1945.

[111] The authors at Potsdam highlight the difficulty in obtaining accurate personnel strength data for all the services which is concurrent. In order to chart the change in strengths, different archival sources had to be used, and sometimes even different sources for different services for the same period. Hence the anomalies in the table.

[112] E.g., M. Harrison, et al, The Economics of WWII: Six Great Powers in International Comparison, Cambridge University Press, Cambridge, UK, 2000, Table 1.5, p, 14. Also, The Oxford Companion to WWII, Oxford University Press, New York, 2001, p. 370. Also, N. Davies, Europe at War 1939-1945, Pan Books, London, 2007, p. 216.

[113] Kroener, B. R., et al, Table III.IV.9.

[114] B. Mueller-Hillebrand, *Das Heer* 1933-1945, Volume 2, Frankfurt, 1956, p. 102.

However, in order to validate the June 1941 figures further, and to gain a deeper understanding of the personnel distribution, it is worthwhile examining the breakdown of personnel within each major branch of service. In general the combined figure of 4,120,000 personnel in the Field Army (*Feldheer* - 3,960,000) and Waffen SS (160,000) appears consistent with the numbers and types of combat units fielded. From the German Deployment Matrix we can see that these men were deployed in 208 divisions (including 3 SS motorised and 1 police division), which equates to around 19,800 men per division. When the many non-divisional combat units are included, as well as the many non-divisional support units (including HQs), this average drops to around 13,500 men per division. This is close to what we would expect, although, if anything, it is on the low side: we would really expect 14-15,000 men per division as the only really small 'divisions' fielded by the Germans in 1941 were the nine security divisions.

At the same time, the personnel figure of 1,240,000 in the Replacement/Training Army appears rather high. First of all there were only 31 replacement divisions in the various *Wehrkreise* (military districts) of the Replacement Army. This equates to around 40,000 personnel per division. Even though we would expect the proportion of non-divisional units in the Replacement Army to be considerably higher than the Field Army, this figure still seems high. This is especially true when one considers that the average replacement division was significantly smaller than the average Field Army division: the replacement divisions were light on heavy weapons, transport, supply and support units (they weren't large and mobile combat units and therefore had a smaller 'divisional slice'). In addition, other German sources state that just prior to Operation Barbarossa the field replacement battalions, which contained the actual troops earmarked as Replacements (R) for Operation Barbarossa, comprised 90,000 men already being transferred, and an additional 475,000 men (of which the Luftwaffe claimed 90,000).[115] It is hard to believe the remaining 625,000 men were all army instructors or other permanent Replacement Army support personnel. The question is then, where did the additional personnel come from? There are several possible explanations which include the following.

- A number of regular army combat units were in Germany in June 1941 undergoing formation, refresher training, refitting, etc. These units were temporarily under the Commander Replacement Army. For example, on 22nd June 1941 the XXXX Motorised Corps HQ along with the 2nd and 5th Panzer Divisions, and the 60th Motorised Division, were refitting in the Replacement Army.[116] In all there were around 115,000 Field Army regulars and Waffen SS personnel in the Replacement Army in late June 1941. Note, in the German FILARM model they are considered Deployed (D) combat units and counted as Field Army personnel.

- In addition to its primary role, on 22nd June 1941 the *Ersatzarmee* also controlled four *Ersatz* security brigades, 361 *Landesschützen* (LS - local defence force militia) battalions, 2 *Wacht* (guard militia) battalions and 1 *Wacht* company.[117] The LS battalions were usually (but not always) organised under a 'security division for special purpose HQ' (zbV), which in turn reported to the *Wehrkreise* commander. The approximately 210,000 men in these units were responsible for certain rear area and line-of-communication security functions. One of their primary functions was to provide guards and security infrastructure for the large number of POW camps dotted around greater Germany. Their primary role was not training replacements for the Field Army or Luftwaffe, and they were essentially deployed as combat units (albeit of very limited combat power). Whether or not these troops are Field Army or Replacement Army personnel is somewhat a grey area. There is no doubt that in June 1941 the 363 *Landesschützen* and *Wacht* battalions reporting to the Replacement Army Commander are included in the 1,240,000 personnel figure. However, on 22nd June 1941 there were 181 additional *Landesschützen* battalions deployed under Field Army control (outside of Germany and the *Wehrkreise* System territories), and these units are definitely included in the Field Army personnel figures. Regardless, in the German FILARM model all the *Landesschützen* and *Wacht* units are considered Deployed (D) combat units, and are then individually allocated to the historical (June 1941) HQ.

- A third possible reason for the 'high' Replacement Army numbers is that this is most likely where armed forces auxiliary (*Wehrmachtsgefolge*) personnel would appear. They were used in the direct employment, assistance or aid of the Wehrmacht, but were not considered part of the *Heer*, *Luftwaffe*, *Kriegsmarine* or *Waffen* SS. They included personnel from organisations such as the: National Socialist Motor Corps (*Nationalsozialistisches Kraftfahr-Korps* – NSKK), Air Protection Warning Service (*Luftschutzwarendienst* - LSW), National Air Raid Protection League (*Reichsluftschutzbund* - RLB), Security and Assistance Service (*Sicherheits und Hilfdienst*), Todt Organisation (*Organisation Todt* – OT) and the Reich Labour Service

---

[115] H. Boog, et al, German Research Institute for Military History at Potsdam, Germany and the Second World War-Volume IV, The Attack on the Soviet Union, Clarendon Press (Oxford University Press), New York, 1996, p. 317. Also, R.H.S. Stolfi, Hitler's Panzers East: WWII Reinterpreted, University of Oklahoma Press, Norman and London, 1991, p. 155.

[116] Refer Volume IIB 4. 7) a. - 'The German Army and the *Wehrkreise* System' for more details on the units in the Replacement Army in June 1941.

[117] Ibid.

(*Reichsarbeitsdienst* – RAD). It is unknown how many of these 'auxiliary personnel' were considered part of the Replacement Army in June 1941.

***

Taking into account the above facts, the overall personnel distribution within the Replacement Army in June 1941 was as follows.[118]

Distribution of Personnel Strength within the Replacement Army, June 1941		
570,400	Regular personnel army agencies with local defence units. Comprised:	
	115,000	Field Army temporarily under command of the Replacement Army.
	210,000	LS & Guard Battalions under command of the Replacement Army.
	245,400	Regular personnel army agencies (e.g., permanent training staff, schools, etc.)
108,000	Available replacement troops for the Luftwaffe and Navy.	
561,600	Available replacement troops for the Army (i.e. not Luftwaffe, Navy or Waffen SS). Comprised	
	90,000	Already in the divisional Field Replacement Battalions at the front.
	275,000	Intended for loss replacement in the Frontier Battles for July-August 1941.
	46,600	Intended for loss replacement in September 1941.
	150,000	Additional Army troops for foreseen losses through disease, unfitness for service, etc.
1,240,000	Total in the Replacement (*Ersatz*) Army*	
* Excludes 92,000 regular personnel in Luftwaffe and Navy agencies.		© Nigel Askey, 2018

***

Best estimates of Luftwaffe personnel strengths from May to December 1941 are as follows.[119]

Luftwaffe Personnel Strength and Distribution in 1941*			
	20th May 1941	22nd June 1941	1st December 1941
Aircrew	32,000	33,000	35,000
Air Troops	494,000	496,000	553,000
Air Signals Troops	243,000	244,000	296,000
Home Defence Units	36,000	36,000	38,000
Flak Troops	500,000	502,000	571,000
Luft Construction Units	153,000	154,000	146,000
Auxiliary organisations*	79,000	80,000	111,000
Total	**1,537,000**	**1,545,000**	**1,750,000**
* Includes personel in *Fallschirmjager* – parachute/airborne forces.			© Nigel Askey, 2018

In general terms, Luftwaffe can be divided into two major parts: the Luftwaffe ground forces, and Luftwaffe flight and flight support personnel. By far the largest component of the Luftwaffe ground forces was the Luftwaffe Flak forces, because this force was responsible for the (ground-based) strategic air-defence of the Reich, especially in Germany and Austria. By August 1940 the Luftwaffe's flak arm already had 791 heavy flak batteries, 686 light flak batteries and 221 searchlight batteries.[120] By June 1941 this force had expanded to 923 heavy flak batteries,

---

[118] Compiled from: Ibid, note 115, and Kroener, B. R., et al, Table III.IV.9. Ref ; Report by Buhle to Halder: Halder War Diaries, 16 June 1941; conference at OKW/WFSt/L with representatives of the Wehrmacht branches on 11 June 1941, BA-MA RW 19/267; WiRuAmt/Stab, KTB, discussion at Chef OKW with Munich (L II) and Wagner (Ru II) on 19 May 1941, BA-MA RW 19/165; Fromm discussion with Halder: Halder War Diaries, 20 May 1941.
[119] Compiled from: Kroener, B. R., et al, Diagram III.V.139. Ref: *Sammlung Greffrath*/MGFA, H. Boog, et al, pp. 818-819, E. B. Westermann, Flak: German Anti-Aircraft Defences 1941-1945, University Press of Kansas, Lawrence, Kansas, 2001, p. 272, and The Oxford Companion to WWII, Oxford University Press, New York, 2001, p. 370.
[120] E.B. Westermann, Flak: German Anti-Aircraft Defences 1941-1945, University Press of Kansas, Lawrence, Kansas, 2001, p. 272. Westermann states these forces had 528,000 personnel, but Westermann's figures include the searchlight batteries and possibly some Home Defence Troops.

752 light flak batteries and around 254 searchlight batteries. They were organised into 2 Flak Corps HQs, 59 Luftwaffe flak regiment HQs, 308 mixed flak battalions and 46 Luftwaffe light flak battalions.[121]

A further breakdown of Luftwaffe personnel in June 1941 reveals the following personnel distribution.

Luftwaffe Personnel Distribution in June 1941	
33,000	Aircrew, including those in Luftwaffe training and replacement agencies.
229,000	Air Troops: flight operations support and airfield support personnel (e.g., ground-crews).
267,000	Air Trps: Motorised Supply Units (inc. supply to air units and forward airfields, i.e. SDE functions).
214,000	Air Signals Troops: radar, communication HQs and other strategic air-defence ground forces.
30,000	Air Signals Trps: in army liaison role (usually embedded in Field Army units, incl local liason HQs).
502,000	Flak Troops (excluding Searchlight Batteries).
154,000	Luftwaffe Construction Units.
36,000	Luftwaffe Home Defence units.
55,000	Other Auxiliary Luftwaffe Organisations.*
25,000	Airborne Forces (part of the Luftwaffe, but mostly under Army operational control).
1,545,000	**Total, Luftwaffe.**
* Auxiliary organisations: e.g.. the Reich Air Protection League, Technical Emergency Aid and Auxiliary Security Service.	
	© Nigel Askey, 2018

Of special note (in the above) are the Luftwaffe Air Signals troops who were often embedded in Field Army units. These troops operated in forward positions and were primarily responsible for the Luftwaffe side of coordinating Luftwaffe attacks with local Army ground operations. Most famously this included close air support from Stuka units at regimental and battalion level. At higher HQ levels it also included coordination of major air-interdiction operations with major offensive operations. It is not generally appreciated that from 1939 to at least 1942 the German Army and Luftwaffe easily led the world in this type of cooperation, and especially in the application of 'close air support'.

To a large extent this was simply an extension of the overall view in the Wehrmacht that the Luftwaffe was primarily a tactical air-force whose main function was the support of the Army, and not a strategic force designed to destroy an enemy's industrial capability. This was also the reason why the Germans built the types of aircraft they did. Whatever the reason, it wasn't until 1943-44 that the Western Allies developed their Army-Air Force cooperation techniques to match this level of sophistication, and it is apparent that the WWII Red Army never did. By late 1944 the Luftwaffe had lost air-parity, but in the period 1939-1942 the close cooperation between the German Army and Luftwaffe enabled the Germans to achieve some phenomenal results with remarkably few aircraft.

From the above figures we can see that there were approximately 529,000 air-crew or personnel involved in the direct support of air-operations. These comprised around 33,000 aircrew, including all those in training units, and another 496,000 'Air Troops'. The latter included airfield ground crews responsible for all aspects of aircraft supply, maintenance and repair, personnel involved in all other aspects of flight operations support, and the Luftwaffe's motorised supply and logistics organisations.

On 22nd June 1941 the Luftwaffe had 5,882 front line aircraft (including 4,948 combat aircraft) and around 3,000 training aircraft.[122] If we exclude the Luftwaffe motorised supply and logistics organisations (which mainly comprised personnel and trucks moving supplies to the airfields), then these aircraft were crewed or directly supported by 262,000 personnel. This equates to around 29 personnel supporting each aircraft and around 7 men per aircrew member. This figure is generally in accordance with other western air forces during 1941, but is considerably more men per aircraft and per aircrew than the VVS (the Soviet air force) was fielding in June 1941.

***

---

[121] Refer Volume IIB 1. – 'The German Deployment Matrix' for more details on Luftwaffe flak deployments.
[122] Refer Volume IIB 5. – 'The Luftwaffe in 1941' for details.

Finally we come to the German Navy (*Kriegsmarine*), which experienced the personnel growth shown in the table below from August 1939 to June 1941.[123]

Personnel Strength of the Kriegsmarine, August 1939 - June 1941				
	1st Aug. 1939	1st Oct. 1939	1st March 1941	15th June 1941
Officers	4,500	8,400	11,200	12,120
Petty officers & enlisted men	73,943	128,188	309,534	391,880
Total	**78,443**	**136,588**	**320,734**	**404,000**

According to these figures, the *Kriegsmarine* grew by an amazing 296% from October 1939 to June 1941. As the October 1939 figure already reflects the mobilisation of personnel due to going from peacetime establishment strength to a war footing, and as there was no corresponding increase in the number of naval vessels from 1939 to 1941, the question is what were all these 'additional' personnel doing as part of the Wehrmacht? By way of illustration, consider that the comparatively small *Kriegsmarine* had similar numbers of personnel in 1941 as the two largest navies in the world when they entered WWII: namely the Royal Navy and US Navy! [124] One clue in the above figures is the changing proportion of officers to other ranks. In October 1939 over 6% of Navy personnel were officers, but by June 1941 this ratio had declined to only 3%. As the standards of officer training had not changed, and the proportion of officers on ships had not changed, then one can only conclude that most of the personnel mobilised after October 1939 were less well trained shore-based personnel fulfilling less demanding roles than crewing warships.

In 1941 the *Kriegsmarine* had the usual fleet and shore based commands. The fleet itself was divided into three basic categories: the High Seas Fleet (*Flottenstreitkrafte*), the Naval Security Forces (*Sicherungsstreitkrafte*) and the U-Boat arm. The High Seas Fleet included all battleships, cruisers, destroyers, torpedo-boats, fast attack craft (S-boats), auxiliary cruisers (including commerce raiders), supply ships and training ships. The Security Forces were concerned with the defence of coastal waters and encompassed minesweepers, patrol and coastal defence boats, submarine hunters and escorts.

In June 1941 the High Seas Fleet and Naval Security Forces comprised: 1 battleship, 2 obsolete pre WWI battleships, 2 battle cruisers, 4 heavy cruisers (including two so called 'pocket-battleships'), 4 light cruisers, 5 old pre WWI light cruises (used as accommodation ships only), 8 commerce raiders (converted merchant ships), 18 destroyers (including three still fitting out), 5 old pre-WWI destroyers, 27 torpedo-boats, 10 old pre WWI torpedo-boats, 9 small escorts, 79 minesweepers, 31 old WWI era minesweepers, 11 minelayers, 10 hospital ships, around 120 S-boats (*Schnellboot* - often called E-boats in western literature), around 117 R-boats (*Raumboote* - small motor minesweepers/seagoing launches), and 15 other miscellaneous vessels (tenders for U-boats, S-boats and seaplanes, gunnery and fleet tenders, one oceanographic survey vessel and one ice-breaker).[125] The entire ship-borne complement for all the above (assuming they were all simultaneously at sea and fully operational) amounted to approximately 65,000 men.[126] It is reasonable to assume that if we include all the sailors and other naval personnel in shore based training schools, on leave, replacements, in dockside support, in naval intelligence and in supply, then the High Seas Fleet and Naval Security Forces comprised, at most, around 130,000 personnel.

The U-boat arm, easily the most dangerous offensive element of the *Kriegsmarine,* had 136 U-boats in the period April to June 1941, and 182 in the period July to September 1941.[127] Of these, only around 17% were actually on operations (on patrol) at any given time.[128] The large majority of these U-boats were type VIIB or VIIC with a complement of 44 men each, so the total number of sailors earmarked for the actual U-boats in July-September 1941

---

[123] Data compiled from: Kroener, B. R., et al, Table III.V.6. Ref; *Marinekommandant* A IIb, 615/41 g.Kdos., 4 Apr 1941, BA-MA RM 7/1206. B. Mueller-Hillebrand, *Das Heer* 1933-1945, Volume 2, Frankfurt, 1956, p. 102. The Oxford Companion to WWII, Oxford University Press, New York, 2001, p. 370.

[124] The Royal Navy had around 161,000 personnel in September 1939, while the US Navy had 382,000 in December 1941. J. Ellis, WWII a Statistical Survey, Facts on File Inc, New York, 1993, Table 9, p. 228.

[125] Data analysed from Conway's All The World's Fighting Ships 1922-1946, Conway Maritime Press, London, 1980, pp. 222 – 254. Also includes an analysis of ships in the Navy prior to 1922 which served in WWII. Excludes a few small Dutch and French ships captured in 1940. Some of these ships were pressed into service but few of these had been recommissioned into the *Kriegsmarine* by 1941.

[126] Ibid. Conway lists the full complement of each ship or ship type.

[127] J. Costello, T. Hughes, The Battle of the Atlantic, Fontana/Collins, Glasgow, 1980, p. 328.

[128] Ibid.

was around 9,000. In total the U-boat arm had around 30,000 personnel in June 1941. This large number relative to the number at sea, reflected the rapid expansion of the U-boat arm at this time, with large numbers entering training and in support functions.

In terms of shore based commands the *Kriegsmarine's* most important responsibility, and its largest commitment of resources, was the operation and maintenance of the Reich's coastal artillery force. On 1st June 1941 there were 73 coastal artillery batteries outside of Norway and 98 coastal artillery batteries in Norway.[129] This force had approximately 1,160 100-280mm coastal artillery pieces.[130] To control these batteries the *Kriegsmarine* formed coastal artillery battalions, and by June 1941 this force contained around 51,000 men. This equates to around 300 men per battery or around 44 men per coastal gun. The total of 51,000 men included the supply, maintenance, fire control-spotting (observer) and radar functions (such as shore based *Seetakt* systems) of the coastal artillery battalions and batteries. Many of these batteries also had Luftwaffe personnel manning anti-aircraft defences around the batteries, and Army personnel in support functions and/or manning local defence points.

The only other significant shore based commands were a handful of naval infantry battalions, naval intelligence and a small *Marine Küstenpolizei*. The latter were a sort of naval *Feldgendarmerie* whose duties included guarding key coastal installations, shore patrols, and maintaining order and discipline in coastal towns where naval personnel were located. However, these organisations fielded no more than 15-20,000 men in total. Finally it is worth noting that unlike most other navies, including the Soviet Navy, the *Kriegsmarine* did not have its own air arm. This was mainly due to Goring insisting that he and the Luftwaffe control all combat air units no matter what their role. Even if Germany's one laid down aircraft carrier, the Graf Zeppelin, had entered service, her aircraft and aircrews would probably have belonged to the Luftwaffe.

Adding all the personnel in all the above *Kriegsmarine* branches, we still arrive at a maximum of approximately 231,000 men in June 1941. This is still 173,000 short of the 404,000 personnel commonly reported. It therefore seems very likely that close to 40% of the personnel in the latter figure were from various auxiliary organisations, which were either not strictly part of the Wehrmacht or were seconded from civilian organisations and listed as part of the *Kriegsmarine*.

One very likely source was the German merchant marine which was under the direct control of the *Kriegsmarine* until May 1942.[131] The sizeable German merchant marine started the war with 4.5 million gross tons of shipping, and the *Kriegsmarine* frequently used their ships (and crews) as blockade runners, supply ships and occasionally auxiliary cruisers. In addition, organisations like the *Organisation Todt* were building some impressive naval infrastructures for the *Kriegsmarine* in France and Germany at this time: most notably the massive U-boat pens in several key ports. Again, it is possible that a portion of these organisations' personnel are included in the 404,000 total (above), especially as they were working so closely with the *Kriegsmarine* and under their supervision.

***

[129] Refer Volume IIB 1. - 'The German Deployment Matrix'. Also, Kroener, B. R., et al, Table III.V.7.
[130] Refer Table 'Ger Total Deployed (D) 2'.
[131] In May 1942 *Gauleiter* Karl Kaufmann was named Reich Commissioner of Shipping.

3) The Proportion of Total Available Resources which were in a Deployed (D) State in the Reich from 22nd June to 4th July 1941

We are now in a position to establish the proportion of total personnel and equipment (resources) which were in a Deployed (D) state in the Reich from 22nd June to 4th July 1941. This is essentially a comparison of the relevant data between tables Ger Total Deployed (D) 2 and the data from the previous section, i.e. 'The Total Available Personnel and Equipment in the Reich on 1st June 1941'. However, before we do this we need to manipulate the data somewhat because the two data streams are not completely compatible: the total available personnel and equipment in the Reich on 1st June 1941 is determined from historical records, but the rows in table Ger Total Deployed (D) 2 are derived directly from the 'German Personnel and Equipment Resource Database'.[132]

For example, there is no historical record of the number of infantry squads in the German Army at a particular time because such a unit varied depending on definition, size, allocated equipment and parent organisation (e.g. infantry squads in infantry divisions, *Schützen* squads in panzer division, etc.). However there was such a thing as a typical or average infantry squad type at a particular time (in this case established using the 'German Personnel and Equipment Resource Database'), and there are historical records of the personnel and equipment available which made up the infantry squad types. Another example is machine guns (MGs) used as heavy machine guns (HMGs). The German Army was unique at this time in that it was equipped with the world's first general purpose machine gun (GPMG): the MG 34 could be used as a squad LMG with a bipod or a HMG mounted on a tripod. Thus the specific number of HMGs in the Reich was not recorded, but the total number of MGs of all types was recorded. Consequently we group all types of MG from the 'German Personnel and Equipment Resource Database' together to ascertain the percentage of all MGs that were allocated to combat units and Deployed (D) in June 1941. In this case it was 66% (including MGs mounted on AFVs and all old pre-MG 34 MGs).

Table % of Ger Resources Deployed (D) (pages 96-99) shows the results of comparing all the resources allocated to Deployed (D) combat units to the total available resources in the Reich. The comparison is made after grouping the total equipment allocated to combat units into appropriate equipment or weapon subtypes. The data for the first column 'Total resources allocated to Deployed (D) combat units' comes directly from table Ger Total Deployed (D) 2 (pages 82-85). The next column indicates the number and type of small arms most commonly used by each database unit in the first column. This information is identical to the small arms distribution used in 'The German Personnel and Equipment Resource Database' to calculate the combat parameters for each database unit.[133] The third column groups the resources into relevant subtypes ready for comparison purposes. It also indicates the total small arms used by all the database units in the first column, which are all the small arms used by all Deployed (D) combat units. The data for 'Total available resources in the Reich on 1st June 1941' is all derived from the previous section.

Finally we come to the last column in table % of Ger Resources Deployed (D) which shows the percentage of total available resources allocated to Deployed (D) combat units from 22nd June to 4th July 1941. A brief analysis of this data reveals some expected results, as well as some more surprising (and thus perhaps more illuminating) results.

- It is immediately apparent that in June 1941 the Wehrmacht had a large proportion of its personnel in non-combat units fulfilling a multitude of rear-area support functions or were part of the Replacement Army. We can see that only 58% of Wehrmacht and Waffen SS personnel were allocated to combat units in the German Army, Waffen SS, Luftwaffe ground forces and naval coastal artillery. If the 7,234,000 figure from *Das Heer* 1933-1945 is used, then the proportion allocated to combat units is still only 59%.[134] This means that approximately 3,069,000 personnel were: supporting **rear area functions** outside those performed by the existing combat units, earmarked as replacements, in basic or advanced training, manning or supporting the Luftwaffe's aircraft and the Kriegsmarine's ships, or were unassigned.

Examples of the extensive nature of these units are shown in the following tables relating to support units in the German Army.[135] Note, these units are **not** considered Deployed (D) combat units on 22nd June 1941.

---

[132] Refer to Volume I Part II and Volume IIA 2. – 'The German Personnel and Equipment Resource Database', for details on what the Resources Database is and how its values are calculated.

[133] Refer to Volume IIA 2. 2) – 'The German Personnel and Equipment Resource Database - German Squads Equipped with Light Infantry Weapons', for typical small arms distribution in German squads in 1941.

[134] B. Mueller-Hillebrand, *Das Heer* 1933-1945, Volume 2, Frankfurt, 1956, p. 102.

[135] Data compiled from: L.W.G. Niehorster, German WWII Organisational Series, Volume 3/III, Waffen SS Mechanised Formations and GHQ Service Units (22.06.1941), The Military Press, Milton Keynes, UK, 2008, pp. 36 - 110. L.W.G. Niehorster, German WWII Organisational Series, Volume 3/V, Military Government, Security, and Provost Marshal Forces; Prisoner-Of-War Administration (22.06.1941), The Military Press, Milton Keynes, UK, 2010, pp. 10 - 69.

Table GHQ Ser Units 1

Army GHQ Ancillary Service Units, which are not considered Deployed (D) Combat Units. Unit Description	No Existing 22/06/1941	Motor-ised	SM or HD
Special Motor Transport Regiment HQ (zbV)	6	M	
Special Motor Transport Battalion (zbV) (up to 2 500 tons load capacity)	15	M	
Motor Transport Battalion (up to 3 000 tons load capacity)	15	M	
Motorised Special Supply Battalion HQ (zbV)	24	M	
Semi-Motorised Supply Battalion	60		SM
Motorised Special Supply Column Battalion HQ (zbV)	9	M	
Motorised Supply Column Battalion	34	M	
Motorised Independent Supply Columns	170	M	
Horse-Drawn Supply Column Battalion (up to 480 ton capacity)	6		HD
Horse-Drawn Supply Columns (up to 60 ton capacity)	30		HD
Semi-Motorised Ammunition Service Company	23		SM
Motorised Fuel Service Company	8	M	
Armoured Vehicle Repair Battalion	4	M	
Motor Vehicle Repair Battalion HQ	15	M	
Motor Vehicle Repair Company	70	M	
Mobile Tyre Supply Detachment	18	M	
Mobile Tyre Repair Detachment	11	M	
Fuel Examination Office (Company echelon unit)	22	M	
Gasoline Leading Section	20	M	
Mobile Motor Vehicle Parts Supply Detachment	30	M	
Motor Vehicle Parts Supply Depot (Company echelon unit)	9	M	
Motor Vehicle Recovery Detachment	3	M	
Motor Towing Platoon for Railway Vehicles	11	M	
Motorised Meteorological Platoon	16	M	
Motorised Light Calibration Section	16	M	
Motorised Heavy Muzzle Velocity Calibration Platoon	12	M	
Motorised Map and Survey Battalion	13	M	
Motorised Commander of Technical Troops HQ	5	M	
Motorised Technical (TN) Battalion	11	M	
Motorised Technical Battalion	10	M	
Motorised Technical Battalion for Oil	2	M	
Motorised Propaganda Company	18	M	
Higher Ordnance HQ (Brigade echelon unit)	6	M	
Special Ordnance HQ (zbV) (Battalion echelon unit)	25	M	
Ordnance Battalion	26	M	
Ordnance Field Motor Column	26	M	
Motorised Field Workshop Company	22	M	
Food Registration HQ	14	M	
Commissary Office (Company echelon unit)	38	M	
Static Commissary Station (Company echelon unit)	63	M	
Motorised Butcher Battalion	7	M	
Motorised Butcher Company	59	M	
Baker Company	58		SM
Motorised GHQ and Army Clothing Depot (Company echelon unit)	22	M	
Semi-Motorised Supply and Clothing Company	9		SM
Infantry Equipment Park (Company echelon unit)	10	M	

SM - Semi-Motorised (predominantly motorised)

HD - Predominantly horse-drawn

© Nigel Askey, 2018

Table GHQ Ser Units 2			
Army GHQ Ancillary Service Units, which are not considered Deployed (D) Combat Units. Unit Description	No Existing 22/06/1941	Motor-ised	SM or HD
Artillery Equipment Park (Company echelon unit)	10	M	
Chemical Warfare Equipment Park (Company echelon unit)	10	M	
Signal and Armoured Signal Equipment Park (Company echelon unit)	14	M	
Engineer Equipment Park (Battalion echelon unit)	12	M	
Engineer Park Company	22		SM
Motorised Engineer Machine Platoon	9	M	
Army Transport and Equipment Park (Company echelon unit)	10	M	
GHQ Motor Vehicle Park and Motor Vehicle Park (Battalion echelon unit)	26	M	
Motor Vehicle Park Company	22	M	
Motorised Army Medical Battalion HQ (Regiment echelon unit)	16	M	
Motorised Casualty Transport Battalion	24	M	
Motorised Military Hospital Battalion	27	M	
Motorised Field Hospital (Battalion echelon unit)	89	M	
Field Hospital (Battalion echelon unit)	15		HD
Motorised Medical Company	24	M	
Motor Ambulance Platoon	92	M	
Motorised Personnel Decontamination Company	19	M	
Hospital Train (Battalion echelon unit)	58	M	
Medical Equipment Park (Battalion echelon unit)	17	M	
Veterinary Company	17		HD
Motorised Horse Transport Column	65	M	
Veterinary Hospital	40		SM
Mobile Animal Blood Examination Station (Company echelon unit)	24	M	
Veterinary Equipment Park (Battalion echelon unit)	17	M	
Remount Equipment Park (Regimental echelon unit)	27		HD
Motorised Field Post Office (Company echelon unit)	121	M	
Army Post Office (Battalion echelon unit)	17	M	
Field Post Forwarding Office (Battalion echelon unit)	16	M	
SM - Semi-Motorised (predominantly motorised)			
HD - Predominantly horse-drawn			© Nigel Askey, 2018

***

Table Rear Area Units 1			
Military Government, Security, Provost Marshal and POW Admin Units, which are not considered Deployed (D) Combat Units. **Unit Description**	**No Existing 22/06/1941**	Motor-ised	SM or HD
German Armed Forces Governor HQ (*Wehrmachtbefehlshaber*)*.^	2	M	
German Armed Forces Governor of the Netherlands HQ*	1	M	
Military Commander in the General Government HQ (in Poland)*	1	M	
Military Governor of Belgium and Northern France HQ (in Brussels)*	1	M	
Military Governor of France HQ (in Paris)*	1	M	
Chief of the Military Government District HQ (all in France)*, **	4	M	
Commandant of Greater Paris HQ*	1	M	
Military Government Area HQ (Administrative)*	12		SM
Commandant of the Army Rear Area HQ*,*^	12	M	
Military Government Commandants*,^^	530	M	
Secret Field Police Group^*	83	M	
Front Forward Collection Point (for troops: battalion echelon unit)	41		SM
Separate HQ, Militia Division (z.b.V.)***	18	M	
Separate HQ, Militia Regiment (z.b.V.)**^	43		SM
Military District Commander for Prisoners of War (POWs)	17	M	
Regional Commandant for Prisoners of War (POWs)	14		SM
Prisoners of War (POW) Forward Collection Camp (*Dulag*)*^^	63		SM
Prisoners of War (POW) Camp for Officers (*Oflag*)	60		SM
Prisoners of War (POW) Camp for Enlisted Men (*Stalag*)	116		HD
Prisoners of War (POW) Construction and Labour Battalion	42		HD
Prisoners of War (POW) Roofer Battalion	4		SM
Prisoners of War (POW) Glazier Battalion	4		SM

* Includes all supporting Command, Administration, Quartermaster, Adjutant, Judge Advocate and Signal Elements.

^ WB *Sudost*, and WB *Norwegen*.

** Subordinate to the Military Governor of France HQ (*Militarbefehlshaber In Frankreich*)

*^ 8 were supporting Armies on the East Front (inc OKH Res), 1 was with the DAK, and 3 were in the West.

^^ 125 were attached to the Security Divisions on the East Front on 22nd June 1941.

^* 27 were attached to the Security Divisions on the East Front, and an additional 11 were on the East Front.

*** All 18 were in the Replacement Army: refer 'Table Rep Army' for detail on deployments.

**^ 19 were in the Replacement Army: refer 'Table Rep Army' for detail on deployments. An additional 24 were in the Field Army, and, of these, 9 with the Security Divisions on the East Front.

*^^ 24 were assigned to the Security Divisions on the East Front (refer 'Table Sec Ass June 1941', Volume IIA).

SM - Semi-Motorised (predominantly motorised)

HD - Predominantly horse-drawn

© Nigel Askey, 2018

***

The overall results show that the Wehrmacht in 1941 was reasonably balanced in terms of resources allocation: it was neither too 'front heavy' or too 'back heavy' in its organisation. In this context, 'front heavy' means the bulk of resources were in combat units at potential fronts and relatively few were in non-combat support roles, while 'back heavy' means the opposite. There is little doubt that the Red Army in 1941 was excessively front heavy in June 1941, while it is arguable that the Western Allied armies from 1943 onwards were somewhat too back heavy.[136] By 1941 the German's 'balanced' strategy seemed to have permeated right through the Wehrmacht and into most army corps and divisional structures. These units also had strong up front fighting elements as well as relatively strong internal support structures.

[136] Refer Volume IIIB 1. 15) – 'The Actual Strength of all Soviet Land Combat Units in a Deployed (D) State on 22nd June 1941 - The Proportion of Total Available Resources which were in a Deployed (D) State in the USSR on 22nd June 1941' for more on the front-heavy nature of the Red Army in June 1941.

The 'front heavy' and 'back heavy' nature of modern-day armed forces has been the subject of much discourse in the post WWII years. Both configurations have advantages and disadvantages.

The advantages of a front heavy configuration include more combat units in the field at any given time, which in turn leads to numerical superiority on the battlefield at the tactical and operational level. In addition, massive front heavy armies are much easier and quicker to mobilise. This is because fewer highly trained rear-area specialists are required along with less specialised rear-area equipment. The disadvantages are that the combat units themselves tend to be far more 'fragile' and less durable during prolonged combat operations: they have a much greater tendency to 'wear out', lose cohesion or even disintegrate completely. As a result, excessively front heavy armed forces tend to suffer much heavier casualties as a proportion of the total force fielded (particularly at the operational level).

In general the advantages and disadvantages of back heavy armed forces are the opposite of the above. Interestingly, however, there comes a point where a progressively (and hence excessively) back heavy configuration also leads to more rapidly 'worn out' combat units and more overall casualties. This also occurs after prolonged combat operations because those 'few' combat units fielded soon become exhausted and battle fatigued, while receiving a continuous stream of inexperienced (i.e. have seen no combat) replacements. It is a case of pouring too much experience and knowledge into a steadily declining group of individuals. No combat unit can sustain prolonged combat indefinitely; but if too few divisions are fielded, then the relevant commands have no choice but to maintain those units it has at the front.[137]

Obviously the changing strategic situation during WWII forced the various combatants (especially the Germans and the Soviets) to mobilise their forces in different modes as WWII progressed. In 1941 - 42 the Soviets had little choice but to mobilise massive front heavy armies because anything else would have likely led to defeat on the Eastern Front. This should not, however, excuse them from having a balanced armed force in June 1941: they had had ample time to prepare for war prior to Operation Barbarossa. They chose instead to build a massive front heavy Red Army with far more divisions and weapons in the field than anyone else. The Germans on the other hand had a far more experienced and balanced armed force in June 1941. But as the war proceeded, the Germans were forced to field more and more combat units with progressively less training and equipment, and fewer and less effective rear-area support units. The Wehrmacht became progressively more front heavy. By 1945 most of the rear-area units had been sucked into the conflagration as 'combat units', while new units and the replacements consisted of little more than untrained teenagers and older civilians.

***

- From table <u>% of Ger Resources Deployed (D)</u> (pages 96-99), we can see that the Germans had 'used up' (or assigned) the bulk of their stockpiled small arms and MGs. Specifically they had already assigned 91%, 72%, 99.5% and 66% of their inventory of pistols-revolvers, rifles-carbines, SMGs and MGs, respectively, on 22nd June 1941. The % figures for rifles and MGs are considerably lower only because these weapon stockpiles contained a much higher proportion of old WWI era weapons. Many of these older weapons were still stockpiled or assigned to: training units in the Replacement Army, armed forces auxiliary (*Wehrmachtsgefolge*) forces, or other rear-area formations.

This is in contrast to the corresponding Soviet figures of 37%, 31%, 71% and 67-71% (LMGs and MMGs): only the Soviet LMG-MMG figure was worse.[138] This means that even if the Germans had wanted to mobilise large numbers of new lightly-armed infantry divisions in the second half of 1941 (which Hitler and the OKW didn't feel was necessary), they would have been hard pressed to arm the infantry squads in these units with anything except old rifles and MGs. In contrast, the Soviets used their abundance of available small arms to equip the huge mass of newly Mobilised and Deployed (MD) rifle units formed after June 1941 (albeit with mainly light and older weapons). These figures also explain why the majority of newly mobilised Soviet rifle squads had no LMG in 1941, as well as the overall shortage of MGs in new Red Army units.

---

[137] In the post WWII period, the relentless advance of technology has meant the more sophisticated armies of the world have become progressively more 'back heavy'. This is largely due to the time needed to train personnel on extremely sophisticated and complex weapons systems and their support organisations. However, it is very apparent, even today, that if most modern armies get involved in a prolonged and intense military campaign, then their ability to sustain combat operations rapidly diminishes and their casualty rate tends to increase. Most modern forces rely on (and are geared for) a rapid knockout punch to ensure a short campaign.

[138] Refer Volume IIIB 1. 15) – 'The Actual Strength of all Soviet Land Combat Units in a Deployed (D) State on 22nd June 1941 - The Proportion of Total Available Resources which were in a Deployed (D) State in the USSR on 22nd June 1941',

- In most other key areas the Germans had also already assigned the bulk of their stockpiled equipment. The most critical weapons in this category were: light and medium tanks (82-96%, except Pz Is), assault guns (94%), all types of armoured cars (87-100%), all types of self-propelled weapons, armoured personnel carriers (90%), 5cm anti-tank guns (89% - needed to deal with the latest generation of tanks), 7.5-15cm infantry guns (77-82%), 10.5cm light field howitzers (86%), 15cm heavy field howitzers (80%), heavy 10cm guns (67%) and heavy 21cm howitzers (77%). These weapons formed the backbone of German panzer divisions, infantry divisions and corps artillery units. The fact that most of this equipment was already utilised, coupled with the fact that some of it was difficult to mass produce (such as heavy artillery), had a marked effect on the number and type of new units the Germans could mobilise (as well as the type of Replacements (R) available) from June to December 1941.

- Somewhat surprisingly, one group of effective weapons that the Germans had not fully deployed in June 1941 was their range of medium to heavy bombardment rockets. These consisted of the 15cm *Nebelwerfer* 41, 32cm *Wurfkörper Flamm* (Flame Mortar) and 28cm *Wurfkörper Spreng* (HE Mortar). The fact that only around 38% of the existing stock was Deployed (D) was probably due to these weapons still being relatively new and untried, and the high equipment attrition rate in the existing rocket units. Despite the availability of these weapons, the Germans did not mobilise any new rocket launcher regiments (*Nebelwerfer*-regiments) from June to December 1941, although a large amount of replacement equipment and rocket 'ammunition' was issued to the exiting rocket troops in the field.

- Other areas where the Germans had yet to fully utilise their available stockpiles were 3.7cm anti-aircraft guns (51%) and 20mm 2cm *Flakvierling* 38 (18%). It is unclear why these excellent weapons appear to have been underutilised. It is known the Luftwaffe was hording the 3.7cm Flak guns for their rapidly expanding flak arm, while the 2cm *Flakvierling* was still a new weapon and the Kriegsmarine was largely earmarking early production weapons for their use.

- It is generally well known that the German Army's infantry divisions used a great deal of horse-drawn transport during WWII. This is verified by the fact that approximately two thirds of the available horses were assigned to Deployed (D) units.

- Table % of Ger Resources Deployed (D) shows that the majority of available trucks (56%) were assigned to either Deployed (D) combat units or rear-area support units (SDE). On face value this doesn't appear too bad. However, the reader should note that the remaining trucks had to support the Reich's economic and transport needs, and the best and heaviest vehicles (including the large majority of German produced vehicles) had already been assigned to the Wehrmacht. This shortage of suitable motor vehicles was largely due to the army's ever hungry mechanised forces, and the fact that almost all the branches of the armed forces and security services had been rapidly expanding since 1939.

In addition, we can also see that around 67% of the motorcycles produced since 1938, and 84-99% of the available light-medium halftracks, were already assigned. This means that the Germans were going to struggle to find suitable motorised vehicles to equip any newly mobilised motorised units during 1941. They would have to rely on new production to meet any additional motorisation needs during Operation Barbarossa, or commandeer even more vehicles from the civilian economy and live with the associated economic penalty.[139]

Finally, it is worth noting that only around 9% of the available 'light-transports' in the Reich were assigned to Deployed (D) combat units. Unfortunately (for the Germans) light-transports included just about every type of commercial car in the Reich, including large numbers of old and foreign vehicles. Most of these vehicles were unsuitable and/or too unreliable for military use, were incapable of carrying significant quantities of supplies, and would have exacerbated an already difficult spare parts and maintenance (logistical) situation. Furthermore, light-transports included all types of commercial vans, etc, which were already needed for the Reich's economy. In many cases these vehicles were already filling the transport 'gaps' left in the economy by the absence of sufficient numbers of trucks.

***

[139] It should be noted here however, that the overall motorisation situation in the German Army from June to December 1941 was far better than the equivalent situation in the Red Army. Refer Volume IIIB 4. – 'The Supply Distribution Efficiency (SDE) for the Soviet Armed Forces from 22nd June to 31st December 1941' and Volume IIB 6. – 'The Supply Distribution Efficiency (SDE) for the Wehrmacht on the East Front from 22nd June to 31st December 1941'.

4. German Mobilisation after 22nd June 1941: the Actual Strength of German Land Combat Units Mobilised from 22nd June to 31st December 1941

In Volume IIB 3. we focused on the German ground forces that existed and were Deployed (D) from 22nd June to 4th July 1941, the first two weeks of Operation Barbarossa. In this chapter we will focus on the new German ground forces that were mobilised between 22nd June and 31st December 1941. It would be reasonable to say that in general the German's mobilisation effort during the second half of 1941 was almost the exact opposite of the Soviet's mobilisation effort. While the Soviets embarked on what became the largest and fastest war mobilisation effort ever carried out by a single country, the Germans appeared confident (and in the end over-confident) that their existing forces in the East would crush the USSR by year's end.[140] Consequently, the German forces Mobilised and Deployed (MD - see below for definitions) on the East Front from June to December 1941 bordered on non-existent compared to the Red Army's MD forces.

1) Definition of Deployed (D), Mobilised and Deployed (MD), and Mobilised and Not Deployed (MND) in the German FILARM Model

In this study of German ground force mobilisation after 22nd June 1941 the following definitions of Deployed (D), Mobilised and Deployed (MD), and Mobilised and Not Deployed (MND) combat units are used in the German FILARM model.

- **Deployed, (D)**: the unit is deployed with a TOE anywhere in the armed forces on the 1st day of the campaign, in this case 22nd June 1941. The unit may be deployed at a fraction of its full TOE strength and it may be allocated to any military district or army. The details and assignments of all units in a Deployed (D) status are detailed in the German Deployment Matrix.

- **Mobilised and Deployed, (MD)**: the unit is mobilised with a TOE after the first day of the campaign, in this case 22nd June 1941, and allocated (or assigned) to an active front or army HQ. For Germany and Finland, an 'active army HQ' is **any** operational army HQ in the armed forces. Note, Germany had multiple theatres of war (or active fronts) in 1941, all with active army HQs. Even occupying forces (such as those in France, Norway and the Balkans) were still in active war fronts. These units were organised and operated on a war footing, and in most cases were carrying out military and security operations. Hence newly mobilised Wehrmacht units which were allocated to HQs in these theatres are considered to have been Mobilised and Deployed (MD).

- **Mobilised and Not Deployed, (MND)**: the unit is mobilised with a TOE after the first day of the campaign, in this case 22nd June 1941, and not allocated (or assigned) to an active front or army HQ. An active front or army HQ is as defined for the MD state above.

In addition a unit which is created by a simple name change from an old unit without the addition of any new subunits from reserves (that is any newly mobilised regiments or battalions) is considered a Mobilised and Not Deployed (MND) unit. This is because the unit in question is already deployed on the battlefield and simply changes its name. In so doing the 'old' unit ceases to exist. In effect the new unit becomes deployed, but the old unit it is replacing simultaneously becomes 'un-deployed'. If there is no additional personnel and equipment added from reserves, **then the net effect is that the deployment of new reserves is zero.**

For example, on 1st August 1941, the already Deployed (D) 5th Light Division (already with the 5th Panzer Regiment) was officially designated the 21st Panzer Division. In order to enable this 'field conversion', the 15th Panzer Division was ordered to hand over its 104th Motorised Infantry (*Schützen*) Regiment and 15th Motorcycle Infantry Battalion to the 21st Panzer Division.[141] In return, the 21st Panzer Division handed over the Staff 200th Infantry Regiment and the 2nd Machine Gun Battalion to the 15th Panzer Division. Neither panzer division received a second *Schützen* regiment, so during 1941 they were both weaker than contemporary panzer divisions in terms of infantry support. The conversion of the 5th Light Division to the 21st Panzer Division amounted to a reshuffle of the forces already within the *Afrika-Korps*: the only new unit used in the 'creation' of the 21st Panzer Division was the 200th Armoured Signal Battalion which arrived in early August 1941. Therefore in the German FILARM model the 21st Panzer Division is an MND unit, and only the 200th Armoured Signal Battalion is a true MD unit.

---

[140] Refer Volume IIIB 2. – 'Soviet Mobilisation After 22nd June 1941: the Actual Strength of all Soviet Land Combat Units Mobilised from 22nd June to 31st December 1941'.
[141] In 1942 the 15th Motorcycle Infantry Battalion became the III./104th *Panzergrenadier* Regiment.

It should be carefully noted here that all D, MD and MND combat units may still receive newly mobilised personnel and equipment (i.e. reserve forces) via the Replacement (R) process. In the FILARM model the **Replacement (R) process is a separate process to creating completely new combat units**.[142] In this way combat units which are considered 'newly mobilised' but were in fact merely old units with a simple name change, can still build up their strength to their TOE given enough time and priority treatment.

***

2) German Land Combat Units Mobilised from 22nd June to 31st December 1941

The German land combat units mobilised from 22nd June to 31st December 1941 are shown in table Ger MD & MND Units (pages 132 - 133). Also shown for each unit is: the approximate date that mobilisation can be considered to have started, whether or not it was Deployed (i.e. MD or MND), if it was sent to the East Front, and a brief historical description. The TOE and peak strength (during 1941) of all the combat units shown in this table are covered in the relevant sections of Volume IIA 3. [143]

Excluded from the table are the following panzer forces.

- The panzer forces used in refurbishing the Deployed (D) 3rd Panzer Regiment/2nd Panzer Division and 31st Panzer Regiment/5th Panzer Division from June to August-September 1941. Both these Deployed (D) divisions which transferred to the East Front in September 1941.

- The assault guns needed to bring the Deployed (D) *Sturmgeschütze* Battalions 177, 189, 202, 209, 244 and 245 to full strength. All these units were sent to the East Front from July 1941 to January 1942. The *Sturmgeschütze* Battalion 249 remained forming in the West during 1941.

- The Pz.Kpfw 35R tanks added to the Deployed (D) Panzer-*Kompanie Paris* in July 1941.

The reader should refer to the next section (The German Tank MD and MND Matrix) for details of the German AFVs allocated to the above units from 22nd June to 31st December 1941. These units are not included in table Ger MD & MND Units because they were all already Deployed (D) units on 22nd June 1941; albeit it not at full strength.

***

---

[142] Refer Volume I Part I 3. 3) c. i. - 'The Structure of the Fully Integrated Land and Air Resource Model (FILARM) - Resource Allocation States inside the FILARM Model - Reserves and Replacements (R) - Replacements (R)', and Volume I Part I 3. 4) – 'Combat Unit Processes inside the FILARM Model' for details of how this process simulates replacements in the FILARM model.

[143] Refer Volume IIA 3.- 'The Tables of Organisation and Equipment (TOE) for German Land Combat Units from 22nd June to 31st December 1941, and The Unit's Actual Organisation and Equipment in 1941'.

Table Ger MD & MND Units

German Land Combat Units Mobilised from 22nd June to 31st December 1941

Unit Description	Date Mobilisation Started	MND	MD	East Front	Description
Infantry Forces					
250th Infantry Division (Spanish Blue Division)	20th July 1941		Yes	Yes	Sent to the East Front in September, Army Group North.
328th Infantry Division	19th December 1941	Yes			17th wave infantry division, still incompletely formed by the end of 1941.
329th Infantry Division	17th December 1941	Yes			17th wave infantry division, still incompletely formed by the end of 1941.
330th Infantry Division	19th December 1941	Yes			17th wave infantry division, still incompletely formed by the end of 1941.
331st Infantry Division	15th December 1941	Yes			17th wave infantry division, still incompletely formed by the end of 1941.
416th Infantry Division	20th December 1941	Yes			Formed for occupation duties in Denmark.
369th Reinforced (Croat) Infantry Regiment	July 1941		Yes	Yes	Sent to the East Front in August, AGS, attached to 100th Light Division.
638th Separate (French) Infantry Regiment	27th August 1941		Yes	Yes	Sent to the East Front in October, AGC, attached to 7th Infantry Division.
373rd 'Wallonian' Infantry Battalion	8th August 1941		Yes	Yes	Sent to the East Front in October, AGS, attached to 101st Light Division.
Panzer Forces*					
21st Panzer Division	1st August 1941	Yes			Organised almost entirely from the existing 5th Light and 15th Panzer Divisions.
22nd Panzer Division	25th September 1941	Yes			Remained forming in Germany, still incompletely formed by the end of 1941.
23rd Panzer Division	21st September 1941	Yes			Remained forming in Germany, still incompletely formed by the end of 1941.
24th Panzer Division	28th November 1941	Yes			Formed from the 1st Cavalry Division. Still very incomplete by the end of 1941.
203rd Panzer Regiment	5th July 1941		Yes	Yes	Sent to the East Front in December 1941 as a separate Heerestruppen unit.
212th Panzer Battalion	10th July 1941		Yes		Formed on Crete for occupation duties on Crete and in the Balkans.
213th Panzer Battalion	17th November 41		Yes		Formed for occupation duties on Jersey and Guernsey.
78th Armoured Signal Battalion	June 1941		Yes		Used as a replacement unit for the 15th Panzer Division in North Africa.
200th Armoured Signal Battalion	July 1941		Yes		Used in converting the 5th Light Division to 21st Panzer Division in North Africa.
Panzer Kompanie FG z.b.V.12	22nd June 1941		Yes		Formed for occupation duties in France (equipped with French tanks).
5th Armoured Rec Battalion AC Company	1st July 1941.		Yes	Yes	Used as a Replacement (R) unit in the 2nd Panzer Division on the East Front.
Waffen SS Forces					
SS Freiwilligen Legion Niederlande	12th July 1941	Yes			Transferred to the East Front in January 1942.
SS Freiwilligen Legion Flandern	12th July 1941		Yes	Yes	Sent to the East Front in November, OKH, assigned to the 2nd SS RFB.
Finnisches Freiwilligen Bataillon der Waffen SS	May 1941	Yes			Transferred to the East Front in early January 1942.
SS Freiwilligen Verband Danemark	8th July 1941	Yes			Transferred to the East Front in May 1942.
SS Freiwilligen Legion Norwegen	29th June 1941	Yes			Transferred to the East Front in January-February 1942.

Table Ger MD & MND Units (cont.)

German Land Combat Units Mobilised from 22nd June to 31st December 1941

Unit Description	Date Mobilisation Started	MND	MD	East Front	Description
Misc GHQ, Security and Corps Forces					
Panzer Group Africa HQ	1st September 1941		Yes		Panzergruppe Afrika did not get a mot panzer group signal regiment in 1941.
27 Landesschutzen Security Battalions	July 1941		Yes	Yes	Used as security units on the East Front during 1941.
2 Ukrainian Nationalist Militia Battalions	July 1941		Yes	Yes	Used as security units on the East Front during 1941.
5 Estonian Nationalist Militia (ERNA) Battalions	August 1941		Yes	Yes	Used as security units on the East Front during 1941.
Artillery Battalion II./Lehr-Rgt. 2	July-August 1941		Yes	Yes	Sent to the East Front in September. Assigned to 11th Army, AGS.
Artillery Battery 999	September 1941		Yes	Yes	Assigned to Norway Mountain Corps, Norway-Finland, in September 1941.
7 Leichtgeschutz Artillery Batteries	October 1941	Yes			Batteries 423, 424, 425, 426, 429, 433 and 443. Remained in the West.
Railroad Artillery Battery 693	Aug-Sept 1941		Yes	Yes	Sent to the East Front in September. Assigned to Army Group North.
Railroad Artillery Battery 459	November 1941		Yes	Yes	Sent to the East Front in December. Went to the Crimea in 1941/42.
Army Light Flak Battalion 616	June-July 1941		Yes	Yes	Sent to the East Front in August.
Motorised Special Engineer Regiment HQ 623	November 1941		Yes	Yes	Sent to the East Front in November. Assigned to 9th Army, AGC.
Motorised Special Engineer Regiment HQ 605	December 1941		Yes	Yes	Sent to the East Front in December. Assigned to 4th Panzer Group, AGC.
78 Motorised Snow Clearing Sections	October 1941		Yes	Yes	Usually attached to road construction companies on the East Front.
15./800zbV (Brandenburgers Company)	July-August 1941		Yes	Yes	Assigned to Norway Mountain Corps, North-Finland, in December 1941.
Luftwaffe Flak Units					
1st - 11th Flak Division HQs	1st September 1941		Yes		Remained in the west defending Germany and occupied Europe.
1 Luftwaffe Flak Regiment HQ	June-July 1941		Yes		Remained in the west defending Germany and occupied Europe.
5 Luftwaffe Flak Regiment HQs	June 1941		Yes	Yes	Transferred to the East Front from July to December 1941.
16 Luftwaffe Mixed Flak Battalions (full mobility)	June 1941		Yes	Yes	Transferred to the East Front from July to December 1941.
13 Luftwaffe Mixed Flak Battalions (red mobility)	June-July 1941		Yes		Remained in the west defending Germany and occupied Europe.
5 Luftwaffe Light Flak Battalions (type 1)	June 1941		Yes	Yes	Transferred to the East Front from July to December 1941.
49 Barrier Fire Batteries	September 1941		Yes		Remained in the west defending Germany and occupied Europe.

* Excludes the panzer forces used in refurbishing the Deployed (D) 3rd Panzer Regiment/2nd Panzer Division and 31st Panzer Regiment/5th Panzer Division from June to August-September 1941. Both these Deployed (D) divisions transferred to the East Front in September 1941. Also excludes the assault guns needed to bring the Deployed (D) Sturmgeschutze Battalions 177, 189, 202, 209, 244 and 245 to full strength. All were sent East from July 1941 to January 1942 (the Sturmgeschutze Battalion 249 remained forming in the west during 1941). Also excludes PzKpfw 35R tanks added to the Panzer-Kompanie Paris in July 1941. Refer table 'Ger Tank MD & MND Matrix' for details of German tank (and selected AFV) allocation to Wehrmacht MD and MND units from 22nd June to 31st December 1941.

© Nigel Askey, 2018

At this point it is instructive to briefly compare the German and Soviet forces Mobilised and Deployed (MD) during the second half of 1941. From the Soviet FILARM model we know that the **Soviets Mobilised and Deployed (MD), against the Axis forces in the Western USSR**, the following principal combat units from 23rd June to 31st December 1941.[144]

11 new Front HQs	41 new Army HQs	182 rifle divisions
43 militia rifle divisions	8 tank divisions	3 mechanised divisions
62 tank brigades	55 rifle brigades	50 cavalry divisions
1 mountain cavalry division	1 mountain rifle division	31 airborne brigades
11 naval infantry brigades	21 naval rifle brigades	3 NKVD rifle divisions
3 NKVD motorised rifle divisions	20 NKVD border regiments	57 anti-aircraft battalions
2 NKVD security (rifle) brigades	73 anti-tank regiments	38 RVGK artillery regiments
11 Mortar Battalions	1 Mortar Brigade	40 Armoured Trains

34 RVGK rocket artillery regiments and battalions   38 engineer and construction battalions

approximately 600 militia fighter battalions.

In short, this massive force represents the largest and fastest war mobilisation effort ever carried out by a single country.

***

From table <u>Ger MD & MND Units</u> we can see that the **Germans Mobilised and Deployed (MD), against the Soviet forces on the East Front**, the following principal combat units from 23rd June to 31st December 1941.

1 infantry division	2 infantry regiments	2 infantry battalions (inc.1 Waffen SS battalion)
1 panzer regiment	1 artillery battalion	1 reconnaissance armoured car company
3 artillery batteries	1 army flak battalion	21 Luftwaffe flak battalions
27 *Landesschützen* (militia) security battalions		7 nationalist militia battalions

***

Most telling of all is that the Germans Mobilised and Deployed (MD) a paltry single infantry division, and even this used Spanish volunteers! In fact all the separate infantry regiments and battalions Mobilised and Deployed were built around foreign (non-Germanic) volunteers who were joining the 'crusade' in the East. The four 17th wave infantry divisions were belatedly mobilised after the Soviet winter counter offensive had commenced, and were not close to being combat ready in 1941. Similarly, the 22nd and 23rd Panzer Divisions only started mobilising in late September 1941. Even though very few of the new Soviet 'divisions' and 'brigades' were in actuality divisional or brigade sized units, and even though many of them were barely trained, the German's mobilisation effort hardly compares to the phenomenal 243 rifle, tank and mechanised divisions mobilised against the Axis forces by the Red Army and NKVD during 1941.[145]

Note, the above discussion only covers forces mobilised by the combatants after hostilities had commenced. They **do not** include additional Deployed (D) Soviet forces transferred from the Central and the Eastern USSR to the Western USSR, or the Deployed (D) German forces transferred from the Western Fronts to the East Front, during the second half of 1941. These forces are covered separately in other sections.[146]

***

---

[144] Refer Volume IIIB 2. – 'Soviet Mobilisation After 22nd June 1941: the Actual Strength of all Soviet Land Combat Units Mobilised from 22nd June to 31st December 1941'. The Soviets also **Mobilised and Not Deployed (MND)** the following (principal) combat units from 23rd June to 31st December 1941: 4 Front HQs, 4 Army HQs, 96 rifle divisions, 3 militia rifle divisions, 3 tank divisions, 26 tank brigades, 79 rifle brigades, 35 cavalry divisions, 1 mountain cavalry division, 5 naval infantry brigades, 7 naval rifle brigades, 1 NKVD motorised rifle division, 17 NKVD border regiments, and 1 NKVD security (rifle) brigade.

[145] The newly mobilised Soviet cavalry and mountain cavalry 'divisions' are excluded from this total because they were, in reality, regimental sized units.

[146] Refer to Volume IIIA 5. 'The Transfer Schedule of Soviet Land Combat Units, which were in a Deployed (D) State, to the Western Fronts from 23rd June to 31st December 1941', and Volume IIB 2. 'German Land Combat Unit Reinforcements on the East Front from 5th July to 31st December 1941'.

a. The German Tank MD and MND Matrix

In this section we are concerned with building a detailed picture of the tanks, assault guns and armoured self-propelled guns (all called AFVs here), allocated to newly mobilised combat units from 22nd June to 31st December 1941. The 'Tank MD and MND Matrix' has to take account of the long time frame involved, i.e. it is not a 'static' picture of the AFVs present at a fixed point in time. During the time period concerned, several panzer units changed (altered their TOE) or were disbanded before ever seeing combat. The resultant AFVs then became available for use by newly mobilising panzer units or to be used as replacements. This means some AFVs were allocated to more than one combat unit in the Wehrmacht during 1941. The Tank MD and MND Matrix therefore has to ensure that double counting of the available AFVs doesn't occur, and that released/refurbished 'old' AFVs are included. For these reasons the German Tank MD and MND Matrix is divided into two parts.

The first part shows the numbers and types of AFVs allocated to all the major panzer units mobilised from 22nd June to the 31st December 1941. All MD and MND panzer units are included regardless of where they were deployed because we want to ensure all available German AFVs in the Reich in the second half of 1941 are included. The results of this analysis are shown in table Ger Tank MD & MND Matrix. All the panzer units detailed in table Ger MD & MND Units, which received new AFVs, are included. In addition, the AFVs allocated to panzer units Deployed (D) on 22nd June 1941 but not yet fully formed, and the AFVs allocated to refurbished/reorganised Deployed (D) panzer units, are also included. The former category includes the *Sturmgeschütze* Battalions 177, 189, 202, 209, 244 and 245, while the latter category includes the 3rd Panzer Regiment/2nd Panzer Division and 31st Panzer Regiment/5th Panzer Division.

The second part of the German Tank MD and MND Matrix is an analysis of AFVs that became available to the German Army's new mobilising units and the source of these vehicles. The results of this analysis are shown in table Ger Tanks Available Jun Dec 41, which shows that the available German AFVs came from one of the three following sources.

- **AFVs existing on 22nd June 1941 that were not allocated to any Deployed (D) unit (hence were not Deployed (D) themselves), and which became serviceable and available before 31st December 1941**. This data is compiled from table % of Ger Resources Deployed (D) (pages 96-99).[147] It includes all categories of serviceable AFVs in depots, in rear area training schools, in transit and in test facilities.

- **AFVs that became available after the disbandment or reorganisation of units which were Deployed (D) on 22nd June 1941**. This mainly involved older German tanks and captured French tanks, which became available when these units upgraded to newer model tanks.

- **Newly manufactured AFVs which were ready for issue from 22nd June to 31st December 1941**. This data is taken from Appendix A, Table IV (for panzers and assault guns) and Volume IIB 4. 4) b. (for other AFV types).

***

One of the most significant operational and strategic failures of the German High Command during 1941 was their failure to send adequate AFV Replacements (R) to their panzer divisions in the East. This was especially true in the critical period August to November1941: the period when Operation Barbarossa came closest to strategic success. The German high command's stockpiling of its available AFVs in Germany, especially tanks and assault guns, is even more puzzling when one examines the operational tank strengths of the panzer divisions on the East Front from June 1941 onwards. By October 1941 most of the panzer divisions and assault gun battalions on the East Front (along with their associated corps HQs) were 'crying out' for significant AFV replacements in order to maintain the operational tempo of the summer months.

Traditionally, the main reason for this failure has been attributed (by historians) to the relatively low rate of German tank production from 1939 to 1942. This argument is then usually strengthened by direct statistical comparisons of German and Soviet tank production from 1941 to 1945. However, the German Tank MD and MND Matrix reveals one very surprising and important result: **specifically that the figures for available AFVs do not correlate at all with the actual German AFV replacements sent East in support of Operation Barbarossa.** In other words, the reasons why the panzer divisions did not receive adequate AFV replacements had more to do with political policy than the actual availability of new tanks and assault guns. Using some of the results of the German Tank MD and MND Matrix, we will examine this in more detail in Volume IIB 4. 7) – 'The Resource Replacements (R) Available to the German Army, Waffen SS, Luftwaffe Ground Forces and Naval Coastal Artillery, from 22nd June to 31st December 1941'.

---

[147] The values in the 4th column minus the values in the 3rd column of table % of Ger Resources Deployed (D).

Table Ger Tank MD & MND Matrix

The German Tank MD & MND Matrix

Tank (and selected AFV) allocation to Wehrmacht MD and MND units from 22nd June to 31st December 1941

Panzer Unit	Pz Reg 201*	Pz Reg 203^	Pz Reg 204**	Pz Reg 3*^	Pz Reg 31^^	Pz Bat 212*~	Pz Bat 213^*	PzCo FG zbV.12-~	Pz Co 'Paris'.~*	StuG Bats.***	78th Sig Bat**^	200th Sig Bat**^	Total Tanks
Pz Kpfw I	1		1										2
Kleine Pz Bef Wg I													
Pz Kpfw II	18	45	24	63	55	5							210
Pz Kpfw III (37mm)						17							17
Pz Kpfw III (50mm)	56	71	105	105									337
Pz Bef Wg III	6		6	6							2	2	22
Pz Kpfw IV	16	20	10	20	20								86
Pz Kpfw 38(t)			39										39
Pz Kpfw 35(t)													
StuG III Assault Gun										84			84
15cm sIG33 SP Guns													
Pz Jager I (47mm)													
47mm, Pz Kpfw 35R(f)								20	27				47
SP 88 mm AAG													
105mm K18 Pz Sfl IVa													
Pz Kpfw II (F)								26					26
Pz Kpfw B2								10					10
Pz Kpfw B2 (F)							10	7					17
Pz Kpfw 35-S								24					24
Pz Kpfw 38H													
Pz Kpfw I (Pio)	10		10										20
													941

* Assigned to the 100th Panzer Brigade in June 1941. Converted to German Panzers in December 1941, and assigned to the newly forming 23rd Panzer Division. Not ready to transfer East until March 1942. Also includes 1x Pz Mk 1, 1x Pz Mk II and 10x Pz I (Pio) in the 23rd Panzer Division's 51st Pionier Battalion.

^ Assigned to the 101st Panzer Brigade in June 1941. Converted to German Panzers. It was sent East in December 1941 as a separate unit.

** Assigned to the 101st Panzer Brigade in June 1941. Converted to German-Czech Panzers and was assigned to the newly forming 22nd Panzer Division. Not ready to transfer East until February 1942. Also includes 1x Pz Mk 1, 1x Pz Mk II and 10x Pz I (Pio) in the 22nd Panzer Division's 50th Pionier Battalion.

*^ Tanks added to the refurbished **Deployed (D)** 3rd Panzer Regiment, which was part of the 2nd Panzer Division sent East in September 1941.

^^ Tanks added to the refurbished **Deployed (D)** 31st Panzer Regiment, which was part of the 5th Panzer Division sent East in September 1941.

^* Formed 17th November 1941; occupation duties on Jersey and Guernsey. 10 tanks were *Flammwagen auf Panzerkampfwagen B-2(f)* (French Char B-1 bis medium tanks modified with German flamethrower armament).

*~ Formed 10th July 1941 on Crete; occupation duties Crete/Balkans.

~~ Formed 22nd June 41; occupation duties France (formed from several 'independent' Panzer Platoons equipped with French tanks)

~* Ad hoc **Deployed (D)** unit, but incomplete on 22nd June 1941. Officially formed 8th July 41 when it received 27 Panzerkampfwagen 35R 731(f) (captured French Renault 35R light tanks). Used for occupation duties around Paris.

*** Assault guns needed to bring the **Deployed (D)** Sturmgeschutze Battalions 177, 189, 202, 209, 244 and 245 to full strength. All sent East from July 1941 to January 1942.

**^ 78th and 200th Armoured Signal Battalions. Formed June-July 1941 and sent to North Africa (DAK). Used in the 15th Panzer Division to replace a lost unit, and the 5th Light Division when converted to the 21st Panzer Division.

© Nigel Askey, 2018

Table Ger Tanks Available Jun-Dec 41

The German Tank MD & MND Matrix

German tanks (and selected AFVs) available to Wehrmacht MD and MND units, and available as replacements from 22nd June to 31st December 1941

Panzer Unit	Existing tanks not Deployed (D) on 22nd June 1941, and which were available (& serviceable) from 22nd June to 31st December 1941.	Tanks available after disbanding and reorganisation of units which were Deployed (D) on 22nd June 1941.						New tanks manufactured (incl converted French tanks) and ready for issue, from 22nd June to 31st December 1941.	Total tanks available, 22nd June to 31st Dec 1941	German tanks available to the Wehrmacht as Replacements (R) from 22nd June to the 31st December 1941 (tanks not used in MD or MND combat units)
		Pz Reg 201:	Pz Reg 203^	Pz Reg 204**	Pz Reg 3*^	Pz Reg 31^^	Pz Co 5./31 ^*			
Pz Kpfw I	422				8				430	408
Kleine Pz Bef Wg I	30								30	30
Pz Kpfw II	97		22	35	5			181	340	130
Pz Kpfw III (37mm)	45		14		17				76	59
Pz kpfw III (50mm)	193		21		17			1201	1432	1095
Pz Bef Wg III	23		6		5			33	67	45
Pz Kpfw IV	22		10		6			330	368	282
Pz Kpfw 38(t)	69							401	470	431
Pz Kpfw 35(t)	10								10	10
StuG III Assault Gun	21							348	369	285
15cm sIG33 SP Guns										
Pz Jager I (47mm)	4								4	4
47mm, Pz Kpfw 35R(f)	0							93	93	93
Pz Kpfw 35R	14							at least 80 refurb.	94	47
SP 88 mm AAG	14								14	14
105mm K18 Pz Sfl IVa										
Pz Kpfw II (F)	6							36	42	42
Pz Kpfw B2	unknown							at least 26 refurb.	26	
Pz Kpfw B2 (F)								10	10	
Pz Kpfw 35-S	unknown	43		5		5		at least 53 refurb.	53	36
Pz Kpfw 38H	unknown	95		12		12		at least 119 refurb.	119	95

* French tanks left over when the Deployed (D) 201st Panzer Regiment (assigned to the 100th Panzer Brigade in June 1941) converted to German Panzers in December 1941. It was assigned to the new 23rd Panzer Division.

^ French tanks left over when the Deployed (D) 203rd Panzer Regiment (assigned to the 101st Panzer Brigade in June 1941) converted to German Panzers. It was assigned sent East in December 1941 as a separate unit.

** French tanks left over when the Deployed (D) 204th Pz Regiment (assigned to the 101st Panzer Brigade in June 1941) converted to German-Czech Panzers. It was assigned to the new 22nd Panzer Division.

*^ Tanks left over when the Deployed (D) 3rd Panzer Regiment/2nd Panzer Division was refurbished/reorganised. 3rd Panzer Regiment was sent East with the 2nd Panzer Division in September 1941.

^^ Tanks left over when the Deployed (D) 31st Panzer Regiment/5th Panzer Division was refurbished/reorganised. 31st Panzer Regiment was sent East with the 5th Panzer Division in September 1941.

^* Tanks left over when the Deployed (D) 5th Company/3rd Pz Regiment (on Crete and redesignated 1.Kompanie/Panzer-Abteilung Kreta) became part of the new 212th Pz Battali. ©Nigel Askey, 2018

3) The Total Resources Allocated to Newly Mobilised Combat Units from 22nd June to 31st December 1941

In this chapter we have, so far, established the German land combat units mobilised from 22nd June to 31st December 1941. In Volume IIA 3. we established the actual strength of each German land combat unit mobilised from 22nd June to 31st December 1941.[148] We are therefore now in a position to ascertain the total resources allocated to all Mobilised and Deployed (MD) units, and Mobilised and Not Deployed (MND) units, from 22nd June to 31st December 1941.

The results of this process are shown in the first column of table Ger Resources in MD & MND Units in 1941 (pages 140-143). Included in this column is the personnel and resources used in all the German land combat units mobilised from 22nd June to 31st December 1941, i.e. in all the combat units shown in table Ger MD & MND Units (pages 132-133).[149]

As before, we need to manipulate the data presented in terms of the Barbarossa simulation's resource database to be comparable to data obtained from historical records of personnel and equipment.[150] This is accomplished in the second and third columns of table Ger Resources in MD & MND Units in 1941. The 'small arms distribution' column indicates the number and type of small arms used by each database unit in the first column. This information is identical to the small arms distribution used in the 'German Personnel and Equipment Resource Database' to calculate the combat parameters for each database unit.[151]

The third column groups the resources into relevant subtypes ready for comparison purposes. It also indicates the total small arms used by all the database units in the first column, i.e. all the small arms used by all MD and MND combat units from 22nd June to 31st December 1941.

***

---

[148] This includes Mobilised and Deployed (MD), and Mobilised and Not Deployed (MND) units. Refer Volume IIA 3. - 'The Table of Organisation and Equipment (TOE) for the German Land Combat Units from 22nd June 1941 to 31st December 1941, and the Unit's Actual Organisation and Equipment in 1941'. All the Wehrmacht and Waffen SS units fielded in 1941 are included in this chapter, including all the units mobilised after 22nd June 1941.

[149] Additional notes for this table column. Total equipment allocated to MD and MND combat units excludes 43 Panhard 178 armoured cars which ran on railway lines. These vehicles were issued as rail-protection vehicles.

[150] This was done in Volume IIB 3. 3) - 'The Proportion of Total Available Resources which were in a Deployed (D) State in the Reich from 22nd June to 4th July 1941' table % of Ger Resources Deployed (D).

[151] Refer Volume IIA 2. 2) – 'The German Personnel and Equipment Resource Database - German Squads Equipped with Light Infantry Weapons', for details on typical small arms distribution in German squads in 1941.

a. Rear Area Transport Available for Supply Distribution from 22nd June to 31st December 1941

As mentioned previously, one of the main objectives of the Fully Integrated Land and Air Resource Model (FILARM) is to enable an accurate calculation of the maximum efficiency of any supporting infrastructure to the armed forces in the field. This is accomplished by calculating the relative Supply Distribution Efficiency (SDE).[152] Exactly as for the Deployed (D) units on 22nd June 1941, we need to calculate the average SDE for MD and MND units in the second half of 1941.

As part of calculating the German's SDE in 1941, we need to know the amount of motorised transport that became available in the second half of 1941 and that was **not** allocated directly to D, MD and MND combat units. Based on the total motorised transport produced or commandeered in the second half of 1941 (section below), and knowing the amount allocated to MD and MND combat units (above), we can estimate the amount of additional 'rear-area motorised transport' that became available to the German armed forces in the second half of 1941. Of this total, at least 33,000 additional motor vehicles (including around 3,000 light transports) were supplied to the German ground forces on the East Front from June to December 1941, excluding those allocated to MD combat units. To determine the average SDE, we are interested in the available rear area transport that was **also available** to support SDE related functions. This is determined using the following:

- 95% of trucks which were unallocated to combat units. 'Trucks' are any motor vehicles with Kfz number from 23 to 100 (inclusive).

- 0% of halftracks which were unallocated to combat units.

- 50% of light transports which were unallocated to combat units. 'Light transports' are any motor vehicles with Kfz number from 1 to 21 (inclusive).

This information has been extracted and displayed in the bottom two rows of table Ger Resources in MD & MND Units in 1941. All the rear area transport thus indicated, as well as part of the transport allocated to MD combat units (i.e. part of the transport in the combat unit's internal support organisations), will be used in calculating the SDE for the Wehrmacht on the East Front from 22nd June to 31st December 1941.[153]

***

---

[152] Refer Volume I Part I 8. - 'Supply Distribution Efficiency (SDE)'.

[153] Refer Volume IIB 6. – 'The Supply Distribution Efficiency (SDE) for the Wehrmacht on the East Front from 22nd June to 31st December 1941'.

Table Ger Resources in MD & MND Units in 1941

Total resources allocated to MD and MND units from 22nd June to 31st Dec 1941, and the percentage of total available resources allocated to D, MD and MND units

Database unit	Total resources allocated to MD combat and MND units: 22nd June to 31st Dec 1941	Small arms distribution (usage) by database units				Total equipment allocated to MD and MND combat units from 22nd June to 31st Dec 1941: grouped by equipment type (i.e. with weapon sub groupings)		Total available resources in the Reich unallocated to Deployed (D) units from 22nd June to 4th July 1941	New resources produced and received in the Reich from June to 31st Dec 1941	Resources unallocated to any D, MD or MND units in 1941: available to the Wehrmacht as Replacements (R)*	Percentage of total available resources in 1941 which were allocated to D, MD & MND combat units.
		Pi	Ri	SMG	LMG						
Allocated Manpower	274,025							3,068,665	792,000	669,600	56%
Heavy Rifle Sqd	2,088	2	7	1	1	Total small arms used by all units					
Light Rifle Sqd	94	2	9	1		Pistols and Revolvers (Pi)	34,823	71,746	290,206	327,129	70%
Motor Cycle Sqd	1,329	2	7	1		Rifles and Carbines (Ri)	190,532	1,629,100	659,111	2,097,679	67%
Bicycle Sqd	703	2	9	1		Sub Machine Guns (SMG)	8,090	960	125,500	118,370	63%
Cavalry Sqd	21	2	9	1							
Eng Sqd	299	2	8	4	1	MGs (incl AFV mounted)	7,522	71,645	38,244	102,367	59%
Light Eng Sqd	226	2	12	2							
Ferry Bridging Sqd	40	1	5			Motorcycles (including sidecars	10,632	112,792	28,025	130,185	64%
Military Police Sqd	4	2	3	2		and Sd.Kfz.2s)					
Irregular Sqd	1,088	1	10								
Rail Repair Sqd	0	1	5								
HMG	826	2	2		1						
LMG	2,871	2	2		1						
AT Rifle	450	1	1			AT Rifle	450	10,179	13,458	23,187	40%
50mm Mor	561	1	2			50mm Mor	561	2,061	2,983	4,483	77%
81mm Mor	492	1	3			81mm Mor	492	3,400	1,278	4,186	68%
Horse Team	7,421		3			Horse Team	7,421	92,182	11,400	96,161	68%
Unit Trucks	9,689		3			Unit and rear area trucks	38,189	493,659	52,754	508,224	57%
Light Transport	6,264	1	2			Unit and rear area light tranpts.	7,764	2,018,030	15,772	2,026,038	9%
Light Halftrack	172	1	2			Light Halftrack (incl SP AA)	172	1,223	2,461	3,512	65%
Medium Halftrack	495	1	4			Medium Halftrack (incl SP AA)	510	48	951	489	93%
Heavy Halftrack	66	1	6			Heavy Halftrack	66	431	631	996	59%

Weapon								%
37mm ATG	342	2	4	342	5,021	555	5,234	67%
50mm ATG	24	2	5	24	115	1,463	1,554	38%
47mm ATG (PaK(t) only)	0	2	4	0	602	159	761	19%
28mm sPzb 41	0	2	2	0	102		102	44%
75mm Inf G	62	2	4	62	971	584	1,493	69%
150mm Inf G	14	2	6	14	158	274	418	64%
75mm Gun (Incl 7.5cm GebG 36)	0	2	6	0	191	60	251	51%
105mm How	208	2	6	208	1,011	533	1,336	82%
105mm IG40	0	2	6	0	73	107	180	2%
150mm How	56	2	8	56	585	255	784	75%
105mm Gun	0	2	8	0	248	41	289	64%
150mm Gun	9	2	14	9	27	40	58	55%
210mm How	0	2	14	0	88	125	213	58%
210mm Gun	0	2	16	0	0	23	23	34%
240mm How	0	2	16	0	2	0	2	80%
240mm Gun	0	2	22	0	0	0	0	100%
305mm How	0	2	26	0	7	0	7	70%
355mm How	0	2	26	0	0	0	0	100%
600mm How	0	4	32	0	0	2	2	67%
150-200 mm Rail Guns	0	4	14	0	23	0	23	28%
210-280 mm Rail Guns	0	6	28	0	3	3	6	85%
380+mm Rail Gun/Mor	4	8	32	4	1	3	0	100%
100-280mm Coastal Guns	0	2	8	0				
Nebelwerfer 35 and 40	0	1	4	0	427	321	748	17%
Nebelwerfer 40 →	0	1	4	0				
Nebelwerfer 41	0	2	6	0	346	407	753	22%
28/32cm Rocket systems^	0	1	2	0	0	0	81500^	

* For 'Manpower' in Replacements (R), the number of available replacement troops in the Replacements Army in June 1941 is used. These comprised 561,600 earmarked for the Army (Heer), and 108,000 for the Luftwaffe and Kriegsmarine.

^ The approximate number of 28cm Wurfkorper Spreng (High Explosive Mortar) and 32cm Wurfkorper Flamm (Flame) rockets produced. 'Rocket systems' above includes only 'frame launchers', but the rockets could be fired individually.

© Nigel Askey, 2018

Table Ger Resources in MD & MND Units in 1941 (cont)

Total resources allocated to MD and MND units from 22nd June to 31st Dec 1941, and the percentage of total available resources allocated to D, MD and MND units

Database unit	Total resources allocated to MD and MND combat units: 22nd June to 31st Dec 1941	Pi	Ri	SMG	LMG	Total equipment allocated to MD and MND combat units from 22nd June to 31st Dec 1941: grouped by equipment type (i.e. with weapon sub groupings)	Total available resources in the Reich unallocated to Deployed (D) units from 22nd June to 4th July 1941	New resources produced and received in the Reich from June to 31st Dec 1941	Resources unallocated to any D, MD or MND units in 1941: available to the Wehrmacht as Replacements (R)*	Percentage of total available resources in 1941 which were allocated to D, MD & MND combat units.
Sd Kfz 250 APC	0	1		1	1	Sd Kfz 250 APC	0	350	350	10%
Sd Kfz 251 APC	25	1		2	1	Sd Kfz 251 APC	75	212	262	73%
Sd Kfz 254 AOP	4	2	2	3	1	Sd Kfz 254 AOP	5	0	1	99%
Sd Kfz 221 A Cars	0	1		2	1	Sd Kfz 221 A Cars	6	0	6	98%
Sd Kfz 222 A Cars	28	1		2	1	Sd Kfz 222 A Cars	43	90	105	76%
Sd Kfz 260/261 A Cars	51	2		3		Sd Kfz 260/261 A Cars	3	77	29	84%
Sd Kfz 223 A Cars	6	1		2	1	Sd Kfz 223 A Cars	5	56	55	84%
Sd Kfz 231/232 A Cars	9	2	1	3	1	Sd Kfz 231/232 A Cars	0	47	38	84%
Sd Kfz 263 A Cars	0	2	1	3	1	Sd Kfz 263 A Cars	0	0	0	100%
Sd Kfz 247 A Cars	5	2	1	3	1	Sd Kfz 247 A Cars	1	54	50	22%
Panhard 178 **	0	1	1	2	1	Panhard 178 **	0	0	0	100%
Pz Kpfw I	2	1		1	2	Pz Kpfw I and Pz Kpfw I (Pio)	422	0	408	54%
Kleine Pz Bef I	0	1		2	1	*Kleine* Pz Bef I	30	0	30	76%
Pz Kpfw II	210	1		2	1	Pz Kpfw II	97	181	130	90%
Pz Kpfw III (37mm)	17	2	1	2	2	Pz Kpfw III (37mm)	45	0	59	85%
Pz Kpfw III (50mm)	337	2	1	2	2	Pz Kpfw III (50mm)	193	1,201	1,095	53%
Pz Bef III (*Gross*)	22	2	1	3	1	Pz Bef III (*Gross*)	23	33	45	83%
Pz Kpfw IV	86	2	1	2	2	Pz Kpfw IV	22	330	282	67%
Pz Kpfw 38(t)	39	2		2	2	Pz Kpfw 38(t) and Pz Bef 38(t) →	69	401	431	62%
Pz Bef 38(t)	0	2		2	1					
Pz Kpfw 35(t)	0	2		2	2	Pz Kpfw 35(t) and Pz Bef 35(t) →	10	0	10	94%
Pz Bef 35(t)	0	2		2	1					

Equipment	R1							%
StuG III Assault Gun	84	2	2		21	348	285	61%
Sdkfz 252	0	1	1	1	58	160	218	47%
Sdkfz 253	8	2	2	1	6	33	32	89%
15cm sIG33 SP Guns	0	2	4	2	0	0	0	100%
Pz Jager I (47mm)	0	1	2		4	0	4	98%
47mm, Pz Kpfw 35R(f)	0	1	2		0	93	93	47%
Pz Kpfw 35R(f) (Bef+ other types)	47	1	2	1	14	at least 80 refurb.	at least 47	56%
SP 88 mm AAG	0	2	6	2	14	0	14	30%
105mm K18 Pz Sfl IVa	0	2	1	2	0	0	0	100%
Pz Kpfw II (F)	0	1	2	1	6	36	42	67%
Pz Kpfw B2	26	2	2	1	unknown	at least 26 refurb.	0	
Pz Kpfw B2 (F)	10	2	2	1	0	0	0	100%
Pz Kpfw 35-S	17	1	2	1	unknown	at least 53 refurb.	at least 36	
Pz Kpfw 38H	24	1	1	2	unknown	at least 119 refurb.	at least 95	
Pz Kpfw I (Pio) — (Inc in Pz Kpfw I Figures)	20	1	2					
Sd Kfz 300 (type B II)	0				49	0	49	52%
Pz IV Bridge Layer	0	1	2		1	1	1	80%
Pz IV Ammo Carrier	0	1	2		6	4	10	44%
Armoured Train	0	10	40	12	0	0	0	100%
20 mm AAG (all types incl SP)	1,124	1	2		2,191	3,690	4,757	73%
20mm Quad AAG (all types incl SP)	6	1	4		406	184	584	14%
37 mm AAG (all types incl SP)	40	1	4		603	341	889	44%
88-105mm AAG (all types incl SP)	544	1	6		583	1,370	1,409	76%
Truck 20mm AAG — (Inc in 20 mm AAG Figures)	0	1	4					
Sd Kfz 10/4	0	2	5		6	46	52	90%
Sd Kfz 6/2	15	2	5		19	51	54	71%
Sd Kfz 7/1	0	2	8		3	32	35	58%
AA Searchlights	292	1	6					
Rear Area SDE Truck	28,500	0	2					
Rear Area SDE Lt Lt	1,500	0	2					

** Excludes 43 Panhard 178s issued as rail protection vehicles which ran on railway lines.

4) The Total Resources in the Reich that were Available for Use by Newly Mobilised Units from 22nd June to 31st December 1941

The next step is to determine the total resources in the Reich that were available in the second half of 1941 for use by MD and MND units. This means we need to determine how many resources were **not** already used by Deployed (D) units between 22nd June and 4th July 1941, and how many new resources were produced (manufactured) and received in the Reich from 22nd June to 31st December 1941. This is accomplished in the fourth and fifth columns in table Ger Resources in MD & MND Units in 1941.

a. Total Available Resources in the Reich Unallocated to Deployed (D) Units from 22nd June to 4th July 1941

The data in column 'Total available resources in the Reich unallocated to Deployed (D) units from 22nd June to 4th July 1941' is obtained directly from table % of Ger Resources Deployed (D) (pages 96-99).[154] The values shown are the differences between values shown in the column 'Total available resources in the Reich on 1st June 1941' minus the values shown in the column 'Total equipment allocated to Deployed (D) combat units (with weapon sub groupings)'.

***

b. New Resources Produced and Received in the Reich from June to 31st December 1941

The data in column 'New resources produced and received in the Reich from June to 31st December 1941' shows the amount of new manpower mobilised (recruited or conscripted, and having undergone at least basic training), and the amount of new equipment manufactured or/and received in the Reich, during the last seven months of 1941.[155]

i. Small Arms and Other Infantry Weapons

The following table shows the small arms and other selected infantry weapons produced by the Germans from June to December 1941.[156]

	Monthly production, June to December 1941							Total Production
	June	July	Aug.	Sept.	Oct.	Nov.	Dec.	June - Dec. 1941
Pistols	32,466	41,935	33,879	42,211	43,649	45,813	50,253	**290,206**
Rifles and Carbines	123,959	105,063	101,479	106,647	78,884	66,514	76,565	**659,111**
Sub Machine Guns*	17,250	20,050	19,600	18,500	19,000	19,000	19,000	**132,400**
MGs	6,620	6,377	6,304	5,733	5,853	3,933	3,424	**38,244**
50mm Mortars^	751	795	677	289	182	144	145	**2,983**
81mm Mortars	322	341	290	124	78	62	62	**1,278**
7.5cm Infantry Guns**	117	134	100	65	83	40	45	**584**
15cm Infantry Guns	46	64	48	24	19	46	27	**274**

* SMGs available on 22nd June include approximately 40% of June 1941 production.
^ 50mm mortars represented approximately 70% of June-December 1941 mortar production.
** 7.5cm infantry guns represented approximately 68% of 1941 infantry gun production.

[154] Refer Volume IIB 3. 3) – 'The Proportion of Total Available Resources which were in a Deployed (D) State in the Reich from 22nd June to 4th July 1941'.

[155] Additional notes for this table column. The 81 500 28/32cm Rocket Systems produced from June to December 1941 is the approximate number of 28cm *Wurfkörper Spreng* (High Explosive Mortar) and 32cm *Wurfkörper Flamm* (Flame) rockets produced. This type of rocket 'system' usually only includes 'frame launchers', but in this case the rockets could be fired individually.

[156] Appendix A, Table II. Kroener, B. R., et al, Germany and the Second World War; Volume I, Organisation and Mobilisation of the German Sphere of Power, Part 1, Wartime Administration, Economy and Manpower Resources 1939-1941, Clarendon Press (Oxford University Press), Oxford, 2000, Table II.VII.3. Ref: Reports on overall state of armaments, BA-MA RH 8/v. IO35ff. Further breakdown of infantry gun data is from: Boog, H., et al., Germany and the Second World War, Volume IV: The Attack on the Soviet Union, Clarendon Press (Oxford University Press), New York, 1996, Table II.VI.I., pp. 1120-1122. Ref: *Uberblick uber den Rustungsstand des Heeres (Waffen und Gerät) Juni 1941-Januar 1942*, BA-MA RH 8/v. 1090, 1091.

Note, 40% of the SMGs produced in June 1941 are not included in table Ger Resources in MD & MND Units in 1941. These are included in table % of Ger Resources Deployed (D) and are assumed to have been available to Deployed (D) combat units on 22nd June 1941.

ii. Anti-Tank Weapons

The following table shows the anti-tank weapons produced by the Germans from June to December 1941.[157]

	Monthly production, June to December 1941							Total Production June - Dec. 1941
	June	July	Aug.	Sept.	Oct.	Nov.	Dec.	
7.92mm PzB 39	2,780	2,967	3,010	2,510	2,133	0	58	13,458
2.8cm sPzb 41	0	0	0	0	0	0	0	n/a
3.7cm Pak 36	183	100	135	95	39	3	0	555
5cm Pak 38	163	220	250	152	241	212	225	1,463
4.7cm Pak (t)	26	11	14	8	28	28	44	159

As we would expect (from the various weapons' performance), by September 1941 production of the 3.7cm *Panzerabwehrkanone* 36 (PaK 36) was being wound down due to its inability to deal with the latest model Soviet tanks. Similarly, by November 1941 production of the 7.92mm *Panzerbüchse* 39 (PzB 39) anti-tank rifle had stopped. By this time it was obvious to the German Army that anti-tank rifles in general were obsolete: even the best of them struggled to make an impression on even light tanks. It is interesting to note here that while almost all other armies had come to the same conclusion, the Red Army either didn't agree or didn't care. The Red Army had only just introduced the PTRD 1941 anti-tank rifle into service in mid-1941, and the Soviets persisted with producing and issuing large numbers of anti-tank rifles until the end of the war.

Unfortunately for the Germans, production of the outstanding 2.8cm *schwere Panzerbüchse* 41 (sPzB 41) had also stopped by June 1941 due to the shortage of tungsten cored ammunition. Ultimately, this proved to be the downfall of all the German WWII taper bore anti-tank weapons.

This left only the excellent 5cm *Panzerabwehrkanone* 38 (PaK 38) and a few good Czech 4.7cm *Panzerabwehrkanone* (t) anti-tank guns. During 1941 the 5cm Pak 38 was one of the few general issue anti-tank weapons capable of stopping the T-34 at anything like medium combat ranges. As a result the front line divisions were soon clamoring to replace their Pak 36s with Pak 38s (or, preferably, with even heavier anti-tank guns). However with a production rate of only around 210 guns per month during 1941, the 3.7cm Pak 36 would remain the German Army's most common anti-tank gun until 1943.

***

[157] Appendix A, Table II. Kroener, B. R., et al, Germany and the Second World War; Volume I, Organisation and Mobilisation of the German Sphere of Power, Part 1, Wartime Administration, Economy and Manpower Resources 1939-1941, Clarendon Press (Oxford University Press), Oxford, 2000, Table II.VII.3. Their ref: Reports on overall state of armaments, BA-MA RH 8/v. IO35ff. Pak 36 and 38 data from: Boog, H., et al., Germany and the Second World War, Volume IV: The Attack on the Soviet Union, Clarendon Press (Oxford University Press), New York, 1996, Table II.VI.I., pp. 1120-1122. Ref: *Uberblick uber den Rustungsstand des Heeres (Waffen und Gerät)* Juni 1941-*Januar* 1942, BA-MA RH 8/v. 1090, 1091.

iii. Artillery Pieces

The following table shows the most important artillery types produced by the Germans from June to December 1941.[158] These types were present in almost all divisional artillery units, as well as forming the backbone of the separate corps artillery battalions.

	Monthly production, June to December 1941							Total Production
	June	July	Aug.	Sept.	Oct.	Nov.	Dec.	June - Dec. 1941
7.5cm GebG 36	9	0	1	0	25	1	0	36
7.5cm leFK 18	24	0	0	0	0	0	0	24
10.5cm le FH	89	100	130	79	45	45	45	533
15cm s FH 18	48	66	51	32	39	10	9	255
10.5cm K 18	5	13	9	5	0	9	0	41
15cm K 18 and 39	7	7	10	8	1	3	4	40
21cm Mor 18	22	21	17	21	14	14	16	125
Nebelwerfer 40	33	21	44	31	79	60	53	321
Nebelwerfer 41*	43	27	55	39	101	75	67	407
* Nebelwerfer 41 launchers represented approximately 56% of 1941 rocket artillery launcher production.								

It is clear from these figures that the Germans still felt that the 10.5cm howitzer was the best weapon for light divisional artillery (as did the US Army in 1941). Consequently, very few 7.5cm calibre guns were produced. 7.5cm *leichte Feldkanone* 18 (le FK 18) production ended in July 1941, while the outstanding 7.5cm *Gebirgsgeschütz* 36 (Geb G 36) mountain gun was a specialised weapon which was only ever going to be produced in small numbers.[159]

Also apparent from the above figures is the high (for the Germans) production rate of their *Nebelwerfer* rocket systems. These weapons were relatively cheap and easy to produce compared to artillery, and they continued to be extremely effective in their specialised 'smoke laying' and 'rocket bombardment' roles. In total, approximately 417,250 15cm *Wurfgranate Spreng* (HE) and *Wurfgranate wKH Nebel* (smoke) rockets were produced in 1941 for the 15cm *Nebelwerfer* 41 rocket launchers.[160]

In addition to their rocket artillery using launchers (the *Nebelwerfer*), the Germans expanded their production of the standalone 28cm *Wurfkörper Spreng* (HE Mortar) and 32cm *Wurfkörper Flamm* (Flame Mortar) bombardment rockets. In 1941 77,150 *Wurfkörper Spreng* and 62,550 *Wurfkörper Flamm* rockets were produced.[161] Assuming a linear rate of rocket production through 1941, then from June to December 1941 the Germans produced approximately 45,000 28cm *Wurfkörper Spreng* and 36,500 32cm *Wurfkörper Flamm* bombardment rockets.

***

In the field of super heavy and railway artillery the Germans produced very few weapons in the second half of 1941. The table below is a summary of the artillery weapons in service and produced by the Germans during this period, which are **not** shown in the previous table.[162]

---

[158] Appendix A, Table II. Kroener, B. R., et al, Germany and the Second World War; Volume I, Organisation and Mobilisation of the German Sphere of Power, Part 1, Wartime Administration, Economy and Manpower Resources 1939-1941, Clarendon Press (Oxford University Press), Oxford, 2000, Table II.VII.3, pp. 725-727. Their ref: Reports on overall state of armaments, BA-MA RH 8/v. IO35ff. 10.5cm leFH, 15cm sFH 18 and 10.5cm K 18 data from: Boog, H., et al., Germany and the Second World War, Volume IV: The Attack on the Soviet Union, Clarendon Press (Oxford University Press), New York, 1996, Table II.VI.I., pp. 1120-1122. Ref: *Uberblick uber den Rustungsstand des Heeres (Waffen und Gerät)* Juni 1941-*Januar* 1942, BA-MA RH 8/v. 1090, 1091.

[159] Production of the old 7.5cm FK 16nA had long since ceased, and around 80 7.5cm FK 38s were completed in 1942. I.V. Hogg, German Artillery of WWII, Greenhill Books, London, 1997, pp. 38 and 42.

[160] F. Haun, *Waffen und Geheimwaffen des deutschen Herres* (Weapons and secret Weapons of the German Army) 1933-1945, Bernard & Graefe Verlag GmbH, Monch, 1998.

[161] Ibid.

[162] Data compiled from: I.V. Hogg, German Artillery of WWII, Greenhill Books, London, 1997. F. Haun, *Waffen und Geheimwaffen des deutschen Herres* (Weapons and secret Weapons of the German Army) 1933-1945, Bernard & Graefe Verlag GmbH, Monch, 1998. T. Gander, P. Chamberlain, Weapons of the Third Reich; an Encyclopedic Survey of all Small Arms, Artillery and Special Weapons of the German Land Forces 1939-1945, Doubleday and Company Inc, New York, 1979. P. Chamberlain, H. Doyle, T. L. Jentz, Encyclopedia pf German Tanks of WWII, Arms and Armour Press, London, 1993, p. 158.

	Total Production June - Dec. 1941
7.5cm LG 40	0
10.5cm LG 41*	107
15cm SK C/28M	0
21cm K 38 and K 39*^	23
24cm H 39	0
24cm K (t)^	0
24cm K L/46	0
24cm K 3	0
30.5cm Mor (t))	0
35.5cm H M1	0
60cm Gerat	2
28cm K 5 (E)^	3
Materiel de 400 mod 15, 16^	3
40.6cm Adolf K (E)**	1
80cm K (E)**	1
* Recoilless artillery.	
*^ K 39 also sometimes desig. K 39/40 and 39/41.	
^ Railroad artillery, entered service in 1941.	
** Railroad artillery, entered service in 1942.	

All the relevant weapons in service are shown in the above table, even though **most underwent no new production** from June to December 1941. These are included to illustrate how long it took to manufacture these sometimes massive weapons, how few were produced, and that most originated from the pre-war period. As an example, the 1,350 metric ton 80cm *Kanone in Eisenbahnlafette* 'Gustav Gerät' (80cm K (E)) remains the largest artillery weapon ever built.

***

iv. Anti-Aircraft Weapons

The following table shows the anti-aircraft weapons produced by the Germans from June to December 1941.[163]

	Monthly production, June to December 1941							Total Production June - Dec. 1941
	June	July	Aug.	Sept.	Oct.	Nov.	Dec.	
2cm Flak 38*	414	399	559	548	455	634	681	3,690
3.7cm Flak 36^	39	50	63	36	54	45	54	341
2cm Flakvierling 38**	67	11	12	27	13	37	17	184
5cm Flak 41	2	5	7	0	3	6	0	23
8.8cm Flak 36 & 37*^	168	179	197	151	192	192	175	1,254
10.5cm Flak 38 & 39^	16	16	19	10	15	22	18	116
Sd Kfz 10/4				46				46
Sd Kfz 6/2				51				51
Sd Kfz 7/1				32				32
* At least 873 2cm Flak were supplied to the Army in 1941.								
^ The large majority of 3.7cm Flak guns were supplied to the Luftwaffe, as were all the 10.5cm Flak guns.								
** Mostly supplied to the Army, comprised four barrels per weapon system.								
*^ At least 126 8.8cm Flak were supplied to the Army in 1941.								

---

[163] Appendix A, Table II. Kroener, B. R., et al, Germany and the Second World War; Volume I, Organisation and Mobilisation of the German Sphere of Power, Part 1, Wartime Administration, Economy and Manpower Resources 1939-1941, Clarendon Press (Oxford University Press), Oxford, 2000, Table II.VII.3., pp. 725-727. SP Flak vehicle data calculated from P. Chamberlain, H. Doyle, T. L. Jentz, Encyclopedia pf German Tanks of WWII, Arms and Armour Press, London, 1993, pp. 181, 183, 184 and 262.

Anti-aircraft weapons were one of the few areas where the Germans actually out-produced both the Soviets and the Western Allies during the early war years; up to and including 1941.[164] However the large majority of these weapons never found their way to the East Front during 1941 (and during WWII in general). Most of these weapons were incorporated into the Luftwaffe Flak batteries which formed part of the German's strategic anti-aircraft defences in Germany and occupied Europe.[165] Note, the 5cm *Flugabwehrkanone* 41 (5cm Flak 41) was still a semi-experimental weapon which was attempting to bridge the perceived 'altitude gap' between 3.7cm and 8.8cm flak guns. It turned out to be a relatively unsuccessful design and only around 200 were ever produced, including prototype and pre-production weapons. As far as is known all these guns were issued to Luftwaffe flak batteries in the West during WWII.

***

v. Tanks and other AFVs

The following table shows the German tanks and assault guns produced **and ready for issue** to the *Panzer Truppen* and *Sturmartillerie*, from June to December 1941.[166]

Newly Manufactured German Tanks and Assault Guns Ready for Issue, June-December 1941								Total Ready for Issue, June - Dec. 1941
	June	July	Aug.	Sept.	Oct.	Nov.	Dec.	
Pz Kpfw I	No longer produced							
(Pz I) Kleine Pz Bef *	No longer produced							
Pz Kpfw II	5	27	9	26	23	50	41	181
Pz Kpfw III (37mm)	No longer produced							
Pz Kpfw III (50mm)	88	176	185	182	174	198	198	1,201
(Pz III) Gross Pz Bef *		14	5	2			12	33
Pz Kpfw IV	29	55	43	49	40	58	56	330
Pz Kpfw 38(t)^	29	80	64	63	66	50	49	401
Pz Kpfw 35(t)^	No longer produced							
StuG III Assault Gun	56	47	50	38	71	46	40	348
* MG armed command tanks based on Pz Kpfw I and Pz Kpfw III tanks.							**Total**	**2,494**
^ Includes all tanks used as command tanks.								

The AFVs in the above table were easily the most vital reinforcements and replacements that the German Army on the East Front could have received during Operation Barbarossa. The reader should note that the vehicles shown above were produced **and 'ready for issue'** to Wehrmacht combat units in 1941. This means they had been manufactured, tested for quality control (which was still comparatively very stringent) and accepted by the Army's representatives.

In total, almost 2,500 new tanks and assault guns were available, of which 1,932 (77%) were the best main battle tanks and assault guns available to the Germans. This includes Pz Kpfw III (with 50mm guns), Pz Kpfw IV (with 75mm guns) and StuG III assault Guns (with 75mm guns). Yet, despite the availability and vital importance of these weapons to the ultimate success or failure of Operation Barbarossa and Operation Typhoon, we shall see in chapter 4. 7) that relatively few of them found their way to the East Front as replacements or reinforcements during the second half of 1941.[167]

---

[164] The Soviets produced 1,700 25-40mm AA guns and 1,700 76-90mm AA Guns from June to December 1941. G.F. Krivosheev, et al, Soviet Casualties and Combat Losses in the Twentieth Century, ed. Colonel General G.F. Krivosheev, Greenhill Books, London, 1997, Table 95. II, p. 248.

[165] Refer Volume IIA 3. 11) – 'Luftwaffe Anti-Aircraft (Flak) Units' and Volume IIA 3. 11) b. – 'Luftwaffe Mixed Flak Battalions' for more on the Luftwaffe's strategic air defences.

[166] Appendix A, Table IV; includes German tank and assault gun losses, rebuilt and inventories for 1941. Data from: T. L. Jentz, *Panzer Truppen* Volume 1: The Complete Guide to the Creation and Combat Deployment of Germany's Tank Force – 1933-1942, Schiffer Military History, Atglen, PA, 1996, pp. 254, 256, 258, 260, 262, 264, 266 and 270. StuG data from: Germany and the Second World War, Volume IV: The Attack on the Soviet Union, Boog, H., et al., Clarendon Press (Oxford University Press), New York, 1996, Table II.VI.I., pp. 1120-1122. Ref: *Uberblick uber den Rustungsstand des Heeres (Waffen und Gerät) Juni 1941-Januar 1942*, BA-MA RH 8/v. 1090, 1091.

[167] Refer Volume IIB 4. 7) – 'The Resource Replacements (R) Available to the German Army, Waffen SS, Luftwaffe Ground Forces and Naval Coastal Artillery, from 22nd June to 31st December 1941'. Also refer Volume IIB 4. 2) a. - 'The German Tank MD and MND Matrix' for details on German tank deployments in newly mobilised units in 1941.

In addition to tanks and assault guns, the Germans also manufactured the following specialised AFVs from June to December 1941.[168]

Armoured semi-tracks	Total Production June - Dec. 1941	Armoured self-propelled guns	Total Production June - Dec. 1941
Sd Kfz 250 APC*	350	15cm sIG33 SP Guns	No longer produced
Sd Kfz 251 APC	212	PzJager I (47mm)	No longer produced
Sd Kfz 254 AOP	No longer produced	47mm, Pz.Kpfw 35R(f) **^	93
Sd Kfz 252^	160	Pz.Kpfw 35R(f) (Bef+ other types)*^^	At least 80
Sd Kfz 253**	33	SP 88 mm AAG	No longer produced
Armoured cars		105mm K18 Pz Sfl IVa	No longer produced
Sd Kfz 221 A Cars	No longer produced	**Armoured flame-thrower vehicles**	
Sd Kfz 222 A Cars	90	Pz.Kpfw II (F)	36
Sd Kfz 260/261 A Cars	77	Pz.Kpfw B2 (F)	10
Sd Kfz 223 A Cars	56	**Armoured pionier vehicles**	
Sd Kfz 231/232 A Cars	47	Sd Kfz 300 (expendable AFVs)	No longer produced
Sd Kfz 263 A Cars	0	Pz IV Bridge Layer	No longer produced
Sd Kfz 247 A Cars*^	54	Pz IV Ammo Carrier	4
Panhard 178 A Cars***	No longer produced		
* Series production commenced in June 1941.			
^ Production ended in September 1941.			
** Production ended in June 1941.			
*^ Produced from July 1941. Production ended in January 1942.			
*** Captured French vehicles. 43 were converted to run on rail lines as railway protection vehicles.			
**^ Production ended in October 1941.			
*^^ Some used as command vehicles for units equipped with the 4.7cm Pz Kpfw 35R(f).			

Evident from these figures is the fact that the Germans focused most of their 'specialised AFV' production capacity on armoured semi-tracked vehicles, especially the Sd Kfz 251 and the smaller Sd Kfz 250 armoured personnel carriers. Out of 1,221 AFVs in the above table (excluding those using the French 35R chassis), 755 (62%) were armoured semi-tracked vehicles. Production of these vehicles would only increase in later war years; with 15,252 Sd Kfz 251s and 6,628 Sd Kfz 250s being produced by war's end.[169]

It is interesting to note here that these 21,880 semi-tracked APCs are almost never mentioned in discussions comparing German and Soviet wartime tank production. The Soviets produced no significant APCs during WWII; relying on US APCs (over 5,000) and military trucks supplied under lend lease. They are at the same time credited with producing 14,923 light tanks; the large majority being T-60s and T-70s. However, a T-60 M1942 weighed only 5,150kg and a T-70 M1942 weighed 9,950kg. In comparison, a standard Sd Kfz 251/1 was a larger vehicle which weighed around 9,000kg. In addition the Sd Kfz 251's steering and power transmission systems were more effective and complex than those in the T-60 and T-70. In other words the German semi-tracked APCs are not included in German 'tank' and 'AFV' production figures purely because they were not fully-tracked vehicles.

In reality, they consumed similar resources (to produce) as a Soviet T-60 or T-70 light tank, were much more useful on the battlefield, and had similar overall combat power. The latter was especially true later in the war when everything from flame-throwers to heavy 7.5cm anti-tank guns were mounted on these vehicles. By 1944 specialised versions of the Sd Kfz 251 and Sd Kfz 250 were fulfilling almost all the roles required in panzer and panzer grenadier divisions which did not require tanks or assault guns. These included armoured infantry transport, armoured reconnaissance, armoured signals, combat *pionier*, and artillery observation and control.

---

[168] Data collated from: P. Chamberlain, H. Doyle, T. L. Jentz, Encyclopedia pf German Tanks of WWII, Arms and Armour Press, London, 1993, pp. 24, 25, 34, 106, 114, 115, 117, 150, 162, 168, 169-178, 179, 186, 191, 192, 194, 196, 198, 201, 205, 213, 214, 220, 226, 261-263. T. Jentz, H. Doyle, P. Sarson, *Flammpanzer*: German Flamethrowers 1941-1945, Osprey Military, Reed International Books Ltd, London, 1995, pp. 7, 13 and 16. Dr. F. M. von Senger und Etterlin, German Tanks of WWII, Galahad Books, New York, 1969, pp. 193, 211, 212.

[169] P. Chamberlain, H. Doyle, T. L. Jentz, Encyclopedia pf German Tanks of WWII, Arms and Armour Press, London, 1993, p.262.

Also evident from the table above is the very slow rate of armoured car production; a total of only around 320 armoured cars being manufactured during the second half of 1941. This meant that only elite panzer and Waffen SS units continued to receive these vehicles (as authorised by their TOE), and replacements were few and far between. In the meantime most other motorised units had to improvise with various types of especially adapted military trucks.

***

vi. Motor Vehicles and Other Transport Types

The following table shows the **military-standard** motor vehicles produced by the Germans from June to December 1941.[170]

Military Vehicle Type	Total Production June - Dec. 1941
Motor Cycles	20,625
Approx. No. of Motor Cycles with Side Cars	7,200
Sd Kfz 2 *Kleines Kettenkraftrad*	c 200
Light Staff Car	8,217
Medium Staff Car	5,626
Heavy Staff Car	1,929
Light Truck	5,122
Medium Truck	15,502
Heavy Truck	3,287
Specialised Truck *	5,843
Sd Kfz 10 (1t) Half-Track ^	1,552
Sd Kfz 11 (3t) Half-Track	909
Sd Kfz 6 (5t) Half-Track **	199
Sd Kfz 7 (8t) Half-Track *^	752
Sd Kfz 8 (12t) Half-Track	460
Sd Kfz 9 (18t) Half-Track	171
* E.g. radio trucks, ambulances, AA weapon mounts, breakdown trucks with cranes and or winches, etc. ^ Includes 46 Sd Kfz 10/4 SP Flak Vehicles. ** Includes 51 Sd Kfz 6/2 SP Flak Vehicles. *^ Includes 32 Sd Kfz 7/1 SP Flak Vehicles.	

Alternative sources indicate German military truck output at 3,479 in June, 1,383 in July, 3,174 in August, 2,905 in September, 3,741 in October 3,765 in November and 3,278 in December (a total of 21,725 from June-December 1941).[171] These figures are slightly lower than those indicated above, but are less comprehensive and do not appear to include specialised trucks. However, we can see there is a reasonable correlation between sources, and the figures are in line with overall German military-truck production in 1941.[172]

Using the data in Appendix A Table V, we can see that around 52% of the military trucks produced in 1941 (45,687) were produced in the last seven months of the year. At the same time it is apparent that German military

---

[170] Data compiled from: Appendix A, Table V. Kroener, B. R., et al, Germany and the Second World War; Volume I, Organisation and Mobilisation of the German Sphere of Power, Part 1, Wartime Administration, Economy and Manpower Resources 1939-1941, Clarendon Press (Oxford University Press), Oxford, 2000, Table II.VII.7. Ref: Compiled from Survey of State Armaments, BA MA RH8/v. 1035ff. R. Michulec, Wehrmacht Support Vehicles, Concord Publications Co, Hong Kong, 1999, p. 4. R. Frank, German Light Half-Tracked Prime Movers 1934-1945, Schiffer Military History, Atglen, PA, 1997, pp. 3 and 23. R. Frank, German Medium Half-Tracked Prime Movers 1934-1945, Schiffer Military History, Atglen, PA, 1997, pp. 4 and 23. R. Frank, German Heavy Half-Tracked Prime Movers 1934-1945, Schiffer Military/Aviation History, Atglen, PA, 1996, pp. 3 and 31.

[171] Boog, H., et al., Germany and the Second World War, Volume IV: The Attack on the Soviet Union, Clarendon Press (Oxford University Press), New York, 1996, Table II.VI.I., pp. 1120-1122. Ref: *Uberblick uber den Rustungsstand des Heeres (Waffen und Gerät)* Juni 1941-*Januar* 1942, BA-MA RH 8/v. 1090, 1091.

[172] E.g., J. Ellis, World War II: A Statistical Survey, Facts on File Inc, New York, 1993, Table 91, p. 278, states German military truck production was 53,348, 51,085, 58,049 and 74,181, in 1940, 1941, 1942 and 1943, respectively.

truck production in 1942 was only slightly higher than that achieved in 1941. If there is a pattern in these figures it is (arguably) that they appear to reinforce the thesis regarding the German High Command's strategic overconfidence during the invasion of the USSR. Next to tanks and assault guns, military trucks were one of the most important pieces of equipment that the German Army needed on the East Front during Operation Barbarossa and Operation Typhoon. Yet, according to these figures they actually reduced military truck production during the critical August-September 1941 period, and even in December 1941 they were producing fewer military trucks than in June 1941 (i.e., 2,903 in December compared to 3,479 in June).

However, as ever, the whole story is not quite as simple as indicated above. This is because of three additional factors which should be considered.

- Firstly, the figures above only include superior quality military vehicles and do not include all truck production in Germany, Austria and the annexed territories. As we have seen previously, total German 1941 truck production amounted to 84,727 vehicles with an average payload of around 2.5 tonnes.[173] This means at least another 39,040 trucks were produced in 1941, which were not considered 'military vehicles'. In the German FILARM model it is assumed that these vehicles were **not used** by German military forces, and were exclusively used in the German economy or were exported.

- Secondly, large numbers of vehicles were being produced in the occupied territories. In 1941, 39,574 trucks were delivered from the occupied territories (mainly France), and in 1942 this figure was 37,163.[174] A considerable number of these trucks, especially the French medium-heavy trucks originally meant for their military, were relatively robust vehicles which were used by the Wehrmacht for the duration of WWII. The main French manufacturers were Renault, Peugeot, Citroen, Panhard, Berliet, Saurer and Laffly (building Ford trucks and Ford spare parts).

In the German FILARM model it is assumed that around 40% of the trucks manufactured in the occupied territories from June to December 1941, were made available to the Wehrmacht from June to December 1941. This equates to approximately 9,200 medium and heavy trucks, with an average payload of around 2.5 tonnes. This is a conservative estimate and the figure was probably higher (than 40%).

- Thirdly, the figures take no account of the 'war booty' vehicles captured by the Germans in 1941. Records indicate that 52,238 serviceable trucks, artillery-tractors and staff cars were captured by German forces on the East Front from 22nd June to 31st December 1941.[175] The condition of these vehicles is unclear; but given the state of the Red Army's truck park in June 1941, it probably wasn't great. In addition they were predominantly civilian types like the rest of the vehicles in the Red Army. Nevertheless, very few of these vehicles found their way into the German economy in 1941, and the large majority of serviceable vehicles were immediately pressed into service with the Wehrmacht on the East Front. Most were used to bolster the motorised transport columns in rear areas and/or supplement the transport in security and military-police forces.

In the German FILARM model it is estimated that around two-thirds of the 'war booty' vehicles were trucks, and approximately 40% of these made a significant contribution to the Wehrmacht's truck inventory from June to December 1941. This takes into account that: many trucks needed major repairs and servicing, significant numbers were cannibalised for spare parts, and the average lift capacity of these trucks was lower than the average German truck's lift capacity (1.99 tonnes vs. 2.49 tonnes). This equates to approximately 13,800 trucks with an average payload of around 2.5 tonnes.

***

Given all the above, it is fair to estimate that the Wehrmacht and Waffen SS had at least 52,800 additional trucks between 22nd June 1941 and 31st December 1941, made up of 39,000 new German and foreign (mainly French) trucks, and 13,800 second-hand Soviet trucks in reasonable working order.

In addition to new trucks, we can see from the above table that the manufacture of half-track prime movers continued at a brisk pace (unless of course, you compare this to US auto production). A total of 4,043 military grade half-track prime movers were produced from June to December 1941: an average of 578 half-tracks per month or 21 halftracks per day. Especially important was that 951 of these were Sd Kfz 6 and 7 machines (capable of towing

---

[173] Refer Volume IIB 3. 2) f. - 'Review of Motor Vehicles and Other Transport Types (in June 1941)', table showing German Truck Production and Exports, 1940-1942.
[174] Ibid.
[175] Kroener, B. R., et al, Germany and the Second World War; Volume I, Organisation and Mobilisation of the German Sphere of Power, Part 1, Wartime Administration, Economy and Manpower Resources 1939-1941, Clarendon Press (Oxford University Press), Oxford, 2000, Table II.VII.4. Ref: Ten-day reports of the quartermaster-general, BA MA RW 19/1379 ff.

very heavy artillery), while another 631 were the very powerful Sd Kfz 8 and 9 machines (capable of towing the heaviest artillery or recovering the heaviest of tanks). Considering the complexity and size of these vehicles, this is actually an impressive production figure. Nevertheless, this rate of production was largely due to the fact that the Sd Kfz 6 to 10 production lines had all been in production since before the war. Although the Sd Kfz 6 to 9 machines were probably the finest half-track prime movers ever produced, they were arguably over engineered for their primary task and were always costly. Furthermore all the German half-track types, and especially the medium and heavy models, were complex vehicles which were never suited to true mass production.

***

In addition to the motor vehicles, approximately 45,000 horses were commandeered from the Reich's economy and the occupied territories from June to December 1941, and of these around 5,000 were riding horses. The latter were predominantly used by cavalry formations and were few in number because the German Army's cavalry forces were rapidly diminishing. Non-riding horses went into 'horse teams', and the German FILARM model's database uses an average of 3.5 per horse team. Note, horse teams include artillery hitches and limbers: a horse team can be a single horse cart or eight horses pulling a heavy artillery piece.

***

vii. Newly Conscripted Wehrmacht and Waffen SS Personnel

From section 3. 2) g. we ascertained that the strength of the Wehrmacht and Waffen SS on 15th June 1941 was approximately 7,309,000 personnel.[176] In addition, by 4th January 1942 these same organisations had grown to a strength of 7,648,000 personnel.[177] This growth in overall strength occurred despite a large number of casualties being sustained from June to December 1941, and with a very large proportion of these casualties being irrecoverable (permanent) loses.

Chapter 8. contains an in depth analysis of all the casualties (killed, wounded, missing, POW and unfit/sick) that occurred in the Wehrmacht and Waffen SS from June 1941 to February 1942.[178] It includes records of all the casualties suffered on the East Front as well as those from the western fronts. In addition, the proportion of wounded and unfit/sick casualties that were recuperated and remained in the Wehrmacht is studied (based on the OKW medical records). From this data, we are able to calculate the number of (mostly conscripted) new recruits that were needed to enable the Wehrmacht and Waffen SS to grow by around 331,000 persons from 22nd June 1941 to 31st December 1941. The results of this analysis are summarised in the following table.

Overall Wehrmacht and Waffen SS Strength Change from June to December 1941	
Army, Luftwaffe, Navy and Waffen SS Strength, 22nd June 1941.	7,309,000
Army, Luftwaffe, Navy and Waffen SS Strength, 31st Dec 1941.*	7,640,000
Total casualties on the East Front.	1,277,587
Casualties who remained in the Wehrmacht and Waffen SS.	822,540
Irrecoverable losses on the East Front.	455,047
Total casualties on other Fronts.^	15,900
Casualties who remained in the Wehrmacht and Waffen SS.	10,200
Irrecoverable losses on other Fronts.	5,700
Newly Mobilised Recruits	792,000
* Estimated, based on the strength 4 days later, i.e. the strength on 4th Jan. 1942 was 7,648,000 personnel.	
^ Based on precise figures for killed, wounded, missing and POW; and an analogous estimate of unfit. © Nigel Askey, 2018	

The figure of 792,000 newly mobilised recruits is used in table <u>Ger Resources in MD & MND Units in 1941</u> (pages 140-143) for 'New (manpower) resources produced and received in the Reich from June to 31st Dec. 1941'.

---

[176] Refer Volume IIB 3. 2) g. - 'Review of Available Wehrmacht Personnel'.
[177] Ibid.
[178] Refer Volume IIB 8. - 'Wehrmacht and Waffen SS Casualties from June 1941 to February 1942'.

5) Resources Unallocated to any Deployed (D), MD or MND Units in 1941

Having determined the total resources used in all German Deployed (D), Mobilised and Deployed (MD), and Mobilised and Not Deployed (MND) combat units in 1941, and having determined the total resources in the Reich that were available in 1941, we can now easily calculate the resources that were 'left over'. For weapons and equipment, this is simply the result of subtracting the total resources allocated to MD and MND units from the total resources in the Reich that were available in the second half of 1941 (i.e. subtracting the values in column three from the sum of the values in columns four and five in table Ger Resources in MD & MND Units in 1941 (pages 140-143). For personnel and AFVs the process is slightly more involved (see paragraphs below).

The reader should note that resources allocated to Deployed (D) units from 22nd June to 4th July 1941 are already taken into account because only resources **not** allocated to Deployed (D) units are considered as being available to MD and MND units in 1941. These 'left over' resources represent the available Replacements (R) in 1941: these were the resources available to replace attrition losses in existing Wehrmacht units from June to December 1941. The sixth column in table Ger Resources in MD & MND Units in 1941 titled 'Resources unallocated to any D, MD or MND units in 1941' shows the results of these calculations. Further discussion on the **actual German Replacements (R) sent to the East Front in 1941** is covered in a separate section (refer Volume IIB 4. 7).

***

As discussed previously, German sources show that there were 1,240,000 personnel in the Replacement/Training Army (*Ersatzarmee*) in June 1941, and they were distributed as follows.[179]

Distribution of Personnel Strength within the Replacement Army, June 1941		
570,400	Regular personnel army agencies with local defence units. Comprised:	
	115,000	Field Army temporarily under command of the Replacement Army.
	210,000	LS & Guard Battalions under command of the Replacement Army.
	245,400	Regular personnel army agencies (e.g., permanent training staff, schools, etc).
108,000	Available replacement troops for the Luftwaffe and Navy.	
561,600	Available replacement troops for the Army (i.e. not Luftwaffe, Navy or Waffen SS). Comprised	
	90,000	Already in the divisional Field Replacement Battalions at the front.
	275,000	Intended for loss replacement in the Frontier Battles for July-August 1941.
	46,600	Intended for loss replacement in September 1941.
	150,000	Additional Army troops for foreseen losses through disease, unfitness for service, etc.
1,240,000	Total in the Replacement (*Ersatz*) Army*	
* Excludes 92,000 regular personnel in Luftwaffe and Navy agencies.		© Nigel Askey, 2018

Therefore, on 22nd June 1941 there were at least 669,600 personnel, with at least basic training, who were earmarked as potential Replacements (R) for combat and attrition losses. These comprised 561,600 personnel earmarked for the Army (*Heer*), and 108,000 for the *Luftwaffe* and *Kriegsmarine*. This is the figure for 'unallocated manpower' used in the sixth column of table Ger Resources in MD & MND Units in 1941. Note, however, that all 1,240,000 personnel in the Replacement Army are already included in the overall Wehrmacht and Waffen SS strength on 22nd June 1941 (i.e. are included in the 7,309,000 June 1941 strength).

We also know that at least 792,000 new personnel were mobilised (mostly conscripted) from 22nd June to 31st December 1941, and that in the German Army in 1941 the basic training course for enlisted men took at least three months.[180] Therefore it is reasonable to assume that around half of the new personnel, or 396,000 personnel, were available in 1941 for assignment to the Field Army. We also know that around 274,000 personnel were allocated to newly mobilised combat units (MD and MND units), which means around 122,000 additional 'trained' personnel were available in 1941 if the German High Command had wanted to use them as Replacements (R).

---

[179] Refer Volume IIB 3. 2) g. - 'Review of Available Wehrmacht and Waffen SS Personnel'.
[180] The pre-war trained reservist pool was still not exhausted in June 1941, so it is likely a proportion of the new personnel already had some form of basic training. Obviously, completion of officer training took much longer. Note, even 3-4 months of training was far in excess of that received by the average Red Army soldier being conscripted in 1941.

In the event, it is likely these personnel were used in rear area non-combat support units (i.e. was added to that sides' Supply Distribution Efficiency (SDE)).

Another way to look at these figures is as follows. From previous sections (Volume IIB 3. 3)), we know that approximately 42% of the Wehrmacht and Waffen SS personnel in the Reich were **not allocated** to Deployed (D) units from 22nd June to 4th July 1941.[181] This means that approximately 3,069,000 personnel were: supporting rear area functions outside those performed by the existing combat units, earmarked as replacements, in basic or advanced training, manning or supporting the Luftwaffe's aircraft and the Kriegsmarine's ships, or were unassigned. From table Ger Resources in MD & MND Units in 1941 we can see that when averaged over the entire period 22nd June to 31st December 1941, this figure increases to around 44%. That is, approximately 44% of the Wehrmacht and Waffen SS personnel in the Reich were **not allocated** to Deployed (D), MD or MND units from 22nd June to 31st December 1941.

***

In addition to the personnel situation (above), the German AFVs unallocated to any Deployed (D), MD or MND units in 1941 also requires clarifying. As well as newly manufactured AFVs, a number of older AFVs also became available due to the disbanding and reorganisation of panzer units which were Deployed (D) on 22nd June 1941. These units and their strengths are detailed in 'The German Tank MD and MND Matrix' shown in section 4. 2) a.[182] Furthermore, a number of foreign AFVs also became available from refurbished captured stock.

The tanks 'released' included:

- 8 *Panzerkampfwagen* I
- 62 *Panzerkampfwagen* II
- 31 *Panzerkampfwagen* III (37mm)
- 38 *Panzerkampfwagen* III (50mm)
- 11 *Panzerbefehlswagen AusF* E or *Ausf* H
- 16 *Panzerkampfwagen* IV
- at least 80 *Panzerkampfwagen* 35-R 731(f)
- at least 26 *Panzerkampfwagen* B-2 740(f)
- at least 53 *Panzerkampfwagen* 35-S 739(f)
- at least 119 *Panzerkampfwagen* 38-H 735(f) tanks.

These tanks are included in the 'Resources unallocated to any D, MD or MND units in 1941' column in table Ger Resources in MD & MND Units in 1941. Although very few of these tanks found their way into combat units on the East Front in 1941, they were used in panzer training units and as replacements in several occupation units in the West.

***

---

[181] Refer Volume IIB 3. 3) – 'The Total Personnel and Equipment in a Deployed (D) State in the Reich from 22nd June to 4th July 1941 - The Proportion of Total Available Resources which were in a Deployed (D) State in the Reich from 22nd June to 4th July 1941' table % of Ger Resources Deployed (D). 4,240,000 of 7,309,000 were assigned to Deployed (D) units.
[182] Refer Volume IIB 4. 2) a. – 'German Land Combat Units Mobilised from 22nd June to 31st December 1941 - The German Tank MD and MND Matrix' table Ger Tanks Available Jun-Dec 41.

6) The Proportion of Total Available Resources Allocated to Deployed (D) and Newly Mobilised Units in 1941

We are now in a position to establish the proportion of total personnel and equipment (resources) available to the Reich in the whole of 1941, which were used in Deployed (D), Mobilised and Deployed (MD), and Mobilised and Not Deployed (MND) combat units.

From the previous chapter we know the total available resources in the Reich on 1st June 1941, and the total resources allocated to Deployed (D) combat units from 22nd June to 4th July 1941.[183] From the above analysis we know the quantity of new resources produced and received in the Reich from June to 31st December 1941, and the total resources allocated to MD and MND units from 22nd June to 31st December 1941. Therefore we can determine the **percentage of total available resources in 1941 which were allocated to D, MD and MND combat units** during 1941.[184] The results of this analysis are shown in the last column of table Ger Resources in MD & MND Units in 1941 (pages 140-143).

***

a. A Comparison of the Percentages of German and Soviet Resources which were allocated to D, MD and MND Combat Units During 1941

In the Soviet FILARM model we examine in detail the proportion of total available resources which were allocated to Soviet combat units during 1941.[185] This analysis is very instructive because it highlights the weaknesses, bottlenecks and constraints in the Soviet mobilisation process during the second half of 1941.[186] This occurred because, shortly after the Axis invasion, the USSR embarked on what became the largest and fastest war mobilisation effort ever carried out by a single country: the USSR went flat out mobilising its personnel and material resources in order to literally replace the Red Army that existed in June 1941. In these circumstances the factors which limited the Soviet's mobilisation effort were physical, i.e. the number of available personnel and amount of equipment. As it turned out the most severe limiting factors were the lack of certain types of weapons and almost all forms of transport. The number of available 'trained reservists' and raw conscripts was not the most severe limiting factor (at least during 1941).[187]

As mentioned previously, in general, the German's mobilisation effort during the second half of 1941 was almost the exact opposite of the Soviet's mobilisation effort: the Germans appeared confident that their existing forces in the East would crush any serious resistance in the USSR by year's end. Consequently, the new German forces mobilised from June to December 1941 bordered on non-existent compared to the Red Army's newly mobilised forces. In other words, the primary limiting factors for the German's mobilisation effort were political, i.e. they were **not** primarily the number of available personnel and amount of equipment. In this circumstance an analysis of the German resources allocated to D, MD and MND combat units during 1941 has limited value, except to demonstrate the 'under-mobilisation' which resulted from their strategic policy decisions.

A good way to demonstrate the differences between the German and Soviet mobilisation programmes and policies during 1941 (apart from the obvious; a look at the units mobilised), is to compare the percentages of German

---

[183] Refer Volume IIA 3. 3) - 'The Proportion of Total Available Resources which were in a Deployed (D) State in the Reich from 22nd June to 4th July 1941' table % of Ger resources Deployed (D).

[184] This is calculated by dividing the 'Total resources allocated to Deployed (D) combat units' (from table % of Ger Resources Deployed (D)) plus the 'Total resources allocated to MD and MND combat units from 22nd June to 31st Dec 1941', by the total resources available to the Reich in the whole of 1941. The latter is calculated by adding the 'Total available resources in the Reich on 1st June 1941' (from table % of Ger resources Deployed (D)) to the 'New resources produced and received in the Reich from June to 31st December 1941'.

[185] Refer Volume IIIB 2. 17) – 'Soviet Mobilisation After 22nd June 1941: the Actual Strength of all Soviet Land Combat Units Mobilised from 22nd June to 31st December 1941 - The Proportion of Total Available Resources Allocated to Deployed (D) and Newly Mobilised Units in 1941'.

[186] Ibid. Volume IIIB 2. 17) a. – 'Conclusions in Regard to the Weaknesses, Bottlenecks and Constraints on the Soviet Mobilisation Process in 1941'.

[187] Between 22nd June and 31st December 1941 the Soviets called up 5,500,000 of its reservists and conscripts into active service. In addition, another 4,000,000 men and women 'volunteered' for militia or volunteer units, and most of these eventually ended up in the Red Army. Arguably, the Soviets actually 'over mobilised' because a proportion of these personnel had to be returned to the economy in 1941, and by the end of the year only about 2,000,000 people (out of the additional 4,000,000 'volunteers') actually joined the fighting troops via the people's militia. At least 1,000,000 of the original 'volunteers' were still in training with very little equipment. Refer Volume IIIB 2. 17) for details.

and Soviet resources which were allocated to D, MD and MND combat units during 1941. This is done in the following table, after some manipulation of the data to ensure that 'apples are compared with apples'.[188]

	Proportion of total available resources in 1941 which were allocated to D, MD & MND combat units.		Soviet % minus German %
	German	Soviet	
Pistols and revolvers	70%	67%	-3%
Rifles and carbines	67%	60%	-7%
Sub machine guns (SMGs)	63%	85%	22%
Machine guns (MGs) ^	59%	91%	32%
50 - 82mm mortars	72%	85%	13%
37 - 57mm anti-tank guns *	53%	83%	30%
75-152mm divisional artillery *	68%	83%	14%
100-210mm corps artillery *	53%	84%	31%
Rocket artillery *	19%	76%	57%
Armoured cars (all types) *	81%	100%	19%
Light tanks *	75%	99%	23%
Medium and heavy tanks *	70%	80%	10%
12.7 - 40mm anti-aircraft guns	58%	97%	38%
76 - 105mm anti-aircraft guns	76%	99%	23%
Horse teams	68%	80%+	12%
Unit and rear area trucks	57%	64%	7%
Unit and rear area prime movers *	72%	95%	23%
* Refer to text for an explanation of the weapons and equipment included for each side. ^ For the Germans, MGs include AFV mounted MGs. For the Soviets, MGs do not include AFV mounted MGs (i.e. the Soviet used % was even higher than 91%). © Nigel Askey, 2018			

The reader should take note, carefully, that the above table takes no account of the **relative numbers** of weapons and amount of equipment involved. For example, the German's light tanks 'percentage used' is 75% and the Soviet's light tank 'percentage used' is 99%. However, the German light tank inventory during 1941 (i.e. the total available resources in that category) involved only 3,609 tanks, while the Soviet light tank inventory during 1941 (see below for the types included) involved the massive number of 23,358 tanks![189] The percentages shown in the table above are therefore only indicative of how 'stretched' that country was in order to meet the demands of its mobilisation policy.

Some of the equipment and weapon categories are self-explanatory and all the relevant weapon types are included. However, the following categories require further explanation and/or clarification.

- **Machine guns (MGs)**. German MGs include light machine guns (LMGs) and general purpose machine guns (GPMGs) which doubled as heavy machine guns (HMGs). German MGs also include MGs mounted on tanks and other AFVs. Soviet MGs include LMGs, medium machine guns (MMGs) and quad MMG mountings, but exclude 12.7mm heavy anti-aircraft machine guns (AAMGs). The latter are included in the light anti-aircraft

---

[188] The data is taken from table <u>Ger Resources in MD & MND Units in 1941</u> (for the Germans) and table <u>Sov Resources in MD & MND units in 1941</u> (for the Soviets). The latter is detailed in Volume IIIB 7. 17). The percentages shown in this table are not absolute percentages for the German and Soviet resources which were allocated to D, MD and MND combat units during 1941: they are an average of the relevant 'weapon-type' percentages shown in the tables above. For example, the Germans used 77% of their available 50mm mortars and 68% of their available 81mm mortars. Therefore this is shown as an average of 72% of 50 - 82mm mortars used in the table. Weapons which cause an unrealistic deviation of this 'average percentage' are excluded, and these are highlighted in the text. These are usually very new weapons, the bulk of which had not yet been released to the armed forces, and rare or semi-experimental weapons which were only ever issued in small numbers.

[189] Refer Volume IIIB 1. 12) - 'The Soviet Tank Deployment Matrix' and Volume IIIB 2. 13) - 'The Soviet Tank MD and MND Matrix'. Includes all tanks that existed on 22nd June 1941 and tanks manufactured from 23rd June to 31st December 1941.

weapon category. Soviet MGs <u>exclude</u> those mounted on tanks and other AFVs, so the Soviet 'percentage used' in the table above was probably significantly higher than the 91% indicated.[190]

- **37 - 57mm anti-tank guns**. Captured French 47mm anti-tank guns and Czech manufactured 47mm anti-tank guns are excluded from the German figures. If included, the German 'percentage used' drops even further.

- **75-152mm divisional artillery**. German divisional artillery includes 75mm infantry guns, 150mm infantry guns, 75mm field guns, 75mm mountain guns, 75mm recoilless artillery guns, 105mm howitzers and 150mm howitzers. Soviet divisional artillery includes 76mm infantry guns, 76mm mountain guns, 76mm field guns, 120mm howitzers and 152mm howitzers.

- **100-210mm corps artillery**. German corps artillery includes 105mm guns (or cannon), 150mm guns, 210mm howitzers and 210mm guns. Soviet corps artillery includes 100mm guns, 107mm guns, 122mm guns, 152mm gun/howitzers and 203mm howitzers.

- **Rocket artillery**. German rocket artillery includes *Nebelwerfer* 35, 40 and 41 rocket systems. Soviet rocket artillery includes BM-8 and BM-13 rocket systems.

- **Armoured cars**. German armoured cars include: Sd Kfz 221, 222, 260, 261, 223, 231, 232, 263 and 247 armoured cars, and captured French Panhard 178s. Soviet armoured cars include: BA-27/27M, D-8, D-12, D-13, FAI/FAI-M, BA-20/20M, BAI, BA-3, BA-6/6M and BA-10/10M types.

- **Light tanks**. German light tanks include: Pz Kpfw I, Pz Kpfw I (pionier), Pz Kpfw I command tanks (*Kleine Pz Bef*), Pz Kpfw II, Pz Kpfw 35(t), Pz Kpfw 35(t) command tanks, Pz Kpfw 38(t) and Pz Kpfw 38(t) command tanks. Soviet light tanks include: T-26, OT-26, T-27, T-37, T-38, T-40, T-50, T-60 (only produced after June 1941), BT-2, BT-5, BT-7 and BT-7M tanks (and all sub-types). Note, the Soviets classified the BT tank series as fast 'cavalry tanks': their weight, armament and performance (especially the BT-7 series) meant they were arguably 'medium tanks'. However, they are classified as light tanks for this purpose.

- **Medium and heavy tanks**. German medium tanks include Pz Kpfw III (37mm guns), Pz Kpfw III (50mm guns), Pz Kpfw III command tanks (*Gross Pz Bef*), Pz Kpfw IV and StuG III assault guns (even though the latter were not strictly tanks). The Germans had no general issue heavy tanks in 1941. The Soviet medium and heavy tanks include T-28, T-35, T-34, KV-1 and KV-2 tanks (and all sub-types).

- **Prime movers**. German prime movers include Sd Kfz 6, 7, 8, 9, 10 and 11 halftracks. Soviet prime movers include all types of semi-tracked, fully-tracked or wheeled prime movers (e.g. tractors) with at least a 1 ton towing capacity.

***

We can see from the table above that the only area that the Germans 'used up' a higher proportion of their resources was rifles, and, to a lesser extent, handguns. There were three reasons for this. Firstly, the USSR possessed around 1.35 times as many rifles and carbines in June 1941 (approximately 7,740,000 vs 5,743,000). Secondly, the USSR produced around 2.38 times as many rifles and carbines in the second half of 1941 (approximately 1,570,000 vs 659,000). And thirdly, the German Army's rear area 'non-combat' units were armed to much higher degree than their Red Army counterparts. For example, most personnel in the German Army's GHQ service and supply units were armed with handguns and/or rifles. In the Red Army in 1941, the large majority of small arms were reserved for Red Army combat units or the various Soviet security forces. Soviet personnel in supply, maintenance, engineering, etc, would be lucky to have had any significant weapons. In the German FILARM model this is epitomised by around 1,043,000 rifles and carbines being allocated to rear area non-combat units during 1941. By comparison, the Soviet FILARM model has only around 392,000 rifles and carbines in rear area non-combat units during 1941. Nevertheless, the Germans still had around 2,098,000 rifles and carbines available for its Replacement Army, for any new combat units mobilised over and above those historically mobilised during 1941, and for use as Replacements (R) for attrition losses during 1941.

In every other category of weapon or equipment we can see that the USSR was far more 'stretched' to meet the demands of its mobilisation policy than the Germans; which is hardly surprising considering the scale of new Soviet forces mobilised from June to December 1941. In general, if the proportion of a particular weapon type allocated to combat units reaches 80%, then that country is in real danger of running out of that resource. This is because a proportion of the resources are always going to be unavailable or/and unserviceable, and at the same time any Replacements (R) for attrition losses also has to come out of the remaining 20%. In addition, the more complex a

---

[190] Data for Soviet MG inventories for 1941 is from G.F. Krivosheev, et al, Soviet Casualties and Combat Losses in the Twentieth Century, ed. Colonel General G.F. Krivosheev, Greenhill Books, London, 1997, p. 246, table 95. This current Russian based source excludes MGs on AFVs.

piece of equipment then the higher the proportion routinely out of service. For example, a higher proportion of existing tanks would always be in unserviceable condition compared to mortars.

For motorised transport (particularly trucks) this critical figure is closer to 50-60%. This is because these vehicles were also required to service the civilian war-economy, and in general the better vehicles went into the military (both for the Germans and the Soviets). Both the Soviets and Germans experienced shortages of trucks on the East Front in 1941-42, but in absolute terms the Germans fielded many more vehicles in their respective armed forces and war economies. In addition the average truck fielded in the Wehrmacht, and in the Reich generally, had a significantly heavier lift capacity than its Soviet counterpart.[191] Conventionally, most historians focus exclusively on the shortages of motorised transport experienced by the Wehrmacht on the East front in 1941, while at the same time ignoring, and not making no attempt to analyse, the same phenomenon in the Red Army.[192] Chapter 6. of this volume (and the relevant chapter from Volume IIIB) examines the **relative effect** of transport shortages on the forces on the East Front in detail.[193]

***

From the table above we can see that for the Germans only armoured cars reached the 80% figure. But for the Soviets only handguns, rifles and rocket artillery **did not** reach or exceed the 80% figure! In some areas the Soviets did not have anywhere near enough resources to meet the immense demands of their massive mobilisation programme. These areas included: machine guns, armoured cars, light tanks, anti-aircraft weapons, horse-drawn transport and (vitally) all forms of motorised transport. This is why a much higher proportion of Red Army combat units went into battle during 1941 well below their equipment TOE strength, why the TOEs for newly mobilised units were dramatically reduced, and why some Red Army units were equipped with old equipment in relatively poor condition.[194]

However, another way to look at the results of this analysis is that the Soviets made much greater use of their available resources than the Germans did. While the Soviets immediately embarked on what became the largest and fastest war-time mobilisation effort ever, the Germans apparently remained almost oblivious to the scale of the forces being generated against them. It was the Soviets who more quickly understood the nature of the 'war of annihilation' on the East Front, while the Germans were gambling on a victory in six months with their existing forces: a remarkable misjudgement at the strategic level. For example, we can see from the above table that even though Germany was conducting the largest invasion in history against the largest country in the world, and at the same time maintaining a war against the British Empire, they still allocated less than three quarters of their available tanks and assault guns to combat units during 1941.

Obviously, because the Germans did not mobilise many new combat units from June to December 1941, this meant that there were a lot more resources available for use as replacements for attrition and combat losses on the East Front. If this had been the primary (operational-strategic) reason for the German's paltry 1941 mobilisation programme, then it arguably could have made strategic sense. In the next section however, we will see that most of these available resources **did not** go the East Front in the second half of 1941 as Replacements (R), which only serves to compound the nonsensical nature of the German High Command's strategic policy in regards to mobilising for total war during 1941.

***

---

[191] For example, the most common truck in the USSR in 1941 was the 4x2 1.5 ton GAZ-AA (a Soviet version of the Ford AA commercial light-truck produced under licence).

[192] E.g., D. Stahel, Operation Barbarossa and Germany's Defeat in the East, Cambridge University Press, New York, 2009. Throughout this work, the author spends a great deal of effort illustrating the equipment and transport shortages within the German Army in the East in 1941. Unfortunately the entire discourse is conducted in a 'relativity vacuum': the reader is left with a feeling of amazement that the German Army made any progress at all, and with absolutely no idea of the state of the opposing Soviet forces (which, if attempting to understand Operation Barbarossa at all, is vital to comprehend).

[193] Refer Volume IIB 6. - 'The Supply Distribution Efficiency (SDE) for the Wehrmacht on the East Front from 22nd June to 31st December 1941'. Also, Volume IIIB 4. 'The Supply Distribution Efficiency (SDE) for the Soviet Armed Forces from 22nd June to 31st December 1941'.

[194] Refer Part IV 7. 17) a. – 'The Proportion of Total Available Resources Allocated to Deployed (D) and Newly Mobilised Units in 1941 - Conclusions in Regard to the Weaknesses, Bottlenecks and Constraints on the Soviet Mobilisation Process in 1941' for detail on this.

7) The Resource Replacements (R) Available to the German Army, Waffen SS, Luftwaffe Ground Forces and Naval Coastal Artillery, from 22nd June to 31st December 1941

a. The German Replacement Army (*Ersatzheer*) and the Military-Districts (*Wehrkreise*) System

Before we examine the personnel and equipment replacements available to the Wehrmacht during the second half of 1941, it is worthwhile (for reasons of context) to briefly examine the structure and function of the German Replacement Army during WWII. The German Replacement Army (*Ersatzheer* - strictly translated as the Reserve Army) was built around the so called *Wehrkreise* (military-districts) system in Germany and some of the annexed territories. The *Wehrkreise* system had special significance for the German Army because these military districts dated back to imperial times and each German division was normally associated with a single *Wehrkreis*. A particular *Wehrkreis* was often responsible for recruiting, drafting and inducting the bulk of the personnel for a newly formed division, as well as the division's initial training and the training of its replacements.

In 1935, two years after Hitler came to power, the *Reichswehr* (the armed forces of the Weimer Republic) was dissolved and replaced by the *Wehrmacht* with four high commands: the OKH, OKL, OKM and OKW.[195] However Hitler had the foresight to retain the *Wehrkreise* system, which already had contingency plans in place for the expansion of the German Army. Prior to the war, each *Wehrkreis* HQ had two components: a tactical component and a second, or deputy, component. Upon general mobilisation in 1939, the tactical HQ component became an active army corps HQ while the secondary HQ remained at home to direct training and replacement activities in the territory. The latter HQ usually included older and experienced soldiers who were no longer able to serve in front line units but were well trained and perfectly capable of efficiently administrating the *Wehrkreis* territory. In 1941-42 the average *Wehrkreis* commander was a General in his mid-sixties, which was ten to twelve years older than a typical front-line corps commander of the same rank.[196]

The various *Wehrkreise* initially reported directly to the High Command of the Army (OKH), but on 26th August 1939 the Replacement Army HQ was created in Berlin to oversee, direct and coordinate the activities of the *Wehrkreise*. The Replacement Army was commanded by Colonel General Freidrick 'Fritz' Fromm until 20th July 1944 (when it was taken over by Reichsführer SS Heinrich Himmler). Prior to the war, three *Wehrkreise* were special function HQs which had no territorial responsibilities or secondary components. Wehrkreis XIV supported the administration and training of the motorised infantry divisions, Wehrkreis XV supported the light divisions and Wehrkreis XVI supported the panzer divisions. All these HQs were upgraded to army corps HQs in mid-1939 so these *Wehrkreise* HQs ceased to exist as such, and their training and replacement functions were taken over by the remaining *Wehrkreise*. By September 1939 the number of *Wehrkreise* had increased from seven (in 1932) to sixteen; including the protectorate of Bohemia and Moravia with its HQ in Prague. During 1940 Wehrkreis XX with its HQ in Danzig and Wehrkreis XXI with its HQ in Posen were added, so the total number of *Wehrkreise* was now increased to eighteen.

On 22nd June 1941 the overall structure and status of the Replacement Army was as shown in table Rep Army. Also included in this table is Denmark because the Commander of the Replacement Army (*Chef Heeresrustung und Befehlshaber der Ersatzarmee* - Chef H.Rust. u. B.d.E.) was also the Commander of German troops in Denmark (*Befehlshaber der Deutch Truppen Danmark*).[197] Table Rep Army shows the numbered *Wehrkreise*, the relevant HQ city, the approximate German/Austrian population, the approximate area and the principal units in each *Wehrkreis*.[198] Most of the many smaller units under each *Wehrkreis*, which had no significant ground combat capability (i.e. were rear-area support units), are **not** shown. These included an assortment of: medical units and hospitals, veterinarian units, POW units and POW camps, horse training and riding schools, various vehicle and maintenance parks, MP and punishment units, and various ancillary training organisations.

---

[195] OKH (*Oberkommando des Heeres* – High Command of the Army), OKL (*Oberkommando des Luftwaffe* – High Command of the Air Force), OKM (*Oberkommando des Marine* – High Command of the Navy), and OKW (*Oberkommando des Wehrmacht* – High Command of the Armed Forces). The OKL was officially formed in 1935, and the OKW was formed in February 1938 from the War (formerly Defence) Ministry.
[196] S. W. Mitcham, Jr., German Order of Battle Volume One: 1st -290th Infantry Divisions in WWII, Stackpole Books, Mechanicsburg, PA, 2007, pp. 26-28, table 3.
[197] The territory *Militärbefehlshaber im General-Gouvernement*, covering an area of western Poland, is commonly included on diagrams showing the *Wehrkreise* system. However, this territory was separately administered in 1941 and was not (at least yet) under the control of the Chef H.Rust. u. B.d.E.
[198] Except for Wehrkreis XX, Wehrkreis XXI, Bohemia and Moravia, and MiG, the population figures relate to German and Austrian nationalities.

German Army combat units which were temporarily under the control of the Commander of the Replacement Army are shown. Most notably these included the XXXX Motorised Corps HQ, the 2nd and 5th Panzer Divisions, the 60th Motorised Division, and the 707th, 713th and 218th Infantry Divisions. The motorised and panzer divisions were refitting in Germany. Note, all German 'combat units' in the Replacement Army (including *Landesschützen* and *Wach* Battalions) are considered to be Deployed (D) units in the German FILARM model (i.e. they **are included** on the 'German Deployment Matrix' under the 'Replacement Army').

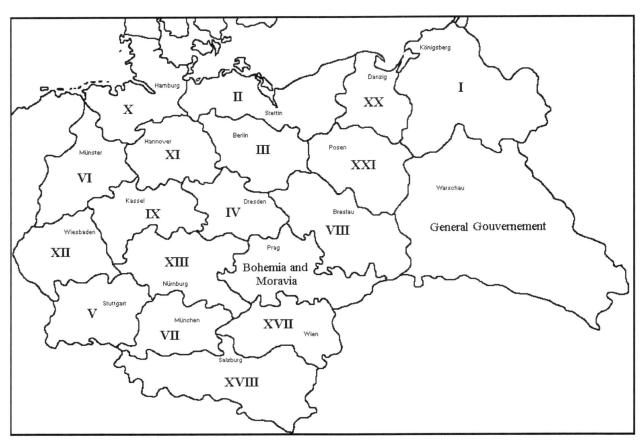

The *Wehrkreise* (military-districts) in June 1941

***

Table Rep Army	The Replacement Army, 22nd June 1941			
	Chef H.Rust. u. B.d.E. (Chef Heeresrustung und Befehlshaber der Ersatzarmee)			
Wehrkreis	Wehrkreis I	Wehrkreis II	Wehrkreis III	Wehrkreis IV
HQ City	Konigsberg	Stettin	Berlin	Dresden
Approx. Ger Population	3,967,000	3,051,000	6,950,000	7,475,000
Approx. Area (square km)	79,000	54,000	39,000	30,000
Territory	East Prussia; extended in 1939 to incl. Memel and part of Nth Poland.	Mecklenburg and Pomerania.	Altmark, Neumark, and Brandenburg.	Saxony & part of Thuringia. Later inc. part of Nth Bohemia.

	Main Units	No	Main Units	No	Main Units	No	Main Units	No
Panzer Corps HQs								
Infantry Divisions								
Panzer Divisions					5*	1		
Mot Divisions								
Replacement Divisions	141*, 151*	2	152, 192	2	143, 153	2	154, 174	2
Artillery HQs, Harko & Arko								
Ersatz-Brigades					Ers Brig. 203	1		
Guard (Wach) Battalions					722, (Wach. Kp 709)	1 1/3		
Sep HQ, Militia Divisions	401 z.b.V.	1	402 z.b.V.	1			404 z.b.V.	1
Sep HQ, Militia Regiment			23 z.b.V.	1	25 z.b.V.	1		
Landesschutzen Battalions	201, 202, 203, 206, 208, 211, 213, 215, 216, 218, 223, 224, 236, 237, 238, 239, 240, 337, 469, 555, 617, 854, 894	23	251, 252, 253, 255, 256, 260, 261, 262, 263, 267, 269, 275, 276, 280, 281, 632, 975, 976, 977, 978, 979, 980, 981, 982	24	303, 305, 307, 311, 313, 314, 316, 319, 320, 325, 326, 332, 333, 334, 336, 343, 344, 345, 346, 347, 348, 940	22	351, 353, 355, 358, 359, 360, 361, 362, 364, 365, 367, 368, 369, 371, 375, 376, 379, 383, 384, 393, 394, 395, 396, 399, 400, 942, 984, 986	28
(Mixed) Pionier Battalions								
Luft Light Flak Battalions								
Notes	* In Bohemia and Moravia 'Protektorat' Area in June 1941.				* Part of OKH Reserves.			

Wehrkreis	Wehrkreis V	Wehrkreis VI	Wehrkreis VII	Wehrkreis VIII
HQ City	Stuttgart	Munster	Munich	Breslau
Approx. Ger Population	4,640,000	11,400,000	3,000,000	8,041,000
Approx. Area (square km)	39,000	40,000	32,000	56,000
Territory	Wuerttemberg & part of Baden. In 1940 also incl. Alsace.	Westphalia and Rhineland. Also incl. part of East Belgium.	Southern Bavaria.	Silesia and the Sudetenland. Also inc. part of Moravia.

	Main Units	No	Main Units	No	Main Units	No	Main Units	No
Panzer Corps HQs								
Infantry Divisions					707*	1		
Panzer Divisions					2*	1		
Mot Divisions								
Replacement Divisions	155, 158, 165	3	156, 166	2	147, 157	2	178	1
Artillery HQs, Harko & Arko								
Ersatz-Brigades								
Guard (Wach) Battalions								
Sep HQ, Militia Divisions (+)	405 z.b.V.	1	406 z.b.V., 526(G)*	2	407 z.b.V.	1	408 z.b.V., 432 z.b.V.	2
Sep HQ, Militia Regiment	51, 55 z.b.V.	2	33, 172, 183 z.b.V.	3	71, 74, 77 z.b.V.	3	41, 84, 87 z.b.V.	3
Landesschutzen Battalions	403, 404, 406, 408, 409, 410, 411, 413, 422, 423, 424, 426, 447, 463, 473, 506, 747, 970	18	217, 254, 308, 357, 456, 460, 461, 462, 464, 465, 466, 468, 470, 471, 472, 474, 477, 478, 479, 486, 487, 488, 489, 490, 491, 492, 493, 494, 495, 857, 871, 902, 909	33	428, 435, 436, 437, 439, 440, 441, 442, 443, 444, 445, 501, 507, 510, 512, 513, 529, 530, 531, 532, 542, 543, 544,	23	370, 398, 553, 554, 556, 557, 559, 560, 561, 565, 567, 568, 584, 585, 586, 590, 593, 594, 595, 707, 752	21
(Mixed) Pionier Battalions			Bridge Guard^	5				
Luft Light Flak Battalions								
			* POW and Guard Division, w the 33rd & 76th LS Regs. ^ 15x Bridge Guard/Eng Companies (1./VI - 15./VI).		* Part of OKH Reserves.			

Table Rep Army	The Replacement Army, 22nd June 1941			
	Chef H.Rust. u. B.d.E. (Chef Heeresrustung und Befehlshaber der Ersatzarmee)			
Wehrkreis	**Wehrkreis IX**	**Wehrkreis X**	**Wehrkreis XI**	**Wehrkreis XII**
HQ City	Kassel	Hamburg	Hannover	Wiesbaden
Approx. Ger Population	5,112,000	5,100,000	3,849,000	5,540,000
Approx. Area (square km)	38,000	39,000	33,000	36,000
Territory	Hessen and part of Thuringia.	Schleswig-Holstein and Nth Hanover. Also incl. part of Danish Slesvig.	Braunschweig, Anhalt, and most of Hanover.	Eifel, the Palatinate, the Saar, part of Hesse, & Lorraine (after 1940).
	Main Units — **No**	**Main Units** — **No**	**Main Units** — **No**	**Main Units** — **No**
Panzer Corps HQs				
Infantry Divisions				
Panzer Divisions				
Mot Divisions				
Replacement Divisions	159, 179 — 2	180, 190 — 2	171, 191 — 2	148, 172, 182 — 3
Artillery HQs, Harko & Arko				
Ersatz- Brigades	Ers Brig. 201 — 1			Ers Brig. 202 — 1
Guard (*Wach*) Battalions				
Sep HQ, Militia Divisions	409 z.b.V. — 1	410 z.b.V. — 1	411 z.b.V. — 1	
Sep HQ, Militia Regiment			111 z.b.V. — 1	
Landesschutzen Battalions	602, 603, 604, 606, 608, 609, 612, 613, 614, 616, 619, 620 621, 622, 624, 631, 633, 634, 635, 642, 643 — 21	232, 233, 234, 496, 497, 498, 499, 653 655, 659, 660, 661, 664, 665, 666, 675, 676, 679, 680, 681, 682, 683 — 22	701, 704, 706, 708, 710, 711, 712, 715, 716, 718, 719, 720, 721, 739, 740, 741 — 16	432, 433, 434, 446, 24 759, 765, 775, 776, 777, 778, 779, 780, 781, 782, 783, 784, 785, 786, 787, 788, 789, 861, 880, 881
(Mixed) Pionier Battalions				Bridge Guard* — 5
Luft Light Flak Battalions				
Notes				* 15x Bridge Guard/Eng Companies, (1./XII - 15./XII).

Wehrkreis	**Wehrkreis XIII**	**Wehrkreis XVII**	**Wehrkreis XVIII**	**Wehrkreis XX**
HQ City	Nuremberg	Vienna	Salzburg	Danzig
Approx. Ger Population^	4,371,000	4,404,000	2,800,000	2,159,000
Approx. Area (square km)	50,000	34,000	53,000	26,000
Territory	Northern Bavaria, and part of western Bohemia.	Northern Austria, and part of southern Moravia.	Southern Austria,	Fmr Danzig Free State, and the western part of East Prussia.
	Main Units — **No**	**Main Units** — **No**	**Main Units** — **No**	**Main Units** — **No**
Panzer Corps HQs		40* — 1		
Infantry Divisions	713* — 1			
Panzer Divisions				
Mot Divisions		60^,** — 1		
Replacement Divisions	173, 193 — 2	177, 187 — 2	188 — 1	
Artillery HQs, Harko & Arko		128^ — 1		
Ersatz- Brigades		Ers Brig. 204 — 1		
Guard (*Wach*) Battalions				603 — 1
Sep HQ, Militia Divisions	413 z.b.V. — 1	417 z.b.V. — 1		428 z.b.V. — 1
Sep HQ, Militia Regiment		174 z.b.V. — 1		
Landesschutzen Battalions	801, 804, 805, 806, 807, 810, 814, 819, 820, 823, 824, 825, 826, 827, 828, 829, 840, 841, 842, 843, 844 — 21	851, 856, 862, 864, 866, 870, 872, 873, 875, 876, 878, 879, 890, 891, 892, 893, 896, 897, 898, 899 — 20	877, 895, 910, 921, 5 922	259, 265, 354, 363, 9 397, 713, 714, 717, 985
(Mixed) Pionier Battalions		(Vienna and Krems) Br 1		
Luft Light Flak Battalions		76^ — 1		
Notes	* Part of OKH Reserves, sent to Crete in 1941.	* Part of OKH Reserves. ^ Attached to 40th Pz Corps ** Had the 660 Mot Bridging Column B attached.		^ Mostly Polish population.

Table Rep Army	The Replacement Army, 22nd June 1941			
	Chef H.Rust. u. B.d.E. (Chef Heeresrustung und Befehlshaber der Ersatzarmee)			
Wehrkreis	Wehrkreis XXI	Bohemia & Moravia*	Danemark	Totals
HQ City	Posen	Prague	Copenhagen	
Approx. Population^	4,535,000	7,200,000		93,594,000^
Approx. Area (square km)	44,000	49,000		771,000
Territory	The Polish Corridor	German occupied part of Czechoslovakia.		
	Main Units　No	Main Units　No	Main Units　No	
Panzer Corps HQs				1
Infantry Divisions			218　1	3
Panzer Divisions				2
Mot Divisions				1
Replacement Divisions			160　1	31
Artillery HQs, Harko & Arko				1
Ersatz-Brigades				4
Guard (Wach) Battalions				2 1/3
Sep HQ, Militia Divisions (+)	429 z.b.V., 431 z.b.V.　2	539 z.b.V., 540 z.b.V.　2		19
Sep HQ, Militia Regiment	53 z.b.V.　1	72, 182 z.b.V.　2		19
Landesschutzen Battalions	301, 310, 312, 317, 342, 356, 475, 476, 610, 662, 723, 821　12	373, 374, 504, 618, 822, 855, 905, 911, 912, 983　10		361
(Mixed) Pionier Battalions				11
Luft Light Flak Battalions				1
Notes	Mostly Polish population.	* Bohemia and Moravia 'Protektorat': the German occupied part of Czechoslovakia.		^ German & Austrian population, c 80,100,000

	MB im General-Gouvernement* (also abbreviated MiG)	MB Frankreich*	
HQ City	Warsaw		
Approx. Pol Population	c 18,000,000		
Approx. Area (square km)	142,000		
Territory	Occupied Poland		
	Main Units　No	Main Units　No	
Panzer Corps HQs			
Infantry Divisions			
Panzer Divisions			
Mot Divisions			
Replacement Divisions			
Artillery HQs, Harko & Arko			
Ersatz-Brigades			
Guard (Wach) Battalions			
Sep HQ, Militia Divisions			
Sep HQ, Militia Regiment*	103 z.b.V.　1		
Landesschutzen Battalions*	268, 377, 405, 515, 709, 818, 874　7	381, 392　2	* MB im General-Gouvernement (Occupied Poland, also abbreviated MiG), and MB Frankreich (Military Governor in France), did not report directly to the Chef H.Rust. u. B.d.E., but the LS units listed here were in these districts and were part of the Replacement Army (Ersatzarmee) on 22nd June 1941.
(Mixed) Pionier Battalions			
Luft Light Flak Battalions			^ Except for Wehrkreis XX, Wehrkreis XXI, Bohemia & Moravia, and MiG, the population figures relate to German and Austrian nationalities.
Notes			

In June 1941 the Replacement Army's troop training and replacement activities was centred around 31 replacement divisions, and to a lesser extent, 18 special purpose (zbV) infantry division HQs. The replacement divisions were non-combat formations, but were still organised along traditional army lines. They were large formations which typically included the following.

- A divisional HQ.

- Around four replacement (*Ersatz*) regiments, each with up to four replacement infantry battalions.

- A replacement artillery regiment with up to five replacement artillery battalions and a replacement artillery observation battalion.

- A replacement reconnaissance regiment HQ with two or more replacement mounted-infantry battalions and/or replacement bicycle infantry battalions.

- A replacement engineering (*pionier*) battalion (which was sometimes fully motorised).

- A fully motorised replacement anti-tank battalion (which was sometimes horse-drawn).

- A replacement signals battalion (which was sometimes fully motorised).

- A replacement maintenance and supply battalion.

- Sometimes, a replacement construction battalion attached.

- Sometimes, one or more *Landesschützen* (LS - local defence force/militia) battalions attached.

The special purpose (zbV) infantry division HQs usually only controlled *Landesschützen* battalions, although they sometimes had up to 25 of these LS battalions attached.

The German *Wehrkreise* system has traditionally received little attention from WWII historians. This is most likely due to the fact that it operated quietly and effectively in the background for almost the whole of WWII. It was actually a highly evolved and efficient mechanism for mobilising and training new divisions, as well as generating and training their replacements. The *Wehrkreise* system functioned so well that the Army did very little to change its actual operations from the beginning of the war until late 1942. From late 1942 the *Wehrkreise* HQs lost some of their training functions, but they remained the primary source of replacements for German divisions. Equally important was that the *Wehrkreise* remained responsible for the rebuilding and refitting of shattered and worn out divisions: a responsibility that became progressively more vital and difficult as the war wore on.

The achievements of the Replacement Army and the *Wehrkreise* system speaks for itself: consider the following table.[199]

German Army and Waffen SS Strength Change from 1935 to 1944			
	Army	**Waffen SS**	**Total**
Strength 1935	100,000		**100,000**
Strength 1939	3,740,000	23,000	**3,763,000**
Strength 1942	5,750,000	190,000	**5,940,000**
Strength 1944	6,510,000	590,000	**7,100,000**
Strength 1945	5,300,000	c 500,000	**5,800,000**
Army and Waffen SS Casualties: 1st Sep. 1939 to 31st Jan. 1945*			**Total**
Dead through enemy action.			**1,622,561**
Dead from other causes.			**160,347**
Wounded.			**4,145,863**
Missing and POW			**1,646,316**
Approx. casualties who remained in the Wehrmacht and Waffen SS.			**2,736,270**
Total irrecoverable losses for the duration of the war.			**4,838,817**
Army and Waffen SS Recruits; Mobilised			**6,876,000**
from 1st September 1939 to 31st January 1945			
* Includes Luftwaffe field divisions, parachute units and foreign volunteer units.			

[199] Compiled from: The Oxford Companion to WWII, Dear, I.C.B. (ed.), Oxford University Press, New York, 2001, Tables 8 and 9, pp. 370 -371. Ref: *Bundesarchiv-Militararchiv*, RM 7/810 D, OKW/WFSt/Org (V b) Nr. 743/45 v. 17.3.1945.

Despite sustaining horrendous casualties, the German Army and Waffen SS grew from around 3,763,000 personnel to around 7,100,000 in the space of five years.[200] If we assume two thirds of the wounded returned to some sort of active service, and around one million non-German/Austrian nationals served in the Wehrmacht and Waffen SS, then the *Wehrkreise* system 'generated' at least 5,876,000 (mostly trained) soldiers from September 1939 to January 1945! Even this staggering number is a low estimate because it excludes *Luftwaffe* aircrew and *Kriegsmarine* losses, although these losses were far lower and their replacements tended to come from specialised training schools. It is also likely that a large proportion of the foreign nationals serving in the Wehrmacht and Waffen SS received their initial training via the *Wehrkreise* system.

In fact, the German Replacement Army and *Wehrkreise* system was probably one of the few German military-economic organisations that proved more efficient and effective than its Western Allied counterparts. This is illustrated by several points. Firstly, Germany's and Austria's pre-war population was only around 79,700,000.[201] Secondly, the UK, with a pre-war population of over 47,000,000, sustained only 755,400 military casualties during WWII; and yet from 1943 onwards the various British Army commands repeatedly complained about the lack of trained replacements and were always concerned about casualties and manpower shortages.[202] Thirdly, the US, with a pre-war population of over 133,400,000, sustained 1,215,900 military casualties during WWII.[203] Clearly, the UK and US replacement systems were nowhere near as stretched as those of the Germans, and yet their forces too often expressed difficulty finding suitable trained replacements for their combat losses. It is no exaggeration to state that, had it not been for the *Wehrkreise* system the Third Reich would never have been able to keep its forces in the field for anything like as long as it did.

As a last comment (and food for thought) on this line of reasoning, consider the following. The USSR had a pre-war population of around 209,300,000 people, suffered an incredible 29,629,205 military casualties (with at least 11,285,057 irrecoverable), and still fielded a Red Army with over 6,461,000 men and women in January 1945.[204] According to these numbers alone, it was the Soviet mobilisation and replacement systems that were the most 'successful' and 'effective'. However very few regimes had the coercive powers of the Soviet state; and given the casualty numbers above and the (training) condition of many Red Army soldiers thrown into the front line, I will let the reader draw their own conclusions about the Soviet 'personnel replacement systems' during WWII.

***

---

[200] The Oxford Companion figures for the Waffen SS in 1944 and 1945 (600,000 and 830,000, respectively) have not been used. These figures, and Waffen SS figures in general after 1942, appear to contain a great many ancillary and SS police personnel. It is probable Himmler was trying to grow his 'empire' and boost his prestige in the Nazi hierarchy, but by 1944 the large majority of the SS personnel were not the elite Waffen SS soldiers they had been from 1939 to 1943.

[201] US Library of Congress. Results of German 1939 census.

[202] The Oxford Companion to WWII, Dear, I.C.B. (ed.), Oxford University Press, New York, 2001, UK tables 1 and 5, pp. 884 and 898. Also J. Ellis, WWII a Statistical Survey, Facts on File Inc, New York, 1993, table 51, p. 254.

[203] J. Ellis, WWII a Statistical Survey, Facts on File Inc, New York, 1993, table 51, p. 254.

[204] G.F. Krivosheev, et al, Soviet Casualties and Combat Losses in the Twentieth Century, Colonel General G.F. Krivosheev (ed.), Greenhill Books, London, 1997. Tables 69 and 72, pp. 97 and 101. Also, B.V. Sokolov, The Journal of Slavic Military Studies, Volume 9 March 1996 No 1, Frank Cass, London, pp. 168-171. Also, an additional 16-17 million Soviet civilians died in WWII. Note, the Red Army was the only army in WWII to field significant numbers of women in their front line combat units.

i. German Armed-Forces Auxiliary (*Wehrmachtsgefolge*) Organizations

As a final aside to this section, it is also worth reviewing some of the German armed-forces auxiliary (*Wehrmachtsgefolge*) organizations. This is because these organisations tended to facilitate the work and aims of the Replacement Army (often with initial military training), or otherwise worked directly with the Replacement Army on Germany's home front. In addition, in the desperate days of late 1944-45 a great many of the personnel in the *Wehrmachtsgefolge* suddenly found themselves to be fully fledged members of the Wehrmacht.

During WWII there was an extensive network of these auxiliary organizations, and their role was to provide the ancillary services (in support of the war effort) that normally fell outside the responsibility of the Wehrmacht or Waffen-SS. These functions included: security, garrison, air-raid civil defence, air-raid early warning, anti-aircraft support, ambulance-medical, fire-fighting, munitions distribution, transportation, construction, combat-engineering assistance, and railroad repair. Many of these organizations also included a significant proportion of women; these included communication specialists, red-cross workers and civil defence volunteers. The organisations listed below were by no means all such organizations that existed during WWII, but they are those that most directly supported the Wehrmacht and the war in general during WWII.

Organisations that were officially *Wehrmachtsgefolge* in 1941 included:

- **The Air Protection Warning Service (*Luftschutzwarendienst* - LSW).**

The Air Protection Warning Service (*Luftschutzwarndienst*, LSW) functioned as part of the Civil Air Defence (*Ziviler Luftschutz*) forces. It was responsible for the timely warning of incoming air-raids and functioned 24 hours a day. Reports were taken from its members, from the Flight Warning Service (*Flugmeldedienst*), and from various related security forces. This information was then processed, and air-raid sirens were activated prior to an expected attack.

Additional activities included observation (and reporting of) of enemy bomber formations, assistance in searchlight operation and helping to keep order among civilians affected by the bombing raids. Most LSW volunteers (including many women) were assembled in the cities and towns that held the highest risk of being bombed. These population centres were divided into area 'blocks' with unit leaders assigned to each individual section of a city. The LSW volunteer teams were expected to operate rotating shifts and sleep in large concrete bunkers that held all the provisions and amenities of a regular fortification. These also included the huge flak towers built around German cities upon which anti-aircraft batteries were stationed. In 1942, the LSW organisation was incorporated into the Luftwaffe.

- **The National Air Raid Protection League (*Reichsluftschutzbund* - RLB)**

The National Air Protection League (*Reichsluftschutzbund*, RLB) was formed in April 1933 and was officially announced in June of that year. Its purpose was to build the framework for a large civilian-population based air-defence organisation, and soon several hundred thousand German citizens had volunteered. The role of the RLB was to provide services related to air raid civil-defence. These included fire-fighting, setting up smoke-screens, establishing ground decoys, setting up camouflage screens and responding to any other damaging effects of air raids.

Until 1942, the organization of the RLB was divided into two main branches. These included the Self Protection Service (*Selbschutz*) and the Extended Self-Protection Service (*Erweiterter-Selbschutz*). The former encompassed all the responsibilities related to protecting families and citizens through the management of air raid shelters and fire prevention patrols. The Extended Self-Protection Service was responsible for overseeing individual buildings and facilities that did not have their own air raid protection teams. In these cases, members of the Self-Protection Service were often employees or workers who normally worked in these buildings or institutions. Overall, the RLB augmented the additional services provided by the Fire Brigade Police (*Feuerwehrpolizei*), the Security and Assistance Service (*Sicherheits und Hilfdienst*, SHD), and after 1941, the Air Protection Police (*Luftschutzpolizei*, LSP) (see below).

- **The Security and Assistance Service (*Sicherheits und Hilfdienst* - SHD)**

The Security and Assistance Service (*Sicherheits und Hilfdienst*, SHD) was formed in 1935 for the purpose of providing security, fire-fighting, decontamination, first aid, reconstruction assistance and similar services for the major population centres that were at high risk from air-raids. It contained a mobile (motorised) workforce that moved within a designated area, but was ultimately under the control of the local Order Police (*Ordungspolizei*). Following the outbreak of war, the existing SHD volunteers were conscripted as reservists who were stationed in their home cities, but who were required to rotate duty and live in temporary barracks as needed.

As the bombing raids on Germany increased in frequency and intensity, it became necessary to reorganise and enlarge the SHD. In April 1942 the new organization was renamed the Air Protection Police (*Luftschutzpolizei*, LSP). The SHD security related personnel were generally assigned to the new LSP and served directly under the Order Police (*Ordungspolizei*). Other members of the SHD were incorporated into fire-fighting, rescue, and damage control/clearing battalions that served in specialized *Luftwaffe* regiments.

- **The National Socialist Motor Corps (*Nationalsozialistischen Kraftfahrkorps* - NSKK)**

The origins of the National Socialist Motor Corps (*Nationalsozialistischen Kraftfahrkorps*, NSKK) can be traced as far back as 1923 when the SA (*Sturmabteilung* - the 'Brown Shirts') introduced a SA Motor Section (SA *Kraftfahr Abteilung*) to transport NSDAP and SA personnel to rallies and meetings.[205] In 1928 the SA Motor Section was expanded and given the title SA Motor Squadrons (*Kraftfahrstaffeln*), and in 1930 an attempt was made to create a national SA motor corps. At this time automobiles were still a luxury item in Germany and relatively few people could afford them. By requisitioning their use through volunteers and other organisations willing to support the NSDAP, the SA avoided the need to acquire funds for their purchase. The 'new' organisation was formed on 1st April 1930 and was called the National Socialist Automobile Corps (*Nationalsozialistischen Automobile Korps*, NSAK).

In early 1931 Adolf Huhnlein was appointed chief of the NSAK, and he proposed a name change to the National Socialist Motor Corps (*Nationalsozialistischen Kraftfahrkorps*, NSKK). This title became official on 1st May 1931. In June 1934 the SA leadership was 'purged' in the so called 'Night of the Long Knives', and the NSKK was promptly 'promoted' to be an official NSDAP auxiliary organization. By August 1934 the NSKK had absorbed the NSDAP's own motor pool and was given independent organisational status within the party. By 1938 the NSKK was administered across five districts and had grown to around 500,000 voluntary members. By this time the NSKK had expanded its role to include mechanics training, and promotion and understanding of motor vehicles across the Reich and in the military. In addition, many NSKK members were employed in duties that supported the local Order Police (*Ordungspolizei*) in cities where traffic control was needed.

Organisationally, the NSKK also encompassed two smaller branches within its structure: the Motor Hitler Youth (Motor-*Hitlerjugend*, HJ) and the Naval NSKK (*Marine*-NSKK). The Hitler Youth branch served to train young men in the disciplines of vehicle use and maintenance as a precursor to military service, while the Naval branch assisted the German Army with training related to small boat operations including that of landing and assault craft. Starting in September 1939, the bulk of the NSKK was organized into transport companies that moved German troops, ammunition and supplies to various locations (including directly to the front lines). In this regard they were controlled by the Wehrmacht, although the NSKK remained a party auxiliary organisation. Throughout the war the NSKK operated across Germany as well as in the occupied territories, and by late 1944 NSKK units were being dragged into front-line combat.[206]

***

Organisations that were not officially *Wehrmachtsgefolge* (at least in 1941), but were armed-forces auxiliary in nature, included:

- **The Reich Labour Service (*Reichsarbeitsdienst* - RAD)**

The Reich Labour Service (*Reichsarbeitsdienst*, RAD) was formed in June 1935 as an organisation designed to mitigate the effects of mass unemployment on the German economy.[207] It was also seen as an effective way to indoctrinate the labour force with the Nazi ideology, and accordingly it became law for all men between the ages of 18 and 24 to serve a minimum of six months in the RAD prior to their military service. In the pre-war period, the RAD was instrumental in helping to build infrastructure such as highways (the *autobahns*), airfields, military complexes, bridges and railroads.

After the invasion of Poland, the RAD became a training ground for young Germans who would be inducted into the Wehrmacht when their term of service was complete. Thus the RAD labour camps also facilitated familiarisation with military protocols and some initial military training. During the war some members of the

---

[205] NSDAP (*Nationalsozialistische Deutsche Arbeiterpartei* or National Socialist German Workers' Party, or Nazi party). The SA was the first para-military organisation to support the NSDAP (in effect an integral part of the party), and during the Nazi rise to power its tasks included providing protection for NSDAP rallies and assemblies, disrupting the meetings of the opposing parties, and violent attacks on other parties and minority groups.
[206] E.g., In September 1944, several NSKK units participated directly in the battles around Arnhem in the Netherlands during the Allied operation Market Garden.
[207] The RAD had its roots in the National Socialist Volunteer Labour Service (*Freiwillige Arbeitsdienst*, NS) which was formed in 1931.

RAD also served in the occupied countries and near the front lines. Combat related duties often included pontoon bridge construction, mine laying, bringing up ammunition, guarding prisoners, and virtually any duty normally assigned to an auxiliary unit. Later in the war (in 1944-45) many RAD units received basic combat training, and in the closing months of WWII six RAD' combat divisions' were formed for the defence of Germany.

- **The Hitler Youth (*Hitlerjugend* - HJ)**

The Hitler Youth (*Hitlerjugend*, HJ) was a National Socialist (Nazi) movement formed as early as 1922. By 1933 the HJ had embraced most of the other 'youth movements' in Germany, and had become one of the primary mechanisms for indoctrination into the Nazi ideology. The HJ organisation was a mainstay of the Nazi regime; by 1933 it already had 2.3 million members and this had increased to 7.7 million by 1939.[208] Membership of the HJ became compulsory in 1940 for all boys between the ages of ten and nineteen, while girls were required to serve until the age of twenty-one. Like the RAD, the HJ also provided the opportunity for initial military training.

As the war wore on, the young HJ members were increasingly involved in war-related duties. By 1940 these duties included assisting anti-aircraft batteries, serving as fire-fighting personnel, and working as special armed assistants of the Order Police (Ordnungspolizei). It became so common to find young HJ members in flak units that they soon became known as the 'the Flak Generation'. In the last months of WWII it was mainly the HJ which (tragically) supplied most of the children soldiers (many as young as 14) for the German *Volkssturm* units.

- **The German Red Cross (*Deutsches Rotes Kreuz* - DRK)**

The German Red Cross (*Deutsches Rote Kreuz*, DRK) was officially recognized in Geneva, Switzerland, on 27th July 1929. Like other Red Cross organizations, the DRK was responsible for providing humanitarian aid and medical assistance to the German population. In December 1937 Hitler and the NSDAP took control of the DRK, and (unfortunately) it became a legally recognized organization of the NSDAP. On 1st January 1938 the DRK established rank, insignia and uniform guidelines for the organization, and at the end of 1938 the German Red Cross officially came under the control of the Ministry of the Interior's Social Welfare Organization; becoming a de facto Nazi entity.

During WWII the DRK mostly functioned in its original humanitarian aid and medical assistance role. However, in addition to helping the civilian population and Allied POWs, it also supplied the Wehrmacht with medical facilities and ambulance services throughout the war.

- **The Todt Organisation (*Organisation Todt* - OT)**

According to a 1945 British Intelligence report, in scarcely five years the Organisation Todt (OT) carried out the most impressive construction programme since the Roman Empire.[209] More than 1,400,000 men built everything from roads, bunkers, bridges, military-buildings, industrial plants, air-fields, oil tanks, rocket launching ramps and air-raid shelters (some extremely large), to the massive U boat pens, Flak towers, and fortified defences on the Atlantic and West Wall. Amazingly, the OT remained fundamentally an engineering-construction organisation during WWII, and somehow it maintained its (relative) independence from both the NSDAP and the Wehrmacht. It was also the only organisation in the Third Reich, apart from the Hitler Youth, to bear the name of a member of the party elite.

Fritz Todt (born 1891) was Hitler's chief engineer and architect, and in 1938 he was given the task of supervising the completion of the German *Westwall* defences along the German-French frontier. To facilitate this, in June 1938 a civilian workforce was established (the OT) to provide construction labour and technical assistance to the West Wall project as well as a number of other engineering projects that were designed to develop Germany's infrastructure. The labour was sourced from a mixture of gangs from the newly built *autobahns*, the Reich Labour Service (*Reichsarbeitsdienst*, RAD) and Wehrmacht construction battalions. In short order the OT built no less than 5,000 bunkers (with some 500,000 workers) along the German-French frontier; helping to convince the French and British armies to remained where they were during 1939 and into 1940.

Until September 1939 the Organization Todt (OT) workforce consisted mainly of civilian contracted engineers, bricklayers, carpenters, and industrial machinists, who wore standard construction clothing and equipment. Following the invasion of Poland, OT members were militarized and given uniforms specifically designed to denote their OT affiliation. During 1940 and 1941 the OT followed the conquering Wehrmacht

---

[208] The Oxford Companion to WWII, Dear, I.C.B. (ed.), Oxford University Press, New York, 2001, p. 425.
[209] Ibid, p. 870.

across Europe; repairing railroads, bridges, dams, road systems and bombed factories. In the Balkans it even took responsibility for the mining or ore needed by the war effort. Leadership in the field was often provided by members of the RAD or a particular Wehrmacht branch, depending on the nature of the construction project. On 17th March 1940 Todt was appointed Reich Minister for Armaments and Munitions (*Reichsminister für Bewaffnung und Munition*) while continuing his role as head of the OT. In effect, his appointment was an effort to increase the flow of arms and equipment to the Wehrmacht through improved industrial coordination. Members of the OT continued to serve in construction related projects but were now also involved in the engineering and construction support of weapon manufacturing facilities.

After mid-1940, progressively more foreign workers joined (or were forced to join) the OT. In this regard the OT became key to exploiting the 'labour' that became available in the occupied territories. The OT labour force soon grew to include foreign volunteers (sold on the clever German propaganda), POWs (mainly Soviet ones) and a great many slave (forced) labourers. Late in the war many of the OT construction sites were little more than forced labour camps. At its peak some 80% of the OT consisted of young non-Germans, and the relatively few Germans employed by the OT had an average age of 53.[210]

On 8th February 1942, Todt was killed in an air crash shortly after take-off from the Wolf's Lair (*Wolfsschanze*) airfield near Rastenburg. Hitler then appointed Albert Speer as head of all industrial manufacturing within Germany and this included leadership of the OT. Under Albert Speer's guidance the German industrial system was completely overhauled, and this did result in increased production and more efficient distribution of arms and material to the Wehrmacht. Also, under Speer's leadership, the OT grew to its maximum size. However, by 1944 the OT had become little more than a vehicle to manage and enforce the slave labour then being used all around the Reich. In the autumn of 1944 the organisation was renamed the 'Front-OT' (a token gesture) and some elements were armed and committed to the defence of the Reich. Even then, the Organization Todt was never fully integrated into either the party or the military infrastructure, and maintained its relative independence to the end.

***

---

[210] Ibid.

b. Replacements (R) available to the Wehrmacht from June to December 1941

In the FILARM model, Replacements (R) are defined as personnel and equipment allocated to rebuild units which are in a D, MD or MND state, to the current authorised TOE (Table of Organisation and Equipment) level. A unit may be below TOE strength due to loss of resources from: combat attrition, training and rear-area attrition (operational loses), or scrapping. Alternatively it may be below strength in its initial peacetime deployment and require newly mobilised resources to bring it up to full strength. The FILARM model dictates that resources allocated to D, MD or MND units cannot be used as Replacements (R) unless they go through the combat or attrition process.[211] **Here we are interested in the Reich's resources that were never initially assigned to any D, MD or MND units in 1941, but were first used as new resources to bring existing combat units up to their authorised TOE strength.**

From the previous section we established the available personnel and resources that remained unallocated to any D, MD or MND units in 1941.[212] The results of this analysis are shown in the sixth column of table Ger Resources in MD & MND Units in 1941 (pages 140-143). These are the resources (including personnel) that were available to the German ground forces as Replacements (R) from 22nd June to 31st December 1941. Obviously Replacements (R) generated from the recycled remnants of almost destroyed combat units are **not** included here.[213]

The resources shown in the above table are expressed in terms of historical records of personnel and equipment. However, we need the German replacements to be expressed in terms of the 'German Personnel and Equipment Resource Database' because these will then be the values used for German Replacements (R) in any simulation of Operation Barbarossa. This process is the reverse of the process where data presented in terms of the Barbarossa Simulation's Resource Database is made comparable to data obtained from historical records of personnel and equipment.[214] The first column in table Ger Replacements 1941 (shown below, on pages 172-175) shows the resources and personnel available as Replacements (R) expressed in terms of the German Personnel and Equipment Resource Database.[215]

***

[211] Refer Volume I Part I 3. - 'The Concepts and General Structure of the Integrated Land and Air Resource Model - The Structure of the Fully Integrated Land and Air Resource Model (FILARM)', for a full description of the Replacement (R) component of the FILARM model, and the 'combat', 'attrition' and 'disband-shatter' processes.

[212] Refer Volume IIB 4. 5) – 'Resources Unallocated to any Deployed (D), MD or MND Units in 1941'.

[213] Note, that the FILARM model enables additional Replacements (R) to be formed from resources left over from almost destroyed combat units. This process is integrated into the FILARM model's structure, and the number of these additional Replacements (R) will depend on the strategic and operational success or failure of the German/Soviet player-commander. Refer Volume I Part I 3., the 'combat', 'attrition' and 'disband-shatter' process in the FILARM model.

[214] Refer Volume IIB 3. 3) – 'The Total Personnel and Equipment in a Deployed (D) State in the Reich from 22nd June to 4th July 1941 - The Proportion of Total Available Resources which were in a Deployed (D) State in the Reich from 22nd June to 4th July 1941' for details.

[215] The data for the first column is from Volume IIB 4. 5), table Ger Resources in MD & MND Units in 1941; sixth column.

Table Ger Replacements 1941

The Resource Replacements (R) Available to the German Army, Waffen SS, Luftwaffe Ground Forces and Naval Coastal Artillery, from 22nd June to 31st December 1941

Database unit	Replacements (R), available to the Wehrmacht; 22nd June to 31st Dec 1941	% of available Replacements (R) sent to the East Front during 1941	East Front Replacements (R) from 22nd June to 31st Dec 1941	Small arms distribution (usage) by database units — Pi	Ri	SMG	LMG	Personnel used by each type of Replacement (R)	Average No. of new personnel used in each Replacement (R) unit	Average number of Replacements (R) / day 22/6/41 to 31/12/41	Begin day	End day
Allocated Manpower	669,600	93%	626,000									
Heavy Rifle Sqd			29,720	2	7	1	1	297,200	10	154	1	194
Light Rifle Sqd			1,740	2	9	1		17,400	10	9	1	194
Motor Cycle Sqd			4,830	2	7	1		38,640	8	25	1	194
Bicycle Sqd			970	2	9	1		9,700	10	5	1	194
Cavalry Sqd			770	2	9	1		7,700	10	4	1	194
Eng Sqd			2,900	2	8	4	2	40,600	14	15	1	194
Light Eng Sqd			1,160	2	12	2		16,240	14	6	1	194
Ferry Bridging Sqd			970	1	5			4,850	5	5	1	194
Military Police Sqd			770	2	3	2		3,850	5	4	1	194
Irregular Sqd			970	1	10			9,700	10	5	1	194
Rail Repair Sqd			770	1	5			3,850	5	4	1	194
HMG	102,367		12,740	2	2			25,480	2	66	1	194
LMG	▼ MGs		19,300	2	2			19,300	1	100	1	194
AT Rifle	23,187	24%	5,536	1	1			5,536	1	30	1	186
50mm Mor	4,483	69%	3,088	1	2			6,176	2	16	1	194
81mm Mor	4,186	65%	2,702	1	3			10,808	4	14	1	194
Horse Team	96,161	6%	5,597		3			11,194	2	29	1	194
Unit Trucks	508,224	2%	11,580		3			23,160	2	60	1	194
Light Transport	2,026,038	0.3%	5,790	1	2			5,790	1	30	1	194
Light Halftrack	3,512	77%	2,702	1	2			5,404	2	14	1	194
Medium Halftrack	489	79%	386	1	4			772	2	2	1	194
Heavy Halftrack	996	78%	772	1	6			2,316	3	4	1	194

% of all available small arms (and motorcycles) allocated to D, MD, MND and R units from 22nd June to 31st Dec 1941

	Total	%
Total small arms used by all (R) units		
Pistols and Revolvers (Pi)	196,986	88%
Rifles and Carbines (Ri)	507,399	75%
Sub Machine Guns (SMG)	56,629	81%
MGs (incl AFV mounted)	67,048	86%
Motorcycles used by all (R) units:		
Motorcycles (including sidecars and Sd.Kfz.2s)	38,640	75%

37mm ATG	5,234	63%	3,281	2	4	3	9,843	17	1	194
50mm ATG	1,554	87%	1,351	2	5	4	5,404	7	1	194
47mm ATG	761	76%	579	2	4	4	2,316	3	1	194
28mm sPzb 41	102	57%	58	2	2	2	116	1	1	59
75mm Inf G	1,493	65%	965	2	4	3	2,895	5	1	194
150mm Inf G	418	56%	234	2	6	6	1,404	2	1	118
75mm Gun	251	22%	55	2	6	4	220	1	1	56
105mm How	1,336	72%	965	2	6	8	7,720	5	1	194
105mm IG40	180	11%	20	2	6	4	80	1	41	61
150mm How	784	74%	579	2	8	12	6,948	3	1	194
105mm Gun	289	73%	210	2	8	12	2,520	2	1	106
150mm Gun	58	59%	34	2	14	14	476	1	10	44
210mm How	213	73%	156	2	14	17	2,652	1	14	170
210mm Gun	23	39%	9	2	16	20	180	1	19	28
240mm How	2	100%	2	2	16	25	50	1	41	43
240mm Gun	0			2	22	30	0			
305mm How	7	43%	3	2	26	40	120	1	41	44
355mm How	0			2	26	40	0			
600mm How	2	0%	0	4	32	60	0			
150-200mm Rail G	23	0%	0	4	14	20	0			
210-280mm Rail G	6	33%	2	6	28	40	80	1	50	52
380+mm Rail G/M	0			8	32	40	0			
100-280mm Coast G			Estimate 12	2	8	10	120	1	72	84
Nebelwerfer 35	748 →	77%	191	1	4	3	573	1	1	192
Nebelwerfer 40			386	1	4	3	1,158	2	1	194
Nebelwerfer 41	753	77%	579	2	6	7	4,053	3	1	194
28/32cm Rockets			Est 110,000 *	1	2	0	0	570	1	194

The Resource Replacements (R) Available to the German Army, Waffen SS, Luftwaffe Ground Forces and Naval Coastal Artillery, from 22nd June to 31st December 1941

Database unit	Replacements (R), available to the Wehrmacht; 22nd June to 31st Dec 1941	% of available Replacements (R) sent to the East Front during 1941	East Front Replacements (R) from 22nd June to 31st Dec 1941	Pi	Ri	SMG	LMG	Average No. of new personnel used in each Replacement (R) unit	Personnel used by each type of Replacement (R)	Average number of Replacements (R) / day	Begin day	End day
Sd Kfz 250 APC	350	82%	286	1	1	1	1	2	572	2	51	194
Sd Kfz 251 APC	262	84%	220	1		2	1	2	440	2	10	120
Sd Kfz 254 AOP	1			2	2	3	1	2	0	2		
Sd Kfz 221 A Cars	6			1		2	1	2	0	2		
Sd Kfz 222 A Cars	105	62%	65	1		2	1	2	130	1	10	75
Sd Kfz 260/261 AC	29	83%	24	2		3		2	48	1	10	34
Sd Kfz 223 A Cars	55	69%	38	1		2	1	2	76	1	1	39
Sd Kfz 231/232 AC	38	73%	28	2	1	3	1	2	56	1	20	48
Sd Kfz 263 A Cars	0			2	1	3	1	3	0			
Sd Kfz 247 A Cars	50	48%	24	2	1	3		3	72	1	121	145
Panhard 178	0			1	1	2	1	2	0			
Pz Kpfw I	408	10%	42	1	1	1	2	1	42	1	133	175
Kleine Pz Bef I	30			1	1	2	1	2	0			
Pz Kpfw II	130	53%	69	1	1	2	1	2	138	1	41	110
Pz Kpfw III (37mm)	59			2	1	2	2	3	0			
Pz Kpfw III (50mm)	1,095	35%	388	2	1	2	2	3	1,164	2	1	194
Pz Bef III (*Gross*)	45	56%	25	2	1	3	1	3	75	1	41	66
Pz Kpfw IV	282	36%	102	2	1	2	2	3	306	1	10	112
Pz Kpfw 38(t)	431	56%	241	2		2	2	2	482	2	10	131
Pz Bef 38(t)	10 →			2		2	1	2	0			
Pz Kpfw 35(t)	10 →	40%	4	2		2	2	2	8	1	41	45
Pz Bef 35(t)				2		2	1	2	0			
StuG III Assault Gun	285	5%	15	2		2		2	30	1	24	39
Sd Kfz 252	218	32%	70	1	1	1	1	2	140	1	24	94
Sd Kfz 253	32	89%	28	2		2	1	2	56	1	1	29

Small arms distribution (usage) by database units: Pi, Ri, SMG, LMG

Tank Replacements (R) sent to DAK; 1st June 1941 to Dec 1941*

Pz Kpfw II	29
Pz Kpfw III (50mm)	135
Pz Bef Wg III	3
Pz Kpfw IV	11

* Note, 11 Pz II and 34 Pz III were sunk en route to North Africa. Also 54 Panzers arrived 5th January 1942 (but were shipped in December 1941).

Item	Total	%									
15cm sIG33 SP Guns	0			2	4	2	3	0			
Pz Jager I (47mm)	4	100%	4	1		2	2	8	1	1	5
47mm, Pz Kpfw 35R(f)	93	39%	36	1		2	2	72	1	1	37
Pz Kpfw 35R(f)	at least 47	11%	5	1	2	1	1	5	1	1	6
SP 88 mm AAG	14	29%	4	2	6	2	8	32	1	41	45
105mm K18 Pz Sfl IVa	0			2	1	2	3	0			
Pz Kpfw II (F)	42			1	2	1	2	0			
Pz Kpfw B2	0			2	2	1	2	0			
Pz Kpfw B2 (F)	0			2	2	1	2	0			
Pz Kpfw 35-S	at least 36			1	2	1	2	0			
Pz Kpfw 38H	at least 95			1	1	1	1	0			
Pz I (Pio)	(Inc in Pz Kpfw I Figures)			1	1	2	1	0			
Sd Kfz 300	49	100%	49				0	0	49	1	2
Pz IV Bridge Layer	1			1	2		2	0			
Pz IV Ammo Carrier	10			1	2		2	0			
Armoured Train	0			10	40	12	200	0			
20 mm AAG	4,757	28%	1,158	1	2		2	2,316	6	1	194
20mm Quad AAG	584	9%	24	1	4		4	96	1	10	34
37 mm AAG	889	19%	124	1	4		3	372	1	10	134
88-105mm AAG	1,409	28%	386	1	6		8	3,088	2	1	194
Truck 20mm AAG	(Inc in 20 mm AAG Figures)	100%	120	1	4		2	240	1	1	121
Sd Kfz 10/4	52		52	2	5		3	156	1	41	93
Sd Kfz 6/2	54	81%	44	2	5		4	176	1	41	85
Sd Kfz 7/1	35	86%	30	2	8		5	150	1	41	71
AA Searchlights	86		86	1	6		10	860	1	72	158
Tot. Personnel	**626,000**										

^ The approximate no. of 28cm *Wurfkorper Spreng* (High Explosive Mortar) and 32cm *Wurfkorper Flamm* (Flame) rockets supplied. The rockets could be mounted and fired individually.

© Nigel Askey, 2018

c. Replacements (R) Actually Issued to the German Ground Forces on the East Front During 1941

In the previous section, and from the Soviet FILARM model, we have seen clear evidence that the Soviet High Command (the Stavka) quickly grasped the seriousness of the situation facing the USSR in June-July 1941, and almost immediately embarked on a massive mobilisation program.[216] It was the Soviets who more quickly understood the nature of the 'war of annihilation' (and attrition) on the East Front, while the Germans were essentially gambling on a victory in six months with their existing forces. One consequence of this for the Soviets was that any resources not allocated to any D, MD or MND combat units, were **available and almost entirely used** as Replacements (R): the resources that remained unallocated were relatively insignificant. This is reflected in the Soviet FILARM model.

For the Germans, however, not all the resources that remained unallocated to any D, MD or MND combat units were used as Replacements (R): a great many were retained in the West during 1941. In the event, the availability of some of these resources (such as tanks and assault guns) was especially critical to the success of the 1941 campaign in the East. This state of affairs is shown in the second two columns of table Ger Replacements 1941. The second column shows the proportion of available Replacements (R) that were dispatched to the East Front from June to December 1941.

***

i. German Personnel Losses (Casualties) and Replacements

As discussed previously, German sources show that there were 1,240,000 personnel in the Replacement/Training Army (*Ersatzarmee*) in June 1941, and they were distributed as follows.[217]

Distribution of Personnel Strength within the Replacement Army, June 1941		
570,400	Regular personnel army agencies with local defence units. Comprised:	
	115,000	Field Army temporarily under command of the Replacement Army.
	210,000	LS & Guard Battalions under command of the Replacement Army.
	245,400	Regular personnel army agencies (e.g., permanent training staff, schools, etc).
108,000	Available replacement troops for the Luftwaffe and Navy.	
561,600	Available replacement troops for the Army (i.e. not Luftwaffe, Navy or Waffen SS). Comprised	
	90,000	Already in the divisional Field Replacement Battalions at the front.
	275,000	Intended for loss replacement in the Frontier Battles for July-August 1941.
	46,600	Intended for loss replacement in September 1941.
	150,000	Additional Army troops for foreseen losses through disease, unfitness for service, etc.
1,240,000	Total in the Replacement (*Ersatz*) Army*	
* Excludes 92,000 regular personnel in Luftwaffe and Navy agencies.		© Nigel Askey, 2018

Therefore, on 22nd June 1941 there were at least 669,600 personnel, with at least basic training, who were earmarked as potential Replacements (R) for combat and attrition losses. These comprised 561,600 personnel earmarked for the Army (*Heer*), and 108,000 for the *Luftwaffe* and *Kriegsmarine*.

In general, these figures concur with other sources. The German High Command's planners for Operation Barbarossa ensured there were already 90,000 men in the field replacement battalions already at the front on 22nd June or in the process of being transferred.[218] In addition, they envisaged another 275,000 casualties in the period July to August 1941; by which time they expected the 'road to Moscow to be open' and the USSR to be on the verge of collapse.[219] The Germans also made contingency plans for an additional 200,000 casualties in the month of September 1941, when the battle for the Moscow-Gorki space was initially planned to occur.[220]

---

[216] Volume IIB 4. 6) and Volume IIIB 2. - 'Soviet Mobilisation After 22nd June 1941'.

[217] Volume IIB 3. 2) g. - 'Review of Available Wehrmacht and Waffen SS Personnel'.

[218] Boog, H., et al., Germany and the Second World War, Volume IV: The Attack on the Soviet Union, Clarendon Press (Oxford University Press), New York, 1996, p. 317.

[219] Ibid. Also, R. H. S. Stolfi, Hitler's Panzers East: WWII Reinterpreted, University of Oklahoma Press, Norman and London, 1991, p. 155.

[220] Ibid. (Boog, H., et al, and R. H. S. Stolfi).

Of these total replacements, the Luftwaffe claimed 90,000.[221]. If we assume that there were 18,000 replacements reserved for the *Kriegsmarine* (i.e. 108,000 minus 90,000), then the above figures indicate that the OKW had had set aside at least 583,000 replacements to support military operations from June to October 1941, or 87% of the replacements available in the Replacement Army in June 1941.

***

Chapter 8. of this volume contains an analysis of the casualties (killed, wounded, missing, POW and unfit/sick) that occurred in the Wehrmacht and Waffen SS from June 1941 to February 1942. It includes records of all the casualties suffered on the East Front as well as those from the western fronts. The table below shows the German casualties suffered on the East Front from 22nd June to 31st December 1941.[222]

Table Total Casualties East Front 1941								
Wehrmacht and Waffen SS* Personnel Killed, Wounded, Missing, POW and Unfit^ on the East Front from 22nd June to 31st Dec. 1941 (including *Befehlsstelle Finnland* forces on the East Front).								
	22nd June-30th June	July	Aug.	Sept.	Oct.	Nov.	Dec.	Total, 22nd June - 31st Dec. 41*
Killed	9,503	38,669	41,592	30,089	24,987	18,327	15,285	**186,452**
Wounded	30,482	128,250	149,298	108,485	89,688	67,693	59,283	**655,179**
MIA & POW	2,995	9,619	8,129	5,177	3,974	3,381	4,882	**40,157**
Unfit^	54,000	17,000	31,000	56,800	62,000	73,092	90,907	**395,799**
Tot., Armed Services	**96,980**	**193,538**	**230,019**	**200,551**	**180,649**	**162,493**	**170,357**	**1,277,587**

* To the Total is added 43,000 Waffen SS casualties; made up of 8,000 killed, 22,000 wounded, 2,000 missing & POW and 11,000 unfit. These casualties represented 27% of the Waffen SS strength in June 1941 (compared to 23% for the Army (*Heer*)).

^ Includes personnel made unfit due to sickness, disease, accidents and frostbite (i.e., losses not directly attributable to enemy action). Excludes 'unfit' personnel which were not transported out of the Army Group sectors for treatment.   © Nigel Askey, 2018

Chapter 8. also includes an analysis of the proportion of wounded and unfit/sick casualties that were recuperated and remained in the Wehrmacht based on the OKW medical records. These records indicate Wehrmacht casualties and Army (*Heer*) recuperated from June 1941 to March 1942, and are shown in table Casualties East 41, Recup and Rep (below).[223]

In regards to casualties sustained during the first year of war in the East, the medical conclusions that were drawn from this analysis (that are relevant here) are as follows:

- Around 66% of the wounded remained in the Wehrmacht or Waffen SS, and approximately 56% returned to active duty (i.e. were capable of front-line duty) later in the war.

- Around 60% of 1941 wounded returned to active service within six months.[224]

- On average it took 98 days for a 'wound' casualty to return to active service.

- Around 98% of the 'unfit' personnel remained in the Wehrmacht or Waffen SS, and approximately 93% returned to active duty (i.e. were capable of front-line duty) later in the war.

- Around 49% of the 'unfit' personnel were fit again after one month, 23% were fit again after two months, and around 85% were fit for active service after twelve months.[225]

- On average it took 27 days for a casualty initially classified as 'unfit' to return to active service.

---

[221] Ibid.
[222] Refer Volume IIB 8. - 'Wehrmacht and Waffen SS Casualties from June 1941 to February 1942'.
[223] Ibid.
[224] Ibid.
[225] Ibid.

Table Casualties East 41, Recup and Rep

Wehrmacht and Waffen SS Casualties (Killed, Missing, Wounded and Unfit) in the East, and Army (Heer) Recuperated and Replacements in the East; 22nd June 1941-31 December 1941 (including *Befehlsstelle Finnland*; German forces on the East Front in Norway and Finland).

	June	July	Aug.	Sept.	Oct.	Nov.	Dec.	Total (plus Waffen SS)^^ June - Dec. 41
Killed	9,503	38,669	41,592	30,089	24,987	18,327	15,285	186,452
Missing/POW	2,995	9,619	8,129	5,177	3,974	3,381	4,882	40,157
Wounded*	30,482	128,250	149,298	108,485	89,688	67,693	59,283	655,179
Unfit^	54,000	17,000	c 31,000	56,800	c 62,000	73,092	90,907	395,799
Total Casualties	96,980	193,538	230,019	200,551	180,649	162,493	170,357	1,277,587
Recuperated**	n/a	65,000	110,000	102,000	78,000	55,000	99,000	509,000
New Replacements*^	40,000	110,000	124,000	90,000	70,000	45,000	66,000	545,000
Net Change	-56,980	-18,538	3,981	-8,551	-32,649	-62,493	-5,357	-223,587

* Around 66% of the wounded remained in the Wehrmacht or Waffen SS, and approximately 56% returned to active duty at a Front later in the war. Refer table Cas Ratio-Ret to Service. Medical records indicate around 60% of 1941 wounded returned to active service within six months, and on average it took 98 days for a 'wound' casualty to return to active service.

^ Includes personnel made unfit due to sickness, disease, accidents and frostbite (i.e., losses not directly attributable to enemy action). Excludes 'unfit' personnel which were not transported out of the Army Group sectors for treatment. These personnel were usually treated by local divisional and army medical facilities, and were returned to duty after relatively short periods. Around 98% of the 'unfit' personnel listed above remained in the Wehrmacht or Waffen SS, and returned to active duty at a Front later in the war. Refer table Cas Ratio-Ret to Service. Medical records indicate that around 49% were fit again after one month, 23% were fit again after two months, and around 85% were fit for active service after twelve months. On average it took 27 days for a casualty initially classified as 'unfit' to return to active service.

** Comprises recuperated personnel who returned to duty on the East Front in 1941. Excludes recuperated personnel that remained in the Wehrmacht, and who returned to active duty (in the Field Army or the Replacement Army) later in the war (refer text).

*^ 90,000 Replacements (R) were released in June 1941. These were already in the divisional Field Replacement Battalions on the East Front (part of the Replacement Army). The Replacements distribution is based on the number of Army troop replacements available in June 1941 (from the Replacement Army), and their movements East in 1941. Excludes *Luftwaffe & Kriegsmarine* Replacements. There were 108,000 additional replacement troops, for the Luftwaffe and Kriegsmarine, in the Replacement Army in June.

^^ To the Total is added 43,000 Waffen SS casualties; made up of 8,000 killed, 22,000 wounded, 2,000 missing & POW and 11,000 unfit. These casualties represented 27% of the Waffen SS strength in June 1941 (compared to 23% for the Army (Heer)).   © Nigel Askey, 2018

The total casualties (including unfit) from 22nd June to 30th Sep. 1941 (101 days) was 742,600, which was 58% of the total. (assumes half the 1941 Waffen SS casualties).
The total casualties (including unfit) from 1st Oct. to 31st Dec. 1941 (92 days) was 535,000; 42% of the total (assumes half of the 1941 Waffen SS casualties)

In terms of maintaining the strength of the army at the front, it turns out that the original German planners were close to the mark for June to August, and significantly overestimated their casualties for September.

From 22nd June to 31st August 1941 the Wehrmacht and Waffen SS suffered 89,764 killed, 308,030 wounded, 20,743 missing and POW, and 102,000 unfit. From the data we can (conservatively) estimate that around one third of the wounded were relatively lightly wounded and returned to their units within the month (most of these wounded would have received treatment from their local divisional medical units). This means approximately 205,000 wounded effectively left the front area (i.e. were evacuated, died of their wounds, etc).[226] From the data we can also see that 49% of the 'unfit' personnel were fit again after one month, which meant approximately 52,000 unfit personnel effectively left the front area (i.e. were evacuated seriously ill, died of their illness or accident, etc). This means around 71% of the total casualties suffered from 22nd June to 31st August 1941 were either still not recuperated or were irrecoverably lost. This equates to a reduction in Wehrmacht front-line strength in the East of approximately **368,000 men**. The data from table Casualties East, Recup and Rep indicates that in the event around 175,000 were actually recuperated, which equates to a reduction in Wehrmacht front-line strength in the East of only **346,000 men**. Both these figures are close to the 365,000 Replacements (R) that the OKW had planned for.

During September 1941 the Wehrmacht and Waffen SS suffered 30,089 killed, 108,485 wounded, 5,177 missing and POW, and 56,800 unfit. If we again estimate that around one third of the wounded were relatively lightly wounded and returned to their units within the month, then approximately 72,000 wounded effectively left the front area. Similarly, if around 49% of the 'unfit' personnel were fit again after one month, then approximately 29,000 unfit personnel effectively left the front area. This means around 68% of the total casualties suffered during September 1941 were either still not recuperated or were irrecoverably lost, which equates to a reduction in Wehrmacht front-line strength in the East of approximately **136,000 men**. The data from table Casualties East, Recup and Rep indicates that in the event around 102,000 were recuperated, which equates to a reduction in Wehrmacht front-line strength in the East of only **99,000 men**. The significant difference in these figures stems from the higher than expected number of 'recuperated' in September 1941. This was most likely due to a high proportion of the 54,000 unfit casualties suffered in June 1941 (which was unusually high) returning to duty after over two months of recuperating. Either way, both these figures are much lower than the 200,000 Replacements (R) that the OKW had planned for in September.

Taken over the period 22nd June to 31st September 1941, then the net reduction in Wehrmacht front-line strength in the East was approximately 504,000 men or 445,000 men (depending on source data used). This was **61,000 to 120,000 fewer than the OKW had planned for** and had Replacements (R) for. These figures are important because they **do not** support the conventional view amongst many current authors that the German High Command was somehow 'surprised' by the number of Wehrmacht casualties it suffered from June to October 1941, and that its original plans were somehow 'thrown off stride' by these casualties. In fact we can see that the OKW planning in this regard was quite conservative, and that they had sufficient Replacement (R) earmarked to replace their losses until at least late October 1941.

***

It was therefore not the German casualty rate (or their logistical supply problems, as we shall see in Volume IIB 6.) that caused their original plans to go awry by November 1941. To find the real reasons for this, we need to dig much deeper. The problem facing the German High Command was that it was 'gambling' on a decisive campaign victory before the onset of the 1941-42 winter. For any real chance of this to occur, the OKW, OKH and OKL needed to all agree, and to have clear strategic objectives at the outset. These objectives needed to ensure near fatal damage to the USSR's war effort, and they had to be pursued relentlessly, without distraction and with maximum effort. 'Maximum effort' in this context included not only military operations, but also timely recruitment and the timely issuing of Replacements (R) of men and equipment. In other words, an appreciation and respect for the ability of the USSR (and Red Army) to recover if its principal strategic production facilities and mobilisation base remained intact.

However, what occurred in the OKW from late July to September 1941 can, at best, be described as inept leadership across the whole strategic-military and political spectrum. It has become apparent that as the campaign progressed, basic disagreements occurred at the highest levels of the German command structure. Vital strategic

---

[226] These figures were typical of most large scale WWII land campaigns. It was typical for around a third of the wounded to return to service quickly, around a third to return to some sort of active service eventually, and around a third to be irrecoverably lost from military service. Obviously, the better the medical support units, the higher the wounded recovery rate. The Red Army, and possibly the Chinese Army, were the worst organizations in this regard during WWII. US Army figures for wounded returned to service were around two thirds of all wounded. US Army estimates of German wounded were about the same. G. A. Harrison, et al, Cross Channel Attack, The Center of Military History, United States Army, Washington, 1951, p. 142, and note 49.

objectives became progressively more confused and less well defined, or/and were actually changed (in some cases they were changed several times within a few months!). Consequently key operational decisions were repeatedly delayed or were simply wrong, distractions due to military objectives of little or no import abounded, and the completion of any pre-invasion objectives (as they were) were severely delayed.

It is clear the German High Command completely failed to understand, and set, the clear strategic objectives for the campaign. By example, Army Group Centre (by far the strongest army group) was halted in its planned advance on Moscow in early August, while its offensive units were turned southwards and northwards towards Kiev and Leningrad.[227] Key senior Army commanders at OKW, and especially those within Army Group Centre, were so opposed to this new directive that they systematically created administrative and operational hurdles to hinder the execution of the new directive. All this vacillation was to no avail, but it did contribute to creating further delay and confusion. Later, when Leningrad was threatened, the strategic objectives were again changed (and, again, before the completion of the most recent strategic directives). This time Army Group North's offensive units, as well as those on 'loan' from Army Group Centre, were now turned southwards to support the belated advance towards Moscow. All this meant that Army Group Centre's original tank and motorised divisions had now travelled several thousand kilometres (on relatively poor roads) further than they had needed to in order to reach Gorki, let alone Moscow! The resultant wear and tear (i.e. the operational losses) were thus far higher than they needed to be, even before any offensive towards Moscow was launched. In the meantime the strategic import of Leningrad was always insignificant compared to that of the Moscow-Gorki region. In addition it is now clear that the Red Army in the Donbass (also far less strategically significant than the Moscow-Gorki region) would almost certainly not have contained Army Group South during September-October 1941, even without any assistance from Army Group Centre's forces. We cannot go further here into the extensive ongoing discourse about these various OKW directives, but it is sufficient to note here that the 'battle for the Moscow-Gorki space' could now not start until October/November 1941.

The Germans had therefore effectively 'expended' most of their ready Replacements (R) by late October 1941 without achieving their primary pre-war objectives and while the USSR was still not near collapse. Even worse, the Red Army west of Moscow (where the bulk of the Red Army had been deployed since August) had had almost two months to mobilise new forces and prepare their defences, whilst at the same time launching some heavy counterattacks against the relatively immobile and depleted Army Group Centre (which held without too much problem).[228] Given that the Soviets had already embarked on the largest mobilisation programme in history, that **around a third of the newly mobilised divisions came from the Moscow-Gorki area**, and that almost **all the factories in this area in June 1941 remained in this area or were moved eastwards in August-September 1941**, two free months was a fatally long time.[229] In addition, as is well known, the weather around Moscow was now much less suitable for almost any type of offensive operation.

***

The Germans had also compounded their deteriorating strategic situation in October and November 1941 by: failing to significantly reinforce their forces on the East Front with existing Deployed (D) infantry divisions still in the West, failing to mobilise significant new forces (almost no new MD or MND infantry units were initiated), failing to plan adequately for new trained Replacements (R), and in some cases failing to issue critical equipment Replacements (R) even though they were available (see 'tanks and assault guns' in the following section). For example, only three infantry divisions (the 212th, 215th and 223rd) were transferred east during the whole of October and November 1941, and only one new infantry division was mobilised before December 1941 (the 250th with Spanish volunteers).[230] Clearly the German High Command had underestimated the Soviet's mobilisation capacity and erred in identifying the most important Soviet mobilisation base, had completely underestimated the approaching weather, and felt their existing forces in the East could finish the job; albeit now two months behind schedule.

---

[227] Literature abounds on the apparent reasons for this. They include: unexpectedly heavy German casualties, logistics problems due to shortages of trucks, shortages of tanks (a relatively recent favorite), strong resistance and/or counterattacks from Soviet forces east of Smolensk, and Army Group South needing help to secure the Donbass region. However, all these 'hypotheses' struggle to stand up to even moderate scrutiny. Furthermore, as we shall systematically prove in this series, they definitely do not stand up to any serious quantitative (statistical) based analysis.

[228] In his various works on Barbarossa, D. M. Glantz has maintained that these offensives by the Soviet Western, Reserve and Bryansk Fronts cost the Red Army so dearly that these Fronts were considerably weaker when Operation Typhoon was finally launched in October 1941.

[229] Refer Volume IIIB 2. - 'Soviet Mobilisation After 22nd June 1941'. The geographic location (district) where each new Soviet division was mobilised is shown, and the number started and completed in the Moscow-Gorki space is shown.

[230] The 250th Infantry Division - the Spanish Blue Division.

***

In June-July 1941 the next German wave of recruits scheduled to be called up was the class of 1922. Incredibly, the powers that be didn't want to call up this group until November 1941, when it was envisaged manpower from the Eastern Army would be released for German industry![231] What better illustration of the German High Command's strategic mindset at the highest levels?

The overall result of all this strategic mismanagement was that the Germans didn't start mobilising any new infantry divisions until mid-December 1941, and the corresponding conscription of able-bodied personnel was also very belated. From the section on newly conscripted Wehrmacht and Waffen SS personnel in 1941, we ascertained that approximately 792,000 recruits were newly mobilised and considered to be on Wehrmacht strength between 22nd June and 31st December 1941.[232] This resulted in a net increase in Wehrmacht and Waffen SS strength of some 331,000 persons (from 7,309,000 to 7,640,000). However, like their Western Allied counterparts, the German Army insisted (with good reason) on giving new recruits at least three-four months training. As most of these recruits arrived after October 1941 they were not going to be available until 1942. In addition, probably only around 60% of the 792,000 new recruits were destined to fill the ranks of ground combat units (the figure includes all new personnel destined for the Luftwaffe and Kriegsmarine, as well as any rear area support units and the Replacement Army). It is worth noting here that a huge proportion of the Soviet recruits being used to fill the ranks of the Red Army in 1941 had next to no training at all.

For all these reasons, **in the German FILARM model, the only Replacements (R) available to the German forces during 1941 are the ready replacements that were actually available in the Replacement Army in June 1941.** This force comprised 561,600 replacement troops for the Army (i.e. not Luftwaffe, or Kriegsmarine, and possibly not Waffen SS), and 108,000 replacement troops for the Luftwaffe and Kriegsmarine. By doing this we are ensuring that in any military-simulation of Operation Barbarossa the German commanders (players) are facing the same Replacements (R) problems faced by the actual German commanders on the East Front during 1941. For our purposes it is assumed the Replacements (R) sent to the East Front were as follows.

	Wehrmacht Replacements (R) Sent East, June to December 1941		
	Available, June 41	Sent East	% Sent East
Army (Heer)*	561,600	545,000	97%
Luftwaffe	90,000	77,000	85%
Kriegsmarine	18,000	4,000	20%
	669,600	**626,000**	**93%**
* Possibly includes some Waffen SS.			

This is a conservative estimate because we are assuming none of the 792,000 newly mobilised Wehrmacht and Waffen SS recruits were sent East in 1941 as Replacements (R), and we are assuming the Waffen SS replacements available in 1941 are included in with the Army's June figure. In all probability there was an additional 60-90,000 Army and Waffen SS Replacements (R) sent east, but this is unknown. The proportion of Luftwaffe replacements sent east is high because this includes all types of Luftwaffe ground forces (including Flak and airborne infantry). In the second half of 1941 the only theatre where Luftwaffe ground forces were heavily engaged in direct combat with enemy ground forces was the East Front: aircrew constituted only a small proportion of the total Luftwaffe losses and replacements.[233] The bulk of the Kriegsmarine forces remained in the West for the duration of the war, but several very significant naval operations were carried out by the Kriegsmarine in the Baltic during 1941.[234] The bulk of the Kriegsmarine replacements went into naval forces in the Baltic, the few naval coastal artillery units sent east, and several naval security units. As we have seen, there is little doubt that had the Germans mobilised their potential manpower for total war in June 1941, and had they used the available replacements already

---

[231] Boog, H., et al, Germany and the Second World War-Volume IV, The Attack on the Soviet Union, Clarendon Press (Oxford University Press), New York, 1996, p. 317.
[232] Refer Volume IIB 4. 4) b. vii. - 'New Resources Produced and Received in the Reich from June to 31st December 1941 - Newly Conscripted Wehrmacht Personnel'.
[233] Luftwaffe aircrew losses in the East in 1941 amounted to 4 404 killed, wounded and missing. Boog, H., et al, p. 818.
[234] Refer Volume IIB 7. 4) -'A History of German Naval Operations in the Baltic: June to December 1941'.

in the Replacement Army on 22nd June 1941, then they could have easily doubled the number of armed personnel Replacements (R) sent to the East Front from June to December 1941.

ii. German Tank and Assault Gun Losses and Replacements

In view of the German High Command's strategic mindset during Operation Barbarossa (as discussed above), it is worth examining the story regarding tank replacements on the East Front from June to December 1941. There are two important reasons for doing this. Firstly, AFVs, especially tanks and assault guns, were critical to the whole German method of war during Operation Barbarossa. They constituted one of the main strengths of the panzer divisions (but by no means the only strength, refer note 235 below), and the panzer divisions were at the heart of the *blitzkrieg* method of rapid mobile warfare. Secondly, in most current literature regarding Operation Barbarossa there is a common perception that the panzer regiments in the panzer divisions were 'worn out' by December 1941, and that the main reason for this was that German tank and assault gun production could not meet the demand for replacement vehicles.

As a first step it is worth examining the state of the panzer divisions on the East Front in regards to their tank losses and tanks under repair. The table below shows the overall tank status in the panzer divisions on the East Front around September 1941.[235] This time period is appropriate because it was at the height of the battle around Kiev, and sometime after Army Group Centre's panzer units had turned and pushed southwards and northwards, towards Kiev and Leningrad in early August 1941. The tank status of the panzer divisions (shown below) is therefore very close to what they would have been if Army Group Centre had been ordered to invade the Moscow-Gorki space in early August 1941 and subsequently reached Moscow in late August or September 1941.

The Tank Status within the Panzer Divisions, September 1941									
Panzer Division	**1st**	**3rd**	**4th**	**6th**	**7th**	**8th**	**9th**	**10th**	**11th**
Date	10/9	4/9	9/9	10/9	6/9	10/9	5/9	4/9	5/9
Main tank type	Pz III	Pz III	Pz III	Pz 35t	Pz 38t	Pz 38t	Pz III	Pz III	Pz III
Operational tanks	99	54	83	181	130	154	62	153	60
Being repaired	24	107	79	15	87	33	67	22	75
Total losses	33	70	50	62	82	36	28	25	40
Replacements	0	2	0	2	21	0	3	0	9
Panzer Div	**12th***	**13th**	**14th**	**16th**	**17th**	**18th**	**19th***	**20th***	**Totals**
Date	26/8	28/8	6/9	22/8	10/9	9/9	25/8	25/8	
Main tank type	Pz 38t	Pz III	Pz III	Pz III	Pz III	Pz III	Pz 38t	Pz 38t	
Operational tanks	103	93	112	62	68	93	102	88	**1,697**
Being repaired	35	34	24	26	76	114	47	62	**927**
Total losses	101	33	27	70	72	47	90	104	**970**
Replacements	7	3	5	0	0	25	0	14	**91**
* 12th, 19th and 20th Panzer Divisions' total losses include 42 Pz I, 47 Pz I and 51 Pz I light tanks, respectively.									

There are several key inferences that can be drawn from this table.

- Army Group Centre's tank losses from the battles around Minsk, across the Dnieper River and around Smolensk, **did not lead to unusually heavy tank losses** and **did not leave Army Group Centre's panzer divisions in an unreasonable state of operational readiness**. The figures show that of the 3,594 tanks deployed in the 17 panzer divisions on the East Front from 22nd June to early September 1941, 47% were fully operational, 26% were in field workshops (the large majority in the panzer divisions' mobile field workshops) and 27% were total write-offs.

The proportion of tanks undergoing repair was not particularly unusual as it was normal for any WWII armoured division to have 10-15% of its tanks out of service, even under peacetime conditions.

---

[235] Data collated from T. L. Jentz, *Panzer Truppen* Volume 1: The Complete Guide to the Creation and Combat Deployment of Germany's Tank Force – 1933-1942, Schiffer Military History, Atglen, PA, 1996, pp. 190-193 and 206.

Furthermore, 1941 panzer divisions with as little as 30% of the combat elements of the divisions (i.e. excluding the rear-area divisional support units) and as few as 50 tanks, routinely demonstrated that they had enough striking power to be capable of conducting very effective offensive operations.[236] This is a dimension of 1941 panzer divisions that few authors seem to understand (especially those with an academic and non-military background).[237] In view of these facts, it is apparent that Army Group Centre's panzer and motorised divisions would have encircled Moscow in September 1941 while still in a relatively high state of operational readiness.

- After almost two and a half months of continuous campaigning against the largest army in the world (also with by far the most tanks), the 17 panzer divisions on the East Front had received a paltry 91 tank replacements! This represented less than 3% of the tanks deployed since 22nd June 1941 and a net loss in strength of 879 tanks.[238] No matter what level of tactical and operational skill the panzer divisions exhibited, without adequate tank Replacements (R) it was only a matter of time before the combat power of the panzer regiments in these divisions was completely diminished. The panzer divisions should have been receiving significant tank replacements within days, or at most weeks, of initiating the campaign. Was this another example of the German's apparent strategic-level overconfidence that the existing forces could finish the job, or were the tanks simply unavailable (see below)?

- It is apparent from the figures that the panzer divisions equipped with lighter Pz Kpfw I, Pz Kpfw 35(t) and Pz Kpfw 38(t) tanks sustained a higher 'total loss' rate than those predominantly equipped with Pz Kpfw III tanks. For example, of the 295 tanks written-off in the 12th, 19th and 20th Panzer Divisions, 140 (47%) were Pz Kpfw Is which were obsolete MG armed light tanks originally intended for training duties. These panzer divisions were all predominantly equipped with Pz Kpfw 38(t) light tanks. On the upside, these panzer divisions had more tanks to start with because their panzer regiments each had three panzer battalions versus normally two.

***

---

[236] R.H.S. Stolfi, German Panzers on the Offensive, Schiffer Military History, Atglen, PA, 2003, p. 79. This book is highly recommended. It demonstrates why panzer divisions were do effective, even in a 'weakened' state, the sophistication of their structure as a modern combined-arms force, and their unique (for the period) and very flexible command and control structure (and training). Similar organisations and training are used today in the divisions of the best modern armies.

[237] E.g., D. Stahel, Operation Barbarossa and Germany's Defeat in the East, Cambridge University Press, New York, 2009. A principal (and often repeated) premise of this work is that Barbarossa failed due to the decline in the panzer division's offensive abilities due to their tank losses. The author assumes the panzer division's entire offensive capability was directly proportional to the number of operational tanks at a particular point in time. It is as though the rest of the division didn't exist and the only element worth considering is the operational tanks in the division's panzer regiment. This could not be further from the truth. Stahel makes no effort to consider factors such as how quickly the support elements of an average 1941 panzer division (which had major field workshop and tank recovery facilities integrated into the divisional infrastructure) could return tanks under repair to service. In many cases, panzer divisions managed to get 30-40% of the panzer regiment's entire tank strength operational in a matter of 3-4 days. Other factors not even considered are the very potent offensive abilities of the panzer division's armoured infantry battalions, motorised infantry battalions, armoured reconnaissance battalions (which were in themselves combined arms formations with heavy weapon companies), motorised anti-tank battalions, motorised combat engineer battalions, motorised artillery battalions, etc. In fact, when the combat power of these divisional elements are analysed (refer sections Volume IIA 3. 3) a.) i. and ii.) we find the panzer regiment alone represented a minor part of the panzer division's overall combat power. In practice, the none-armoured elements of a panzer division often embarked on offensive operations without any part of the panzer regiment being present at all.

This is also the reason why German Army 1941 motorised divisions, and the Waffen SS motorised divisions, (both of which had no panzer regiment at all) were able to operate in the spearhead-offensive role in the USSR during 1941-42. Throughout the campaign in the USSR during 1941, these divisions operated alongside (and not behind) the panzer divisions, broke their own 'enemy-ground' in the advance, and were always able to defend a similar length of 'frontage' as the panzer divisions. For example, it was the 29th Motorised Division, without a single tank to its name, that spearheaded the XXXXVII Motorised Corps advance south of Orsha and captured Smolensk on 16-17th July 1941. Notably, it had the 17th and 18th Panzer Divisions to the north and behind (further west), and another motorised division, the SS Das Reich, spearheading the XXXXVI Motorised Corps to the south.

[238] This net loss was somewhat offset by the arrival of the 2nd and 5th Panzer Divisions, which were shipped east in early September 1941. These powerful units were at full strength, and had 380 tanks in their 3rd and 31st Panzer Regiments.

The next step in this story is to ascertain if the Germans could have replaced their tank and assault gun losses on the East Front during 1941. The table opposite (page 185) shows how the overall tank and assault gun inventory changed from June to December 1941.[239] Included are German tank and assault gun losses, newly manufactured tanks and assault guns which were ready for issue to the Wehrmacht, and tanks and assault guns that were rebuilt (in factories) from damaged vehicles and were ready for reissue. The latter also includes tanks which were upgraded during a rebuild, e.g. replacing the 37mm gun type used on an early model Pz Kpfw III with a 50mm gun type used on later models. The loss figures above include around 240 tank losses suffered by the DAK in North Africa, as well any losses on other fronts and losses due to accidents or scrapping.[240] Consequently, the German AFV loss figures above are significantly higher than those only reporting losses on the East Front.

The German Research Institute for Military History at Potsdam places German Pz Kpfw I, Pz Kpfw II, Pz Kpfw III, Pz Kpfw IV, Pz Kpfw 35(t), Pz Kpfw 38(t), command tanks, StuG III assault guns and Pz Kpfw II(F) Flame tank losses at **2,839 from June to 31st December 1941 on the East Front**.[241] Monthly losses in this instance were reported as 118 in June, 732 in July, 638 in August, 257 in September, 337 in October, 382 in November and 375 in December.

Another source states German tank losses on the East Front from June to 31st December 1941 were: 428 Pz Kpfw I, 424 Pz Kpfw II and II(F), 660 Pz Kpfw III, 348 Pz Kpfw IV, 796 Pz Kpfw 35(t) and 38(t), and 79 command tanks.[242] This totals to 2,735 tanks. If we add the 104 assault gun losses, then this **totals to 2,839**; exactly the same figure as above. In this case the tanks were reported as total write-offs or no longer repairable by the divisional field workshops. A proportion of these tanks were shipped back to Germany or Czechoslovakia where they were either rebuilt, rebuilt and upgraded, or scrapped. Note, if we add the 424 Pz Kpfw II and II(F) losses above, and the 67 Pz Kpfw II lost in North Africa, then this totals to 491 Pz Kpfw II and II(F) lost. This is 33 AFVs more than shown in the table above, and this is most likely the number of Pz Kpfw II(F) Flame tank lost (which are not included in the table above).[243]

Other sources have lower figures for German tank total-losses from 22nd June to 31st December 1941. These sources state the Germans lost 2,758 tanks during this period, including tank losses suffered by the DAK in North Africa.[244] If we add the 104 assault gun losses, then this figure still totals to only 2,862. This figure is very close to the losses on the East Front only (2,839). On balance, it is therefore likely that these sources are mistaken (at least regarding the 1941 figure), and the losses shown only apply to the East Front. Just in case the reader thinks these were German tank losses were high, **the corresponding Red Army tank losses during the same period amounted to 20,500 total-losses**, while the Commonwealth forces in North Africa suffered approximately 600 tank total-losses in the second half of 1941.[245] This equates to a German tank kill-loss ratio of over 7.2 to 1 against the Soviets and around 2.5 to 1 against the Commonwealth forces, during the second half of 1941.

---

[239] Data collated from: T. L. Jentz, *Panzer Truppen* Volume 1: The Complete Guide to the Creation and Combat Deployment of Germany's Tank Force – 1933-1942, Schiffer Military History, Atglen, PA, 1996, pp. 254-270. Assault gun data is from, H. Boog, et al, Germany and the Second World War-Volume IV: The Attack on the Soviet Union, Clarendon Press (Oxford University Press), New York, 1996, Table II.VII.1., pp. 1120-1122. This also correlates with annual production data of all AFV types, as shown in P. Chamberlain, H. Doyle, T. L. Jentz, Encyclopedia of German Tanks of WWII, Arms and Armour Press, London, 1993, Appendix VII –German AFV production, pp. 261-263. Pz Kpfw 35(t) losses are averaged over the period June to November 1941, with only 6 left in the 6th Panzer Division on 1st December 1941 (total 162 lost).

[240] These losses break down as 67 Pz Kpfw II, 139 Pz Kpfw III, 29 Pz Kpfw IV and 5 Pz Bef Wg. This includes 11 Pz Kpfw II and 34 Pz Kpfw III tanks sunk en route to North Africa on 19th December (probably by Royal Navy submarines). T. Jentz, Panzer Truppen, The Complete Guide To The Creation And Combat Deployment of Germany's Tank Force 1933-1942, Schiffer Military History, Atglen PA, 1996, p. 174.

[241] H. Boog, et al, Germany and the Second World War-Volume IV, The Attack on the Soviet Union, Clarendon Press (Oxford University Press), New York, 1996, Diagram II.VI.2., p. 1129.

[242] T. L. Jentz, *Panzer Truppen* Volume 1: The Complete Guide to the Creation and Combat Deployment of Germany's Tank Force – 1933-1942, Schiffer Military History, Atglen, PA, 1996, p. 209.

[243] There were 90 Pz Kpfw II *Flamm* (F) Flame tanks (Sd Kfz 122) available on 1st June 1941, of which 84 were deployed in support of Operation Barbarossa.

[244] S. J. Zaloga, L. S. Ness, Red Army Handbook 1939-1945, Sutton Publishing Ltd, Stroud, Gloucestershire, UK, 1998, Table 6.3., p. 181. Also, T. Bean, W. Fowler, Russian Tanks of WWII – Stalin's Armoured Might, Ian Allen Publishing, London, 2002, Appendix, p. 170.

[245] G.F. Krivosheev, et al, Soviet Casualties and Combat Losses in the Twentieth Century, ed. Colonel General G.F. Krivosheev, Greenhill Books, London, 1997, Table 95, p. 252. Also, S. J. Zaloga, L. S. Ness, Red Army Handbook 1939-1945, Sutton Publishing Ltd, Stroud, Gloucestershire, UK, 1998, Table 6.3., p. 181. Also, T. Bean, W. Fowler, Russian Tanks of WWII – Stalin's Armoured Might, Ian Allen Publishing, London, 2002, Appendix, p. 170.
The Commonwealth 8th Army (in North Africa) lost 98 tanks in Operation Battleaxe (15th June 1941) and around 400 tanks in Operation Crusader (18th November 1941), alone. T. L. Jentz, Tank Combat in North Africa; The Opening Rounds, Schiffer Military History, Atglen PA, 1998.

German Tank and Assault Gun Losses, Production, Rebuilt and Inventory: June-December 1941

German Tank and Assault Gun Losses, June-December 1941 ^^

	June	July	Aug.	Sept.	Oct.	Nov.	Dec.	Total
Pz I *	34	146	171	7	18	33	19	**428**
Pz II ^	16	117	106	32	65	30	92	**458**
Pz 35(t) **	26	26	26	26	26	26	6	**162**
Pz 38(t)	33	182	183	62	85	149	102	**796**
Pz III (37mm)	23	59	25	16	11	13	29	**176**
Pz III (50mm)	27	164	78	104	79	116	208	**776**
StuG III	3	11	26	12	23	10	19	**104**
Pz IV	16	111	70	23	55	38	65	**378**
Pz Bef *^	1	18	12	17	14	6	28	**96**
	179	**834**	**697**	**299**	**376**	**421**	**568**	**3,374**

* Includes Pz I *pionier* vehicles and ammunition carriers (i.e. all types).   ^ Excludes Pz II Flame Tanks (Sd Kfz 122).
** Comprises 157xPz 35(t) and 5xPZ35(t) Bef, all in the 6th Pz. Division. Average taken for losses each month.
*^ *Panzerbefehlswagen* (command tanks). Incls. Pz I *Kleine* Pz Bef (Sd Kfz 265) & Pz III *Gross* Pz Bef (Sd Kfz 266 - 268).
^^ Includes 240 plus tank losses in North Africa (mainly Pz II, III and IV).

Newly Manufactured German Tanks and Assault Guns Ready for Issue, June-December 1941

	June	July	Aug.	Sept.	Oct.	Nov.	Dec.	Total
Pz I	No longer produced							
Pz II	5	27	9	26	23	50	41	**181**
Pz 35(t)	No longer produced							
Pz 38(t) *	29	80	64	63	66	50	49	**401**
Pz III (37mm)	No longer produced							
Pz III (50mm)	88	176	185	182	174	198	198	**1,201**
StuG III	56	47	50	38	71	46	40	**348**
Pz IV	29	55	43	49	40	58	56	**330**
Pz Bef III		14	5	2			12	**33**
	207	**399**	**356**	**360**	**374**	**402**	**396**	**2,494**

* Includes all tanks used as command tanks.

German Tank and Assault Gun Losses, Production, Rebuilt and Inventory: June-December 1941

Factory Rebuilt German Tanks and Assault Guns Ready for Issue, June-December 1941

	June	July	Aug.	Sept.	Oct.	Nov.	Dec.	Total
Pz I *		74	42	46	54	44	14	**274**
Pz II ^	4	8	12	2	5	2	7	**40**
Pz 35(t)	2		2			1	5	**10**
Pz 38(t)	13	74	1	3		5		**96**
Pz III (37mm)	Rebuilt with 50mm guns (inc in Pz III (50mm) figures)							
Pz III (50mm)	23	25	10	13	13	13	22	**119**
StuG III **	◄------------------------------ 13 ------------------------------►							**13**
Pz IV	1	13	9	3	1	6	11	**44**
Pz Bef *^	2	4	11	8	1	9	5	**40**
	45	**198**	**87**	**88**	**74**	**80**	**64**	**636**

* Includes Pz I *pionier* vehicles and ammunition carriers (i.e. all types).   ^ Excludes Pz II Flame Tanks (Sd Kfz 122).
** Unknown, but estimated at 12-13% of losses (as per the Pz III and IV).
*^ Includes Pz I *Kleine* Pz Bef (Sd Kfz 265), but mostly Pz III *Gross* Pz Bef (Sd Kfz 266 - 268).

German Tank and Assault Gun Inventories, June-December 1941

	1st June	1st July	1st Aug.	1st Sept.	1st Oct.	1st Nov.	1st Dec.	Six Month Change
Pz I *	877	843	771	642	681	717	728	-149
Pz II ^	1,074	1,067	985	900	896	859	881	-193
Pz 35(t) **	170						19	-151
Pz 38(t)	746	755	727	609	613	594	500	-246
Pz III (37mm)	350	327	268	243	227	216	203	-147
Pz III (50mm)	1,090	1,174	1,211	1,328	1,419	1,527	1,622	532
StuG III	377						634	257
Pz IV	517	531	488	470	499	485	511	-6
Pz Bef *^	330	331	331	335	328	315	318	-12
Net change in the German tank and ass-gun inventory from 1st June 1941 to 1st Dec 1941								**-115**

* Includes Pz I *pionier* vehicles and ammunition carriers (i.e. all types except command tanks).
^ Excludes Pz II Flame Tanks (Sd Kfz 122), of which 90 were available on 1st June 1941. ** Dec. inv. is for 11th Dec.
*^ Comprised of 160 Pz I *Kleine* Pz Bef (Sd Kfz 265) and 170 Pz III *Gross* Pz Bef (Sd Kfz 266 - 268).

The following table compares the German tanks manufactured to those ready for issue (from the above table), from June to December 1941. [246]

German Tanks Manufactured, June-December 1941								Total Produced June - Dec. 41	Total Ready for Issue June - Dec. 41
	June	July	Aug.	Sept.	Oct.	Nov.	Dec.		
Pz I	No longer produced								
Pz II	15	21	25	25	38	40	35	199	181
Pz 35(t)	No longer produced								
Pz 38(t) *	65	65	64	76	53	50	50	423	401
Pz III (37mm)	No longer produced								
Pz III (50mm)	133	127	179	178	164	206	171	1,158	1,201
StuG III ^	56	47	50	38	71	46	40	348	348
Pz IV	38	38	44	46	51	52	61	330	330
Pz Bef III	5	13		2			16	36	33
	312	311	362	365	377	394	373	2,494	2,494

* Includes all tanks used as command tanks.

^ Exact no. manufactured is unknown. Figures used are the same as 'ready for issue'.   © Nigel Askey, 2018

The difference between 'manufactured' tanks and 'ready for issue' tanks is an important consideration here. This is because from 1939 to at least early 1943 the Germans had the toughest quality control of any of the combatants in relation to weapons production; particularly tank production. In fact, one of the criticisms levelled at German industry during the early war years is that they unnecessarily enforced strict quality control measures. This meant that critical weapons, such as tanks, were often initially 'rejected' and sent back to the factory when they had comparatively minor problems which could have been rectified in the divisional field workshops. The result was a reduction in overall production rate. This was almost a non-event in the USSR and the Red Army during WWII, especially prior to 1943. Despite the German's (arguably) unnecessarily restrictive quality and testing procedures, we see from the above table that around 2,500 new tanks and assault guns were issued to the Wehrmacht from June to December 1941. At least we know these vehicles were in excellent condition and without many problems.

***

From the main table (on page 184), we can see that the net German tank and assault gun inventory went down by only 115 vehicles from 1st June to 1st December 1941. This is a rather surprising result. According to these figures the German Field Army should have been able to replace most of its tank losses during 1941: although German tank production was significantly lower than Soviet production, it was still significantly higher than commonly perceived.

Furthermore, we can see that the newly produced tanks were predominantly much more powerful (and harder to produce) medium tanks, while most of the total-losses were attributed to much less powerful (and easier to produce) light tanks. For example, from June to December 1941, 56% of German tank losses were Pz Kpfw I, Pz Kpfw II, Pz Kpfw 35(t), Pz Kpfw 38(t) and *Kleine* Pz Bef I light tanks, while 44% were Pz Kpfw III, Pz Kpfw IV, Pz Bef III (*Gross*) and StuG III medium tanks and assault guns. [247] During the same period only 23% of the new 'ready for issue' tanks were light tanks (as above), while 77% were medium tanks and assault guns. In other words, **not only should the German Field Army have been able to replace most of its tank losses during 1941, but it should have been able to replace them with much better tanks**.

So the question is, what happened and how many tank replacements were actually sent to the East Front forces and the DAK during the second half of 1941? The tables below show the number (and schedule) of German

---

[246] Data collated from: T. L. Jentz, *Panzer Truppen* Volume 1: The Complete Guide to the Creation and Combat Deployment of Germany's Tank Force – 1933-1942, Schiffer Military History, Atglen, PA, 1996, pp. 254-270. Assault gun data from, H. Boog, et al, Germany and the Second World War-Volume IV: The Attack on the Soviet Union, Clarendon Press (Oxford University Press), New York, 1996, Table II.VII.1., pp. 1120-1122. This also correlates with annual production data of all AFV types, as shown in P. Chamberlain, H. Doyle, T. L. Jentz, Encyclopedia of German Tanks of WWII, Arms and Armour Press, London, 1993, Appendix VII –German AFV production, pp. 261-263.

[247] Assumes around half of the Pz Bef (command tanks) lost were *Kleine* Pz Bef I light tanks..

tank and assault gun Replacements (R) sent to the East Front and North Africa from June to December 1941/January 1942.[248]

German Tank & Assault Gun Replacements (R) sent to the East Front, June to Dec. 1941/Jan. 1942								Total
	June	July	Aug.	Sep.	Oct.	Nov.	Dec./Jan.	Replacements
Pz Kpfw I						12	30	**42**
Pz Kpfw II			1	20	1	16	31	**69**
Pz Kpfw III (50mm)		45		62	187	39	55	**388**
Pz Bef Wg III			2			5	18	**25**
Pz Kpfw IV		15		2	56	7	22	**102**
Pz Kpfw 38(t) *		27	8	45	72	44	45	**241**
Pz Kpfw 35(t)			4					**4**
StuG III Ass. Gun		4			7		4	**15**
Totals		**91**	**15**	**129**	**323**	**123**	**205**	**886**

* Includes Pz Kpfw 38(t) used as command tanks.   © Nigel Askey, 2018

German Tank Replacements (R) sent to the D.A.K (North Africa), 1st June to Dec. 1941								Total
Date	4/06*	30/06*	10/07*	19/12^	19/12**	19/12*^	5/01/42^^	Replacements
Pz Bef Wg III							3	**3**
Pz Kpfw II		4		5	6	11	3	**29**
Pz Kpfw III (50mm)	15	6	4	17	17	34	42	**135**
Pz Kpfw IV	5						6	**11**
							Total	**178**

* Replacements issued to the 5th Panzer Regiment/5th Light Division.
^ Arrived at Benghazi and assigned to the 3rd Company/8th Panzer Regiment/15th Panzer Division.
** Arrived at Tripoli and assigned to the 7th Company/8th Panzer Regiment/15th Panzer Division.
*^ Assigned to the 3rd & 7th C0/5th Pz Reg/5th Light Division. These tanks were all sunk en route to N. Africa.
^^ Convoy arrived at Tripoli on 5th January 1942 but the tanks were shipped in December 1941.

© Nigel Askey, 2018

The tables above show replacements reaching the front until December 1941/January 1942, and not just December 1941. The main reason for this is that there appears to be inconsistencies in the timing of these replacements: there is evidence that many of the tank replacements started travelling East in December 1941 but arrived at the front in January 1942. In addition, an analysis of the changing strength data for some tank types, taking into account their initial strengths and monthly losses, indicates that some replacements must have arrived in 1941 even though they are reported as arriving in early 1942. Furthermore, it is sometimes difficult to differentiate the vehicles which arrived as part of reinforcement units (arriving at the front) and those that were Replacements (R) for existing combat units. For example, the refurbished 2nd and 5th Panzer Divisions were transferred to the East Front in September 1941, and at this time they had a total of 404 tanks on strength.[249] However, some strength returns for German tanks on the East Front show the 2nd and 5th Panzer Divisions arriving in early October 1941, resulting in an increase in overall tank strength of 450 tanks.[250]

---

[248] East Front data is mostly from H. Boog, et al, Germany and the Second World War-Volume IV, The Attack on the Soviet Union, Clarendon Press (Oxford University Press), New York, 1996, Table II.VI.I., pp. 1120-1122, and Diagram II.VI.2., p. 1129. Note, Boog attributes 450 tanks to the 2nd and 5th Panzer Divisions in September, but these divisions actually had only 404 tanks on strength in their respective panzer regiments and within other elements of the divisions. Also, the Boog data relating to Pz 35(t) and Pz 38(t) replacements appears completely incorrect for some of the months: it does not match the monthly strength data for these vehicles at the front after their initial strengths and monthly losses are taken into account. Also, some data (especially relating to Pz 35(t) and Pz 38(t)) is collated from: T. L. Jentz, Panzer Truppen Volume 1: The Complete Guide to the Creation and Combat Deployment of Germany's Tank Force – 1933-1942, Schiffer Military History, Atglen, PA, 1996, pp. 186-211. North Africa data is collated from Jentz, pp. 167 to 174.

[249] There were 380 tanks in the 3rd and 31st Panzer Regiments, and an additional 12 light tanks in each division's pionier battalion. Refer Volume IIA 3. 3) a. v. and viii. - '2nd and 5th Panzer Divisions, Actual Organisation and Equipment'. Also, T. L. Jentz, Panzer Truppen Volume 1: The Complete Guide to the Creation and Combat Deployment of Germany's Tank Force – 1933-1942, Schiffer Military History, Atglen, PA, 1996, p. 212.

[250] E.g., H. Boog, et al, Germany and the Second World War-Volume IV, The Attack on the Soviet Union, Clarendon Press (Oxford University Press), New York, 1996, Diagram II.VI.2., p. 1129.

Even giving the Germans the benefit of the doubt regarding tank replacements arriving in December or/and January 1941, it is very apparent from the above that the tank replacements received during the most of the critical months (for Operation Barbarossa's success) were few and far between. From 22nd June to the end of September 1941 the German panzer forces on the East Front received a paltry 231 tanks and 4 assault guns. From the German tank losses and (tanks rebuilt) table, we can see that during the same period the Germans lost 1,552 tanks and 39 assault guns as irrecoverable total-losses: a net loss in strength of 1,356 AFVs.[251] At the same time the Wehrmacht was issued 1,322 new tanks and assault guns from German industry. In other words, the German High Command had the opportunity to replace the large majority of the tank and assault guns losses on the East Front during the decisive June to September 1941 period; and yet it appears to have completely failed to understand the strategic importance of doing so. This is yet more strong evidence of the German High Command's underestimation (at the strategic level) of the task facing the Wehrmacht when it invaded the USSR.

Even after September 1941 it appears that the Germans continued to allow their panzer forces in the East to decline: they continued to believe the existing forces on the East Front could achieve a decisive strategic victory over the USSR in 1941. By the end of 1941 and early 1942, only 886 tank and assault gun replacements had been sent to the East Front. This represented only 36% of the 2,494 new tanks and assault guns received from German industry in the same period. Even if we take account of the 178 tanks sent to North Africa as replacements (see above table), this still **left 1,430 brand new tanks which could easily have been used as ready replacements for the embattled East Front panzer forces.** Furthermore, most of these would have been the very good Pz Kpfw III medium tanks with 50mm guns. Interestingly, the German DAK in North Africa received more tank replacements during 1941, pro rata to the number available in June 1941, than the panzer forces on the East Front. And yet, Hitler made several statements to the effect that North Africa was a 'backwater' and that the DAK was essentially there to prop up the Italian effort.

***

By the end of 1941 the overall Replacement (R) story, including that for tanks and other AFVs, was as shown in table Ger Replacements 1941 (pages 172-175). Because this table is generated from the German FILARN model, it **takes into account those tanks and assault guns used in mobilising new panzer and *Sturmgeschütz* (assault gun) units from 22nd June to 31st December 1941.** These newly mobilised combat units included the 22nd and 23rd Panzer Divisions, the separate 203rd Panzer Regiment, and various other separate panzer brigades, battalions and companies. In addition the tanks used in refurbishing large panzer units which were Deployed (D) on 22nd June 1941, such as the 2nd and 5th Panzer Divisions, are taken into account. The details of the tanks 'used' in forming these units is shown in the German Tank MD & MND Matrix (pages 136-137).[252] The German Tank MD & MND Matrix, and therefore table Ger Replacements 1941, also takes account of any unallocated and serviceable tanks on 22nd June 1941, as well as older tanks which became available due to the disbandment or reorganisation of Deployed (D) panzer units from 22nd June to 31st December 1941.[253]

From table Ger Replacements 1941 we can see that only 10% of available Pz Kpfw I and 53% of available Pz Kpfw II light tanks were sent east as Replacements (R). This was reasonable as the Pz Kpfw I was completely obsolete by June 1941 (production had already ceased), and the Pz Kpfw II was really only useful for armoured reconnaissance work. Both these types were by now more suited to panzer training schools in the Replacement Army.

Around 56% of available Pz Kpfw 38(t) light tanks were also sent east, and this is where the mystery starts. Although the Pz Kpfw 38(t) was bordering on obsolescence and was completely outclassed by the T-34, in 1941 it still represented the 'main battle tank' in the 7th, 8th, 12th, 19th and 20th Panzer Divisions on the East Front. These divisions all remained in the front line, under intense combat conditions, and all started to desperately need replacement tanks by October 1941. In addition, few Pz Kpfw 38(t) were being 'reserved' for new units because it was obvious the Pz Kpfw 38(t)'s days were numbered: there was therefore really no good reason at all to keep close to half of new production back in Germany/Czechoslovakia during 1941.

The most important and powerful AFVs fielded by the German Army during 1941 were their Pz Kpfw III and Pz Kpfw IV medium tanks, and StuG III assault guns. These AFVs represented the backbone of the Wehrmacht's panzer and assault artillery forces. However, we can see from table Ger Replacements 1941 that only 35% of

---

[251] This assumes all the tank losses shown were on the East Front. This is reasonable because during late June to the end of September 1941, both the DAK and British 8th Army in North Africa were consolidating their forces (there were no major offensives) and tank losses during this period were minimal.

[252] Refer Volume IIB 4. 2) a. – 'German Land Combat Units Mobilised from 22nd June to 31st December 1941 - The German Tank MD and MND Matrix', Table Ger Tank MD & MND Matrix.

[253] Ibid. Table Ger Tanks Available Jun-Dec 41.

available Pz Kpfw III (50mm) tanks, 36% of available Pz Kpfw IV tanks, and a pitiful 5% of the available StuG III assault guns were sent east as Replacements (R) from 22nd June to 31st December 1941. Even if we include the tank Replacements (R) sent to North Africa, which was not strategically vital in 1941, then: 52% of available Pz Kpfw III (50mm) tanks, 60% of available Pz Kpfw IV tanks, 40% of available Pz Kpfw 38(t), and a staggering 95% of available StuG III assault guns remained in the West. Excluding captured French tanks and AFVs based on French chassis, over 1,750 German and Czech tanks remained in Germany and the Replacement Army in the second half of 1941. Astonishingly, this included **572 Pz Kpfw III (50mm) tanks, 169 Pz Kpfw IV tanks, 190 Pz Kpfw 38(t) tanks and 270 StuG III assault guns**. Most of these AFVs were newly produced vehicles: they remained unused by any existing (Deployed (D)) combat units or by any new mobilising combat units (MD of MND units), and were not used as Replacements (R), during 1941.

Considering that the German Army was embroiled in the largest land invasion in history and the outcome of WWII effectively hung on its outcome, this replacement policy made absolutely no strategic sense. It would have caused almost no hardship on German industry or its population (or on the troops in North Africa, or on the new panzer unit mobilisation schedule) to have doubled the number of medium tank replacements on the East Front during 1941, and multiplied the assault gun replacements by an order of magnitude.

***

It is easy to attribute the blame for the German High Command's strategically incomprehensible strategy regarding replacements and reinforcements (during Operation Barbarossa) on Hitler himself. There are several reasons for this. Firstly, Hitler was certainly the instigator and driving force in the fateful decision to divert Army Group Centre away from the Moscow axis in late July and early August 1941. Reading different accounts of this decision making process and the events that led up to it, it is not difficult to see how Hitler's sheer force of will and his position of absolute power could overcome any operational or strategic objections from the OKW. Secondly, it is well documented that Hitler became obsessed with having more panzer divisions (and divisions in general) than fewer better equipped and trained divisions. As the war wore on this desire became ever more acute, and by 1945 many of Hitler's 'divisions' were paper organisations or battalion strength units. An example of this during Operation Barbarossa was the remarkable decision to form the 22nd and 23rd Panzer Divisions in September 1941. Neither of these units could be ready for operations until February-March 1942 at the earliest. They were therefore irrelevant to the outcome of Operation Barbarossa at the operational level, but had a severely detrimental impact at the strategic level: i.e. they consumed valuable resources which could otherwise have found their way in to existing panzer units as Replacements (R) during the most critical phase of Operation Barbarossa. Thirdly, Hitler continuously exhibited a micromanagement style in relation to military-logistical matters which should never have concerned him. For example, Guderian (in his memoirs Panzer Leader) recounts an incident in August 1941 in which Field Marshal Fedor von Bock (Army Group Centre's commander) implored Hitler for tank replacements; but the only concession he could get was a handful of spare tank engines!

However, it has also arguably been too convenient to blame Hitler for the logistical and planning failures of the German Army's High Command. The failure to mobilise Germany for total war, and the astonishing strategic failure to even fully utilise available and critical assets such as tanks and assault guns, must be borne in part by the OKW and OKH staff officers and chief planners. These were the military professionals who were responsible for the supply and support of their field army no matter what situation that army found itself in operationally. It is hard to believe (but not impossible to believe) that a whole entourage of strong willed and intelligent staff officers could not influence Hitler in matters of longer term logistics management and contingency planning.

At the beginning of this section it was stated that there is a common perception in most literature regarding Operation Barbarossa that the panzer regiments in the panzer divisions were 'worn out' by December 1941, and that the main reason for this was that German tank and assault gun production could not meet the demand for replacement vehicles. From the analysis above, we can now conclude that **there were in fact sufficient new tanks and assault guns released to the Wehrmacht from German industry to replace almost all their combat losses during the second half of 1941**. Not only that, but the replacement AFVs would have mostly consisted of more powerful medium Pz Kpfw III and Pz Kpfw IV tanks, and the Wehrmacht could have simultaneously maintained its historically modest mobilisation programme. In the event most of the panzer regiments in the East were close to being worn out by the end of December 1941. However, this was **not** due to the failure of German industry to produce sufficient AFV replacements (as commonly perceived). It was almost entirely due to the almost unbelievable strategic ineptitude of the German High Command in keeping these AFVs in the West while the panzer and assault artillery forces on the East Front attritted through 1941. This was especially incomprehensible during the most critical period for Operation Barbarossa's success; namely July to October 1941.

d. Small Arms Used by all Ground Combat Units in the Reich in 1941, including Replacements (R)

The 'small arms distribution' column (the fourth column) in table <u>Ger Replacements 1941</u> (pages 172-175) indicates the number and type of small arms used by each database unit. This information is identical to the small arms distribution used in the German Personnel and Equipment Resource Database to calculate the combat parameters for each database unit.[254] The fifth column of this table displays the total small arms used by all the database units in the third column: that is the small arms used by all Replacements (R) sent to the East Front from 22nd June to 31st December 1941. Also included in the fifth column (for convenience) is the total motorcycles used by all the database units in the third column: that is the motorcycles (including sidecars and Sd.Kfz.2s) used by all Replacements (R).

Adjacent to this is shown the percentage of available small arms (and motorcycles) used by all D, MD, MND and R combat units from 22nd June to 31st December 1941.[255] It is quite revealing to compare these percentages with the corresponding figures in the Soviet FILARM model. The German figures for handguns, rifles and carbines, SMGs and MGs are 88%, 75%, 81% and 86%, respectively. The German figure for MGs includes all LMGs, GPMGs (general purpose machine guns) used as LMGs in infantry squads, GPMGs used as MMGs and HMGs (medium and heavy machine guns), and MGs mounted on AFVs.[256] The Soviet figures for handguns, rifles and carbines, SMGs and LMGs are 93%, 85%, 100% and 100%, respectively. The Soviet LMGs exclude MMGs, HMGs and AFV mounted MGs.[257]

In all categories, the German war effort used far fewer of their available small arms than the Soviet war effort did. This is especially true for SMGs and LMGs (or GPMG-LMG equivalents). This explains why the majority of Soviet Replacements (R) were 'light rifle squads' and 'irregular squads' as opposed to 'rifle squads', and why 54% of the rifle squads authorised in the July 1941 TOE rifle division were also light rifle squads. Soviet light rifle squads had no LMGs and almost no SMGs because there simply weren't any available (indicated by the 100% used). The figures for other types of small arms also indicate that the vast majority of hand guns and rifles in the Soviet inventory were also 'used up': over 93% of pistols-revolvers and 85% of rifles-carbines had been allocated to combat units by the end of 1941. When one considers that the Soviet June 1941 small-arms inventory included large numbers of old weapons dating back to the 19th century, and that the percentages above don't include a large proportion of the armed rear area support troops, then it becomes obvious that a large proportion of the newly mobilised Soviet soldiers were barely armed during 1941.[258] The real significance of these figures is that they show that the USSR immediately mobilised for total war (from July 1941) to a much higher degree than the Germans. Even if the Soviets had called up more personnel than they did historically, they had nothing to arm them with. In fact, these figures suggest the USSR may have even over-mobilised. This is because unarmed (and usually untrained) personnel in the Red Army contributed less to the Soviet war effort than personnel remaining in productive roles in the Soviet economy.[259]

By contrast the German infantry squads, and especially their motorised infantry squads, were very well armed. Nearly all infantry squads were equipped with a MG 34 GPMG and at least one SMG each, while motorised infantry (*Schützen*) squads had two MG 34 GPMGs each. There were of course far fewer German infantry squads fielded during 1941 (and WWII in general) than Soviet rifle and light rifle squads. The significance of the lower German 'small-arms usage' figures in table <u>Ger Replacements 1941</u> is that they, again, indicate that the Germans did **not** fully mobilise for total war during 1941. The Germans still had around 25% of their available rifles, 19% of their available SMGs and 14% of their available MGs unallocated to combat units in 1941.

---

[254] Refer Volume IIA 2. 2) - 'The German Personnel and Equipment Resource Database - German Squads Equipped with Light Infantry Weapons', for details on typical small arms distribution in German squads in 1941.

[255] These are calculated by adding all the small arms used in D, MD, MND and R units from the relevant tables, and dividing by the sum of all available small arms in the Reich on 22nd June 1941 plus all the small arms produced from June to the end of December 1941, also derived from the relevant tables.

[256] This is because the German Army was the only army in WWII to use GPMGs (general purpose machine guns), namely the MG 34 and later MG 42. These served as LMGs, MMGs and HMGs. All other armies, including the Red Army, used an LMG (or an equivalent air cooled weapon) in their rifle/infantry squads, and much heavier MG types as MMGs and HMGs.

[257] Ibid.

[258] This was particularly true for the irregular squads (in the so called 'fighter battalions') because they had the lowest priority for receiving new weapons. In addition militia type units were often equipped with whatever local weapons and equipment were available and that hadn't already been commandeered into the Red Army. Also, in 1941 the Soviet rear area support troops (but not their NKVD security units) were much less well armed than their Axis counterparts.

[259] Refer Volume IIIB 2. 17) a. – 'The Proportion of Total Available Resources Allocated to Deployed (D) and Newly Mobilised Units in 1941 - Conclusions in Regard to the Weaknesses, Bottlenecks and Constraints on the Soviet Mobilisation Process in 1941'. Also, Volume IIIB 2. 18) – 'The Resource Replacements (R) Available to the Red Army, NKVD, PVO and Soviet Militia from 22nd June to 31st December 1941'.

In terms of absolute numbers this equates to approximately 130,000 handguns, 1,590,000 rifles and carbines, 62,000 SMGs and 35,000 MGs.[260] This was sufficient small arms to fully equip an additional 35,000 heavy infantry/rifle squads, and still have over 1,340,000 rifles and carbines on hand! We can see from table Ger Replacements 1941 that only around 29,700 heavy rifle squads were actually sent to the East Front as Replacements (R) during 1941. Given the manpower situation discussed in the previous section 'German Personnel Losses and Replacements', it is clear that the German High Command could have easily doubled the number of heavy rifle squad replacements sent to the East Front from June to December 1941.[261]

The overall findings of this examination are very much in line with those from the previous two sections ('German Personnel Losses and Replacements' and 'German Tank and Assault Gun Losses and Replacements'). In these sections it is evident that the bottleneck in the German's mobilisation process was not physical and economical (as it was with the Soviets), but was political and the result of strategic policy. In this case the constraint on German infantry squad replacements sent to the East Front in 1941 was **not** due to any failure of German industry to produce sufficient small arms, nor was it due to shortages of available manpower: it was (again) due to the strategic policy dictated by the German High Command.

***

e. Personnel Used by all Types of Replacements (R)

We now come to the distribution of available replacement personnel used by the various types of Replacements (R). Even though the majority of German Army Replacements (R) went into the various infantry type units as infantrymen, a major proportion were needed to crew and support the various weapons and other equipment also used as Replacements (R).

The sixth column of table Ger Replacements 1941 indicates the average number of personnel required for the German ground forces to replace a similar database unit lost in tactical combat. For infantry type squads it is assumed the new Replacement (R) required a full complement of personnel to be replaced; i.e. a 10 man infantry squad required 10 Replacement (R) personnel. For weapon systems and other equipment, the Replacement (R) personnel required is an estimate based on the size of the crew required to man and support the weapon type, and the proportion of the original crew likely to have been killed, wounded or missing in combat when that weapon system was destroyed.

For example, the Pz Kpfw III and Pz Kpfw IV tanks had a crew of five who were immediately vulnerable if the tank was destroyed. On average around half the tank crew were killed or wounded when a penetrative hit occurred on a typical WWII tank.[262] Obviously the rear area personnel supporting the tank were unaffected by

---

[260] Collated from the data in tables '% of Ger Resources Deployed (D)', 'Ger Resources in MD & MND Units in 1941' and 'Ger Replacements 1941', rounded to the nearest thousand.

[261] Refer Volume IIB 4. 7) c. i. – 'Replacements (R) Actually Issued to the German Ground Forces on the East Front During 1941 - German Personnel Losses (Casualties) and Replacements'.

[262] This fact, and the consequential loss of trained tank crewmen, is conveniently ignored in most WWII literature that praises Soviet and Western Allied mass production of lighter and more vulnerable 'medium' tanks. The Germans are often criticised for focusing on fewer heavier tanks, like the Tiger and Panther, instead of cheaper and easier to produce tanks. However, all these tanks had 4-5 crewmen and, on average, a little over half of them became casualties when the tank was destroyed by a direct hit. Let us take the Tiger I and II tanks as an example. The detailed history of every Tiger battalion shows that, on average, they destroyed 12 enemy tanks for every Tiger destroyed in tactical combat (i.e. when they were actually shooting at each other or other targets), which is when the casualties occurred. This ratio dropped to around 5.4 to 1 when all operational losses are included (i.e. including Tigers abandoned due to fuel shortages, lost in large pockets, etc). This does not include the additional kill ratio that these same Tigers achieved against enemy anti-tank guns and artillery, which, in fact, destroyed more Tigers in combat than enemy tanks did. E.g. the 502nd Tiger Battalion destroyed 1,400 tanks, but even more impressive is that it also destroyed around 2,000 anti-tank guns and artillery pieces. (Ref: W. Wilbeck, Sledgehammers, The Aberjona Press, Bedford, Pen, 2004, p. 186. Also, W. Schneider, Tigers in Combat; Volume I and II, J.J. Fedorowicz Publishing Inc, Winnipeg, Canada, 1994 and 1998.) Limiting ourselves to only the tanks destroyed; if 12 Soviet or Western Allied tanks (the large majority being T-34s and Shermans) were destroyed in combat for each Tiger destroyed in combat, then this equates to around 36 trained Allied tank crewmen being killed or wounded for every 3 German. If we include the many other personnel and weapons destroyed by these same Tigers, such as the literally thousands of artillery pieces, anti-tank guns and infantry units, then this figure probably doubles in the German's favour! Apart from the incredible waste of human life, it should be remembered that it takes just as long to train a tank crew to operate a weak tank as it does a superior tank. As the saying goes, "it takes a few weeks to build a tank, but it takes 20 years to build a tank crew". Although the overall figures for Panther tanks are not as extreme as those for the Tiger, they are still similarly stark.

However it gets even worse than this. The chances of a tank crew surviving in a weaker tank suffering a penetrative hit from a powerful anti-tank weapon were considerably less than the chances of a tank crew surviving in a strong tank suffering a penetrative hit from a weaker anti-tank weapon. In other words Tiger and Panther crews more often escaped unscathed from penetrative hits by T-34 and Sherman tanks (and similarly powerful anti-tank guns), while entire T-34 and Sherman crews were

tactical combat, so on average three new Replacement (R) crew were required along with a new Pz Kpfw III or Pz Kpfw IV to replace the loss.

Another example is a divisional artillery regiment which contained the gun-howitzer crews as well as a large numbers of personnel to support them. For example, a German 1st wave infantry division's artillery regiment was authorised 2,872 men, and contained 36 10.5cm leFH light field howitzers and 12 15cm sFH heavy field howitzers.[263] The crew servicing these weapons, including those bringing up the 'ready ammunition' and in local fire direction (signals), ranged from 24 to 36 men. The rest of the men in the regiment fulfilled a multitude of supply and support functions. In tactical combat the howitzer would most commonly have been destroyed by an enemy high explosive shell or bomb, or by direct infantry assault. In this case it is assumed that on average approximately a third of the howitzer crew became casualties. Again, it is assumed that the rear area personnel supporting the artillery were largely unaffected. Therefore to replace a typical 10.5cm leFH light field howitzer required, on average, eight new Replacement (R) personnel along with a new artillery piece. Similarly, to replace a typical 15cm sFH heavy field howitzer required, on average, twelve new Replacement (R) personnel along with a new artillery piece.

It should be noted here that defeat at the tactical combat level can (and often did) lead to much larger operational level losses. For example, loss of a tank regiment's tanks might lead to the bulk of the tank regiment, including its support personnel and rear area units, being overrun or surrounded. In this case the tank regiment itself was lost and this was a much more difficult entity to replace than simply the tanks themselves. This is taken into account in the FILARM model by the loss of the entire combat unit: it is withdrawn from the simulation map and is no longer Deployed (D). Replacements (R) are only issued to combat units which are Deployed (D) and hence have most of their supporting infrastructure intact. For a completely destroyed combat unit to be rebuilt it requires the support equipment and personnel to be rebuilt as well as all the weapons. In this case the combat unit needs to be Mobilised and Deployed (MD) again. If a combat unit is destroyed but a portion is saved, then the FILARM model takes the saved resources into account via the 'Disband and Shatter Process' detailed in 'The Structure of the Fully Integrated Land and Air Resource Model (FILARM)'.[264] In this process all recoverable losses from disbanded or shattered units are allocated to the campaign reserves and then into newly mobilising units.

Having determined the average personnel used in each Replacement (R) database unit, we can ascertain the total personnel used by each type of replacement. This is displayed in the seventh column of table Ger Replacements 1941. In total approximately 626,000 personnel were allocated as Replacements (R) from 22nd June to 31st December 1941, of which around 60% were in infantry squads, bicycle infantry squads, motorcycle infantry squads or irregular squads.

***

---

often killed outright by the much more destructive guns on Tigers and Panthers. Thus the ratio of 'lives lost' was even less in the Allied favour than above. Furthermore, as the Tiger and Panther crews tended to survive longer they had more opportunity to improve on their basic training with combat experience (and hence they became even more lethal on the battlefield). Conversely, many more Soviet and Western Allied tank crews never had the opportunity to improve with battlefield experience because they simply didn't live long enough. This tragic cost in human life and loss of highly trained personnel is rarely mentioned in literature discussing the 'high financial and production cost' of German tanks. Usually the focus is exclusively on the (apparently obvious) strategic success of mass producing cheaper and lighter tanks: the fact that the German Army didn't have the luxury of unlimited numbers of personnel that they could 'expend' in less survivable and cheaper tanks is ignored.

As a (related) aside, it should also be noted that all the German medium and heavy tanks from WWII (from the Pz III upwards) were the easiest tanks to get out of in an emergency. In terms of the numbers and positioning of escape hatches, they were all superior to the M4 Sherman, and vastly superior to all the main Soviet types (especially the T-34 and IS series; both of which were 'death traps' for most of the crew positions if a penetrating hit occurred. The IS-2 being easily the worst medium - heavy tank, in this regard, to see significant combat during WWII). Of course, having more properly designed escape hatches on every tank means a slower production rate (mainly due to the extra work needed to cut and shape the armour plates).

Ironically, when Israel designed the Merkava main battle tank, every consideration (almost regardless of expense) was given to crew survivability: a reflection on the fact that for Israel the tank crew were far more valuable than the tank itself. This wasn't sentiment, but simply that Israel did not have the luxury of unlimited manpower: the tank could be replaced far more easily than a trained tank crew. Today, virtually all western MBTs have very expensive and extensive crew saving features for similar reasons. Why is it that this same AFV characteristic (so sought after in the post-war period and today) is totally ignored in discussions on the pros and cons of producing Tigers and Panthers during WWII; when Germany had far more limited human resources than the Soviets or Western Allies?

[263] A. Buchner, The German Infantry Handbook 1939-1945, Schiffer Military History, Atglen, PA, 1991, p. 85. These comprised 114 officers, 10 administrators, 427 non-commissioned officers and 2,321 enlisted men.

[264] Refer Volume I Part I 3. - 'The Concepts and General Structure of the Integrated Land and Air Resource Model - The Structure of the Fully Integrated Land and Air Resource Model (FILARM)'.

5. The Luftwaffe in 1941

1) The Structure of the Luftwaffe: June to December 1941

a. The *Geschwader* and *Gruppe*

The overall authorised structure of the Luftwaffe's air combat units in June 1941 was as shown in the accompanying diagram <u>Luft TOE</u>. The basic unit in the Luftwaffe at the operational level (as opposed to the tactical-combat level) was the *Geschwader* (Aviation wing). The commander of the *Geschwader* was usually a *Major, Oberstleutnant* or *Oberst*, and he was given the honorary title *Geschwaderkommodore* or *Kommodore*.[265] Fighter and bomber *Geschwader* were authorised 164 aircraft each, while air-transport *Geschwader* were authorised 216 aircraft each. The approximate organisational equivalent in the Western Allied forces was the RAF Group and the USAAF Wing.

Individual *Geschwader* were identified by a number with an abbreviated prefix according to its branch of service. These prefixes were as follows:

- JG - *Jagdgeschwader* – Fighter aviation wing (e.g., JG 54).
- NJG - *Nachtjagdgeschwader* – Night fighter aviation wing (e.g., NJG 1).
- ZG - *Zerstörergeschwader* – Heavy fighter aviation wing (e.g., ZG 26).
- SchG - *Schlachtgeschwader* – Ground attack aviation wing (e.g., SchG 2).
- StG - *Sturzkampfgeschwader* – Dive-bomber aviation wing (e.g., StG 77).
- SKG - *Schnellkampfgeschwader* – High-speed bomber aviation wing (e.g., SKG 210).
- KG - *Kampfgeschwader* - Bomber aviation wing (e.g., KG 51).
- KG zbV - *Kampfgeschwader zu besonderen Verwendung* – Special purpose (transport) bomber aviation wing (e.g., KG zbV 1).[266]
- LLG - *Luftlandegeschwader* – Air-landing (airborne and glider) aviation wing (e.g., LLG 1).
- LG - *Lehrgeschwader* – Operational training aviation wing (e.g., LG 2).

Several *Geschwader* were given honorary titles as well as their alpha numeric designation. For example, the JG 54 *Grunherz* (Green Heart) and the ZG 26 *Horst Wessel*.

Each *Geschwader* was normally comprised of three or four *Gruppen* (Aviation groups), which were designated with Roman characters. For example,

III./ JG 54 was the third *Gruppe* of *Jagdgeschwader* 54.

I./ KG 51 was the first *Gruppe* of *Kampfgeschwader* 51.

In addition to the three or four *Gruppen*, the *Geschwaderstab* (Aviation wing staff) was also authorised a *Stabstaffel* with four aircraft. These were often used by the *Geschwaderkommodore* and his staff, and it was not uncommon for the *Stabstaffel* aircraft to be used in combat.

The commander of a *Gruppe* was usually a *Major* or *Hauptmann*, and he was given the title *Gruppenkommandeur* or *Kommandeur*.[267] The individual *Gruppe* was usually organised with three (occasionally four) *Staffeln*, which were numbered with Arabic numerals. For example,

9. / JG 54 was the ninth *Staffel* of *Jagdgeschwader* 54 (under III./ JG 54).

1. / KG 51 was the first *Staffel* of *Kampfgeschwader* 51 (under I./ KG 51).

Apart from the three *Staffeln*, the *Gruppenstab* (Group staff) was also authorised a *Stabsschwarm* with four aircraft. These were used by the *Gruppenkommandeur* and his staff, and it normal practise for the *Stabsschwarm* to be used on combat missions.

***

---

[265] These Wehrmacht ranks equate to that of Major, Lieutenant Colonel and Colonel, respectively, in the West.

[266] Note, KGr zbV (as opposed to the very similar KG zbV) were separate air-transport groups, designated *Kampfgruppe zu besonderen Verwendung* – Special purpose (transport) bomber aviation group. E.g., KGr zbV 172. Later in the war the Luftwaffe's air-transport units were redesignated as *Transportgeschwader* and *Transportfliegergruppe*.

[267] These Wehrmacht ranks equate to that of Major or Captain, respectively, in the West.

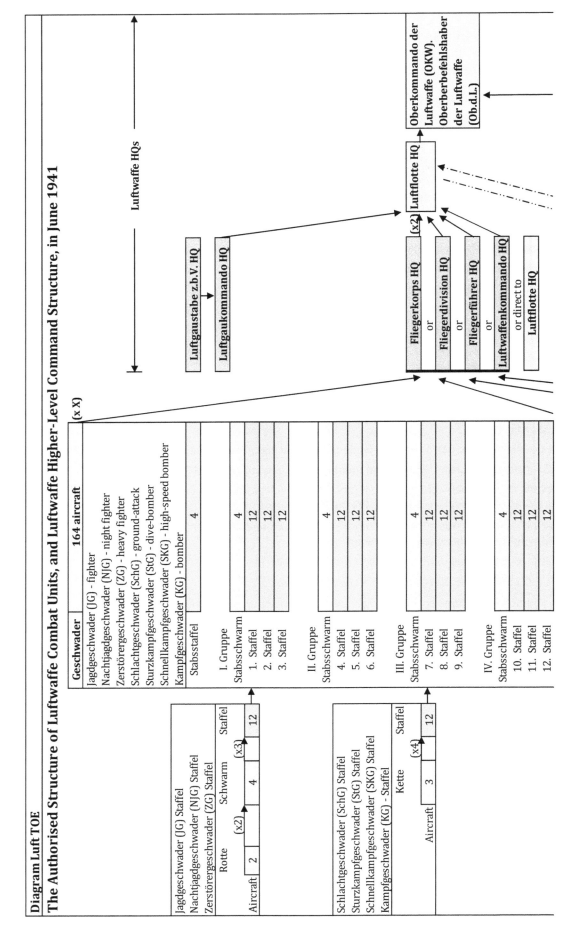

Diagram Luft TOE

The Authorised Structure of Luftwaffe Combat Units, and Luftwaffe Higher-Level Command Structure, in June 1941

Luftwaffe HQs

Luftgaustabe z.b.V. HQ

Luftgaukommando HQ

Fliegerkorps HQ

or

Fliegerdivision HQ

or

Fliegerführer HQ

or

Luftwaffenkommando HQ

or direct to

Luftflotte HQ

Luftflotte HQ (x2)

Oberkommando der Luftwaffe (OKW). Oberberfehlshaber der Luftwaffe (Ob.d.L.)

(x X)

Geschwader	164 aircraft

Jagdgeschwader (JG) - fighter
Nachtjagdgeschwader (NJG) - night fighter
Zerstörergeschwader (ZG) - heavy fighter
Schlachtgeschwader (SchG) - ground-attack
Sturzkampfgeschwader (StG) - dive-bomber
Schnellkampfgeschwader (SKG) - high-speed bomber
Kampfgeschwader (KG) - bomber

Stabsstaffel	4
I. Gruppe Stabsschwarm	4
1. Staffel	12
2. Staffel	12
3. Staffel	12
II. Gruppe Stabsschwarm	4
4. Staffel	12
5. Staffel	12
6. Staffel	12
III. Gruppe Stabsschwarm	4
7. Staffel	12
8. Staffel	12
9. Staffel	12
IV. Gruppe Stabsschwarm	4
10. Staffel	12
11. Staffel	12
12. Staffel	12

Jagdgeschwader (JG) Staffel
Nachtjagdgeschwader (NJG) Staffel
Zerstörergeschwader (ZG) Staffel

	Rotte	Schwarm (x2)	Staffel (x3)
Aircraft	2	4	12

Schlachtgeschwader (SchG) Staffel
Sturzkampfgeschwader (StG) Staffel
Schnellkampfgeschwader (SKG) Staffel
Kampfgeschwader (KG) - Staffel

	Kette	Staffel (x4)
Aircraft	3	12

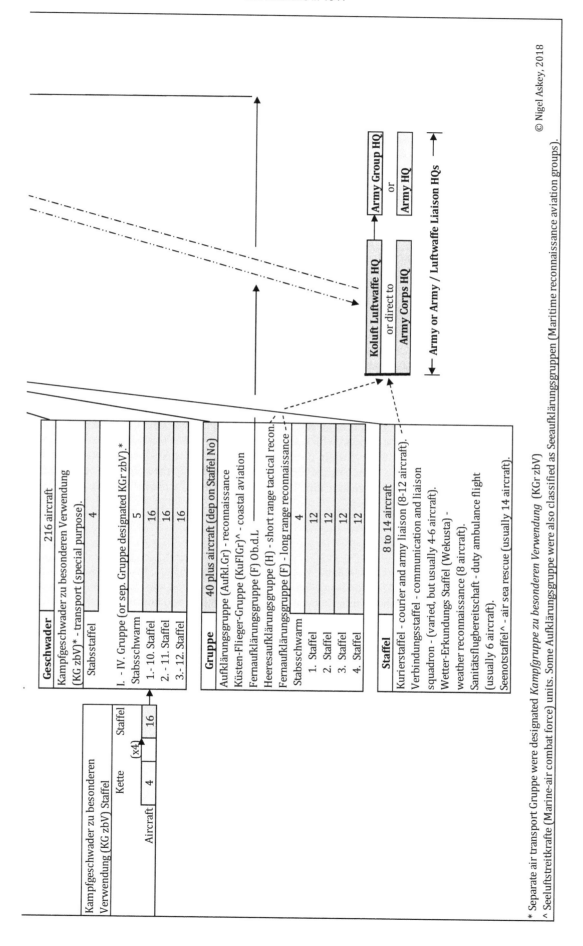

© Nigel Askey, 2018

* Separate air transport Gruppe were designated *Kampfgruppe zu besonderen Verwendung* (KGr zbV).
^ Seeluftstreitkrafte (Marine-air combat force) units. Some Aufklärungsgruppe were also classified as Seeaufklärungsgruppen (Maritime reconnaissance aviation groups).

The exceptions, to being organised into Geschwader, were the reconnaissance and coastal aviation forces. These were generally organised into separate *Gruppen*, and used an abbreviated prefix according to the aviation group's long-range strategic or short-range tactical (army support) role. These prefixes were as follows:

- Aufkl.Gr - *Aufklärungsgruppe* – Reconnaissance aviation group (e.g., Aufkl.Gr 125).

- F - *Fernaufklärungsgruppe* - Long range reconnaissance aviation group (e.g., (F)/122).

- H - *Heeresaufklärungsgruppe* - Short range army reconnaissance aviation group (e.g., (H)/10).

- Pz - *Panzeraufklärungsgruppe* - Short range army reconnaissance aviation group attached to a motorised (panzer) corps (e.g., (Pz)/11).

- Ku.Fl.Gr (or sometimes KGr) - *Küstenfliegergruppe* - Coastal aviation group (e.g., Ku.Fl.Gr 806).

- Bo.Fl.Gr - *Bordfliegergruppe* - Ship based aviation group (e.g., Bo.Fl.Gr 196).

In these cases the individual *Staffel* was still designated with numbered Arabic numerals. For example,

3./Aufkl.Gr 125 was the third *Staffel* of *Aufklärungsgruppe* 125.

4.(F)/122 was the fourth *Staffel* of *Fernaufklärungsgruppe* 122.

2.(H)/10 was the second *Staffel* of *Heeresaufklärungsgruppe* 10.

A particular reconnaissance group was the *Aufklärungsgruppe Oberbefehlshaber der Luftwaffe* (AufklObdL) which was directly subordinate to the overall commander of the Luftwaffe; namely *Reichsmarschall* Hermann Goring.

It is appropriate to note here the Luftwaffe's doctrine on conducting 'aggressive' reconnaissance. This most often entailed reconnaissance aircraft taking advantage of any 'targets of opportunity' during missions (unless ordered otherwise for security reasons). With that in mind the *Aufklärungsgruppe* and *Fernaufklärungsgruppe* were often equipped with slightly modified long range bombers or twin engine fighter-bombers, and the relatively elite crews in these units were trained to attack targets quickly and then evade any enemy response. In addition, the name given to these units was not always a clear indication of their equipment or primary function. For example, on 22nd June 1941, Aufkl.Gr 125 was wholly equipped with seaplanes so one would reasonably expect it to have had a coastal aviation designation. Similarly, Ku.Fl.Gr 806 (in the same area of the Baltic Sea) was wholly equipped with fast Ju 88 bombers so one might expect it to have had a KG designation. Obviously the seaplanes of Aufkl.Gr 125 were used for naval reconnaissance work and also attacking naval targets, while the bombers of Ku.Fl.Gr 806 also patrolled over land areas and attacked land targets.

*** *

b. The Staffel

The *Staffel* was the basic unit in the Luftwaffe at the tactical-combat level (as opposed to the operational level) and was roughly equivalent to an RAF Squadron. The commander of a *Staffel* was usually a *Hauptmann*, *Oberleutnant* or *Leutnant*, and he was given the title *Staffelkapitan*.[268] All fighter and bomber *Staffel* were authorised 12 aircraft each, while transport *Staffel* were authorised 16 aircraft each, and some specialised *Staffel* had 8-14 aircraft each.

Fighter *Staffel* in *Jagdgeschwader*, *Nachtjagdgeschwader* and *Zerstörergeschwader* were made up of three tactical formations: the *Schwarm* with four aircraft each. Each *Schwarm* was in turn divided into two basic tactical formations: the *Rotte* with two aircraft each. The significance of the *Rotte* (the basic leader and wingman tactical formation) and the *Schwarm* (the mutually supporting pair) may not be understood by the casual reader, but will not be lost on those knowledgeable about the history of aircraft dog-fighting.

During the pre-war period the best tactical fighter formation was widely thought to be the so called three aircraft V, or 'Vic', formation. As the name implies, this formation comprised a leader and two wingmen. It was championed by the RAF during the initial war period and was the standard formation adopted by the Western Allied air-forces during 1939 and well into 1940. However the Luftwaffe fighter forces were the first to develop and adopt the classic 'finger four' and 'two pairs' tactical air combat formation. This was the direct result of their dog fighting experiences in Spain and was largely due to the efforts of Werner Molders.[269] The Luftwaffe pilots had found several critical weaknesses with the Vic formation. The wingmen were so busy keeping station with their leader and each

---

[268] These Wehrmacht ranks equate to that of Captain, Lieutenant (1st Lieutenant in the US) and 2nd Lieutenant, respectively, in the West.

[269] Significantly, Soviet fighter pilots in Spain, opposing the Condor Legion, do not seem to have learnt the same lesson. If they did then they were not at all successful in conveying these lessons back to the VVS.

other that their opportunity to search the sky for hostile aircraft was vastly reduced. The leader, whose job was to also search the sky and select enemy targets, relied on the wingmen to protect the rear. The result was that almost no one was regularly looking behind and this was where the enemy would probably strike. In addition, the leader had to be careful not to make sudden movements without warning his wingmen because one or other of them could easily collide with him. This resulted in loss of valuable seconds in starting any sudden manoeuvre. Of course the Vic formation always did look good, and was very suitable for peacetime manoeuvres and air displays. The failure of the Luftwaffe's fighter opponents to immediately copy the *Rotte* and *Schwarm* (with two *Rotte* mutually supporting each other) placed them at a disadvantage during air to air combat. The RAF had learnt this lesson the hard way in France in 1940, but by June 1941 the Soviet VVS still had to go through the same learning experience (as demonstrated by their fighter *Zveno* still having three aircraft). It is noteworthy that the basic two aircraft tactical formation (leader and wingman) and the 'mutually supporting pair' remained the preferred tactical fighter formation in Korea, Vietnam and beyond. To this day it remains the standard tactical fighter formation for close in combat and manoeuvre.

Bomber *Staffel* in *Kampfgeschwader*, *Schnellkampfgeschwader*, *Schlachtgeschwader* and *Sturzkampfgeschwade* were made up of four tactical formations: the *Kette* (chain) with three aircraft each. The *Kette* employed a leader and two followers, although Luftwaffe bomber crews were trained and equipped (with a navigator, radios, etc) to operate independently if necessary. In general it was found the *Kette* could provide good mutual defensive fire support for bomber formations, and several *Kette* could support each other in larger formations.

The *Kampfgeschwader zu besonderen Verwendung* (KG zbV - transport) *Staffeln* were organised similarly to the bomber units with four *Kette* per *Staffel*. However the KG zbV *Kette* had four aircraft each (vs. three in the bomber *Kette*), while the KG zbV *Stabsschwarm* had five aircraft (vs. four). This meant that each KG zbV *Staffel* was authorised 16 aircraft, each KG zbV *Gruppe* was authorised 53 aircraft, and a KG zbV unit with four *Gruppen* and a *Stabsstaffel* (with 4 aircraft) was therefore authorised a total of 216 aircraft.

***

In addition to fighter, bomber and air-transport *Staffeln*, there were several types of independent (separate) *Staffel* employed in the Luftwaffe which fulfilled specialised functions. The most significant of these (which are also included in the Luftwaffe OOB in the succeeding sections of this work), included the following types.

- *Wettererkundungsstaffel* - Wekusta - Meteorological reconnaissance aviation squadron (e.g., Wekusta 26).[270]

- *Kurierstaffel* - Courier and liaison squadron (e.g., Kurierstaffel 3.).

- *Verbindungsstaffel* - Communication and liaison squadron (e.g., Verbindungsstaffel 52.).

- *Sanitätsflugbereitschaft* - Duty Ambulance flight (e.g., Sanitätsflugbereitschaft 2.).

- *Seenotstaffel* - Sea rescue squadron (e.g., Seenotstaffeln 9.).

- *Wüstennotstaffel* - Desert rescue squadron (e.g., Wüstennotstaffel 1.).

The Wekusta *Staffeln* were authorised 8 aircraft each, although they were rarely at full strength. These incongruously named units were somewhat deceptive in that they were also frequently used for long-range strategic reconnaissance. They were usually equipped with long range bombers which were armed (depending on the mission range) and could also attack any targets of opportunity.

The *Kurierstaffeln* were authorised 8 - 12 aircraft each (depending on their assignment) and were usually equipped with short-range battlefield reconnaissance and transport aircraft: the most famous of these being the outstanding Fieseler Fi 156 *Storch* (Stork) STOL aircraft. A particular *Kurierstaffel* usually reported directly to an Army or Army Corps HQ (see below) although it was still a Luftwaffe unit with primarily Luftwaffe personnel. The *Kurierstaffel* were mostly used for transporting important command personnel around the battlefield, communication and air-ambulance duties. However in some circumstances, where no *Heeresaufklärungsgruppe* units were available, the *Kurierstaffel* would also fulfil the role of short-range army reconnaissance.

The *Verbindungsstaffeln* (usually authorised 4-6 aircraft each) had a similar function, and performed in a similar fashion, to the *Kurierstaffeln*. The large majority of these units were formed from April to May 1941 in recognition of the fact that the Wehrmacht now had many disparate units spread across Europe and North Africa, and was about to invade the huge expanse of the USSR. The *Verbindungsstaffeln* were seen as temporary units that could be quickly formed in order to meet the rapidly expanding liaison and communication needs of both the Army and Luftwaffe, especially in the East where Operation Barbarossa was about to commence.[271] They were mostly formed

---

[270] Depending on source, these units are also sometimes listed as *Wetter-Erkundungs Staffel* (abbreviated as Wekusta) or *Wetter-Fernerkundungs-Staffel* (abbreviated as Westa (F)).

[271] There was also a *Flugbereitschaft* (Standby (duty) flight) attached to some higher HQs. In some cases a HQ did not have a *Stabsschwarm*, *Stabskette* or *Kurierstaffel* assigned; or the assigned *Stabsschwarm* was not considered large enough to meet that

from the various Luftwaffe training schools and replacement units.[272] In November and December 1941 most of the *Verbindungsstaffeln* on the East Front were temporarily disbanded, and their aircraft and crews returned to their parent training schools. Most of these units were again reformed in April 1942 in preparation for the German summer offensive in the East. The *Verbindungsstaffeln* operated a variety of second line aircraft such as the: Arado Ar 66 and Ar 96, Caudron C.445, Fieseler Fi 156, Focke-Wulf Fw 58, Gotha Go 145, Junkers W 34, Klemm Kl 35 and Siebel Fh 104.

The *Sanitätsflugbereitschaften* were created to transport the sick and wounded to medical facilities further in the rear which could not be easily reached by train or road. Most of the existing *Sanitätsflugbereitschaften* were formed in March 1941, specifically in preparation for Operation Barbarossa. At this time each *Sanitätsflugbereitschaft* was authorised 6 Junkers Ju 52 aircraft, which were fitted to accommodate up to 12 patients on stretchers and medical staff. Later in 1941 each *Sanitätsflugbereitschaft* was authorised an additional 4 Fieseler Fi 146 STOL aircraft. Combat experience had shown that an aircraft was needed which could pick up wounded directly from the front line (or as close as practical) and fly them to the rear for further transport. The unit's TOE also included a ground ambulance section (*Krankenkraftwagenzug*) with 12 ambulances and/or buses, as well medical staff and the usual (aircraft) ground support infrastructure. In 1941 most of the *Sanitätsflugbereitschaften* reported directly to a *Fliegerkorps* or a *Luftflotte* HQ.

The *Seenotstaffeln* were normally authorised 14 aircraft each and were usually equipped with seaplanes such as the Heinkel He 59, and floatplanes such as the Dornier Do 18 and Do 24. As their name implies, the *Seenotstaffeln* were used for air sea rescue; mainly of downed pilots. However like most other separate Luftwaffe *Staffeln*, the *Seenotstaffeln* often found themselves fulfilling several roles. In this case it included long-range maritime reconnaissance and interdiction, and less well known, the *Seenotstaffeln* specialised in clandestine air-sea-land operations at night off the enemy's coast. The latter usually involved dropping off and picking up agents, or laying mines in narrow shipping channels.

The *Wüstennotstaffel* was a very specialised unit which was formed to rescue downed pilots in the desert terrain in North Africa. *Wüstennotstaffel* 1. was formed in June 1941 with the only aircraft really able to perform this task well: namely the Fieseler Fi 146 *Storch* STOL aircraft. The problems associated with rescuing a pilot in the desert were similar to those posed in an air-sea rescue. First, the downed aircrew had to be found in the trackless and barren landscape with few (if any) landmarks. Thus any rescue aircraft had to be able to 'loiter' in the search area for some time, whilst being able to navigate on instruments and have good downward visibility for the pilot and/or observer. If the aircrew were found, the aircraft then had to be able to land relatively safely on unprepared ground. As far as is known, *Wüstennotstaffel* 1. was authorised 12 Fi 146 aircraft in 1941, and it operated very successfully throughout the rest of 1941 and through 1942.

***

HQ's communication and liaison requirements. In this case a *Flugbereitschaft* was sometimes formed (usually on a temporary basis) which incorporated the aircraft of any assigned *Stabsschwarm* or *Stabskette. Flugbereitschaften* were generally ad hoc units formed and disbanded as the demand arose. *Flugbereitschaften* were more common after 1941, and the largest such unit known to exist in 1941 was Flugber./Luftflotte 2 which operated some 30-40 aircraft on the East Front from June to November 1941.
[272] Servicing and technical support for the aircraft in the *Verbindungsstaffel* was normally provided by the ground support personnel of other Luftwaffe units stationed at the same airfield.

c. Luftwaffe Higher-Level Command Structure

The overall Luftwaffe higher-level command structure, in June 1941, was as shown on the right side of the accompanying diagram Luft TOE (pages 194-195).

The highest command HQ in the Luftwaffe was the ***Oberkommando der Luftwaffe*** (**OKL** - Luftwaffe High Command) which was led by the *Oberbefehlshaber der Luftwaffe* (ObdL. – Commander-in-chief of the Luftwaffe). During WWII this was Reichsmarschall Hermann Goring. Note, the rank of *Reichsmarschall* was especially created for Goring and was in reality a political rank: it had no equivalent in other military forces. The ObdL reported directly to the Führer (the supreme commander: Hitler) with a 'dotted line' report to the *Oberkommando der Wehrmacht* (OKW - High Command of the Armed Forces).

The highest Luftwaffe command at the operational-strategic level was usually a ***Luftflotte*** (Air fleet). A *Luftflotte,* which was roughly the organisational equivalent of a numbered US Army Air Force, was designated with an Arabic numeral (e.g., Luftflotte 4.). In broad terms a single *Luftflotte* would normally provide the air support for a single Army Group. Depending on the overall strategic and operational situation, there were several types of subordinate HQ assigned to each *Luftflotte*. These were as follows.

- ***Fliegerkorps*** (Aviation corps). A *Fliegerkorps* was the principal organisational HQ used to control larger concentrations of *Geschwader* and (separate) *Staffeln* for offensive operations. They were designated with a Roman numeral (e.g., VIII. Fliegerkorps), and no more than two *Fliegerkorps* were normally assigned to a particular *Luftflotte*.

  A separate *Fliegerkorps*, i.e. one not attached to any *Luftflotte*, would normally report directly to the ObdL. For example, in June 1941 the X. Fliegerkorps in the Mediterranean reported directly to the ObdL and was not assigned to a *Luftflotte*.

  In 1941 a *Fliegerkorps* HQ (the XI. Fliegerkorps) was also used to control and coordinate German airborne operations. This was because all *Fallschirmjäger* units still belonged to the Luftwaffe, even though they came under the tactical-operational control of the Army. For airborne operations the *Fliegerkorps* included *Fallschirmjäger* troops, air-transport groups, a glider group and a reconnaissance squadron.[273]

- ***Fliegerdivision*** (Aviation division). A *Fliegerdivision* was essentially a scaled down version of the *Fliegerkorps*. It was designated with an Arabic numeral (e.g., Fliegerdivision 1.) and usually controlled 2-4 *Geschwader* and (separate) *Staffel.* The *Fliegerdivision* was a relatively rare organisational entity in the Luftwaffe, and in June 1941 none were listed in the Luftwaffe's order of battle.

- ***Fliegerführer*** (Aviation command or leader). A *Fliegerführer* was a lower level Luftwaffe command HQ which was used to control the aviation forces within a defined geographical area. As a result it was usually designated with the name of the area concerned (e.g., Fliegerführer Ostsee – Aviation Command Baltic Sea). If the geographical area's name was not used in the designation then an Arabic numeral was used. *Fliegerführer* HQs usually controlled 0-2 *Geschwader*, along with numerous (separate) *Gruppen* and *Staffeln*.

  A *Fliegerführer* HQ was usually used to control the air-forces required to fulfil a specialised task, such as control of a particular sea area. It was also commonly used to control the air-forces required to defend a particular area using a primarily defensive posture, whilst still being capable of limited offensive operations. If the *Fliegerführer* HQ only controlled fighter units it was usually designated a *Jagdfliegerführer* (e.g., Jagdfliegerführer 2.).

- ***Luftwaffenkommando*** (Air force command). A *Luftwaffenkommando* was very similar to a *Fliegerführer* (above) although not as common. It was also generally used to control the aviation forces within a defined geographical area, and was also designated with the name of the area concerned (e.g., Luftwaffenkommando Kirkenes).

- ***Luftgaukommando*** (Air district command). A *Luftgaukommando* was a Luftwaffe HQ responsible for the ground organisations supporting the air operations within a defined geographical area. They were designated with a Roman numeral and, in most cases, a location name in the geographical area concerned (e.g., Luftgaukommando VIII. Breslau). Usually one *Luftgaukommando* HQ was assigned to a particular *Luftflotte*, but for major offensive operations several subordinate *Luftgaukommando* HQs could also be assigned. In such cases the additional *Luftgaukommando* HQs were designated *Luftgaustabe z.b.V.* (Air district staff for special purpose) and designated with an Arabic numeral (e.g., Luftgaustabe z.b.V. 10.).

---

[273] The XI. Fliegerkorps became the I. Fallschirmkorps (I Parachute Corps) in January 1944. German Army 1933-1945, An Order of Battle Volume V, Ed., L. Cole, Military Press International, Milton Keynes, UK, 1999, p. 68.

The *Luftgaukommando* HQs managed such things as: building and enlarging airfields, managing the field repair and maintenance facilities, organising the motorised logistical supply of all air-combat units, and organising the flying in of replacement (reserve) aircraft. In some instances the *Ergänzungsgruppen* (Training and replacement *Gruppen* which were sometimes also used operationally) reported directly to the *Luftgaukommando* HQ. For example, on 22nd June 1941, Erg./JG 3 and Erg./JG 27 reported directly to Luftgaukommando VIII, which in turn reported to Luftflotte 4.

- **Koluft** – ***Kommandeur der Luftwaffe*** (Air force commander) or ***Kommandeur der Luftstreitkrafte*** (Air combat force commander). A Koluft was a Luftwaffe command and coordinating HQ which was assigned to a particular Army Group or Army. As such it was usually designated with the name of its 'parent' Army HQ. For example, Koluft Mitte (Centre) was the Luftwaffe command HQ reporting directly to Army Group Centre's HQ, and Koluft 18 was the Luftwaffe command HQ subordinate to the 18th Army's HQ.

The Koluft HQs were important units within the overall Wehrmacht command and control framework, and performed several critically important functions:

1. They controlled and coordinated any *Fernaufklärungsstaffeln* (Long range reconnaissance squadrons), *Heeresaufklärungsstaffeln* (Short range army reconnaissance squadrons) and *Kurierstaffeln* (Courier and army liaison squadrons) attached directly to that Army Group or Army HQ. For example, in June 1941 Koluft 4 was attached to the 4th Army and controlled the operations of 1.(F)/33, Kurierstaffel 11 and 2 (H) Signals, which were assigned to the 4th Army's HQ. In effect this meant that German Army Group and Army commanders (and often Corps commanders) had immediate access to 'their own' aviation resources which they could use for all types of reconnaissance and utility work. In addition the Army Group and Army HQs were not burdened with the complexities and logistics of operating (and communicating with) aviation squadrons.

2. The Koluft HQs provided the link between the German Army Group and Army HQs, and their supporting *Luftflotte* and *Fliegerkorps*. The most powerful air-combat units needed for close air-support of friendly ground units, and interdiction of enemy ground units, were normally concentrated in the *Luftflotte*'s *Fliegerkorps*. However it was the German Army's HQs which controlled the day to day ground operations, and ultimately set the operational and strategic objectives. There therefore needed to be rapid and clear communication and control between the various army HQs and their supporting *Luftflotte*'s *Fliegerkorps*. The Koluft HQs provided the command and control functions required to ensure this occurred. The available supporting *Geschwader*, *Gruppen* and *Staffeln* were 'released' (by the supporting *Luftflotte*) for ground support operations to the appropriate Koluft HQ. At the operational level, the Koluft HQ then allocated ground targets and attack schedules as instructed by the relevant army HQs.

3. The Koluft HQ included staff officers from the Luftwaffe's Flak artillery. Their job was to assist in the assignment and coordination of any Luftwaffe Flak units attached to the Army or Army Group.

***

In addition to the Luftwaffe forces reporting via the Koluft HQs to Army Group and Army HQs, in June 1941 most of the infantry and motorised corps HQs on the East Front also had a dedicated *Heeresaufklärungsstaffel* (Short range army reconnaissance squadron) attached. For example, on 22nd June 1941 the VII Corps HQ in 4th Army had the 1.(H)/10 attached, while the IX Corps HQ in 4th Army had the 2.(H)/41 attached. This meant that the corps commanders had dedicated aviation reconnaissance assets, in direct communication with the corps HQ, which could update the corps commander of enemy movements and dispositions almost immediately.[274]

Furthermore, apart from the Koluft personnel, there were Luftwaffe staff and signals personnel embedded in almost every German Field Army HQ from divisional level upwards. These Luftwaffe personnel had the job of coordinating any close air-support when it arrived. These small Luftwaffe units (of squad to platoon size) operated near or on the front line, and were in direct communication with the supporting *Gruppen* and *Staffeln*. They then provided the latest targeting information at the tactical-combat level, ensuring extremely effective close air support for the German ground troops. So effective was this close air-support that there are numerous combat reports of German infantry moving forward to attack a bombed enemy position before the debris from the Stuka's bombs had even settled!

---

[274] These *Heeresaufklärungsstaffeln* usually also had a 'secondary reporting' function to the Army's Koluft HQ.

Interestingly, some WWII commentators criticise the Luftwaffe as being little more than "flying artillery for the German Army" and bemoan the lack of strategic bombing capability.[275] In actual fact this is not a criticism but an inadvertent compliment: to be more precise, the Luftwaffe was 'very accurate flying heavy artillery, which worked with German ground forces in a true combined arms fashion'. It took the US Army Air Force and the RAF until mid-1944 to achieve this level of combined arms sophistication, while **none** of the other army and air forces fielded during WWII managed it.

***

---

[275] Many so-called 'documentaries' and WWII commentators claim it was a strategic mistake for the Germans not to produce a large strategic bomber force, and that it was a mistake for the Luftwaffe to focus on being a tactical air-force (mainly to support the German Army's ground operations). In actuality, the Luftwaffe was never going to be big enough to be all things to all men, and authors which criticise the Luftwaffe's lack off strategic bombing capability forget that it took the US and UK years of uninterrupted and massive production to produce their huge strategic bomber forces by 1944. A small German strategic bombing force (the only type they could have realistically produced if Germany was to also produce anything like adequate ground forces) would have made almost no difference to the war in the West or East. Germany simply never had the production capacity or resources to produce anything like the 7,377 Lancasters, 6,176 Halifaxs, 12,731 B-17s, 18,482 B-24s and 3,960 B-29s produced by the Western Allies. Production of these aircraft types, alone, amounted to almost 49,000 four engine heavy bombers! For comparison, by far the most produced German bomber of the WWII era was the Ju 88, with 14,980 of all types produced (including large numbers of night-fighters and other specialised types). In addition, a typical Ju 88 used only around a third of the material and production capacity required for a four-engine heavy bomber (and probably only a quarter of that required to produce a B-29), so total Ju 88 production was barely equivalent to that required to produce 5,000 four engine heavy bombers.

On top of all this, heavy strategic bombers use an immense amount of fuel (more than any other type of WWII weapon system, pro rata to the overall combat power). To this day, no one has ever produced any sort of satisfactory explanation about where a very large Luftwaffe strategic bomber force (i.e., one sufficiently large enough to affect the course of WWII) was going to get its fuel from. The Germans had to carefully manage their fuel situation as far back as September 1939. A strategic bomber force on the needed scale was always going to burn an order of magnitude more fuel than even the largest panzer force Germany could ever produce (or even a massive, but a predominantly tactical, air force).

Consider that the Allies produced a staggering 1,043,000,000 metric tons of crude oil during WWII (USA, 833.2; USSR, 110.6; UK and British colonies abroad, 90.8; Canada, 8.4; m. metric tons). This was sufficient to fuel the massive number of over 49,000 four engine heavy bombers produced (in addition to the many thousands of two engine and single engine types). Compare this to the entire Axis production of only 67,000,000 metric tons of crude oil during WWII (Germany, 33.4 (with 23.4 from synthetic production plants); Italy, 0.17; Hungary, 3.2; Rumania, 25; Japan, 5.2; m. metric tons). The Allies (including the USSR) produced close to 16 times as much crude oil as all the Axis powers combined, with almost 80% being produced by the USA! Anyone who still believes the USSR and UK could have won WWII in Europe without any assistance from the US would have huge difficulties getting past even this basic start statistic!

Some claim the Axis oil shortages were directly due to the Western Allied strategic bombing campaign. Well, no, not really; this is only partially true (especially before 1945). Total Axis crude oil production (including the Rumanian oil fields) in 1940, 1941, 1942, 1943 and 1944 amounted to 10.1, 11.7, 14.8, 16 and 11.1 m. metric tons, respectively. It is apparent that even from 1941 to 1943, when peak production was achieved and oil-production degradation due to Allied bombing was minor, that the Germans never had the fuel to operate a large strategic bomber force as well as their other forces. They barely had enough fuel to operate the moderately sized (by Western Allied standards) tactical air-force they did produce. In addition, almost all the Allied oil production and refinery was conducted outside the European zone (along with most military production), so even a large German strategic bombing force (using 1940s technology) would have had very little impact on the Allied oil-production industry. Essentially, the Allies had identified oil as the Achilles heel in the Axis war economy (it was rather obvious), and focused on it accordingly. Despite this, German - Rumanian oil production remained at a reasonable level, until it was really smashed in 1945. The Allied strategic bombing campaign only made a bad oil-production situation worse, and only 'much worse' by 1945.

It is very clear that even a moderate Luftwaffe strategic bomber force (by Western Allied standards), even in 1940-42, would have been wishful thinking. As early as January 1944, the entire Luftwaffe fighter force (which had always used far less fuel than even a small strategic bomber force) had to dramatically curtail all its training programmes (i.e., fewer pilot training flights and training flight hours) as there was insufficient fuel available. This was the primary reason for the degradation in Luftwaffe fighter pilot training-standards later in the war. Even U-boat training, and newly commissioned U boat shakedown cruises in the Baltic, were being curtailed by this time for the same reason. In fact, further analysis (based around weapon type effectiveness per litre of fuel consumed) indicates that had the Germans spent a lot of time and scarce resources building and operating a large strategic four-engine bomber force in 1939-42, then this would have actually accelerated their final defeat due to the weakening of their other forces (particularly their much more strategically significant motorised ground forces).

Oil data from: J. Ellis, World War II: A Statistical Survey, Facts on File Inc, New York, 1993, pp. 275, table 81. Also, J. Ellis, Brute Force: Allied Strategy and Tactics in the Second World War, Andre Deutsch Ltd, London, 1990, Appendix, table 50.

2) The Order of Battle and Actual Strength of all Luftwaffe Air Combat Units in a Deployed (D) State on 21st June 1941

a. Luftwaffe Higher Level Organisation and Deployment on 21st June 1941

The Luftwaffe higher-level organisation and chain of command, on the eve of Operation Barbarossa, was as shown in diagram Luft CofC (pages 204-205). There were five *Luftflotte* in existence at this time, of which three and a half were deployed in the East. These were Luftflotte 1, 2, 4 and around half of Luftflotte 5, which represented 67% of the Luftwaffe's total combat-aircraft strength.[276] This means that the Luftwaffe was only able to field around two thirds of its total front-line air strength against the principal enemy in 1941: the USSR.

For Operation Barbarossa the Luftwaffe's initial deployment area extended behind an approximately 1,600km broad front, encompassing the front-lines of the German, Hungarian and Rumanian Armies. It was aimed at an enemy front line roughly 2,400km long between Odessa and Leningrad. Added to this was the Finnish-German front line of about 1,000kms. The Luftwaffe's deployment was adapted to meet the operational and strategic objectives of the German Army, with three primary tasks. These were: the initial elimination of the Soviet Air Force (the VVS) in the Western Military Districts (by destroying them on the ground), protecting German ground forces by destroying VVS bomber units in the air and maintaining air-superiority over the front lines, and direct support of the army on the battlefield. Essentially, each Army Group had a *Luftflotte* assigned to it, and each Army or Panzer Group at the points of main effort had a *Fliegerkorps* assigned to it.

Of vital importance to the Luftwaffe's preparation and deployment in the East, and its ability to maintain ongoing offensive operations, was the work of the *Luftgaukommandos* (Air district commands). These HQs were responsible for the Luftwaffe's ground forces supporting the air operations: an efficient and effective ground organisation was a prerequisite for successful operations by the air formations. The *Luftgaukommando* HQs in the East cooperated closely with the staffs in their assigned *Luftflotte* and *Fliegerkorps*. As well as managing the logistical supply of the air-combat units, the *Luftgaukommando* managed the Luftwaffe construction battalions and the Reich Labour Service (RAD) battalions which built and enlarged the airfields. These units were extremely busy in May 1941 making the final preparations for Operation Barbarossa. For example, Luftgaukommando II enlarged or laid out 105 airfields in preparation for the first phase of the campaign; and it mostly managed to do this while maintaining the security conditions needed for secrecy.[277]

In addition to supporting the initial phase of Operation Barbarossa, the *Luftgaukommandos* had to organise and manage the establishment of the support infrastructures in the newly occupied territories. This included the rapid establishment of new airfields or/and the restoration of captured airfields, supporting the flying units in reconnaissance of new airfields, and moving forward the logistical supply systems to ensure the 'new' airfields were adequately supplied in all respects (especially aviation fuel, ammunition and spare parts). To fulfil this considerable task the Luftwaffe formed two *Luftgaustabe* z.b.V. (Air district staff for special purpose) for each *Luftflotte* supporting Army Groups North, Centre and South. The *Luftgaustabe* z.b.V. and their staffs represented an 'extended arm' of the *Luftgaukommando*, using a system that had been tried and tested, and had proved successful, during previous campaigns.

In practice a *Luftgaustabe* z.b.V. usually worked closely with a particular *Fliegerkorps* as its air-unit bases were moved forward into enemy territory. As we can see from diagram Luft CofC, there were sufficient *Luftgaustabe* z.b.V. for each of the *Fliegerkorps* supporting Army Groups North, Centre and South to be allocated a dedicated support HQ. This was especially critical for *Fliegerkorps* containing *Jagdgeschwader* (Fighter aviation wings), *Sturzkampfgeschwader* (Dive-bomber aviation wings) and *Schlachtgeschwader* (Ground attack aviation wings). This was because of the relatively short operational ranges of these aircraft types, because they used large amounts of fuel and ammunition during offensive operations, and because StG and SchG units provided (by far) the most effective close air-support for the ground troops. The effectiveness of close air-support was greatly enhanced by the air-bases being relatively close to the front lines: the response time (onto target) was reduced and the number of missions per day per aircraft was increased.

The details on each *Luftflotte's* organisation, as well as the details of the air combat units within each *Luftflotte, Fliegerkorps, Fliegerführer* and *Luftwaffenkommando*, are examined in the following sections.

---

[276] 3,297 combat-aircraft out of 4,948 available. This excludes transport aircraft in KGr zbV and LLG Units, and courier, liaison and transport aircraft in *Kurierstaffeln, Verbindungsstaffeln* and *Sanitätsflugbereitschaften*.

[277] The campaign start was initially set for 15th May 1941, so the *Luftgaukommandos* were working to this timeline until April 1941. H. Boog, et al, German Research Institute for Military History at Potsdam, Germany and the Second World War-Volume IV: The Attack on the Soviet Union, Clarendon Press (Oxford University Press), New York, 1996, p. 360.

In addition to the air-combat and air-support units, the Luftwaffe also contributed two Flak Corps to support Operation Barbarossa. These were the 1st Flak Corps supporting Army Group Centre and the 2nd Flak Corps supporting Army Group South. In total, 20% of the Wehrmacht's (Luftwaffe's and Army's) heavy flak batteries, and 15% of all medium and light flak batteries, were deployed in the East in June 1941.[278]

Although the 1st and 2nd Flak Corps reported to Luftflotte 2 and 4, respectively, this was an administrative function: the flak units in the 1st and 2nd Flak Corps were under the tactical and operational control of the German Army. As such they were used in much the same way as the army's flak units. The Luftwaffe flak batteries were fully motorised so they could operate with the army's motorised (panzer) corps; and they were used to engage ground targets (including, most famously, T-34 and KV tanks) whilst providing anti-aircraft protection for ground troops and supply lines near the front lines.

For Operation Barbarossa the 1st Flak Corps was primarily assigned to support the 2nd and 3rd Panzer Groups, while the 2nd Flak Corps was assigned to support the 1st Panzer Group. The Luftwaffe flak corps HQs, flak regiments and flak battalions are treated as German ground combat units in the German FILARM model, in exactly the same way as the German Army's flak units.

***

---

[278] H. Boog, et al, German Research Institute for Military History at Potsdam, Germany and the Second World War-Volume IV: The Attack on the Soviet Union, Clarendon Press (Oxford University Press), New York, 1996, Table I.IV.8., p. 376.

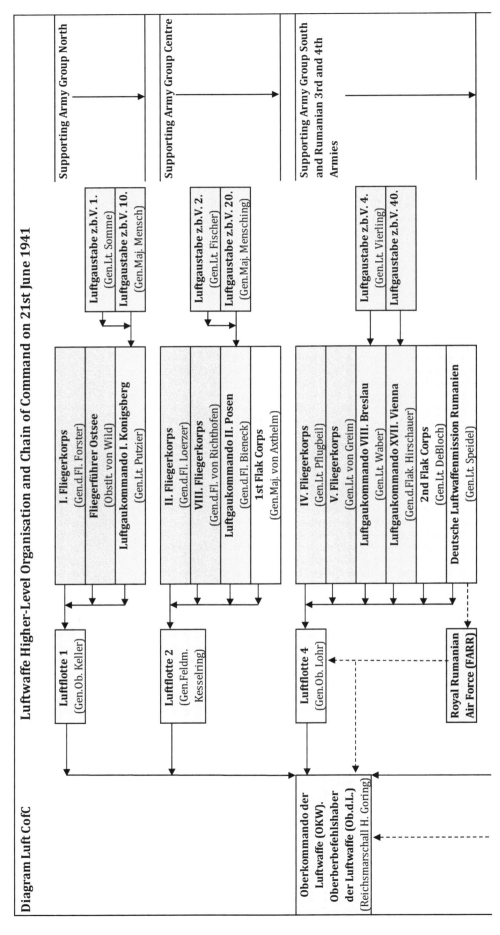

Diagram Luft CofC

Luftwaffe Higher-Level Organisation and Chain of Command on 21st June 1941

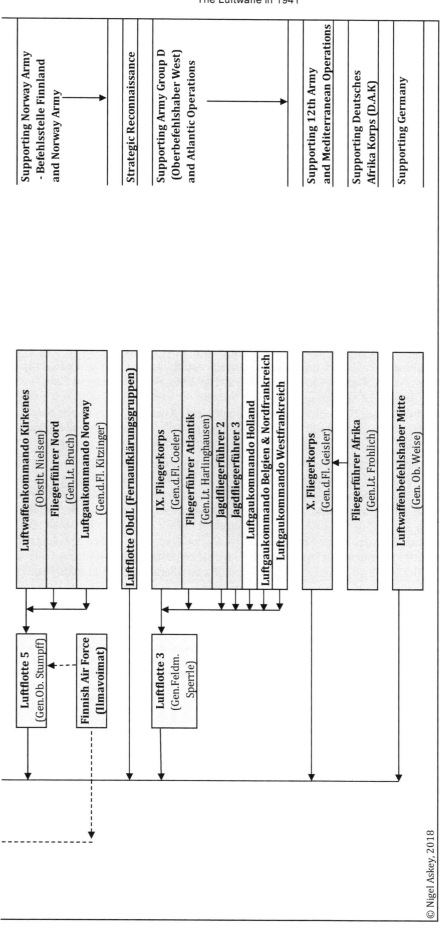

b. Luftflotte 1

On 21st June 1941, Luftflotte 1, commanded by Generaloberst Alfred Keller, was deployed in East Prussia with orders to support Army Group North. The distribution of available and serviceable aircraft in Luftflotte 1, and the units they were assigned to on 21st June 1941, are shown in table Luft 1.[279]

The principal air-support for Army Group North's 18th Army, 16th Army and 4th Panzer Group was to be provided by the I. Fliegerkorps, commanded by General der Flieger Helmuth Forster. I. Fliegerkorps was to support the Operations of Army Group North from East Prussia towards the Dvina River and then further on towards Leningrad. It was ordered to cooperate especially closely with 4th Panzer Group during its drive towards Leningrad. The main striking power of I. Fliegerkorps initially resided in only 159 fighters and 241 medium bombers, which was a small force when one considers that I. Fliegerkorps' operational area consisted of a 200km front extending eastwards to a depth of around 850km (to Leningrad). Even worse was the fact that I. Fliegerkorps had no close-support units: all the bomber *Geschwader* contained Ju 88 aircraft. The Ju 88 was a fast medium bomber and was not designed to provide close-air support to ground troops. It was only the outstanding design of this aircraft and its suitably trained crews, which gave the Ju 88 enough flexibility to be used in this role (albeit imperfectly). The only concession to providing 4th Panzer Group with any really effective close air support was to issue two of the supporting *Kampfgeschwader* with anti-personnel fragmentation bombs.[280]

As far as Operation Barbarossa was concerned the most important naval area was the Baltic Sea. This was because Army Group North's objectives included the invasion and control of Latvia and Estonia, both with extensive Baltic Sea coastlines on Army Group North's northern flank. In addition the Germans needed to protect their iron ore supplies, coming from Sweden via the Baltic Sea, from attack by the Soviet Baltic Red Banner Fleet. On 22nd June 1941 this force included two old battleships, a heavy cruiser, a light cruiser, 19 destroyers of varying age and size and (most dangerously) 65 submarines.[281] With this force the Soviets could interdict the German supply convoys and interfere with any planed German naval activity in the Baltic Sea. The *Kriegsmarine* (German Navy) could only commit minimal resources in support of Operation Barbarossa because the vast majority of its resources were already committed to fighting the Royal Navy in the North Sea and North Atlantic. For example, only five small coastal U-boats were available for use in the Baltic Sea on 22nd June 1941.[282] Therefore in order to gain control of the Baltic Sea the Germans relied on two things; extensive naval minefields and naval-air power.

For controlling Baltic Sea operations, Luftflotte 1 formed the Fliegerführer Ostsee (Aviation command Baltic Sea) under the command of Oberstleutnant Wolfgang von Wild.[283] Fliegerführer Ostsee's initial duties included: guarding the coastal flank from surprise attacks by Soviet naval units, interdicting any Soviet naval operations (especially those by enemy submarines), protecting convoys east of 13° East, and mining the ports of Kronshtadt and Leningrad (in the Gulf of Finland). Later Fliegerführer Ostsee would also be called upon to mine the Neva River as far as Shlisselburg and the White Sea Canal, attack the locks on Lake Onega, and support the army in the capture of the Baltic Islands. The main striking power of Fliegerführer Ostsee, against enemy ships, came from *Küstenfliegergruppe* 806 (KuFlGr 806 – Coastal aviation group 806): another unit in the *Luftflotte* equipped with the

---

[279] Primary sources include: Bundesarchiv-Militararchiv (BA-MA) RL 2 III/700-734, Survey of target, stock, commitment, losses and reserves of flying formations (also BA-MA RL 2 III/736). Some summaries of these records can be found at the Public Records Office in the UK as AIR 40/1207 'The German Air Force: first line strength at three monthly intervals during the European War 1939-1945'. USAF Historical Research Agency, Alabama, HRA 137.306-14 on microfilm A1128. Bundesarchiv-Militararchiv (BA-MA) RL 2 III/713, Report on the combat-readiness of the flying formations, 21st June 1941, GenSt GenQu 6. Abt. (1), 24th June 1941. Bundesarchiv-Militararchiv (BA-MA) o.S. 234, Wall chart of the Ob.d.L as of 20th June 1941. Bundesarchiv-Militararchiv (BA-MA) RH 11 III/32, OKH GenStdH/Op Abt (III) (o.D.), Pruf-Nr. 15819.
Published sources include: H. Boog, et al, German Research Institute for Military History at Potsdam, Germany and the Second World War-Volume IV, The Attack on the Soviet Union, Clarendon Press, New York, 1996, Tables, I.IV.5, and I.IV.6, pp. 364-370. H. L. de Zeng IV, D. G. Stankey, Dive Bomber and Ground-Attack Units of the Luftwaffe 1933-1945: Volumes 1 and 2, Ian Allan Publishing, Hersham, Surrey, 2009 and 2013. H. L. de Zeng IV, D. J. Stankey, E. J. Creek, Bomber Units of the Luftwaffe 1933-1945: A reference Source Volumes 1 and 2, Ian Allan Publishing, Hinckley, UK, 2007 and 2008. J. R. Smith, E. J. Creek, Kampfflieger: Bombers of the Luftwaffe July 1940-December 1941, Classic-Ian Allan Publishing, Hersham UK, 2004, pp. 170 - 171. B. Rosch, Luftwaffe Support Units: 1993-1945, Classic-Ian Allan Publishing, Hersham UK, 2009. H. Plocher, The German Air Force versus Russia - 1941, USAF Historical Studies 153, New York, 1968. A great deal of secondary information on individual unit history and strength data was also collated piece by piece from many of the Luftwaffe sources listed in the Bibliography.
[280] H. Boog, et al, German Research Institute for Military History at Potsdam, Germany and the Second World War-Volume IV, The Attack on the Soviet Union, Clarendon Press (Oxford University Press), New York, 1996, p. 367.
[281] Refer Volume IIIB 6. – 'Soviet Naval Forces: June to December 1941'.
[282] Only five small Type IID coastal U-boats were available for use in the Baltic Sea on 22nd June 1941. These were U-140, U-142, U-144, U-145 and U-149. Refer Volume IIB 7. - 'German Naval Forces on the East Front: June to December 1941'.
[283] Fliegerführer Ostsee was formed in March 1941 from Fliegerführer Osten (East).

ever versatile Ju 88. The maritime patrol and anti-submarine aircraft were supplied by *Aufklärungsgruppe* 125 (Aufkl.Gr 125 –Reconnaissance group (naval) 125) and *Seenotstaffel* 9 (Air-sea rescue squadron 9), together equipped with 48 seaplanes.[284] Fliegerführer Ostsee fielded a total of only 89 aircraft on 21st June 1941, and on this date all its air-units were concentrated in the immediate vicinity north and east of Konigsberg.

From table Luft 1 we can see that on 21st June 1941 Luftflotte 1 contained 822 combat and transport aircraft, but this included only 213 fighters and 271 twin engine bombers. The remaining 338 aircraft were all short range reconnaissance (army tactical) or long range reconnaissance aircraft, army cooperation/liaison aircraft, transport aircraft or seaplanes. Of the latter, 204 aircraft were under the operational and tactical control of ground units in Army Group North.[285] These comprised aircraft in the *Fernaufklärungsgruppen* (except those in 2.(F)/Ob.d.L), the *Heeresaufklärungsgruppen*, the *Panzeraufklärungsgruppen*, the *Kurierstaffeln* and the *Verbindungsstaffeln* (shown in grey on table Luft 1). Excluding the aircraft in KGr zbV units, *Kurierstaffeln*, *Verbindungsstaffeln* and *Sanitätsflugbereitschaften*, *Luftflotte* 1 contained a total 689 'combat aircraft' (551 serviceable).

Of the total of 822 aircraft in Luftflotte 1, around 78% were serviceable. Noticeably a higher proportion of fighter and bomber aircraft were serviceable (83% and 78%, respectively), whilst transport aircraft exhibited the lowest degree of readiness (41%). It is probable that the KGr zbV units were still recovering from Operation Mercury (the airborne invasion of Crete), and had very recently been working hard transporting critical material eastwards in preparation for Operation Barbarossa. It is worth diverging here to mention that in 1941 the Luftwaffe's daily and weekly reports for serviceable aircraft were generally much more accurate than similar reports from their VVS counterparts, and especially reports from the immediate pre-Barbarossa period. It is not unreasonable to interpret 'serviceable' as 'operational'; that is to say by simply arming and fuelling these aircraft they were ready to fly combat missions. However the term 'serviceable' for aircraft is very subjective. It could mean anything from 'immediately ready for aerial combat' to 'can get off the ground after some extensive maintenance'. For a variety of internal reasons, which are discussed in the Soviet FILARM (air) model, VVS officer reports tended to exaggerate the number of serviceable/operational aircraft during most of 1941.[286]

It is instructive to compare Luftflotte 1 against its immediate opponents in June 1941; namely the VVS-Baltic Special Military District (Northwestern Front from 22nd June 1941). The latter had 1,262 combat aircraft on 22nd June 1941, of which 1,078 were reported as 'serviceable'.[287] This total included 744 fighters (including 140 modern Mig1/3 fighters) and 458 bombers and assault (ground-attack) aircraft. Therefore on the eve of Operations Barbarossa, Luftflotte 1 was outnumbered by its VVS opponent by 1.8 to 1 in combat aircraft. In terms of fighters and bombers the numerical disparity was 3.5 to 1 for fighters and 1.7 to 1 for bombers, in the Soviet's favour. In terms of reconnaissance (all types) and army-cooperation aircraft, *Luftflotte* 1 outnumbered the VVS-Baltic Special Military District by 3.7 to 1. The latter is indicative of how important the German Army considered battlefield reconnaissance to be, and how closely the Luftwaffe was designed and organised to operate with the army.

To make matters worse for Luftflotte 1, most of the 1,336 combat aircraft initially in the VVS-Leningrad Military District (Northern Front from 24th June 1941) transferred south to face Army Group North in July 1941. This meant that even though the VVS forces originally in the Baltic Special Military District were effectively wiped out within the first week of war (around 85% of aircraft were destroyed or severely damaged), the newly formed VVS-Northwestern Zone still had a substantial numerical superiority (in combat-aircraft) over *Luftflotte* 1 during July and early August 1941. Refer to the Soviet FILARM air-model (Volume IIIB 3. 2)) for details on the air battles and losses over the Baltic States in June and July 1941.[288]

***

---

[284] In addition, air-sea rescue missions, and probably most clandestine air-sea-land operations, were to be conducted by the seaplanes of *Seenotstaffel* 9. Note, strictly speaking, seaplanes are aircraft with floats attached to their wings and fuselage, while flying boats are aircraft which use their fuselage to displace the water and usually have small floats on the wings.

[285] H. Boog, et al, Table, I.IV.5, p. 364, shows 176 aircraft (143 serviceable) under Army control. This only includes the *Fernaufklärungsgruppen* (52), *Heeresaufklärungsgruppen* (87) and *Kurierstaffeln (37)*, as per the data in table Luft 1.

[286] Many VVS status reports for June 1941 claimed that an average of 80-95% of their combat aircraft were serviceable and hence could be considered operational. However, there is little doubt that these reports were based on overly optimistic VVS commander assessments in the period prior to June 1941. Refer Volume IIIB 3. 2) a. – 'The Soviet Air Forces in 1941 - The Order of Battle and Actual Strength of all Soviet Air Combat Units in a Deployed (D) State on 22nd June 1941 - Aircraft Serviceability and Numbers of Operational Aircraft'.

[287] Refer Volume IIIB 3. 2) c. – 'The Soviet Air Forces in 1941 - The Order of Battle and Actual Strength of all Soviet Air Combat Units in a Deployed (D) State on 22nd June 1941 - VVS-Baltic Special Military District'.

[288] Refer Volume IIIB 3. 2) c. – 'VVS-Baltic Special Military District' and Volume IIIB 3. 2) b. – 'VVS-Leningrad Military District'.

Table Luft 1 — Deployment and Composition of Luftwaffe Air Units, 21st June 1941

	Luftflotte 1											
	I. Fliegerkorps				Fliegerführer Ostsee*							
	Description	No x Type/Auth	Av	Sv	Description	No x Type/Auth	Av	Sv	Description	No x Type/Auth	Av	Sv
JG (Jagdgeschwader) Fighter.	Stab/JG 54	4xBf-109F	4	3					Erg./JG 52^**	16xBf-109E	30	19
	I./JG 54	40xBf-109F	40	34					Erg./JG 54^**	16xBf-109E/F	24	19
	II./JG 54	40xBf-109E/F	40	33								
	III./JG 54	40xBf-109F	40	35								
	4.,5./ JG 53*	28xBf-109F	35	33								
KG (Kampfgeschwader) Bomber.	Stab/KG 1^	4xHe111H^/Ju-88A	1	1								
	II./KG 1**	40xJu-88A	29	27								
	III./KG 1	40xJu-88A	30	29								
	Stab/KG 76	4xJu-88A	1	0								
	I./KG 76	40xJu-88A	30	22								
	II./KG 76	40xJu-88A	30	25								
	III./KG 76	40xJu-88A	29	22								
	Stab/KG 77*^	4xJu-88A	1	1								
	I./KG 77^^	40xJu-88A	30	23								
	II./KG 77^*	40xJu-88A	31	23								
	III./KG 77***	40xJu-88A	29	20								
Aufkl Gr (Aufklärungsgruppe) Reconnaissance.					1./Aufkl.Gr 125 (S)*^	12xHe-114, He-60	12	10				
					Stab, 2./Aufkl.Gr 125 (S)^^	16xHe-114, He-60	15	13				
					3./Aufkl.Gr 125 (S)**, *^	12xAr-95A	8	7				
H (Heeresaufklärungsgruppe) Short Range Tactical Reconnaissance.									2.(H)/21**	4xHs126	8	6
									7.(H)/21*^	12xHs-126	7	6
									4.(H)/21^^	12xHs-126	7	6
									2.(Pz)/23***	12xHs-126	9	9
									3.(Pz)/23***	12xHs-126/Fw-189	10	8
									4.(H)/31***	12xFw-189 (pos some Do-17P)	7	5
									3.(H)/32**^	12xHs-126	8	5
									3.(Pz)/41**^	12xHs-126	10	8
									1.(H)/12*^^	12xFw-189	7	6
									2.(H)/13^^^	12xHs-126/Fw-189	7	6
									4.(H)/23^^*	12xHs-126	7	5
F (Fernaufklärungsgruppe) Long Range Strategic Reconnaissance.	5.(F)/122	12x (see note **^)	10	8	3.(F)/22	12x (see note ^*)	11	9	2.(F)/Ob.d.L*	12x (see note *)	4,3,1,2	7
									3.(F)/Nacht^	12xDo-215B, Do-17P, He-111H	9	7
									1.(F)/22^	12xJu-88A/D	11	8
									4.(F)/33^*	12xBf-110C/E	11	9
KGr zbV (Kampfgeschwader zu besonderen Verwendung) Transport.	I. Korps Tr.Sta	16xJu-52	18	14					KGr zbV 106	53xJu-52	44	8

Unit	Aircraft type		
Wekusta (Wettererkundungsstaffel) Weather Observation.	8xJu-88A/D, He-111J, Ju-52/3m	8	6
Wekusta 1			
KuFlGr (Küstenfliegergruppe) Coastal Aviation.			
KGr 806 (KuFlGr 806)^	52xJu-88A	30	18
(Seenotstaffel) Air-Sea Rescue.			
9. Seenotstaffel	14xHe-59	13	10
(Kurierstaffel) Courier/Liaison.			
Kurierkette PzGrp 4^*	Fi-156	9	6
Kurierstaffel 12**	Fi-156, Fw-58	9	8
Kurierstaffel 9^*	Fi-156, Fw-44 and W-34	10	10
Kurierstaffel 2*^^	Fi-156, Fw-58 and W-34	9	8
(Verbindungsstaffel) Communication/Liaison.			
Verbindungsstaffel 1~	Misc types (refer text).	6	6
Verbindungsstaffel 52*~	F-156, Ar-66 and Fw-58	4	4
Verbindungsstaffel 53*~	F-156, Ar-66, Fw-58 and W-34	5	5
Verbindungsstaffel 54*~	F-156, Ar-66, Si-202 and W-34	5	4
Verbindungsstaffel 55~~	F-156, W-34, Fw-58 and KI-35	4	4
Verbindungsstaffel 60*~	F-156 and Ar-66	4	4
(Sanitätsflugbereitschaft) Ambulance Flight.			
Sanitätsflugbereitschaft 1	6x Ju-52~*	6	6

* Oberbefehlshaber der Luftwaffe, reports directly to C in C Luftwaffe (Hermann Goring). Possibly still had two BV-142 on strength. One Kette (w Do-215 and He-111) was based at Luonetjarvi, Finland.
Aircraft types: 12xJu-88D, Do-215B, He-111, BV-142.

^ Attached directly to Koluft Nord, Kommandeur der Luftstreitkrafte, (Army Group North Coordinator attached to the Army).

** Attached to Koluft 18. (18th Army).

*^ Attached to I Corps.

^^ Attached to XXVI Corps.

^* Attached to Koluft 4 Pz Gr, (4th Pz Group). Kurierkette PzGrp 4 was formed in June 1941.

*** Attached to Gruft 23, (XXXXI Mot Cps)

**^ Attached to Gruft 13, (LVI Mot. Cps).

*^^ Attached to Koluft 16, (16th Army).

^^^ Attached to II Corps.

^** Attached to XXVIII Corps.

^*** Erganzungs (sometimes operational Training and Replacement) Gruppen, reporting to Luftgaukommando I. (Both Gruppen in reserve at Neuhausen).

~ Disbanded in Nov. 1941. Misc types included early Arado biplanes, C-445, Fi-156, Fw-58, Ju-52, W-34 and KI-35, at various times.

*~ Disbanded in November 1941.

~~ Disbanded in December 1941.

~* 4 Fi-156 were added to the TOE in late 1941 or 1942.

---

* Air Commander Baltic Sea.

^ Comprised Stab., 2. and 3./Kgr 806, and 1. and 2./KGr 106. 1. and 2./K.Gr 106 were withdrawn to France/Holland in July 1941. 1./KGr 806 joined other 806 Staffel in July 1941. KGr 806 was withdrawn to Germany for rest and refit ca 13th Nov. 1941, and then to Sicily with II. Fliegerkorps ca 18th Dec. 1941. KuFlGr 806 was redesignated III./KG 54 on 1st Sep. 1942.

** This was the only unit with the Ar-95, with 8 on strength on 22nd June 1941.

1 Kette/125 (1 Flight) transferred to Luftflotte 4, by Oct. 1941. After a brief deployment to Finland, 3./Aufkl.Gr 125 (S) reequipped with BV-138C in late 1941, for operations in the Black Sea (based at Constanza). Note, this unit is commonly designated 3.(F)/SAGr. 125.

*^ Reequipped with BV-138Cs in late 1941-42.

^^ Reequipped with Ar-196s in late 1941.

^* Aircraft types: 12x Bf-110C/E, Ju-88D.

---

* 4,5,/JG53 and a Stabsschwarm present only. At this time 6,/JG 53 was at Doberitz.

^ One He-111H was available and in service. Note, I./KG 1 was renamed III./KG 40 on 1st April 1941, and was not reformed until June 1942.

** Unit handed over Ju-88s to III./KG 1 and withdrawn to Insterburg in East Prussia on 12th September 1941 (to refit with Ju-88A-4s). It returned to the East Front (Northern Sector) ca 9th October 1941.

*^ Stab./KG 77 was withdrawn in Dec. 1941. In early January 1942 it was assigned to the II. Fliegerkorps (newly transferred to the Med.) for operations against Malta and over North Africa.

^^ I./KG 77 was withdrawn to Germany for rest and reequipping ca mid-Nov. 1941. It returned to the East Front (Central Sector) ca 7th January 1942.

^* II./KG 77 was withdrawn in Oct/early Nov. 1941. Assigned to II. Fliegerkorps and operated against Malta in Dec. 1941.

*** III./KG 77 was withdrawn in Nov 1941. Assigned to the II. Fliegerkorps and operated against Malta in Jan. 1942.

**^ Aircraft types: 12xJu-88A, BF-110D./E.

Table Luft 1 (cont.)

Luftflotte 1, Totals

Unit Type	No. of Units	No. of Aircraft Avail	Svcble
Jagdgruppen	3 2/3	159	138
Erg.Guppen (JG,ZG)	2	54	38
Schlachtgruppen	0	0	0
zerstörergruppen	0	0	0
Kampfgruppen	9 1/3	271	211
Stukagruppen	0	0	0
(Pz) Staffeln	3	29	25
(H) Staffeln	8	58	45
Luft (F) Staffeln	1	10	7
Heeres (F) Staffeln	5	52	41
KGr zbV	1 1/3	62	22
Wetterstaffeln	1	8	6
Seefliegerstaffeln	3	35	30
Seenotstaffeln	1	13	10
Kurierstaffeln/Verb. Staffeln	10	65	59
Sanitätsflugbereitschaften	1	6	6
		822	638
Number of Aircraft by type:			
Single Engine Fighters		213	176
Twin Eng Fighters / Ftr Bmbrs		0	0
Twin Eng Night Fighters		0	0
Single Eng Fighter Bombers		0	0
Dive Bombers		0	0
Twin Engine Bombers		271	211
Four Engine Bombers		0	0
Long Range Recon*		70	54
SR Recon / Army Coop^		152	129
Seaplanes		48	40
Transport Aircraft**		68	28
		822	638

* Includes Wetterstaffeln aircraft.

^ Includes Courier, Liaison aircraft.

** Includes Sanitätsflugbereitschaften aircraft.

Total Combat Aircraft*		689	551

*Excludes aircraft in KGr zbV, Kurierstaffeln, and Sanitätsflugbereitschaften.

Aircraft Under Tactical Control of the Army			
Long Range Reconnaissance		52	41
Short Range Recon. / Army Coop.^		152	129
		204	170

^ Includes Courier, Liaison Aircraft.

© Nigel Askey, 2018

***

c. Luftflotte 2

Luftflotte 2 was commanded by Generalfeldmarschall Albert Kesselring, and on 21st June 1941 it was deployed in East Poland behind Army Group Centre. Its initial orders were to provide Army Group Centre with any air-support needed during its drive through Belorussia, across the Dnieper River and onto Moscow. As a result of having to support the German Army's main effort during Operation Barbarossa, Luftflotte 2 was by far the strongest air-fleet deployed anywhere in the Reich. On 21st June 1941 it was organised into two powerful *Fliegerkorps*: the II. and VIII. Fliegerkorps. It also had the motorised 1st Flak Corps assigned. The distribution of available and serviceable aircraft in Luftflotte 2, and the units they were assigned to on 21st June 1941, are shown in table Luft 2.[289]

The northern wing of Luftflotte 2 consisted of the VIII. Fliegerkorps, commanded by General der Flieger Dr Wolfram Freiherr von Richthofen. It was to provide the principal air-support for Army Group Centre's 9th Army and 3rd Panzer Group, with orders to cooperate especially closely with 3rd Panzer Group. On 21st June 1941 the VIII. Fliegerkorps was deployed in the region around Suvalki and extending westwards to the area north of Warsaw. The *Fliegerkorps* had very recently played a major part in the capture of Crete and had only transferred to the East Front after 6th June 1941. Consequently the VIII. Fliegerkorps was still short of its full complement of transport vehicles, aircraft, spare parts and communication equipment on the eve of Operation Barbarossa.[290] This hurried move from the Mediterranean theatre is reflected in the relatively low overall readiness: we can see from table Luft 2 that only around 63% of the 616 aircraft in VIII. Fliegerkorps were fully serviceable on 21st June 1941. The main striking power of VIII. Fliegerkorps resided in 201 fighters (including 78 Bf 110 *Zerstörer* or heavy-fighters), 131 twin engine bombers, 180 dive bombers (comprised of 158 Stukas and 22 Hs 123s) and 50 ground attack fighter-bombers. The latter comprised 12 Bf 110s in the *Stab* of the *Sturzkampfgeschwader* 1 and 2, and 38 Bf 109E fighter-bombers in II.(Sch.)/LG 2.

The southern wing of Luftflotte 2 consisted of the II. Fliegerkorps, commanded by General der Flieger Bruno Loerzer. Its objective was to provide the air-support for Army Group Centre's 4th Army and 2nd Panzer Group, with orders to cooperate especially closely with 2nd Panzer Group. On 21st June 1941 the II. Fliegerkorps was deployed in the Warsaw-Brest-Litovsk-Deblin region, with its fighter and dive-bomber units deployed on airfields just west of the Bug River. The II. Fliegerkorps was in a relatively high state of readiness with around 72% of its 630 aircraft fully serviceable on 21st June 1941. Noticeably, the fighter, bomber and dive-bomber units had 76-77% of their aircraft ready for action on this date, while the KGr zbV (air-transport) units had the lowest state of readiness. The combat power of II. Fliegerkorps resided in 160 fighters, 252 twin engine bombers (including 83 Bf 110 high-speed bombers), and 123 dive bombers and ground attack aircraft (comprised of 115 Stukas, 7 Bf 110s in Stab/StG 77, and 1 Bf 110 in II./StG 77). II. Fliegerkorps was also initially able to call upon the services of another powerful fighter unit; namely JG 53. The Stab/JG 53, I./JG 53 and III./JG 53 was an experienced force with 79 Bf 109Fs available on 21st June 1941. Although it reported directly to Luftflotte 2, it was deployed around Rogozn (just west of Brest-Litovsk) on 21st June 1941 and was immediately available to support 4th Army and 2nd Panzer Group in June 1941. II. Fliegerkorps therefore effectively had 239 fighters on hand at the start of Operation Barbarossa.

From table Luft 2 we can see that on 21st June 1941 Luftflotte 2 contained a total of 1,741 combat and transport aircraft. This included 384 single engine fighters, 201 twin engine Bf 110s acting as heavy-fighters (*Zerstörer*) or/and fighter-bombers, 38 single engine fighter-bombers, 295 dive bombers and 300 twin engine bombers. The remaining 523 aircraft were all short range (army tactical) or long range reconnaissance aircraft, or various types of army-cooperation, liaison and transport aircraft. Of the latter, 292 aircraft were under the operational and tactical control of ground units in Army Group Centre.[291] These comprised aircraft in the *Heeresaufklärungsgruppen*, the *Panzeraufklärungsgruppen*, the *Kurierstaffeln*, the *Verbindungsstaffeln* and *Fernaufklärungsgruppen* 2.(F)/Nacht, 2.(F)/33, 4.(F)/14, 1.(F)/33 and 3.(F)/31. Excluding the transport aircraft in KGr zbV units, *Kurierstaffeln*, *Verbindungsstaffel* and *Sanitätsflugbereitschaften*, *Luftflotte* 2 contained a total 1,480 'combat aircraft' (1,065 serviceable) on 21st June 1941.

***

---

[289] Ibid, note 277. Also, P.C. Smith, Luftwaffe Ju 87 Dive Bomber Units 1939-1941, Classic-Ian Allan Publishing, Hersham UK, 2006, p. 85, (for additional details of *Sturzkampfgeschwader* deployments and strengths on 21st June 1941).

[290] It was short 600 motor vehicles. H. Boog, et al, German Research Institute for Military History at Potsdam, Germany and the Second World War-Volume IV, The Attack on the Soviet Union, Clarendon Press (Oxford University Press), New York, 1996, p. 362.

[291] H. Boog, et al, Table, I.IV.5, p. 364, shows 244 aircraft (with 200 serviceable) under Army control. This only includes the *Fernaufklärungsgruppen* (46), *Heeresaufklärungsgruppen* (170) and *Kurierstaffeln* (28), which agrees with the data in table Luft 2.

Table Luft 2 — Deployment and Composition of Luftwaffe Air Units, 21st June 1941

Category	Luftflotte 2^^ — II. Fliegerkorps^^ Description	No x Type/Auth	Av	Sv	VIII. Fliegerkorps Description	No x Type/Auth	Av	Sv	Description	No x Type/Auth	Av	Sv
JG (Jagdgeschwader) Fighter.	Stab/JG 51	4xBf-109F	4	4	Stab/JG 27	4xBf-109E	4	4	Stab/JG 53	4xBf-109F	6	6
	I./JG 51	40xBf-109F	40	38	I./JG 27	40xBf-109E	40	31	I./JG 53	40xBf-109F	35	29
	II./JG 51	40xBf-109F	40	23	III./JG 27	40xBf-109E	40	14	III./JG 53	40xBf-109F	38	36
	III./JG 51	40xBf-109F	38	30	II./JG 52	40xBf-109F	39	37	Erg./JG 51^***	16xBf-109E/F	22	6
	IV./JG 51	40xBf-109F	38	26								
SKG (Schnellkampfgeschwader) High-speed Bomber.	Stab/SKG 210*	4xBf-110D/E	5	4								
	I./SKG 210^	40xBf-110D/E	41	33								
	II./SKG 210**	40xBf-110D/E	37	37								
ZG (Zerstörergeschwader) Heavy Fighter (twin engine).					Stab/ZG 26**	4xBf-110C/E	4	4	Erg./ZG 26^^***	40xBf-110C/E	20	9
					I./ZG 26*^	40xBf-110C/E	38	17				
					II./ZG 26	40xBf-110C/E	36	30				
KG (Kampfgeschwader) Bomber.	Stab/KG 3***	4xJu-88A, 6xDo-17Z	2, 1	2, 0	Stab/KG 2^	4xDo-17Z	11	5				
	I./KG 3***	40xJu-88A	41	32	I./KG 2^	40xDo-17Z	35	19				
	II./KG 3	36xJu-88A, 4xDo-17Z	38, 1	32, 0	III./KG 2^	40xDo-17Z	41	23				
	Stab/KG 53	4xHe-111H	6	4	III./KG 3***	40xDo-17Z	44	18				
	I./KG 53***^	40xHe-111H	28	18								
	II./KG 53	40xHe-111H	21	10								
	III./KG 53	38xHe-111H,2xHe111P	29, 2	20, 2								
StG (Sturzkampfgeschwader) Dive Bomber.	Stab/StG 77	6xBf-110, 4xJu-87B	7,3	6,1	Stab/StG 1**^	6xBf-110, 4xJu-87B	6,3	3,2				
	I./StG 77	40xJu-87B	38	31	II./StG 1	40xJu-87B	39	28				
	II./StG 77*^^	40xJu-87B, Bf-110	39,1	27,1	III./StG 1*^^	40xJu-87B	39	24				
	III./StG 77	40xJu-87B	35	28	Stab/StG 2	6xBf-110, 4xJu-87B	6,3	4,3				
					I./StG 2^^^	40xJu-87B	35	19				
					III./StG 2	40xJu-87R	39	20				
SchG (Schlachtgeschwader) Ground-attack Aircraft.					II.(Sch.)/LG 2*	40xBf-109E	38	37				
					10.(Sch.)/LG 2*, ^*	12xHs-123A	22	17				
H (Heeresaufklärungsgruppe) Short Range Tactical Reconnaissance.									4.(H)/10^	12xHs-126/Fw-189	6	5
									2.(H)/12**	12xHs-126	7	5
									4.(H)/12*^	12xHs-126/BF-110E	6	6
									1.(Pz)/11*^	12xFw-189	9	7
									1.(Pz)/13*^	12xHs-126	9	8
									7.(H)/13^^	12xHs-126	9	6
									3.(Pz)/12^^	12xHs-126/Fw-189	9	7
									2.(Pz)/32^^	12xHs-126/Fw-189	9	8
									1.(H)/31**^	12xFw-189	7	6
									5.(H)/41*^^	12xHs-126/Fw-189	6	6
									1.(H)/10***	12xHs-126	7	6
									2.(H)/41^^^	12xHs-126	6	5
									5.(H)/12****	12xFw-189	6	5
									7.(H)/12***^	12xHs-126	6	6
									1.(H)/21*^^^	12xHs-126	6	5
									7.(H)/32^^^^	12xHs-126/Fw-189	6	6
									6.(Pz)/41^^^^	12xHs-126/Fw-189	9	7
									9.(Pz)/LG2^^^^	12xHs-126/Fw-189	9	8
									6.(H)/31^^^*	12xHs-126	6	6

Type	Unit	Aircraft	Est.	Serv.
F [Fernaufklärungsgruppe] Long Range Strategic Reconnaissance.	1.(F)/122**	12xJu-88A/D,Bf-110E-3	10	9
	2.(F)/11	12xDo-17P	12	8
	1.(F)/122^*			
	3.(Pz)/14^^^^	12xFw-189	8	6
	5.(H)/23^^^^	12xHs-126	7	5
	6.(Pz)/13^^^	12xHs-126/Fw-189	8	7
	6.(Pz)/32^^^	12xHs-126	9	7
	Stab./122	4xJu-88A	3	2
	2.(F)/122	12xJu-88A,Bf-109E,Bf-110	13	9
	2.(F)/Nacht*	12xDo-17M/Do-17Z	8	5
	2.(F)/33^*	12xBf-110C/E	9	6
	4.(F)/14***	12xJu-88D, Bf-110C/E	10	8
	1.(F)/33^^^	12xJu-88A/D	9	7
	3.(F)/31***^^	12xDo-17P, Bf-110D/E	10	7
KGr zbV (Kampfgeschwader zu besonderen Verwendung) Transport.	KGr zbV 102	53xJu-52	43	8
	KGr zbV 9^^	53xJu-52	25	9
	IV./KG zbV 1	53xJu-52	40	38
	KGr zbV 105*^	53xJu-52 (BV-142, Fw 200B)	27	17
	VIII. Korps Tr.Sta	16xJu-52	17	11
	II. Korps Tr.Sta	16xJu-52	15	12
Wekusta (Staffel)	Wekusta 26*~	8xDo-17Z, Bf-110C, Ju88A	8	8
[Kurierstaffel] Courier/Liaison.	Kurierstaffel 3*	Fi-156, Kl-35 and W-34	7	7
	Kurierstaffel 1^*	Fi-156	8	6
	Kurierstaffel 8***	Fi-156, Fw-44 and Kl-35	7	6
	Kurierkette 11^^^	Fi-156, Bu-131, Fw-58 & W-34	6	6
	Kurierkette PzGrp 2**^^	Fi-156, Ju-52	6	6
(Verbindungsstaffel) Communication/Liaison.	Verbindungsstaffel 3~~	Fi-156, Fw-58	5	5
	Verbindungsstaffel 56~	Fi-156, W-34 and Ar-66	5	5
	Verbindungsstaffel 57~	Fi-156 and Fw-58	4	4
	Verbindungsstaffel 58~	Fi-156, Ar-66, Fw-58 & W-34	6	6
	Verbindungsstaffel 62~	Fi-156 and W-34	4	4
	Verbindungsstaffel 63~	Fi-156, Fw-58, Ar-66, Ar-96 ~*	6	5
	Verbindungsstaffel 66~	Fi-156, Fw 58 and Go 145	4	4
	Verbindungsstaffel 67~	Fi-156, Ar-66, W-34	4	4
	Verbindungsstaffel 68~	Fi-156 and W-34	4	4
(Sanitätsflugbereitschaft) Ambulance Flight.	Sanitätsflugbereitschaft 3	6xJu-52	6	6
	Sanitätsflugbereitschaft 4	6xJu-52	6	6
	Sanitätsflugbereitschaft 6	6xJu-52	6	5

Notes (left block):

* Stab./SKG 210 was withdrawn to Ger. for rest and refit ca 26 Nov. 1941. It was redesig. Stab./ZG 1 on 4 Jan. 1942.
^ I./SKG 210 was withdrawn to Ger. for refit from early Oct. to 14 Dec. 1941. It was redesig. I./ZG 1 on 4 Jan. 42.
** II./SKG 210 remained on the East Front until Jan. 1942. It was redesignated II./ZG 1 on 4th Jan. 1942.
*^ KGr zbV 105 transferring from Mediterranean theatre, disbanded XI Fliegerkorps. In Warsaw by June 1941. Pos. still had 1x Fw 200B-1, and 2x BV-142, on strength.
^^ Transferred in late Nov./Dec. 1941 to the Med. Theatre. By this time incl. the following units: II/JG3, Stab., II & III/JG27, Stab., I, II & III/JG53, Stab. & I./KG54, Stab., II. & III. KG77, KGr.806, LG1, 1.(F)/122 & Weku. 26.
^* In transit to Warsaw Area.
*** Stab./KG 3 & I./KG 3 handed over rem. aircraft to II./KG 3, & withdrawn to Ger. for re-equipping, ca 6th Dec. 1941.
*** Withdrawn for approx. 3 weeks for rest in late Dec. 1941.
*** II./StG 77 sent to Sth Poland for refit, 14-24 Nov. 41

Notes (middle block):

* Operating under Stab./StG2. Redes. I./Sch.G. 1 on 13 Jan. 42.
^* Renamed 8. (Pz)/ Sch.G. 1 on 13th January 1942.
^ All these KG2 units were withdrawn from the East Front ca early Nov. 1941, and had converted to Do-217E-2 and E-3 by the end of 1941.
** Stab./ZG 26 redesignated Stab./NJG 3 on 29 Sep. 41.
*^ I./ZG 26 redesignated I./ZG 2 in April 1942.
^^ KGr zbV 9 trans from Med. theatre, X Fliegerkorps.
*** Handed over remaining aircraft to Croation Air Force Legion (5. Bomber Wing was attached to the Gruppe), & sent to Ger. for re-equipping with Ju-88s on 6 Dec. 1941. Croation unit was known as 10./KG 3 in late 1941/42. It appears most of this unit eventually went into the 15./(Kroat.)/KG 3 in June 1943.
*** Stab./StG 1 was withdrawn for rest and refit in Dec. 1941.
*** III./StG 1 was withdrawn for rest and refit ca 6th Dec. 41.
^^^ II./StG 1 was withdrawn for rest & refit ca 6th Dec 1941.

Notes (right block):

* Attached directly to Koluft Mitte, *Kommandeur der Luftstreitkräfte.*
** Attached to VI Corps.
^^ Attached to Gruft 11, (XXXIX Mot Cps, Panzer Divisions).
^^ Attached to Gruft 21, (LVII Mot Cps)   ^ Attached to V Corps.
^^ Attached to Koluft 3 Pz Gr, (3rd Pz Grp). Redesignated Kurierstaffel Oberost in Oct. 1941. Redesignated Kurierstaffel Oberost in October 1941.
*** Attached to Koluft 9, (9th Army).   *** Attached to VIII Corps.
*^ Attached to XX Corps.   ^^^ Attached to Koluft 4, (4th Army).
**** Attached to VII Corps.   ^^^ Attached to IX Corps.
**** Attached to XIII Corps.   **** Attached to XXXIII Corps.
***^^ Attached to Koluft 2 Pz Gr. (2nd Pz Group). Kurierkette PzGrp 2 was formed in June 1941. 3.(F)/31 returned to Germany in 1941.
*^^^ Attached to XII Corps.   ^^^^ Attached to Gruft 10, (XXIV Mot Cps)
^^^ Attached to Gruft 14, (XXXVI Mot Cps)   ^^* Attached to Gruft 31, (XXXXVII Mot Cps)
~ Ergänzungs. (Sometimes operational, Training and Replacement) Gruppen, reporting to Luftgaukommando II, (Both Gruppen in reserve in Poznan area).
~ Wekusta 26 was withdrawn in mid November 1941 for rest and refit (with Ju-88Ds). It was reass. to II. Fliegerkorps (in Sicily) in late 1941. ~ Disbanded in Nov. 1941.
~~ Disbanded in Dec. 1941.   ~* Also operated C-445, Go-145 and Kl-35 at some point.

Table Luft 2 (cont.)

Luftflotte 2, Totals

Unit Type	No. of Units	No. of Aircraft Avail	Svcble
Jagdgruppen	9	362	278
Erg.Guppen (JG and ZG)	2	42	15
Schlachtgruppen	1 1/3	60	54
Zerstörergruppen	2	78	51
Kampfgruppen	8	300	185
Stukagruppen (+) **	9	376	271
(Pz) Staffeln	9	79	65
(H) Staffeln	14	91	77
Luft (F) Staffeln	3	38	28
Heeres (F) Staffeln	5	46	33
KGr zbV	4 2/3	167	95
Wetterstaffeln	1	8	8
Seefliegerstaffeln	0	0	0
Seenotstaffeln	0	0	0
Kurierstaffeln/Verb. Staffeln	14	76	72
Sanitätsflugbereitschaften	3	18	17
		1741	1249
Number of Aircraft by type			
Single Engine Fighters		384	284
Twin Eng Fighters / Ftr Bmbrs **		201	148
Twin Eng Night Fighters		0	0
Single Eng Fighter Bombers		38	37
Dive Bombers		295	200
Twin Engine Bombers		300	185
Four Engine Bombers		0	0
Long Range Recon *		92	69
SR Recon / Army Coop ^		246	214
Seaplanes		0	0
Transport Aircraft *^		185	112
		1741	1249

* Includes Wetterstaffeln.

^ Includes Courier, Liaison aircraft.

** Includes Schnellkampfgeschwader 210.

*^ Includes Sanitätsflugbereitschaften aircraft.

Total Combat Aircraft *		1480	1065

* Excludes aircraft in KGr zbV, Kurierstaffeln, and
  Sanitätsflugbereitschaften.

Aircraft under tactical control of the Army			
Long Range Recon		46	33
SR Recon / Army Coop ^		246	214
		292	247

^ Includes Courier, Liaison Aircraft.

© Nigel Askey, 2018

***

One very significant feature of Luftflotte 2 is that it contained **almost all** the *Sturzkampfgeschwader* (Dive-bomber), *Schlachtgeschwader* (Ground attack) and *Schnellkampfgeschwader* (High-speed bomber) units on the East Front in June 1941. In fact the only similar units deployed anywhere in the Reich were one *Sturzkampfgeschwader Gruppe* (IV.(St)/LG 1) in northern Finland and two *Sturzkampfgeschwader Gruppen* (I./StG 1 and II./StG 2) in Fliegerführer Afrika. In addition, 3 *Kampfgeschwader* (Bomber), 1 *Sturzkampfgeschwader* (Dive-bomber), 1 *Zerstörergeschwader* (Destroyer-heavy Fighter) and 2 *Jagdgeschwader* (Fighter) *Gruppen* in Luftflotte 2 were supplied with devices for dropping 2kg anti-personnel fragmentation bombs for close air support.[292] The sheer concentration of 'close air support' units, and the equipping of even more units to fulfil similar functions, all under Luftflotte 2, clearly demonstrates that the German Army High Command (OKH) didn't want anything to delay Army Group Centre's progress towards Moscow.

***

It is instructive to compare Luftflotte 2 against its main opponent in June 1941; namely the VVS-Western Special Military District (Western Front from 22nd June 1941). The latter had 1,771 combat aircraft on 22nd June 1941, of which 1,539 were reported as 'serviceable'.[293] This total included 1,043 fighters (including 258 modern Mig-1/3 and Yak-1 fighters) and 586 bombers and assault (ground-attack) aircraft. Therefore on the eve of Operations Barbarossa, Luftflotte 2 was outnumbered by its immediate VVS opponent by 1.2 to 1 in combat aircraft. In terms of fighters the numerical disparity was large: the VVS had a 2.2 to 1 numerical superiority (which includes the 98 Bf 110 *Zerstörer* or twin engine heavy-fighters in ZG 26 and Erg./ZG). However, Luftflotte 2 enjoyed an initial numerical superiority of around 1.3 to 1 in bombers and ground attack aircraft, and 2.3 to 1 in all types of army-cooperation and reconnaissance aircraft.

Given the figures above, and the technological and training disparity between the VVS and Luftwaffe in June 1941, it is not too surprising that the VVS-Western Special Military District was virtually wiped out in the first ten days of the war. During this time around 1,270 (72%) of the combat aircraft initially deployed in the VVS-Western Special Military District were destroyed.[294] Luftflotte 2 achieved this despite having to support Luftflotte 1 in the north, despite providing almost continuous close-air support for Army Group Centre, and despite carrying out an effective interdiction campaign on Western Front's deep rear area (mainly against rail lines and major river crossings).

The reader should note that Luftflotte 2's front sector included the whole border with the Western Special Military District and a large portion of the border with the Baltic Special Military District. Hence elements of Luftflotte 2 (mainly from VIII. Fliegerkorps) were expected to engage VVS forces in both these military from the first day of the campaign. On top of this, elements of the II Fliegerkorps/ Luftflotte 2 had to assist Army Group South and Luftflotte 4 in June-July 1941 due to the initial overwhelming VVS numerical superiority in this sector (see below). Refer to the Soviet FILARM air-model (Volume IIIB 3. 2)) for details on the air battles and losses over Eastern Poland, Belorussia and the Ukraine in June-July 1941.[295]

***

---

[292] H. Boog, et al, German Research Institute for Military History at Potsdam, Germany and the Second World War-Volume IV, The Attack on the Soviet Union, Clarendon Press (Oxford University Press), New York, 1996, p. 366.

[293] Refer Volume IIIB 3. 2) d. – 'The Soviet Air Forces in 1941 - The Order of Battle and Actual Strength of all Soviet Air Combat Units in a Deployed (D) State on 22nd June 1941 - VVS-Western Special Military District'.

[294] Ibid. A.G. Fyodorov, *Aviatsiya v bitve pod Moskvoi* [Aviation in the Battle of Moscow] Moscow, Nauka, 1975, gives the losses of VVS-Western Front up to 30th June 1941 as 1 163 aircraft.

[295] Refer Volume IIIB 3. 2) d. – 'The Soviet Air Forces in 1941 - The Order of Battle and Actual Strength of all Soviet Air Combat Units in a Deployed (D) State on 22nd June 1941 - VVS-Western Special Military District', and 3. 2) c. – 'VVS- Baltic Special Military District', and 3. 2) e. – 'VVS-Kiev Special Military District'.

d. Luftflotte 4

Luftflotte 4 was deployed in Army Group South's area on 21st June 1941, commanded by Generaloberst Alexander Lohr. Its task was to assist Army Group South during its attack across South East Poland, the Ukraine and towards Kiev and the Dnieper River. At the same time Luftflotte 4 had to support the German and Rumanian armies in their offensive eastwards across Bessarabia and the Southern Ukraine, whilst also establishing air superiority over the western part of the Black Sea. To accomplish this difficult and diverse set of objectives against what turned out to be the strongest VVS forces, Luftflotte 4 contained the IV. and V. Fliegerkorps, the motorised 2nd Flak Corps, and the *Deutsche Luftwaffenmission Rumanien* (Luftwaffe Mission Rumania). Because of the huge area to be covered, Luftflotte 4's two Fliegerkorps were deployed into two distinct and widely separated (i.e., mutually none-supporting) areas. The distribution of available and serviceable aircraft in Luftflotte 4, and the units they were assigned to on 21st June 1941, are shown in table Luft 4.[296]

The V. Fliegerkorps, commanded by General der Flieger Robert Ritter von Greim, was to provide the principal air-support for Army Group South's 6th Army, 17th Army and 1st Panzer Group, with orders to cooperate especially closely with 1st Panzer Group. On 21st June 1941 the V. Fliegerkorps and 2nd Flak Corps were deployed in South East Poland between Lublin-Chelm and the Slovakian border. The fighters of JG 3 and bombers of KG 54 and KG 55 were based in the Lublin-Zamosc area, while KG 51 was somewhat out on a limb in the south near the Slovakian-Hungarian border (near Krosno). The attack forces of V. Fliegerkorps consisted of only 109 fighters and 247 twin engine bombers. By any standards this was not a large air-force, especially when one considers it was about to attack the strongest VVS force in the USSR (the VVS Kiev Special Military District - see force comparisons below), and that its initial area of operations covered a front roughly 350km wide and over 600km deep. On top of this V. Fliegerkorps did not even have a single *Sturzkampfgeschwader* (Dive-bomber) or *Schlachtgeschwader* (Ground attack) *Staffeln*: yet it was expected to provide close air-support for the northern wing of Army Group South which was about to attack the strongest Red Army Front in the USSR with the (numerically) strongest armoured force concentration anywhere in the world at that time.

The southern wing of Luftflotte 4 consisted of the IV. Fliegerkorps, commanded by Generalleutnant Kurt Pflugbeil. Its primary objective was to provide the air-support for the German 11th Army and the Rumanian 3rd and 4th Armies in their offensive across Bessarabia and the Southern Ukraine, with a secondary objective of helping to establishing air superiority over the Black Sea around Odessa. Accordingly, on 21st June 1941 IV. Fliegerkorps was deployed in Moldavia and eastern Rumania which was over 500km further south and east than the most southerly unit in V. Fliegerkorps.[297] With the Carpathian Mountains and whole of eastern Hungary between them, the two 'adjacent' *Fliegerkorps* in Luftflotte 4 could not mutually support each other's air-operations as they could in Luftflotte 1 and 2 further north. In fact, IV. Fliegerkorps was so far south that its front sector was defended by a completely different VVS command: namely the VVS-Odessa Military District (including 9th Separate Army). This VVS command controlled a relatively strong air-force in its own right. Unsurprisingly, being on the southernmost fringe of the German's East Front, IV. Fliegerkorps was the weakest full *Fliegerkorps* fielded in support of Operation Barbarossa. On 21st June 1941 its attack forces consisted of only 116 fighters and 111 twin engine bombers. It also had no *Sturzkampfgeschwader* (Dive-bomber) or *Schlachtgeschwader* (Ground attack) *Staffeln*.

A third 'air-operations' HQ reporting to Luftflotte 4 in June 1941 was the *Deutsche Luftwaffenmission Rumanien* (DLM - Luftwaffe Mission Rumania). It was commanded by Generalleutnant Hans Speidel and was deployed in the far south around Bucharest. The DLM had three main purposes in June 1941. Firstly, it was used as an administrative HQ for Luftwaffe units and personnel seconded to assist in the training of *Fortele Aeriene Regale ale Romaniei* (FARR - Royal Rumanian Air Force) personnel. The DLM had been steadily increasing its commitment to training FARR personnel since October 1940, when General Antonescu first invited the Germans to send a military mission to Rumania. Secondly, the DLM was used to facilitate cooperation between FARR and Luftwaffe combat units in the lead up to, and during, Operation Barbarossa. And thirdly, the DLM was used to control the Luftwaffe fighter units used to 'stiffen' the FARR air defences in southern and eastern Rumania. On 21st June 1941 the DLM controlled the experienced Stab/JG 52, III./JG 52 and KGr zbV 104; all deployed in the Ploesti-Bucharest region. The 47 Luftwaffe Bf 109F fighters available to the DLM were used to stiffen the FARR air-defences around the strategically vital Ploesti oil fields, which were well within range of Soviet bombers operating out of the Odessa Military District.

---

[296] Ibid, note 277 and 287.
[297] KG.51 was the southernmost unit in V Fliegerkorps, deployed near Krosno. It was approximately 500km from JG.77, the most northern unit in IV Fliegerkorps, deployed around Roman in Moldavia (Rumania). H. Boog, et al, German Research Institute for Military History at Potsdam, Germany and the Second World War-Volume IV, The Attack on the Soviet Union, Clarendon Press (Oxford University Press), New York, 1996, pull-out map 3.

From table <u>Luft 4</u> we can see that on 21st June 1941 Luftflotte 4 contained a total of 1,163 combat and transport aircraft. This included 366 single engine fighters, 2 heavy twin engine fighters and 356 twin engine bombers. The remaining 439 aircraft were all seaplanes, short range (army tactical) or long range reconnaissance aircraft, or various types of army-cooperation, liaison and transport aircraft. Of the latter, 278 aircraft were under the operational and tactical control of ground units in Army Group South.[298] These comprised aircraft in the *Heeresaufklärungsgruppen*, the *Panzeraufklärungsgruppen*, the *Kurierstaffeln*, the *Verbindungsstaffeln* and *Fernaufklärungsgruppen* 1.(F)/Nacht, 3.(F)/10, 3.(F)/11, 7.(F)/LG2 and 2.(F)/22.

Excluding the transport aircraft in KGr zbV units, *Kurierstaffeln*, *Verbindungsstaffel* and *Sanitätsflugbereitschaften*, Luftflotte 4 contained a total 967 combat aircraft (784 serviceable) on 21st June 1941. None of these aircraft belonged to *Sturzkampfgeschwader* (Dive-bomber) or *Schlachtgeschwader* (Ground attack) *Staffeln*, even though the original invasion plans had called for a *Sturzkampfgeschwader* to be deployed with Luftflotte 4. The only attempt to provide any 'close air support' capability was in the equipping of KG 51 and KG 54 (both equipped with Ju 88s) with devices for dropping SD-2 anti-personnel fragmentation bombs.

***

---

[298] H. Boog, et al, Table, I.IV.5, p. 364, shows 239 aircraft (with 208 serviceable) under Army control. This only includes the *Fernaufklärungsgruppen* (48), *Heeresaufklärungsgruppen* (149) and *Kurierstaffeln* (42), which agrees with the data in table <u>Luft 4</u>.

Table Luft 4 — Deployment and Composition of Luftwaffe Air Units, 21st June 1941

Luftflotte 4

IV. Fliegerkorps

Category	Description	No x Type/Auth	Av	Sv
JG (Jagdgeschwader) Fighter.	Stab/JG 77	4xBf-109E	2	2
	II./JG 77	40xBf-109E	39	19
	III./JG 77	40xBf-109E/F	35	20
	I.(Jagd.)/LG 2^	40xBf-109E	40	20
KG (Kampfgeschwader) Bomber.	Stab/KG 27	4xHe-111H	5	5
	I./KG 27	40xHe-111H	30	22
	II./KG 27**	40xHe-111H	24	21
	III./KG 27*^	40xHe-111H	28	25
	II./KG 4*	40xHe-111H	24	8
F (Fernaufklärungsgruppe) Long Range Strategic Reconnaissance.	3.(F)/121	12x (see note^*)	11	8

V. Fliegerkorps

Category	Description	No x Type/Auth	Av	Sv
JG (Jagdgeschwader) Fighter.	Stab/JG 3	4xBf-109F	4	4
	I./JG 3	40xBf-109F	35	28
	II./JG 3	40xBf-109F	35	32
	III./JG 3	40xBf-109F	35	34
KG (Kampfgeschwader) Bomber.	Stab/KG 51	4xJu-88A	2	2
	I./KG 51	40xJu-88A	22	22
	II./KG 51*	40xJu-88A	36	29
	III./KG 51^	40xJu-88A	32	28
	Stab/KG 54**	4xJu-88A	1	1
	I./KG 54*^	40xJu-88A	34	31
	II./KG 54^^	40xJu-88A	36	33
	Stab/KG 55^*	4xHe-111H, Bf-110	6,2	6,1
	I./KG 55***	40xHe-111H	27	27
	II./KG 55**^	40xHe-111H	24	22
	III./KG 55^^	40xHe-111P/H	25	24
F (Fernaufklärungsgruppe) Long Range Strategic Reconnaissance.	4.(F)/121	12xJu-88A/D	10	7

(continued)

Category	Description	No x Type/Auth	Av	Sv
JG (Jagdgeschwader) Fighter.	Stab/JG 52*	4xBf-109F	4	3
	III./JG 52*	40xBf-109F	43	41
	Erg./JG 3****	16xBf-109E	33	26
	Erg./JG 27^***	16xBf-109E	31	24
	Erg./JG 77*****	16xBf-109E	30	19
H (Heeresaufklärungsgruppe) Short Range Tactical Reconnaissance.	6.(H)/21*^	12xHs-126	7	6
	2.(H)/10^^	12xHs-126	7	7
	4.(H)/41**	12xHs-126	8	8
	4.(H)/22**^	12xHs-126	7	6
	4.(Pz)/13**^	12xHs-126	11	10
	5.(Pz)/14**^	12xHs-126	12	10
	5.(H)/21**^	12xHs-126	8	7
	1.(Pz)/23*^^	12xHs-126	10	9
	5.(Pz)/11*^^	12xFw-189	10	10
	3.(Pz)/21^^^	12xHs-126	12	11
	5.(H)/32^^^	12xHs-126	7	7
	5.(H)/31^^^	12xHs-126	7	6
	1.(H)/41****	12xHs-126/Fw-189	7	6
	8.(H)/32***^	12xHs-126	8	8
	4.(H)/32***^^	12xHs-126	7	7
	3.(H)/13^^^^	12xHs-126	7	6
	5.(H)/13^^^*	12xHs-126	7	7
	6.(H)/12^^**	12xHs-126	7	6
F (Fernaufklärungsgruppe) Long Range Strategic Reconnaissance.	4.(F)/122	12xJu-88D/A,Bf-110E	11	7
	1.(F)/Nacht^	12xDo-17P	9	5
	3.(F)/10^	12xDo-17P, Bf-110C/E	10	9

Unit	Aircraft		
3.(F)/11^	12xDo-17P, Bf-110C/E	10	8
7.(F)/LG2***	12xBf-110C/E (Bf-109E?)	10	8
2.(F)/22*^^^	12xJu-88A/D	9	7
KGr zbV 104*	53xJu-52	41	37
KGr zbV 50	53xJu-52	44	24
IV. Korps Tr.Sta 16xJu-52		15	11
V. Korps Tr.Sta 16xJu-52		15	12
Wekusta 76	8xJu-88A/D, He-111H	8	6
8. Seenotstaffel*	14xHe-59	6	3
Kurierstaffel 4^	Fi-156, Ar-66 and W-34	9	7
Kurierstaffel 5**	Fi-156, Ar-66, Bu-131, Kl-35 & W-34	9	7
Kurierstaffel 10***	Fi-156, Bf-108, Bu-131 and W-34	8	7
Kurierstaffel 6***	Fi-156, Bu-131 and W-34	8	6
Kurierstaffel 7*^^^	Fi-156, Ar-66, Kl-35 and W-34	8	7
Verbindungsstaffel 4~	Fi-156, Ar-66 & Fw-58.	6	6
Verbindungsstaffel 59~	Fi-156, Ar-66, Fw-58 (+) ~	5	5
Verbindungsstaffel 61~	Fi-156, Go-145, W-34 and Fw-58	6	5
Verbindungsstaffel 64~	Fi-156, C-445, Fw-58, W-34 (+)~~	6	6
Verbindungsstaffel 65~	Fi-156, Go-145, W-34 & Kl-35	6	5
Verbindungsstaffel 69~	Fi-156, Fw-58, W-34 and Bf-108	4	4
Verbindungsstaffel 70~	Fi-156, Ar-66, Fw-58, Bf-108, & Kl-35	6	6

Row-label descriptions (left column):

- KGr zbV (Kampfgeschwader zu besonderen Verwendung) Transport.
- Wekusta (Wettererkundungsstaffel) Weather Observation.
- (Seenotstaffel) Air-Sea Rescue.
- (Kurierstaffel) Courier/Liaison.
- (Verbindungsstaffel) Communication/Liaison.
- (Sanitätsflugbereitschaft) Ambulance Flight.

* Assigned to Luftflotte 2, ca 10th July 1941, joined Stab, I., and III./KG 4. II./KG 4 was withdrawn to East Prussia for refit in early Oct. 1941. It returned to the East Front ca 21st Dec. 1941. KG 4 units also operated in Northern Area (w Luftflotte 1) in late 1941.

^ Bf-109Es were fighter-bombers but used as a fighter unit reporting to Stab/JG 77. Was also used as a SchG (Schlachtgeschwader - Ground-attack) unit. It was redesignated 1./JG 77 ca 13th January 1942.

** II./KG 27 was withdrawn to Germany for rest and refit, ca early November 1941.

*^ III./KG 27 was withdrawn to Germany for rest and refit (to He-111 H-6) from late August to late October 1941. It returned to the East Front ca 1st November 1941.

^* Aircraft types: 12xJu-88A/D, Bf-110E.

* II./KG 51 was withdrawn to Austria ca 8th Sep. 1941. Returned to East Front (S. Sector) on 4th Dec. 1941.

^ III./KG 51 was withdrawn to Austria ca 18th July 41. Returned to East front (S. Sector) on 30th Aug. 41.

** Stab./KG 54 returned to Germany ca 15th Nov. 1941. It was assigned to the Mediterranean (Sicily and Italy) along with II. Fliegerkorps in Dec. 1941.

*^ I. /KG 54 returned to Germany ca 17th Nov. 1941. It was assigned to the Mediterranean (Sicily and Italy) along with II. Fliegerkorps in Dec. 1941. Made its first attack on Malta on 20th Dec. 1941.

^^ II. /KG 54 withdrawn to East Front ca 30th Dec. 41. Returned to East Front (Cen Sector), 22nd Jan. 1942.

^* Stab./KG 55 was sent to Germany/France for rest and reequipping ca 18th Nov. 1941.

*** I./KG 55 was withdrawn to Austria/France for rest and reequipping ca 1st Oct. 1941.

**^ II./KG 55 was withdrawn to France for rest and reequipping ca 18th Nov. 1941.

*^^ III./KG 55 was withdrawn to France for rest and reequipping in Dec. 1941 (although the original withdrawal orders were given on 18th Nov 1941).

* Attached to the Deutsche Luftwaffenmission Rumanien, (Generalleutnant Hans Speidel).

^ Attached directly to Koluft Sud, Kommandeur der Luftstreitkrafte, (Army Group South Coordinator attached to the Army).

3.(F)/10 received Ju-88D aircraft later in 1941.

** Attached to Koluft 6, (6th Army).   *^ Attached to XVII Corps.

^^ Attached to XXXXIV Corps.   ^* Attached to LV Corps.

*** Attached to Koluft 1 Pz Gr, (1st Pz Group).

**^ Attached to Gruft 12, (III Mot Cps)

*^^ Attached to Gruft 41, (XIV Mot Cps)

^^^ Attached to Gruft 32, (XXXXVIII Mot Cps)

^** Attached to XXIX Corps.   ^^* Attached to Koluft 17, (17th Army).

**** Attached to IV Corps.   ***^ Attached to XXXIX Mountain Corps.

**^* Attached to LII Corps.   *^^^ Attached to Koluft 11, (11th Army).

^^^^ Attached to XI Corps.   ^^^* Attached to XXX Corps.

**^^ Attached to LIV Corps.   ~ Disbanded in November 1941.

^*** Erganzungs, (Sometimes operational Training and Replacement) Gruppen, reporting to Luftgaukommando VIII, (Both Gruppen in reserve in Breslau area).

***** Erganzungs Gruppe reporting to Luftgaukommando XVII, (Gruppe in reserve in Vienna area).

~~ Also operated Go-145 & Bf-108 at some point.

Table Luft 4 (cont.)			
Luftflotte 4, Totals			
	No. of	No. of Aircraft	
Unit Type	Units	Avail	Svcble
Jagdgruppen	7	272	203
Erg.Guppen (JG,ZG)	3	94	69
Schlachtgruppen	0	0	0
Zerstörergruppen	0	0	0
Kampfgruppen	12	358	307
Stukagruppen	0	0	0
(Pz) Staffeln	5	55	50
(H) Staffeln	13	94	87
Luft (F) Staffeln	3	32	22
Heeres (F) Staffeln	5	48	37
KGr zbV	2 2/3	115	84
Wetterstaffeln	1	8	6
Seefliegerstaffeln	0	0	0
Seenotstaffeln	1	6	3
Kurierstaffeln/Verb. Staffeln	12	81	71
Sanitätsflugbereitschaften	0	0	0
		1163	939
Number of Aircraft by type			
Single Engine Fighters		366	272
Twin Eng Fighters / Ftr Bmbrs		2	1
Twin Eng Night Fighters		0	0
Single Eng Fighter Bombers		0	0
Dive Bombers		0	0
Twin Engine Bombers		356	306
Four Engine Bombers		0	0
Long Range Recon*		88	65
SR Recon / Army Coop^		230	208
Seaplanes		6	3
Transport Aircraft**		115	84
		1163	939
* Includes Wetterstaffeln aircraft.			
^ Includes Courier, Liaison aircraft.			
** Includes Sanitätsflugbereitschaften aircraft.			
Total Combat Aircraft*		967	784
*Excludes aircraft in KGr zbV, Kurierstaffeln, and Sanitätsflugbereitschaften.			
Aircraft under tactical control of the Army			
Long Range Recon		48	37
SR Recon / Army Coop^		230	208
		278	245
^ Includes Courier, Liaison Aircraft			
© Nigel Askey, 2018			

***

It is very revealing to compare Luftflotte 4 against its main opponents in June 1941; namely the VVS-Kiev Special Military District (facing V. Fliegerkorps) and the VVS-Odessa Military District (facing IV. Fliegerkorps, the DLM and the FARR).

The VVS-Kiev Special Military District had no less than 2,059 combat aircraft on 22nd June 1941, of which 1,759 were reported as 'serviceable'.[299] This total included 1,341 fighters (with 253 modern MiG-1/3 and Yak-1 fighters) and 570 bombers and assault (ground-attack) aircraft. In terms of numbers of fighters, numbers of modern aircraft, and training and readiness, the VVS-Kiev Special Military District was the strongest VVS force in the western USSR.

Therefore on the eve of Operations Barbarossa, V. Fliegerkorps was outnumbered by its immediate VVS opponent by a staggering 12.3 to 1 (1,341 vs 109) in fighters and 2.3 to 1 (570 vs 247) in bombers and ground attack (assault) aircraft. If all of V Fliegerkorps aircraft are included, all other aircraft in Luftflotte 4 which were deployed in Poland and Hungary on 22nd June 1941 are included, and all reserve aircraft in Erg./JG 3 and Erg./JG 27 are included, then the total Luftwaffe force potentially available to attack the VVS-Kiev Special Military District contained 683 'combat' aircraft. This figure excludes Ju 52 transports, but includes all aircraft in the *Kurierstaffeln* and *Verbindungsstaffeln* deployed in or anywhere near Poland and Hungary.[300] This potential force comprised 173 single engine fighters, 247 twin engine bombers, 68 long range reconnaissance aircraft, and 195 short range reconnaissance and army-cooperation/liaison aircraft.

Therefore, on the morning of 22nd June 1941 the VVS-Kiev Special Military District outnumbered the force that could possibly be fielded against it by at least 3 to 1 in combat aircraft. In terms of aircraft types, the **VVS-Kiev Special Military District initially outnumbered its opponent by a huge 7.8 to 1 in fighters and 2.3 to 1 in bombers and ground attack (assault) aircraft**, while the VVS-Kiev Special Military District was in turn outnumbered by 1.8 to 1 in reconnaissance and army-cooperation/liaison aircraft.

Further analysis shows that the VVS-Kiev Special Military District initially had 253 modern MiG-1/3 and Yak-1 fighters on strength. This means the VVS in this sector actually had at least 80 more MiG-3s and Yak-1s than the Luftwaffe had Bf 109s (a 1.5 to 1 superiority in modern fighters even if we include the older Bf 109Es in the German reserve/training units, Erg./JG 3 and Erg./JG 27). This does not support the general perception that the VVS's best fighters were only encountered further east later in the war, and it does not support the perception that the Bf 109 only came up against obsolete fighter types in June-July 1941.

Furthermore, the VVS-Kiev Special Military District included 455 I-16s: more than any other VVS-KA force in the Western Military Districts. Although not really a match for the Bf 109 E or F, the I-16 was highly manoeuvrable and still a capable fighter in 1941. Given these numbers it is probable that German pre-war intelligence severely underestimated the overall strength (especially the fighter strength) of the VVS-Kiev Special Military District, and would have allocated more Luftwaffe resources to this sector if they had known the full extent of the Kiev Special Military District's forces.

The bottom line of all these figures is that **on 21st June 1941 Luftflotte 4 probably faced the highest odds ever faced by an air-force which was about to launch a major strategic air-offensive!** Given this, and according to current theories of modern air warfare, 22nd June 1941 and the following days should have been a disaster for Luftflotte 4. In the event, V. Fliegerkorps still managed to decimate the VVS forces defending the northern Ukraine in late June 1941. How it achieved victory against such odds remains a lesson in surprise, skill imparted by training, exploiting an initial advantage to the full, and in not allowing a hard fought for initiative to pass back to an opponent. Refer to the Soviet FILARM air-model for more details on the air battles and losses over the northern Ukraine in June-July 1941.[301]

***

---

[299] Refer Volume IIIB 3. 2) e. – 'The Soviet Air Forces in 1941 - The Order of Battle and Actual Strength of all Soviet Air Combat Units in a Deployed (D) State on 22nd June 1941 - VVS-Kiev Special Military District'.

[300] 'Erg' refers to *Ergänzungsgruppe* (Replacement Aviation Group): Erg./JG 3 and Erg./JG 27 were essentially 'training and replacement units' which were sometimes also operational, depending in the situation. Including Erg./JG 3 and Erg./JG 27 with 64 fighters is really overestimating the fighters immediately available to *Luftflotte* 4 because they were based in reserve in the Breslau area and were not available for operations on 22nd June 1941. However they reported to Luftgaukommando VIII and are included in the German fighter figures so no one can say the German fighter figures are underestimated.

[301] Refer Volume IIIB 3. 2) e. – 'The Soviet Air Forces in 1941 - The Order of Battle and Actual Strength of all Soviet Air Combat Units in a Deployed (D) State on 22nd June 1941 - VVS-Kiev Special Military District'.

It is also worth looking briefly at the German allied air forces committed in this sector in June-July 1941. This is mainly because old Soviet sources (and some sources today) make great play of the fact that the Luftwaffe was supported by the Hungarian, Slovakian and Rumanian air forces in the south.

From 27th June 1941 the *Magyar Kiralyi Honved Legiero* (**MKH - Hungarian Air Force**) contributed a single air force brigade to support the Hungarians' Carpathian Army Group which was moving to support Army Group South. The 1. Field Brigade (Carpathian Army Group) consisted of 48 biplane fighters (Fiat C.R. 32s and C.R. 42s), 40 twin engine bombers (Caproni Ca 135bis and Ju 86Ks) and 29 reconnaissance aircraft (total 117 aircraft).[302] The C.R.32s and 42s were obsolescent fighters which were of limited value to Army Group South, but the bombers were a useful contribution to the Axis forces attacking into the Ukraine.

Also, from 7th July 1941 the tiny *Slovenske Vzdusne Zbrane* (**SVZ - Slovakian Air Force**) contributed 71 aircraft to support the Axis forces in the Ukraine. These consisted of 33 Avia-B534s biplane fighters, 37 biplane reconnaissance aircraft (mostly Letov S-328s), and one transport.[303] The Avia-B534s were obsolete fighters and were barely able to match the I-153 or I-153bis by June 1941. The fact that the Hungarian and Slovakian Air Forces had around 650 aircraft in their entire air forces is sometimes quoted in current literature on Operation Barbarossa: the misleading implication is that around this number was available to support the Axis forces. In fact the vast majority of these aircraft were obsolete types used as trainers, transports, liaison, etc, and were totally unsuitable, or were simply unable, to perform combat missions. The total MKH (Hungarian) and SVZ (Slovakian) air forces actually committed to support Operation Barbarossa contained only 188 aircraft, and these were all obsolete or semi-obsolete types.

***

On Luftflotte 4's southern wing things were not as dire for the IV. Fliegerkorps. This was largely due to the presence of the *Fortele Aeriene Regale ale Romaniei* (FARR - Royal Rumanian Air Force). Facing the Axis forces was the VVS KA (*VVS Krasnaya Armiya* or VVS Red Army) forces in the VVS-Odessa Military District, and the VVS VMF (*VVS Voyenno-Morskoy Flot* SSSR or VVS Naval Forces of the USSR) forces in the VVS-ChF (*Chernomorskiy Flot* or Black Sea Fleet). On 22nd June 1941 the VVS KA and VSS VMF forces in the Odessa Military District possessed a total of 1,685 combat aircraft, of which 1,399 were reported as 'serviceable'.[304] This total included 1,050 fighters (including 201 of the latest Mig-1/3 fighters) and 454 bombers and assault (ground-attack) aircraft. It turns out that the VVS-Odessa Military District was in fact the fourth strongest VVS force in the Western Military Districts. It was numerically stronger and with more modern fighters than the Baltic Special Military District, and it only had 86 fewer combat aircraft than the vital Western Special Military District.

If all of IV. Fliegerkorps aircraft are included, all other aircraft in Luftflotte 4 which were deployed in Rumania on 22nd June 1941 are included, and all reserve aircraft in Erg./JG 77 are included, then the total Luftwaffe force initially available to attack the VVS-Odessa Military District contained 365 combat aircraft. This figure excludes Ju 52 transports, but includes all aircraft in the *Kurierstaffeln* and *Verbindungsstaffeln* deployed in or anywhere near Rumania.[305] This number was made up of 193 single engine fighters (mostly older Bf 109Es), 111 twin engine bombers (all He 111s), 20 long range reconnaissance aircraft, 35 short range reconnaissance and army-cooperation/liaison aircraft, and six seaplanes.

Therefore on 22nd June 1941 the VVS-Odessa Military District outnumbered its Luftwaffe opponents only (excluding FARR forces, see below) by 4.6 to 1 in combat aircraft, 4.1 to 1 in bombers and assault aircraft, and, most critically, by 5.4 to 1 in fighters. In addition the VVS-Odessa Military District had more MiG-3s (a fighter produced in the period 1940-41) than Luftflotte 4 had Bf 109E/Fs (mostly fighters produced in the period 1939-1940). In this sector the VVS could not complain that they were overmatched by more modern Luftwaffe fighters and, on paper at least, they had some advantage in this regard.

***

---

[302] Refer Volume IV - The Hungarian PILARM model for a detailed breakdown of the MKH aircraft on 27th June 1941.
[303] Refer Volume IV - The Slovakian PILARM model for a detailed breakdown of the SVZ aircraft in June 1941.
[304] Refer Volume IIIB 3. 2) f. – 'The Soviet Air Forces in 1941 - The Order of Battle and Actual Strength of all Soviet Air Combat Units in a Deployed (D) State on 22nd June 1941 - VVS-Odessa Military District, Including 9th Separate Army'.
[305] 'Erg.' refers to *Ergänzungsgruppe* (Replacement Aviation Group). Erg./JG 77 was actually in the Vienna area on 22nd June 1941 and so strictly shouldn't be included in the initial Luftwaffe figures.

Fortunately for Luftflotte 4's IV. Fliegerkorps it was supported by the *Fortele Aeriene Regale ale Romaniei* **(FARR or ARR - Royal Rumanian Air Force)**, which, apart from the Luftwaffe, was the largest Axis air force committed to support Operation Barbarossa.[306]

In June 1941 the FARR was organised under three main commands: the GAL (*Gruparea Aeriana de Lupta* or Combat Air Grouping), the 3rd and 4th Rumanian Army's local air support, and the Rumanian home defences. By far the most important grouping was the GAL (Combat Air Grouping) which comprised most of the FARR's strength and was to be used in offensive operations in support of Operation Barbarossa. On 22nd June 1941 the GAL contained 253 aircraft made up of: 88 low wing mono-plane fighters, 89 twin engine bombers, 9 older light 'reconnaissance' bombers, 10 long range reconnaissance aircraft and 57 short range reconnaissance and army-cooperation aircraft.[307] The remaining FARR groups included 134 fighters (with only 10 Hurricane I 'modern' fighters), 21 long range reconnaissance aircraft, 143 short range reconnaissance and army cooperation aircraft, 21 seaplanes and 20 transports. Thus the total number of combat aircraft that the FARR could possibly bring to bear on the VVS-Odessa Military District on 22nd June 1941 was 572 (excluding 20 transports). These consisted of 222 fighters, 89 twin engine bombers, 31 long range reconnaissance aircraft (Blenheim Is), 209 short range reconnaissance and army cooperation aircraft (mostly older biplanes) and 21 seaplanes.[308]

Therefore, the combined forces of Luftflotte 4 and the FARR opposing the VVS-Odessa Military District on 22nd June 1941 contained 937 combat aircraft (excluding transports). These comprised 415 fighters, 200 twin engine bombers, 51 long range reconnaissance aircraft, 244 short range reconnaissance and army-cooperation/liaison aircraft (mostly older biplanes) and 27 seaplanes. Thus on 22nd June 1941 the **VVS-Odessa Military District outnumbered its combined Axis opponents by 1.8 to one in combat aircraft overall; 2.5 to one in fighters, and 2.3 to one in bombers and assault aircraft**. These odds were considerably better than those faced by V. Fliegerkorps / Luftflotte 4 in its upcoming battle with the VVS-Kiev Special Military District (see previous section).

Arguably, a more accurate comparison would only include the forces of IV. Fliegerkorps / Luftflotte 4 and the FARR GAL (Combat Air Grouping) aircraft, because this was the Axis attack force on 22nd June 1941. In this case the VVS-Odessa Military District outnumbered the Axis force by 2.7 to 1 in combat aircraft overall, 3.7 to 1 in fighters, and 2.3 to 1 in bombers and assault aircraft. These odds were still considerably better than those faced by V. Fliegerkorps (further north) in June 1941. However, the VVS started flying offensive missions into Rumania from almost the first day of the war, and they continued to attack Rumania almost daily during the Bessarabian Campaign.[309] When considering the overall air battle in June-July 1941 over Bessarabia, Rumania and the Southern Front, it is thus probably fairer to include all the FARR commands.

On balance the VVS forces in the VVS-Southern Front, which contained almost all the original air units from the Odessa Military District, put up the best fight (by the VVS) in any district in June-July 1941. Despite this and its initial numerical advantages, the VVS-Odessa Military District (Southern Front) lost at least 60% of its initially deployed force in the first 18 days of war. Appalling as these losses were, it is incredible to think they were considerably better than the similar figures for the VVS-Northwestern, Western and Southwestern Fronts in June-July 1941. By August 1941 the Luftwaffe and FARR units in this sector were preparing for the battle of Odessa, and it is true to say that by this time they had achieved air parity bordering on air superiority in this front sector. This was despite the VVS-Southern Front receiving substantial VVS reinforcements from the Far East and the internal military districts. Refer to the Soviet FILARM air-model for more details on the air battles and losses over Bessarabia and the southern Ukraine in June-July 1941.[310]

***

---

[306] The abbreviation ARR (*Aeronautica Regala Romana* or Royal Rumanian Aeronautics) was apparently used in official Rumanian Air Force documents. However the abbreviation FARR is more commonly used internationally (especially in the West) and in most published Rumanian sources. D. Bernad, Rumanian Air Force: The Prime Decade, 1938-1947, Squadron Signal Publications, Carrollton, Texas, 1999, p. 3.

[307] The fighters were comprised of 36 Bf 109Es, 28 He 112B and 24 IAR 80/80As. The bombers were comprised of 15 PZL P.37, 27 He 111H, 17 Potez 633, 8 Bloch 210, 22 S.M. 79B, and 9 IAR 37. The long range reconnaissance aircraft consisted of 10 Blenheim I, and the short range reconnaissance and army-cooperation aircraft were all IAR 38 and IAR 39 aircraft. Refer Volume IV - The Rumanian PILARM model for a detailed breakdown of the FARR figures on 22nd June 1941.

[308] Refer Volume IV - 'The Rumanian PILARM model'. The FARR had an additional 238 transport and other aircraft types in its inventory (excluding small training types).

[309] D. Bernad, Rumanian Air Force: The Prime Decade, 1938-1947, Squadron Signal Publications, Carrollton, Texas 1999, p. 6.

[310] Refer Volume IIIB 3. 2) f. – 'VVS-Odessa Military District, Including 9th Separate Army'.

e. Luftflotte 5

On 21st June 1941 Luftflotte 5, commanded by Generaloberst Hans-Jurgen Stumpff, was deployed in Norway and northern Finland. Its primary objectives were to support the German forces in northern Finland in their attacks towards Murmansk and the Kola Peninsula, to interdict the Soviet Northern Fleet, to protect German supply routes along the Norwegian coast, and to garrison the Norwegian coast against British naval forces. To accomplish these tasks Luftflotte 5 was essentially split into two commands: Luftwaffenkommando Kirkenes and Fliegerführer Nord. The distribution of available and serviceable aircraft in Luftflotte 5, and the units they were assigned to on 21st June 1941, are shown in the two tables Luft 5 EF and Luft 5 Nor.[311]

In the far north was Luftwaffenkommando Kirkenes commanded by Oberstleutnant Andreas Nielsen. Based around Banak and Kirkenes in the northern tip of Norway, Luftwaffenkommando Kirkenes constituted Luftflotte 5's direct support for Operation Barbarossa. Its primary task was to support the German Army's Norway Mountain Corps (*Gebirgskorps*) and XXXVI Special Corps (HoH. Kdo XXXVI) during their offensive across harsh terrain towards Murmansk and further south (through Salla) to cut the Murmansk railroad.[312] It was also expected to conduct operations against the Soviet Northern Fleet operating in the Barents and White Seas, including attacking shipping in and around the port of Murmansk, as well as interdicting the important rail junctions at Murmansk and Archangel.

From table Luft 5 EF it is apparent that the initial striking power of Luftwaffenkommando Kirkenes resided in only 16 fighters (barely more than a single *Staffel*), 22 medium bombers, 42 dive-bombers and 9 seaplanes. Fortunately, additional fighter elements from Jagdgruppe Kirkenes were also on hand to support air operations in this sector (although they were deployed under Fliegerführer Nord, see next section). This force comprised 1./JG 77 and 14./JG 77 (together with 17 Bf 109E based at Kirkenes), and 1.(Z)/JG 77 (with 12 Bf 110 C/D based at Kirkenes). This at least increased the available fighters to 29 Bf 109 fighters and 16 Bf 110 heavy fighters.

However it is readily apparent from the small size of Luftwaffenkommando Kirkenes that the Luftwaffe considered its commitments to Operation Barbarossa in northern Finland as minimal at best, and bordering on token. Even with support from Jagdgruppe Kirkenes (with 29 fighters), only 139 combat aircraft were available for combat operations across the whole Kola Peninsula.[313] This excludes a handful of transport aircraft in KGr zbV units, *Kurierstaffeln* and *Verbindungsstaffel*n. By any assessment, to accomplish the formidable set of tasks laid out (above) would have required a considerably larger Luftwaffe force. This is especially apparent when one compares the Luftwaffe and Kriegsmarine strengths in the region against those of the VVS-Leningrad Military District and the Soviet Northern Fleet (see below).

The only real exception to this was the presence of *Sturzkampfgeschwader Gruppe* IV.(St)/LG 1 with 42 Ju 87 Stukas. This was a very dangerous unit for both Red Army fortifications and enemy naval units operating in the Barents Sea. It has to be said, however, that in the overall scheme of Operation Barbarossa IV. (St)/LG 1 would have better served the German cause if it had been deployed with I. Fliegerkorps/ Luftflotte 1 supporting Army Group North, or V. Fliegerkorps/ Luftflotte 4 supporting Army Group South. The strategically vital Luftflotte 1 and Luftflotte 4 did not have a single *Sturzkampfgeschwader* (Dive-bomber) or *Schlachtgeschwader* (Ground attack) *Staffel* between them! And yet, Army Group South (for example) was attacking the numerically strongest armoured concentration in the world supported by the strongest VVS forces in the western USSR.

***

---

[311] Ibid, note 277 and 287. Also, Boog, et al, p. 372. P.C. Smith, Luftwaffe Ju 87 Dive Bomber Units 1939-1941, Classic-Ian Allan Publishing, Hersham UK, 2006, p. 85, for IV.(St)/LG 1 strengths on 21st June 1941. C. Bergstrom, A. Mikhailov, Black Cross Red Star, The Air War Over the Eastern Front: Volume 1, Pacifica Military History, Pacifica, California, 2000, p. 166, for selected Luftwaffenkommando Kirkenes unit strengths on 21st June 1941.

[312] The HoH. Kdo XXXVI was redesignated XXXVI *Gebirgskorps* on 18th November 1941.

[313] 4./KG 30 with 9 Ju 88s moved from Stavanger in Norway to reinforce Luftwaffenkommando Kirkenes in late June 1941.

Table Luft 5 EF	Deployment and Composition of Luftwaffe Air Units, 21st June 1941			
	Luftflotte 5 (East Front only)			
	Luftwaffenkommando Kirkenes*			
	Description	No x Type/Auth	Av	Sv
JG (Jagdgeschwader)	Stab/Jafu Norwegen (Stab/ZG 76) ^	4xBf-110	4	4
Fighter.	13./JG 77 **	12xBf-109E	12	12
KG (Kampfgeschwader)	Stab II./KG 30, 5./KG30, 6./KG30 *^	28xJu-88A	22	17
Bomber.				
StG (Sturzkampfgeschwader)	IV.(St)/LG 1 ^^	40xJu-87B/R	42	36
Dive Bomber.				
H (Heeresaufklärungsgruppe)	1.(H)/32 ***	12xHs-126/Do-17P (Fi-156)	7, 3	6, 3
Short Range Tactical				
Reconnaissance.				
F (Fernaufklärungsgruppe)	1.(F)/124 **^	12xJu-88A/D	7	5
Long Range Strategic				
Reconnaissance.				
KGr zbV (Kampfgeschwader	Trans Staffel/Fliegerführer Nord *^^	16xJu-52	11	6
zu besonderen Verwendung)				
Transport.				
Wekusta (Wettererkundungs	Wekusta 5	8xJu-88D, He-111H	2, 2	1, 2
staffel) Weather Observation.				
KuFlGr (Küstenfliegergruppe)	1./KuFlGr 406 ^^^	12xHe-115B/C	9	4
Coastal Aviation.				
(Verbindungsstaffel)	Verbindungsstaffel 2 ~	Ar-96, Fw-58 & Ju-52.	5	5
Communication/Liaison.				

* Luftwaffenkommando Kirkenes was responsible for operations
  against Murmansk and the Kola Peninsula, in the Soviet Union
  from 22nd June 41. (Commander: Oberstleutnant Nielsen).
^ Stab/ZG 76 (at Kirkenes), was acting in this role.
  It was formally renamed Jagdfliegerführer Norwegen on 1st Aug. 41.
** 13./JG 77 recently based at Stavanger, under Jagdgruppe Stavanger
   (Moved to Kirkenes as part of Luftwaffenkommando Kirkenes).
*^ Stab II./KG 30 and 5./KG 30 (10 Ju-88s) based at Banak, Norway,
   6./KG 30 based at Kirkenes (8 Ju 88s).
   The whole of II./KG 30 transferred to Luftflotte 1, VIII. Fliegerkorps,
   in December 1941.
^^ IV.(St)/LG 1 based at Rovaniemi, Finland
   (Moved to Kirkenes as part of Luftwaffenkommando Kirkenes).
   Renamed I./StG 5 on 27th January 1942.
*** Attached to Luftwaffenkommando Kirkenes. 1.(H)/32 based at
    Kemijarvi and Rovaniemi with 7xHs-126 and 3xDo-17Ps. This unit
    may also have had one or more Fi-156 on strength (or seconded).
**^ 1.(F)/124 based at Kirkenes, Norway (possibly still some Do-215B
    on strength).
*^^ Formed from Kurierstaffel z.b.V./ X Fliegerkorps in April 1941. Temporarily
    attached to Luftwaffenkommando Kirkenes from Fliegerführer Nord.
^^^ Based at Tromso, Norway, under Stab./KuFlGr 706.
    (Moved to Banak as part of Luftwaffenkommando Kirkenes).
~ Disbanded in November 1941. Also called Verbindungsstaffel Norwegen.

© Nigel Askey, 2018

***

Table Luft 5 EF (cont.)			
Luftflotte 5 (East Front only)			
	No. of	No. of Aircraft	
Unit Type	Units	Avail	Svcble
Jagdgruppen	1/3	16	16
Erg.Guppen (JG,ZG)	0	0	0
Schlachtgruppen	0	0	0
Zerstörergruppen	0	0	0
Kampfgruppen	2/3	22	17
Stukagruppen	1	42	36
(Pz) Staffeln	0	0	0
(H) Staffeln	1	10	9
Luft (F) Staffeln	1	7	5
Heeres (F) Staffeln	0	0	0
KGr zbV	1/3	11	6
Wetterstaffeln	1	4	3
Seefliegerstaffeln	1	9	4
Seenotstaffeln	0	0	0
Kurierstaffeln/Verb. Staffeln	1	5	5
Sanitätsflugbereitschaften	0	0	0
		126	101
Number of Aircraft by type			
Single Engine Fighters		12	12
Twin Eng Fighters / Ftr Bmbrs		4	4
Twin Eng Night Fighters		0	0
Single Eng Fighter Bombers		0	0
Dive Bombers		42	36
Twin Engine Bombers		22	17
Four Engine Bombers		0	0
Long Range Recon*		11	8
SR Recon / Army Coop^		15	14
Seaplanes		9	4
Transport Aircraft**		11	6
		126	101

* Includes Wetterstaffeln aircraft.
^ Includes Courier, Liaison aircraft.
** Includes Sanitätsflugbereitschaften aircraft.

Total Combat Aircraft*		110	90

* Excludes aircraft in KGr zbV, Kurierstaffeln/Verbindungsstaffeln, and Sanitätsflugbereitschaften.

Aircraft under tactical control of the Army			
Long Range Recon		0	0
SR Recon / Army Coop^		15	14
		15	14

^ Includes Courier, Liaison Aircraft.

© Nigel Askey, 2018

***

The remaining forces in Luftflotte 5 were deployed across the length and breadth of Norway, and extending as far south as Denmark. Their main purpose was to: protect German supply ships moving along the Norwegian coast against Royal Navy surface ship and submarine attack, garrison the Norwegian coast against superior British naval and naval-air (carrier) forces, deter any British amphibious raids into Norway, and carry out reconnaissance and interdiction raids against British shipping in the North and Norwegian Sea.

The fighter and bomber units were grouped under Fliegerführer Nord, commanded by Generalleutnant Bruch. The fighter units were grouped under the Stab/ZG 76 (at Kirkenes) which was acting as the *Jagdfliegerführer* for fighter units in Norway.[314] Due to the large distances involved, the fighter units were further split into two controlling HQs: Jagdgruppe (Fighter Group) Stavanger in southern Norway and Jagdgruppe Kirkenes in northern Norway. On 22nd June 1941, 2./JG 77, 3./JG 77 and 4./JG 77 reported to Jagdgruppe Stavanger, while 1./JG 77, 14./JG 77 and 1.(Z)/JG 77 (*Zerstörer*) reported to Jagdgruppe Kirkenes. The bomber units, I./KG 26 and elements of II./KG 30 reported directly to Fliegerführer Nord. On 21st June 1941 there were 152 combat aircraft in Luftflotte 5 defending Norway, not including those in Luftwaffenkommando Kirkenes. These comprised 52 fighters (including 12 long-range *Zerstörer*), 46 twin engine bombers, 40 seaplanes, 6 long-range reconnaissance aircraft and 8 short-range tactical reconnaissance aircraft. The seaplanes were mostly in *Seeluftstreitkrafte* units in four *Küstenfliegergruppen*. Although these aircraft were largely used for reconnaissance, they were armed with bombs, torpedoes, depth charges or/and mines, were capable of long range operations, and were effective anti-shipping and anti-submarine aircraft.[315]

From tables Luft 5 EF and Luft 5 Nor (together) we can see that on 21st June 1941 Luftflotte 5 contained a total of 313 aircraft. These comprised 68 fighters (including 16 *Zerstörer*), 42 dive bombers, 68 twin engine bombers, 49 seaplanes and 86 reconnaissance, transport and army-cooperation/liaison aircraft. Of the latter, 32 aircraft were short-range tactical reconnaissance and army-cooperation/liaison aircraft under the operational control of the ground units in the Norway Army.[316] These comprised aircraft in the *Heeresaufklärungsgruppen Kurierstaffeln* and *Verbindungsstaffel*n. Excluding the transport aircraft in KGr zbV units, *Kurierstaffeln* and *Verbindungsstaffel*n, Luftflotte 5 contained a total 262 'combat' aircraft of which 176 (67%) were serviceable. Unsurprisingly, on 21st June 1941 a higher proportion of the combat aircraft under Luftwaffenkommando Kirkenes were serviceable (82%) than in Fliegerführer Nord and the rest of Luftflotte 5 in Norway (57%).

***

Facing Luftwaffe 5 and the Finnish Air Force (*Ilmavoimat*, see below) on 22nd June 1941 was the VVS forces in the Leningrad Military District. These forces covered an area south of Soltsy and Lake Ilmen, as far west of Leningrad as Narva and Pskov, and as far north as the USSR's coastline on the Barents Sea. They included the VVS-KA Leningrad Military District, the VVS-SF (*Severnyy Flot* or Northern Fleet) and the VVS-KBF (*Krasnoznamyonnyy Baltiyskiy Flot* or Red Banner Baltic Fleet).

On 22nd June 1941 the VVS KA (army) and VSS VMF (naval) forces in the Leningrad Military District possessed a total of 2,159 combat aircraft, of which 823 were in the VVS-VMF.[317] This force included 1,312 fighters (including 208 modern MiG-3s, LaGG-3s and Yak-1s), 585 twin engine bombers, and 262 reconnaissance and army-cooperation aircraft. This made the VVS-Leningrad Military District one of the strongest VVS forces in the USSR, and in purely numerical terms, the strongest in the western USSR: it had 100 more combat aircraft than even the VVS-Kiev Special Military District.

***

---

[314] Stab/ZG 76 was acting in this role and was formally renamed Jagdfliegerführer Norwegen on 1st August 1941. It was attached to Luftwaffenkommando Kirkenes on 21st June 1941.

[315] The twin engine He 115C was an especially capable attack seaplane. It was durable, able of operate in heavy seas, was reasonably fast with a 2,800km range, was heavily armed with a 15mm cannon and 4 MGs, and could attack with 1,250kg of bombs, torpedoes or mines. Production continued until mid-1944.

[316] H. Boog, et al, Table, I.IV.5, p. 364, shows 10 aircraft (with 9 serviceable) under Army control. This only includes the *Heeresaufklärungsgruppen* (10) in Luftwaffenkommando Kirkenes, which agrees with the data in table Luft 5 EF.

[317] Refer Volume IIIB 3. 2) b. – 'The Soviet Air Forces in 1941 - The Order of Battle and Actual Strength of all Soviet Air Combat Units in a Deployed (D) State on 22nd June 1941 - VVS-Leningrad Military District'.

Table Luft 5 Nor	Deployment and Composition of Luftwaffe Air Units, 21st June 1941							
	Luftflotte 5 (Norway and Finland)							
	Fliegerführer Nord^^							
	Description	No x Type/Auth	Av	Sv	Description	No x Type/Auth	Av	Sv
JG (Jagdgeschwader) Fighter.	2.,3.,4./JG 77*	40xBf-109E/T/D	23	5				
	1.,14./JG 77^	24xBf-109E	17	9				
ZG (Zerstörergeschwader) Heavy fighter (twin engine).	1.(Z)/JG 77^	12xBf-110C/D	12	7				
KG (Kampfgeschwader) Bomber.	I./KG 26**	40xHe-111H	31	26				
	4./KG30*^	12xJu-88A	9	5				
H (Heeresaufklärungsgruppe) Short Range Tactical Reconnaissance.					2.(H)/31	12xHs-126/Fw-189	8	5
F (Fernaufklärungsgruppe) Long Range Strategic Reconnaissance.					1.(F)/120	12xJu-88A/D,Bf-110***	6	4
KGr zbV (Kampfgeschwader zu besonderen Verwendung) Transport.					KGr zbV 108*	53xJu-52,He-111, (Ha 139, BV-222)	26	17
Wekusta (Wettererkundungs staffel) Weather Observation.								
KuFlGr (Küstenfliegergruppe) Coastal Aviation.					Stab/ KuFlGr 706	4xHe115/Bv138	2	1
					2./KuFlGr 406^	12xBv-138B	7	5
					3./KuFlGr 406^,^*	12xDo-18D/G	8	5
					1./KGr 806 (1./KuFlGr 806)^^	12xJu-88A	6	5
					3./KuFlGr 906**	12xDo-18, He-115/BV-138	9	5
(Seenotstaffel) Air-Sea Rescue.					2x"Undes" Sta	28xHe-59, Do-18 (later, Do-24N)	14	4
(Kurierstaffel) Courier/Liaison.					Kurierkette Lappland*^	Fi-156/(+ pos He-60s during 1941)	9	4

* 2./JG 77 based at Lister, Norway.
3./JG 77 based at Herdla, Norway.
4./JG 77 based at Stavanger, Norway.
Together known as **Jagdgruppe Stavanger**.
1.,2.,3./JG 77 were redesignated I./JG 5 on 25th January 1942, in Stavanger.
4.,14./JG 77 were redesignated part of II./JG 5 on 25th January 1942, in Petsamo.

^ 1./JG 77 based at Kirkenes, Norway.
14./JG 77 based at Kirkenes, Norway.
1.(Z)/JG 77 (Zerstörer) based at Kirkenes, Norway
Together known as **Jagdgruppe Kirkenes**. This group directly supported Luftwaffenkommando Kirkenes during Operation Barbarossa (see text).

** 1./KG 26 based at Aalborg, Denmark.
2. and 3./KG 26 based at Stavanger, Norway.

*^ 4./KG 30 based in Stavanger, Norway.
4./KG 30 reinforced 'Luftwaffenkommando Kirkenes' in late June 1941.
The whole of II./KG 30 transferred to Luftflotte 1, VIII Fliegerkorps, in December 1941.

^^ Stab. KG 26 was redesignated Stab./Fliegerführer Nord, ca 12th March 1941.

* KGr zbV 108 based at Oslo, Norway (possibly had 3x Ha-139s).
Also appears to have had the BV-222 V1 (Viking) prototype, which flew its first mission to Norway on 10th July 1941.
The BV-222 V1, V2 and V3 operated in the Mediterranean later in 1941. (It is possible BV-222 V2 was temporarily attached to Fliegerführer Atlantik).

^ Based at Trondheim, Norway, under Stab./KuFlGr 706.

^^ 1./KGr 806 was based at Marvi, Finland, under Stab./KuFlGr 706.
This unit mined the Stalin Canal on 22nd June 1941, and attacked Kronstadt harbour in June 1941. It transferred to Riga in July 1941 to join the rest of KGr 806.

** Based at Tromso, Norway, under Stab./KuFlGr 706.
Still operated Do-18G/D from June to August 1941.
Received BV-138Cs in late 1941-42.

*^ Attached to Koluft Norwegen, Norway Army. Based at Petsamo.

^^ Started reequipping with BV-138s later in 1941.

*** Possibly still had some Do-17P and/or Do-215B on strength.

Table Luft 5 Nor (cont.)			
Luftflotte 5 (Norway and Finland)			
	No. of	No. of Aircraft	
Unit Type	Units	Avail	Svcble
Jagdgruppen	1 2/3	40	14
Erg.Guppen (JG,ZG)	0	0	0
Schlachtgruppen	0	0	0
Zerstörergruppen	1/3	12	7
Kampfgruppen	1 2/3	46	36
Stukagruppen	0	0	0
(Pz) Staffeln	0	0	0
(H) Staffeln	1	8	5
Luft (F) Staffeln	1	6	4
Heeres (F) Staffeln	0	0	0
KGr zbV	1	26	17
Wetterstaffeln	0	0	0
Seefliegerstaffeln	3	26	16
Seenotstaffeln	2	14	4
Kurierstaffeln/Verb. Staffeln	1/3	9	4
Sanitätsflugbereitschaften	0	0	0
		187	107
Number of Aircraft by type			
Single Engine Fighters		40	14
Twin Eng Fighters / Ftr Bmbrs		12	7
Twin Eng Night Fighters		0	0
Single Eng Fighter Bombers		0	0
Dive Bombers		0	0
Twin Engine Bombers		46	36
Four Engine Bombers		0	0
Long Range Recon*		6	4
SR Recon / Army Coop^		17	9
Seaplanes*^		40	20
Transport Aircraft**		26	17
		187	107

* Includes Wetterstaffeln aircraft.

^ Includes Courier, Liaison aircraft.

** Includes Sanitätsflugbereitschaften aircraft.

*^ Excludes 3 Ha 139s with KGr zbV 108, used as transports.

Total Combat Aircraft*		152	86

*Excludes aircraft in KGr zbV, Kurierstaffeln/Verbindungsstaffeln, and Sanitätsflugbereitschaften.

Aircraft under tactical control of the Army			
Long Range Recon		0	0
SR Recon / Army Coop^		17	9
		17	9

^ Includes Courier, Liaison Aircraft

***

Alongside the Luftwaffe in the north was the **Finnish Air Force (***Ilmavoimat***)**, which was an effective and well trained force. However the whole Finnish Air force only contained 374 combat and transport aircraft, and of these, 226 were deployed on the Soviet-Finnish front by 25th June 1941.[318] The forces deployed in the East included 160 single engine fighters, only 22 twin engine bombers (mostly Bristol Blenheims), 9 long-range reconnaissance aircraft, 27 short-range (army-tactical) reconnaissance aircraft, 4 seaplanes and 4 transport aircraft. How Finland managed to cobble together this force is, in itself, a remarkable story. But it is sufficient to say here that their aircraft came from all over Europe, North America and the USSR. For example, the fighter aircraft being operated by the Finnish Air Force included the: Curtis Hawk 75A, Gloster Gladiator II, Brewster Buffalo 239, Morane-Saulnier MS 406, Fiat G. 50, Hawker Hurricane I and Fokker D.XXI!

Therefore, in broad terms, this meant the **VVS-Leningrad Military District forces outnumbered their immediate Axis opponents by 5.9 to 1 (2,159 vs 365) in combat aircraft across the Soviet-Finnish front** in late June 1941.[319] This included an overall superiority of 6.4 to 1 (1,312 vs 205) in fighters, and 6.8 to 1 (585 vs 86) in bombers and ground attack aircraft.

Such a small Axis force with so few bombers could not provide much in the way of ground support to the Finnish or German armies in the Karelia, and it obviously had no chance of winning air superiority in direct combat or via airfield attacks. Nevertheless, through late June and early July 1941 Luftwaffenkommando Kirkenes carried out numerous successful offensive operations. These included raids on Soviet VVS-KA and VVS-SF airfields around Murmansk and the Kola Peninsula after 24th June, destruction of the Red Army fortifications in the battle for Salla (particularly by the Stukas of IV.(St)/LG 1), and numerous raids against the ports and railroad junctions of Murmansk and Archangel.[320] At the same time the Finnish Air Force's fighter units consistently inflicted heavy losses on Soviet bomber units (which were often unescorted) attempting operations over the Karelia, the Karelian Isthmus and Helsinki.

Fortunately for the Axis air forces in Finland, the bulk of the Leningrad Military District's (called Northern Front from 24th June) air assets remained defending Leningrad, or were rapidly moved further south and became embroiled with Luftwaffe units involved in the German advance against the Leningrad and Northwestern Fronts. After the German ground offensive in the north had failed to capture Murmansk and the front had become more of less static in the last quarter of 1941, Luftwaffenkommando Kirkenes spent most of its time interdicting the Kirov railroad between Murmansk and the Soviet mainland, and attacking shipping in the Barents Sea and in the port of Murmansk.

In the meantime Luftwaffe 5 was forced to maintain its 'aerial garrison' over Norway by British naval activity; particularly after July 1941. Most notably a Royal Navy task force mounted a major attack against the German port and airfields at Kirkenes on 30th July 1941. This surprise attack involved two aircraft carriers and supporting surface units, but was successfully beaten off with minimal damage.[321] Nevertheless, the appearance of powerful British naval forces off the north Norwegian coast continued to pose a serious threat to the small German naval forces in the area and the supply routes along the coast to northern Norway. In addition the British sent seven convoys (PQ 1 to PQ 7) to Murmansk from September to December 1941, all of which were escorted by heavy surface and/or carrier units.[322] Luftwaffe 5 in northern Norway simply lacked the air units and the maritime aircraft types needed to effectively attack these convoys in 1941. As a consequence these convoys were able to get through relatively unmolested, and this situation remained unchanged until 1942.

***

---

[318] Refer Volume IV - The Finnish FILARM model for a detailed breakdown of the *Ilmavoimat* figures on 22nd June 1941.
[319] This includes the 29 fighters supplied by Jagdgruppe Kirkenes in support of Luftwaffenkommando Kirkenes.
[320] Unlike the rest of the East Front, Luftwaffenkommando Kirkenes could not carry out effective airfield attacks on 22nd and 23rd of June due to bad weather. C. Bergstrom, A. Mikhailov, Black Cross Red Star, The Air War Over the Eastern Front: Volume 1, Pacifica Military History, Pacifica, California, 2000, p. 167.
[321] H. Boog, et al, p. 957. The two carriers involved were HMS Furious and HMS Victorious.
[322] The first convoy (PQ 1) left Britain on 26th September 1941. By the end of 1941 the Western Allies had sent 750 tanks, 800 fighters, 1,400 other vehicles and around 100,000 tons of stores via Murmansk. C. Messenger, WWII Chronological Atlas, Bloomsbury Publishing, London, 1989, p. 108.

f. Luftflotte 3

On 21st June 1941 Luftflotte 3, commanded by Generalfeldmarschall H. Sperrle, was deployed across France and the Low Countries. By this time the majority of the Luftwaffe's forces had been transferred east to support Operation Barbarossa, which left Luftflotte 3 as the only full 'air-fleet' still deployed in the West. Although now considered a secondary theatre for air operations, the Luftwaffe forces that remained in the West, including in the Mediterranean theatre (see next section), were still considerable. In addition the Luftwaffe units that remained in the West generally contained the latest aircraft types along with many of the most highly trained aircrews. This was particularly true for fighter units and fighter pilots, but also applied to some bomber types (see below on Fw 190 deployments in 1941/42). During 1941 this was almost entirely due to the quality and quantity of RAF aircraft and aircrew, particularly their fighters.[323]

The distribution of available and serviceable aircraft in Luftflotte 3, and the units they were assigned to on 21st June 1941, are shown in the tables Luft 3 (pages 234 - 238).[324] Luftflotte 3 was split into four commands: Jagdfliegerführer 2, Jagdfliegerführer 3, Fliegerführer Atlantik and IX. Fliegerkorps. These commands were focused on a particular set of objectives for most of 1941 and 1942 as follows:

1. To provide air-defence against RAF raids into France and northwest Europe. The responsibility for countering these attacks during 1941/42 fell to Jagdfliegerführer 2 (headquartered at Pas-de-Calais) and Jagdfliegerführer 3 (headquartered at Brest).

2. To attack Allied convoys and naval forces in the Atlantic (the Battle of the Atlantic), and assist the Kriegsmarine (German Navy) with reconnaissance in said tasks. The responsibility for these maritime operations fell to Fliegerführer Atlantik.

3. To continue a scaled down night bombing offensive against Britain, and conduct 'hit and run' attacks on selected targets. The KG units controlled by IX. Fliegerkorps had the responsibility for most of these attacks in June 1941, although many of the bomber units in Fliegerführer Atlantik participated in these missions as 1941 wore on.

4. To deter and counter any amphibious raids across the English Channel. Although the Commonwealth forces in Britain were not strong enough to launch a major land invasion of France, they were still capable of conducting major amphibious operations against selected targets in occupied Western Europe. The most famous of these being the Dieppe raid on 19th August 1942. The responsibility for countering such attacks fell to the Jagdfliegerführer and whatever bomber units Luftflotte 3 could muster.

From table Luft 3 we can see that on 21st June 1941 Luftflotte 3 contained 818 aircraft. These comprised: 312 fighters, 351 twin engine bombers, 25 four engine bombers, 62 seaplanes (including flying-boats), 44 long range reconnaissance aircraft, and 24 transport and army-cooperation/liaison aircraft.[325] Excluding the aircraft in KGr zbV units, *Kurierstaffeln*, *Verbindungsstaffeln* and *Sanitätsflugbereitschaften*, Luftflotte 3 contained a total of 794 'combat' aircraft of which 510 (64%) were serviceable. Also, we can see that around 80% of the fighters in Luftflotte 3 were serviceable compared to only 50% of the bombers.

***

When examining the Luftwaffe forces on the East Front in June 1941 (in previous sections), it is very revealing to examine the opposing VVS forces as well as some details on the air battles over Eastern Poland and the USSR June-July 1941.[326] For the purposes of completeness, and because it is also instructive, it is worth examining how the Luftwaffe forces that remained in France and the Low Countries fared during 1941-42.

In June 1941 the RAF had approximately 2,860 combat aircraft in the UK, of which approximately 1,480 were fighters (including night fighters), 1,290 were bombers, torpedo bombers and reconnaissance aircraft, and 90 were flying boats.[327] This included at least 700 aircraft in RAF Bomber Command and 550 in RAF Coastal Command. In addition, the RN Air Fleet Arm had around 330 combat aircraft which were mostly reserved for carrier

---

[323] Interestingly, this was the opposite of the situation facing the German Army in 1941/42: the army could send their best units to support Operation Barbarossa, while using 2nd and 3rd line (static) divisions to garrison France.

[324] Ibid, notes 277 and 287, for primary sources.

[325] There were additional transport, courier and liaison aircraft in Luftflotte 3, which were in other types of rear-area support units. H. Boog, et al, p. 372, states that Luftflotte 3 had 861 aircraft (582 serviceable). This is 43 aircraft more than shown in table Luft 3, and these were very likely the additional misc. aircraft types in unidentified and/or ad hoc support units.

[326] Refer to the Soviet FILARM air-model Volume IIIB 3. 2) – 'The Soviet Air Forces in 1941 - The Order of Battle and Actual Strength of all Soviet Air Combat Units in a Deployed (D) State on 22nd June 1941'.

[327] J. Ellis, World War II: A Statistical Survey, Facts on File Inc, New York, 1993, pp. 231-242, tables 17, 37, and 39. Note, care should be taken with WWII RAF strength and casualty figures because they often only include certain commands. Most often Coastal Command aircraft are excluded.

operations and were part of the Royal Navy.[328] The Wehrmacht had no equivalent to the RN Air Fleet Arm, and this relatively small (though highly trained) naval-air force is excluded here for the purposes of this discussion.[329]

By June 1941 the RAF had around 191 operational squadrons comprised of 99 fighter squadrons, 47 Bomber Command squadrons, 10 other medium and heavy bomber squadrons, 21 'light' bomber squadrons, 8 torpedo bomber squadrons and 6 flying boat squadrons.[330] Despite heavy losses on offensive operations over occupied Europe (see below), the RAF forces in the UK continued to expand. By December 1941 the RAF forces in the UK had increased to approximately 3,210 aircraft in 214 RAF squadrons; comprised of 114 fighter squadrons, 50 Bomber Command squadrons, 12 other medium and heavy bomber squadrons, 22 'light' bomber squadrons, 9 torpedo bomber squadrons and 7 flying boat squadrons.

Comparing the figures for the RAF in the UK with Luftflotte 3 shows that for air-operations over France and the Low Countries the RAF enjoyed an overall numerical superiority of around 3.6 to 1 on 21st June 1941 (2,860 vs 794). **This included a huge fighter superiority of over 4.7 to 1 (1,480 vs 312), and a bomber and reconnaissance aircraft superiority of around 3.1 to 1 (1,290 vs 420).** It should be noted here that in 1941-42 Luftflotte 3 was the only Luftwaffe force which could operate fighter units over the UK, France and Belgium, or bomber units over the same areas and the North Atlantic. All the other Luftwaffe units were not only out of operational range, but had no command authority to operate in these areas.

This numerical disparity only increased further in the RAF's favour from June to December 1941. This was because the RAF mobilised and deployed in the UK a further 23 RAF squadrons, while the *Jagdwaffe* in Luftflotte 3 received no new fighter unit reinforcements. At the same time, table Luft 3 shows that no less than 85% of the bomber units in IX. Fliegerkorps transferred to the East Front or Norway during this period. The only front line fighter units in Luftflotte 3 remained JG 2, JG 26 and a *Staffel* of JG 1. 1./JG 52 was transferred to the East Front in September 1941.

On 26th July 1941 there were only 238 Luftwaffe fighters on the Western Front with the large majority being Bf 109Es and Fs.[331] To put it another way; during the second half of 1941, Luftflotte 3's fighters, on average, faced between 2 and 3 times the numerical odds that the RAF fighters had faced during the Battle of Britain in the previous year.

***

---

[328] J. Ellis, World War II: A Statistical Survey, Facts on File Inc, New York, 1993, p 242, table 40.
[329] It is arguable that they should be included because the aircraft of Fliegerführer Atlantik came up against RN aircraft carriers when attacking important convoys, and later Sea Hurricanes which were launched from merchant ships. On the whole, however, the RN Air Fleet Arm was much a much more prominent force in the Mediterranean.
[330] RAF fighter and bomber squadrons were authorised 12 to 24 aircraft, depending on type and deployment. Coastal Command squadrons had between 6 and 10 aircraft each. Squadrons were usually divided into 3 Flights and reported to a Wing or Sector. These then reported to a Group, which in turn reported to a Command. The latter included Bomber Command, Fighter Command, Coastal Command, Middle East Command and the SEAC.
[331] N. Franks, Aircraft versus Aircraft, Grub Street Books, London, 1998, p. 96.

Table Luft 3	Deployment and Composition of Luftwaffe Air Units, 21st June 1941							
	Luftflotte 3							
	IX. Fliegerkorps				**Fliegerführer Atlantik^***			
	Description	No x Type/Auth	Av	Sv	Description	No x Type/Auth	Av	Sv
JG (Jagdgeschwader) Fighter.								
KG (Kampfgeschwader) Bomber.	Stab./KG 4^	4xHe-111H	3	2	Stab./Fl.Fu.Atl	4xHe-111H	2	1
	I./KG 4^	40xHe-111H	29	19	Stab./KG 40	4xFw-200C	4	0
	III./KG 4^	40xHe-111H	25	15	I./KG 40	40xFw-200C-0 and C-1	21	4
	Stab./KG 28*^	4xHe-111H	3	1	II./KG 40^^	28xDo-217E-1,12xHe-111H	12, 10	5, 5
	I./KG 28*^	40xHe-111H	31	17	III./KG 40	40xHe-111H	22	14
	III./KG 26^^	40xHe-111H	30	12				
	Stab./KG 30^*	4xJu-88A	2	1				
	I./KG 30^*	40xJu-88A	34	19				
	III./KG 30^*	40xJu-88A	45	18				
	Erp St./KG 30**^	12xJu-88A	7	2				
	KGr 100*	40xHe-111H-3	19	14				
	II./KG 2	40xDo-217E-2/3	31	23				
F (Fernaufklärungsgruppe) Long Range Strategic Reconnaissance.					3.(F)/122	12xJu-88A/D,Bf-110C/E	9	8
KGr zbV (Kampfgeschwader zu besonderen Verwendung) Transport.	IX. Korps Tr.Sta	16xJu-52	7	4				

Category	Unit	Aircraft		
Wekusta (Wettererkundungsstaffel) Weather Observation.				
KuFlGr (Küstenfliegergruppe) Coastal Aviation.	KGr 106 (KuFlGr 106)*	24xJu-88A	17	4
	KuFlGr 406^	28xHe115 (Stab w Do-18 & 2xDo-26)	18	9
	KGr 606 (KuFlGr 606)*^	40xJu-88A (few Do-17Z)	29	13
	5./BoFlGr 196**	24xAr-196A	26	19
(Seenotstaffel) Air-Sea Rescue.	1x'Undes' Staffel	14xDo-18,Do-24,He-59	10	6
	1. Seenotstaffel	14xBre.521**, (later, Do-24N).	8	5
(Kurierstaffel) Courier/Liaison. (Sanitätsflugbereitschaft)	Kurierstaffel W*** Fi-156		6	4

Notes (Coastal Aviation etc.):

* Redesignated K.Gr 106 ca 1st February 1941, when conv from He-115s to Ju-88. Includes only Stab./K.Gr 106 and 3./K.Gr 106 (Ju-88s) at Amsterdam-Schiphol.

^ Includes Stab./KuFlGr 406 (Stab with a few Do-18 and two Do-26), 2./KuFlGr 506 (still with He-115s), and 1./KuFlGr 906 (He-115s). 5./BoFlGr 196 was also controlled by Stab./KuFlGr 406. 2./KuFlGr 506 was redesignated 2./KuFlGr 906 on 6th October 1941.

*^ Includes Stab./KuFlGr 606, 1./KuFlGr 606, 2./KuFlGr 606 and 3./KuFlGr 606. Had almost completely converted from Do-17Z to Ju-88s (Commenced March 1941). Transferred to II. Fliegerkorps (Luftflotte 2) in Sicily ca 1st Dec. 1941.

** (Bordfliegerstaffeln) Ship Based Aviation Squadron. 5./BoFlGr 196 was attached to KuFlGr 406 (above). Redesignated 1./SAGr 128 in 1942-43.

^^ II./KG 40 equipping and training to be able to use air-drop torpedoes.

^* Some sources show Fliegerführer Atlantik also controlled KuFlGr 506, KuFlGr 906 and 1./BoFlGr 196 in 1941. However, these units had been withdrawn from France and the Low Countries by June 1941, and were based in Germany and Denmark (some were refitting with new aircraft types). Refer to Luftwaffenbefehlshaber Mitte for more details on the Staffel and equipment in these units, and their bases.

*** Bre.521 - captured French Breguet 521 Bizerte flying boats.

Notes (Courier/Liaison etc.):

* KGr 100 'Pathfinders', transferred to Luftflotte 2 II Fliegerkorps, under Stab/KG 28, ca 19th July 1941. Renamed I./KG 100 on 15th December 1941.

^ Stab, I., III./KG 4 all transferred to Luftflotte 2, (East Prussia) from 19th July 1941. III./KG 4 was withdrawn on 6th Dec. 1941 for rest and refit

*^ Stab./KG 28 and I./KG 28 transferred to Luftflotte 2 II Fliegerkorps, 20th July to 2nd Aug. 1941. Stab./KG 28 and I./KG 28 were redesignated Stab./KG 26 and III./KG 26 (respectively) on 15th Dec. 1941.

^^ III./KG 26 transferred to Brest-Litovsk 20th July 41. It moved to Bobruisk in August-September 41. III./KG 26 was redesignated II./KG 100 on 15th Dec. 1941, but it was reformed on the same date from I./KG 28. The new 8./KG 26 was formed from 1./Ku.Fl.Gr 906.

^* Stab./KG 30 moved to Norway ca 24th January 1942. I./KG 30 Moved to Northern Norway in early Aug. 1941. III./KG 30 moved to Holland in Aug. 1941 and to Norway ca 24th Jan. 1942.

**^ Officially formed July 1941. Transferred Norway ca 24th Jan. 1942 with Stab./KG 30.

*** Kurierstaffel Westfrankreich (OKH, based at Paris).

Table Luft 3 (cont.)　Deployment and Composition of Luftwaffe Air Units, 21st June 1941

	Jagdfliegerführer 2				Jagdfliegerführer 3					Description	No x Type/Auth	Av	Sv
	Description	No x Type/Auth	Av	Sv	Description	No x Type/Auth	Av	Sv					
JG (Jagdgeschwader) Fighter.	Stab./Jafu 2	4xBf-109E	1	1	Stab./Jafu 3	4xBf-109E	2	1					
	Stab./JG 26	4xBf-109E/F	4	3	Stab./JG 2	4xBf-109F	4	4					
	I./JG 26	40xBf-109E	31	27	I./JG 2	40xBf-109E	36	30					
	II./JG 26**	40xBf-109E, Fw-190A	34	22	II./JG 2	40xBf-109F	40	36					
	8,9,/JG 26*	28xBf-109F	26	23	III./JG 2	40xBf-109F	37	32					
	Erg./JG 26	16xBf-109E	10	6	Erg./JG 2	16xBf-109E	18	14					
	I./JG 52^	40xBf-109E/F	38	28	Erg./JG 53*	16xBf-109E/F	20	12					
	1./JG 1	12xBf-109F	11	10									
KG (Kampfgeschwader) Bomber.													
F (Fernaufklärungsgruppe) Long Range Strategic Reconnaissance.										Stab./123	4xJu-88A/D, Bf-110D/E	2	2
										3.(F)/123	12xJu-88A/D, Bf-110D/E	6,6	3,3
										1.(F)/123	12xJu-88A,Ju-86P,Bf-110D/E	9	8
KGr-zbV (Kampfgeschwader zu besonderen Verwendung) Transport.													

Unit Type	Unit	Aircraft		
Wekusta (Wettererkundungs staffel) Weather Observation.	Wekusta 51	8xDo-17Z, He-111H/J, Ju-88D	7	5
	Wekusta 2. Ob.d.L	8x Ju-88D, He111H	5	4
KuFlGr (Küstenfliegergruppe) Coastal Aviation.				
(Seenotstaffel) Air-Sea Rescue.				
(Kurierstaffel) Courier/Liaison.	Verbindungsstaffel 51* Fi-156, Kl-35 and W-34		5	4
(Sanitätsflugbereitschaft)	San. Flug. 11^	6xJu-52	6	4

* Disbanded in November 1941.

^ Sanitätsflugbereitschaft 11. Transferred to the East Front under V. Fliegerkorps in December 1941.

* Erg./JG 53 was in reserve in the West, based at La Rochelle-La Leu. Combat capable and provided replacements to JG53.

* Staffels 8. and 9./JG 26 present, only. Staffel 7./JG 26 was in Libya.

^ 1./JG 52 was stationed in Holland. 1./JG 52 transferred to Luftflotte 2, VIII Fliegerkorps, under Stab/JG 27, from 27th September 1941.

** II./JG 26 had converted to Fw-190A-1s by early September 1941. III./JG 26 and most of I./JG 26 had converted to Fw-190A-1 and A-2 by late December 1941. Some test Fw-190s were delivered to II./JG 26 in February 1941 for evaluation.

© Nigel Askey, 2018

Table Luft 3 (cont).			
Luftflotte 3, Totals			
	No. of	No. of Aircraft	
Unit Type	Units	Avail	Svcble
Jagdgruppen	7	264	217
Erg.Guppen (JG,ZG)	3	48	32
Schlachtgruppen	0	0	0
Zerstörergruppen	0	0	0
Kampfgruppen**	12 2/3	376	189
Stukagruppen	0	0	0
(Pz) Staffeln	0	0	0
(H) Staffeln	0	0	0
Luft (F) Staffeln	3	32	24
Heeres (F) Staffeln	0	0	0
KGr zbV	1/3	7	4
Wetterstaffeln	2	12	9
Seefliegerstaffeln	3	44	28
Seenotstaffeln	2	18	11
Kurierstaffeln/Verb. Staffeln	2	11	8
Sanitätsflugbereitschaften	1	6	4
		818	526
Number of Aircraft by type			
Single Engine Fighters		312	249
Twin Eng Fighters / Ftr Bmbrs		0	0
Twin Eng Night Fighters		0	0
Single Eng Fighter Bombers		0	0
Dive Bombers		0	0
Twin Engine Bombers		351	185
Four Engine Bombers		25	4
Long Range Recon*		44	33
SR Recon / Army Coop^		11	8
Seaplanes		62	39
Transport Aircraft*^		13	8
		818	526

* Includes Wetterstaffeln aircraft
^ Includes Courier, Liaison aircraft
** Includes KGr 106 and KGr 606.
  (equipped with twin engine bombers; Ju 88s and a few Do-17Zs)
*^ Includes Sanitätsflugbereitschaften aircraft.

Total Combat Aircraft*	794	510

*Excludes aircraft in KGr zbV, Kurierstaffeln/Verbindungsstaffeln,
  and Sanitätsflugbereitschaften.

© Nigel Askey, 2018

***

From late 1940 Bomber Command (with over 700 bombers in June 1941) was already largely committed to raiding Germany by night. This meant their heaviest bombers skirted around the short range fighters in Luftflotte 3 via the North Sea, and became embroiled with the night-fighters of Luftwaffenbefehlshaber Mitte defending Germany. Even in this regard Bomber Command (alone) had a significant numerical advantage because Luftwaffenbefehlshaber Mitte had only 189 night-fighters available on 21st June 1941 (refer following sections).

Starting in December 1940, the RAF commenced progressively larger daylight raids over France with the objective of tying down and destroying as many Luftwaffe resources in occupied Western Europe as possible. After Operation Barbarossa was launched these objectives became even more paramount: the RAF raids were one of the few ways the Commonwealth forces could directly and immediately help the USSR. Bomber Command's heaviest bombers were already committed to night operations, so only the RAF's 'light' bomber force was available to support the daylight raids. This was just as well because all the slower RAF 'heavy' bomber types had already shown themselves to be very vulnerable to German fighters in daylight. However, virtually the whole of Fighter Command was available so the RAF devised tactics specifically aimed at attacking the Luftwaffe over France. These raids were often large, involving up to 500 aircraft (sometimes as many as 300 fighters and 200 medium bombers) and were colourfully designated as follows.[332]

- **Circus operations**. A small force of fast bombers, usually aircraft like the twin engine Blenheim IV and Beaufort I/II, would entice the German fighters into the air. Then up to ten fighter squadrons would be used to cover the bombers and ambush any German fighters endeavouring to intercept the bombers. The RAF fighter cover was designed to be very intense and had four elements. 'Close escort' fighters stayed close to the bomber formations. 'Escort cover' fighters covered the close escort fighters. 'High cover' fighters flew well above the whole operation and prevented German fighters from positioning themselves above the bombers and their escorts. 'Top cover' fighters flew high above the planned route and had a roving commission to seek out enemy fighters in the proximity to the bombers' route.

- **Ramrod operations**. A similar operation to the Circus, but in which the prime objective was also the destruction by bombers of a specific target. The target in this case could be an airfield, a factory, a capital ship in harbour, U-boat facilities or anything in-between. The only prerequisite was that the target was well within range of the fighters. If anything, the bombers in Ramrod operations had even more fighter escorts than during Circus operations. The Germans of course had no idea that there was any difference between a Ramrod and Circus operation.

- **Rodeo operations**. An attack by fighters over enemy territory without bombers, which may have also included strafing attacks on airfields or other targets. All such operations (without bombers) were collectively termed **Rhubarb operations**.

- **Sweep operations**. A general term for a fighter group mounting an offensive mission over enemy territory. It differed specifically from a Rodeo operation in that it was flown in support of a Circus or Ramrod operation. In this case the fighters would cover the area which the bombers would be shortly attacking, and was designed to 'sweep' the sky of any hostile aircraft.

***

So all this begs the question; what happened? During 1941 the RAF admitted to the loss of 849 fighters in addition to a number of medium bombers (mainly from 2 Group) while involved in the above operations.[333] Luftflotte 3's fighter pilots claimed about 950 kills during this period (including enemy bombers), so their claims were fairly accurate.[334] However, RAF Fighter Command claimed 909 kills over France during this period but the Luftwaffe actually lost only 183 aircraft from all causes![335] The RAF thus claimed almost five times as many aircraft destroyed as was actually achieved, which ranks as one of the worst 'over claims' of its type during WWII.

---

[332] The Oxford Companion to WWII, Oxford University Press, New York, 2001, pp. 189 and 739.

[333] N. Franks, Aircraft versus Aircraft, Grub Street, London 1998, p. 96. Also, Jane's Fighting Aircraft of WWII, The Random House Group Ltd: Studio, London, 2001, pp. 31 and 32 (RAF Statistics on Cease Fire in Europe). Also, D. Wadmann, M. Pegg, Jagdwaffe: Holding the West 1941-1943, Ian Allan Publishing (Classic), Surrey, 2003, pp. 2-10.

[334] For any air-force fighting over enemy territory, confirming kills is much more difficult than over friendly territory. In this case, Luftflotte 3 could confirm most kills (i.e. those that didn't crash into the sea on the way home) by the viewing any wreckage on the ground. In fact, it was Luftwaffe policy to confirm kills with at least one approved wreckage report (if possible) or, alternatively, with at least two separate eye witness reports (from either ground or air-crew). In addition Luftwaffe fighter pilots were not allowed to 'share' the credit for a kill, as was the practice in the RAF and USAAF during WWII, and were not allowed to tally 'probables' as a kill. G. Williamson, Aces of the Reich, Arms and Armour Press, London, 1989, pp. 92-93.

[335] N. Franks, Aircraft versus Aircraft, Grub Street Books, London, 1998, p. 96. The Luftwaffe losses include losses due to accidents, which were significant.

This rather embarrassing propensity to over claim continued. In 1942 the RAF lost around 900 fighters in Circus type operations while Luftflotte 3's fighters claimed 972 aircraft (including bombers) destroyed. At the same time the RAF claimed some 500 kills over France while actual Luftwaffe losses from all causes (including accidents) were just 272. Therefore, **through 1941 and 1942 the Luftwaffe day fighter pilots on the Western Front averaged a kill to loss ratio against allied fighters of almost 4 to 1.**

Another way to look at these numbers is this. When the RAF attempted daylight operations with medium bombers over the English Channel during 1941-42 as the Luftwaffe had done in 1940, it fared over twice as badly as the Luftwaffe did during the Battle of Britain.[336] In fact it is even worse than this: the RAF in 1941-42 enjoyed a fighter numerical superiority over three times that enjoyed by the Luftwaffe in the summer of 1940, and most RAF fighters had superior range (compared to Bf 109s) so they could operate over France and the Low Countries for longer periods than the Bf 109Es could operate over the UK in 1940. On top of their fighter losses, the Commonwealth forces lost an additional 2,944 bombers and 691 coastal aircraft during 1941 and 1942, which includes Bomber Command's night losses over Germany.[337]

In summary we can see that although the RAF continuously took the war to the Germans during 1941-42, the daylight campaign over France and the Low Countries was, on balance, a major RAF defeat. This campaign cost around 1,950 RAF aircraft (including around 200 bombers), whilst the Luftwaffe lost around 460 fighters from all causes (including accidents). Furthermore, it failed to force the Luftwaffe to transfer significant combat units away from the East Front which was one of its primary objectives. However as the RAF claimed over 1,400 aerial victories, they thought they were, at the very least, inflicting heavy casualties on their opponents.

***

In June 1941 the Luftwaffe still envisaged continuing its own limited night bombing campaign against Britain, which mainly fell to the 260 odd bombers left in IX. Fliegerkorps. But with the advent of more efficient RAF night fighters such as the Beaufighter IIF, these operations became increasingly dangerous whilst having little strategic benefit. The OKL soon realised that these KG units would be better employed elsewhere, and in July 1941 Stab./KG 28, I./KG 28, III./KG 26 and KGr 100 were all transferred to the East Front. In August 1941 these were followed by Stab./KG 4, I./KG 4 and III./KG 4, which also transferred to the East Front. In addition Stab./KG 30, I./KG 30 and III./KG 30 were transferred piecemeal to Norway. This meant that by September 1941 around 85% of the bombers that were in IX. Fliegerkorps on 21st June 1941 had been transferred (or was being transferred) to the East Front or Norway. This left only one full *Kampfgeschwader Gruppe* in IX. Fliegerkorps (II./KG 2), and even this was soon switched to anti-shipping operations. This meant that for most of the second half of 1941 the RAF's night fighters were left with little to do. As a result some RAF night fighter units soon started night 'intruder' raids over occupied Europe.

***

In the meantime the Battle of the Atlantic raged on, and although the U-Boats were the Wehrmacht's primary offensive weapon in this vital battle, the aircraft in Fliegerführer Atlantik made a very significant contribution. Fliegerführer Atlantik was formed on 31st March 1941 under the command of anti-shipping specialist Generalmajor Martin Harlinghausen. On 21st June 1941 the Fliegerführer Atlantik contained 188 aircraft made up of 117 bombers, 62 seaplanes and flying-boats, and 9 long-range reconnaissance/bomber aircraft. Its anti-shipping operations were sometimes supplemented by units from IX. Fliegerkorps prior to July 1941, although the KG and KGr units in Fliegerführer Atlantik also sometimes participated in night bombing attacks on land targets in the UK. The latter occurred more often as the KG units in IX. Fliegerkorps were transferred east (see above).

Despite its limited resources, Fliegerführer Atlantik was able to carry out 2,750 anti-shipping sorties, 1,947 mine-laying sorties and an unknown number of reconnaissance sorties from June to December 1941, inclusive.[338] This resulted in the sinking of at least 329,000 tons of shipping, as well as untold damage from assisting

---

[336] The RAF achieved a 1.8 to 1 kill-loss ratio from 10th July to 31st October 1940, including bombers (1,065 RAF vs. 1,922 Luftwaffe losses). J. Ellis, WWII: A Statistical Survey, Facts On File Inc, New York 1993, p. 259, table 61. For some years after WWII various histories of the Battle of Britain claimed the RAF had achieved a 3-4 to 1 kill-loss ratio in this battle. These claims were, again, based almost entirely on inadequately verified RAF pilot claims, and were not verified by either ground wreckage or recorded Luftwaffe losses. These RAF claims, and the resultant figures, are now discredited in almost all up to date works on the subject.

[337] N. Franks, Aircraft versus Aircraft, Grub Street, London 1998, p. 98. Also, Jane's Fighting Aircraft of WWII, The Random House Group Ltd: Studio, London, 2001, pp. 31 and 32 (RAF Statistics on Cease Fire in Europe).

[338] J. R. Smith, E. J. Creek, Kampfflieger: Bombers of the Luftwaffe July 1940-December 1941, Classic-Ian Allan Publishing, Hersham UK, 2004, pp. 138 and 145.

the U-Boat wolf packs to find and attack convoys.[339] Most of the anti-shipping strikes were carried out by KG 40, KuFlGr 106 (KGr 106), KuFlGr 606 (KGr 606) and KuFLGr 406. However the most famous unit was probably I./KG 40 which operated the long range Focke-Wulf 200 Condor: capable of operating far out to see beyond the range of shore based fighters. By June 1941 I./KG 40 had already sunk 450-500,000 tons of Allied shipping in the North Sea and Atlantic using Fw 200s, which had earned this aircraft the "scourge of the Atlantic" title bestowed by Winston Churchill.[340] However, by June 1941 the Condor threat was already being countered by more heavily armed and longer range RAF Coastal Command aircraft, increasing numbers of escort carriers, and CAM (Catapult Armed Merchantmen) ships with an expendable Hurricane fighter on board. This meant the relatively vulnerable Fw 200s were forced to attack from progressively higher altitudes, which dramatically reduced their effectiveness during the second half of 1941. They did however remain very effective at long range reconnaissance, and convoys spotted by a Condor learnt to expect U-Boat attacks shortly thereafter.

***

As we have seen, the RAF daylight campaign against the Luftwaffe in France and the Low Countries during 1941 and 1942 was not successful. However there is one respect in which the RAF (and later the USAAF) was successful in 1941, and, for the most part, for the rest of WWII. This is that they forced the Luftwaffe to commit their most technologically advanced aircraft and air-launched weapons on the Western Fronts. The aircraft types deployed in Luftflotte 3 on 21st June 1941 are a good example of this. In June 1941 the best available German fighter was the recently introduced Focke-Wulf (Fw) 190A-2, and the only unit in the Luftwaffe equipped with this aircraft was II./JG 26. The Fw 190 entered operational service in May 1941, although trial aircraft were first issued to JG 26 in February 1941. By mid-1941 the Fw 190A-2/3 was easily the best and most powerful fighter in the world, even outclassing the Supermarine Spitfire V (an aircraft evenly matched with the Bf 109F).[341] The Fw 190A would retain this position until July 1942 and the introduction of the Spitfire IX; against which it was evenly matched.[342]

The remarkable thing here is that while the Fw 190A rapidly became the fighter of choice among the *Jagdgeschwader* in occupied Europe, **no Fw 190s went to the Eastern Front until JG 51 received some in November 1942!** In other words the Germans felt that the threat posed by the superior RAF fighters in 1941 and almost all of 1942 was sufficient for them maintain hundreds of Fw 190s in the West; even though the Wehrmacht's main effort and most critical campaigns were elsewhere. Even the 'strategically blind' German High Command would have not done this if the 'inferior' Bf 109F hadn't proved more than capable of maintaining air superiority in the East. Note, however, that the reader should **not** attribute the approximately 4 to 1 kill-loss ratio achieved against the RAF during 1941-42 as due to the superiority of the Fw 190. Although this was a factor, the large majority of fighters in France during 1941 were Messerschmitt Bf 109Es and Fs, and even in 1942 the majority were Bf 109Fs and Gs.[343]

---

[339] J. Costello, T. Hughes, The Battle of the Atlantic, Fontana/Collins, Glasgow, 1980, p. 330, table 4. From June to December 1941 the Allies lost 126,000 tons of shipping to sea-mines. The above figure assumes that half of these losses were due to mines laid by the aircraft of Fliegerführer Atlantik, although it was very probably more because most U-Boats were generally too valuable to risk in this role. In total the Allies lost 1,017,000 tons of shipping due to direct attack from aircraft and 231,000 tons of shipping from mines in 1941.

[340] J. R. Smith, E. J. Creek, Kampfflieger: Bombers of the Luftwaffe July 1940-December 1941, Classic-Ian Allan Publishing, Hersham UK, 2004, p. 142. Staffel 1./KG 40 alone was credited with sinking 145,200 tons of shipping by 22nd February 1941.

[341] N. Franks, Aircraft versus Aircraft, Grub Street, London 1998, p. 121. Also S. Wilson, Aircraft of WWII, Aerospace Publications Ltd, Australia 1998, p. 155. In June 1941 the five best fighters in the world, in order of decreasing overall combat power, were: the Focke-Wulf 190A-1/3, Supermarine Spitfire V, Messerschmitt Bf 109F, Mitsubishi A6M2 'Zero' and Yakovlev Yak-1. The order listed above is 'arguable' in that different aircraft had different outstanding attributes, which made them compatible (e.g. victory in air to air combat between the Spitfire V and Bf 109F was usually determined by circumstance and pilot skill, rather than any obvious technical advantage). However, in terms of overall combat power, the Fw 190A-1/3 was simply unmatched as a fighter in 1941 and for most of 1942. For example, it could outrun, outdive, outclimb and outgun the Spitfire V. Noticeably missing from this list are any US fighters. The best US fighter available in June 1941 was the Curtiss P-40C, which was introduced in April 1941 (it was a superior fighter to the Bell P-39C/D Airacobra which saw limited US service). However the P-40C struggled to match the older Bf 109E, or the flawed MiG-3 and LaGG-3, as an all-round fighter.

[342] N. Franks, Aircraft versus Aircraft, Grub Street, London 1998, p. 124. The RAF conducted flight tests comparing a captured Fw 190A-3, Spitfire V and Spitfire IX in 1942. The Spitfire V was essentially outclassed. The Spitfire IX (from July 1942) was slower at 2-5,000ft and 18-21,000ft. The Fw 190A was faster than the Spitfire IX in the dive, had a superior rate of role, and was generally more maneuverable. The Spitfire IX still had a faster turn rate, while the climb rates were effectively equal. If caught by a Spitfire IX attack in a turn, the Fw 190A's superior role rate enabled it to flick over into a diving turn in the opposite direction, which was "almost impossible for any Spitfire to follow".

[343] The Messerschmitt Bf 109G-1 and G-2 first appeared in operational units in the summer of 1942. The G-6 was the first mass produced G version and it appeared in late 1942. As with the Fw 190, the *Jagdgeschwader* in occupied Europe were equipped with these aircraft before units on the East Front.

Another example (of the Germans keeping their most advanced aerospace technology in the West) in June 1941 is the presence of the Dornier (Do) 217E bomber in Luftflotte 3. The Do 217E was a complete reengineering of the old Do 17Z design, to the point that it was a completely new aircraft. It entered operational service in late 1940 and soon developed into a family of fast and versatile bombers, strike aircraft and even night fighters. Its overall performance was similar to the outstanding Ju 88 series, and yet in June 1941 the only Luftwaffe units equipped with Do 217Es were II./KG 2 and II./KG 40; both of which remained in the West. In the meantime Luftflotte 2 on the East Front had to make do with three *Kampfgeschwader* equipped with the much inferior Do 17Z. This is remarkable when one considers that Luftflotte 2 was strategically supporting Army Group Centre in the largest land invasion ever, and upon which the outcome of WWII would be decided.

Again, the conclusion is that the OKL must have been confident the Do 17Z could survive reasonably well against the Soviet fighters in 1941-42, but stood little chance against the superior RAF types. Nevertheless, one cannot help but feel that these excellent bombers and strike aircraft would have better served the German cause (strategically) by being focused on their point of main effort (i.e. the East Front). In this sense the RAF succeeded: **although it failed (in 1941-42) to force the Luftwaffe to focus in the West in numerical terms, it did so in terms of aircraft quality** right from the start of Operation Barbarossa. Considering the damage to the Soviet VVS actually inflicted by the 'inferior' Bf 109F, the Fw 190A-2/3 would have been absolutely devastating against Soviet VVS fighter and bomber types during 1941 and most of 1942.

***

g. X. Fliegerkorps

Due to Mussolini's problems in Greece and North Africa, Hitler was obliged to come to the aid of his ally from December 1940 to January 1941. Assistance took the form of a small land force called the Deutsches Afrikakorps (DAK) and the X. Fliegerkorps. The latter was a specialised anti-shipping unit commanded by Generalleutnant Hans Geisler. It was transferred from Norway and the bulk of its strength (129 Ju 88s and He 111s) had redeployed to Sicily by 10th January 1941.[344] In April 1941 X. Fliegerkorps was attached to Luftflotte 4 and participated in the Balkans campaign, as well as the invasion of Crete in May 1941. After Luftflotte 4 was transferred east in preparation for Operations Barbarossa, X. Fliegerkorps was left in control of all Luftwaffe air units left in the Mediterranean theatre, with General der Flieger Hans Geisler as its commander (he was promoted in June 1941).

The distribution of available and serviceable aircraft in X. Fliegerkorps, and the units they were assigned to on 21st June 1941, are shown in the table X FCps.[345] X. Fliegerkorps was essentially split into two commands: X. Fliegerkorps covering the central Mediterranean and western Balkans including Sicily, southern Italy and Crete, and Fliegerführer Afrika covering North Africa. In June 1941 these commands were focused on a particular set of objectives as follows:

1. To attack Allied convoys and naval forces in the central Mediterranean, with a particular emphasis on attacking convoys supplying Malta and the naval base at Malta. The responsibility for these maritime operations fell to X. Fliegerkorps.

2. To continue supporting the 12th Army in the Balkans and Crete as required. This responsibility also fell to X. Fliegerkorps and by this time mostly involved air-transport and reconnaissance operations.

3. To provide air-support for the Axis ground forces in Tunisia and Libya, and interdict the Allied overland supply routes in Libya and Egypt. The responsibility for these operations fell to Fliegerführer Afrika, which was first formed in February 1941 under the command of Generalleutnant S Frohlich. Although technically subordinate to X. Fliegerkorps, Fliegerführer Afrika was under the day to day operational and tactical control of the German Army's DAK.

***

From table X FCps we can see that on 21st June 1941 X. Fliegerkorps contained 566 aircraft. These were comprised of: 87 fighters, fighter-bombers and night-fighters (including 36 Bf 110 *Zerstörer*), 137 twin engine bombers, 85 dive bombers, 32 seaplanes and flying boats, 13 long-range reconnaissance aircraft, 37 short-range (tactical) reconnaissance and army cooperation/liaison aircraft, and 175 transport aircraft. Excluding the transport aircraft in KGr zbV units, *Kurierstaffeln*, *Verbindungsstaffeln*, *Sanitätsflugbereitschaften* and *Wüstennotstaffel* 1, X. Fliegerkorps contained a total of 367 combat aircraft of which 216 (59%) were serviceable. The disproportionately high number of transport aircraft in X. Fliegerkorps on 21st June 1941 was a 'hangover' from the recently completed Operation Mercury: the airborne invasion of Crete. Most of these KG and KGr zbZ (air-transport) units were recovering and preparing to be transferred to the East Front, which they did in the following weeks.

Fliegerführer Afrika itself, the only Luftwaffe force in position to support Rommel's DAK, had only 182 combat aircraft on 21st June 1941. These included 83 fighters, fighter-bombers and night-fighters (including 32 Bf 110 *Zerstörer*), 27 bombers, 52 dive bombers and 20 reconnaissance aircraft. The most dangerous aircraft for Allied ships operating off the North African coast, and for Allied ground forces in Libya, were the Ju 87s from I./StG 1 and II./StG 2. The diversion of these units away from the East Front represented a significant dilution of the Luftwaffe forces available to support Operation Barbarossa. As we have seen in previous sections, the strategically far more important Luftflotte 1 and Luftflotte 4 had no StG units at all.

In addition to X. Fliegerkorps, the Axis air-forces in the Mediterranean included those of the Regia Aeronautica (Italian Air Force). In June 1941 there were around 550 Italian combat aircraft in Sicily, Sardinia and North Africa, of which around 380 (69%) were serviceable.[346] These were comprised of approximately 360 fighters, 60 ground attack aircraft and 130 bombers. Of this force covering the Mediterranean, 90 fighters, 10 ground attack aircraft and 28 bombers were based in Libya in June 1941, in a position to support the Axis ground forces in North Africa.[347]

***

[344] J. R. Smith, E. J. Creek, Kampfflieger: Bombers of the Luftwaffe July 1940-December 1941, Classic-Ian Allan Publishing, Hersham UK, 2004, p. 150.

[345] Ibid, notes 277 and 287, for primary sources.

[346] J. Ellis, WWII: A Statistical Survey, Facts On File Inc, New York 1993, pp. 232 and 239, tables 19, 30 and 31.

[347] Ibid, table 31. The Regia Aeronautica also dispatched 104 aircraft to the East Front from July to November 1941.

Table X FCps — Deployment and Composition of Luftwaffe Air Units, 21st June 1941

Category	X. Fliegerkorps Description	No x Type/Auth	Av	Sv	Fliegerführer Afrika Description	No x Type/Auth	Av	Sv
JG (Jagdgeschwader) Fighter.					I./JG 27	40xBf-109E-7(T)	34	25
					7./JG 26	12xBf-109E-7	17	13
					1./NJG 3	12xBf-110E-1^^	7	4
ZG (Zerstörergeschwader) Heavy fighter (twin engine).					III./ZG 26	40xBf-110D/E	25	22
KG (Kampfgeschwader) Bomber.	Stab/LG 1	4xJu-88A	1	1	III.(K)/LG 1	40xJu-88A-4(T)	27	11
	I.(K)/LG 1	40xJu-88A-4	35	4				
	II.(K)/LG 1	40xJu-88A	25	11				
	II./KG 26*^	40xHe-111H-3/6	28	5				
	11./Erg Gr./LG 1	12xJu-88A	10	7				
	12./Erg Gr./LG 2	12xJu-88A	11	6				
StG (Sturzkampfgeschwader) Dive Bomber.	Stab/StG 3***	6xBf-110, 4xJu-87B	4, 3	0, 3	I./StG 1^	40xJu-87B/R	25	21
	I./StG 3**^	40xJu-87R	30	13	II./StG 2**	40xJu-87B/R	27	27
Aufkl Gr (aufklärungsgruppe) Reconnaissance.	Aufkl.Gr 126 (S)	40xHe-60, Ar-196, Bv-138 Fokker T.VIII-W	18	13				
H (Heeresaufklärungsgruppe) Short Range Tactical Reconnaissance.					2.(H)/14*	12xBf-110C/E, Hs-126s	13	13
F (Fernaufklärungsgruppe) Long Range Strategic Reconnaissance.	1.(F)/121	12xJu-88D, Bf-110E, Do-215E	6	6	2.(F)/123	12xJu-88D-1/5	7	2
KGr zbV (Kampfgeschwader zu besonderen Verwendung) Transport.	Stab/KGr zbV 1	4xJu-88A/Ju52*	2	1				
	I./KG zbV 1^^	53xJu-52	27	14				
	II./KG zbV 1**	53xJu-52	39	19				
	III./KG zbV 1	53xJu-52	41	29				
	KGr zbV 172^	53xJu-52	44	8				
	I./LLG 1^*	22xJu-52, 36xDFS-230	11, 22	3, 20				

Category	Unit	Aircraft		
(Seenotstaffel) Air-Sea Rescue.	6. Seenotstaffel	14xDo-18	8	6
	7. Seenotstaffel(?)	14xDo-18/He-59/Ar-196	6	3
(Kurierstaffel) Courier/Liaison.	Verbindungsstaffel 5~	Fi-156, Misc Types	4	3
(Wüstennotstaffel) Des. Rescue.	Sanitätsflugbereitschaft 2~*	6xJu-52 (+ 4 Fi-156, 1941)	6	4
(Sanitätsflugbereitschaft) Ambulance Flight.	Sanitätsflugbereitschaft 7	6xJu-52	5	4
	Kurierstaffel Fliegerführer A*^	Various types, ref notes	8	7
	Wüstennotstaffel 1^**	Fi-156	12	9

* Ju 52's available

^ I./KGr zbV 172 transferred to Luftflotte 1 in Sep. 1941.

** II./KG zbV 1 transferred to Luftflotte 2, II Fliegerkorps, in Aug./Sep.1941.

*^ 6./KG 26 was equipped with He-111H-6 torpedo bombers, and was detached to Luftflotte 4, Rumania. Arrived ca 1st Sep. 1941. 4 and 5./KG 26 remained in the Med, moved to Athens-Eleusis/ Greece.

^^ I./KG zbV 1 transferred to Luftflotte 4 in Aug./Sep. 1941.

^* Gruppe I, Luftlandegeschwader (Air Landing), with 3 Staffel. Transferred to Luftflotte 2, VIII. Fliegerkorps, in Sep. 1941.

*** Transferred to Fliegerführer Afrika in late July-Aug. 1941.

***^ Transferred to Fliegerführer Afrika in mid Nov. 1941.

~ Redesignated Flugbereitschaft Luftflotte 2 in Oct. 1941.

~* Renamed from Sanitätsflugbereitschaft/X. Fliegerkorps on 7th July 1941, when it was based at Athens. Transferred to Fliegerführer Afrika (Libya) in 1941 (with some Fi-156s added)

* Attached to 5th Light Division.

^ I./StG 1 redesignated II./StG 3 on 13th Jan. 1942.

** II./StG 2 redesignated III./StG 3 on 13th Jan. 1942.

*^ Kurierstaffel Fliegerführer Afrika (tropical) and Utility, mostly Fi-156. Also used Bf-108, C-445, He-111 and Ju-52 at various times. Also known as Kurierstaffel Afrika.

^^ Probably Me110E-1/U1 night fighters with infrared sensors.

^* A special (and well known) unit for rescuing air-crew forced down in the desert. It was officially formed on 28th June 1941, but appears to have initially used local resources, and is included here for completeness.

© Nigel Askey, 2018

Table X FCps (cont.)			
X. Fliegerkorps, Totals			
	No. of	No. of Aircraft	
Unit Type	Units	Avail	Svcble
Nacht-Jagdgruppen	1/3	7	4
Jagdgruppen	1 1/3	51	38
Erg.Guppen (JG,ZG)	0	0	0
Schlachtgruppen	0	0	0
Zerstörergruppen	1	25	22
Kampfgruppen	4 2/3	137	45
Stukagruppen	3	89	64
(Pz) Staffeln	0	0	0
(H) Staffeln	1	13	13
Luft (F) Staffeln	2	13	8
Heeres (F) Staffeln	0	0	0
KGr zbV (and LLG)**	5	164	74
Wetterstaffeln	0	0	0
Seefliegerstaffeln	3	18	13
Seenotstaffeln	2	14	9
Kurierstaffeln/Verb. Staffeln/Wust. 1	2	24	19
Sanitätsflugbereitschaften	2	11	8
		566	317
Number of Aircraft by type			
Single Engine Fighters		51	38
Twin Eng Fighters / Ftr Bmbrs		29	22
Twin Eng Night Fighters		7	4
Single Eng Fighter Bombers		0	0
Dive Bombers		85	64
Twin Engine Bombers		137	45
Four Engine Bombers		0	0
Long Range Recon*		13	8
SR Recon /Army Coop^		37	32
Seaplanes		32	22
Transport Aircraft**		175	82
		566	317

* Includes Wetterstaffeln aircraft.
^ Includes Courier, Liaison and Desert-Rescue aircraft.
** Includes LLG and Sanitätsflugbereitschaften aircraft.

Total Combat Aircraft*		367	216

*Excludes aircraft in KGr zbV, Kurierstaffeln/Verbindungsstaffeln, Sanitätsflugbereitschaften and Wüstennotstaffel 1.

© Nigel Askey, 2018

***

By June 1941 the only RAF bases left in the central and eastern Mediterranean were on Malta, in eastern Libya and in Egypt. This meant that the only opposition to Axis aircraft operating in the central Mediterranean came from a few RAF fighter squadrons based on Malta, and Royal Navy aircraft carriers escorting convoys to Malta. Consequently the Royal Navy and merchant navy had to constantly run the gauntlet of Axis bombers whenever they supplied Malta from Gibraltar or Alexandria, and (until well into 1942) this was the primary activity of the X. Fliegerkorps and Regia Aeronautica aircraft based on Sicily and Sardinia. As a result, the only significant air to air battles in the Mediterranean theatre during the second half of 1941 occurred between the Axis forces under Fliegerführer Afrika and the Commonwealth's Desert Air Force (the DAF - headquartered in Alexandria).[348]

In June 1941 the RAF (including the South African Air Force) had approximately 570 combat aircraft in the Middle East, of which approximately 290 were fighters, 240 were bombers, torpedo bombers and reconnaissance aircraft, and 40 were flying boats. This force was deployed across 38 operational squadrons in the Middle East, made up of: 19 fighter squadrons, 5 medium bomber squadrons, 9 'light' bomber squadrons, 2 torpedo bomber squadrons and 3 flying boat squadrons.[349] Comparing the figures for the RAF in Libya and Egypt (there were six squadrons on Malta) with those of Fliegerführer Afrika, we find that for air-operations over Libya and Egypt the RAF enjoyed an overall numerical superiority of around 2.6 to 1 (480 vs 182) on 21st June 1941. This included a fighter superiority of around 2.8 to 1 (230 vs 83).

However, if we include the Regia Aeronautica aircraft based in North Africa, the RAF's overall numerical superiority dropped to around 1.5 to 1 (480 vs 310), with a fighter superiority of only 1.3 to 1 (230 vs 173). Therefore, although the Axis forces were still somewhat outnumbered, **in June 1941 Fliegerführer Afrika faced better overall odds than any other Luftwaffe force anywhere!** In the event these were the best odds Fliegerführer Afrika would ever achieve during the entire North African campaign. This was because the RAF's Desert Air Force was reinforced at a progressively higher rate than Fliegerführer Afrika and the Regia Aeronautica in North Africa. From June to November 1941 the Desert Air Force received 13 new squadrons and a large numbers of replacement aircraft, while Fliegerführer Afrika's first reinforcements arrived in October/November 1941. Around this time, Stab. JG27, II./JG27 and III./JG27 were transferred from the East Front, while I./JG27 was rotated back to Germany for reequipping. By December 1941 the RAF forces in the Middle East had increased to approximately 830 combat aircraft in 51 squadrons. These comprised 29 fighter squadrons, 7 medium bomber squadrons, 10 'light' bomber squadrons, 2 torpedo bomber squadrons and 3 flying boat squadrons.[350] Most of these aircraft had arrived in time to take part in Operation Crusader on 18th November 1941, which was the major Allied offensive to relieve the Tobruk garrison and drive the Axis forces out of Libya.

Despite being progressively more outnumbered, and despite fuel shortages which often became chronic, it is generally acknowledged that Fliegerführer Afrika was able to achieve a measure of air-superiority over the desert for most of 1941 and (arguably) even into early 1942. This was largely due to the experience and skill of the fighter pilots in I./JG 27, commanded by Hauptmann Eduard Neumann. I./JG 27 was a battle-hardened unit which achieved a kill to loss ratio against enemy fighters of better than 4 to 1 during 1941.[351] It produced some of the Luftwaffe's best 'Western Front aces' including Hauptmann Hans-Joachim Marseille (with 151 kills over North Africa), Oberleutnant Hans-Arnold Stahlschmidt (59 North Africa kills), Leutnant Gunter Steinhausen (40 North Africa kills), and Oberleutnant Ludwig Franzisket (24 North Africa kills, from 43 total).[352] *Staffel* 7./JG 26 also performed extremely well, producing several very high scoring aces such as Major Joachim Muncheberg (with 135 kills, including at least 46 Spitfires, mostly in the Mediterranean theatre).

***

Many current histories of the North African campaign attribute the Commonwealth DAF's mediocre performance during 1941 and early 1942 to "being forced to use inferior second line fighters, and inexperienced and under-trained pilots". However, an analysis of the aircraft types available to both sides, and the history leading up to the air-battles over the North African desert, does not support this view (or at least means it needs to be heavily qualified).

---

[348] Also known (chronologically) as the Air Headquarters Western Desert, the Air Headquarters Libya, the Western Desert Air Force (WDAF), and the First Tactical Air Force (1 TAF).
[349] J. Ellis, World War II: A Statistical Survey, Facts on File Inc, New York, 1993, pp. 232-241, tables 19 and 37.
[350] Ibid. Fliegerführer Afrika's strength at this time is estimated at around 280 aircraft.
[351] I./JG 27 claimed 588 kills from April 1941 to November 1942. Total claims in North Africa for JG 27 were 1,166 aircraft, and total JG 27 losses during this period were approximately 200 Bf 109s.
[352] All with I./JG 27 in North Africa. N. Franks, Aircraft versus Aircraft, Grub Street, London 1998, p. 99. Also C. Bishop, Luftwaffe Squadrons 1939-45, Amber Books Ltd, London, 2006, pp. 55, 56 and 59. Also G. Williamson, Aces of the Reich, Arms and Armour Press, London, 1989, p. 192.

The principal fighter and fighter-bomber types used by the DAF during 1941 were the Hawker Hurricane I, Hurricane IIA, Hurricane IIB, Tomahawk IIA (renamed from the Curtiss P-40B) and Tomahawk IIB (renamed from the Curtiss P-40C). These aircraft can be considered 'second line' in that they were inferior fighters (though not necessarily inferior at ground attack) to the Supermarine Spitfire V, which was the mainstay of RAF Fighter Command in the UK during the second half of 1941. The principal fighter and fighter-bomber types used by the Axis forces in North Africa during 1941 were the Messerschmitt Bf 109E-7, Messerschmitt Bf 110D and E, Fiat G.50 Freccia and Macchi MC 200 Saetta. Although the G.50 and MC 200 were still considered first line fighters in the Regia Aeronautica, the G.50 was obsolescent as a front line fighter, while the MC 200 was inferior to all the Allied types fielded in North Africa during 1941. In addition the twin engine Bf 110 had already been withdrawn from engaging with any Allied single engine fighters if possible, while the Bf 109E-7 was well and truly a 'second line' fighter as far as the Luftwaffe were concerned. By June 1941 the Bf 109E had been supplanted by the Bf 109F and Focke-Wulf (Fw) 190A in most *Jagdgeschwader*. As far as is known, on 21st June 1941 there wasn't a single Bf 109F or Fw 190A in the entire Mediterranean theatre, and this situation didn't change until late 1941.

From table X FCps we can see that there were only 51 Bf 109Es in Fliegerführer Afrika on 21st June 1941. This represented only 29% of the Axis fighters in North Africa: the remaining 122 fighters were all Bf 110s, G.50s and MC 200s. Therefore, **the principal Allied fighter types fielded in June 1941 were actually superior fighters to the large majority of Axis fighters fielded**. Furthermore, the 'second line' Hurricane IIA and Tomahawk II models were only marginally inferior (as pure fighters) to the 'second line' Bf 109E-7s. In late 1941 and into 1942 better Axis fighters started to appear in North Africa, such as the Bf 109F and Macchi C 202 Folgore. However by this time the DAF was receiving increasing numbers of Spitfire Vs, Hurricane IICs, and Kittyhawk IAs (renamed from the Curtiss P-40D Warhawk).

So what about training and experience? There is no doubt that the *Jagdwaffe* units in North Africa were well trained and combat experienced. However the DAF was also a very experienced force by 1941; and with far more experience than any Luftwaffe unit in operating in harsh desert conditions. Fliegerführer Afrika had only been formed in February 1941 with the first fighter units arriving in North Africa in April 1941. The DAF had been operating in one form or another in the Middle East since before the war, and in September 1939 the RAF forces in the Middle East already had 18 squadrons on strength (including 6 fighter squadrons).[353] Furthermore, from June 1940 the RAF in the Middle East had been in almost continuous action against the Italian air, ground and naval forces. Recent campaigns included: the air-defence of Malta, the defence of Egypt against an Italian invasion, the very successful Allied offensive to clear Cyrenaica in eastern Libya (Operation Compass), the air-defence of Greece and the successful conquest of Italian East Africa.

Some of the RAF's most successful wartime aces racked up their 'scores' in the Middle East during this period. They included probably the highest scoring RAF pilot of WWII: Squadron Leader M T St John 'Pat' Pattle with 40+ kills, all achieved in the Middle East and mostly against Italian aircraft from June 1940 to April 1941.[354] Other aces included Flight Lieutenant G F Beurling (26 Malta kills, from 31 total) the fifth highest scoring RAF ace of WWII, Squadron Leader V C Woodward (22 Middle East kills) and Squadron Leader C R Caldwell (20 kills over the desert from 28+ total).[355] Furthermore, the average training period (including flying hours) for pilots in the DAF was no different to those sent to RAF commands in Europe, and after December 1940 (when it had become apparent an invasion of the UK was not imminent) a large number of fighter pilots in Fighter Command (in the UK) were transferred to the Middle East and the DAF.

It would therefore be true to say the DAF in 1941 and 1942 was far from having mostly 'inexperienced and under-trained pilots'. It was in fact at least as well trained, and with as much experience, as any command in the RAF, and with some of the most highly decorated pilots in the entire Commonwealth.

***

---

[353] J. Ellis, WWII: A Statistical Survey, Facts On File Inc, New York 1993, p. 2401 table 37.
[354] N. Franks, Aircraft versus Aircraft, Grub Street, London 1998, pp. 99, 101, and 155. Pattle's final score could be as high as 51 (excluding shared kills).
[355] Ibid.

h. Luftwaffenbefehlshaber Mitte

Luftwaffenbefehlshaber Mitte (Air Force Commander Centre), commanded by Generaloberst Hubert Weise, was responsible for the air-defence of Germany and its immediate approaches. Later in the war when the Allied strategic air offensive became a serious threat to the German industrial base, this command was expanded into the Luftflotte Reich, controlling the XII. Fliegerkorps. The distribution of available and serviceable aircraft in Luftwaffenbefehlshaber Mitte, and the units they were assigned to on 21st June 1941, are shown in table LuftM.[356] From this table we can see that on 21st June 1941 Luftwaffenbefehlshaber Mitte contained 397 aircraft comprised of: 72 day-fighters (including 34 Bf 110 *Zerstörer*), 189 night-fighters, 20 twin engine bombers, 47 seaplanes and flying boats, 10 reconnaissance aircraft, and 59 transport and courier/liaison aircraft. Excluding the transport aircraft in KGr zbV, LLG, *Kurierstaffeln* and *Sanitätsflugbereitschaften* units, Luftwaffenbefehlshaber Mitte contained a total of 338 'combat' aircraft of which 233 (69%) were serviceable. Luftwaffenbefehlshaber Mitte also had operational control of the Luftwaffe's flak and searchlight forces defending Germany.

As early as the spring of 1940 the RAF had demonstrated that it was unable to bomb targets in Germany during daylight without suffering prohibitive losses. RAF Bomber Command (responsible for strategic bombing) had therefore quickly switched to night bombing, and by June 1941 this force had grown to 47 squadrons with some 700 aircraft.[357] The large majority of these aircraft were twin-engine medium bombers; specifically Vickers Wellingtons, Handley Page Hampdens, Bristol Blenheims, Armstrong Whitworth Whitleys and a few Avro Manchesters. Interestingly, although these aircraft were of the same vintage as the German Junkers 88 and Heinkel 111, the British bombers of this period had proved much more vulnerable to Bf 109 fighters in daylight than the German bombers had been against Spitfires and Hurricanes during the summer of 1940.[358] The Wellington was the most common type with 21 operational squadrons, followed by the Hampden with 10 operational squadrons, all based in the UK.[359] Only a handful of the four engine RAF 'heavies' had entered service by June 1941: the Short Stirling recorded its first combat mission in February 1941, while the Handley Page Halifax went into combat for the first time in March 1941. Despite their larger crews and heavier defensive armament, these aircraft were almost as vulnerable to daylight fighter interception as the older medium bombers, mainly due to the fact that they were less manoeuvrable. After a few 'experimental' daylight sorties, the RAF 'heavies' also quickly reverted to night bombing.[360]

The heart of the German air-defence system by mid-1941 was the so called Kammhuber Line (named after its organiser and commander).[361] Started in 1940, the Kammhuber Line consisted of a radar network stretching from the French coast, through Germany and north into Denmark. By 1941 it had evolved into a system which the Germans termed *Raumnachtjagd* (sector night fighting, or box system). The entire defensive area was divided into overlapping sectors, and each sector or 'box' was scanned by a Wurzburg radar set which could scan an area around 30km (18.6 miles) by 30km. As enemy bombers entered its sector, the radar set relayed the information to a controller who plotted the bomber formation's course, speed and altitude on a plotting table. At the same time, one or two night fighters would be circling a radio beacon within a particular sector, and they would be directed by their controller onto an interception course. Once the night fighter got within range of its own on board sensors (which was still only a few miles in 1940-41), the night fighter would engage the target or targets as it saw fit.

This was very different from daylight operations were large groups of fighters in formation would be directed to intercept enemy bomber formations. Interception at night involved one or two night fighters attacking at a time. Note, the technology of the radar and/or infra-red sensors on night-fighters in 1941 did not allow them to distinguish between an enemy or a friendly aircraft. There was therefore a real danger of night fighters engaging each other if too many operated within a sector, or they strayed too far from their 'home' sector. The downside of the *Raumnachtjagd* for Allied bomber crews was that they could be attacked without warning by a night fighter at any point within the defended area, as they approached the target as well as on their way home.

***

---

[356] Ibid, notes 277 and 287, for primary sources. Also, J. Scutts, German Night Fighter Aces of WWII, Osprey Publishing Ltd, Oxford, 1998.

[357] J. Ellis, World War II: A Statistical Survey, Facts on File Inc, New York, 1993, p. 241, tables 37 and 38.

[358] Some have attributed this to the fact that the Bf 109E was normally armed with 2 20mm cannon, while the Spitfire I/IA/IIA and Hurricane I had only MGs. There is little doubt however, that the Ju 88 was a superior all-round aircraft to the RAF twin engine bombers being fielded during 1939-1941.

[359] Ibid, note 355. Also, S. Stewart, Aircraft of WWII, Aerospace Publications Ltd, Fyshwick, Australia, 1998, pp. 81 &161.

[360] S. Stewart, Aircraft of WWII, Aerospace Publications Ltd, Fyshwick, Australia, 1998, p. 153.

[361] *Generalmajor* Josef Kammhuber, who also oversaw the establishment of *Nachtjagdgeschwader* 1 and was its first commander. He was promoted to *Generalleutnant* on 1st October 1941 and to *General der Flieger* on 1 January 1943.

Table LuftM	Deployment and Composition of Luftwaffe Air Units, 21st June 1941			
	Luftwaffenbefehlshaber Mitte			
	Description	No x Type/Auth	Av	Sv
JG (Jagdgeschwader)	Stab/Jafu Holland	4xBf-109E	2	1
Fighter.	Stab/Jafu Dt Bucht	4xBf-109E	1	1
NJG (Nachtjagdgeschwader)	Stab/Jafu Mitte Dt	4xBf-109B/E	2	1
Night fighter.	Stab/JG 1	4xBf-109E/F	4	4
	2./JG 1*	12xBf-109E	15	2
	Stab/NJG 1	4xBf-110C/E	4	2
	I./NJG 1	40xBf-110C/D/E	37	28
	II./NJG 1	40xBf-110D/E, Do-215B-5	32, 5	21, 2
	III./NJG 1	40xBf-109E, Bf-110C/D/E	11, 34	9, 28
	Stab/NJG 2	4xJu-88C	4	4
	I./NJG 2	40xJu-88C, Do-17Z-10	32	15
	4./NJG 2	12xDo-17Z-10	6	4
	Stab/NJG 3	4xBf-110C/D/E	3	3
	2.,3./NJG 3^	28xBf-110C/D/E	30	28
	Stab/NJG 4	4xBf-110D/E	2	2
	6./JG 53	12xBf-109F	3	3
ZG (Zerstörergeschwader)	II./ZG 76**	40xBf-110D-F	34	21
Heavy fighter (twin engine).				
H (Heeresaufklärungsgruppe)	1.(H)/14^^	12xHs-126	5	5
Short Range Tactical				
Reconnaissance.				
KGr zbV (Kampfgeschwader	ObdM	4xJu-52 (1x Fw 200 V3)	3	2
zu besonderen Verwendung)	Stab/LLG 1	4xDo-17, 4x DFS-230	2, 2	1, 2
Transport.	II./LLG 1*^	22xJu-52, 36xDFS-230/Go-242	6, 25	2, 23
	III./LLG 1	22xHs-126, 36xDFS-230	4, 24	2, 22
Wekusta (Wettererkundungs	Wekusta 1. Ob.d.L	20x Ju-88D, He111H	5	4
staffel) Weather Observation.				
KuFlGr (Küstenfliegergruppe)	KuFlGr 506^*	40xJu-88, (He-115)	20, (8)	12 (6)
Coastal Aviation.	KuFlGr 906***	16xHe115, Ar-196	14	10
	1./BoFlGr 196**^	24xAr-196	10	7
(Seenotstaffel) Air-Sea Rescue.	1x'Undes' Staffel	12xDo-18/He-59	15	10
(Kurierstaffel) Courier/Liaison.	Führer Kurierstaffel*^^	Ju-52, Fw-200, He-111, Fw-58, Fh-104 (+)*^^	7	5
(Sanitätsflugbereitschaft)	Kurierstaffel Ob.d.L	Ju-52, Fi-156, Fw-58, Ju-88, Do-215	9	8
Ambulance Flight.	Kurierstaffel O.K.W	Ju-52, Fi-156, Fw-58, C-445.	9	7
	Kurierstaffel Ob.d.M	Ju-52, Fi-156, He-111, Fw-58, W-34, C-445.	8	4
	Sanitätsflugbereitschaft 8~	6xJu-52	6	6
	Sanitätsflugbereitschaft 17	6xJu-52	5	5
	* 2./JG 1 forming (until 5th July 41). 3./JG 1 was not formed until March 42. ^ 2.,3./NJG 3 present only. 1./NJG 3 was in X. Fliegerkorps. ** II./ZG 76 redesignated III./NJG 3 on 1st November 1941. Already performing night/day bomber interception missions. 4./ZG 76 was dispatched to Mosul, Iraq in April/May to June 1941. Stab/ZG 76 was acting Jagdfliegerführer Norwegen. It was formally renamed Jagdfliegerführer Norwegen on 1st August 1941. *^ 6./LLG 1 moved to Dunaburg in July 41, and Pernau by Sep. 1941. Used in attack on Osel. ^^ Transferred to the East Front, (Grodno) after 9th Sep. 41. ^* Includes Stab./KuFlGr 506, 1./KuFlGr 506, 3./KuFlGr 506 (conv He-115s to Ju-88s), and 2./KuFlGr 906. Based at Westerland (German Coast) in June 1941. 2./KuFlGr 906 was redesignated 2./KuFlGr 506 on 6th October 1941. Transferred to Luftflotte 1, Fl. Fu. Ostsee, by 21st September 41, based in Riga. Had returned to Westerland by 18th Oct 1941 (and later, went West) Was redesignated K.Gr 506 on 19th October 1941. *** Includes Stab./KuFlGr 906 and 1./KuFlGr 706 (He-115 and Ar 196). Based at Aalborg in Denmark in June 1941. **^ (Bordfliegerstaffeln) Ship Based Aviation Squadron. Based at Wilhelmshaven in June 1941. On 25th August 1941 around half the Staffel (with 15 aircraft) transferred to Stavanger, Norway, under Luftflotte 5. *^^ Also called the Fliegerstaffel des Führer; originally formed 26th Aug. 1939. On 20th June 1941 its base was moved to Rastenburg (from Berlin-Staaken), at which time it appears to have been more commonly called the Führer Kurierstaffel. It is also known to have operated Do-217, Ju-88, Bf-108 and Fi-156 during its time. ~ Transferred to Luftflotte 5 on 11th July 1941 (and based at Bardufoss).

Table LuftM (cont.)		
Luftwaffenbefehlshaber Mitte, Totals		
	No. of	No. of Aircraft
Unit Type	Units	Avail	Svcble
Nacht-Jagdgruppen	5	200	146
Jagdgruppen	2/3	27	12
Erg.Guppen (JG,ZG)	0	0	0
Schlachtgruppen	0	0	0
Zerstörergruppen	1	34	21
Kampfgruppen	0	0	0
Stukagruppen	0	0	0
(Pz) Staffeln	0	0	0
(H) Staffeln	1	5	5
Luft (F) Staffeln	0	0	0
Heeres (F) Staffeln	0	0	0
KGr zbV (and LLG)**	2	15	7
Wetterstaffeln	1	5	4
Seefliegerstaffeln	5	52	35
Seenotstaffeln	1	15	10
Kurierstaffeln/Verb. Staffeln	4	33	24
Sanitätsflugbereitschaften	2	11	11
		397	275
Number of Aircraft by type			
Single Engine Fighters		38	21
Twin Eng Fighters / Ftr Bmbrs		34	21
Twin Eng Night Fighters		189	137
Single Eng Fighter Bombers		0	0
Dive Bombers		0	0
Twin Engine Bombers		20	12
Four Engine Bombers		0	0
Long Range Recon*		5	4
SR Recon /Army Coop^		5	5
Seaplanes		47	33
Transport Aircraft **		59	42
		397	275
* Includes Wetterstaffeln aircraft.			
^ Includes Courier, Liaison aircraft.			
** Includes Kurierstaffel, LLG and Sanitätsflugbereitschaften aircraft.			
Total Combat Aircraft*		338	233
* Excludes aircraft in KGr zbV, LLG, Kurierstaffeln, and Sanitätsflugbereitschaften.			
© Nigel Askey, 2018			

***

By June 1941 the operational German night fighter types included various Messerschmitt Bf 110 C, D and E marks, very small numbers of Dornier 17Z-10s and 215B-5s, and a few early model Junkers 88Cs (Ju 88 C-1/4). The most numerous types were those built around the Bf 110, which was enjoying something of a renaissance as a night fighter after its failure as a long range day fighter (*Zerstörer*).

The equipment on these fighters included Lichtenstein BC or C-1 radar, FuG 202 or 212 interception radar, nose mounted infrared detectors and 2-6 20mm cannon. The radar on these aircraft was not able to function at ranges less than around 200 metres, which was just within visual range on a dark night. Therefore night fighters still had to get a visual lock in the last stage of an approach in order to effectively engage an enemy bomber. On balance, the combination of the Kammhuber Line radar, flak and night fighters was able to provide a very effective air-defence during 1941 and 1942. The RAF lost 1,328 bombers in 1941 and another 1,616 during 1942: the large majority from Bomber Command on night operations.[362] Things got so bad that by mid-1942 a Bomber Command aircrew had less than a 50% chance of surviving its first tour of operations.[363]

***

In addition to its air-defence role, Luftwaffenbefehlshaber Mitte was also responsible for patrolling the sea areas around Denmark, the southern North Sea and the southern Baltic Sea. To accomplish this, Luftwaffenbefehlshaber Mitte had 67 bombers, seaplanes and flying boats available on 21st June 1941. The bombers (Ju 88s) were grouped under Stab./KuFlGr 506, and included 1./KuFlGr 506, 3./KuFlGr 506 and 2./KuFlGr 906. 3./KuFlGr 506 was still in the process of converting from seaplanes to Ju 88s and so still had its He 115s on strength. The patrol and attack-seaplanes were grouped under Stab./KuFlGr 906, and included 1./KuFlGr 706 with He 115s and Ar 196s. This unit was based in Aalborg and was largely responsible for anti-submarine patrols around the coast of Denmark and southern Sweden (mainly to protect coastal shipping and to hinder Royal Navy submarines from entering the Baltic).

The 1./BoFlGr 196 was based at Wilhelmshaven, and was the immediate unit responsible for supplying catapult capable seaplanes (the Ar 196) and suitably trained pilots to the Kriegsmarine for use on their larger warships. However, BoFlGr 196 spent most of its time and resources on active patrols, probably working with Stab./KuFlGr 906. The *Seenotstaffeln* operated obsolescent Do 18 flying boats and a few He 59 seaplanes, and were responsible for rescuing downed pilots in the North Sea. No doubt they also conducted a 'few' clandestine operations at night off the coast of Scotland and England.

***

Also shown in table <u>Luft M</u> are the transport *Staffeln* used by the various Wehrmacht high commands. These included the following:

- The Führer Kurierstaffel.[364]

- Kurierstaffel O.K.W.

- Kurierstaffel Ob.d.M.

- Kurierstaffel Ob.d.L.

These *Staffeln* contained a small number of transport aircraft for Hitler's personnel use, and for use by the most senior members of the Nazi Party, the Wehrmacht and the SS. For example, both Hitler and Himmler had a VIP Fw 200 Condor for their personnel use. Note, Kurierstaffel 110 (under Luftflotte ObdL, refer next section) was acting as the Kurierstaffel Ob.d.H. It was officially redesignated Kurierstaffel Ob.d.H. in October 1941.

---

[362] N. Franks, Aircraft versus Aircraft, Grub Street, London 1998, p. 98. Also, Jane's Fighting Aircraft of WWII, The Random House Group Ltd: Studio, London, 2001, pp. 31 and 32 (RAF Statistics on Cease Fire in Europe). RAF Bomber Command did manage to drop 31,704 tons of bombs in 1941, and 45,561 tons in 1942. P. Moyes, Bomber Squadrons of the RAF and their Aircraft, MacDonald Aviation Books, 1964, Appendix 28, p. 327.

[363] C. Bishop, Luftwaffe Squadrons 1939-45, Amber Books Ltd, London, 2006, p. 138. By war's end RAF Bomber Command had suffered 74,000 casualties (55,750 killed) and admitted to the loss of 10,255 aircraft (1,600 by accident). R. A. Freeman, Raiding the Reich: The Allied Strategic Offensive in Europe, Arms and Armour Press, Cassell Group, London, 1997, p. 160. Another well researched source places RAF Bomber Command's losses at 10,724 aircraft (with 1,604 due to accidents). This total included 6,931 four-engine heavy bombers (and 57 aircraft lost while operating with Coastal Command). P. Moyes, Bomber Squadrons of the RAF and their Aircraft, MacDonald Aviation Books, 1964, Appendix 28, p. 327. Even this statistic seems a low estimate: this equates to 5.2 men being killed for every single aircraft shot down or lost in accidents (55,750 killed/10,724 aircraft lost). Even the largest types (Lancaster, Halifax and Stirling Bombers) normally had a crew of only 7 men, and only occasionally carried 8 if on special missions (such as a pathfinding mission). The other mainstay aircraft, the Vickers Wellington, only had a 5-6 man crew, and a large proportion of the bombers lost had a crew of only 3-5. Just considering the heaviest bombers and the Wellingtons, this would mean that, on average, at least 74-87% of these crews were killed outright when their aircraft was shot down! This is before we even consider the many aircraft types lost which had fewer than 5 crewmen. There is something very wrong here, and it is not the number of deaths which is very well recorded and documented (as opposed to the aircraft numbers and types lost). To put it bluntly, Bomber Command's personnel casualty and admitted aircraft loss figures **do not** match up at all, even if we attribute a significant number of deaths to ground personnel. If we assume around 3.5 deaths per aircraft lost (which is still a high estimate), and around 4,000 RAF ground-crew personnel were killed while on the ground, then Bomber Command likely lost around 14,800 aircraft during WWII. This figure also agrees much more closely with an analysis of the total bombers produced during WWII (of the types used by only Bomber Command), and those on strength at war's end in May 1945. These figures correlate closely even after assuming 20% of war-production never went on any combat operations, and ignoring any pre-war production.

[364] Also called the *Fliegerstaffel des Führer*; originally formed 26th August 1939. On 20th June 1941 its base was moved to Rastenburg (from Berlin-Staaken), at which time it appears to have been more commonly called the *Führer Kurierstaffel*. It is also known to have operated Do 217, Ju 88, Bf 108 and Fi 156 during its time.

i. Luftflotte ObdL

The Luftflotte ObdL (*Luftflotte Oberbefehlshaber der Luftwaffe* – Air Fleet Commander-in-Chief of the Luftwaffe) was a small and specialised command which reported directly to the OKL (*Oberkommando der Luftwaffe* - Luftwaffe High Command). Its primary function was strategic reconnaissance for the German High Command (OKW). The distribution of available and serviceable aircraft in Luftflotte ObdL, and the units they were assigned to on 21st June 1941, are shown in table <u>Luft ObdL</u>.[365]

From this table we can see that on 21st June 1941 Luftflotte ObdL contained 62 aircraft, comprised of 51 long-range reconnaissance aircraft in five *Fernaufklärungsgruppen*, and 11 transport and courier/liaison aircraft. Excluding the aircraft in *Kurierstaffel* 110, Luftflotte ObdL contained a total of 51 'combat aircraft' of which 32 (63%) were serviceable.

Probably the most famous unit operated by Luftflotte ObdL in 1941 was 4.(F)/ObdL. This was because it operated the handful of the very high altitude Junkers Ju 86Ps available to the Luftwaffe.[366] The Ju 86P had a very large wing area and turbocharged engines which enabled it to reach 15,088 metres (49,500ft) in an emergency. It first appeared over Britain in late 1940 and immediately proved to be immune from interception by RAF fighters due to the very high altitude at which it normally operated. During 1941 it appeared over the Mediterranean and North Africa, photographing Allied troop and shipping movements at will; much to the chagrin of the RAF and senior Allied commanders. The high altitude at which this plane operated also made it difficult to detect, and the existence of the aircraft was not even officially acknowledged in Britain until mid-1942.

Arguably the Ju 86P's most significant contribution to Germany's war effort was the repeated deep reconnaissance missions made into the USSR immediately prior to Operation Barbarossa. It is not known how many sorties were flown, but a very large area of the western USSR was extensively photographed. The particulars of Ju 86P deep reconnaissance missions over the USSR after 22nd June 1941 are not known, but it is fair to assume they continued after this date as the VVS was unable to prevent them.[367]

The Ju 86P continued to roam freely across Europe for almost two years (late 1940 to mid-1942) before the Allies were able to fix the problem; at least in the West. A version of the Spitfire V was produced that was specifically adapted for Ju 86P interception, and from mid-1942 to late-1942 three Ju 86Ps were shot down over the Mediterranean. This included the highest ever kill recorded by an unpressurised aircraft flown by a pilot not wearing a pressure suit, when it claimed a Ju 86P at a staggering 49,500ft.

***

---

[365] Ibid, notes 277 and 287. H. Boog, et al, German Research Institute for Military History at Potsdam, Germany and the Second World War-Volume IV, The Attack on the Soviet Union, Oxford University Press, New York, 1996, tables, I.IV.5, p. 364, for total reconnaissance aircraft in Luftflotte ObdL.

[366] It is possible that other *Fernaufklärungsgruppen* operated the Ju 86P in 1941. However, 4.(F)/ObdL is known to have been operating Ju 86Ps on this date.

[367] The best high altitude interceptor available to the VVS in 1941 was the MiG-3 and this aircraft's service ceiling was 12,000 metres (39,370ft), well below that required to intercept a Ju 86P.

Table Luft ObdL — Deployment and Composition of Luftwaffe Air Units, 21st June 1941

Luftflotte ObdL*

Description	No x Type/Auth	Av	Sv
F (Fernaufklärungsgruppe) Long Range Strategic Reconnaissance.			
4.(F)/11	12xJu-88A/D, Do-17P	12	6
3.(F)/33^*	12xJu-88A/D	12	8
1.(F)/Ob.d.L^	12xJu-88D,Do-215B,Bf-110E, Do-217A-0	11	8
3.(F)/Ob.d.L**	12xJu-88D,Do-215B, Do-217A-0	10	7
4.(F)/Ob.d.L*^	12xJu-86P-2,Do-215B	6	3
(Kurierstaffel) Courier/Liaison.			
Kurierstaffel 110^^	Fi-156, C-445 and W-34^^	11	10

* Oberbefehlshaber der Luftwaffe: reported directly to C in C Luftwaffe (Hermann Goring).

^ 1.(F)/Ob.d.L transferred to Luftflotte 2 in July 1941. This unit also operated a few of the rare Ju-88B in 1941.

** 3.(F)/Ob.d.L transferred to Luftflotte 4, IV. Fliegerkorps, in July 1941.

*^ 4.(F)/Ob.d.L transferred East in Dec 41/Jan 42. Also known as the *Versuchsstelle fur Hohenfluge* (high altitude test centre).

^^ Kurierstaffel 110 was redesignated Kurierstaffel Ob.d.H. in October 1941. It also operated Ju-52 and He-111 at various times.

*^ 3.(F)/33 had transferred East (Army Group Centre) by November or December 1941.

Luftflotte ObdL, Totals

Unit Type	No. of Units	No. of Aircraft Avail	No. of Aircraft Svcble
Jagdgruppen	0	0	0
Erg.Guppen (JG,ZG)	0	0	0
Schlachtgruppen	0	0	0
Zerstörergruppen	0	0	0
Kampfgruppen	0	0	0
Stukagruppen	0	0	0
(Pz) Staffeln	0	0	0
(H) Staffeln	0	0	0
Luft (F) Staffeln	5	51	32
Heeres (F) Staffeln	0	0	0
KGr zbV	0	0	0
Wetterstaffeln	0	0	0
Seefliegerstaffeln	0	0	0
Seenotstaffeln	0	0	0
Kurierstaffeln	1	11	10
Sanitätsflugbereitschaften	0	0	0
		62	42
Number of Aircraft by type			
Single Engine Fighters		0	0
Twin Eng Fighters / Ftr Bmbrs		0	0
Twin Eng Night Fighters		0	0
Single Eng Fighter Bombers		0	0
Dive Bombers		0	0
Twin Engine Bombers		0	0
Four Engine Bombers		0	0
Long Range Recon		51	32
SR Recon / Army Coop^		11	10
Seaplanes		0	0
Transport Aircraft		0	0
		62	42

^ Includes Courier, Liaison aircraft.

Total Combat Aircraft*		51	32

*Excludes aircraft in Kurierstaffeln.

Nigel Askey, © 2018

j. Luftwaffe Seeluftstreitkrafte and Küstenfliegergruppen

By the outbreak of World War II the German strategic planning had concentrated almost exclusively on attaining air-superiority (in continental Europe) and building the Luftwaffe as a tactical air-force focused on land based offensive operations. As a consequence relatively little development of the Luftwaffe's maritime warfare capability had occurred. To compound this situation, Goring insisted that the Luftwaffe (and he as its ObdL) control all aviation assets in the Reich. The *Oberkommando der Heeres* (OKH – Army High Command) did not mind this state of affairs because the Luftwaffe's primary mission in life was already to support the army's ground offensives. The navy, however, came off worst: it was never strategically important enough to enable the *Oberkommando der Kriegsmarine* (OKM – Navy High Command) to gain complete control of its own maritime aviation forces. The compromise reached was that the Luftwaffe would set up a special service branch devoted to maritime warfare: the *Seeluftstreitkrafte* (Marine-air combat force). The *Seeluftstreitkrafte* had a dedicated commander (the *Führer der Seeluftstreitkrafte*) and supposedly reported to the OKM via the *General der Luftwaffe beim Oberkommando der Kriegsmarine*.

In reality, the *Seeluftstreitkrafte* remained a branch of the Luftwaffe and the Kriegsmarine had little say in either its organisation or day to day operations. In this regard Germany never developed the equivalent of the RAF Coastal Command or the Soviet VVS VMF (*VVS Voyenno-Morskoy Flot* SSSR or VVS Naval Forces of the USSR). These organisations were large air-forces in their own right. In addition these restrictions meant that the Kriegsmarine never developed the equivalent of the Royal Navy's Fleet Air Arm, or the carrier-borne forces of the US and Imperial Japanese navies. This means that if the Graf Zeppelin aircraft carrier had been commissioned in mid-1940 as planned, then the 40-50 aircraft on it would still have belonged to the Luftwaffe and not the Kriegsmarine.

By June 1941 the *Seeluftstreitkrafte* was comprised of *Küstenfliegergruppen* (Coastal aviation groups) which had seaplanes or twin-engine bombers, a few *Seenotstaffeln* (Air-sea rescue squadrons) and *Seeaufklärungsgruppen* (Maritime reconnaissance aviation groups), and one *Bordfliegergruppe* (Ship based aviation group). The *Seeluftstreitkrafte* units were mainly concentrated in certain areas and under the following commands.

- Fliegerführer Ostsee (Aviation command Baltic Sea) reporting to Luftflotte 1.

- Luftflotte 5 (Air Fleet 5) covering Norway and North Finland. This included Luftwaffenkommando Kirkenes (Air force command Kirkenes) which reported to Luftflotte 5.

- Fliegerführer Atlantik (Aviation command Atlantic) reporting to Luftflotte 3.

- X. Fliegerkorps (X Aviation corps) covering the central Mediterranean.

***

The overall deployment and aircraft status of the various *Küstenfliegergruppen* in June 1941 was as shown in the following table. From this table we can see that no less than four out of the seven *Küstenfliegergruppen* in the Luftwaffe (i.e. KuFlGr 106, 506, 606 and 806) were either equipped with Ju 88s or were in the process of equipping with this aircraft. These units generally had their designations changed from KuFlGr to KGr, and could operate against naval targets or like the Luftwaffe's *Kampfgeschwader* (KG, Bomber) units.[368] The KGr units that found themselves on the East Front spent the large majority of their time and resources operating as bomber units supporting the army's ground operations.

KuFlGr 406, 706 and 906 retained their seaplanes and floatplanes. They were mostly equipped with He 115, Bv 138 and Ar 196 aircraft. These *Gruppen* were more often split into their component *Staffeln*, which then operated as small units under whichever Luftwaffe command needed their maritime capabilities. For more details on these units in June 1941, as well as the *Seeluftstreitkrafte Seenotstaffeln* and *Bordfliegergruppe* 196, refer to the previous sections.

***

---

[368] Several sources use the designations KuFlGr and KGr interchangeably. However it appears the KGr designation became more common later in the war (after 1941).

K.Gr and Ku.Fl.Gr. (Küstenfliegergruppen), June 1941

	KGr 106 (KuFlGr 106)*	KuFlGr 406	KuFlGr 506 (KGr 506)*	KGr 606 (KuFlGr 606)*	KuFlGr 706	KGr 806 (KuFlGr 806)*	KuFlGr 906
Stab.	Stab./KGr 106 4xJu-88A Fliegerführer Atlantik Luftflotte 3	Stab./KuFlGr 406 4xDo-18, (incl 2xDo-26) Fliegerführer Atlantik Luftflotte 3	Stab./KuFlGr 506 4xJu-88A Luftwaffenbefehlshaber Mitte	Stab./KGr 606 4xJu-88A Fliegerführer Atlantik Luftflotte 3	Stab./KuFlGr 706 4xHe-115 / Bv-138 Luftflotte 5	Stab./KGr 806 4xJu-88A Fliegerführer Ostsee Luftflotte 1	Stab./KuFlGr 906 4xHe-115, Ar-196 Luftwaffenbefehlshaber Mitte
1./	1./KGr 106 12xHe-115B/C Fliegerführer Ostsee Luftflotte 1	1./KuFlGr 406 12xHe-115B/C Luft.wa.kom. Kirkenes Luftflotte 5	1./KuFlGr 506 12xJu-88A Luftwaffenbefehlshaber Mitte	1./KGr 606 12xJu-88A (few Do-17Z) Fliegerführer Atlantik Luftflotte 3	1./KuFlGr 706 12xHe-115, Ar-196 Luftwaffenbefehlshaber Mitte	1./KGr 806 12xJu-88A Luftflotte 5	1./KuFlGr 906^ 12xHe-115B/C Fliegerführer Atlantik Luftflotte 3
2./	2./KGr 106 12xJu-88A Fliegerführer Atlantik Luftflotte 1	2./KuFlGr 406 12xBv-138B Fliegerführer Ostsee Luftflotte 1	2./KuFlGr 506 ^ 12xHe115B/C Fliegerführer Atlantik Luftflotte 3	2./KGr 606 12xJu-88A (few Do-17Z) Fliegerführer Atlantik Luftflotte 3		2./KGr 806 12xJu-88A Fliegerführer Ostsee Luftflotte 1	2./KuFlGr 906* 12xJu-88A Luftwaffenbefehlshaber Mitte
3./	3./KGr 106 12xJu-88A Fliegerführer Atlantik Luftflotte 3	3./KuFlGr 406* 12xDo-18D/G Luftflotte 5	3./KuFlGr 506** 12xHe-115 / Ju-88s Luftwaffenbefehlshaber Mitte	3./KGr 606 12xJu-88A (few Do-17Z) Fliegerführer Atlantik Luftflotte 3		3./KGr 806 12xJu-88A Fliegerführer Ostsee Luftflotte 1	3./KuFlGr 906 12xDo-18, He-115, BV-138 Luftflotte 5
	* Renamed KGr 106 ca 1st Feb. 1941.	* Started reequipping with BV-138s later in 1941.	* Renamed K.Gr 506 on 19th Oct. 1941. ^ Was redesignated 2./KuFlGr 906 on 6th Oct 1941. Conv to Ju-88s in Oct. and Nov. 1941. ** Had started converting to Ju-88s.	* Renamed K.Gr 606, ca Nov. 1939.		* Renamed KGr 806 ca 8th July 1940.	* Was redesignated 2./KuFlGr 506 on 6th Oct 1941. ^ 1./KuFlGr 906 was converted to He-111, and by Dec. 1941 was redesignated 8./KG 26.

Fliegerführer Ostsee
Fliegerführer Atlantik
Luftwaffenkommando Kirkenes and Luftflotte 5
Luftwaffenbefehlshaber Mitte

3) Luftwaffe Strengths on 21st June 1941

a. Luftwaffe Strength Available to Support Operation Barbarossa on 21st June 1941

From the preceding sections it is now possible to obtain a complete picture of the Luftwaffe strength available to support Operation Barbarossa in June and early July 1941. The forces available comprised those in Luftflotte 1, Luftflotte 2, Luftflotte 4, Luftflotte ObdL, and Luftwaffenkommando Kirkenes which was part of Luftflotte 5.[369] The result of adding together the forces in these commands are displayed in table Luft Total EF. The total aircraft obtained (as well as the general breakdown by type) is very close to most current reputable published sources.[370]

From this table we can see that the Luftwaffe had 3,297 combat aircraft available to support Operation Barbarossa on 21st June 1941. These consisted of 1,013 single engine fighters and fighter bombers, 207 twin engine fighter and fighter bombers (Bf 110s), 337 dive bombers, 949 twin engine bombers, 63 seaplanes and flying-boats, and 728 long and short range reconnaissance aircraft. An additional 617 non-combat aircraft were also committed in the East, made up of 238 smaller army cooperation/liaison aircraft and 379 larger transport aircraft.

In terms of readiness, approximately 2,522 combat aircraft (76%) were fully operational on 21st June 1941. This included 77% of single engine fighters and fighter bombers, 74% of twin engine fighter and fighter bombers, 70% of dive bombers, and 76% of twin engine bombers. The least ready aircraft type was transport aircraft with only 61% fully operational. This was probably due to the large numbers damaged during Operation Mercury (the airborne invasion of Crete) in May, and the fact that these aircraft were heavily used in late May and early June in transporting personnel and equipment eastwards in preparation for Operation Barbarossa.

***

---

[369] Jagdgruppe Kirkenes, with its 29 fighter aircraft, is excluded as this unit reported to Luftflotte 5.

[370] E.g., H. Boog, et al, German Research Institute for Military History at Potsdam, Germany and the Second World War-Volume IV, The Attack on the Soviet Union, Clarendon Press (Oxford University Press), New York, 1996, table I.IV.5, p. 364, indicates 3904 aircraft on 21st June 1941. This includes non-combat aircraft on the East Front.
C. Bergstrom, A. Mikhailov, Black Cross Red Star, The Air War Over the Eastern Front: Volume 1, Pacifica Military History, Pacifica, California, 2000, pp. 263-266, states there were 2,598 (1,939 serviceable) combat aircraft available, excluding aircraft in: Luftflotte 5 in Norway/Finland, transport units, army reconnaissance units, courier/liaison units, ambulance flights and air-sea rescue units. The same analysis from table Luft Total EF reveals 2,616 combat aircraft (1,959 serviceable).

Table Luft Total EF			
Luftwaffe Strength Supporting Operation Barbarossa on 21st June 1941			
Total Luftwaffe Forces, East Front, 21st June 1941.			
Unit Type	No. of Units	No. of Aircraft Available	Serviceable
Jagdgruppen	20	809	635
Erg.Guppen (JG,ZG)	7	190	122
Schlachtgruppen	1 1/3	60	54
Zerstörergruppen	2	78	51
Kampfgruppen	30	951	720
Stukagruppen	10	418	307
(Pz) Staffeln	17	163	140
(H) Staffeln	36	253	218
Luft (F) Staffeln	13	138	94
Heeres (F) Staffeln	15	146	111
KGr zbV	9	355	207
Wetterstaffeln	4	28	23
Seefliegerstaffeln	4	44	34
Seenotstaffeln	2	19	13
Kurierstaffeln/Verb. Staffeln	38	238	217
Sanitätsflugbereitschaften	4	24	23
		3,914	**2,969**
Number of Aircraft by type			
Single Engine Fighters		975	744
Twin Eng Fighters / Ftr Bmbrs		207	153
Twin Eng Night Fighters		0	0
Single Eng Fighter Bombers		38	37
Dive Bombers		337	236
Twin Engine Bombers		949	719
Four Engine Bombers		0	0
Long Range Recon*		312	228
SR Recon / Army Coop^		654	575
Seaplanes		63	47
Transport Aircraft		379	230
		3,914	**2,969**
* Includes Wetterstaffeln aircraft.			
^ Includes Courier, Liaison aircraft.			

Total Aircraft, East Front (all types)		3,914	2,969
Total Combat Aircraft, East Front *		**3,297**	**2,522**

* Excluding transport aircraft in KGr zbV and LLG Units, and courier/liaison and transport aircraft in Kurierstaffeln, Verbindungsstaffeln and Sanitätsflugbereitschaften.

© Nigel Askey, 2018

***

b. A Comparison of Luftwaffe Forces Supporting Operation Barbarossa and VVS Strengths in the Western Special Military Districts on 22nd June 1941

It is instructive to compare the invading Luftwaffe forces with the opposing VVS forces in the Soviet Western Military Districts on 22nd June 1941. From the Soviet FILARM model we know that the Soviet VVS KA (Army), VVS VMF (Naval) and PVO (Home Air Defence) Air Forces had 8,936 combat aircraft in the Western Military Districts on 22nd June 1941.[371] This force consisted of 5,490 fighters, 2,426 bombers, 227 ground attack (assault) aircraft, and 793 reconnaissance and army-cooperation aircraft.

The figures (above) **exclude** VVS-DBA (Long Range Bomber Aviation) forces, a very large proportion of which were also stationed in the Western Military Districts. On 22nd June 1941 the VVS-DBA forces in the Western Military Districts contained 1,515 combat aircraft (nearly all bombers), which included 1, 2, 3 and 4 BAK. Note, 5 BAK DBA (with 392 aircraft) was in the Far East at this time. Thus, when the Wehrmacht invaded the USSR on 22nd June 1941, the combined VVS forces immediately available to meet the invasion forces contained 10,451 combat aircraft. In addition to this force, there was approximately 8,300 combat aircraft assigned to VVS air-units in the Internal Military Districts and the Far Eastern Front on 22nd June 1941.[372]

Therefore, on the eve of Operation Barbarossa the VVS forces in the Western Military Districts enjoyed a numerical superiority of 3.2 to 1 in combat aircraft (10,451 vs 3,297). This included a huge fighter superiority of 4.6 to 1 (5,642 vs 1,220), and a similarly huge bomber superiority of 4 to 1 (3,783 vs 949). The Luftwaffe had a marginal superiority of 1.5 to 1 in ground attack/assault aircraft (337 vs 227); while the two sides were almost equal in numbers of reconnaissance aircraft and seaplanes (799 VVS vs 791 Luftwaffe). Given these numbers alone, it is remarkable that the Luftwaffe was able to conduct effective offensive operations at all without being annihilated, and even more remarkable that they rapidly established air superiority along most of the East Front. There are, of course, many reasons why this occurred which have little to do with the numerical disparity. These reasons included: the initial surprise attacks and initial deployment of the VVS forces, aircrew training and combat experience, efficient ground and logistical support (which enabled the Luftwaffe to maintain units at a higher state of readiness), effective command and control (especially in relation to **not** sending vulnerable bombers against heavily defended targets in broad daylight as the VVS-DBA repeatedly did), and lastly, the overall state of the respective air-force's aviation technology.

In all these categories the Luftwaffe enjoyed an advantage during 1941. However, during the course of researching this work it became apparent that in most pertain works it is the last factor (above) that is given overriding consideration. These works state or imply that the main reason the Luftwaffe was successful was that the VVS were forced to fly obsolete aircraft, and it was only in late 1941 that Luftwaffe fighters encountered significant numbers of 'modern' VVS fighters. As we now have the actual numbers on hand, it is worth examining this belief in more detail to at least get a qualification of this view. In the Soviet FILARM model there is a detailed analysis of the numbers and deployment of modern aircraft in the VVS on 1st June 1941, and comparisons are made with the invading Luftwaffe force.[373] This analysis indicates the following:

- On 1st June 1941 the VVS had approximately 1,860 modern single-engine (air superiority) fighters in service; namely LaGG-3s, MiG-1/3s and Yak-1s. This means it actually had almost 1.3 times more modern single-engine (air superiority) fighters in service than the Luftwaffe, which had approximately 1,450 Bf 109 and Fw 190 fighters and fighter-bombers in service.[374] More importantly, the VVS had more modern single-engine fighters in the Western Special Military Districts than the entire attacking Luftwaffe force (1,060 vs 1,013).[375] If we include the VVS forces in the Moscow Military District, then the number of modern VVS single-engine fighters rises to around 1,230, or almost 1.2 times the number in the attacking Luftwaffe force. This is significant because the large majority of the VVS's modern fighters, which were initially deployed outside the Western Special Military Districts, were thrown into the air battles over Smolensk in July 1941.

At the same time Luftflotte 1, 2 and 4 received very few air-unit reinforcements and only small numbers of replacement aircraft. Conversely, from June to December 1941 the Soviets manufactured or received 5,355 LaGG-3s, MiG-3s, Yak-1s, Yak-7s, Hurricane IIBs and P-40s, of which the majority reached VVS

[371] Refer Volume IIIB 3. 3) a. – 'The Soviet Air Forces in 1941 - The Soviet Aircraft Deployment Matrix - The Composition of the Soviet VVS KA, VVS VMF and PVO Air Forces on 22nd June 1941'.
[372] Ibid. There was also approximately 1,690 aircraft available to the VVS, but as yet unallocated (to air-combat units). They were still at factories, in depots, at test and research facilities, in transit or being rebuilt for units in rear areas.
[373] Refer Volume IIIB Part IV 8. 3) b. – 'The Soviet Air Forces in 1941 - The Soviet Aircraft Deployment Matrix - Numbers and Deployment of Modern Aircraft in the VVS on 22nd June 1941, and comparison to the Luftwaffe's invasion forces'.
[374] This includes all Bf 109Es used as fighter-bombers on the East Front.
[375] Ibid.

combat units (mainly in the central sector) before the end of the year.[376] This was far more aircraft than the Luftwaffe in the East received over the same period; and, to compound this, by December 1941 most of the fighters in II. Fliegerkorps/Luftflotte 2 had already transferred to the West. These numbers provide conclusive evidence that the Bf 109s extremely high kill to loss ratio during 1941 was not solely (or even primarily) due to it being up against the obsolete 1-15s or inferior I-16s (there were no Fw 190s in the East until late 1942). Although it was technologically superior, the main reason why the Bf 109 was able to maintain such a high kill to loss ratio against **all** VVS fighter types was the average Luftwaffe fighter pilot's more extensive training and experience, as well as the air-combat tactics they employed.

It is noteworthy that until late 1941, the average Luftwaffe fighter or dive-bomber pilot received around 13 months of relatively intense training (and selection) before they were assigned to any *Ergänzungseinheiten* (operational training units; one *Ergänzungsgruppe* was normally attached to each *Geschwader*). This included around 200 flying hours. The average Luftwaffe bomber or reconnaissance pilot received around 20 months training with 250-270 flying hours, before being assigned to their *Ergänzungseinheit*. It almost goes without saying that this initial training was far more extensive than any VVS pilot training, especially VVS pilots who joined after June 1941. Despite the Luftwaffe's 'extensive' training programme, the replacement system actually surpassed losses in 1941. On 21st June 1941 the Luftwaffe had 5,875 trained 'aircrews' and on 27th December 1941 this number had increased to 6,149.[377] Individual aircrew personnel losses in the East during this period amounted 3,010 killed, missing or captured (including 664 officers).[378]

- On 1st June 1941 the VVS had 366 modern ground attack (or assault) aircraft in the Western Special Military Districts; namely Su-2s, Il-2s and Ar 2s. Another 193 of these aircraft types were deployed near Kharkov and Moscow, and 40 were unallocated in reserve. In all, almost 600 modern assault and close support aircraft were in the western USSR (none were in the Far East), all of which were committed to the initial border battles or the Battle of Smolensk in July 1941. The entire Luftwaffe forces initially committed to Operation Barbarossa contained 337 dive bombers, including the redoubtable little Henschel Hs 123 biplanes (which were considerably less than 'modern').[379] If we include all Bf 110 fighter-bombers in all *Schnellkampfgeschwader* (High speed bomber) units and all Bf 110s in all *Sturzkampfgeschwader* (Dive bomber) units, this adds 103 twin engine fighter-bombers. Thus the Luftwaffe's total dedicated 'ground attack' or 'close support' force committed to Operation Barbarossa amounted to only 440 aircraft; a number considerably lower than the number of modern equivalent VVS aircraft committed to battle in June-July 1941.[380] The Luftwaffe definitely did not outnumber the VVS in modern 'ground attack' or 'close support' aircraft.

- On 1st June 1941 the VVS had 1,607 modern medium and heavy bombers in the Western Special Military Districts; namely DB-3/IL-4s, Pe-2s, TB-7s and Yak-2/4s.[381] This includes DBA forces deployed in the Western Military Districts (with 1,157 DB3/IL-4), which were used on the first day of the war and were immediately available to meet the German invasion. Very significantly, 72% of the VVS's modern bomber force in the Western Military Districts were DBA forces, and these were deployed on airfields to the rear and well away from the borders. These forces therefore emerged unscathed from the initial Luftwaffe onslaught on VVS airfields. Another 322 modern bombers were available in the Leningrad, Moscow, Kharkov and Orel Military Districts (including 151 DB-3 in DBA reserve units deployed within these districts). Thus at least 1,929 modern bombers were available to the VVS in the western USSR in June-early July 1941.

It is also very arguable that the SB-2bis, the most numerous bomber type in the VVS, should be classified as 'modern' because of its on-paper performance and the fact that the SB-2bis prototype had first flown in October 1936 (only three years before WWII started). This meant it was of the same vintage as many of the German bomber types (see below). However, for the sake of argument we will call the SB-2bis obsolescent in

---

[376] Refer Volume IIIB 3. 5) - 'Overall Soviet Combat Aircraft Usage, Production and Replacements (R): 22nd June to 31st December 1941'.

[377] H. Boog, et al, German Research Institute for Military History at Potsdam, Germany and the Second World War-Volume IV, The Attack on the Soviet Union, Clarendon Press (Oxford University Press), New York, 1996, pp. 818 and 819. Note, an 'aircrew' in this context can range from a fighter pilot to a complete bomber aircrew.

[378] Ibid, p. 818. This represented a fifth of aircrew losses since the start of the war in 1939. As the war wore on, the standard of Luftwaffe aircrew training progressively declined. By February 1945, most new German day-fighter pilots were being committed to combat with less than 20 hours of flying training! The primary reason for this was lack of fuel, which actually curtailed training flights during 1944-45 far more than lack of training or combat aircraft.

[379] Includes 42 Ju 87s from IV.(St)/LG 1 / Luftwaffenkommando Kirkenes / Luftflotte 5 in northern Norway.

[380] Even if we include all 104 Bf 110 heavy fighters from all other unit types and throw them in as potential fighter-bombers, the Luftwaffe still only had 544 possible 'ground attack' or 'close support' aircraft in the East on 22nd June 1941.

[381] The DB-3F version of the DB-3 went into production in 1940, and was soon designated the IL-4.

June 1941 for the purposes of this discussion. Conveniently for the VVS figures this immediately removes over 3,500 possible bombers from the VVS's 'modern bomber' tally.

The mainstay of the Luftwaffe's bomber fleet during Operation Barbarossa was made up of the He 111H (first flown in 1938), He 111P (first flown in 1937/38), Do 17Z (first flown in 1938) and the Ju 88A (first flown in 1936). If we assume that **all** German bombers involved in Operation Barbarossa were 'modern' (which is very debatable), then the entire Luftwaffe force that attacked the USSR on 22nd June 1941 contained 949 modern bombers.[382] If we include all the Luftwaffe's long range strategic reconnaissance (*Fernaufklärungsgruppe)* and weather observation (*Wekusta*) aircraft, which were usually derivatives of German twin engine bombers and fighter bombers, then the maximum possible number of modern Luftwaffe bombers comes to 1,261.[383] This is not totally unreasonable because the Luftwaffe often conducted armed long range reconnaissance missions where the reconnaissance aircraft attacked a target of opportunity in the enemy's deep rear.

Therefore, even after classifying well over half the VVS's bomber force as obsolete and including 312 German reconnaissance aircraft as 'bombers', the VVS forces in the Western USSR still outnumbered the Luftwaffe in modern bombers by over 1.5 to 1 in June 1941: that is 1,929 VVS bombers vs 1,261 Luftwaffe bombers and reconnaissance/bombers in the western USSR during June 1941.

***

The unavoidable conclusion from the above figures is that the main reason the Luftwaffe was successful in 1941 was definitely not solely (or even primarily) due to the VVS being forced to fly obsolete aircraft. In fact the VVS forces in the Western Special Military Districts fielded considerably more 'modern' combat aircraft than the Luftwaffe did in June and July 1941. In this context, 'modern' means at least of the same (development) vintage as the attacking German aircraft, and, in many cases, with as good or better on-paper performance. The fact that the VVS operated huge numbers of older aircraft should not obscure the fact that they simultaneously operated very large numbers of 'modern' aircraft.

The reasons why the VVS suffered such a catastrophic defeat in 1941 are much more complex than simple technology, and had much more to do with overall state of the VVS as an organisation. Essentially it suffered from the same debilitating pre-war conditions that afflicted the Red Army, and this is discussed further in the Soviet FILARM model.[384]

***

---

[382] Includes 22 Ju 88As from Stab II./KG 30, 5./KG30 and 6./KG30 / Luftwaffenkommando Kirkenes / Luftflotte 5 in northern Norway.
[383] Includes 312 long range strategic reconnaissance aircraft. This includes aircraft in all *Fernaufklärungsgruppen* and *Wekusta* (*Wetter-Erkundungs Staffeln*). Includes 7 Ju 88A/D from 1.(F)/124 and 4 Ju 88D/He 111H from *Wekusta* 5 in *Luftflotte* 5 in northern Norway.
[384] Refer Volume IIIB 3. 3) b. and 3. 5) a.

c. An Assessment of the Actual Luftwaffe Forces Available to Support German Ground Operations during Operation Barbarossa

When one reads Red Army officers' accounts of Red Army operations during Operation Barbarossa, it is striking how often German air support is credited with destroying and/or disrupting a particular defence line or attack formation. In many cases the impression is given that the failure of this or that Red Army ground assault was due to enemy air-attack, that no Red Army units could move in daylight without being attacked by dive-bombers, and that supply was almost always being severely disrupted. These reports are strikingly similar to those from the British and French Armies following the German invasion of France in May-June 1940, and those from the German Army following the Normandy campaign in June-July 1944 (the Allied Operation Overlord).

However, any objective analysis of the Luftwaffe strengths available to support Operation Barbarossa, along with some other pertinent facts, shows conclusively that it would have been **physically impossible for the Luftwaffe to have achieved the level of air interdiction or air support claimed by the Red Army in 1941.** This is a rather strong statement, so in order to illustrate this point we will briefly look at the 'air interdiction and ground support intensity' in the aforementioned campaigns. The results of this process are shown in the table below.

Aircraft Interdiction and Ground Support Intensity in Selected Campaigns					
Campaign	Nationality considered	Number of available bombers, ground attack aircraft & ftr-bombers*	Men to support per aircraft	Men to attack per aircraft	Front area in km2 to cover per aircraft
Western USSR, June-July 1941	German	1,427	2,354	2,320	488
France, May-June 1940	German	1,530	1,307	1,503	45
Normandy, June-July 1944	Allied	6,360	322	91	1
* Numbers at start of the campaign.					© Nigel Askey, 2014

For the French campaign (the German Operation Case Yellow - *Fall Gelb*) the Luftwaffe had 410 dive-bombers and 1,120 twin engine bombers available (out of a total of 3,385 combat aircraft).[385] This means that for Operation Barbarossa the Luftwaffe actually had around 100 fewer ground-attack aircraft, bombers and fighter-bombers than it had for Operation Fall Gelb over a year earlier. Operation Barbarossa may have been the largest land invasion in history, but from the German point of view it certainly wasn't the largest air invasion! This was primarily due to three factors: the Luftwaffe's loss of 961 dive-bombers and bombers over Britain from 10th July to 31st October 1940, the commitment of significant dive-bomber and bomber units to the Mediterranean theatre and in France, and the rather remarkable failure of the German aerospace industry to gear up for total war (which it didn't manage until 1943).[386] The Luftwaffe figure used in the table above for Operation Barbarossa also includes all Bf 109Es used as fighter-bombers, all Bf 110 fighter-bombers in all *Schnellkampfgeschwader* (High speed bomber) units, and all Bf 110s in all *Sturzkampfgeschwader* (Dive bomber) units. During the Battle of France it was still hoped that the Bf 110 would be able to perform in its designed role of long-range fighter (*Zerstörer*), but by June 1941 it had been largely relegated to the ground attack role.

The RAF and USAAF figures for Operation Overlord are, in comparison, nothing short of astonishing: the size of this force dwarfs the entire Luftwaffe during 1940/41 and for that matter at any time during WWII. For Operation Overlord the Allies assembled the Allied Expeditionary Air Force with the combined forces of the RAF 2nd Tactical Air Force, the US 9th Air Force, and large elements of RAF Fighter Command, RAF Bomber Command and the US 8th Air Force. Throughout most of the June to July 1944 period, the heavy bombers in RAF Bomber Command and the US 8th Air Force were mostly diverted from their strategic bombing campaigns against Germany to support the invasion of France. These bombers contributed to the pre-invasion interdiction attacks on all infrastructure in northern France, and were mostly responsible for the massive 'carpet bombing' operations (each involving 500 to 1000+ bombers) during the Normandy Campaign. Examples included Operation Goodwood, Operation Totalise, Operation Epsom and Operation Cobra. By June 1941 the RAF and USAAF forces supporting Overlord had 112 fighter-bomber squadrons (excluding another 113 fighter squadrons), 79 medium and light bomber squadrons, 233 heavy bomber squadrons, and at least another 63 squadrons of transport and reconnaissance aircraft.[387] In June 1944 this force contained at least 6,360 first-line bombers and ground-attack aircraft, out of a total

---

[385] Includes 640 long and short range reconnaissance aircraft. J. Ellis, WWII: A Statistical Survey, Facts On File Inc, New York, 1993, p. 238, table 28.

[386] Ibid, p. 259, table 61.

[387] S. Badsey, Normandy 1944, Osprey Military, Reed International Books Ltd, London, 1990, p. 21.

of more than 12,000 combat aircraft.[388] These figures are supported by the respective air-force strength returns for 1944: in December 1944 the RAF reported a strength of 8,395 front-line combat aircraft, while the US Army Air Force (alone) reported a strength of 19,892 first-line combat aircraft deployed overseas.[389]

The 'men to support' and 'men to attack' columns give an indication of the size of ground force the respective air-forces had to support and attack during a particular campaign. The manpower figures used are based on the peak manpower fielded during the campaign, except for Operation Barbarossa were the initial Red Army figure on 22nd June 1941 is used. For the Battle of France the Germans fielded close to 2,000,000 men in 117 divisions and support units, while the Allies (the French, British, Dutch, and Belgium Armies) fielded around 2,300,000 men in 136 divisions.[390] The Germans invaded the USSR with around 3,359,000 men (strength from 22nd June to 4th July 1941), while the Red Army in the Western Special Military Districts had around 3,310,000 personnel on 22nd June 1941.[391] The Allied Armies in Normandy grew to over 2,050,000 men, while the accumulated German strength in Normandy never exceeded 580,000 (contrary to many poorly researched accounts which still state the Wehrmacht had over 1,000,000 men in Normandy).[392]

The 'front area' column is to give an indication of the geographical area that the respective air-forces were forced to cover during a particular campaign. The relevant data is derived from the maps shown in the West Point Atlas for WWII.[393] The French campaign in May 1940 involved an area of approximately 69,000 square kilometres, Operation Barbarossa in June and July 1941 involved a massive front and an area in excess of 696,000 square kilometres, while the Battle for Normandy in June and July 1944 was fought in the relatively tiny area of around 7,000 square kilometres.

All this data is used in the table above, and reveals some startling results. Most obvious is the fact that the Luftwaffe forces fielded in support of Operation Barbarossa were relatively small by WWII standards, and were in fact minimal when one considers the magnitude of the task facing them. In 1941 the Luftwaffe was expected to support close to twice as many men per (ground attack) aircraft as during their French campaign, while the equivalent RAF and USAAF figure in Normandy was over seven times smaller. To put it another way: in the USSR a single Luftwaffe (ground attack) aircraft was available to support the equivalent of around a regiment, in France a single Luftwaffe aircraft was available to support the equivalent of say two battalions, while in Normandy a single Allied aircraft was available to support every company fielded.

In terms of targets (to be attacked), we find that in the USSR an average of around 2,300 Red Army soldiers (around a regiment) faced an enemy aircraft, in France an average of 1,500 Allied soldiers faced an enemy aircraft, while in Normandy an Allied (ground attack) aircraft was available to attack every 90 German soldiers! In other words, in order to achieve a similar level of air interdiction and air-support, each Luftwaffe (ground attack) aircraft in the USSR in June/July 1941 would have had to attack around 25 times more enemy soldiers than their counterparts in the RAF and USAAF during the Normandy campaign.

The final nail in the coffin of any argument that the Red Army suffered from unusually heavy air attacks is the geographic area concerned. In France the Luftwaffe's forward bases were for the most part concentrated in western Germany, and were within easy range of Holland, Belgium and northern France. Similarly, the RAF and USAAF bases were mostly in southern England and Normandy was just across the channel. Even fighters of the 1944 period were able to loiter around the battlefield looking for targets, while the fighter-bombers literally lined up in 'cab-rank' fashion and attacked targets whenever and wherever the Allied ground forces required. The Normandy battlefield was so small that it didn't take long for any area to be covered by air-support when needed. From the table we can see that in Normandy an Allied (ground attack) aircraft was literally available for every square kilometre of battlefield! Similarly, in France a Luftwaffe bomber or dive-bomber was available for almost every 45 square kilometres of battlefield.

[388] Ibid. Also J. Ellis, WWII: A Statistical Survey, Facts On File Inc, New York, 1993, pp. 231-243.

[389] J. Ellis, WWII: A Statistical Survey, Facts On File Inc, New York 1993, p. 231, table 17, and p. 242, table 42. This equates to around 28,300 combat aircraft of which around 5,000 were in the Mediterranean theatre (mainly Italy) and several thousand in the Pacific. Note, the US Navy and Marine Corps reported a strength of 13,065 combat aircraft in the Pacific theatre in December 1944 (which is in addition to the US Army Air Force strength).

[390] The German figures include their reserve of 42 infantry divisions. J. Delaney, The Blitzkrieg Campaigns, Caxton Editions, London, 2000, p. 76. Allied divisions included 94 French, 10 British, 10 Dutch and 22 Belgian divisions. A. Shepperd, France 1940, Osprey Military, Reed International Books Ltd, London, 1993, p. 13.

[391] Data from the German and Soviet FILARM models. Includes personnel in the Stavka Reserves deployed within the Western Special Military Districts on 22nd June 1941.

[392] N. Zetterling, Normandy 1944: German Military Organisation, Combat Power and Organisational Effectiveness, J.J. Fedorowicz Publishing Inc, Winnipeg, Canada, 2000, p. 31, diagram 4.1.

[393] The West Point Atlas for the Second World War: Europe and the Mediterranean, Ed. T.E. Griess, Square One Publishers Inc, New York, 2002, maps 11, 12, 13, 19, 58, 59 and 63.

The contrast to the situation facing the Luftwaffe in Operation Barbarossa could not be starker. In this case the Luftwaffe was deployed along a front stretching from the Baltic Sea to the Black Sea, a distance of over 1,450 kilometres. The thousands of additional square kilometres covered by Luftflotte 5 on the Norway-Finland-USSR border is ignored for this purpose. In addition the VVS and Red Army forces were deployed in depth; up to 480 kilometres to the east. The distances involved were so great that the various Luftflotte commands along the front were unable to effectively support each other, and as the front rapidly moved east the distances aircraft had to fly to reach their targets rapidly increased. This meant individual airbases had to disrupt their air operations to move forward, increased the overall flying time and wear and tear on aircraft, and limited the number of possible missions per day. From the table above we see that the average Luftwaffe (ground attack) aircraft during Operation Barbarossa had to 'cover' around 11 times as much area as in France in 1940, and a staggering 488 times as much area as an RAF or USAAF aircraft in Normandy.

On top of all this, the Luftwaffe bombers in Operation Barbarossa had to contend with neutralizing the largest air-force in the world in 1941 (the Soviet VVS which started with approximately 20,450 combat aircraft), before they could even think about serious ground support and interdiction attacks. This meant they were initially operating under conditions of air parity bordering on inferiority, and only later under conditions of air superiority. The Luftwaffe in France started in a similar situation, although it won air superiority fairly quickly (the Allies started the campaign with around 1,200 French, 600 British, and several hundred Dutch and Belgian combat aircraft).[394] In contrast, the RAF and USAAF started the Normandy campaign with complete air-supremacy over northern France (a condition never achieved by the Luftwaffe on the East Front): Luftflotte 3 had only 891 aircraft (including 315 day fighters and 64 transports) on 30th May 1944, of which 497 were serviceable.[395]

Lastly, it is again worth pointing out that **all** the German *Sturzkampfgeschwader* (Dive Bomber) units in the East on 22nd June 1941 were concentrated in Luftflotte 2, except for IV.(St)/LG 1 with 42 Ju 87s in *Luftwaffenkommando Kirkenes* (northern Norway). Even then, Luftflotte 2 had only 273 Ju 87 and 22 Hs 123A dive-bombers on 21st June 1941. This number is a very far cry from the 'hordes of Stuka's acting as flying artillery' impression obtained when reading accounts of Red Army battles in 1941, especially when one considers they were spread out over a 1,450km front line.

It gets worse. Luftflotte 4, attacking against the far stronger Red Army forces in the Kiev Special and Odessa Military Districts, initially had no dedicated ground attack aircraft at all. This meant that it had to use its already over-stretched and far less effective high level medium bombers in this role. And yet, many Red Army mechanised corps commanders in the Kiev Special Military District (Southwestern Front) reported "heavy tank losses due to air strikes" and "devastating enemy close air-support" in the huge tank battles across the Ukraine in June-July 1941.[396] The question is therefore; what possible aircraft were the Germans using to destroy Soviet tanks in Southwestern Front in June-July 1941? Bf 109 fighters, Ju 88s and He 111s were very poor to the point of useless in this role! This is all apart from the multitude of other tasks these aircraft were meant to be simultaneously doing.

In conclusion, it is therefore very hard to believe the many Red Army records for 1941 which repeatedly refer to attacks being 'spoiled' or 'broken up' or 'hindered', etc, by German air power. It seems much more probable that Red Army officers could explain away their own (and their army's) shortcomings by attributing them to enemy air power. If German air power was the main cause of defeat, then this was outside the realm of the Red Army and hence the responsibility for failure was not on their (the Red Army officers') shoulders. It should always be borne in mind that in 1940-41 any admission of failure by a Red Army officer, no matter how small, had potentially fatal consequences. This was very true in 1939-40 following Stalin's purges, and this fear continued to grip and hence debilitate all levels of command within the Red Army (and VVS) well into 1942.

It is of course equally arguable that German Army officers in Normandy could use the same 'excuse' regarding Allied air power in the summer of 1944. However, as we have seen from the data presented here, it was unusual for the average Red Army soldier to even see a German bomber during 1941; while it is remarkable that the German ground forces in Normandy weren't simply obliterated by Allied airpower alone in a matter of weeks.

*****

[394] A. Shepperd, France 1940, Osprey Military, Reed International Books Ltd, London, 1993, p. 15.

[395] S. Badsey, Normandy 1944, Osprey Military, Reed International Books Ltd, London, 1990, p. 17.

[396] E.g., D.M. Glantz, Barbarossa, Hitler's Invasion of Russia 1941, Tempus Publishing, Stroud, Gloucestershire, 2001. Also, B.I. Fugate, Operation Barbarossa, Presidio Press, Novato, CA, 1984. Also, C. Pleshakov, Stalin's Folly, Houghton Mifflin Company, New York, 2005.

d. Overall Luftwaffe Strength on 21st June 1941

The total Luftwaffe strength in 21st June 1941 is shown in table <u>Luft Total</u>. This includes all aircraft in Luftflotte 1, Luftflotte 2, Luftflotte 3, Luftflotte 4, Luftflotte 5, X. Fliegerkorps, Luftwaffenbefehlshaber Mitte and Luftflotte ObdL. The following aircraft are not included in this table.

- Training aircraft, particularly the large number available for pilot training; most commonly the Arado Ar 96 advanced trainer.[397] Other types which became important training aircraft were the Ar 68, Ar 76, Bu 131 (*Jungmann*), Bu 133 (*Jungmeister*), Bu 181 (*Bestmann*), Fw 44 (*Stieglitz*), Fw 56 (*Stosser*), Fw 58 (*Weihe*), Go 145, Kl 35 and Bf 108.

- Combat aircraft in most *Ergänzungsgruppen* (Erg or ErgGr – Replacement/training aviation groups). Some Erg groups **are** included because on 21st June 1941 a number of these units were classified as operational in the Luftwaffe's order of battle, and capable of conducting combat operations. These were nearly always fighter *Ergänzungsgruppen* (Erg./JG or Erg./ZG). The specific units included are: Erg./JG 3, Erg./JG 27, Erg./JG 51, Erg./JG 52, Erg./JG 54, Erg./JG 77 and Erg./ZG 26 deployed on the East Front, and Erg./JG 2, Erg./JG 26 and Erg./JG 53 deployed in the West. All these units were equipped with Bf 109E and Fs, or Bf 110s.

- Additional liaison and/or transport aircraft in additional *Flugbereitschaften* (Duty on-call flights). These were usually small ad hoc units formed in order to meet the courier and communication needs of some HQs. They were usually formed if a HQ did not have an assigned *Stabskette* or *Stabsschwarm*. If it did, then the aircraft in these units were incorporated into the *Flugbereitschafte* for that HQ.

- Aircraft in other support organisations, such as the: *Fliegerforstschützverband*, *Luftzeuggruppen*, *Luftzeugamter*, *Flugzeuguberfuhrungsgeschwader Gruppen* and *Kommandos* (aircraft ferrying to front line units and other areas), and *Luftdienst* (air target towing).

***

From this table we can see that the Luftwaffe had a total of 4,948 combat aircraft available on 21st June 1941. These consisted of 1,454 single engine fighters and fighter bombers, 282 twin engine fighters and fighter bombers (Bf 110s), 196 twin engine night-fighters, 422 dive bombers, 1,503 twin engine bombers, 25 four engine bombers, 244 seaplanes, and 822 long and short range reconnaissance aircraft. There were an additional 934 non-combat aircraft in KGr zbV, LLG, *Kurierstaffeln*, *Verbindungsstaffeln* and *Sanitätsflugbereitschaften* units which are also shown. The total aircraft obtained (as well as the general breakdown by type) is very close to most current reputable sources.[398]

In terms of readiness, approximately 3,567 combat aircraft (72%) were operational on 21st June 1941. This included 76% of single engine fighters and fighter bombers, 72% of twin engine fighters and fighter bombers, 72% of night fighters, 71% of dive bombers, and 66% of twin and four engine bombers. The least ready aircraft type was transport aircraft with only 58% fully operational. This was probably due to the large numbers damaged during Operation Mercury (the airborne invasion of Crete) in May, and the fact that these aircraft were heavily used in late May and early June in moving units eastwards in preparation for Operation Barbarossa.

Table <u>Luft Total</u> also shows that, even at the start of Operation Barbarossa, considerable Luftwaffe forces remained in the West. In total around 33% (one third) of all available combat aircraft remained in the West (including in the Mediterranean theatre). These forces included 31% of all single engine fighters, 27% of twin engine fighters and fighter bombers, 100% of night fighters, 20% of dive bombers, 37% of twin engine bombers, 100% of four engine bombers, 74% of seaplanes, 18% of long range reconnaissance aircraft, 10% of short range/army cooperation aircraft, and 42% of transport aircraft.

The importance that the German Army attached to aerial reconnaissance and army cooperation/liaison is obvious from these figures, with relatively few reconnaissance units of any type remaining in the West. Probably the most striking figure here is the 20% of dive bombers (one fifth) which remained in the West. This is a high figure considering the importance of this aircraft type in providing close air-support, and considering that Luftflotte 1 and 4 in the East had no close-air support aircraft at all. Unfortunately for the Germans the Ju 87 (Stuka) was also their best

---

[397] The large number of 11,546 Ar 96s were produced pre-war and during WWII, as the standard Luftwaffe two seat primary and advanced training aircraft. S. Wilson, Aircraft of WWII, Aerospace Publications Ltd, Fyshwick, Australia, 1998, p. 13.
[398] For example, H. Boog, et al, German Research Institute for Military History at Potsdam, Germany and the Second World War- Volume IV, The Attack on the Soviet Union, Clarendon Press (Oxford University Press), New York, 1996, p. 817, states there were 5,570 front-line aircraft (including transports) in the Luftwaffe on 22nd June 1941, of which 3,812 were operational. However, their figures are also not entirely consistent: on pp. 364 and 372, it is shown in tables that there were 5,680 front-line aircraft (including transports) in the Luftwaffe on 22nd June 1941, of which at least 3,977 were operational.

aircraft for sinking enemy ships in 1941. As a result, all the Stukas that remained in the West were deployed in the Mediterranean theatre attacking allied naval supply convoys as well as supporting Rommel's DAK.

***

Table Luft Total
Overall Luftwaffe Strength on 21st June 1941
Total Luftwaffe Forces, all Fronts, 21st June 1941

Unit Type	No. of Units	No. of Aircraft Available	Serviceable	Percentage Operational	Percentage on the East Front
Nacht-Jagdgruppen	5 1/3	207	150	72%	0%
Jagdgruppen	30 2/3	1,191	916	77%	68%
Erg.Guppen (JG,ZG)	10	238	154	65%	80%
Schlachtgruppen	1 1/3	60	54	90%	100%
Zerstörergruppen	4 1/3	149	101	68%	52%
Kampfgruppen*^	49	1,510	990	66%	63%
Stukagruppen (+)^^	13	507	371	73%	82%
(Pz) Staffeln	17	163	140	86%	100%
(H) Staffeln	39	279	241	86%	91%
Luft (F) Staffeln	19	189	130	69%	73%
Heeres (F) Staffeln	15	146	111	76%	100%
KGr zbV (and LLG)**	17 1/3	567	309	54%	63%
Wetterstaffeln	7	45	36	80%	62%
Seefliegerstaffeln	18	184	126	68%	24%
Seenotstaffeln	9	80	47	59%	24%
Kurierstaffeln/Verb. Staffeln	46 1/3	315	272	86%	76%
Sanitätsflugbereitschaften	9	52	46	88%	46%
		5,882	4,194		
Number of Aircraft by type					
Single Engine Fighters		1,416	1,066	75%	69%
Twin Eng Fighters / Ftr Bmbrs		282	203	72%	73%
Twin Eng Night Fighters		196	141	72%	0%
Single Eng Fighter Bombers		38	37	97%	100%
Dive Bombers		422	300	71%	80%
Twin Engine Bombers		1,503	997	66%	63%
Four Engine Bombers		25	4	16%	0%
Long Range Recon*		380	277	73%	82%
SR Recon /Army Coop^		724	629	87%	90%
Seaplanes		244	161	66%	26%
Transport Aircraft***		652	379	58%	58%
Total		5,882	4,194	71%	67%
Total number of Combat Aircraft^*	**4,948**	**3,567**	**72%**	**67%**

* Includes aircraft in Wetterstaffeln.
^ Includes courier/liaison aircraft.
** Includes Luftlandegeschwader (Air Landing - LLG).
*^ Includes Küstenfliegergruppen (Coastal aviation - KuFlGr) with Ju-88s.
^^ Includes Schnellkampfgeschwader 210 (SKG 210).
^* Excluding transport aircraft in KGr zbV and LLG Units, and courier/liaison and transport aircraft in Kurierstaffeln (including Verbindungsstaffeln) and Sanitätsflugbereitschaften.
*** Includes Sanitätsflugbereitschaften aircraft.
© Nigel Askey, 2018

***

4) Luftwaffe Air Combat Unit Reinforcements: June to December 1941

In this section we will examine the movements of Luftwaffe air combat units deployed on 21st June 1941 (i.e. Deployed (D)) between the western fronts and the Eastern Front, and vice versa, as well as units that were newly mobilised from June to December 1941. Newly mobilised units include new formations as well as units formed after 22nd June 1941 from existing training units.

Information in the following sections is based primarily on individual unit histories at the *Geschwader Gruppen*, and sometimes *Staffeln,* level. The following sections concentrate on the numbers of combat aircraft, and no effort is made to correlate these numbers with available and trained aircrew. However the Luftwaffe maintained a very high standard of aircrew training throughout the 1939-1942 period and before losses outstripped adequately trained replacements.[399] It is therefore reasonable to assume that most of the Luftwaffe units that transferred east had experienced and trained aircrew, including the relatively few newly mobilised units. It should be noted here that this was **not** the situation in the opposing VVS forces during 1941. In their case the pre-war air units that transferred from the eastern USSR probably had experienced and trained aircrew, but the much larger number of newly mobilised VVS air units had inadequately trained aircrew at best. This was primarily due to the VVS's debacle in the Western Military Districts in June-August 1941, which resulted in huge losses amongst experienced aircrew (especially bomber aircrew) during this period.

a. The Transfer of Deployed (D) and Newly Mobilised Air Combat Units to the Eastern Front: June to December 1941

Tables <u>Luft Rein 1</u> and <u>Luft Rein 2</u> show the air unit reinforcements for Luftflotte 1, 2, 4 and Luftwaffenkommando Kirkenes, from June/July 1941 to December 1941. The units which were Deployed (D) in the West and later transferred to the Eastern Front are shown in normal type, while the units which were newly mobilised after 22nd June 1941 and which then transferred to the East Front are **highlighted in bold**. Footnotes for each unit provide additional information. In many cases the unit's exact strength and readiness when it transferred the East Front is unknown. In these cases the strength on 21st June 1941 is used, and it is assumed the unit was in a heightened state of readiness. This is not an unreasonable assumption because most Luftwaffe units in the West were maintained at an average state of readiness during 1941-42 (averaging around 60% operational for bomber groups and 70% for fighter groups). In addition most of the units transferred to the East were withdrawn from combat operations for a short period prior to being transferred (at least in 1941).

From tables <u>Luft Rein 1</u> and <u>Luft Rein 2</u> we can see that the Luftwaffe never transferred units to the East Front in earnest during the second half of 1941, with the possible exception of transport aircraft in December 1941. Starting in July 1941, only 115, 134, 177, 73, none and 160 aircraft arrived in reinforcing units in each consecutive month until December 1941. This amounts to a total of 659 aircraft, of which over half were non-combat aircraft. It included 62 fighters, 246 twin engine bombers, 9 reconnaissance aircraft and 342 transport aircraft. The only fighter units transferred East were the I./JG 52 (from Jagdfliegerführer 2 in France) and the newly mobilised *Staffeln* 15 (Span)./JG 27 and 15 (Kroat)./JG 52. Both of the latter used pilots and other personnel from Spain and Croatia, and were equipped with older Bf 109Es. Considerably more bomber units transferred east than fighter units. These mainly came from Luftflotte 3 (in France) as it wound down its night bombing campaign against Britain almost completely. The units transferred included the bulk of KG 4, and parts of KG 26 (6./KG 26 came from the Mediterranean) and KG 28. Smaller bomber units transferred east included the crack KGr 100 'Pathfinders' and KuFlGr 506 (KGr 506).

The long range reconnaissance units 'transferred east' came from three *Fernaufklärungsgruppe Staffeln*, initially reporting to Luftflotte ObdL on 22nd June 1941. These were 1.(F)/ObdL, 3.(F)/ObdL and 4.(F)/ObdL. These units are tricky to handle in the FILARM model because they were officially under the control of the Luftflotte ObdL, but the bulk of their operations were certainly conducted over the East Front for most of 1941. They did however also conduct secret missions over Britain and in the Mediterranean theatre. For this reason their aircraft strengths on 21st June 1941 are already included in the total Luftwaffe strength available to support Operation Barbarossa.[400] However, in order to bolster the reconnaissance forces in the East, these rather elite units came under the control of various Luftwaffe commands on the East Front during 1941. For example, 1.(F)/ObdL reported to Luftflotte 2 and 3.(F)/ObdL reported to Luftflotte 4/IV. Fliegerkorps by early August 1941.[401]

---

[399] On 27th December 1941 the Luftwaffe had 6,149 front-line aircrews and an actual strength of 5,167 front-line aircraft. This was 274 more aircrews than on 21st June 1941. H. Boog, et al, German Research Institute for Military history at Potsdam, Germany and the Second World War, Volume IV, Clarendon Press (Oxford University Press), New York, 1996, p. 819.

[400] Refer Volume IIB 5. 3) a. – 'Luftwaffe Strength Available to Support Operation Barbarossa on 21st June 1941'.

[401] H. Boog, et al, German Research Institute for Military history at Potsdam, Germany and the Second World War, Volume IV: The Attack on the Soviet Union. Clarendon Press (Oxford University Press), New York, 1996, table II.I.2, p. 772.

Table Luft Rein 1 — Air Unit Reinforcements for Luftflotte 1, 2, 4 and Luftwaffenkommando Kirkenes; from June/July to September 1941

Category	July Description	July No x Type/Auth	July Av	July Sv	August Description	August No x Type/Auth	August Av	August Sv	September Description	September No x Type/Auth	September Av	September Sv
JG (Jagdgeschwader) Fighter.									15 (Span)./JG 27^^	12xBf-109E	12	12
									I./JG 52^^	40xBf-109F	38	36
KG (Kampfgeschwader) Bomber.	III./KG 26**	40xHe-111H	30	26	Stab/KG 4*	4xHe-111H	3	3	6./KG 26***	12xHe-111H-6	12	11
	Stab/KG 28*^	4xHe-111H	3	3	I./KG 4*	40xHe-111H	29	23				
	I./KG 28*^	40xHe-111H	31	30	III./KG 4*	40xHe-111H	25	22				
	KGr 100***	40xHe-111H-3	36 (17 new)	34								
	4./KG30^^	12xJu-88A	9	5								
H (Heeresaufklärungsgruppe) Short Range Tactical Reconnaissance.									1.(H)/14*^^	12xHs-126	9 (4 new)	8
F (Fernaufklärungsgruppe) Long Range Strategic Reconnaissance.	1.(F)/Ob.d.L*	12xJu-88D, Do-215B	Already op in the East									
	3.(F)/Ob.d.L^	12xJu-88D, Do-215B	Already op in the East									
KGr zbV (Kampfgeschwader zu besonderen Verwendung) Transport.					II./KG zbV 1^^	53xJu-52	39	36	I./KGr zbV 172 *	53xJu-52	44	35
					I./KG zbV 1*^	53xJu-52	38 (11 new)	35	I./LLG 1^	22xJu-52, 36xDFS-230/Go-242	19 (8 new), 30	17, 30
									6./LLG 1**^	6xJu-52, 12xDFS-230/Go-242	5, 10	5, 10
KuFlGr (Küstenfliegergruppe) Coastal Aviation.	1./KGr 806**^	12xJu-88A	6	6					KuFlGr 506** (KGr 506)	40xJu-88A	38 (18 new)	36
(Sanitätsflugbereitschaft) Ambulance Flight.												

July notes:

* Also had Bf-110Es. Officially attached to Luftflotte 2.
^ Officially attached to Luftflotte 4, IV. Fliegerkorps.
** I./KG 26 transferred to Brest-Litovsk 20th July 41. It moved to Bobruisk in August-September 41. III./KG 26 was redesignated II./KG 100 on 15th Dec 41, but it was reformed on the same date from I./KG 28. The new 8./KG 26 was formed from 1./Ku.Fl.Gr 906.
*^ Stab./KG 28 and I./KG 28 transferred to Luftflotte 2 II Fliegerkorps, 20th July to 2nd Aug 1941. Stab./KG 28 and I./KG 28 were redesignated Stab./KG 26 and I./KG 26 (respectively) on 15th Dec. 1941. 1./KG28 (one *Staffel*) was detached to X. Fliegerkorps (based Athens-Kalamaki), and equipped with aerial torpedoes), by 28th Nov. 1941.
*** KGr 100 was redesignated I./KG 100 on 15th Dec. 41.
^^ 4./KG 30 reinforced 'Luftwaffenkommando Kirkenes' in late June 1941 (mov from Stavanger, Nor)
**^ 1./KGr 806 (ex 1./KuFlGr 806) transferred from Marvi/Finland to Riga with KGr 806. However, it conducted combat operations in the East from 22nd June 1941.

August notes:

* Attached to Luftflotte 2. III./KG 4 (deployed in the West on 22/6/41) was withdrawn on 6th Dec. 1941 for rest and refit.
*^ Attached to Luftflotte 4.
^^ Attached to Luftflotte 2, II. Fliegerkorps.

September notes:

* Attached to Luftflotte 1.
** Includes Stab./KuFlGr 506, 1./KuFlGr 506, 3./KuFlGr 506 and 2./KuFlGr 906 (Ju-88s). 2./KuFlGr 906 was redesignated 2./KuFlGr 506 on 6th Oct. 1941. Transferred to Luftflotte 1, Fl. Fu. Ostsee, by 21st Sep. 41, based at Riga. Had returned to Westerland by 18th Oct 1941. Was redesignated K.Gr 506 on 19th Oct 1941.
^ Gruppe I, Luftlandegeschwader, (Air Landing). Attached to Luftflotte 2, VIII. Fliegerkorps.
^^ Attached to Luftflotte 2, VIII Fliegerkorps, Stab./JG 27. 1./JG 52 based at Ponjatowka from 27th Sep. 1941. 15 (Span)./JG 27 based at Moschna from 24th Sep. 1941.
*^ Attached to Luftflotte 4, V. Fliegerkorps, under Stab./KG 54.
*** Based at Buzau/Rumania and then at Focsani, and then Saki /Crimea. 6./KG 26 was equipped with He-111H-6 torpedo bombers.
**^ 6./LLG 1 based at Dunaburg, used in attack on Osel.
*^^ 1.(H)/14 based near Grodno.

Table Luft Rein 2 — Air Unit Reinforcements for Luftflotte 1, 2, 4 and Luftwaffenkommando Kirkenes; from October to December 1941

	October			December			
	Description	No x Type/Auth	Av	Sv	Description	No x Type/Auth	Av	Sv
JG (Jagdgeschwader) Fighter.	15 (Kroat)./JG 52 ^^	12xBf-109E	12	11				
KG (Kampfgeschwader) Bomber.					II./KG 30*	40xJu-88A	Already Deployed	
					10./KG 3 (Kroat)^	12xDo-17Z (using 2nd hand a/c)^	12^	10
					KG 100***	Redesignated Gruppen	Already Deployed	
					IV.(Erg)/KG 100***^	24xHe-111H-3	24	18
H (Heeresaufklärungsgruppe) Short Range Tactical Reconnaissance.								
F (Fernaufklärungsgruppe) Long Range Strategic Reconnaissance.					4.(F)/Ob.d.L.	26xJu-88,Ju-86P,Do-215,He-111	Already op in the East	
					3.(F)/33	12xJu-88A/D	Already op in the East	
KGr zbV (Kampfgeschwader zu besonderen Verwendung) Transport.	LGL 1 *	6xMe-321, 12xMe110	6,9	6,8	KGr zbV 600**	53xJu-52	28	25
	LGL 2, 22 ^	12xMe-321, 24xMe110	12,18	11,16	KGr zbV 700***	53xJu-52	25	23
	LGL 4 **	6xMe-321, 12xMe110	6,10	6,9	KGr zbV 800*^	53xJu-52	29	26
					KGr zbV 900**^	53xJu-52	24	22
					KGr zbV 999^^	53xJu-52	24	23
KuFlGr (Küstenfliegergruppe) Coastal Aviation.								
(Sanitätsflugbereitschaft) Ambulance Flight.					Sanitätsflugbereitschaft 1	6xJu-52	6	6

Total Aircraft Used in Reinforcing Air Combat Units, from July to December 1941 *

Single Engine Fighters	62
Twin Eng Fighters / Ftr	0
Twin Eng Night Fighter	0
Single Eng Fighter Bom	0
Dive Bombers	0
Twin Engine Bombers	246
Four Engine Bombers	0
Long Range Recon	0
SR Recon /Army Coop	9
Seaplanes	0
Transport Aircraft	342
	659

* Comprised:
362 aircraft in Deployed (D) air combat units which subsequently transferred to the East Front.
58 new aircraft received as Replacements (R) by Deployed (D) units prior to the latter's transfer to the East Front.
239 new aircraft in newly Mobilised and Deployed (MD) air combat units. Note, total numbers exclude the Do-17Z handed over to 10./KG 3 (Kroat) from III./KG3 (already in the East).

October notes:
* Grossraumlastenseglerstaffel 1, (Special Large Glider Staffel 1). Attached to Luftflotte 1. Normally 3x110s are required to tow 1 Me-321. Possibly also had some Go 242 gliders on strength.
^ Grossraumlastenseglerstaffel 2, 22, (Special Large Glider Staffel 2, 22), Attached to Luftflotte 2. Possibly also had some Go 242 gliders on strength.
** Grossraumlastenseglerstaffel 4, (Special Large Glider Staffel 4), Attached to Luftflotte 4. Possibly also had some Go 242 gliders on strength.
^^ Attached to Luftflotte 4, V. Fliegerkorps. 15 (Kroat)./JG 52 based at Poltava from 10th Oct 1941.

December notes:
* II./KG30 already on East Front (dispersed in Luftflotte 5 in Finland/N Norway). However it moved South in December 41, VIII. Fliegerkorps, based at Orscha by 22nd Dec. 41. 4./KG 30 in transit arriving later.
^ Luftwaffe unit, attached to Luftflotte 1, Nahkampfführer 2, (Close Support Leader 2). Absorbed into 15./(Kroat)/KG 3 in 1943 (after a short re-training period). In Dec. 1941, received left over Do-17Z from III./KG3 (which conv to Ju-88s).
** Formed 17th Dec. 41. Based near Orscha.
*^ Formed 17th Dec. 41. Based near Vitebsk.
^^ Formed 17th Dec. 41. Based near Pleskau.
*** Note. KG 100 'Wiking' is sometimes stated to have arrived in Dec. 1941 with 3 "New" Gruppen. However, 2 of the Gruppen were simply renamed units on the East Front. The newly mobilising Stab remained in the West in 1941. Stab KG 100 (new), was mobilised on 29th Nov. 41, at Chartres (comp Apr. 1942). KGr 100 (already in the East), was redesignated I./KG 100 on 15th Dec. 41. III./KG 26 (already in the East), was redesignated II./KG 100 on 15th Dec. 41. III./KG 100 was not mobilised until 20th Sep. 1942.
***^ Mobilised on 29th Nov. 1941 with 10.(Erg) and 11.(Erg)/KG 100 (using Erg Staffel). It was used to airlift supplies from Latvia into the Demyansk and Kholm 'pockets' in Dec 1941.

The air-transport units transferred east from July to December 1941, and which contained over half the total aircraft transferred east in reinforcing units during this period (i.e. excluding Replacement aircraft (R) to existing units), arrived in two main waves and from two sources. They were mainly units initially deployed in X. Fliegerkorps in the Mediterranean theatre and new units which were mobilised in December 1941. The disproportionately high number of transport aircraft in X. Fliegerkorps on 21st June 1941 was due to the recently completed airborne invasion of Crete (Operation Mercury). Most of these air-transport units were recovering and preparing to be transferred to the East Front, which they did in the following months.

The second wave of air-transport units occurred in December after the OKW and Hitler belatedly realised the seriousness of the winter supply situation on the East Front.[402] This was especially ironic because only a month earlier Hitler had, remarkably, ordered major air assets away from the East Front to the Mediterranean (see next section). The 'new' KGr zbV units were created by taking the last Ju 52s from the chief of training and by the plundering of any 'spare' Ju 52s in commands and staffs. All these units were officially mobilised on 17th December 1941 and hurriedly dispatched to the East Front (mainly supporting Army Group Centre).

***

---

[402] H. Boog, et al, German Research Institute for Military history at Potsdam, Germany and the Second World War, Volume IV: The Attack on the Soviet Union. Clarendon Press (Oxford University Press), New York, 1996, table II.I.2, p. 798.

b. The Transfer of Deployed (D) Air Combat Units from the Eastern Front to the West: June to December 1941

It is unclear when exactly Hitler made the (very poor strategic) decision to withdraw major air assets away from the East Front, but Luftflotte 2 (along with the bulk of its II. Fliegerkorps) were already in the process of redeploying to the Mediterranean theatre by November 1941.[403] What made this decision so extraordinary is that it was made while Operation Typhoon (the strategically vital assault by Army Group Centre towards Moscow) was at a critical phase and was still nowhere near complete.

The decision appears to have been made (or at least implemented) immediately after the closure of the massive Vyazma and Bryansk pockets in late October 1941: the size of this success (with around 658,000 POWs) possibly reassuring Hitler that Moscow's fall would soon inevitably follow. This does, however, fit the pattern of extraordinarily bad strategic decisions made after July 1941. As discussed in previous chapters, these included: the failure to allow Army Group Centre to advance on Moscow in August-September, the failure to mobilise new infantry divisions (and even prematurely disband some), and the failure to send available tank Replacements (R) to the panzer divisions in the East.[404]

The principal Luftwaffe air combat units withdrawn from the East Front during the second half of 1941 are shown in table Luft Tran (over page).[405] The notes below this table provide additional information on timing, destination and reorganisation (refitting) of important units (mainly the bomber and dive-bomber/ground attack units). The units highlighted in grey (in the notes) returned to the East Front before the end of 1941: these units are **not** included in table Luft Tran.

Some of these units were withdrawn to re-equip with more modern aircraft types. For example, Stab./KG2, I./KG2 and III./KG2 spent the rest of 1941 re-equipping and training on the much improved Do 217E. However, the majority of the units withdrawn from the East Front were fully operational and were soon in action in the West. For example, the following units were transferred straight to the Mediterranean area and almost immediately initiated combat operations against Allied forces in this theatre.[406]

Luftwaffe Air Units Sent from the East Front directly to the Mediterranean Theatre: November-December 1941	
Unit	**Notes**
Luftflotte 2	HQ established in Sicily by January 1942.
II. Fliegerkorps	Sent to Sicily and southern Italy.
II/JG3	Southern Italy.
Stab., II. and III./JG27	Joined I./JG 27 in Libya-Egypt.
Stab., I., II. and III./JG53	Stab., I. & II./JG53 Sicily. 1./JG53 Greece & Crete.
Stab. and I./KG54,	Sent to Sicily.
Stab., II. and III./KG77	Sent to Sicily.
KGr 806 (ex KuFlGr 806)	Sent to Sicily.
LG1	Sent to southern Italy.
1.(F)/122	Sent to Sicily.
Wekusta 26	Sent to Sicily.

By mid-January 1942 Luftflotte 2 was well established in Sicily and commanded by Generalfeldmarschall Albert Kesselring. It now controlled II Fliegerkorps, X Fliegerkorps and Fliegerführer Afrika, and had orders to focus on supporting the DAK, cover the supply routes to North Africa and renew operations against Malta.

---

[403] H. Boog, et al, German Research Institute for Military history at Potsdam, Germany and the Second World War, Volume IV: The Attack on the Soviet Union. Clarendon Press (Oxford University Press), New York, 1996, table II.I.2, p. 795.
[404] Refer Volume IIB 4. 2) – 'German Land Combat Units Mobilised from 22nd June to 31st December 1941'.
Also, Volume IIB 4. 7) c. - 'Replacements (R) Actually Issued to the German Ground Forces on the East Front During 1941'.
[405] H. Boog, et al, German Research Institute for Military history at Potsdam, Germany and the Second World War, Volume IV: The Attack on the Soviet Union. Clarendon Press (Oxford University Press), New York, 1996, tables II.I.2, II.I.3 and II.I.4, pp. 772-797, and p. 801. Also, J. R. Smith, E. J. Creek, Kampfflieger: Bombers of the Luftwaffe July 1940-December 1941, Classic-Ian Allan Publishing, Hersham UK, 2004, p. 165.
[406] In addition, KGr 606 (ex KuFlGr 606) had transferred from Fliegerführer Atlantik (in France) to Luftflotte 2 in Sicily by early December 1941, equipped with Ju 88s.

Table Luft Tran

Principal Luftwaffe Air Combat Units withdrawn from the East Front, August-December 1941.*

Luftflotte 2

II. Fliegerkorps

Fighter Units

Description	No x Type/Auth
Stab/JG 53	4xBf-109F
I./JG 53	40xBf-109F
II./JG 53	40xBf-109F
III./JG 53	40xBf-109F
II./JG 54	40xBf-109F
Stab/JG 27	4xBf-109E/F
II./JG 27	40xBf-109E/F
III./JG 27	40xBf-109E/F
Stab/JG 3	4xBf-109F
I./JG 3	40xBf-109F
II./JG 3	40xBf-109F
III./JG 3	40xBf-109F
Stab/ZG 26	4xBf-110C/E
I./ZG 26	40xBf-110C/E
II./JG 77	40xBf-109E/F

Bomber Units

Description	No x Type/Auth
Stab/KG 77	4xJu-88A
I./KG 77	40xJu-88A
II./KG 77	40xJu-88A
III./KG 77	40xJu-88A
KGr 806	40xJu-88A
Stab/KG 3	6xDo-17Z, 4xJu-88A
I./KG 3	40xJu-88A
III./KG 3	40xJu-88A
I./KG 53	40xHe-111H
Stab/KG 2	4xDo-17Z
I./KG 2	40xDo-17Z
III./KG 2	40xDo-17Z
II./KG 27	40xHe-111H
1./KG 28	12xHe-111H
Stab/KG 54	4xJu-88A
I./KG 54	40xJu-88A
II./KG 54	40xJu-88A
Stab/KG 55	4xHe-111H
I./KG 55	40xHe-111H
II./KG 55	40xHe-111H
III./KG 55	40xHe-111H
III./KG 4	40xHe-111H
KuFlGr 506 (KGr 506)	40xJu-88A
Aufkl.Gr 125 (S)	40xHe-114/Bv-138/Ar-95A
1. and 2./KGr 106	24xJu-88

Dive-Bomber / Ground Attack Units

Description	No x Type/Auth
Stab/SKG 210	4xBf-110D/E
I./SKG 210	40xBf-110D/E
Stab/StG 1	6xBf-110, 4xJu-87B
III./StG 1	40xJu-87B
I./StG 2	40xJu-87B

Long Range Reconnaissance Units

2.(F)/Ob.d.L	12xDo-215B
1.(F)/122	12xJu-88A,Bf-110E-3
2.(F)/122	12xJu-88A,Bf-110
Wekusta 26	12xJu88A/D
4.(F)/121	12xJu-88A
3.(F)/31	12xDo-17P, Bf-110C/E

(Verbindungsstaffel) Communication.

Verbindungsstaffeln	1, 2, 3, 4, 52, 53, 54, 55, 56, 57, 58, 59, 60, 61, 62, 63, 64, 65, 66, 67, 68, 69, 70

© Nigel Askey, 2018

* Excludes Heeresaufklarungsgruppe (H), KGr.zbV and Seenotstaffel (around 100 additional aircraft).

II./KG 1 handed over Ju-88s to III./KG 1 & withdrawn to Insterburg, East Prussia on 12th Sep. 1941 (refit w Ju-88A-4s). Returned to the East Front (Nth Sector) ca 9th Oct. 1941.

Stab/KG 2, I./KG 2, III./KG 2 had withdrawn from the East Front by early November 1941, and had converted to Do-217E-2 and E-3 by the end of 1941.

Stab/KG 3 and I./KG 3 handed over remaining aircraft to II./KG 3, and withdrawn to Germany for re-equipping ca 6th December 1941.

III./KG 3 Handed over remaining aircraft to Croation Air Force Legion (5. Bomber Wing was attached to the Gruppe), and withdrawn to Ger. for refit with Ju-88s on 6th Dec 1941.

III./KG 4 (deployed in the West on 22nd June 1941) was withdrawn to Germany on 6th December 1941 for rest and refit

II./KG 27 was withdrawn to Germany for rest and refit ca early November 1941.

III./KG 27 was withdrawn to Germany for rest/refit (to He-111 H-6) from late August to late October 1941, It returned to the East Front ca 1st November 1941.

1./KG28 (one Staffel) was detached to X. Fliegerkorps (based Athens-Kalamaki, and equipped with aerial torpedoes), by 28th November 1941.

II./KG 51 was withdrawn to Austria ca 8th September for a rest/refit. It returned to the Southern Sector of the East Front on 4th December 1941.

III./KG 51 was withdrawn to Austria ca 18th July 1941 for a rest/refit. It returned to the Southern Sector of the East Front on 30th August 1941.

I./KG 53 was withdrawn for 2-3 few weeks for rest in late December 1941. Returned to the East Front (Central and then Northern Sectors) ca mid January 1942.

Stab./KG 54 returned to Germany ca 15th November 1941. It was assigned to the Mediterranean Theatre (Sicily and Italy) along with II. Fliegerkorps in December 1941.

I. /KG 54 returned to Ger. ca 17th Nov. 1941. It was assigned to the Med. Theatre (Sicily and Italy) along with II. Fliegerkorps in Dec. 1941. First attack on Malta 20th Dec. 1941.

II. /KG 54 withdrawn to East Prussia ca 30th December 1941 for rest and refit. Returned to the East Front (Central Sector) ca 22nd January 1942.

Stab./KG 55 was withdrawn to Germany/France for rest and reequipping ca 18th November 1941.

I./KG 55 was withdrawn to Austria/France for rest and reequipping ca 1st October 1941. Returned to the East Front (Southern Sector) in early January 1942.

II./KG 55 was withdrawn to France for rest and reequipping ca 18th November 1941.

III./KG 55 was withdrawn to France for rest and reequipping in December 1941 (although the original withdrawal orders were given on 18th November 1941).

Stab./KG 77 was withdrawn in Dec. 1941. In Jan. 1942 it was assigned to II. Fliegerkorps (newly transferred to the Med Theatre) for operations against Malta & over Nth Africa.

I./KG 77 was withdrawn to Germany for rest and reequipping ca mid-November 1941. It returned to the East Front (Central Sector) ca 7th January 1942.

II./KG 77 was withdrawn in Oct./early Nov. 1941. Assigned to the II. Fliegerkorps (newly transferred to the Mediterranean Theatre) and operated against Malta in Dec. 1941.

III./KG 77 was withdrawn in November 1941. Assigned to the II. Fliegerkorps (newly transferred to the Mediterranean Theatre) and operated against Malta in January 1942.

KGr 100 was withdrawn for refit 13-22 Nov. 1941. It returned to the East Front ca 11th Dec. 1941 (Poland & then Sth Sector), and was redesignated I./KG 100 on 15th Dec. 1941.

1. and 2./KGr 106 were withdrawn to France/Holland in July 1941 and operated as part of KGr 106 under Fliegerfuhrer Atlantik.

KuFlGr 506 was redesignated KGr 506 on 19th Oct. 1941. It was withdrawn to Westerland by 18th Oct. 1941. In Nov. and Dec. 1941, K.Gr. 506 operated over UK and the Nth Sea.

KGr 806 was withdrawn to Germany for rest and refit ca 13th November 1941, and then to Sicily with II. Fliegerkorps ca 18th December 1941.

Stab/StG 1 was withdrawn for rest and refit in December 1941.

III./StG 1 was withdrawn for rest and refit ca 6th December 1941.

I./StG 2 was withdrawn for rest and refit ca 6th December 1941.

Stab./SKG 210 was withdrawn to Germany for rest and refit ca 26th November 1941. It was redesignated Stab./ZG 1 on 4th January 1942.

I./SKG 210 was gradually withdrawn to Germany for refit from early October to 14th Dec 1941. It was redesignated I./ZG 1 on 4th January 1942.

II./SKG 210 remained on the East front until January 1942. It was redesignated II./ZG 1 on 4th January 1942.

Wekusta 26 was withdrawn in mid November 1941 for rest and refit (with Ju-88Ds). It was reassigned to II. Fliegerkorps (in the Med) in late December 1941.

3.(F)/31 was withdrawn to Germany in December 1941.

The majority of the Verbindungsstaffeln were disbanded in Nov.-Dec. 1941, and their personnel and aircraft were reassigned (mostly back to the A/B training schools).

© Nigel Askey, 2018

The precise strength of most of the Luftwaffe units when they were withdrawn from the East Front in 1941 is unknown. However, based on known unit strengths in October 1941, and the overall losses and replacements up to that time, it is reasonable to assume that they averaged around 75% of their authorised strength when they transferred.[407] From table Luft Tran, this means that around 1,080 fighters, bombers, dive-bombers and long-range reconnaissance aircraft were withdrawn from the East Front: most of which were withdrawn from late October to early December 1941. Around 500 of these aircraft were used to reinforce Luftflotte 2, which was establishing its HQ on Sicily.[408] If we include the aircraft in *Ergänzungs* (Erg), *Heeresaufklärungsgruppen* (H), KGr zbV, *Seenotstaffeln*, *Kurierstaffeln*, *Verbindungsstaffeln* and *Sanitätsflugbereitschaften*, then the total number of aircraft withdrawn from the East Front during 1941 was around 1,380.[409] This is an extraordinary number considering that in late 1941 the German Army was about to face a Russian winter and its greatest crisis since 1918.

By 27th December 1941 the Luftwaffe strength on the East Front had declined to approximately 2,000 aircraft, while the total Luftwaffe strength had declined to approximately 5,480 first-line aircraft.[410] This represented a net reduction in overall Luftwaffe strength of 402 first-line aircraft from 21st June to 27th December 1941.[411] This meant that only around one third (36%) of the Luftwaffe's existing strength was available to support the German forces in the East during the first month of the Soviet 1941/42 winter counter-offensive. In comparison, six months earlier (on 21st June 1941) around two thirds (67%) of the Luftwaffe's existing strength had been available to support Operation Barbarossa (3,914 aircraft out of a total strength of 5,882).

Therefore, although the Luftwaffe's overall strength had only declined by around 400 aircraft, the Luftwaffe's strength in the East had declined by approximately 1,910 aircraft (i.e. from 3, 914 aircraft to around 2,000 aircraft). The remarkable finding here is that the decline in strength in the East was not primarily attributable to combat losses, despite the ferocious fighting on the East Front (refer IIB 5. 5) b. - 'Review of the Luftwaffe Aircraft Losses in 1941'): it was mostly due to strategic misjudgement at the highest level of the Wehrmacht command. This withdrawal of crucial air-formations at a critical juncture of the East Front campaign is especially mystifying when one considers that there was no significant pressure on the Reich in the West, or from the Western Allied air-forces, at this time.[412]

***

In the meantime the Luftwaffe forces in the East had been reorganised. On 27th October 1941 the Fliegerführer Ostsee command (under Luftflotte 1) was disbanded after its tasks in the Baltic Sea area had been largely achieved. Its staff was transferred to the Crimea to form the Fliegerführer *Suden* (Aviation leader South): a small command covering the Black Sea. Most of its air units were transferred west and the remaining units were taken over by I. Fliegerkorps.

VIII Fliegerkorps took over command of the air units remaining in the central sector of the East Front on 30th November 1941, and then came under the control of Luftflotte 1. By 20th December 1941 there were now only three Luftflotte with forces on the East Front, of which one was small. These were as follows.

- Luftflotte 1 controlling I Fliegerkorps, VIII Fliegerkorps and a newly formed command called Schlachtflieger Führer 2 (Ground-attack Leader 2).

- Luftflotte 4 controlling IV Fliegerkorps, Fliegerführer Suden and the Deutsche Luftwaffenmission Rumanien.

- Part of Luftflotte 5 controlling Luftwaffenkommando Kirkenes (in north Finland/Norway).

---

[407] Refer Volume IIB 5. 5) for more on Luftwaffe losses and Replacements (R) on the East Front during 1941.

[408] C. Bishop, Luftwaffe Squadrons 1939-45, Amber Books Ltd, London, 2006, p. 58.

[409] Note, the majority of the *Verbindungsstaffeln* (which were mostly formed specifically to support Operation Barbarossa) were disbanded in November-December 1941. Their personnel and aircraft were reassigned to other units (mostly back to the A/B training schools). Many of these units were reformed in 1942 to support the German summer offensive in the East.

[410] H. Boog, et al, German Research Institute for Military history at Potsdam, Germany and the Second World War, Volume IV: The Attack on the Soviet Union, Clarendon Press (Oxford University Press), New York, 1996, p. 817, states the Luftwaffe had 1,900 'front-line' aircraft on the East Front out of a total Luftwaffe strength of 5,167 'first-line' aircraft (for 27th December 1941). These figures apparently include Ju 52 transport aircraft, but exclude training aircraft and appear to exclude liaison/light-transport aircraft in *Kurierstaffeln*, *Verbindungsstaffeln* and *Sanitätsflugbereitschaften*. These amounted to at least 310 aircraft, of which around 100 remained on the East Front in December 1941. These aircraft types are not considered 'front-line' or even 'first-line' aircraft in the context used by H. Boog, et al, (e.g. as in Table I.IV.5 on p. 364).

[411] Ibid, p. 817.

[412] The Allies did launch Operation Crusader in North Africa on 18th November 1941. However the decision to transfer major air-assets from the East was made well before this time. In addition, the size and strategic importance of this offensive hardly justified the transfer of critical air assets from the East, and the very large majority of air units transferred (from the East) never went to assist Rommel or the DAK anyway.

c. Newly Mobilised Luftwaffe Air Combat Units: June to December 1941

We now come to the Luftwaffe air units which were newly mobilised from 22nd June to 31st December 1941. These are shown in table Luft MD and MND. The units shown in bold with a grey background were Mobilised and Deployed (MD) on the East Front. These units are also shown on tables Luft Rein 1 and Luft Rein 2 as units sent as reinforcements to the East Front.

The remaining units were Mobilised and Deployed (MD) on the various western fronts, or were Mobilised and Not Deployed (MND). The latter units were deployed to an active theatre after 1941 or were deployed to unknown locations in the West.

The first obvious thing about this table is how few units are actually on it; especially compared to the equivalent VVS and RAF mobilisation tables of the same period.[413] The total strength of all the new aircraft shown in this table comes to only 477, of which 76 were fighters, 105 were bombers and reconnaissance aircraft, and 296 (62%) were transport and liaison aircraft. These figures **exclude** the aircraft in 10./KG3 (Kroat) which received left over Do 17Zs from III./KG3 when that unit was withdrawn from the East Front to convert to Ju 88s in December 1941. This is because the Do 17Zs involved were already Deployed (D) on the East Front in June 1941.

The air units newly Mobilised and Deployed (MD) in the East contained 239 aircraft, made up of 24 fighters (in two *Staffeln*), 12 bombers (in one *Staffel*), and 191 transport aircraft (in 5 separate air-transport *Gruppen* and 4 special large glider *Staffeln*). It is apparent from these figures that most of the new aircraft and pilots sent to the East Front in 1941 arrived as Replacements (R) to existing units already deployed, and not in newly mobilised air combat units (refer next section).

***

---

[413] Refer Volume IIIB 3. 4) b. – 'Newly Mobilised VVS KA, VVS VMF and PVO Air Combat Units: June 1941 to January 1942'.

Table Luft MD and MND	Luftwaffe Air Units Mobilised and Deployed on the East Front, Mobilised and Deployed in the 'West' (Germany, Western Europe, Mediterranean Theatre, or Norway), and Mobilised and Not Deployed; from July 1941 to December 1941			
	Description	No x Type/Auth	Avail	Svcble
JG (Jagdgeschwader) Fighter.	15 (Span)./JG 27*	12xBf-109E	12	12
	15 (Kroat)./JG 52^	12xBf-109E	12	11
NJG (Nachtjagdgeschwader) Night fighter.	Stab/NJG 2**	4xJu-88C	4	2
	5..6./NJG 2**	24xJu-88C	20	16
	II./NJG 3*^	40xBf-110D/E	35	30
	Jagdlehrer Uber.St.	16xBf-109D/E/F	17	12
KG (Kampfgeschwader) Bomber.	10./KG3 (Kroat) ^*	12xDo-17Z	12	10
	Stab/KG 100	4xHe-111H	4	3
	IV.(Erg)/KG 100^^	24xHe-111H	24	18
F (Fernaufklärungsgruppe) Long Range Strategic Reconnaissance.	F-Kette Lappland	4xDo-17Z	4	2
Wekusta (Wettererkundungs staffel) Weather Observation.	W-Kette Sudnorwegen*~~	4xJu-88D	4	4
KGr zbV (Kampfgeschwader zu besonderen Verwendung) Transport.	KGr zbV 400***	53xJu-52	40	26
	Tr.Gr 111***	32xJu-52	24	8
	KGr zbV 300**^	65xHe-111	45	35
	KGr zbV 500*^^	53xJu-52	41	35
	LGL 1*~	6xMe-321, 12xMe110	6, 9	6, 8
	LGL 2, 22~~	12xMe-321, 24xMe110	12, 18	11, 16
	LGL 4*~~	6xMe-321, 12xMe110	6, 10	6, 9
	KGr zbV 600^^^	53xJu-52	28	25
	KGr zbV 700^^^	53xJu-52	25	23
	KGr zbV 800^**	53xJu-52	29	26
	KGr zbV 900^**	53xJu-52	24	22
	KGr zbV 999^^*	53xJu-52	24	23

* Attached to Luftflotte 2, VIII Fliegerkorps (under Stab/JG 27), by Sep. 1941.

^ Attached to Luftflotte 4, V. Fliegerkorps, by October 1941.

** Formed 1st November 1941.

*^ Formed 1st September 1941.

^* Attached to Luftflotte 1, Nahkampfführer 2 (Close Support Leader 2) Dec. 1941. In Dec. 1941, received left over Do-17Z from III./KG3 (which conv to Ju-88s).

^^ IV.(Erg)/KG 100 mobilised on 29th November 1941 (from Erg Staffel), at Bourges. Moved to Luneburg from 1st January 1942.

*** KGr zbV 400 formed 10th Dec 41. Deployed to Luftflotte 2, (Tripoli), in January 42 . Tr.Gr. 111 Disbanded by Feb 1942.

**^ Formed November 41 with 5 Staffel. Deployed Athens.

*^^ Formed 10th December 1941. Remained at Brindisi till 15th January 1942, then moved to Pleskau-West.

*~ Grossraumlastenseglerstaffel 1, (Special Large Glider Staffel 1), Attached to Luftflotte 1 by October 1941.

~~ Grossraumlastenseglerstaffel 2, 22, (Special Large Glider Staffel 2, 22), Attached to Luftflotte 2 by October 1941.

*~~ Grossraumlastenseglerstaffel 4, (Special Large Glider Staffel 4), Attached to Luftflotte 4 by October 1941.

^^^ Formed 17th Dec 41. Based near Orscha.

^** Formed 17th Dec 41. Based near Vitebsk.

^^* Formed 17th Dec 41. Based near Pleskau.

*~~ Formed in late 1941 as a detachment of Wekusta 1 Ob.d.L.

5) Overall Luftwaffe Combat Aircraft Usage, Production and Replacements (R): 22nd June to 31st December 1941

We now come to the final chapter relating to the Luftwaffe component of the German FILARM model. This is to ascertain the number of combat aircraft that were available to newly mobilising Luftwaffe units in 1941, and the number of Replacement (R) aircraft available, and issued, to existing Luftwaffe units that were Deployed (D) in the front lines.

From the previous section we determined the total number and type of combat aircraft allocated to newly mobilised Luftwaffe air combat units from 22nd June to 31st December 1941. The results of this analysis are displayed in the first three columns of table Ger Air Usage 1941 (over page). We find that approximately 477 combat aircraft were issued to newly mobilised Luftwaffe air units, of which around 343 (72%) went into Mobilised and Deployed (MD) units on the East Front and in the West during 1941.

Also shown in this table is the relevant German aircraft production from June to December 1941, the proportion used as Replacements (R) on the East and Western Fronts, and the number that remained in rear area support and training units or (for various reasons) were not yet assigned to 'front-line' Luftwaffe air units. The figures used in these columns are discussed and reviewed in the subsequent sections.

***

Table Ger Air Usage 1941 | German New Aircraft Production, Usage and Replacements (R): 22nd June to 31st December 1941

| | German combat aircraft utilised by newly mobilised air combat units; 22nd June to 31st December 1941 | | | German combat aircraft available; June to December 1941** | German combat aircraft Replacements (R) from 22nd June to 27th December 1941 | | New aircraft production used in Erg (Replacement) units, training units, depots, in transit, still in factories, other rear area organisations, and/or not yet released to the supply and replacement office of the Luftwaffe; 22nd June to 31st December 1941 |
	Mobilised and Deployed (MD) on the East Front	Mobilised and Deployed (MD) in the West^	Mobilised and not Deployed (MND)	New Production, June to December 1941	Replacements (R) aircraft issued to forces in the West'^*	Replacement (R) aircraft issued to forces on the East Front***	
Fighters, Ftr-Bombers*							
Bf-109F	24		17	1478	354	889	194
Bf-110D/E/F		35		268	143	80	10
Me-210				67	108		67
Fw-190A				182			74
	24	35	17	1995	605	969	345
Bombers, Long Range Recon.							
Ju-88A/C/D	24	24	4	1617	383	740	466
He111 H		45	4	551	110	329	39
Do-17Z/215B			4	(20)^^			16
Do-217E				225	80		145
Fw-200C				37	23		14
Ju-86P/R				4	1	2	1
	24	69	12	2454	597	1071	681
Ground Attack							
Ju-87R/D				316	76	204	36
Hs-123A				(35)*^		35	
HS-129				7			7
				358	76	239	43

Short Range Recon., Liaison							
Fw-189A						130	19
Hs-126A/B				157	8		
				157	**8**	**130**	**19**
Seaplanes, Floatplanes							
Ar-196				59	33	10	16
Bv-138				52	31	6	15
Do-24				15	14		1
Do-18							
He-115C				18	16		2
He-114							
He-60							
He-59							
				144	**94**	**16**	**34**
Transport, Courier, Liaison							
Ju-52	130			291	12	36	8
Me-321	24			82			58
Fi-156	37		105	271	68	113	53
	191	**0**	**105**	**644**	**80**	**149**	**119**
Total aircraft	**239**	**104**	**134**	**5752 (55)**,^^**	**1460**	**2574**	**1241**

* Includes Messerschmitt BF110E-3 used for Long Range Reconnaissance.

^ 'West' includes Germany, Western Europe, the Mediterranean Theatre, or Norway (except Luftwaffenkommando Kirkenes).

** Does **not** include aircraft produced prior to June 1941 which were still in transit to Luftwaffe units, or which were still in depots/factories.

Also does **not** include Ju52s removed from bomber and training units in October-December 1941, to form Air Transport Units on the East Front.

*^ The 35 Hs-123As were not 'new production': they were pre-war aircraft commandeered from training units and depots, and sent East.

^^ The Do-17Z/215B ceased production in May 1941. The 'new' aircraft used in units with this aircraft type, were actually from existing pre-June 1941 stock.

^* Includes 58 new aircraft received as Replacement (R) by Deployed (D) units prior to the latter's transfer to the East Front.

*** Does not include 58 new aircraft received as Replacement (R) by Deployed (D) units (in the West) prior to the latter's transfer to the East Front.

a. German Aircraft Production and Replacements (R) in 1941

There are several reputable sources which supply reasonably accurate figures for German aircraft production during WWII. Unfortunately the information provided is often too general in nature for our needs: i.e. annual (and sometimes monthly) production figures by aircraft type (e.g., all fighters, all bombers, etc.). For the purposes of this work we are interested in 1941 production, and the numbers and specific types produced from June to December 1941. Having surveyed the available sources, the following tables contain the consolidated and (where possible) reconciled information relating to German aircraft production during 1941.[414]

Overall German Military Aircraft Production in 1941									
Reconnaissance*	Fighters^	G Attack**	Bombers*^	Transports^^	Naval^*	Trainers***	Liaison**^	Gliders *^^ (plus some transport)	**Total**
1,079	3,744	507	3,373	502	183	1,121	431	836	11,776

* Comprised of Bf-110, Ju-88, Me-210, Do-215, Fw-200, Fw-189 & Hs-126 production. Excludes a handful of Ju-86P/R produced.
^ Comprised of Bf-109, Fw-190, Me-210, Bf-110 Night Fighter and Ju-88 Night Fighter production.
** Comprised of Ju-87 and Hs-129 production.
*^ Comprised of Ju-88, He-111, Do-217 production.
^^ Comprised of Ju-52 production only.
^* Seaplanes and flying boats. Comprised of Ar-196, Bv-138 and some Do-24 production. Does not include limited He-115, and additional Dutch or French Do-24 production, or limited (initial) BV-222 production.
*** Comprised mainly of A-96 and Bu-181, but also includes other primary and advanced trainers. This figure may also include some light transport types.
**^ Comprised of Fi-156 production only.
*^^ Comprised of DFS-230, Go-242 and Me-321 production. Also includes misc. light transport types such as the Fw-58 (134 produced in 1941) and Kl-35. It is unlikely that these figures include the light transport aircraft manufactured by conquered countries for Germany during WWII. Examples include the C-445M and C-449 (349 eventually built), which were manufactured specifically for German service by Renault and Caudron in France.

German Monthly Aircraft Production, by Category, in 1941						
	Fighters	Bombers & LR Recon.	Transports & Liaison	Trainers	Other (inc. Gliders)	**Total**
January	136	255	70	89	83	**633**
February	255	326	72	76	142	**871**
March	424	392	85	118	155	**1,174**
April	476	355	92	76	130	**1,129**
May	446	269	88	62	172	**1,037**
Total Jan.-May	**1,737**	**1,597**	**407**	**421**	**682**	**4,844**
June	376	325	74	61	204	**1,040**
July	320	446	72	78	138	**1,054**
August	285	454	75	56	151	**1,021**
September	258	416	62	64	187	**987**
October	261	382	101	77	136	**957**
November	232	331	93	77	162	**895**
December	263	399	85	55	176	**978**
Total June-Dec.	**1,995**	**2,753**	**562**	**468**	**1,154**	**6,932**
Total 1941	**3,732**	**4,350**	**969**	**889**	**1,836**	**11,776**

[414] Compiled from the following primary sources: F. A. Vajda, P. Dancey, German Aircraft Industry and Production 1933-1945; Illustrated Edition, Society of Automotive Engineers Inc, Warrendale, PA, 1998, table 8-B (p. 133), table 8-D (p. 134), table 8-E (p. 135), table 8-G (p. 136), table 8-Q (p. 146) and table 8-H (p. 138).
H. Boog, et al, German Research Institute for Military history at Potsdam, Germany and the Second World War, Volume IV: The Attack on the Soviet Union, Clarendon Press (Oxford University Press), New York, 1996, pp. 818 and 819 (for total aircraft and single-engine fighter production June-Dec. 41; excluding seaplanes, gliders and courier aircraft).
J. Ellis, WWII: A Statistical Survey, Facts On File Inc, New York 1993, table 93, pp. 278-279, (annual production by type).
S.M. Pavelec, WWII Data Book, The Luftwaffe 1933-1945, Amber Books Ltd, London, 2010, pp. 34-37.
S. Wilson, Aircraft of WWII, Aerospace Publications Ltd, Fyshwick, Australia 1998, pp. 9, 14, 25, 52, 53, 54, 68, 70, 73, 86, 87, 88, 90, 91, 94, 95, 96, 97, 118, 120 and 123.
W. Green, G. Swanborough, The Complete Book of Fighters, Greenwich Editions, London, 2004, pp. 214, 375, 376 and 378.
Purnell's Illustrated Encyclopedia of Modern Weapons and Warfare, Phoebus Publishing Co/BPC Publishing Ltd, London, 1971/77/78/79/80, pp. 613, 1235, 1236, 1238, 1239, 1241, 1242, 1323, 1325, 1450, 1454-1459 and 1461-1465.
W. Green, Aircraft of the Luftwaffe, Volume One, Aerospace Publishing Ltd, London, 2010.

German Military Aircraft Production by Type in 1941		As Night-Fighters	As Recon Aircraft*
Bf-109F	2,764		
Bf-110D/E/F		594^	190
Me 210	94		2
Fw-190A	226^^		
Ju-88A/C/D	2,146	66**	568
He111 H	950		
Do-215B			6
Do-217E	277		
Fw-200C			58
Ju-86P/R			8
Ju-87R/D	500		
Hs-129	7		
Fw-189A			250
Hs-126A/B			5
Ar-196	94		
Bv-138	82		
Do-24*^	18		
He-115C	36		
Ju-52	502		
Me-321	90		
Fi-156	431		
Total aircraft	**8,217**	**660**	**1,087**

* Although designated reconnaissance aircraft, these types were capable of limited operations as naval attack, bombers or ground-attack aircraft.
^ Monthly production from Jan. to Dec. 1941 was: 50, 123, 119, 83, 53, 73, 29, 22, 15, 15, 11, 1. An additional 13 Bf 110s were rebuilt as night fighters.
** Monthly production from Jan to May 1941 was: 9, 12, 27, 15 and 3. An additional 280 Ju-88s were rebuilt as night fighters.
*^ Includes Do-24s from Dutch assembly lines (Aviolanda and De Schelde).
^^ Includes 124 Fw190A-2 in 1941.   © Nigel Askey, 2018

**

From the data above, we are able to ascertain (with considerable accuracy) the German military aircraft production by model type for the period June to December 1941. This information is presented in the fourth column in table Ger Air Usage 1941 (pages 278 - 279). For the German FILARM model this represents the maximum number of additional combat aircraft available from June to December 1941.

However, this is a conservative (low) estimate because it excludes aircraft manufactured prior to June 1941 which were still in transit to Luftwaffe units, or which were still in depots and factories. Also, it does not include pre-Barbarossa Ju 52s, which were removed from bomber training units in October-December 1941 to hurriedly form five new separate air-transport *Gruppen* for the East Front. The only exceptions to this are the inclusion of 35 Hs 123As and 20 Do 17Z/215Bs from existing pre-June 1941 stock. The remarkable little Hs 123A biplanes were commandeered from dive-bomber training schools and sent as replacements to Sch. /LG 2 on the East Front. [415] The Do 17Z/215Bs were commandeered mainly from training units to supplement aircraft in some *Fernaufklärungsgruppen* (Long range strategic reconnaissance groups) and KG 2.[416]

Note, in the Soviet FILARM model, aircraft issued to the VVS prior to 22nd June 1941 but which were: still at factories, in depots, in transit, being rebuilt in rear areas, and brand new aircraft which were manufactured prior to

[415] Production of the Hs 123A dive-bombing biplane stopped in October 1938. However it was so successful in the close support role that as late as January 1943 there were still serious calls to reinstate the Hs 123 in production. The tooling had been scrapped in 1940, after 610 had been produced, and this was found to be impractical. Consequently, Hs 123 aircraft which had been sent to training schools, and sometimes even to derelict depots, were recalled and issued to front-line *Schlachtgeschwader* units. Remarkably the 'obsolete' little Hs 123 soldered on and was able to conduct daylight operations until late 1944: gradually declining until there were simply none left.
[416] Production of the Do 215 ceased in May 1941, and the Do 17Z/215B was out of front-line bomber service by 1941/42. However, they still operated as a useful long-range reconnaissance aircraft into 1943.

22nd June 1941 but which were not yet issued to any VVS or PVO unit, **are all included**. This is because the VVS was still largely on a peacetime aircraft deployment on 21st June 1941, while the Luftwaffe had already been at war since 1939. Consequently the VVS had far more aircraft available in 'rear areas', in transit, etc, than the Luftwaffe did in June 1941.[417]

In total the Luftwaffe had approximately 5,752 aircraft available for reinforcements and Replacements (R) from 22nd June to 31st December 1941. These comprised approximately 1,660 single engine fighters, 335 twin engine fighters/fighter bombers (including night fighters), 2,454 twin engine bombers and long-range reconnaissance aircraft, 358 dive bombers and ground-attack aircraft, 157 short range (army) tactical reconnaissance aircraft, 144 seaplanes and floatplanes, and 644 transport and courier/liaison aircraft.[418]

**

So the question remains; how many of these aircraft were used as Replacements (R) for air-units Deployed (D) in the East and the West during the second half or 1941? We know that on 21st June 1941 the Luftwaffe had a total strength of 5,882 aircraft (excluding training aircraft, but including transport aircraft in KGr zbV and LLG units, and courier/liaison/transport aircraft in *Kurierstaffeln*, *Verbindungsstaffeln* and *Sanitätsflugbereitschaften*).[419] We also know that on 27th December 1941, after over six months of combat on the East Front, the Luftwaffe had a total strength of around 5.480 aircraft (excluding training aircraft, but including transport aircraft in KGr zbV and LLG units, and courier/liaison/transport aircraft in *Kurierstaffeln*, *Verbindungsstaffeln* and *Sanitätsflugbereitschaften*).[420] In addition, from the next section 'Review of the Luftwaffe Aircraft Losses and Casualties in 1941' we know that the total losses suffered by air-combat units during this period amounted to approximately 4,913 aircraft.[421] This includes aircraft totally destroyed as well as those written off as too badly damaged to repair, and includes all combat as well as operational (accidental) losses. This means that in order to maintain its strength the Luftwaffe received at least 4,511 aircraft between 21st June and 27th December 1941 as Replacements (R) or within newly mobilised air units (excluding training aircraft, but including transport aircraft in KGr zbV and LLG units, and courier/liaison/transport aircraft in *Kurierstaffeln*, *Verbindungsstaffeln* and *Sanitätsflugbereitschaften*). However, from the previous section 'Newly Mobilised Luftwaffe Air Combat Units: June to December 1941' we know that approximately 477 aircraft went into newly mobilised units.[422] Therefore around **4,034 aircraft were used as Replacement (R) aircraft** in front-line units (on all fronts) from 22nd June to 27th December 1941.

On 21st June 1941 the Luftwaffe strength on the East Front was 3,914 aircraft (excluding training aircraft, but including transport aircraft in KGr zbV and LLG units, and courier/liaison/transport aircraft in *Kurierstaffeln*, *Verbindungsstaffeln* and *Sanitätsflugbereitschaften*).[423] By 27th December 1941 the Luftwaffe strength on the East Front had declined to approximately 2,000 aircraft (excluding training aircraft, but including transport aircraft in KGr zbV and LLG units, and courier/liaison/transport aircraft in *Kurierstaffeln*, *Verbindungsstaffeln* and *Sanitätsflugbereitschaften*).[424] From June to December 1941 the Luftwaffe forces in the East were reinforced with 659 aircraft in reinforcing units transferred from the West (including aircraft in newly mobilised units).[425] Unfortunately for the Wehrmacht forces in the USSR, during the same period around 1,380 aircraft were withdrawn from the East Front and transferred to the West.[426] In addition, Luftwaffe aircraft losses on the East Front from 22nd June to 27th December 1941 amounted to approximately 3,767 aircraft.[427] This includes aircraft totally destroyed as well as those written off as too badly damaged to repair, and includes all combat as well as operational

---

[417] Refer Volume IIIB 3. 5) – 'Overall Soviet Combat Aircraft Usage, Production and Replacements (R): 22nd June to 31st December 1941'.

[418] Counting all Ju 88s as bombers and reconnaissance aircraft. 66 of the Ju 88s produced in 1941 were new night-fighters, but these were produced from January to May 1941. An additional 280 existing Ju 88s were converted to night-fighters.

[419] Refer Volume IIB 5. 3) d. – 'Overall Luftwaffe Strength on 21st June 1941'.

[420] Refer Volume IIB 5. 4) b. – 'The Transfer of Deployed (D) Air Combat Units from the Eastern Front to the West: June to December 1941'.

[421] Refer Volume IIB 5. 5) b. – 'Review of the Luftwaffe Aircraft Losses and Casualties in 1941'.

[422] Refer Volume IIB 5. 4) c. – 'Newly Mobilised Luftwaffe Air Combat Units: June to December 1941'.

[423] Refer Volume IIB 5. 3) a. – 'Luftwaffe Strength Available to Support Operation Barbarossa on 21st June 1941'.

[424] Refer Volume IIB 5. 4) b. Also, H. Boog, et al, German Research Institute for Military history at Potsdam, Germany and the Second World War, Volume IV: The Attack on the Soviet Union. Clarendon Press (Oxford University Press), New York, 1996, p. 817.

[425] Refer Volume IIB 5. 4) a. – 'The Transfer of Deployed (D) and Newly Mobilised Air Combat Units to the Eastern Front: June to December 1941'.

[426] Refer Volume IIB 5. 4) b. – 'The Transfer of Deployed (D) Air Combat Units from the Eastern Front to the West: December 1941'.

[427] Refer Volume IIB 5. 5) b. – 'Review of the Luftwaffe Aircraft Losses and Casualties in 1941'.

(accidental) losses. Therefore, taking all the above into account, we can ascertain that at least **2,574 aircraft were used as Replacement (R) aircraft** for front-line units on the East Front from 22nd June to 27th December 1941.

The fifth and sixth columns of table <u>Ger Air Usage 1941</u> (pages 278 - 279) include the results of this analysis, and indicate the Replacements (R) by type issued to front-line air units in the East and in the West from 22nd June to 27th December 1941. The last column in this table displays the front-line aircraft that remained in *Ergänzungs* (Erg - Replacement and training) units, or in other rear area organisations, during the second half of 1941. Overall around 45% of the available combat aircraft were sent to the East Front as Replacements (R) from June to December 1941, while at the same time around 25% were used as Replacements (R) to Luftwaffe forces on the Western Fronts. Around 22% (over a fifth of the available new aircraft) remained unassigned in rear areas, or were assigned to training type units, and only 8% went into newly formed units.

***

b. Review of the Luftwaffe Aircraft Losses and Casualties in 1941

Similarly to the Soviet FILARM model, it is necessary here to review the Luftwaffe aircraft losses in 1941.[428] On balance the Luftwaffe's losses and casualties during WWII are relatively well documented: the word 'relatively' being used when considering the post-war 'records' of the Soviet VVS (and, to a lesser extent, some Western Allied air forces).[429] In addition to limited information and/or records, errors often occur when examining aircraft loss figures due to differing air-force practices. In this case air-forces had differing definitions of what constituted a 'slightly' or 'heavily' damaged aircraft, whether or not aircraft destroyed on the ground are included, and whether or not operational (accidental) losses are included. All of these can be used to mislead the reader; accidentally or otherwise.

One German source gives the following information on overall Luftwaffe aircraft losses and replacements during 1941.[430]

Front Line Formation Combat Aircraft Losses, June-December 1941*													Total 1941
	Jan.	Feb.	Mar.	Apr.	May	June	July	Aug.	Sept.	Oct.	Nov.	Dec.	
Total loss (incl. 60% + damage).	127	150	237	366	429	542	640	393	429	387	276	304	**4,280**
Less than 60% damage.	101	125	179	247	345	399	373	256	270	272	229	195	**2,991**
	228	**275**	**416**	**613**	**774**	**941**	**1,013**	**649**	**699**	**659**	**505**	**499**	**7,271**

Front Line Formation Combat Aircraft Issued, June-December 1941*													Total 1941
	Jan.	Feb.	Mar.	Apr.	May	June	July	Aug.	Sept.	Oct.	Nov.	Dec.	
New prod. and major overhaul.	446	669	909	1,019	894	689	807	851	794	758	671	732	**9,239**
From repair shops.	75	157	259	300	248	214	279	296	274	264	265	227	**2,858**
	521	**826**	**1,168**	**1,319**	**1,142**	**903**	**1,086**	**1,147**	**1,068**	**1,022**	**936**	**959**	**12,097**

* Includes combat aircraft in the Kriegsmarine, but excludes all aircraft types in *Kurierstaffeln*, *Verbindungsstaffeln*, *Sanitätsflugbereitschaften* and similar support units.

[428] Refer Volume IIIB 3. 5) a. – 'Review of the VVS Aircraft Losses in 1941'.

[429] For example, the author is yet to find a comprehensive, complete and reputable compendium of RAF aircraft losses during WWII (unpublished or published). It appears that some of this detailed information has never been released by the British government (and definitely not in a comprehensive compendium), and if it has then it has come out piecemeal and in a series of revised forms. Furthermore many published and quoted RAF aircraft loss figures do not reconcile with relevant RAF personnel losses (especially those of Bomber Command), nor do they tally with known aircraft production figures and RAF aircraft strengths. There are some notable exceptions focusing on specialised areas of RAF operations during WWII: the best available works on this topic appears to be the series of volumes by W.R. Chorley on RAF Bomber Command Losses, and N.L.R. Franks, Royal Air Force Fighter Command Losses of the Second World War, Operational Losses Aircraft and Crews 1939-1941; Volume I, Midland Publishing, UK, 2010.

[430] B. R. Kroener, et al, Germany and the Second World War; Volume I, Organisation and Mobilisation of the German Sphere of Power, Part 1, Wartime Administration, Economy and Manpower Resources 1939-1941, German Research Institute for Military History at Potsdam, Clarendon Press (Oxford University Press Inc), New York, 2000, Diagram II.VII.2. Ref: BA-MA RW 19/1379ff, Ten Day reports ObdL/GenQu 6. Abt. (IA). It is unclear if the loss figures in this table also exclude transport aircraft (Ju 52s) in KGr zbV and LLG Units.

The loss figures in this table tend to be on the low side compared to other sources (see below), while the replacements tend to be much higher than used in the previous section (see above). The latter are indicative only, as it is impossible to distinguish the proportion of aircraft that were from new production, what constituted a 'major overhaul' and what constituted a 'repair shop' (i.e. a factory repair facility in Germany or an airfield based maintenance/repair facility). This table indicates that the Luftwaffe lost 2,971 combat aircraft as total losses from June to December 1941, and another 1,994 aircraft suffered less than 60% damage (a total of 4,965 aircraft). However these loss figures are incomplete and of limited value: they do not distinguish losses by either type or cause (i.e. combat or operational), they do not distinguish losses by Front, and they exclude aircraft in support units such as *Kurierstaffeln*, *Verbindungsstaffeln* and *Sanitätsflugbereitschaften*. Many of these support units may not have operated 'combat aircraft' in the traditional sense, but they often operated on, or close to, the front-line and often liaised closely with the German Army's operations on the ground.

***

A more useful and accurate German source places the Luftwaffe's aircraft losses from 22nd June to 27th December 1941 as follows.[431]

Luftwaffe Aircraft Losses From 22nd June to 27th December 1941					
	Aircraft totally written off (including accidental) *	Aircraft significantly damaged (including accidental)	Total; written off and damaged	Estimate of medium and heavily damaged aircraft written off and removed from service ^	**Aircraft Classified as Written Off; Total Losses**
East Front	2,505	1,895	4,400	1,262	**3,767**
Non East Front	779	551	1,330	367	**1,146**
Total all Fronts	**3,284**	**2,446**	**5,730****	**1,629**	**4,913**

* Around 13% of total write off were due to accidents. E.g., 327 of the 2,505 lost in the East were due to accidents.

^ The Germans classified 60% or above damage as total loss. This was roughly equivalent to the RAF's 'Category 3' damage/loss rating. Estimated at 2/3 of damaged aircraft.

** Approximately 1,823 (32%) of these were fighters.

The figures in this table are considerably higher than those in the previous table; but they now include all aircraft types in all aircraft units (including those in support units such as *Kurierstaffeln*, *Verbindungsstaffeln* and *Sanitätsflugbereitschaften*). They also differentiate the losses between the East Front and the Western Fronts. Of the 5,730 aircraft lost or damaged on all fronts from June to December 1941, 1,823 (32%) were fighters of one form or another.[432] Around 36% of the aircraft lost were medium bombers, while the remainder were mostly dive-bombers and short range reconnaissance and army cooperation aircraft which operated over the front-lines.

The 'aircraft totally written-off' column includes those totally destroyed due to combat (being shot down), those destroyed on the ground, and those destroyed due to accidents not directly related to enemy action. The latter are usually called 'operational losses'. For example, 327 of the 2,505 aircraft totally written-off on the East Front were operational losses. Operational losses include crashes while taking off and landing for any reason, training accidents and aircraft lost or damaged in 'ferrying operations'. The latter involved flying replacement aircraft to forward front-line bases and the movement of whole air units from one front to another. As we have seen in previous sections, close to a third of the Luftwaffe strength in the East was transferred west from October to December 1941, and it is unclear whether the operational losses suffered in these operations are attributable to the East Front or the western fronts in the above table.

In the Luftwaffe aircraft damage was classified using a percentage weighting system which took account of critical damage to vital aircraft components. Aircraft with 1-39% damage were generally classified as 'lightly damaged', aircraft with 40-59% damage were generally classified as 'medium damaged', and aircraft with 60-100%

[431] H. Boog, et al, German Research Institute for Military history at Potsdam, Germany and the Second World War, Volume IV: The Attack on the Soviet Union. Clarendon Press (Oxford University Press), New York, 1996, pp. 817-818. Their primary reference is: BA-MA RL 2 III/713, 716, Report on the combat readiness of the flying units as of 21 June 1941, 27 Dec. 1941, *Generalquartiermeister der* Luftwaffe, 6. Abt., 24 June 1941, 30 Dec. 1941. Although a higher
[432] Ibid, p. 819.

damage were generally classified as 'heavily damaged'.[433] Lightly damaged aircraft were normally repaired at the forward airbase, and in most cases they were returned to service within a few days (often overnight if it was only a few holes or a simple problem). It is likely most of the lightly damaged aircraft were not even reported to the higher Luftwaffe commands and only appeared on 'statements of readiness' of the air unit. 100% damaged aircraft were automatically total losses, but in practice the Luftwaffe generally wrote-off any aircraft with 60% or more damage.[434] Obviously these aircraft were cannibalised as far as possible to keep less severely damaged aircraft operational. In the table above, 'aircraft significantly damaged' only includes those which were medium and heavily damaged (i.e. with 40% or more damage). The fourth column in the above table is therefore an estimate of the significantly damaged aircraft which could not be repaired, and which were subsequently written-off and removed from service (and probably cannibalised where possible). Assuming a linear spread of aircraft with 40-100% damage, and assuming aircraft with 60% or more damage were written-off, then an estimated two thirds of medium and heavily damaged aircraft were written-off. These are therefore also classified as 'total losses' in the table above.

The above distinction is important because, as we can see just from the data presented in the above table, the Luftwaffe's aircraft losses could be interpreted to be as low as 3,284 or as high as 5,730.[435] The number of 4,913 aircraft lost is the most reasonable (and accurate) figure because it includes aircraft totally destroyed as well as those written-off as too badly damaged to repair, and it includes all combat as well as operational (accidental) losses. Furthermore, this is precisely the number that we are interested in for the German FILARM model. This is because we are interested in aircraft Replacements (R), and damaged aircraft which were returned to service did not require a Replacement (R) aircraft to maintain the air unit's strength. In any realistic military simulation of Operation Barbarossa, aircraft which sustain damage in the region of 1-59% should eventually be repaired and returned to service (with the time period being dependent on the degree of damage and the supply state of the air force ground unit carrying out the repairs).

Given that the Luftwaffe lost around 3,800 aircraft totally destroyed or written-off as too badly damaged to repair on the East Front during 1941, the big question remains; **did the Luftwaffe succeed in providing the German Army with the preconditions it needed to enable Operation Barbarossa to succeed?**

To put it another way; the German Army needed (at least marginal) air superiority on the main front sectors in order to have any chance of bringing down the USSR in 1941. Therefore, did the Luftwaffe succeed in neutralizing the VVS in 1941 sufficiently for the Army to have the freedom of action it needed to succeed? Any objective analysis indicates the answer to these questions is clearly yes for the following reasons.

1. After the Soviet Red Army (or RKKA), the Soviet Military Air Force (*Voyenno-Vozdushnye Sily* or VVS) constituted the largest single threat to Operation Barbarossa's chances of success. On 22nd June 1941 the VVS (comprising the VVS KA (Army), VVS VMF (Naval), VVS DBA (Long Range Bomber) and PVO (Home Air Defence) forces) was by largest air-force in the world. On this date it had no less than 20,450 combat aircraft on strength. Of this force, around 10,450 combat aircraft were in the Western Special Military Districts and immediately available to meet the Wehrmacht when it attacked the USSR on 22nd June 1941.[436]

   As we have seen, the attacking Luftwaffe forces in the East contained only 3,297 combat aircraft on 21st June 1941, which means that on the eve of Operation Barbarossa the VVS forces in the Western Special Military Districts already enjoyed a numerical superiority of 3.2 to 1 in combat aircraft. Even if the Luftwaffe eliminated this force in short order (which, in the event, it effectively did), the VVS still had thousands of aircraft available in deeper regions of the USSR. The magnitude of the task facing the Luftwaffe forces in June and July 1941 cannot be over stated; especially given that they had to not only neutralize a vastly larger enemy air force, but were being asked to simultaneously provide ground and interdiction support for the Army along a 1,500km front in what was the largest ground invasion in history.[437]

---

[433] In the RAF aircraft damage was classified by category, with 'category 3' as the most severe and likely to result in the aircraft being written off.

[434] J. Ellis, WWII: A Statistical Survey, Facts On File Inc, New York 1993, p. 258.

[435] Sometimes ambiguity and/or carelessness even exist in the same source. E.g., H. Boog, et al, p. 817 states there were "4,400 Luftwaffe aircraft put permanently or temporarily out of action on the East Front in 1941", i.e. this figure includes damaged aircraft which were temporarily out of action. On p. 818 it then states that "Total losses on all fronts since the beginning of the war in the East was therefore 5,730"; i.e. this was the 'total-loss' figure and no attempt is made to understand how many were returned to service. Accordingly, in the next paragraph this figure is then (inappropriately) compared directly to the new aircraft production figures for June to December 1941.

[436] Refer Volume IIIB 3. 3) a. – 'The Composition of the Soviet VVS KA, VVS VMF and PVO Air Forces on 22nd June 1941'. This figure includes those VVS DBA (Long Range Bomber Aviation) units which were Deployed (D) within the Western Special Military Districts on 22nd June 1941.

[437] Refer to Volume IIB 5. 3) c. - 'An Assessment of the Actual Luftwaffe Forces Available to Support German Ground Operations during Operation Barbarossa', to gain an appreciation of the magnitude of this task.

Given these numbers alone, it is rather astonishing the Luftwaffe was able to conduct effective offensive operations at all without being annihilated. This is even truer when one considers that the Luftwaffe was the attacking air force over hostile territory as opposed to a defending fighter force over friendly territory. In fact, it is safe to say that no other air force in WWII faced anything close to the numerical odds, or such diverse strategic objectives, as those faced by the Luftwaffe in the East from June to August 1941. This includes the so called RAF 'few' during the Battle of Britain.[438]

2. Remarkably, the Luftwaffe managed to rapidly establish air superiority along most of the East Front by mid-July 1941.[439] It had established air superiority in almost all the major front sectors by late July, especially in the most critical central and northern sectors, and the approaches to Moscow. Post-war reports by Red Army units in these sectors reveal that they repeatedly complained of enemy air support destroying and/or disrupting a particular defence line or attack formation. It was only in the far south (around Odessa) that the Axis air-forces only achieved what could be described as air parity.

3. This level of air superiority and interdiction against Red Army units was maintained until late October and early November 1941, when Luftflotte 2 and II. Fliegerkorps, along with almost a third of the Luftwaffe strength in the East, was ordered to the West. At the same time German Army reports of VVS activities seriously affecting their ground operations are relatively rare, especially from June to November 1941. In fact the OKH remained far more concerned with Red Army activities during the whole of 1941, and didn't even rate the VVS as a serious threat at the operational level until late 1942. Interestingly, this is also when the first Fw 190 fighters were sent to the East Front, even though they had been operating in the West for almost a year and a half (since mid-1941).

4. Given the previous point, it is apparent that the Luftwaffe achieved all its operational goals in the East in the critical period June to October 1941, especially in the central and northern sectors of the East Front. This meant that the German Army had its needed air superiority in the central sector and the approaches to Moscow during almost the whole 1941 summer-autumn period. When the OKH and OKW chose not to send the German Army against Moscow in August-September 1941, then this decision was **not due** to VVS air power. In other words, the Luftwaffe had succeeded in creating the preconditions needed for the German Army to invade the Moscow-Gorki space in August and September 1941, which was the best chance for Operation Barbarossa to succeed in 1941.

5. The Luftwaffe averaged an incredible kill to loss ratio of over 5.5 to 1 (including aircraft destroyed on the ground) on the East Front from June to December 1941, and it was probably considerably higher. During this time the VVS lost at least 21,200 aircraft as total write offs, while the Luftwaffe lost only around 3,800 aircraft as total write-offs during the same period (including operational losses).[440] Even worse than this is that there is strong evidence that the VVS losses in 1941 actually amounted to some 25,000 aircraft (including operational losses). This is based on the known VVS strengths from June to December 1941, and the aircraft known to have been manufactured and received.[441] On balance, it is almost impossible to imagine how the Luftwaffe could have accomplished what they historically achieved with fewer casualties.

---

[438] The numerical odds in the air alone, far exceeded those faced by the RAF during the Battle of Britain. From 6th July to 28th September 1940 the RAF Fighter Command's strength (in the UK) averaged around 990 serviceable fighters. The entire Luftwaffe strength available to attack the UK on 6th July 1940 was 2,460 aircraft, comprising 760 single engine fighters, 220 twin engine fighters, 280 dive bombers and 1,200 bombers. This gave the Luftwaffe an apparent initial combat aircraft superiority of around 2.5 to 1. Note, however, the parity in numbers of fighters. In addition, if RAF Bomber Command (506 aircraft) and RAF Coastal Command (490 aircraft) are included, the Luftwaffe's initial apparent 'overwhelming numerical superiority' (as it is often referred to) in this battle drops to only around 1.2 combat aircraft to 1. The RAF achieved a 1.8 to 1 kill/loss ratio in this battle from 10th July to 31st October 1940 (1,065 RAF aircraft totally destroyed including 1,004 fighters, vs 1 922 Luftwaffe aircraft totally destroyed including 636 single engine and 243 two engine fighters). Data compiled from J. Ellis, WWII: A Statistical Survey, Facts On File Inc, New York, 1993, pp. 232, 241, 242 and 259, tables 18, 38, 39 and 61.

[439] Note, 'air superiority' is a level down from 'air supremacy'. The side with air superiority can achieve control over a particular airspace when it chooses to; usually in order to fulfil a particular mission. In general, bombers still require escort and protection from enemy fighters. Air supremacy is achieved only when one side effectively achieves complete control of a particular air space for extended periods. In this instance the side with air supremacy can use bombers to attack ground targets at will, usually even without escorts. This condition was achieved by the USAAF and RAF over Normandy in June 1944, and Germany in late 1944 and 1945. In all these situations, enemy Flak remains a very significant threat.

[440] G.F. Krivosheev, et al, Soviet Casualties and Combat Losses in the Twentieth Century, ed. Colonel General G.F. Krivosheev, Greenhill Books, London, 1997, table 95, p. 254. Also, C. Bergstrom, A. Mikhailov, Black Cross Red Star, The Air War Over the Eastern Front: Volume 1, Pacifica Military History, Pacifica, California, 2000, p. 252. Bergstrom and Mikhailov also refer to a 5,240 'unaccounted decrease' in VVS aircraft strength in June and July 1941 (p. 252).

[441] This analysis is carried out in depth in Volume IIIB 3. 5) a. – 'Review of the VVS Aircraft Losses in 1941'.

With this kill to loss ratio the Luftwaffe forces in the East were able to accomplish the daunting tasks set out for them on 22nd June 1941, particularly the virtual elimination of the huge VVS forces that existed in June 1941. The 3,800 aircraft total write-offs, and the approximately 4,400 aircrew personnel casualties suffered in the East in 1941 (see below), were well within the capacity of German industry and Luftwaffe flight training schools to replace. By 27th December 1941 the Luftwaffe's actual front-line aircraft strength had declined by only 403 aircraft (since 21st June 1941) while the number of available front-line aircrew had actually increased by 274 (since 21st June 1941).[442] By comparison the VVS aircraft strength had declined by over 14,200 aircraft (since 22nd June 1941) and, much worse, around 75% of the experienced pre-war aircrews had been irrecoverably lost.[443] The fact that Operation Barbarossa ultimately failed to defeat the USSR in 1941 was not due to the Luftwaffe's lack of results: the blame for this lies squarely elsewhere in the Wehrmacht.

***

Another number which stands out in the 'Luftwaffe Aircraft Losses From 22nd June to 27th December 1941' table (above) is the relatively high number of aircraft lost on the Western Fronts from June to December 1941. Almost a quarter of the total aircraft lost by the Luftwaffe during the second half of 1941 were in the West. This is very significant when one considers that during this whole period the main effort (by far) of the German ground forces was on the Eastern Front where the strategic outcome of WWII was likely being decided, and when the Western Fronts were still considered complete sideshows. Despite this, many of the aircraft lost in the West were the most modern fighters and bombers available, along with some of the best trained fighter pilots and bomber aircrews.[444] As the war progressed into 1942 the proportion of Luftwaffe aircraft lost in the West steadily increased, along with progressively more Luftwaffe strength. As we have seen in previous sections, only around one third of the Luftwaffe's existing strength was available to support the German forces in the East in late December 1941. After July 1943 (the Kursk offensive) the proportion of Luftwaffe aircraft lost on the Western Fronts permanently exceeded 50%, and continued upwards towards the 65-70% mark (especially for fighters and night fighters).

It is sometimes claimed that the largest air war in history was conducted on the East Front during WWII.[445] However this is only a true statement if the measure for a 'large air war' is the total number of aircraft lost by all the belligerents. Due to the fact that the USSR irrecoverably lost 106,400 aircraft during WWII, then the air war in the East may arguably be considered the largest in history.[446] In comparison, the RAF and USAAF irrecoverably lost at least 69,000 aircraft in Europe during WWII.[447] But if the average air-force strengths of the respective air forces over the relevant time period are considered, and if where the Luftwaffe sustained most of its aircraft losses during WWII is considered, then the battles between the Luftwaffe and the RAF and USAAF over Europe actually constituted the largest air war in history.

[442] H. Boog, et al, German Research Institute for Military history at Potsdam, Germany and the Second World War, Volume IV: The Attack on the Soviet Union. Clarendon Press (Oxford University Press), New York, 1996, pp. 817 and 819.
[443] G.F. Krivosheev, et al, Soviet Casualties and Combat Losses in the Twentieth Century, ed. Colonel General G.F. Krivosheev, Greenhill Books, London, 1997, table 95, p. 254. Also Refer Volume IIIB 3. 5) a. – 'Review of the VVS Aircraft Losses in 1941'.
[444] E.g., Fw 190s and Do 217s, neither of which served in the East during 1941.
[445] E.g., C. Bergstrom, A. Mikhailov, Black Cross Red Star, The Air War Over the Eastern Front: Volume 1, Pacifica Military History, Pacifica, California, 2000, p. 255. This series is recommended for anyone wanting a view of the air war on the East Front from the Soviet VVS's perspective. However, this is not due to the excellence of the work, but rather to the dearth of available information on the VVS during 1941. Unfortunately the statistical data presented is unreferenced, and for the Luftwaffe their statistics do not usually stand up to scrutiny (despite the authors, claim it is "the Luftwaffe's own records"). To quote one example of many: on page 255 it is stated that the total number of Luftwaffe aircraft written off and damaged on the East Front from 22nd June to 31st December 1941 was 3,827, which is considerably fewer than the 4,400 figure supplied by the German records in the Bundesarchiv-Militärarchiv (up to 27th Dec. 1941). Furthermore, the work is tainted with an unfortunate tendency to use Soviet-era style rhetoric when describing the apparent outcomes of this or that operation or campaign. It is quite subtle at times but permeates the whole work: the attempt at objectivity is more an illusion than actual. The 'conclusions' chapter is the guiltiest of this: it is as though the authors suddenly revealed their true feelings. Most of the statements in this chapter are misinformed, misleading and nonsensical (unsupported in the book). Most of the figures used are either incorrect or/and presented out of context, and several paragraphs are reminiscent of passages from the Soviet 'History of the Great Patriotic War'. This is unfortunate as the work is otherwise quite good in regard to VVS information. Just ignore the rhetoric, and treat the figures (especially those relating to the Luftwaffe) with extreme caution and in their proper context (i.e. from other accounts of WWII air campaigns if possible).
[446] G.F. Krivosheev, et al, Soviet Casualties and Combat Losses in the Twentieth Century, ed. Colonel General G.F. Krivosheev, Greenhill Books, London, 1997, table 95, p. 254. Includes losses from all causes, with the large majority being single engine aircraft. In the West, over half of the losses were heavy 2-4 engine bomber types.
[447] J. Ellis, WWII: A Statistical Survey, Facts On File Inc, New York 1993, p. 259. This includes a conservative estimate of 32,000 RAF (22,010 combat related and around 10,000 'operational') aircraft and 37,000 USAAF (18,418 combat related and 18,369 'operational') aircraft lost in Europe during WWII. RAF losses are assumed to include all losses from 1939 to 1941, while USAAF losses are from 1942 to 1945.

In addition, it should be borne in mind that the large majority of VVS aircraft lost on the Eastern Front were small single engine fighters and ground attack aircraft (with 1 or 2 man crews), while a huge proportion of the RAF and USAAF aircraft lost were four engine heavy bombers (with 7 to 8 man crews). This explains why the total number of RAF and USAAF casualties, suffered in air combat during WWII, exceeds that of the VVS.[448] By almost any measure, especially those relating to material and production cost and lives lost, each Avro Lancaster, Boeing B-17 or Consolidated B-24 was worth at least 5-6 single engine aircraft.

On top of all this, the Luftwaffe always maintained its best equipped fighter units in the West, even during the height of Operation Barbarossa. This is illustrated in 1941 by the deployment of the Fw 190A-2/3. This was easily the best and most powerful fighter in the world in mid-1941, even outclassing the Supermarine Spitfire V (an aircraft evenly matched with the Bf 109F).[449] Remarkably, while the Fw 190A rapidly became the fighter of choice among the *Jagdgeschwader* in occupied Europe, **no Fw 190s went to the Eastern Front until JG 51 received some in November 1942**. In other words the OKL and OKW felt the threat posed by the superior RAF fighters in 1941 and almost all of 1942, was sufficient for them maintain hundreds of Fw 190s in the West; even though the Wehrmacht's main effort and most critical campaigns were elsewhere. Even the 'strategically blind' German high command would not have done this if the 'inferior' Bf 109F hadn't proved more than capable of maintaining air superiority in the East. This trend remained unchanged throughout WWII. For example, even in 1945, with the Red Army invading Germany itself, <u>all</u> the *Jagdgeschwader* equipped with Me 262 jet fighters were still deployed against the RAF and USAAF in the West. In fact the only Soviet fighter to claim a Me 262 during WWII was a single La-7 in 1945.[450]

There remains no doubt that the largest and bloodiest land war in history easily remains the East Front during WWII: even exceeding by a wide margin all the losses by all the belligerent nations during WWI. Nevertheless, this does not automatically mean the same applied to the air war on the East Front. The Red Army may have broken the back of the German ground forces during WWII, but it was the RAF and USAAF that eventually broke the back of the Luftwaffe, particularly the Luftwaffe's vital fighter arm (the *Jagdwaffe*). However, as can be seen from the various figures in this section, the price paid by the VVS, RAF and USAAF was extremely high.

***

Finally in this section it is worth examining if the Luftwaffe's effectiveness was severely reduced due to loss of trained aircrew by December 1941. This is because this is stated in some pertinent works, which also sometimes go on to list unqualified Luftwaffe personnel casualties during 1941.[451] The Luftwaffe personnel casualties from 22nd June to 27th December 1941, along with aircrew losses on the East Front, can be summarised in the table below.[452]

---

[448] RAF Bomber Command, alone, suffered 74,000 casualties, of which 55,750 were killed. Officially, this occurred in 8,655 aircraft shot down and another 1,600 accidents. Another well researched source places RAF Bomber Command's losses at 10,724 aircraft (with 1,604 due to accidents). This total included 6,931 four-engine heavy bombers (and 57 aircraft lost while operating with Coastal Command). However (as shown in note 363) even this equates to a huge 6.9 casualties (with 5.2 killed) per aircraft lost, which is impossible to believe (e.g., even the Vickers Wellingtons had a crew of only 5 or 6). Even taking into account personnel losses on the ground (mainly due to accidents), it is far more likely that RAF Bomber Command lost at least 14,800 aircraft in WWII. This figure then correlates with the number and types of bombers that were in service in September 1939, the number and types manufactured and received during the war, and the number and types in service in May 1945. These figures correlate closely even after assuming 20% of war-production never went on any combat operations, and ignoring any pre-war production. Like the RAF, the USAAF has never produced precise figures for aircrew losses over Europe in WWII; but the total Commonwealth and American bomber-crew casualties suffered in the 'strategic bombing offensive' definitely exceeded 100,000 (the US 8th Air Force, alone, suffered over 27,000 killed on operations from UK bases). Only German U-Boat crews suffered a higher percentage loss of their personnel. Refer to note 363 for more on this, and the sources used.

[449] N. Franks, Aircraft versus Aircraft, Grub Street, London 1998, p. 121. Also, S. Wilson, Aircraft of WWII, Aerospace Publications Ltd, Fyshwick, Australia 1998, pp. 70 and 155.

[450] S. Wilson, Aircraft of WWII, Aerospace Publications Ltd, Fyshwick, Australia 1998, p. 107.

[451] E.g., C. Bergstrom, A. Mikhailov, Black Cross Red Star, The Air War Over the Eastern Front: Volume 1, Pacifica Military History, Pacifica, California, 2000, p. 255. Quote. "At the end of 1941 it was clear that neither aircraft production nor the flight training schools could keep pace with such heavy attrition (of Luftwaffe aircraft). If the material losses were hard to replace the personnel losses were impossible to replace. From June to December 1941, the Luftwaffe lost 13,742 men, including ground personnel, on the Eastern Front. Of these 3,231 were killed, 2,028 were missing, and 8,453 were injured". This statement is incorrect and misleading in all regards. Firstly, the Luftwaffe casualty figures are incorrect (actually too low) and there is no effort to clarify the proportion which were aircrew (which is meant to be the whole point; another example of a statistic used out of context). Secondly, German aircraft production in 1941 did keep pace with the losses stated and even kept pace with the higher number of 'total write-offs' using other sources (refer Volume IIB 5. 5) for details on aircraft production in 1941 by type). And thirdly, the Luftwaffe's trained aircrew output outstripped their losses in 1941/42 and actually increased from June to December 1941 (refer text).

[452] H. Boog, et al, German Research Institute for Military history at Potsdam, Germany and the Second World War, Volume IV: The Attack on the Soviet Union. Clarendon Press (Oxford University Press), New York, 1996, p. 818. Ref: Bundesarchiv-

Luftwaffe Personnel Casualties From 22nd June to 27th December 1941				
	Killed	MIA & POW	Wounded	Total
Total Personnel *	6,232	2,564	11,424	20,220
Officers *	732	476	831	2,039
Total Aircrew in the East	3,010	⟶	1,394	4,404
Officer Aircrew in the East	664	⟶	344	1,008
* Includes Luftwaffe flying, anti-aircraft and signals branches on all fronts.				

The total Luftwaffe personnel in this table includes all personnel in: flying units (i.e. aircrew and 'air-troops'), signals units, flak units and airborne forces. These forces numbered around 1,300,000 men on 15th June 1941, of which 33,000 were aircrew (including those in training and replacement agencies).[453] The majority of the casualties shown were sustained by selected Luftwaffe flak battalions which were seconded to operate with the German Army in the East during Operation Barbarossa. These units routinely operated in forward areas and often came into contact with first-line Red Army ground troops. They included the Luftwaffe's motorised mixed flak battalions, each with 12 8.8cm flak guns, which proved to be the most effective way of dealing with the Soviet T-34 and KV heavy tanks during 1941.

The most obvious thing about these figures is that **only 22% of the Luftwaffe's total casualties from June to December 1941 were aircrew personnel on the East Front**. The high proportion of officer casualties (49%) is because a very large proportion of aircrew were officers. The 4,404 aircrew casualties represented only 13% of the 33,000 aircrew personnel in the Luftwaffe on 15th June 1941 (including those in training and replacement agencies). The 3,010 aircrew personnel killed, MIA or POW in the East in 1941 represented only one fifth of the flying crews lost in this way since the start of WWII in September 1939.[454]

In other words these casualties were not particularly exceptional. For irrecoverable losses, the aircrew monthly loss rate in the East from 22nd June to 27th December 1941 was around 502 per month (i.e. 3,010 over 6 months), while the aircrew monthly loss rate in the West from September 1939 to 22nd June 1941 was around 547 per month (i.e. 12,040 over 22 months). In fact we can see that the number of aircrew personnel irrecoverably lost (i.e. killed, MIA or POW) in the East in 1941 was significantly fewer than the number of aircraft totally written off (3,010 vs 3,767), and definitely remained well within acceptable limits. The pre-June 1941 attrition rate had already ensured that the Luftwaffe's training schools were geared to produce highly trained flight crews at a high rate before Operation Barbarossa even commenced. In addition, they did this without compromising the quality of flight training and without reducing flight training hours.[455] A typical Luftwaffe fighter pilot in 1940-42 could still expect five months of military training and aviation theory, followed by a year of pilot training before reporting to an air-combat unit.[456]

On 27th December 1941 the Luftwaffe had 6,149 front-line aircrews, which was 274 more aircrews than the Luftwaffe had on 21st June 1941![457] The fact that only around 2,000 Luftwaffe aircraft remained on the East Front by 27th December 1941, out of a total Luftwaffe strength of approximately 5,480 first-line aircraft, had absolutely nothing to do with shortages of Luftwaffe aircrews. It was almost entirely due to the series of extraordinary 'strategic' decisions made by the highest commands of the OKW from August to November 1941.

***

Militararchiv (BA-MA) RL 2 III/702. Also BA-MA RL 2 III/716, Report on the combat readiness of the flying units as of 27 Dec. 1941, Generalquartiermeister der Luftwaffe, 6. Abt., 30 Dec. 1941.

[453] Refer Volume IIB 3. 2) g. - 'Review of Available Wehrmacht and Waffen SS Personnel (22nd June to 4th July 1941)'. It excludes Luftwaffe personnel in Luftwaffe construction units, home defence units and other auxiliary organisations, with around 245,000 personnel on 15th June 1941.

[454] H. Boog, et al, German Research Institute for Military history at Potsdam, Germany and the Second World War, Volume IV: The Attack on the Soviet Union. Clarendon Press (Oxford University Press), New York, 1996, p. 818.

[455] Ibid.

[456] R.F. Toliver, T.J. Constable, The Blond Knight of Germany: a biography of Erich Hartmann, McGraw Hill Inc, Blue Ridge Summit, PA, 1970, pp. 28, 29 and 30. As a typical Luftwaffe fighter pilot starting in 1940-41, Erich Hartmann started his training at Luftwaffe training regiment 10 at Neukuhren on 15th October 1940, and started flight training at Berlin-Gatow in March 1941. He had completed basic flight training by 14th October 1941, advanced flight training by 31st January 1942, and fighter training by 31st March 1942. He first reported to III/ JG 52 in late August 1942.

[457] H. Boog, et al, German Research Institute for Military history at Potsdam, Germany and the Second World War, Volume IV: The Attack on the Soviet Union. Clarendon Press (Oxford University Press), New York, 1996, p. 819.

6. The Supply Distribution Efficiency (SDE) for the Wehrmacht on the East Front from 22nd June to 31st December 1941

In the FILARM model the relative Supply Distribution Efficiency (SDE) is a measure of the ability of support infrastructures to supply and support a specific number of combat unit types, over a fixed distance and terrain, during combat operations. The support infrastructures include divisional and smaller unit internal support organisations, as well as all corps, army and army group level support units. The SDE includes the ability of these same support infrastructures to maintain equipment in an operational condition: this includes maintenance, repair and recovery of equipment.

For the purposes of clarification, in this chapter the term 'Wehrmacht' includes any organisation which fielded ground and/or air combat units in the East during 1941. This includes the Waffen SS which was not hierarchically part of the Wehrmacht. Volume I Part I 8. titled 'The Structure of the Fully Integrated Land and Air Resource Model (FILARM) - Supply Distribution Efficiency (SDE)' details the concepts behind SDE, why it is so important and all equations relating to how the SDE is calculated. The results of applying the methodology detailed in the above to the German FILARM model from 22nd June to 31st December 1941 are displayed in table Ger 1941 SDE (pages 294 - 297).

The Wehrmacht SDE is shown separately (as a percentage figure) for three forces and period between June and December 1941. These are:

- The SDE for all Deployed (D) Land Combat Units on the East Front from 22nd June to 4th July 1941.

- The SDE for all Reinforcement (R) Land Combat Units on the East Front from 5th July to 31st December 1941.

- The SDE for all Deployed (D) and Reinforcement (R) Land Combat Units on the East Front from 22nd June to 31st December 1941.

The individual weapon system's or squad's Supply Demand Factor (SDF) values are calculated and displayed in the tables shown in Volume IIA 2. titled 'The German Personnel and Equipment Resource Database'. The SDF units used are 100kg of 'supply' per day, with supply representing the average ammunition, fuel, food and water that the weapon system or squad would consume per day on normal offensive operations.

$$***$$

For reference, and for those readers who do not have access to Volume I, the following is a summary of the three principal equations used in table Ger 1941 SDE.

$$SDE_{Force}(\%) = \frac{Supply\ Lift_{All\ Support\ Infrastructure}}{Supply\ Demand_{All\ Combat\ Units} * Supply\ Radius_{km}} * C_{Weather} * \frac{1}{10}$$

Where: $Supply\ Lift_{All\ Support\ Infrastructure}$ is the product of the supply mass that can be moved, and the distance it can be moved per day (measured in metric ton kilometres per day) by all support infrastructures. These include divisional and smaller unit internal support organisations, as well as all corps, army and front level support units.

$Supply\ Demand_{All\ Combat\ Units}$ is the supply demand per day of all combat units supported by the above infrastructures, during combat operations (measured in metric tons per day).

$Supply\ Radius_{km}$ is the fixed distance (measured in kilometres) over which the SDE is being measured. In the FILARM and PILARM models this is 100kms.

$C_{Weather}$ is a modifier for the weather during the period the SDE is being considered. In most cases this equation constant is the same for opposing forces so weather effects usually cancel out when considering relative SDE values. In certain circumstances however, one side may have a higher 'weather constant' value due to special conditions. An example of this in Operation Barbarossa was the winter conditions in November/December 1941, when the Soviets were more prepared for supplying units in freezing or blizzard conditions.

The 1/10 is a scaling factor (so the SDE is in the form of a meaningful percentage).

$$***$$

$$Supply\ Lift_{All\ Support\ Infrastructure} = (T_{RA} * L_T * D_T) + (LT_{RA} * L_{LT} * D_{LT}) + (TR_{RA} * L_{TR} * D_{TR}) +$$
$$0.3 * ((T_{TOE} * L_T * D_T) + (LT_{TOE} * L_{LT} * D_{LT}) + (TR_{TOE} * L_{TR} * D_{TR})) + 0.5 * (H_{TOE} * L_H * D_H)$$

Where: The suffix RA is 'Rear Area'. Rear area in this case means not assigned to the TOE for any Deployed (D), Mobilised and Deployed (MD) or Mobilised and Not Deployed (MND) combat unit.

The suffix TOE means 'assigned to a units TOE', that is to say included in the TOE for any Deployed (D), Mobilised and Deployed (MD) or Mobilised and Not Deployed (MND) combat unit.

T is the number of available Trucks. Trucks include non-tracked vehicles with a designed load capacity of one metric ton or over.

LT is the number of available Light Transports. Light Transports include non-tracked vehicles which are not trucks.

TR is the number of available Tractors or prime movers. Prime movers includes fully or half-tracked vehicles, including artillery tractors and recovery vehicles.

H is the number of available Horse teams. Horse teams include artillery hitch and limber teams (4-8 horses each), separate horse drawn vehicles such as carts, wagons or field kitchens, and groups of six pack horses.

L is the average load capacity of the motorised vehicle or horse team, measured in metric tons. The L suffixes T, LT, TR and H denote Truck, Light Transport, Tractor and Horse Team, respectively.

D is average distance the fully loaded motorised vehicle or horse team can move in one day (measured in kilometres per day), over the terrain in which the SDE is being measured. The D suffixes T, LT, TR and H denote Truck, Light Transport, Tractor or Horse Team, respectively.

The supply lift equation means that all 'unassigned' transport in rear areas, as well as 30% of motorised transport and 50% of horse drawn transport in the TOE of combat units, is available for supply and support services. In addition the inclusion of all prime movers ensures support structures include maintenance, repair and recovery equipment.

***

$$Supply\ Demand_{All\ Combat\ Units} = \left(\sum_{x=1}^{x=n} WS - Sqd\ type\,1\,SDF_x\right) * 0.1 + \left(\sum_{x=1}^{x=n} WS - Sqd\ type\,2\,SDF_x\right) * 0.1$$
$$+ \left(\sum_{x=1}^{x=n} WS - Sqd\ type\,3\,SDF_x\right) * 0.1 .... + Ave\ No\ Listed\ Personnel\,/\,1000$$

Where: $WS - Sqd\ type\ SDF$ is the specific weapon system or squad type **Supply Demand Factor** (SDF), calculated using the methodology used for creating the FILARM database (detailed in Part II of Volume I).[458] Note, the Supply Demand Factor (SDF) for individual weapon system or squad types is expressed in units of 100kg per day: hence the 0.1 correction to express the overall Supply Demand in metric tons per day.

n is the total number of specific weapon system or squad types in the force, e.g. the number of heavy infantry squads, or the number of T-34 tanks, or the number of 76mm howitzers, or the number of Bf 109 fighters, etc.

Ave No Listed personnel is the average number of personnel in the overall forces during the period under consideration. For example, if attempting to calculate SDE over a period of months then this should be the average monthly listed strength. This component of the supply demand equation is to account for the relative food and water consumption by the overall force.

***

---

[458] Refer Volume I, Part II 3. 10) - 'The Methodology Used for Analysing Weapon System Effectiveness, and the Structure of the 1941 Soviet and Axis Resource Database - Methodology for Calculating a Weapon System's or Database Unit's Specific Combat Attributes - Supply Demand Factor (SDF)'.

Table Ger 1941 SDE

The Supply Distribution Efficiency (SDE) for the Wehrmacht on the East Front from 22nd June to 31st December 1941

Database unit	Specific weapon system or squad type Supply Demand Factor (SDF)*	SDE for all Deployed (D) units on the East Front; 22nd June 1941 - 4th July 1941		SDE for all Reinforcements (R) units on the East Front; 5th July 1941 - 31st Dec1941		SDE for all (D) and (R) units on the East Front; 22nd June 1941 - 31st Dec1941	
		No allocated to D units	Supply demand**	No allocated to R units	Supply demand**	No allocated to D and R units	Supply demand**
Heavy Rifle Sqd	1.18	37,710	4,445	8,052	949	45,762	5,394
Light Rifle Sqd	0.70	4,120	289	169	12	4,289	301
Motor Cycle Sqd	1.91	21,046	4,011	2,489	474	23,535	4,485
Bicycle Sqd	0.70	3,430	241	991	70	4,421	311
Cavalry Sqd	1.23	1,599	197	81	10	1,680	207
Eng Sqd	2.14	6,932	1,486	973	209	7,905	1,694
Light Eng Sqd	0.98	12,932	1,271	298	29	13,230	1,300
Ferry Bridging Sqd	0.30	3,991	121	119	4	4,110	124
Military Police Sqd	0.41	2,544	104	14	1	2,558	104
Irregular Sqd	0.49	1,344	66	1,088	54	2,432	120
Rail Repair Sqd	0.30	2,901	88	8	0	2,909	88
HMG	0.74	14,981	1,102	2,588	190	17,569	1,292
LMG	0.55	19,984	1,105	4,138	229	24,122	1,334
AT Rifle	0.04	9,287	37	1,965	8	11,252	45
50mm Mor	2.21	10,381	2,290	1,690	373	12,071	2,663
81mm Mor	6.04	6,700	4,049	1,065	644	7,765	4,693
Horse Team	0.26	126,969	3,352	25,574	675	152,543	4,027
Unit Trucks	1.50	150,088	22,453	17,261	2,582	167,349	25,035
Light Transport	0.53	84,880	4,482	9,594	507	94,474	4,988
Light Halftrack	2.30	5,159	1,187	370	85	5,529	1,272
Medium Halftrack	3.22	4,324	1,392	396	128	4,720	1,520
Heavy Halftrack	4.26	1,265	538	60	26	1,325	564

Weapon System	SDF factor						
37mm ATG	1.62	8,118	1,317	1,282	208	9,400	1,526
50mm ATG	4.17	812	339	72	30	884	369
47mm ATG	3.63	177	64	6	2	183	66
28mm sPzb 41	0.34	40	1	40	1	80	3
75mm Inf G	9.45	2,584	2,442	398	376	2,982	2,818
150mm Inf G	25.54	672	1,716	60	153	732	1,869
75mm Gun	9.18	160	147	38	35	198	182
105mm How	17.26	4,293	7,410	772	1,333	5,065	8,743
105mm IG40	17.25	4	7	0	0	4	7
150mm How	29.23	1,972	5,765	222	649	2,194	6,414
105mm Gun	17.65	428	755	8	14	436	769
150mm Gun	28.90	62	179	9	26	71	205
210mm How	33.22	291	967	0	0	291	967
210mm Gun	39.69	12	48	0	0	12	48
240mm How	38.35	8	31	0	0	8	31
240mm Gun	34.97	12	42	0	0	12	42
305mm How	48.55	16	78	0	0	16	78
355mm How	72.45	1	7	0	0	1	7
600mm How	89.25	4	36	0	0	4	36
150-200 mm Rail Guns	28.90	3	9	0	0	3	9
210-280 mm Rail Guns	48.29	21	101	10	48	31	150
380+mm Rail Gun/Mor	84.00	0	0	4	34	4	34
100-280mm Coastal Guns	30.58	177	541	0	0	177	541
Nebelwerfer 35	5.16	72	37	0	0	72	37
Nebelwerfer 40	6.22	72	45	0	0	72	45
Nebelwerfer 41	15.94	210	335	0	0	210	335
28/32cm Rocket Systems	19.33	960	1,856	0	0	960	1,856

* Refer to Volume IIA 2. "The German Personnel and Equipment Resource Database - Supply Demand Factors' for description and values of each weapon system's or squad's SDF factor: shown in units of 100kg per day.

^ The 'Ave No of listed personnel' is the German average monthly listed strength on the East Front from June to December 1941.

** Measured in metric tons per day (refer text)

*^ Measured in metric ton kilometres per day (refer text).

© Nigel Askey, 2018

Table Ger 1941 SDE (cont.)

The Supply Distribution Efficiency (SDE) for the Wehrmacht on the East Front from 22nd June to 31st December 1941

Database unit	Specific weapon system or squad type Supply Demand Factor (SDF)*	SDE for all Deployed (D) units on the East Front; 22nd June 1941 - 4th July 1941		SDE for all Reinforcements (R) units on the East Front; 5th July 1941 - 31st Dec1941		SDE for all (D) and (R) units on the East Front; 22nd June 1941 - 31st Dec1941	
		No allocated to D units	Supply demand**	No allocated to R units	Supply demand**	No allocated to D and R units	Supply demand**
Sd Kfz 250 APC	2.94	39	11	0	0	39	11
Sd Kfz 251 APC	2.94	591	174	55	16	646	190
Sd Kfz 254 AOP	2.15	101	22	7	2	108	23
Sd Kfz 221 A Cars	2.26	277	63	20	5	297	67
Sd Kfz 222 A Cars	2.71	260	71	20	5	280	76
Sd Kfz 260/261 A Cars	1.90	99	19	2	0	101	19
Sd Kfz 223 A Cars	2.26	256	58	11	2	267	60
Sd Kfz 231/232 A Cars	5.02	162	81	12	6	174	87
Sd Kfz 263 A Cars	3.91	114	45	2	1	116	45
Sd Kfz 247 A Cars	2.02	9	2	0	0	9	2
Panhard 178	3.50	190	66	0	0	190	66
Pz Kpfw I	3.08	309	95	2	1	311	96
Kleine Pz Bef I	3.06	119	36	4	1	123	38
Pz Kpfw II	4.52	817	369	172	78	989	447
Pz Kpfw III (37mm)	11.03	274	302	0	0	274	302
Pz Kpfw III (50mm)	13.30	717	953	281	374	998	1327
Pz Bef III (Gross)	7.86	122	96	18	14	140	110
Pz Kpfw IV	20.77	439	912	60	125	499	1036
Pz Kpfw 38(t)	6.22	625	389	17	11	642	400
Pz Bef 38(t)	6.22	35	22	0	0	35	22
Pz Kpfw 35(t)	6.10	155	95	0	0	155	95
Pz Bef 35(t)	6.10	5	3	0	0	5	3
StuG III Assault Gun	19.44	301	585	111	216	412	801
Sdkfz 252	2.94	129	38	48	14	177	52
Sdkfz 253	2.94	195	57	19	5	214	63
15cm sIG33 SP Guns	31.52	24	76	12	38	36	113
PzJager I (47mm)	6.34	150	95	27	17	177	112
47mm, Pz kpfw 35R(f)	5.91	81	48	0	0	81	48

	SDF						
Pz kpfw 35R(f) (Bef only)	4.67	12	6	0	0	12	6
SP 88 mm AAG	22.84	6	14	0	0	6	14
105mm K18 Pz Sfl IVa	28.64	2	6	0	0	2	6
Pz.Kpfw II (F)	47.03	84	395	0	0	84	395
Pz.Kpfw B2	30.26	6	18	0	0	6	18
Pz.Kpfw B2 (F)	61.03	24	146	0	0	24	146
Pz.Kpfw 35-S	9.02	28	25	0	0	28	25
Pz.Kpfw 38H	5.59	24	13	0	0	24	13
Pz I (Pio)	3.08	80	25	20	6	100	31
Sd Kfz 300	0.70	54	4	0	0	54	4
Pz IV Bridge Layer	7.20	4	3	8	6	12	9
Pz IV Ammo Carrier	7.20	8	6	0	0	8	6
Armoured Train	0.00	12	0	0	0	12	0
20 mm AAG	0.61	2371	144	744	45	3115	190
20mm Quad AAG	1.27	22	3	16	2	38	5
37 mm AAG	2.26	152	34	50	11	202	46
88-105mm AAG	16.96	616	1045	192	326	808	1371
Truck 20mm AAG	1.74	60	10	0	0	60	10
Sd Kfz 10/4	2.97	384	114	20	6	404	120
Sd Kfz 6/2	5.12	114	58	15	8	129	66
Sd Kfz 7/1	4.61	44	20	4	2	48	22
AA Searchlights	0.00	584	0	188	0	772	0
Rear Area Trucks	1.50	299912	44867	28500	4264	328412	49130
Rear Area Light Transports	0.53	42328	2235	1500	79	43828	2314
Average number of listed personnel		3359345			500125	^	3341421
Total Supply Demand (all combat units)**		135913			16351		151746
Motorised vehicles available for SDE		415955			38304		454259
Total Supply Lift (all support infrastructure)*^		102486936			10081598		112568535
Total Ground Forces only SDE		75.4%			61.7%		74.18%
Total Ground Force **and Luftwaffe** SDE		71.9%			58.8%		70.72%

© Nigel Askey, 2018

* Refer to Volume IIA 2. "The German Personnel and Equipment Resource Database - Supply Demand Factors' for description and values of each weapon system's or squad's SDF factor: shown in units of 100kg per day.

^ The 'Ave No of listed personnel' is the German average monthly listed strength on the East Front from June to December 1941.

** Measured in metric tons per day (refer text)

*^ Measured in metric ton kilometres per day (refer text).

1) The SDE for all Deployed (D) Land Combat Units on the East Front from 22nd June to 4th July 1941

Columns 3-4 in table Ger 1941 SDE shows the Supply Distribution Efficiency (SDE) for all personnel and equipment allocated to all Deployed (D) land combat units in the German Army, Waffen SS, Luftwaffe Ground Forces and Naval Coastal Artillery, on the East Front from 22nd June to 4th July 1941.

It therefore includes all land combat units shown in 'The German Deployment Matrix' which were in Army Group North, Army Group Centre, Army Group South, Norway Army - Befehlsstelle Finnland (East Front Only), and OKH Reserves.[459] The 'number of database units allocated to Deployed (D) combat units' and the 'average number of listed personnel' is obtained from table Ger Total Deployed (D) 1 (pages 74 - 77).[460]

The overall SDE for all Deployed (D) land combat units on the East Front from 22nd June to 4th July 1941 was approximately **75%**.

***

2) The SDE for all Reinforcement (R) Land Combat Units on the East Front from 5th July to 31st December 1941

Columns 5-6 in table Ger 1941 SDE shows the Supply Distribution Efficiency (SDE) for all personnel and equipment that arrived in land combat unit Reinforcements (R) from 5th July to 31st December 1941.

It includes combat units Deployed (D) in the West on 22nd June 1941 and which were transferred east and arrived on the East Front after 4th July 1941, and newly mobilised combat units which were mobilised after 22nd June 1941 and arrived on the East Front during 1941. Note, the latter are classified as Mobilised and Deployed (MD) combat units in the German FILARM model.

The 'number of database units allocated to (R) combat units' and the 'average number of listed personnel' is calculated from the table German Reinforcement Matrix (pages 68 - 71).[461] This shows the German Army, Waffen SS and Luftwaffe Flak reinforcements to the East Front, each month, from 5th July to 31st December 1941. The values shown in table Ger 1941 SDE are the sum of all the actual equipment and personnel that were in these units (as far as can be ascertained) when they arrived on the East Front during 1941.

The overall SDE for land combat units that arrived as Reinforcements (R) on the East Front from 5th July to 31st December 1941 was approximately **62%**.

The reader should note that this SDE is not a 'real SDE' in that it didn't actually exist at any point in time. This is because the Reinforcement (R) units under question, as well as any additional rear area transport, arrived on the East Front over a period of approximately six months. The SDE shown here is effectively the hypothetical SDE that these Reinforcement (R) units would have had if they had all appeared simultaneously along with any new (reinforcing) rear area transport. Nevertheless, it is not an unreasonable assumption that the monthly arrival of reinforcements on the German's East Front corresponded in general terms with the arrival of additional transport (commandeered from the civilian economy and from new production). Thus the average SDE available to the Reinforcement (R) units over the period June-December 1941 is going to average from 60-70%.

From table Ger 1941 SDE we can see that the SDE for land combat units that arrived as Reinforcements (R) was significantly lower than that for the units already Deployed (D) on the East Front from 22nd June to 4th July 1941. This was because by 22nd June 1941 the Wehrmacht had already commandeered most of the available motor vehicles that could be spared by the German economy, including those from the occupied territories and those captured from defeated enemy forces (particularly French vehicles). Thus the additional rear-area transport sent to the East Front after 4th July 1941 mostly consisted of newly produced motor vehicles.

***

---

[459] Refer Volume IIB 1. – 'The Order of Battle (OOB) of German Land Combat Units from 22nd June to 4th July 1941'.
[460] Refer Volume IIB 3. 1) – 'The Total Personnel and Equipment Allocated to Combat Units and in a Deployed (D) state in the German Army, Waffen SS, Luftwaffe Ground Forces and Naval Coastal Artillery from 22nd June to 4th July 1941'.
[461] Refer Volume IIB 2. – 'German Land Combat Unit Reinforcements on the East Front from 5th July to 31st December 1941'.

3) The SDE for all Deployed (D) and Reinforcement (R) Land Combat Units on the East Front from 22nd June to 31st December 1941

The last two columns in table Ger 1941 SDE shows the Supply Distribution Efficiency (SDE) for all personnel and equipment allocated to all Deployed (D) and Reinforcement (R) land combat units in the German Army, Waffen SS, Luftwaffe Ground Forces and Naval Coastal Artillery, on the East Front from 22nd June to 31st December 1941. It therefore includes all land combat units shown in 'The German Deployment Matrix' which were in Army Group North, Army Group Centre, Army Group South, Norway Army - Befehlsstelle Finnland (East Front Only), and OKH Reserves; and all land combat units shown in the 'German Reinforcement Matrix'.[462]

The 'number of database units allocated to D and R combat units' is the sum of the corresponding values in the previous third and fifth columns. The 'average number of listed personnel' is obtained from table Prof MSG.[463] This is the average monthly listed strength for Wehrmacht personnel facing the Soviet forces from 22nd June to 31st December 1941.

From table Ger 1941 SDE we can finally ascertain that the **overall average SDE available to the Wehrmacht's ground forces on the East Front from June to December 1941 was approximately 74%.**

From this analysis we can see that the German Army's SDE in the East declined only slightly after June 1941, despite relatively few additional motorised transport and supply units arriving at the front. This was because the 'size' of the Reinforcement (R) forces that arrived on the East Front from July to December 1941 was relatively small compared to the size of initial invasion force.

Similarly to the SDE calculation for 'Reinforcement (R) Land Combat Units on the East Front', the SDE calculation for 'Deployed (D) and Reinforcement (R) Land Combat Units on the East Front' is a theoretical value based on the assumption that all units existed simultaneously along with all the rear area transport. It does **not take into account combat and attrition losses, the staggered arrival of new combat units and new transport units, or the average rate of repair of broken down motor vehicles**. In reality, many of the units already at the front were being depleted or possibly even destroyed, while simultaneously new reinforcements and Replacements (R) were continuously arriving over the period under question. In addition, the available rear area transport also fluctuated as the Germans captured large numbers of trucks and tractor prime-movers in the large enveloping attacks of 1941. For example, between 22nd June and 31st December 1941 the German Army captured at least 52,238 Soviet trucks and artillery tractors in working order, and an immense supply of spare parts (mainly from intact vehicles which were not in working order).[464]

However it is again not unreasonable to assume that the loss and gain of combat unit strength (units being destroyed and new units arriving) would have approximately correlated with the loss and gain of transport strength (transport being destroyed and new transport arriving). Thus the overall average SDE available to the Wehrmacht's ground forces on the East Front from June to December 1941 would still have averaged around 74%, plus or minus 2%. With modern levels of commuting power, and if the simulation is sophisticated enough, then it is possible to calculate (using the equations in this chapter) the average SDE across the whole front at the end of each day. The Wehrmacht ground forces operating on the East Front would then start with an SDE of around 75%, and each day all that day's losses and reinforcements/replacements would be taken into account to adjust the overall force SDE for the next day. This would then also account for repaired vehicles returning to service and captured vehicles entering service. To some extent this SDE adjustment is done anyway due to fluctuations in the weather (each day, week or month; depending on the simulation). In this case the SDE modification is applied to both sides equally, unless one side had some advantage in this regard.

On balance, however, if a military simulation or war-game designer needed one value for the Wehrmacht ground forces' SDE (on the East Front) over the period 22nd June to 31st December 1941, then the value of around 74% would be it.

---

[462] Refer Volume IIB 1. – 'The Order of Battle (OOB) of German Land Combat Units from 22nd June to 4th July 1941' and Volume IIB 2. – 'German Land Combat Unit Reinforcements on the East Front from 5th July to 31st December 1941'.

[463] Table Prof MSG (Monthly Strength German). Refer Volume 5. 3. 1) - 'Axis and Soviet Relative Overall Combat Proficiency (ROCP) in 1941 - German Forces: Strength, Casualties, Defensive Posture and Terrain'. This calculation takes into account the German strength in the East on 22nd July 1941, the casualties each month, the Replacements (R) each month and the reinforcements that arrived in the East each month. It may vary slightly as new information is added to the ROCP calculations (in Volume V), but not enough to significantly alter the overall SDE figure for 1941.

[464] Kroener, B. R., et al, German Research Institute for Military History at Potsdam, Germany and the Second World War; Volume I, Part 1, Wartime Administration, Economy and Manpower Resources 1939-1941, Clarendon Press (Oxford University Press Inc), New York, 2000, Table II.VII.4. Ref: BA-MA RW 19/1379 ff, ten-day reports of the quartermaster-general. Also indicated in this list is 13,958 AFVs, armoured scout cars and 'other' vehicles.

4) Inclusion of the Luftwaffe's Air Combat Units in the SDE Calculation

Combat aircraft in WWII had a huge appetite for fuel, ammunition and spare parts, which usually arrived on the airfield in trucks with very little being flown in. If an airfield was located forward with advancing spearheads or was remote from a railhead, this only made the overland (or seaborne) supply system more important. Supplying them purely by air was usually not an option. Obviously vehicles transporting ammunition and fuel to air combat units, and involved in supporting and maintaining them, cannot also have been supplying and supporting land combat units. Naturally the Luftwaffe had a significant amount of dedicated motorised transport to perform this function.

Table Ger 1941 SDE Luft shows the calculation of the additional 'supply demand' on the German's transport infrastructure due to the need to support the Luftwaffe's air combat units on the East Front from 22nd June to 31st December 1941. The aircraft type Supply Demand Factors (SDF) are derived from the methodology detailed in Volume I Part II.[465] The number and type of combat aircraft in a Deployed (D) state on the East Front on 21st June 1941 is taken from table Luft Total EF.[466] In addition, the number and type of combat aircraft that arrived in Reinforcement (R) units on the East Front from June to 31st December 1941 is ascertained from tables Luft Rein 1 and Luft Rein 2.[467] Obviously the geographical area included, and the time period selected, match the Wehrmacht ground forces data used for table Ger 1941 SDE.

Table Ger 1941 SDE Luft							
The Additional 'Supply Demand' for the Luftwaffe's Air Combat Units from 22nd June to 31st December 1941							
Aircraft Type	Aircraft Type Supply Demand Factor (SDF)*	SDE for aircraft Deployed (D) on the East Front, 21st June 1941		SDE for Reinforcements (R) (incl. MD units) on the East Front, June - 31st Dec. 1941		SDE for D, MD and R aircraft on the East Front from 21st June to 31st December 1941	
		No allocated to D units	Supply demand^	No allocated to MD and R units	Supply demand^	No allocated to D, MD and R units	Supply demand^
Single Engine Fighters	10	975	975	62	62	1037	1037
Twin Eng. Ftr. / Ftr. Bmbrs	20	207	414	0	0	207	414
Twin Eng Night Fighters	16	0	0	0	0	0	0
Single Eng. Ftr. Bombers	12	38	46	0	0	38	46
Dive Bombers	24	337	809	0	0	337	809
Twin Engine Bombers	30	949	2847	246	738	1195	3585
Four Engine Bombers	40	0	0	0	0	0	0
Long Range Recon	25	312	780	0	0	312	780
SR Recon / Army Coop	10	654	654	9	9	663	663
Seaplanes	15	63	95	0	0	63	95
Tot. Supply Demand (combat aircraft)^			6619		809		7428
* Refer to Volume IIA 2. 'The German Personnel and Equipment Resource Database' for description and values of aircraft type SDF factors: shown in units of 100kg per day.							
^ Measured in metric tons per day (refer text). © Nigel Askey, 2018							

At the bottom of table Ger 1941 SDE we can now see the average SDE of the Wehrmacht ground forces **and** Luftwaffe air combat units, together. This takes into account the additional trucks and supplies needed to support the Luftwaffe air units operating in the same vicinity and during the same period as the relevant Wehrmacht ground units. The inclusion of the Luftwaffe's air units means that the 'Total Supply Lift' capacity of the Wehrmacht on the East Front used in table Ger 1941 SDE doesn't change, but the 'Total Supply Demand' changes significantly.

This ignores any increase in the available 'Total Supply Lift' due to any Luftwaffe transport aircraft in 1941, which is not unreasonable for three main reasons. Firstly, the Luftwaffe never had huge numbers of transport aircraft available.[468] Secondly, most of the time the available Luftwaffe air-transport units were used to transport troops to

---

[465] Refer Volume I Part II 3. 10) b. – 'Methodology for Calculating a Weapon System's or Database Unit's Specific Combat Attributes - Supply Demand Factor (SDF) - SDF Values for Aircraft'. A few reasons why overland (or seaborne) supply of combat aircraft should be considered in any realistic military simulation, are also discussed.
[466] Refer Volume IIB 5. 3) a. – 'Luftwaffe Strength Available to Support Operation Barbarossa on 21st June 1941'.
[467] Refer Volume IIB 5. 4) a. – 'The Transfer of Deployed (D) and Newly Mobilised Air Combat Units to the Eastern Front: June to December 1941'.
[468] A total of 4,845 Ju 52s, the Luftwaffe's principal transport aircraft throughout the war, were manufactured in Germany and France; including significant pre-war production. S. Wilson, Aircraft of WWII, Aerospace Publications Ltd, Fyshwick, Australia 1998, p. 94. The Luftwaffe forces had only 379 transport aircraft in the East on 21st June 1941 (ref. note 464).

and from the front, including the transport of wounded personnel to rear area hospitals; and there were a lot of wounded on the East Front. Valuable air transport capacity was usually only used for transporting ammunition and fuel to airfields under exceptional (and usually desperate) circumstances. And, thirdly, airlift capacity in WWII was in general far less capable and significant than in modern day air forces.[469]

Having said all this, it should be noted that neglecting air-transport in the respective FILARM models has a much larger negative effect on the German's overall SDE value than on the Soviet's overall SDE value. This is because around 720 Ju 52s (the Luftwaffe's principal dedicated transport aircraft) operated on the East Front at some point between 21st June and 31st December 1941, while the VVS had no equivalent (dedicated) air-transport capability. However the overall impact of neglecting air-transport in the FILARM models is still very small. For example, if we include the 721 Ju 52s in the German FILARM model with the appropriate SDF parameters for the Ju 52, then the overall German SDE value shown in table Ger 1941 SDE only increases by around 0.4%.[470]

German air transport did have a significant supply enhancement effect in certain circumstances, even on the massive East Front. During 1941 it was most notably used to maintain six German divisions, with around 90,000 men, in the 'Demyansk pocket' in minimal supply during the whole 1941/42 winter. It has to be said however, that the so called Demyansk pocket was never a truly isolated pocket: it was more a very narrow necked salient into the Soviet lines with a very tenuous overland supply route. From February to May 1942, using airlift and overland supply, a total of 36,000 wounded were evacuated, and around 31,000 replacements/reinforcements and 65,000 tons of supplies arrived in the pocket.[471]

***

Adding the increase in 'supply demand' due to Luftwaffe air operations in 1941, we find that the overall average SDE for all Wehrmacht combat units on the East Front drops by a few percentage points. Specifically that:

- The overall SDE for all Deployed (D) land and air combat units on the East Front from 22nd June to 4th July 1941 was approximately **72%**.

- The overall SDE for land and air combat units that arrived as Reinforcements (R) on the East Front from 5th July to 31st December 1941 was approximately **59%**.

- The overall average SDE available to the Wehrmacht's ground and air forces on the East Front from June to December 1941 was approximately **71%**.

If a military simulation or war-game designer needed one value for the Wehrmacht ground and air forces' SDE (in the East) over the period 22nd June to 31st December 1941, then the value of around 71% would be the value.

In a more sophisticated simulation the Wehrmacht ground and air units operating on the East Front should start with an SDE of around 72%. This should then decline with Reinforcing (R) units having an SDE of approximately 59%. In reality the transport already on the East Front was used in supplying Deployed (D) units as well as the Reinforcing (R) units, so the actual overall Wehrmacht ground and air force SDE approached the average of 71% (above). As noted in the previous section, with modern levels of commuting power it is possible to calculate (using the equations in this chapter) the average SDE across the whole front at the end of each day. The Wehrmacht ground and air forces operating on the East Front would then start with an SDE of around 72%, and each day all that day's losses and reinforcements/replacements would be taken into account to adjust the overall force SDE for the next day.

Finally, it is worth noting that during 1941 the Luftwaffe air combat units in the East only reduced the overall average SDE by around 3.5%. This is because the Luftwaffe forces that invaded the USSR in 1941 were small compared to the German Army's ground forces, and this ratio only shifted progressively further in the German Army's favour as the war wore on. Even the peak Luftwaffe force that invaded the USSR on 22nd June 1941 was relatively small by WWII standards (contrary to popular perception); especially compared to Western Allied air-forces fielded from 1942 onwards and compared to the opposing VVS force in June 1941.

---

[469] Today large fleets of massive heavy lift aircraft are capable of routinely transporting major supplies and even motorised land forces around the world. The closest to this during WWII was the USAAF's air-transport arm from late 1944. This was mostly due to the abundance of the Douglas C-47. A total of 10,665 Douglas C-47 Skytrain/Dakotas and 1,242 Douglas C-54 Skymasters had been manufactured in the USA by the end of WWII. S. Wilson, Aircraft of WWII, Aerospace Publications Ltd, Fyshwick, Australia 1998, p. 58.

[470] This assumes a Ju 52 SDF of 15, which leads to an increase in overall 'Supply Demand' of 1,082 metric tons per day. It results in increase in 'Supply Lift' of 1,418,928 metric ton kilometres per day (refer Volume I Part II 3. 10)). The latter uses a L (Lift) factor of 3.28 metric tons, and a D (Distance) factor of 600km (i.e. 721 aircraft x 3.28 x 600).

[471] Refer Volume IIA 3. 9) a. ii. – 'Waffen SS Motorised Divisions - SS Totenkopf Motorised Division' for more details on the Demyansk pocket in 1941/42.

5) Parameters Relating Specifically to the Calculation of the Wehrmacht SDE in 1941

In calculating the Supply Distribution Efficiency (SDE) for the Wehrmacht from 22nd June to 31st December 1941, certain specific parameters were used. These relate to the unique conditions or circumstances facing the German Army and Luftwaffe in 1941.

a. Specific Weapon System or Squad Supply Demand Factors (SDFs)

The weapon system or squad SDF factor is a measure of the minimum amount of supply and support needed by a weapon system or squad to remain operational during combat operations. 'Supply' includes factors for ammunition and fuel (simple supply requirements), while 'support' includes a component for maintenance, repair and possible recovery of the weapon system. The very high combat power of certain weapon systems comes at a high price in supply and support infrastructure needed to support them.

The specific weapon system or squad Supply Demand Factors (SDF) shown in table Ger 1941 SDE and table Ger 1941 SDE Luft are calculated using the methodology detailed in Volume I.[472] The results of applying this methodology to German weapon systems and squads in 1941 is detailed in 'The German Personnel and Equipment Resource Database' (tables Ger Res Database 1 to 1A, Ger Res Database 2 to 2B, Ger Res Database 3 to 3B, and Ger Res Database 4 to 4B).[473]

b. Proportion of Available Rear Area Trucks, Tractors (Prime Movers) and Light Transports Allocated to Rear Area SDE functions

i. Proportion Available on 22nd June 1941

From the previous analysis of the total resources allocated to combat units in a Deployed (D) state on 22nd June 1941, we can determine the amount of motorised transport available in the rear areas of the Wehrmacht forces on the East Front.[474] Having determined the total amount of rear area transport available, the following proportions are used in determining the amount of rear area transport that was also available to support SDE related functions on 22nd June 1941.

- 100% of rear area trucks which were unallocated to combat units. 'Trucks' are any motor vehicles with Kfz number from 23 to 100 (inclusive).

- 0% of rear area prime movers which were unallocated to combat units. 'Prime movers' are German Sd.Kfz.6, 7, 8, 9, 10 and 11 half-tracks.

- 65% of rear area light transports which were unallocated to combat units. 'Light transports' are any motor vehicles with Kfz number from 1 to 21 (inclusive).

This assumes that no rear area trucks, all rear area prime movers, and around 35% of rear area light transports (unallocated to combat units on 22nd June 1941) were available to the Wehrmacht as Replacements (R), or to place into new MD or MND combat units. Note, in the FILARM model a **rear-area** database unit (i.e. one not allocated to a combat unit as part of its TOE) cannot be used to enhance SDE **and** later be placed in a combat unit (including in a newly mobilised combat unit, or as a Replacement (R)): **it must do one or the other**. For comparison, in the Soviet FILARM model the figures used to calculate the Soviet armed force's SDE are 100%, 40% and 65% of rear area trucks, tractors (prime movers) and light transports, respectively.[475]

Those Wehrmacht prime movers which were not heavy trucks were nearly all half-tracks, and there were never enough of these valuable vehicles to go round. On 22nd June 1941 almost all available half-tracks were already allocated to Deployed (D) combat units (including engineer, bridging and construction units) or were reserved for new combat units. The available German light to heavy half-tracks were simply too valuable to be wasted on rear area supply functions and were allocated to combat units as prime movers. Some vital functions involved towing artillery, tank recovery, battlefield engineering-construction, transport of bridging equipment and self-propelled AA guns. It should be noted that a very large proportion of the far more numerous Red Army tractors were agricultural in origin (there were notable exceptions, which were excellent military vehicles). These particular

---

[472] Refer Volume I Part II 3. 10) – 'Methodology for Calculating a Weapon System's or Database Unit's Specific Combat Attributes - Supply Demand Factor (SDF)'.

[473] Refer Volume IIA 2. – 'The German Personnel and Equipment Resource Database'.

[474] Refer Volume IIB 3. 1) – 'The Total Personnel and Equipment in a Deployed (D) State in the Reich from 22nd June to 4th July 1941 – The Total Personnel and Equipment Allocated to Combat Units and in a Deployed (D) State in the German Army, Waffen SS, Luftwaffe Ground Forces and Naval Coastal Artillery from 22nd June to 4th July 1941' table Ger Total Deployed (D) 1.

[475] Refer Volume IIIB 4. 6) c. i. – 'Parameters Relating Specifically to the Calculation of Soviet SDE in 1941 - Proportion of Available Rear Area Trucks, Tractors and Light Transports Allocated to Rear Area SDE functions - Proportion Available from the 22nd June 1941' on why these proportions are different for Soviet 'tractors'.

tractor types were much less useful and less well suited to the rigours of a military campaign, compared to the custom designed (but far fewer) German Sd.Kfz.6, 7, 8, 9, 10 and 11 half-tracks. As a result the German half-tracks were generally unavailable for rear-area SDE related functions. The effect of this is that it lowers the Wehrmacht's overall average SDE due to there being less available 'overall supply-lift capacity'.

ii. Proportion Available from 22nd June to 31st December 1941

From the previous analysis of the total resources allocated to MD and MND units from 22nd June to 31st December 1941, it was determined that at least 33,000 additional motor vehicles (including around 3,000 light transports) were supplied to the German ground forces on the East Front from June to December 1941; excluding those allocated to MD combat units.[476] Having determined the total amount of newly arrived rear-area transport available on the East Front, the following proportions are used in determining the amount of rear area transport that was **also available** to support SDE related functions on the East Front from June to December 1941.

- 95% of rear area trucks which were unallocated to combat units. 'Trucks' are any motor vehicles with Kfz number from 23 to 100 (inclusive).

- 0% of rear area halftracks which were unallocated to combat units. 'Prime movers' are German Sd.Kfz.6, 7, 8, 9, 10 and 11 half-tracks.

- 50% of rear area light transports which were unallocated to combat units. 'Light transports' are any motor vehicles with Kfz number from 1 to 21 (inclusive).

This assumes that 5% of rear area trucks, all rear area halftracks (prime movers), and around 50% of rear area light transports (unallocated to combat units on the East Front from 22nd June to 31st December 1941) were available to the Wehrmacht as Replacements (R).

For comparison, in the Soviet FILARM model the equivalent figures used to calculate the Soviet armed force's SDE are 98%, 35% and 55% of rear area trucks, tractors (prime movers) and light transports, respectively.[477] Note, in the Soviet FILARM model all the motorised vehicles that became available to the Soviet armed forces in 1941 are allocated to one of the following functions:

- Allocated directly to D, MD, and MND combat units.

- Allocated directly to SDE related functions (to enhance SDE).

- Allocated as Replacements (R).

In the German FILARM model this is not the case: in the German model the majority of available Replacement (R) trucks and light transports remained in the West during 1941.[478]

The relatively few newly arriving (on the East Front) German half-tracks were generally allocated to reinforcing combat units (including engineer, bridging and construction units) and were therefore unavailable for SDE related functions. The figures above also mean a larger proportion of available German rear-area trucks and light transports were not involved in SDE related functions compared to 22nd June 1941: they were mostly diverted to rear-area engineering-construction and security duties. This diversion of available transport, along with the fact that the Germans kept many available trucks in the West from June to December 1941 (and sent relatively few new trucks to the East Front compared to the Soviets), contributed to the drop in the Wehrmacht's overall SDE by November-December 1941.

***

---

[476] Refer Volume IIB 4. 3) a. – 'German Mobilisation After 22nd June 1941: the Actual Strength of German Land Combat Units Mobilised from 22nd June to 31st December 1941 - The Total Resources Allocated to Newly Mobilised Combat Units from 22nd June to 31st December 1941 - Rear Area Transport Available for Supply Distribution from 22nd June to 31st December 1941', table Ger Resources in MD & MND Units in 1941.

[477] Refer Volume IIIB 4. 6) c. ii. – 'Parameters Relating Specifically to the Calculation of Soviet SDE in 1941 - Proportion of Available Rear Area Trucks, Tractors and Light Transports Allocated to Rear Area SDE functions - Proportion Available from the 22nd June to 31st December 1941'.

[478] Refer Volume IIB 4. 7) c. – 'German Mobilisation After 22nd June 1941: the Actual Strength of German Land Combat Units Mobilised from 22nd June to 31st December 1941 - The Resource Replacements (R) Available to the German Army, Waffen SS, Luftwaffe Ground Forces and Naval Coastal Artillery, from 22nd June to 31st December 1941 - Replacements (R) Actually Issued to the German Ground Forces on the East Front During 1941'.

c. Average Lift Capacity of the Wehrmacht's Motorised Vehicles and Horse Teams: Measured in Metric Ton Kilometres per Day

We now come to an important factor in assessing a side's SDE: the average lift capacity of available trucks, prime movers (including half-tracks and tractors), light transports and horse teams.

As a reminder for the reader, in the FILARM and PILARM models the available Supply Lift per day of a force's support infrastructure is given by the following equation.[479]

$$Supply\ Lift_{All\ SupportInfrastructure} = (T_{RA} * L_T * D_T) + (LT_{RA} * L_{LT} * D_{LT}) + (TR_{RA} * L_{TR} * D_{TR}) +$$
$$0.3 * ((T_{TOE} * L_T * D_T) + (LT_{TOE} * L_{LT} * D_{LT}) + (TR_{TOE} * L_{TR} * D_{TR})) + 0.5 * (H_{TOE} * L_H * D_H)$$

Where: The suffix RA is 'Rear Area'. Rear area in this case means not assigned to the TOE for any Deployed (D), Mobilised and Deployed (MD) or Mobilised and Not Deployed (MND) combat unit.

The suffix TOE means 'assigned to a units TOE', that is to say included in the TOE for any Deployed (D), Mobilised and Deployed (MD) or Mobilised and Not Deployed (MND) combat unit.

T is the number of available Trucks. Trucks include non-tracked vehicles with a designed load capacity of one metric ton or over.

LT is the number of available Light Transports. Light Transports include non-tracked vehicles which are not trucks.

TR is number of available Tractors or prime movers. Prime movers includes fully or half-tracked vehicles, including artillery tractors and recovery vehicles.

H is the number of available Horse teams. Horse teams include artillery hitch and limber teams (4-8 horses each), separate horse drawn vehicles such as carts, wagons or field kitchens, and groups of six pack horses.

L is average load capacity of the motorised vehicle or horse team, measured in metric tons (see below). The L suffixes *T, LT, TR* and *H* denote Truck, Light Transport, Tractor and Horse team, respectively.

D is the average distance the fully loaded motorised vehicle or horse team can move in one day, measured in kilometres, over the terrain in which the SDE is being measured (see below). The D suffixes *T, LT, TR* and *H* denote Truck, Light Transport, Tractor and Horse team, respectively.

In the SDE discussions so far (in this chapter) we have focused on the number of vehicles and horse teams only, which are represented by the T, LT, TR and H parameters in the above equation. However we have not focused on the values of the L or D parameters above, which take into account the load capacity of the average vehicle (including horse teams) and the average distance it could carry this load in one day. For our purposes, L*D is defined as the **'average lift capacity'** of the vehicle type, measured in metric ton kilometres per day.

***

i. Average Transport Load Capacity (L)

On 22nd June 1941 the Wehrmacht had over 828,000 motor vehicles in service, of which around 638,000 were trucks.[480] Of these, approximately 450,000 trucks and 150,000 light transports (600,000 motor vehicles) were deployed in the East in support of Operation Barbarossa.[481] These vehicles were obtained from many different sources as the Reich expanded, which resulted in a bewildering array of different vehicle types being in service by June 1941. These different sources included the following:[482]

- German pre-war production under the *Kraftfahrrustungsprogramm* (motorisation program) initiated in 1927/28 by the German General Staff. The program was finalised in 1929 and formalised the nomenclature, standard specifications and requirements for military transport.

---

[479] Refer to Volume I Part I 8. – 'Supply Distribution Efficiency (SDE)' for details on all the SDE equations.

[480] Refer Volume IIB 3. 1) – 'The Total Personnel and Equipment in a Deployed (D) State in the Reich from 22nd June to 4th July 1941 – The Total Personnel and Equipment Allocated to Combat Units and in a Deployed (D) State in the German Army, Waffen SS, Luftwaffe Ground Forces and Naval Coastal Artillery from 22nd June to 4th July 1941' table Ger Total Deployed (D) 2. Excluding half-tracks and all types of armoured vehicles.

[481] Ibid, table Ger Total Deployed (D) 1. Also, H. Boog, et al, German Research Institute for Military history at Potsdam, Germany and the Second World War, Volume IV: The Attack on the Soviet Union. Clarendon Press (Oxford University Press), New York, 1996, p. 318.

[482] Refer Volume IIA 2. 15) b., c. and d. for more details on German pre-war and wartime vehicle production, as well as the principal vehicle types delivered within each program.

- German pre-war production under the *Einheits* vehicle program, which was initiated in 1934 after Hitler had come to power. This was an attempt to produce a series of standardised vehicles suitable for the military and was part of the Wehrmacht's rearmament program. Although the *Einheits* vehicles were good military vehicles with a cross-county performance superior to most contemporaries, their complexity and quality resulted in relatively slow manufacture.

- German pre-war production under the *Schell* Vehicle Program, which was initiated in 1938 when it was apparent that the *Einheits* Program was not going to meet the future motorisation needs of the German Army. It was named after General Schell, Director of Motorisation for the Wehrmacht. The far sighted *Schell* Program rationalised the number of Einheits and commercial chassis types produced. It also succeeded in providing a limited number of alternative commercial vehicles with all-wheel drive, streamlining production and reducing the number of different spare parts required and hence needing manufacture. The latter also enabled the German Army to commandeer certain civilian vehicles without drastically complicating the spare parts situation. On the down side the more abundant *Schell* Program semi-commercial vehicles did not usually have the durability or cross-country performance of the earlier *Einheits* Program vehicles.

- Pre-war commercial vehicles (as opposed to military or semi-commercial vehicles). These were mostly produced under the *Schell* Vehicle Program (above) and ranged from single-axle drive light vehicles (1.5 ton payload) to multi-axle drive heavy vehicles (9 ton payload). Trucks with over a 5 ton payload capacity were only purchased (for the Army) in commercial versions. A large number of commercial trucks (and cars) which were commandeered by the Wehrmacht, mainly upon the latter's mobilisation in August-September 1939.

- Vehicles from the annexed territories. These were military and commercial trucks from Austria and the German occupied part of Czechoslovakia (the Sudetenland) when those countries were annexed. In addition, many of the relevant factories in these countries maintained their pre-war vehicle production which went into the German war effort, or were re-tooled to produce German military vehicles. For example, Saurer and Steyr manufactured trucks in Austria for the German Army, as did Praga, Tatra and Skoda in Czechoslovakia.

- Vehicles captured from the Polish, Norwegian, Danish, French, Belgium, Dutch and British armed forces (and to a lesser extent the Yugoslavian and Greek forces), and commandeered vehicles from the occupied territories. The majority of captured military-trucks came from the French forces, and, overall, the majority of foreign vehicles came from France (first) and then Belgium, the Netherlands and Denmark

- Commercial trucks and military-trucks manufactured in Germany, and from factories in the occupied territories, during the war years.[483] The largest producer of trucks outside of Germany was France. For example, from 1939 to 1944 Peugeot manufactured 48,813 trucks from 1.2 ton to 6 ton capacity, of which 90% were used by Germany.[484] A similar number were also supplied by Renault.

***

From 1934 onwards the Wehrmacht classified trucks used for general transport purposes as follows:[485]

- Light – *Leichte* - Any approved make with useful load up to 2 tons.

- Medium – *Mittlerer* - Any approved make with useful load above 2 tons and less than 4.5 tons.

- Heavy – *Schwere* - Any approved make with useful load of 4.5 tons or over.

Generally trucks came in two versions: open trucks with a flat bed and (usually) a folding canvas cover, or closed with a body instead of a flatbed (a van). In addition trucks were classified as commercial or military, with military trucks being more robust and having multi-axle drive. Based on pre-war production and wartime production since September 1939, the table below is an estimate of the **average** load capacity within each category above, and the proportion of the overall German truck pool represented by each category during 1941.[486]

---

[483] Refer Volume IIB 3. 2) f. - 'Review of available Motor Vehicles and Other Transport Types' for more on German truck production from 1940-1942. Also refer Appendix A Table V for more on German wartime production of military standard motor vehicles.
[484] R. Michulec, Wehrmacht Support Vehicles, Concord Publications Co, Hong Kong, 1999, p. 3.
[485] C. Ellis, Wheeled Vehicles of the Wehrmacht, Kristall Productions and Avocet Books, Surrey, UK 1988, p. 10.
[486] Ibid, note 481. Also, Volume IIA 2. 15) b., c. and d. Note, the large majority of heavy (*Schwere*) trucks were 4.5t trucks. Only around 20% were 4.6t – 9t trucks.

German Average Truck Load Capacity (L) during 1941		
Average Load Capacity Metric Tons	% of Trucks in the Truck Park	% of Trucks times Load Capacity
1.5	45%	0.68
3	45%	1.35
4.5	8%	0.36
5	2%	0.10
Overall Average Truck Load Capacity - Metric Tons		**2.49**

From this table we can see that **the average truck in the Wehrmacht during the second half of 1941 had a load capacity of approximately 2.49 metric tons**.

As with trucks, the Germans used a large and diverse range of light transports in the Wehrmacht. As part of the Wehrmacht's rearmament program in 1934 (the start of the *Einheits* Vehicle Program) an attempt was made at rationalisation, and cars with or without Kfz numbers were classified as follows:

- Light - *Leichte* - Any approved make up to 1500cc.

- Medium - *Mittlerer* - Any approved make up to 3000cc.

- Heavy - *Schwere* - Any approved make over 3000cc.

Light transports suitable for military use were generally given Kfz numbers. This eventually led to Kfz 1-4s being classified as *Leichte Personenkraftwagen* (Light Passenger/Personnel Cars), Kfz 11-18s being classified as *Mittlerer Personenkraftwagen* (Medium Passenger/Personnel Cars), and Kfz 21s being classified as *Schwerer Personenkraftwagen* (Heavy Passenger/Personnel Cars).[487] Unlike in the Soviet pre-war economy, the German pre-war planners devoted a great deal of effort to developing a range of rugged light vehicles suitable for military use. A whole series of specialised light vehicles were developed, and designated, accordingly. These included several types of specialised radio vehicles and personnel carriers, which were designated light personnel carriers (le. PKW) and medium personnel carriers (m. PKW). Most of these vehicles had multi-axle drive and were suitable for cross country work. Refer to Volume IIA 2. 15) for details on the 'light transports' produced and their classifications in the Wehrmacht.[488]

In comparison, the pre-war Soviet automobile industry was still in early stages of development and growth (although it was expanding very rapidly), which meant there were relatively few cars either in the military or the civil economy in June 1941.[489] Unsurprisingly the Soviets had not devoted much effort to developing or producing light military vehicles and most of the light transports in the Red Army in 1941 were civilian automobiles.

In the German FILARM model a 'light transport' is differentiated from a 'truck' by being defined as any of the following:

- A supply or transport motor vehicle with a lift capacity (payload) less than 1,080kg and having only two axles.

- Any specialised motor vehicle with a lift capacity less than 1,080kg and having only two axles, i.e. a vehicle fulfilling a specialised function such as a radio car or telephone exchange van.

The above definition means that in June 1941 the Wehrmacht motor vehicles with Kfz number from 1 to 21 (inclusive) can be classified as 'light transports'. Based on pre-war production and wartime production since September 1939, for the German SDE calculation in 1941 these **light transports are estimated to have had an average load capacity of approximately 0.6 metric tons**. This is only marginally higher than the 0.5 metric ton average load capacity attributed to Soviet 'light transports' in 1941. This is arguably being over generous in estimating the Red Army's light transport capacity in 1941; in which case the Soviet SDE in the Soviet FILARM model is slightly higher than it was historically.

***

[487] C. Ellis, Wheeled Vehicles of the Wehrmacht, Kristall Productions and Avocet Books, Surrey, UK 1988, p. 5.
[488] Volume IIA 2. 15) c. – 'The German Personnel and Equipment Resource Database - Transports and Prime Movers - Light Transports'. Includes a full description of German soft skinned vehicles defined as 'light transports'.
[489] Refer Volume IIIA 2. 9) - 'The Soviet Personnel and Equipment Database - Transport and Prime Movers' for a history if the Soviet pre-war auto industry. The large American influence is examined, along with the numbers and types of trucks, light transports and tractors (prime-movers) produced up to the end of 1941.

During WWII no other country developed half-tracked vehicles to the same degree as Germany. By June 1941, and during the first three quarters of WWII, almost all of the German Army's prime movers were based on a series of very high quality half-track designs. They formed the basis of several well known German WWII Armoured Personnel Carriers as well as a whole range of prime movers and transports. All these designs originated in the pre-war period, and they were all designed as specialised military vehicles: i.e. they were all given Sd.Kfz. designations which were reserved for military vehicles only (including AFVs).[490] Refer to Volume IIA 2. 15) for details on the different German half-tracks produced, the numbers available, and their classifications within the Wehrmacht.[491] In the German FILARM model the following half-tracks are defined,

- Light half-track. Any unarmed and non-armoured half-track with a towing capacity equal to or less than 3 tons. Note, this excludes half-tracked APCs and self-propelled weapons. It includes the *Leichter Zugkraftwagen* 1-ton (Sd Kfz 10) and the *Leichter Zugkraftwagen* 3-ton (Sd Kfz 11).

- Medium half-track. Any unarmed and non-armoured half-track with a towing capacity greater than 3 tons but equal to or less than 8 tons. It includes the *Mittlerer Zugkraftwagen* 5-ton (Sd Kfz 6) and the *Mittlerer Zugkraftwagen* 8-ton (Sd Kfz 7).

- Heavy half-track. Any unarmed and non-armoured half-track with a towing capacity greater than 8 tons. It includes the *Schwerer Zugkraftwagen* 12-ton (Sd Kfz 8) and the very large *Schwerer Zugkraftwagen* 18-ton (Sd Kfz 9).

Based on the number of halftracks that served on the East Front from 22nd June to 31st December 1941 and the load capacity of the three most common types in service, the table below is an estimate of the average half-track load capacity during 1941.[492]

Principal German Half-Tracks in Service on the East Front During 1941, & the Average Load Capacity			
Type	Most Common Load Capacity, Metric Tons*	Number of Half-track on the East Front in 1941, inc. all (D) and (R) units	Total Load Capacity, Metric Tons
Sd.Kfz. 10 and 11	1	5,529	5,529
Sd.Kfz. 6 and 7	8	4,720	37,760
Sd.Kfz. 8 and 9	12	1,325	15,900
Overall Average Half-Track Load Capacity - Metric Tons		5.11	
* The load capacity of the most common type of half-track in service is used.			

From this table we can see that **the average half-track in the Wehrmacht during the second half of 1941 had a load capacity of approximately 5.11 metric tons**.

Despite the availability of these excellent vehicles, the overall effect on the Wehrmacht's SDE was, however, still very small. There are two reasons for this. Firstly, there were relatively few available as can be seen from the above table. The lift capacity of the approximately 11,600 half-tracks on the East Front was a tiny fraction of the total lift capacity, which mostly stemmed from the over 600,000 motor vehicles and 625,000 horses in the invasion forces. Secondly, the half-tracks that were available were generally too valuable to be used for routine supply functions. This is simulated in the German FILARM model using the TOE transport rules; i.e. transport in rear areas (specifically no German 'rear-area' halftracks allowed), as well as 30% of motorised transport and 50% of horse drawn transport included as part of the TOE of combat units, is available for supply and support services.[493]

---

[490] The Wehrmacht used Sd.Kfz (*Sonder Kraftfahrzeug*) and Kfz (*Kraftfahrzeug)* numbers. The Sd.Kfz numbers applied to 'special purpose motor vehicles' and were designated to vehicles designed and built for the military. The Kfz numbers were reserved for 'soft skinned' vehicles and included vehicles designed for military use as well as commercial vehicles. The only armoured vehicles designated with Kfz numbers were the Kfz 13 and 14, both early armoured cars developed pre-war from 1932 to 1934.

[491] Volume IIA 2. 15) f. g. and h. – 'The German Personnel and Equipment Resource Database - Transports and Prime Movers'. Contains separate sections on light half-tracks, medium half-tracks and heavy half-tracks.

[492] The numbers of half-tracks on the East Front is taken from Volume IIB 6. 3) – 'SDE for all Deployed (D) and Reinforcement (R) Land Combat Units on the East Front from 22nd June to 31st December 1941' table Ger 1941 SDE. For the most common types in service refer to Volume IIA 2. 15) f. g. and h.

[493] Refer Volume I Part I 8. 1) – 'Supply Distribution Efficiency (SDE) - Supply Lift'.

In the case of German half-tracks, Sd.Kfz.6, 7, 8, 9, 10 and 11 half-tracks were **all** allocated to the TOE of combat units and only 30% of these contributed to the German SDE. Therefore the relatively few available German half-tracks contributed only around 0.8% to the overall average Wehrmacht SDE value of 71% during 1941.

Finally, for both the German and Soviet SDE calculations for 1941, **the average 'horse team' is assumed to have had an average load capacity of 1.25 metric tons.**[494]

***

ii. Average Distance Moved Per Day (D)

So what of the D parameter? This is the average distance the fully loaded motorised vehicle or horse team could move in one day over the terrain in which the SDE is being measured. This is essentially a **measure of the relative reliability** of the vehicle in question. The stress here is on 'relative'. We are not particularly interested in the absolute distance a truck could carry its load on a tarmac road. What we are interested in is how far the average German motor vehicle could carry its full load **relative** to how far the average Soviet motor vehicle could carry its full load over the same terrain, without breaking down or getting stuck. Note the terrain and road conditions in question are assumed to be the same for both sides.

The German truck park in June 1941 consisted of a mixed bag of domestic and foreign built vehicles, ranging from excellent quality military vehicles to purely commercial vehicles. Those trucks and light transports built under the Einheits Vehicle Program conformed to relatively luxurious specifications. The standard military light truck accepted for production under this program was the le. E-LKW or the 'Einheits Diesel'. It had all wheel drive (6x6) with self-locking differentials on each axle, was one of the few German vehicles powered by a diesel engine, had a cross-country payload of 2.5 tons, and was produced from 1937.[495] There is little doubt that in 1941 the Einheits Diesel was one of the best performing military trucks in the world. On the downside, the Einheits Diesel was always in short supply because it was expensive and difficult to mass produce.

Another outstanding light military truck available to the German Army in June 1941 was the Krupp model L2H-43 and its almost identical (in appearance) L2H-143. This truck is also commonly referred to as the 'Krupp Protz' and is probably the best known 6x4 military truck used by the Wehrmacht during WWII. Other good 6x4 military truck chassis were manufactured by Daimler-Benz, Büssing-NAG and Magirus (all three manufacturers were asked to modify their truck chassis to produce six wheeled armoured cars). All these six wheeled 'light' trucks were produced from 1934 to 1938, after which they were replaced by vehicles from the *Schell* Vehicle Program.

In the medium class (i.e. with useful load above 2 tons and less than 4.5 tons), good pre *Schell* Program military trucks included the Krupp L3H-63 and L3H-163, Henschel 33-D1 and 33-G1, Magirus 33-G1, Daimler-Benz LG3000 and Büssing-NAG IIIGL6. These vehicles all had 4 wheel drive and were variously in production in the 1930-39 period. The Henschel chassis was the most numerous in this class up to 1941, and remained in production until 1940.

Commercial trucks (as opposed to the military trucks above) were not always given Kfz numbers but were still classified as light, medium or heavy trucks. Trucks with over a 5 ton payload capacity were only purchased in commercial versions. The trucks shown in the table below were the most important commercial trucks used by the Wehrmacht, and most were produced under the *Schell* Vehicle Program.

***

---

[494] Refer Volume IIA 2. 15) a. – 'The German Personnel and Equipment Resource Database - Transports and Prime Movers – Horse Teams' for definitions of what constitutes a 'horse team'.

[495] It was produced by Büssing-NAG, MAN, Daimler-Benz and Borgward, and began replacing the (o.) chassis commercial vehicles on the production lines in 1937.

German Commercial Trucks in Military Use		
Category	Make	Model
up to 2 ton (light)	Adler	W61
	Borgward	LI400
	Daimler-Benz	L1500, L1500S, L1500A
	Phanomen	Granit 25H, 1500S, 1500A
	Opel	Blitz 2, 5 - 32
	Steyr (Ost.Daimler)	1500A/01, 1500A/02, 2000A
3 ton (medium)	Borgward	B3000S, B3000A
	Daimler-Benz	L3000, L3000S, L3000A
	Ford	G21T, V3000, V3000S
	KHD (Magirus)	3000S, 3000A
	MAN	E2, E3000
	Opel	Blitz 3, 6 - 36S, Blitz 6700A
4.5 ton (heavy)	Bussing-NAG	4500S, 4500A
	Daimler-Benz	L4500S, L4500A
	Grafe & Stift	V7DW
	MAN	ML4500S, ML4500A
6.5 ton	Bussing-NAG	6500
	Daimler-Benz	L6500
	Krupp	LD6, 5
	MAN	F4
	Vomag	6LR-647, 6LR-652
	Tatra	6500A
9 ton	Bussing-NAG	801, 802
	Faun	L9000D567

In the light truck class a standard type of chassis with a payload of 1.5 tons was proposed. Usually designated '1500' by builders, the various chassis were produced in two forms: a conventional 4x2 layout was known as Type-S (standard) and a 4x4 military version known as Type-A (*allradantrieb*, all-wheel drive). Aside from the changes necessitated by the driven front axle and different gears etc, the A and S types were mechanically and structurally similar in all respects. The most common vehicle produced in this category used the Phanomen-Granit chassis: the model 25H being in production before 1938. The Phanomen-Granit 25H and 1500A were probably the most common ambulance vehicle used by the Wehrmacht during WWII, and were suited to this role because of their light weight and high road speed. Most of the vehicles in this class were supplied with open or van type bodies and many were used as specialist vehicles such as ambulances, signal trucks, machinery trucks, etc.

For the medium truck class a 3 ton rating was specified in the *Schell* Program. As for the light truck class, A(4x4) and S(4x2) versions were built. In this case manufacturers most commonly designated them 3000A or 3000S. The two most widely produced trucks in this class were possibly the most important truck types produced by Germany during WWII. They were the famous Opel Blitz and less well known Ford V3000S. These trucks were produced in very large numbers and formed the backbone of transportation within the Wehrmacht's divisions. The Opel Blitz was produced in two versions: the original 36S with 4x2 drive and later the *Blitzwagen* model 6700A with 4x4 drive. The Blitz cab was enclosed and the usual body style was a flat cargo bed with canvass cover. In all, over 70,000 Blitz 36S trucks were built.[496] The Ford was only ever produced with the commercial S type chassis, but it was similarly supplied in large numbers and served widely in secondary supply carrying roles. There were over 100 different types of body which could be fitted to the 3 ton class enabling it to be used in almost any transport role. In addition a long wheel base version of the chassis was produced, mainly for use with a bus body (*Wehrmachtbus*). This enabled the 3 ton class to be adapted internally as a personnel carrier, an ambulance, a signals vehicle or even a command vehicle.

In terms of overall lift capacity, **the *Schell* Program medium 3 ton trucks, along with the aforementioned pre *Schell* Program medium military trucks, were by far the most important vehicles available to the Wehrmacht during Operation Barbarossa.** Of the approximately 450,000 trucks available on the East front in June 1941, around 45% were medium military or commercial trucks.

---

[496] I. Hogg, J. Weeks, The Illustrated Encyclopedia of Military Vehicles, Quantum Publishing Ltd, London 2003, p. 282.

In the pre-war years heavy trucks purchased by the Wehrmacht were restricted to conventional commercial types. They were supplemented in 1939-40 by a few heavy military trucks from Austria, Czechoslovakia and France when those countries were annexed or occupied. Standard military heavy class trucks resulted entirely from the *Schell* Program, which specified 4.5 tons as the payload rating. Again, A(4x4) and S(4x2) versions were built and in this case manufacturers most commonly designated them 4500A or 4500S. The most common types produced in this class were the Büssing-NAG 4500A and 4500S, Daimler-Benz L4500S and L4500A, and MAN ML4500S and ML4500A. Around 45,000 4.5 ton trucks were produced from 1941 to 1945.

***

Compared to the Wehrmacht's truck park, the Soviet Red Army's (and VVS's) truck park in 1941 was almost entirely based around commercial vehicles. Table Sov Truck Production (over page) shows the numbers and types of trucks produced in the USSR from the earliest days of the fledgling Soviet auto-industry to the end of 1941.[497] The most common trucks in the USSR were the GAZ AA (1.5t) and the larger ZiS-5 (3t), which together comprised the large bulk of the Red Army's truck park. In the Soviet FILARM model (Volume III) we analyse the Soviet's and Red Army's 1941 truck, light-transport and tractor parks in depth. This analysis shows that the average truck in the Red Army on 22nd June 1941 had a lift capacity of 1.89 tonnes, and this increased to 2.09 tonnes by late December 1941.[498] If we assume a uniform transition of the 'average lift capacity per truck' from June to December 1941, **then the average lift capacity per truck in the Red Army, taken over the second half of 1941, was around 1.99 tonnes.** Note, however, that the vast majority of these vehicles were (4x2) trucks which were designed and produced for use by a civil economy; they were not designed (or modified later) for the rigours of a military campaign, and their cross-country abilities were limited.

The overall situation with 'light transports' (cars or automobiles) was even worse, as demonstrated by the following table.[499] This shows two things. Firstly, there were relatively few automobiles in the USSR, and secondly, the few which were in the employ of the armed forces were almost entirely civilian vehicles.

Soviet Light Transport (Automobile) Production to the End of 1941

Automobile Type	NAMI-1	GAZ-A	GAZ-M1	GAZ-415^^	GAZ-11**	GAZ-61-73	GAZ-64^*	KIM-10***	Other**^
Production Period	1927-30	1932-36	1936-41	1937-41	1939-41	1940-41	1941-42	1934-41	1934-41
Total No. Produced	369	41,900*	c 62,000^	c 5,000	c 3,000	181*^	c 300^*	c 630	11,400
Engine Power	21	40	50	50	76	76	50	30	
Wheels & Drive Type	4x2	4x2	4x2	4x2	4x2	4x4	4x4	4x2	4x2
Passenger Capacity	4	4	5	1 & 400kg	5	5	4	4	4-6

	Totals
Production Period	1927-41
Total No. Produced	c 124,780

* Probably includes a few pickup models of the GAZ-A designated the GAZ-4, and 23 GAZ-TK tri-axle self-propelled guns.
^ Limited production reinstated in 1942-43 from available parts (around 900 additional vehicles made).
^^ Pickup based on the GAZ-M1. Possibly production was as high as 7,000 vehicles.
** Includes GAZ-11-41 pickup version and the GAZ-11-73 sedan version.
*^ Excludes a handful of GAZ-11-40 phaeton vehicles; the number produced is unknown.
^* A total of 646 produced by mid 1942.
*** Includes KIM-10-50, KIM-10-51 and KIM-10-52.
**^ Includes ZIS-101, ZIS-101A, ZIS-101 Sport, ZIS-101C, ZIS-102 and any other misc. automobiles.

© Nigel Askey, 2018

[497] Refer Volume IIIA 2. 9) b. – 'The Soviet Personnel and Equipment Resource Database - Transport and Prime Movers – Trucks', for a detailed history of the pre-war Soviet auto-industry and the motor vehicles produced. Note, for table Sov Truck Prod, the AMO-4, AMO-4lux, ZIS-8, ATUL/AL-2, ZIS-16, ZIS-16S, Ya-6, GAZ-03/30, GAZ-05/193 and GAZ-55 were buses or smaller passenger vehicles produced in limited numbers, and are not included in the table. Also the ZIS-22, ZIS-33 and GAZ-60 were half-tracks based on the relevant truck chassis. Only 5,100 of these vehicles were produced by the end of 1941 and these are considered under the Soviet Prime Movers section. Also, note, the ZIS-5V, ZIS-42, ZIS-42M and ZIS-44 only commenced production from 1942 onwards.
[498] Ibid. Also, refer to Volume IIIB 4. – 'The Supply Distribution Efficiency (SDE) for the Soviet Armed Forces from 22nd June to 31st December 1941'
[499] Refer Volume IIIA 2. 9) c. – 'The Soviet Personnel and Equipment Resource Database - Transport and Prime Movers – Light Transports'. Also, Volume IIIA 2. 9) d. includes a detailed review of the available Soviet tractors (prime-movers).

Table Sov Truck Prod

Soviet Truck Production to the End of 1941 (Excluding Truck Based Half-Tracks and Buses)

Truck Type	AMO-F-15	AMO-2	AMO-3	ZIS-5	ZIS-6	ZIS-10	ZIS-11	ZIS-12	ZIS-13	ZIS-14	ZIS-21	ZIS-32*	ZIS-30	ZIS-31
Production Period	1924-31	1930-31	1931-33	1933-41	1933-41	1934-41	1934-41	1935-41	1936	1936-40	1938-41	1941	1940-41	1939-40
Total No Produced	6,084	1,715	34,969	325,051	21,239	766	3,047	4,223	900	821	15,445	197	45	43
Engine Power	35	60	60	73	73	73	73	73	45	73	48	73*	73	45
Wheels & Drive Type	4x2	4x2	4x2	4x2	6x4	4x2	4x2	4x2	4x2	4x2	4x2	4x4	4x2	4x2
Cargo Capacity (Kg)	1,500	2,500	2,500	3,000	3,500	3,500	3,400	3,400	2,500	3,400	2,500	2,500	2,500	2,500

* Produced with ZiS-5 73hp engine or ZIS-16 82hp engine.

Truck Type	Ya-3	Ya-4	Ya-5	YaG-3	YaG-4	YaG-6	YaG-6M	YaG-6A	YaG-10^	YaG-10M	YaS-1**	YaS-3**
Production Period	1925-28	1928-29	1929-34	1932-34	1934-36	1936-42*	1938-40	1940	1932-40	1938-40	1935-36	1936-42*
Total No Produced	160	137	2,273	2,681	5,348	7,498	50	15	323	10	573	4,425
Engine Power	30	54	93	60	73	73	93	82	93	103	73	73
Wheels & Drive Type	4x2	4x2	4x2	4x2	4x2	4x2	4x2	4x2	6x4	6x4	4x2	4x2
Cargo Capacity (Kg)	3,000	4,000	5,000	5,000	5,000	3,500	3,500	3,500	5,000	5,000	4,000	4,000

* Production to the end of 1941 is shown only. Total YaG-6 production (including 1942 production) was 8075, and total YaS-3 production was 4765.

^ Includes the YaG-12. A few (mainly experimental) YaG-12s were produced which were 8x8 configuration (12t) on a YaG-10 chassis. Produced around 1932.

** YaS-1 and YaS-3, dump trucks based on the YaG-4 and YaG-6 chassis'.

Truck Type	GAZ-AA^	GAZ-AAA	GAZ-MM**	GAZ-410	GAZ-42	GAZ-43	GAZ-44	GAZ-11-51
Production Period	1932-38	1933-43	1938-49	1936-43	1939-46	1939	1939-41	1939-44
Total No Produced*	409,985	30,578	226,200	5,486	12,690	2,000	130	397
Engine Power	40	40 or 50	50	40	30	29	42	85
Wheels & Drive Type	4x2	6x4	4x2	4x2	4x2	4x2	4x2	4x2
Cargo Capacity (Kg)	1,500	2,000	1,500	1,200	1,200	1,250	1,200	2,000

* Production to the end of 1941 is shown only.

^ Constituted 58.5% of the Red Army's Truck Pool on 22nd June 1941. Includes GAZ-4 production, which was based on the GAZ-AA.

** By far the most produced wartime truck; a total of 419,812 produced to 1947. Approximately another 89,400 produced 1948 to 1949, inclusive.

	Totals
Production Period	1924 - Dec. 1941
Total No Produced*	1,125,503
Total Cargo Capacity (t)	2,355,427
Ave Truck Lift Capacity (t)	2.09

© Nigel Askey, 2018

However, the Soviets had additional, even more severe, problems. For example, because of poor repair facilities, shortages of spare parts and tyres, and lack of trained mechanics, 23.1% of the all Red Army motor vehicles were inoperable on the eve of war.[500] In addition an estimated 45% of the entire Soviet truck park (including those in the economy) was inoperable in June 1941, with stocks of tyres meeting only about 25% of demand.

What all this meant was that although the German truck park left a great deal to be desired, it was generally made up of heavier lift capacity and considerably more reliable vehicles than the Soviet truck park. The German truck park also included significant numbers of military designed and specified trucks and light transports. The Germans also used large numbers of captured vehicles (especially French vehicles), and, while not as good as the best German vehicles, they were certainly at least as reliable as the best Soviet vehicles and better than the majority of older ones. Furthermore, the **Germans were no shorter of spare parts for their mixed bag of domestic and foreign built vehicles than the Soviets were for their old home grown or newer licence built ones**. It is perplexing (and completely illogical) that the large majority of current publications on Operation Barbarossa focus exclusively on the weaknesses of the German truck park in 1941, whilst not even mentioning the Soviet truck park let alone actually analysing it. Yet it was the **relative** state of the two truck parks that was a critical factor in the success or failure of the massive manoeuvre war that commenced on the East Front in June 1941.

Based on the overall state of the German motor vehicle inventory in 1941, Wehrmacht trucks, light transports, half-tracks and horse teams are estimated to have D parameters equal to 110km, 110km, 70km and 30km, respectively. This is only marginally greater than the D parameters used for the equivalent Red Army and VVS motor vehicles, which have D parameters around 9% less than the Wehrmacht vehicles. This is, again, very arguably being over generous in estimating the relative reliability of the average Soviet motor vehicle in 1941. In this case the Soviet SDE calculated in the Soviet FILARM model is somewhat higher than it was historically (see below).[501]

***

iii. Comparison of the Average Soviet and German Lift Capacity (L*D)

For comparison purposes, the following is a summary of the average 'lift capacity' used for the various transport types in calculating the Soviet and German SDEs in 1941.

Average lift capacity for Soviet and German transport in 1941						
	Soviet			German		
	L	D	Lift Capacity	L	D	Lift Capacity
	(t)	(km)	(tkm)	(t)	(km)	(tkm)
Trucks	1.99	100	**199**	2.49	110	**274**
Light Transport	0.5	100	**50**	0.6	110	**66**
Tractors-Prime Movers	2	50	**100**	5.11	70	**358**
Horse Teams	1.25	30	**38**	1.25	30	**38**

Of all the parameters shown in this table, the most contentious (and difficult to assess accurately) are the relative D parameters. In the respective FILARM models, **the Wehrmacht D parameters for trucks and light transports are only 10% greater than those used for the Red Army and VVS (110km vs 100km)**. Given the commercial nature and overall state of the Soviet truck park in 1941 (see above), it is very arguable that the D parameters used are too high in the Soviet FILARM model. In this case the Soviet SDE calculated for the Soviet FILARM model is higher than it was historically, as illustrated by the following examples.

- If the Red Army and VVS D parameters for trucks and light transports are reduced to 96km (so the relevant Wehrmacht D parameters are now approximately 15% greater than the Soviet parameters), then the overall Soviet SDE in the Soviet FILARM model is reduced by 0.72% (from 20.6% to 19.88%).[502]

- If the Red Army and VVS D parameters for trucks and light transports are reduced to 92km (so the relevant Wehrmacht D parameters are now approximately 20% greater than the Soviet parameters), then the overall Soviet SDE in the Soviet FILARM model is reduced by 1.44% (from 20.6% to 19.16%).

***

---

[500] D.M. Glantz, Stumbling Colossus, University Press of Kansas, Lawrence, Kansas, 1998, pp. 177-178.
[501] Refer Volume IIIB 4. – 'The Supply Distribution Efficiency (SDE) for the Soviet Armed Forces from 22nd June to 31st December 1941'
[502] Ibid. Assumes all L values remain unchanged, and D values for tractors-prime movers and horse-teams remain unchanged.

6) Conclusions Relating to the Wehrmacht's SDE during 1941

Based purely on the above analysis, it is difficult to draw any detailed conclusions relating to the German SDE in 1941 unless we have something to compare it to. For this reason we need a little data from the Soviet FILARM model and Soviet SDE analysis for 1941. The Soviet FILARM model shows the following data for the Soviet armed forces in 1941.[503]

- The overall SDE for all Soviet Deployed (D) land combat units in the USSR on 22nd June 1941 was approximately 17.4%. If VVS air units are added this drops to 14.6%.

- The overall SDE for all Soviet Deployed (D) land combat units in the Western Military Districts on 22nd June 1941 was approximately 15.5%. If VVS air units are added this drops to 13.7%.

- The overall SDE for all Soviet MD and MND land combat units in the USSR from June to December 1941 was approximately 32.5%. If VVS air units are added this drops to 29.2%.

- The overall average SDE available to the Soviet ground forces from June to December 1941 was approximately 23.9%. If VVS air units are added this drops to 20.6%.

We can now compare these values to the Wehrmacht SDE values for 1941, shown in table Ger 1941 SDE (pages 294 - 297). The first thing that is apparent is that up to 4th July 1941 the invading Wehrmacht ground forces enjoyed a SDE value around 4.3 times greater than in the opposing Red Army forces in the Western Military Districts (i.e. an SDE of 75.4% vs 17.4%). If air units are included this value marginally increases to around 4.9 (71.9% vs 14.6%).[504] This means that if a similar Soviet and German division were fighting **at the same distance from their respective supply sources (such as a railhead or supply dump), had the same amount of supplies available in their respective supply sources, were deployed in the same type of terrain, and the roads were in the same condition, then the German division would normally receive around 4.9 times as much fuel and ammunition per day as the Soviet division**.

All other things being equal, within a relatively short space of time this level of supply difference would be catastrophic for the Soviet unit. Obviously many other factors come into play such as: the fact that attacking units generally use far more supplies, the level of entrenchment of the defending unit, the weather, the local stockpiling of supplies by the defending unit, and the interdiction of any supply routes. However, regardless of all other factors, any force with such weak relative SDE would find it difficult to gain sufficient supply to launch an effective and sustained offensive. Given the SDE difference between opposing forces in Operation Barbarossa in June-early July 1941, the Soviets were in for a hard time regardless of the surprise nature of the German attack or the multitude of other problems afflicting the Red Army at this time. Even prepared Red Army units were going to struggle to obtain sufficient ammunition and fuel to remain a cohesive and operational force. When one also considers that the German forces immediately attacked any supply infrastructure and the supply dumps themselves, then it is not surprising that many Red Army units in the Western Military Districts had soon ran out of almost everything. Even the strongest, most well trained and highly motivated units will not last long under these conditions and under constant enemy pressure.

The second major finding in comparing the opposing forces' SDEs is that between 22nd June and 31st December 1941 the German Army had an average SDE value around 3.1 times greater than the Red Army forces facing them (74.2% vs 23.9%). If Luftwaffe and VVS air units are included this value increases to over 3.4 (70.7% vs 20.6%).

This is still a very substantial difference. It meant that in situations where the Germans had time to consolidate their supply lines and move their railheads forward, they were able to supply their combat units much more quickly than the Red Army. This sustained SDE difference during 1941 goes a long way to explaining how the German Army was usually able to repeatedly launch successful penetrating offensives after only a brief period of rest and movements of supplies (and supply sources) forward. However, for a large part of Operation Barbarossa German divisions (especially those in the motorised corps) were operating 2-8 times further away from their supply sources than most Red Army divisions. This is because they were the attacking force and during major offensives they were continuously moving eastwards, further from their primary supply sources. In general these offensives moved eastwards faster than the supply sources (e.g. railheads) could, and it usually took some time for the 'narrower track'

---

[503] Ibid.

[504] Note, this includes a factor to compensate for the VVS losses on airfields in the first five days of war. The Soviets didn't need to supply these aircraft with fuel and ammunition because they very rapidly ceased to exist. Thus only 80% of the aircraft in the Western Military Districts are considered to have ever needed overland supply. In addition, Soviet VVS DBA (Long Range Aviation) air units which were Deployed (D) in the Western Special Military Districts (on 22nd June 1941) are excluded.

German rail network in the USSR to catch up.[505] Thus **if German divisions were on average operating 3.4 times further from their primary supply source compared to the opposing Red Army divisions, then the amount of supply received per day would have been similar** (assuming all other factors being equal).

***

So what were the main reasons for the large difference in Supply Distribution Efficiency (SDE) between Soviet and German forces in 1941? Examining the relevant data from Soviet and German FILARM models we find the following:

- The **average German ground force's total supply demand** from 22nd June to 31st December, over the **average Soviet ground force's total supply demand** in the same period, was **64%**.[506] This means that on average during 1941, the smaller overall German force needed 64% of the supply that the Soviet force needed to operate at the same level.

- The **average German ground force's total supply lift** from 22nd June to 31st December, over the **average Soviet ground force's total supply lift** in the same period, was **198%**.[507] This means that on average during 1941, the overall German force had almost twice the total supply lift capacity as the opposing Soviet force.

In a nutshell the reason for the large difference in Soviet-German SDE was because of a massive Red Army with fewer trucks operating against a smaller German Army with more trucks. This situation was exacerbated by the relative quality, reliability and size of the Soviet and German truck parks.

The large majority of current publications on Operation Barbarossa carefully point out that the German Army entered the Soviet Union in June 1941 with 625,000 horses. The reader is then usually led (or, more accurately, misled) to the conclusion that: the German Army was almost completely dependent on horse-drawn transport, it suffered from chronic truck shortages and the attrition rate of the 'few' available trucks in the USSR was fatally high due to the poor road conditions, and the outcome of Operation Barbarossa was therefore somehow predetermined.[508] Comparisons even occasion where the German Army in 1941 is compared to the fully motorised US and Commonwealth forces that landed in Normandy in 1944![509] Yet almost none of these publications **compare the German truck and transport situation in 1941 to the only thing that actually mattered; namely, (relative) to the Red Army and Soviet truck and transport situation during 1941**.

In addition, none of these publications actually quantify the statement 'the German Army was mostly reliant on horse transport': it appears sufficient that the German Army used large numbers of horses to justify this statement. Even a simple calculation reveals that this statement is meaningless and misleading when made without proper context. For example, we can see from table Ger 1941 SDE that the Wehrmacht on the East Front (from 22nd June to 31st December 1941) employed around 152,500 horse teams (approximately 686,000 horses) whilst at the same time it employed around 495,800 trucks. Using the figures for 'the average lift capacity of German transport in 1941' (i.e. L*D) we find that **the total lift capacity of the Wehrmacht's trucks on the East Front during 1941 was 24 times the total lift capacity of the Wehrmacht's horses!**[510]

---

[505] The Soviet rail gauge was 8.9cm wider than the standard European gauge so the Germans had to re-gauge the track to use any of their rolling stock. This was relatively easy because it is generally much easier to narrow a rail gauge than widen it. W. S. Dunn. JR. The Soviet Economy and the Red Army, 1930-1945, Praeger Publishers, Westport, CT, 1995, p. 191. During Operation Barbarossa the process of narrowing the Soviet rail gauge was quite rapid. Gercke (chief of German army transportation) had estimated that one railway battalion could re-gauge 20km of track per day. German railway pioneer and construction troops had changed the Russian gauge railway to German gauge 80km towards Minsk by 25th June 1941. By 29th June they had extended German gauge track from Brest to Oranczyce, and by 1st July the track reached Baranovice. These rates were very close to Gercke's pre-war estimate. R.H.S. Stolfi, Hitler's Panzers East, University of Oklahoma Press, Oklahoma, 1991, pp. 174 and 175.
[506] Specifically, 151,748 tonnes per day (Wehrmacht) over 237,042 tonnes per day (Red Army and VVS).
[507] Specifically, 112,568,535 tonnes kilometers per day (Wehrmacht) over 56,717,955 tonnes kilometers per day (Red Army and VVS).
[508] E.g., J. Ellis, Brute Force: Allied Strategy and Tactics in the Second World War, Andre Deutsch Ltd, London, 1990, pp. 39-51. The number of incorrect conclusions and inferences, as well as the factual inaccuracies, drawn in this chapter would in themselves rate an entire article. Also, this is the thrust of H. Boog, et al, (German Research Institute for Military history at Potsdam), Germany and the Second World War, Volume IV: The Attack on the Soviet Union. Oxford University Press, New York, 1996, Equipment of the Eastern Army, pp. tables I. III, 199-224.
[509] E.g., Hitler's Army: The Evolution and Structure of German Forces 1933-1945, Combined Books Inc, PA, 1996, ed. Command Magazine, article by J, Desch, The 1941 German Army/ The 1944 US Army, p. 79-93. The author compares the fully motorized US forces in 1944 to the German Army in 1941. The author even makes the completely ridiculous statement "Even just a few thousand (US) 2.5 ton trucks could have been decisive in the drive on Moscow"; completely forgetting the several hundred thousand German cargo trucks that were actually there.
[510] Specifically, 135,788,938 tonnes kilometers per day (trucks) over 5,720,363 tonnes kilometers per day (horses).

Between 22nd June and 4th July 1941, the German forces invading the USSR contained over 600,000 light-transports and trucks, including approximately 450,000 cargo trucks. On 22nd June 1941 the entire Soviet armed forces contained 272,600 motor-vehicles, of which approximately 193,200 were cargo trucks.[511] This means that at the start of the campaign the Wehrmacht forces on the East Front fielded well over twice as many cargo trucks as the entire Red Army.

Between 22nd June and 31st December 1941 the Red Army received another 204,900 motor vehicles, the vast majority commandeered from the Soviet civilian economy: only around 33,000 of these were newly manufactured trucks.[512] Therefore, the total Soviet vehicles available during the whole of 1941 (including all commandeered vehicles) was around 477,500 (272,600 available on 22nd June 1941 and 204,900 received from June to December 1941). This still only represented around 80% of the vehicles available to the Wehrmacht's invasion forces at the start of the campaign.

In addition, the Red Army lost over 159,000 vehicles due to enemy action in 1941, which represented over a third of all the available Red Army vehicles.[513] This was a much higher proportion of its available transport park than the Wehrmacht lost from all causes, including non-combat attrition losses. On top of all this the average German cargo truck had a considerably higher lift capacity (274 tkm vs. 199 tkm) and was easily as reliable as the average Soviet truck. Furthermore, a much higher proportion of the German vehicles also had superior off road ability, as a significant proportion of them were built to military specifications.

At the same time the German vehicles were supplying a smaller army in the field, as well as a much smaller mechanised force (at least in the first months of the campaign, and until the massive Soviet tank and mechanised division losses took effect). The latter required a disproportionably high number of cargo trucks to supply and support. The Red Army started the war with an incredible 61 tank divisions and 31 mechanised divisions. It is no wonder most of these divisions had barely enough motorised transport to move at all, let alone sustain prolonged combat operations. By comparison, the German invasion forces initially contained only 17 tank (panzer) divisions and 12 motorised divisions (including 3 Waffen SS motorised divisions and excluding SS Brigade Nord and the LSSAH Motorised Brigade).

In other words, bad as the German Supply Distribution Efficiency (SDE) became, at a strategic level it was always much better than the Red Army's SDE during 1941. **This became very apparent when both armies were operating from a supply source (such as a railhead or port) of similar distance for any significant length of time**. Of course the problem for the Germans in 1941 was that they generally had to move their supplies much further to their combat units in the field compared to the Red Army, and the Red Army units were better able to stockpile supplies locally over time as they prepared defensive positions.

Finally it must be pointed out (again) that the SDE analysis in the FILARM models assumes similar terrain and weather for both sides. It also assumes these effects have a similar impact on the respective sides' SDE. For example, accounts of Operation Barbarossa often remind us how bad the Soviet roads were for German transport reliability. What is rarely mentioned is that the Soviets had to use the same roads and cross the same terrain, often in lighter and less robust trucks. In October 1941 the situation started to change dramatically with the autumn rains. The ensuing muddy terrain severely curtailed German offensive operations in late October 1941 because combat and supply units could hardly move. Fortunately for the Germans, the Soviets could handle the mud only marginally better than they could (i.e. the German and Soviet SDEs both fell sharply, but the Soviets were defending and so didn't need to move as many units or as many supplies). When November 1941 came around and the ground froze, the Germans could resume offensive operations at a much reduced level. However, when December 1941 came round with heavy snow and freezing blizzard conditions, the German SDE initially fell dramatically while the Soviet SDE remained at more respectable levels. Obviously the 'constant' used in the SDE equation to represent weather effects was no longer the same for both sides in December 1941.[514]

***

---

[511] Refer Volume IIIB 4. – 'The Supply Distribution Efficiency (SDE) for the Soviet Armed Forces from 22nd June to 31st December 1941' Also, G.F. Krivosheev, et al, Soviet Casualties and Combat Losses in the Twentieth Century, ed. Colonel General G.F. Krivosheev, Greenhill Books, London, 1997, table 95, VI. motor vehicles p. 257.

[512] Refer Volume IIIA, 2. 9). – 'The Soviet Personnel and Equipment Resource Database - Transport and Prime Movers ' for a full analysis of the Soviet trucks, light transports and tractors used during 1941. The best estimate is that the Soviets produced around 33,000 new trucks from 23rd June to 31st December 1941: only around 28% of the total 1941 production. The majority of these trucks were 1.5t GAZ-MMs.

[513] G.F. Krivosheev, et al, Soviet Casualties and Combat Losses in the Twentieth Century, ed. Colonel General G.F. Krivosheev, Greenhill Books, London, 1997, p. page 257, table 95.

[514] Refer to Volume I Part I 8. – 'The Concepts and General Structure of the Integrated Land and Air Resource Model - Supply Distribution Efficiency (SDE)', for details on the SDE equations.

Finally, if there is one overriding conclusion that the reader should draw from the SDE analyses in the Soviet and German FILARM models then it is this. The Wehrmacht enjoyed an average Supply Distribution Efficiency (SDE) advantage on the East Front over 3.4 times that of the Red Army and VVS during the second half of 1941. This was very significant. It means that regardless of who was the attacking force, regardless of the road quality, and regardless of the speed with which the German railheads moved eastwards, the Red Army in 1941 had to stop the German Army in battle: **they could not (and did not) simply retreat eastwards and rely on the German supply situation to slow down their army**.

In short, there was nothing predetermined about the final outcome of Operation Barbarossa due to the respective army's supply and support infrastructures (logistics): the final outcome had to be (and was) determined by combat operations. **The German Army in the East definitely possessed the vehicular transport it needed to inflict fatal damage on the Red Army and the USSR in 1941.**

***

7. German Naval Forces on the East Front; June to December 1941

The various combatant's naval forces are not 'fully integrated' into the German or Soviet Fully Integrated Land and Air Resource Models (FILARMs). This is because the seagoing personnel, smaller pieces of equipment, and dockyard supply and repair infrastructures are not tracked in the naval models. Hence naval personnel and equipment should be seen as additional to those in the FILARM models, with the exception of the following which **are** included in the FILARM models:

- Naval personnel that became naval infantry and fought as ground troops.
- Land based naval aircraft.
- Naval coastal artillery.

This is particularly significant for the Soviets because all aircraft in the Soviet VVS-SF (Northern Fleet), VVS-KBF (Red Banner Baltic Fleet) and VVS-ChF (Black Sea Fleet) are all included in the Soviet FILARM model. These were all significant land based naval air forces, and were primarily involved in air to air and air to ground combat during Operation Barbarossa. In addition, 146,899 Soviet naval personnel transferred to the Red Army in the form of naval infantry in the second half of 1941. These were mostly used in the creation of naval infantry brigades and naval rifle brigades.

Although the naval forces are not fully integrated into the FILARM and PILARM models, the waterborne components of the naval and river forces involved in Operation Barbarossa should still be included in any Operation Barbarossa simulation. Where the majority of a county's naval forces were involved in Operation Barbarossa, then all that country's warships are shown (i.e. a Full (F) naval model). Where only a minor portion of a country's naval forces were involved in Operation Barbarossa, then only the relevant ships which were available for operations in theatre are shown (i.e. a Partial (P) naval model).

***

If the quality of naval training and ship readiness is included, and we exclude the Soviet land-based naval air forces, then the most powerful navy involved in Operation Barbarossa was the *Kriegsmarine* (German Navy). Its approximate strength in May-June 1941 is shown in the following table.[515]

---

[515] B. R. Kroener, et al, tables III.V.6 and III.V.7. Ref: BA-MA RM 7/1206, *Marinekommandant* A IIb, 615/41 g.Kdos, 4 Apr 1941. Also, BA-MA RM 7/395, *Wehrkraft der Wehrmacht im Fruhjahr* 1942, OKW, WFSt/Org. No 22230/42 g.Kdos. Chefs., 6 June 1942.

Personnel Strength of the Kriegsmarine, August 1939 - June 1941				
	1st Aug. 1939	1st Oct. 1939	1st March 1941	15th June 1941
Officers	4,500	8,400	11,200	12,120
Petty officers & enlisted men	73,943	128,188	309,534	391,880
Total	**78,443**	**136,588**	**320,734**	**404,000**

Strength of the Kriegsmarine, May 1941			
Battleships	2	Boom-breaker flotillas	4
Obsolete Battleships	2	Mine-seeker Flotillas	34
Battlecruisers	2	Minesweeper Flotillas	5
Heavy Cruisers	4	Outpost Flotillas	24
Light cruisers	4	Sub Hunter Flotillas	5
Old pre WWI light cruises	5	Harbour protection Flotillas	30
Destroyers	15		
Old pre WWI destroyers	5	**Artillery Batteries**	
Torpedo-boats	18	Heavy Coastal Batteries	25
Motor Torpedo Boats	40	Medium Coastal Batteries	99
Old pre WWI T Boats	10	Heavy AA Batteries	173
Submarines	122	Light AA Batteries	65
Auxiliary Cruisers	6	Searchlight Batteries	53
Minelayers	11		
Hospital Ships	10		

However, the *Kriegsmarine* committed relatively few forces to support Operation Barbarossa because they were busy fighting the Royal Navy and RAF Coastal Command at the time. We will therefore use only a Partial (P) model to study the German naval forces available to support operations on the East Front during 1941.

1) Kriegsmarine High Level Operational Commands: June 1941

In June 1941 the German navy's supreme headquarters was the *Oberkommando der Marine* (OKM) in Berlin, under the command of Grand Admiral Erich Raeder. The OKM reported directly to the *Oberkommando der Wehrmacht* (OKW). The Navy General Staff supporting the OKM was the *Seekriegsleitung* (SKL), which was equivalent to the Army General Staff. Directly subordinate to the OKM were the various operational commands. These were a mixture of fleet and more temporary geographic commands. On 21st June 1941 the most significant naval commands, which were responsible for operations, were as follows:

- The *Flottenstreitkrafte* (High Sees Fleet) headed by the *Flottenchef* (Fleet Commander). The High Seas Fleet included battleships, cruisers, destroyers, torpedo-boats, fast attack craft (S-boats), auxiliary cruisers (including commerce raiders), and supply and training ships. Each of these categories had its own flag officer, and elements of each flag officer's command often came under the operational control of other geographic commands and task forces. This was especially the case for smaller vessels such as torpedo-boats and fast attack craft (S-boats).

- The *Sicherungsstreitkrafte* (Naval Security Forces). The Naval Security Forces were primarily concerned with the defence of coastal waters and encompassed minesweepers, patrol and coastal defence boats, submarine hunters and escorts. They were organised into 11 *Sicherungsdivisionen* (Security divisions) covering all coasts controlled by the Germans, except for Norway. The latter was covered by the *Küstensicherungsverband* (Coastal Security Unit). The Naval Security Forces also often came under the operational control of other geographic commands and task forces.

- The *Unterseeboot* (U-Boat or submarine) forces. The U-Boat forces were organised into operational flotillas, each based on a particular port and reporting to the flag officer for U-Boats.[516] Each U-Boat flotilla numbered up to 20 submarines of which around half were at sea at any one time.

---

[516] In June 1941 this was Vice-Admiral Karl Donitz, and he had his HQ at Lorient on the French Atlantic coast. The HQ Flag Officer for U-Boats was initially at Wilhelmshaven, but after the fall of France Donitz transferred his HQ to Paris and then

- *Marinegruppenkommando West* (Naval Group HQ West). This was a temporary geographic command with its HQ in France, and was responsible for controlling operations in the French Atlantic waters.[517]

- *Marinegruppenkommando Nord* (Naval Group HQ North). This was a temporary geographic command with its HQ in Germany, and was responsible for controlling operations in the German Bight, North Sea, Norwegian waters and the Baltic Sea.[518]

As far as Operation Barbarossa was concerned, the only other sea area of relevance was the Black Sea. Achievement of naval superiority in the Black Sea was ruled out from the start by the OKW and OKM planners. This was because the Soviet Black Sea Fleet was known to be vastly superior to the Rumanian and Bulgarian naval forces, and these could not therefore be expected to engage in offensive action.[519] The *Kriegsmarine* had no naval assets in the Black Sea in June 1941, so during 1941 the Soviet Black Sea Fleet enjoyed such naval superiority as the Luftwaffe units in the area would allow. It wasn't until 1942 that small *Kriegsmarine* naval units found their way down to the Black Sea after a tortuous 1,500 mile inland journey.[520]

2) Orders and Objectives of the German Naval forces in the Baltic in 1941

Directive No. 21 (Hitler's and the OKW's orders concerning Operation Barbarossa) defined the German Navy's main task during 1941 as the continuation of the war against Britain and the Commonwealth. For the Baltic its orders were to safeguard sea transports to Finland and the Gulf of Bothnia, and to conduct defensive mine-laying operations to bottle up the Red Banner Baltic Fleet in Kronshtadt and Leningrad.[521] OKM (specifically Raeder) concurred with this view because it appeared to be the most economical use of the limited naval assets available so as not to jeopardise the German Navy's main effort in the Atlantic.

On 30th January 1941 the naval staff submitted its operations plan. Its central feature was the laying of mine barrages in the Gulf of Finland from bases at Porkkala and Turku (Abo) in southern Finland, with only very limited attacks on enemy naval units. The second principal task was the protection of seaborne traffic to Finland (mainly troop and supply convoys), Sweden (mainly iron ore shipments) and the eastern Baltic ports (mainly supplies for Army Group North), which were yet to be captured. The most serious threat from the Soviet Red Banner Baltic Fleet was seen to be its submarines and mine-laying capabilities: the large enemy surface fleet was viewed as less of a threat due to "low levels of training and readiness, and inadequate command skills". On the other hand, the large number of Soviet submarines in the Baltic (65 on 21st June 1941) were actually expected to cause "temporary disruption of sea communication in the Baltic".[522]

On 26th February 1941 Colonel-General Halder and Admiral Otto Schniewind, chief of staff of the naval war staff, discussed the problem of naval support for Army Group North which was scheduled to invade the Baltic States. Schniewind made it clear that warships were unavailable to support the Army's planned advance along the coast. However, it was envisaged that some seagoing ships and transport barges would be available to supplement rail and road transport capacity; and their use would depend on the developing naval-war situation in the Baltic.

This eventually resulted in 2 ships with food supplies and 4 ships with ammunition being loaded and ready at Memel and Konigsberg by 23rd June 1941. An additional 18 ships were earmarked to supply 18th Army, and these were to be brought up to Libau as soon as possible (after the invasion had started). For transportation across the

---

Lorient. Donitz was promoted to Admiral in 1942 and Grand Admiral in January 1943, when he replaced Raeder as C in C of the German Navy.

[517] In September 1939 *Marinegruppenkommando West* controlled operations in the German Bight and North Sea. After the fall of France, *Marinegruppenkommando West* transferred its HQ to France and became responsible for operations in the French Atlantic waters.

[518] In September 1939 *Marinegruppenkommando Ost* (East) controlled operations in the Baltic. However *Marinegruppenkommando Nord* was formed after the fall of France, and by June 1941 it had overall control of operations in the Baltic Sea. Note, some sources state that the German naval forces in the Baltic were under the control of *Marinegruppenkommando Ost* (East), under the command of Generaladmiral Albrecht. This was the situation at the outbreak of WWII, but both the HQ and commander had changed by June 1941.

[519] H. Boog, et al., German Research Institute for Military History at Potsdam, Germany and the Second World War, Volume IV: The Attack on the Soviet Union, Clarendon Press (Oxford University Press), New York, 1996, p. 382.

[520] During WWII the *Kriegsmarine* brought some 500 small cargo craft and light vessels up the Elbe to Dresden from where they were transported by road and refloated at Ingolstadt on the Danube. They then made their way to the Black Sea. This force included 6 small type IIB U-Boats, 23 minesweepers, 16 S-boats, 50 landing craft and 26 sub-chasers. A. Seaton, The Russo-German War 1941-1945, Presidio Press, Novato, CA, 1971, p. 508.

[521] H. Boog, et al., German Research Institute for Military History at Potsdam, Germany and the Second World War, Volume IV: The Attack on the Soviet Union, Clarendon Press (Oxford University Press), New York, 1996, p. 381.

[522] Ibid, p. 381.

Niemen River near Memel, 2,250 tons of river-barge capacity, laden with ammunition, was readied; and a further 1,250 tons of river-barge capacity was made ready at Konigsberg.[523]

By 22nd June 1941 the *Kriegsmarine* had moved 48 additional small warships into Finnish waters, specifically in preparation for Operation Barbarossa.[524] Overall control of Baltic Sea operations was exercised by *Marinegruppenkommando Nord* under the command of *Generaladmiral* Carls. The operational-tactical commander was the flag officer for cruisers, *Befehlshaber der Kreuzer* (B.d.K), reinforced for this purpose by some of the staff of the *Führer der Torpedoboote* (F.d.T.; Leader of Torpedo-boats).[525]

To ensure these commands (above) could concentrate on offensive operations, the Leader of Mining Vessels from the North Sea Security Area assumed control of routine mine sweeping and patrol services in the southern Baltic area. In addition two temporary naval commands, called 'C' and 'D', were created. These were to advance eastwards with Army Group North and coordinate the army's and navy's organisation and defence of newly captured ports in the Baltic States. Naval Command 'D' also had control of the supply ships concentrating in Libau (see above) bringing seaborne supplies to 18th Army.

In order to ensure liaison with the Finnish Navy, the F.d.T. commander and the rest of his staff were posted to Helsinki as 'Commander of German naval forces in Finland'. The first consultations between German and Finnish naval staff occurred on 28th May 1941, and were followed on 6th June by meetings between the *Marinegruppenkommando Nord* HQ and Finnish naval staff regarding operational engagement plans. The Finnish Navy was relatively important because of the weakness of German naval strength in the Gulf of Finland. Although small, the Finnish Navy included two good coast defence ships (each with four 10-inch guns), four sloops/gunboats, five submarines and, most importantly, 12 small minelayers.[526]

***

---

[523] Ibid, p. 383.
[524] The Oxford Companion to WWII, Ed. I.C.B. Dear, M.R.D. Foot, Oxford University Press, New York, 2001, p. 83.
[525] H. Boog, et al., German Research Institute for Military History at Potsdam, Germany and the Second World War, Volume IV: The Attack on the Soviet Union, Clarendon Press (Oxford University Press), New York, 1996, p. 382.
[526] Refer Volume IV – 'The Finnish, Rumanian, Hungarian, Slovakian and Italian Forces Involved on the East Front in 1941 - Deployment and Composition of the Finnish Navy, 22 June 1941'.

3) The Actual Strength of German Naval Units in the Baltic during 1941

On 22nd June 1941 the deployment of German ships and smaller craft in the Baltic Sea was as shown in table Ger Navy Baltic.[527] The forces were effectively divided into two areas: the Southern Baltic and the Northern Baltic including the Gulf of Finland. In terms of naval forces available for immediate offensive action against the Red Banner Baltic Fleet, only the *Kriegsmarine* forces in the Northern Baltic area should be considered. This includes all naval forces north of an east-west line running from Libau to the island of Oland.

The most important German ships in the Gulf of Finland were the six specially built minelayers, which were initially divided into two groups or task forces. The first group was Mining Group 'Kobra', based in the Porkalla skerries and consisting of the Kaiser, Kobra and Konigin Luise. The second group was Mining Group 'Nord', based in the Turku (Abo) skerries and consisting of the Brummer, Hansestadt Danzig and Tannenberg. As an indication of the shoestring nature of the German force, it is noteworthy that all these minelayers were converted merchant ships, except for the Brummer. The latter was originally a purpose built Norwegian vessel called the Olav Tryggvason. Although these ships were essentially wartime improvisations, the crews on these ships and their commanders were not: they were highly trained and experienced, and had been carefully selected for the job. The table below summarises the capabilities of these vessels.

German Minelayers (*Minenschiffe*) in the North Baltic Sea, 22nd June 1941				
	Launch Date	Displacement (Deep Load, tons)	Speed (knots)	Armament
Kaiser	1905	1,920	16	2x88mm, 2x37mmAA, 8x20mmAA, 200 mines.
Kobra	1926	2,760	17	2x88mm, 2x37mmAA, 2x20mmAA, 180 mines.
Konigin Luise	1934	3,370	16	2x88mm, 1x37mmAA, 2x20mmAA, 240 mines.
Brummer	1932	1,860	21	4x127mm, 2x37mmAA, 4x20mmAA, 280 mines.
Hansestadt Danzig	1926	2,500	20	2x88mm, 4x37mmAA, 6x20mmAA, 360 mines.
Tannenberg	1935	5,700	20	3x150mm, 4x37mmAA, 6x20mmAA, 460 mines.

Mine-sweeping in the Gulf of Finland was the responsibility of the 5th Mine-Clearing Flotilla, with its headquarters at Gotenhafen. For operations in the Gulf of Finland, a detachment of 10 small R-boats (*Raumboote* - Sweeper boats) was sent north. 5 boats were based at Porkkala and the other 5 were based at Turku (Abo). The R-boats were essentially large armed motor launches. They displaced 125 tons, were capable of 20 knots, had a complement of 34 men and were usually armed with a 37mm flak gun or 2 20mm flak guns.[528] They were capable of mine-sweeping, but were also often fitted with stern racks to carry 10 sea-mines for mine-laying. It is unknown if the R-boats in the Gulf of Finland were equipped for mine-laying, but considering the situation it is highly likely they were also used in this fashion in June and July 1941.

***

The minelaying and minesweeping force in the Gulf of Finland was 'covered' by the 1st and 2nd S-Boat Flotillas, based at Porkkala and Turku (Abo), respectively. This force contained 19 S-boats (*Schnellboote* - Fast boats) which are famously known in the West as E-boats. In most post-war literature the generic term motor-torpedo-boat (MTB) is used to describe vessels in this class, and as a result the German S-boats (or E-boats) are thought of as equivalent to the Royal Navy's MTBs and the US Navy's PT boats. While not unreasonable, this disguises the fact that the German S-boats were the largest and most powerful general issue 'MTBs' fielded during WWII, and that the Allies produced very few vessels in this class to match them.

---

[527] Data for this table is compiled from the following sources. H. Boog, et al., German Research Institute for Military History at Potsdam, Germany and the Second World War, Volume IV: The Attack on the Soviet Union, Oxford University Press, New York, 1996, map I.IV.5, p. 384. The Nafziger Collection: The German Fleet in the Baltic (Ostseeraum) 22 June 1941. Conway's All The World's Fighting Ships 1922-1946, Conway Maritime Press, London, 1980, pp. 222 – 254. The Oxford Companion to WWII, Ed. I.C.B. Dear, M.R.D. Foot, Oxford University Press, New York, 2001, p. 83. A. Seaton, The Russo-German War 1941-1945, Presidio Press, Novato, CA, 1971, p. 506. A. Mollo, The Armed forces of WWII, Orbis Publishing, London, 1982, p. 195. K. Wynn, U-Boat Operations of the Second World War: Volume 1, Caxton Editions, Caxton Publishing Group, 2003, pp. 113-116.

[528] Conway's All The World's Fighting Ships 1922-1946, Conway Maritime Press, London, 1980, p. 251. All the R-Boats in the Gulf of Finland in June 1941 were from the R41 production group, launched from 1939 to 1943.

Table Ger Navy Baltic — Deployment and Composition of the German Fleet in the Baltic Sea (Ostseeraum), 22nd June 1941

	Naval Group HQ North (Marinegruppenkommando Nord). Northern Baltic Sea and Gulf of Finland — Description	No	Southern Baltic Sea — Description	No	TOTAL	Reinforcement Units of the German Fleet in the Baltic, July 1941 - 31st Dec. 1941	Tirpitz*
New Battleships						New Battleships	Tirpitz*
Old Battleships*			Schlesien, Schleswig-Holstein*	2	2	Old Battleships	
Heavy Cruisers^			Admiral Scheer^	1	1	Heavy Cruisers	
Light Cruisers**			Emden, Leipzig, Köln, Nürnberg**	4	4	Light Cruisers	
Destroyers*^			Z-25, Z-26, Z-27*^	3	3	Destroyers	
Escorts/Torpedo Boats^^			11th U-Boat Hunter Flotilla^^	4	4	Escorts/Torpedo Boats	
Submarines	U-140, U-142, U-144, U-145, U-149*	5			5	Submarines	
Minelayers^^	(Refer to notes for names)^	6	Preussen, Grille, Versailles, Skagerrak.	4	10	Minelayers	4
Minesweepers***			5th, 10th, 15th, 17th, 31st Minesweeper Flotillas^^	20	20	Minesweepers	8
Motor Minesweepers***^	(R53, R54, R55, R56, R57, R60, R61, R62, R63, R64)**	10	1st Mine-clearing Flotilla	10	20	Motor Minesweepers	12
MTBs (Schnellboote, S-boote)*^^	(S26-S29, S39-S47, S101-S106)^^	19	3rd, 5th and 6th MTB Flotillas***	27	46	MTBs (Schnellboote, S-boote)	36
Patrol Boats			3rd Patrol Boat Flotilla (at Gotenhafen).	12	12	Patrol Boats	
Ocean Tugs (+500t, Armed, AA)	Fohn, Passat, Monsun, Taifun.	4			4	Ocean Tugs (+500t).	
Depot Ships, Sub Tender, (Armed)	Elbe, Tanga, Tsingtau, Carl Peters, Krefeld, Seeburg, Hernosand.	7			7	Depot, Sub Tenders	
Auxiliary Tankers (Armed, AA)	Brummer, Gabelflach, Oderbank, Phonica, Nina, Stellergrund.	6			6	Auxiliary Tankers	
Armed Trawlers (Armed)	"Outpost or Picket Boat" Flotilla	10			10	Armed Trawlers	
Merchant/Supply/Transports/Misc.	^*	20	**^	24	44	Merch./Supply/Trans./Misc.	30
Totals		87		111	198		90

Northern Baltic Sea and Gulf of Finland notes:

* U-140, U-142, U-144, U-145 and U-149 are all Type IID U-Boats, (309t/358t). Attached to the 22nd U-Boat Flotilla, operating North of Libau (but not deployed in the Gulf of Finland).

^ Kaiser, Cobra, Königin Luise, Brummer, Hansestadt Danzig and Tannenberg.

** Kaiser, Cobra and Königin Luise were attached to the Kobra Minelayer Group, (at Porkkala). Brummer, Hansestadt Danzig, Tannenberg were attached to the Nord Minelayer Group, (at Turku (Abo)).

*** Part of the 5th Mine-clearing Flotilla, operating from Porkkala and Turku (Abo). The flotilla HQ was at Gotenhafen.

*^ Attached to the 1st and 2nd MTB Flotillas, at Porkkala and Turku (Abo), respectively.

^* Excludes ships transporting materials to and from Sweden and Merchant Ships not directly involved in military operations (such as transporting supplies to Army Group North along the coast).

Southern Baltic Sea notes:

* Obsolete Battleships, originally launched 1906. Partially modernised in 1930s, secondary armament removed 1939 (accept AA). Schlesien was at the northern end of the Great Belt exit to the Kattegat. Schleswig-Holstein was at southern end of the Sund exit.

^ Recently ret. from Atlantic, at Kiel. Part of the "Baltenflotte" in Sep. 41.

** Köln and Nurnberg were part of the "Baltenflotte" force in Sept 1941. Emden, Leipzig and Köln supported ground operations invading the "Baltic Islands" in Sep. to Oct 41.

*^ Z-25, Z-26, Z-27 were all part of the "Baltenflotte" force in Sep. 1941.

^^ Formed a Sub Hunter Group patrolling behind the "Wartburg" mine barrage between Memel and South of Öland. Based out of Memel and Stolpmunde.

^^ Were based at Gotenhafen, Swinemunde, Pillau, Memel and Memel, respectively.

*** The 3rd, 5th and 6th MTB Flotillas were based at Pillau, Gotenhafen and Sund, respectively.

**^ Includes 20 supply ships (2 loaded with food), and 4 ammunition ships (loaded). The ships were at Memel and Königsberg in readiness to supply 18th Army. The above does not include 2250 tons of river barge transport capacity at Memel loaded with ammunition, or 1250 tons of river barge transport capacity at Königsberg. Excludes ships transporting materials to and from Norway and Sweden, and merchant ships not directly involved in military operations.

Reinforcement Units notes:

* Commissioned 25th Feb. 1941. Completing workup and trials to Aug. 41 in the Southern Baltic. Part of the "Baltenflotte" force in Sep. 1941.

General legend (tonnages):

* 13000 tons standard.
^ 11700 tons standard.
** 5600 - 6700 tons standard.
*^ 3543 tons standard
^^ 712 - 933 tons standard, F class escorts or torpedo boats.
^^ 1596 - 5700 tons standard, armed conversions from merchant ships, except Brummer and Grille.
*** 515-690 tons standard. Mainly Mob type minesweepers, capable of escort, ASW, AA defence, and minelaying.
***^ 115-125 tons standard, Raumboote (R-boote).
*^^ 93 tons standard, Schnellboote (S-boote).

© Nigel Askey, 2018

The S-boats S26 to S29 were from the 'S26 group' produced in 1940, while the remaining S-boats in the North Baltic Sea in June 1941 were from the 'S38 group' produced from 1939 to 1943. These boats displaced 115 ton (deep load), had 6,000bhp diesel engines, could travel at 39.5 knots, had a complement of 21 men, and were armed with 2 internal 533mm (21 inch) torpedo tubes with 4 torpedoes, 2 20mm flak guns and 6 sea-mines (or 12 plus depth charges). The S-boats had over twice the displacement of the Royal Navy's MTBs and the US Navy's PT boats during WWII.[529] In addition, the British MTBs and MGBs, and the US PT boats, used petrol engines which made them both fragile and highly flammable compared to the S-boats with their more powerful and more reliable diesel engines.[530]

From Operation Barbarossa's point of view, the most significant aspects of the S-boats were that they were large enough to carry sea-mines in launch-racks and that they could carry enough fuel to cruise at very fast speeds over long distances. This meant that S-boats could depart the Porkalla skerries just before dusk, reach areas deep inside the Gulf of Finland patrolled by the Red Banner Baltic Fleet, lay their mines, and be back at base by dawn (even in the short northern summer nights). Detection and interception of these craft was difficult enough in daylight, with aircraft being the most effective means of doing this. However the Soviet VVS-VMS (the naval air arm of the Red Navy) did not have the capability to detect or attack these craft at night. The result of this was that Soviet ships and submarines could run into an undetected enemy mine-field almost anywhere west of the island of Suursaari. For the same reasons, Soviet ships and submarines could also come under surprise torpedo attack from S-boats (especially at night) in areas they might have thought safe.

***

It is well known that the principal and most dangerous offensive branch of the *Kriegsmarine* during WWII was the U-boat arm. Operation Barbarossa was not allowed to interfere with ongoing U-boat operations in the 'Battle of the Atlantic'; with the result that no ocean going U-boats were transferred to the Baltic and placed under the control of *Marinegruppenkommando Nord*. The only concession from Raeder and Donitz was the release of five small coastal submarines from the 22nd U-boat Training Flotilla (22 U-*Flottille*) in Gotenhafen in the Southern Baltic. These U-boats continued to be attached to the 22nd U-boat Flotilla and were as follows.[531]

U-Boats Released for Operations in the Baltic During 1941			
U-Boat	Type	Base	Where Deployed on 22nd June 1941
U 140	IID	Gotenhafen	West of Libau and north of Memel.
U 142	IID	Gotenhafen	South of Gotland.
U 144	IID	Gotenhafen	West of Ventspils and Windau.
U 145	IID	Gotenhafen	West of Osel and Dago Islands.
U 149	IID	Gotenhafen	On the entrance to the Gulf of Finland.

The type IID U-boat displaced 358 tons when submerged, had a complement of 25 men, and was armed with three 533mm torpedo tubes with 6 torpedoes and a 20mm flak gun. Although unsuited to the open ocean, these small U-boats were well suited to the relatively tight confines and shallower waters of the Baltic Sea coast.

The remaining ships in the North Baltic Sea were either merchant ships or *Kriegsmarine* auxiliary ships. The latter included ocean tugs (*seeschlepper*) of around 500 tons, depot ships (*begleitschiffe*) and one submarine tender (the Krefeld) in the range 2,000-4,000 tons, supply ships (*versorgunsdampfer*), tankers (*tankschiffe*) and a few converted trawlers. All these ships were usually armed with a few 20mm or 37mm flak guns, while the depot ships and submarine tenders often also had 2-4 88mm or 105mm guns for self-defence.

***

---

[529] The many Royal Navy MTB types launched from 1940 to 1945 displaced from 28-53 tons (deep load), had 1,650-4,050bhp engines, could travel at 33-40 knots, had a complement of 9-17 men, and were typically armed with 2 external 18 inch torpedo tubes, various MG and light flak gun combinations, and up to 4 mines (or 8 depth charges). The US Navy's PT boats displaced from 45-54 tons (deep load), had 3,375-4,050bhp engines, could travel at 38-39 knots, had a complement of 10-17 men, and were typically armed with 2-4 externally mounted 18 inch torpedo tubes, various MG and light flak gun combinations, and sometimes 4.5inch rockets (used later in the war in place of two torpedoes). Conway's All The World's Fighting Ships 1922-1946, Conway Maritime Press, London, 1980, pp. 68, 69, 154, 155, and 248.

[530] M. Stephen, Ed. E. Grove, Sea Battles in Close Up: WWII, Naval Institute Press, Annapolis, Maryland, 1988, p. 126.

[531] K. Wynn, U-Boat Operations of the Second World War: Volume 1, Caxton Editions, Caxton Publishing Group, 2003, pp. 113-116.

For the purposes of this discussion, the 'Southern Baltic' includes the sea area south of an east-west line running from Libau to the island of Oland, and as far west as the Kattegat and the waters around Denmark. This therefore encompasses the home waters of southern Sweden, eastern Denmark and northern Germany; including Copenhagen and the main *Kriegsmarine* home port of Kiel. As such it is not surprising that the German naval forces in the Southern Baltic were far stronger than those in the Northern Baltic and the Gulf of Finland. However, due to Kiel and the Kiel Canal being a major staging area for operations against Britain and the Commonwealth, and due to Raeder's reluctance to release any major surface or submarine units to support what he saw as a dilution of the main naval effort in the West, the naval forces in the Southern Baltic were not available for offensive operations in support of Operation Barbarossa in June and July 1941.[532]

Nevertheless, as we can see from table <u>Ger Navy Baltic</u>, the *Kriegsmarine* did have major naval assets in the Southern Baltic in June 1941. In the event of the Soviet Red Banner Baltic Fleet (the strongest fleet in the Red Navy) breaking out into the open Baltic, then the OKW and OKM would have had no option but to commit their major naval units to battle. The Operation Barbarossa war plan, at both the strategic and operational level, made no allowances for loss of control of the Northern Baltic area. Therefore any comprehensive simulation of Operation Barbarossa has to allow the German 'player' the same freedom of action and options as the OKW had historically; i.e. being able to order the OKM to release the naval assets in the Southern Baltic to confront a potentially rampant Soviet Red Banner Baltic Fleet. In the event of a Soviet naval breakout out into the open Baltic in 1941, this would have been the minimum action ordered: it is likely other naval assets in Wilhelmshaven and Norway would have been released and transferred east as well.

The following table summarises the capabilities of the principal German warships and warship types in the South Baltic Sea on 22nd June 1941.

Principal German Warships and Warship Types in the South Baltic Sea Area, 22nd June 1941				
	Comm. Date	Disp. (Deep Load, tons)	Complement	Speed (knots)	Armament
Tirpitz	Feb. 1941	52,600	2,347	29	8x380mm, 12x150mm, 16x105mm, 16x37mmAA, 20x20mmAA, 6 aircraft.
Admiral Scheer	Nov. 1934	15,900	1,150	28	6x280mm, 8x150mm, 6x105mm, 8x37mmAA, 6x20mmAA, 8x533mmTT, 2 aircraft.
Schlesien	May 1908	14,218	802	18	4x280mm, 2x88mm, 4x37mmAA, 22x20mmAA.
Schleswig-Holstein	July 1908	14,218	771	18	4x280mm, 2x88mm, 4x37mmAA, 22x20mmAA.
Emden	Oct. 1925	6,990	650	29.4	8x150mm, 3x88mm, 4x20mmAA, 4x533mmTT.
Koln	Jan. 1930	8,130	850	32	9x150mm, 4x88mm, 8x37mmAA, 8x20mmAA, 12x533mmTT, 2 aircraft.
Leipzig	Oct. 1931	8,250	850	32	9x150mm, 6x88mm, 8x37mmAA, 6x533mmTT, 2 aircraft.
Nurnberg	Nov 1935	8,380	896	32	9x150mm, 8x88mm, 8x37mmAA, 8x20mmAA, 6x533mmTT, 2 aircraft.
Z-25, Z-26, Z-27	1940/41	3,605	321	38.5	4x150mm, 4x37mmAA, 5x20mm, 8x533mmTT, DCs.
1935 Type T Boats	1939/40	1,088	119	35.5	1x105mm, 1x37mm, 8x20mm. 6x533mmTT, DCs.
F Class Escorts	1935/36	1,028	121	28	2x105mm, 4x37mm, 4x20mm, DCs.
Ex Minelayer, Grille	May 1935	3,430	248	26	3x127mm, 4x37mm, 4x20mm, 240 mines.
(Mob) Minesweepers	1937-41	874	113	18.3	2x105mm, 2x37mm, 2x20mm, DCs.
R-boats	1938-41	125	34	20	1x37mmAA or 2x20mm, 10 mines.
S-boats	1939-41	115	21	39.5	2x20mmAA, 2x533TT, 6 mines (or DCs)

[532] Raeder opposed the idea of Operation Barbarossa and on 27th December 1940 he reiterated his objections to the OKW about embarking on operations in the East before the UK was defeated. He cited the dangers of an undefeated Britain and entry of the USA into the war due to an intensification of the U-boat war, before the USSR could be defeated. In the event this is what happened, although much faster than hoped (by the Germans) and for different reasons. H. Boog, et al. (German Research Institute for Military History at Potsdam), Germany and the Second World War, Volume IV: The Attack on the Soviet Union, Clarendon Press (Oxford University Press), New York, 1996, pp. 376-380.

The battleship Tirpitz had only completed commissioning on 25th February 1941, and was still completing sea-trials and crew shakedown cruises in June-July. It was otherwise operational, and in June 1941 it represented one of the three most powerful surface warships in the world (excluding aircraft carriers). The other two were the US Navy's battleships North Carolina and Washington which were even newer; having just been commissioned on 9th April 1941 and 15th May 1941, respectively.[533] It is safe to say that in late 1941 there wasn't another battleship or battlecruiser anywhere in European waters that could match the fully operational Tirpitz in a one on one gun duel. This includes the Royal Navy's King George V and Nelson class battleships, and (for largely non-technological reasons) the Italian Navy's Littorio class battleships.[534]

There can be little doubt that in any open water battle the Tirpitz would have made short work of the much older and less ready Soviet battleships and cruisers in the Soviet Red Banner Baltic Fleet. This is especially true if any German *Baltenflotte* (Baltic Fleet) included the Tirpitz, Admiral Scheer (see below) and covering light cruisers and destroyers. In the event, the Soviet Red Banner Baltic Fleet was somewhat easily contained within the Gulf of Finland, and one is left to wonder if the Soviet Naval High Command had intelligence of the 'Tirpitz menace' that awaited any Soviet fleet attempting to operate in the open Baltic Sea. It is also possible that Soviet intelligence overestimated the Tirpitz's readiness in mid-1941, because it appears the better informed British Naval Intelligence probably did.[535] The Tirpitz remained in the Baltic until 12th January 1942, when she left for Norwegian waters.

The other powerful surface unit available in the South Baltic was the Admiral Scheer. The Admiral Scheer was originally classified as a *Panzerschiffe* (armoured ship) by the *Kriegsmarine*, but by 1940 it was more conventionally classified as a heavy cruiser. It remained, however, considerably more heavily armed than contemporary heavy cruisers, which is why the term 'pocket battleship' was loosely used (and is still sometimes used today) in the western press to describe this class of ship. Although not in actuality in the same class as a true battleship or battlecruiser, the Admiral Scheer was close to being able to match the Soviet capital ships in the Soviet Red Banner Baltic Fleet: the much older Marat and Oktyabrskaya Revoluciya battleships. Whatever the classification, by June 1941 the Admiral Scheer was one of the most experienced and successful warships anywhere. On 1st April 1941 she had reached Kiel after a gruelling five month commerce raiding voyage, in which she sank or captured 16 merchant ships of 113,233 tons and the large armed merchant cruiser HMS Jervis Bay (an additional 14,164 tons).[536] The Admiral Scheer was overhauled in Kiel and was operational by June-July 1941. She was assigned to the temporary *Baltenflotte* along with the Tirpitz on 21st September 1991 (refer next section), and remained in the Baltic (apart from a short stint in Hamburg for repairs) until February 1942.

---

[533] This is why it is often stated that the Bismarck, which was commissioned on 24th August 1940, was the most powerful battleship in the world in its day. Both the North Carolina and Washington were not fully functional until early 1942, largely due to severe propeller vibration problems. The first of the South Dakota class (smaller and slightly slower than the North Carolina class, and with similar overall protection and firepower) didn't commission until 20th March 1942, while the considerably more powerful Iowa class wasn't commissioned until 22nd February 1943. The first of the Japanese Yamato class wasn't completed until December 1941 and wasn't operational until well into 1942. The Yamato and Iowa class battleships remain the most powerful all-round battleships ever built. Conway's All The World's Fighting Ships 1922-1946, Conway Maritime Press, London, 1980, pp. 97-99, 178 and 224.

[534] Any two of these Royal Navy ship types were, together, certainly more than a match for Tirpitz (even without smashed rudders!); and the Littorio (commissioned on 6th May 1940) was definitely a match on paper. However, the training in the Italian Navy (especially gunnery training and practise), and the quality of fire control systems and damage control, meant it was demonstrably not a match (i.e., in reality). In addition the Littorio class had limited endurance (designed for Mediterranean operations), was found to be a 'wet' ship in heavy weather, and the modern Pugliese underwater torpedo defence system never performed as well as expected. The latter was graphically illustrated by the bottoming of Littorio in Taranto harbor after three 18 inch torpedo hits from Swordfish aircraft. If she had been at sea, it is very likely she would have sunk with this level of damage and inadequate damage control. By comparison, the Bismarck had taken at least three (and very possibly four) such torpedoes as well as three 14 inch shell hits before her final battle, and only one torpedo hit (on the rudders) proved vital. The Royal Navy command in the Mediterranean rated a Littorio class battleship as equivalent to a Queen Elizabeth class battleship in 1941, even though the former was theoretically a much more powerful ship. This is one of the primary reasons why the Royal Navy's most powerful all-round battleships (the five KGVs) spent so little time in the Mediterranean theatre during WWII, even though three Littorio class ships were completed and made operational.

[535] British Intelligence indicated Tirpitz was operational by mid-1941. The Admiralty was concerned enough to have its Home Fleet on alert for a Tirpitz 'breakout', and RAF Bomber Command had standing orders to attack the ship at any opportunity. The first (of many) RAF Bomber Command's attacks on Tirpitz, after it was commissioned at Kiel, occurred as early as 28th February 1941 with 30 Wellingtons from 40, 115, 214 and 218 Squadrons.

[536] The Admiral Scheer sailed 46,419 nautical miles from 23rd October 1940 to 1st April 1941 under the command of Captain Theodor Kranke. She ranged across the North Atlantic, South Atlantic and Indian Ocean, and in this time she evaded numerous hunt and destroy 'nets' cast by several different Royal Navy task forces and commands. The Admiral Scheer went on to become the most successful capital ship commerce raider of WWII. Her success was only exceeded by U-boats (e.g., U-48 sank 54 ships of around 306,000 tons) and several disguised merchant ship commerce raiders (e.g., the Thor which sank or captured 22 ships of around 152,000 tons).

Of the remaining large warships in the *Kriegsmarine*, only the old pre-dreadnoughts Schlesien and Schleswig-Holstein were available for operations in the Baltic Sea during the second half of 1941. Both these ships were launched in 1906 and were still functional mainly due to careful maintenance and several partial refits in the 1930s. By WWII they were really only suitable for training and coastal defence duties. In June 1941 the Schlesien was defending the northern end of the Great Belt (Danish, *Storebaelt*) exit to the Kattegat, while the Schleswig-Holstein was at southern end of The Sound exit (Danish, *Oresund*).

The battlecruisers Scharnhorst and Gneisenau, and the heavy cruiser Prinz Eugen, were in Brest (France) after their respective commerce raiding forays into the North Atlantic.[537] All three ships were under constant threat from RAF bombers and were only able to return to home waters in February 1942 as a result of Operation Cerberus; better known as 'The Channel Dash'. The heavy cruiser Lutzow (renamed from the Deutschland) was in dry dock at Kiel, undergoing repairs after being torpedoed by a RAF Beaufort on 13th June 1941. She was not operational again until 17th January 1942. The last of the German's heavy cruisers, the Admiral Hipper, was also at Kiel undergoing a refit after her second commerce raiding voyage.[538] She had returned to Kiel on 28th March 1941 and spent the next year undergoing a refit, which included the conversion of some of her water tanks to fuel tanks in order to increase her range. The Admiral Hipper was not operational again until March 1942.

In addition to the battleships and heavy cruisers above, the *Kriegsmarine* had four light cruisers in June 1941 and they were all deployed in the Southern Baltic. These were the Emden, Koln, Leipzig and Nurnberg. All these cruisers stemmed from a clause in the Treaty of Versailles which allowed Germany to possess eight 6,000 ton light cruisers, of which six could be in service at any one time. The end result was the four light cruisers above, as well as the Konigsberg and Karlsruhe. The latter two were both sunk in April 1940 during the German invasion of Norway. By 1941 the Emden, the smallest of the German light cruisers, was showing her age and was mainly serving as a training ship for junior officers and cadets.

The other light cruisers all displaced over 6,500 tons (standard) and 8,100 tons (deep load), and they were all armed with three triple turrets with 150mm (6 inch) guns. They were also fast (32 knots), were well armed with torpedo tubes and flak guns, and could each carry two useful Arado Ar 196 seaplanes. On balance these German cruisers were inferior to most contemporary Royal Navy light cruisers, especially in the armour and seakeeping departments. They were nonetheless a very useful addition to the German naval forces in the Baltic during 1941. This was because they were all operational, and, almost equally as important, they were a lot more expendable in Raeder's eyes than the larger surface units; i.e. they could be committed to action in the Baltic Sea without having any significant effect on the *Kriegsmarine's* operations in the North Atlantic.

***

---

[537] Scharnhorst and Gneisenau entered Brest on 22nd March 1941 after a three month raiding cruise in the Atlantic, during which they had sunk 21 merchant ships totalling 105,784 tons. The Prinz Eugen entered Brest on 1st June 1941 after the Bismarck episode. M. Stephen, Ed. E. Grove, Sea Battles in Close Up: WWII, Naval Institute Press, Annapolis, Maryland, 1988, pp. 115 and 116.
[538] On these two voyages the Admiral Hipper sunk at least 9 ships totalling more than 61,000 tons, mostly from convoys W-55A and SLS-64.

4) A History of German Naval Operations in the Baltic: June to December 1941

As a first step in securing the Baltic Sea the Germans needed to ensure the home waters in the southern Baltic were well protected, especially from submarine attack. They therefore declared an exclusion zone which extended from Libau to Memel, westwards across the Baltic, and all the way to the southern part of the Swedish island of Oland and the Swedish coast. This became known as the Wartburg I, II and III mine-barrage with sector I being closest to Libau/Memel and sector III being closest to Sweden. The laying of the extensive mine-barrages within this zone commenced on 18th June 1941, and initially contained 1,500 mines and 1,800 explosive buoys.[539]

The system was completed by a Swedish mine-barrage which was laid to meet German demands in Swedish territorial waters. The Wartburg mine-barrages needed pilots and or escorts to traverse safely, and in June 1941 it was also patrolled by the 11th U-Boat Hunter Flotilla based out of Memel and Stolpmunde. In addition, German protective mine-barrages were laid (before 22nd June 1941) around the ports of Memel, Pillau, Kolberg and Stettin to protect them against penetration by enemy naval forces. At the suggestion of the German naval war staff, a further defensive measure was taken by the Swedish Navy, which laid a mine-barrage between Stockholm and the boundary of Swedish territorial waters off the Aland archipelago (in the central Baltic Sea area).[540]

In the event, the 'defensive' Wartburg mine-barrage, and those around the Baltic ports, possibly caused only friendly shipping losses. At least ten German, Swedish or Finnish merchant ships and two minesweepers were lost on the German mine-barrages during 1941. In addition, a further three minesweepers were lost in the Swedish barrage on 9th July 1941 because the naval war staffs involved failed to advise them of the barrage which had been laid on 28th June 1941. However, it is highly likely that a number of Soviet submarines were also lost in these barrages because several of them disappeared without trace whilst operating in the Southern Baltic during 1941.[541]

***

On 29th May 1941 the *Kriegsmarine's* offensive units started moving to their assigned ports in the central and northern Baltic areas. By 18th June all units had reached their ports, including those in Finland, without incident. After 14th June 1941 German merchant vessels were not permitted to make for Soviet ports, while Soviet ships were detained in German controlled ports using whatever covert means available.

At the western exit to the Gulf of Finland, German mining units had been arriving in the skerries around Turku (Abo) since 14th June 1941. Possibly as early as the 18-19th June the German Nord Minelayer Group started laying mines between the island of Dago (Hiiumaa) and the Finnish Hanko Peninsula (which was occupied by the Soviets as part of the Winter-War ceasefire settlement). On the night of 21-22nd June these mining operations had extended to within 3-5 nautical miles of the coast of Dago. In the meantime the German Kobra Minelayer Group started building another mine-barrage across the Gulf of Finland between Porkkala (in Finland) and Pakerort (in Estonia), supplemented by Finnish submarines and minelayers. Around 980 mines and 1,373 explosive buoys were initially used in these operations.[542] Additional barrages were laid at the entrance to the Bay of Riga (the Irben Strait and the Muhu Sound) to obstruct Soviet shipping until the bases and ports in the area could be captured by the advancing German 18th Army.

It is almost certain that most of these major German mining operations were sighted by Soviet forces and reconnaissance aircraft, but in the event none of the operations was significantly hindered. In addition Soviet ships of all types almost immediately started taking heavy losses from these mine-barrages; including the new heavy cruiser Maxim Gorkiy which was damaged when she lost her bow to a mine on 23rd June 1941.[543] It is something of a mystery as to why the much superior (on paper) Soviet Red Banner Baltic Fleet allowed the German mining operations to proceed for so long without serious interference. During the initial stages at least, the German mining force and the barrages themselves were only protected by a few S-boats of the 1st and 2nd S-Boat Flotillas (based at Porkkala and Turku (Abo), respectively). The apparent 'paralysis' of the Soviet naval commands in the face of the

---

[539] Explosive buoys were devices which destroy or damage mine-sweeping equipment. H. Boog, et al., German Research Institute for Military History at Potsdam, Germany and the Second World War, Volume IV: The Attack on the Soviet Union, Clarendon Press (Oxford University Press), New York, 1996, p. 654.

[540] Ibid, p. 385.

[541] The Soviets admitted to losing 36 submarines in 1941; the majority in the Baltic operating west of the islands of Osel and Dago. The exact number lost and where they were lost is unknown. G.F. Krivosheev, et al, Soviet Casualties and Combat Losses in the Twentieth Century, ed. Colonel General G.F. Krivosheev, Greenhill Books, London, 1997, , table 95 V, p. 256.

[542] H. Boog, et al., German Research Institute for Military History at Potsdam, Germany and the Second World War, Volume IV: The Attack on the Soviet Union, Clarendon Press (Oxford University Press), New York, 1996, p. 655.

[543] The Maxim Gorkiy (9,792 tons, deep load displacement) was only completed on 12th November 1940.

German's offensive naval operations during June and early July 1941 remains something of a mystery, and this phenomenon is discussed further in the Volume IIIB.[544]

***

After the German Army had captured Libau (Liepaja) on the coast of Latvia, the *Kriegsmarine* forces in the Baltic were able to concentrate on their second major task; namely the seaborne supply of 18th Army. These shipments started on 3rd July 1941 using coastal ships and smaller vessels. Only after 6th July did light Soviet surface forces and submarines become more active. Destroyers, patrol-boats and aircraft attempted to interdict the German supply ships headed for Dunamunde but did not achieve much success. Rather ironically, the most successful Soviet naval operations at this time were also mining operations. The Soviets laid their own mine-barrages on the approaches to the Baltic ports, which closed the route along the coast (the safest route from submarine attack) for several days. The Soviet countermeasures necessitated the unwelcome transfer of two additional minesweeper and motor-minesweeper flotillas from the western theatre to the Baltic. The need to protect the supply ships for 18th Army meant that the already overstretched S-boat units and Finnish naval forces in the northern Baltic were unable to effectively interfere with Soviet supply ships moving along the Estonian coast to the Baltic Islands and the islands west of Leningrad. Only the Soviet supply ships to the Hanko Peninsula were thoroughly disrupted; to the point that the Soviet command was forced to resort to submarines for transport purposes.

After 6th August and the capture of the Kunda by 18th Army, the German Kobra Minelayer Group started building another major mine-barrage north of Cape Juminda (east of Tallinn) and was soon joined by additional Finnish vessels. By 31st August these ships had laid a system of 32 different barrages with a total of 1,409 mines and 912 explosive buoys in an area of approximately 768 square nautical miles.[545] What became known as the 'Juminda barrage' represented a considerable obstacle to Soviet naval movement in the Gulf of Finland; especially any ships attempting to move to and from Tallinn, the large Baltic Islands and Hanko. The Red Army and the Red Banner Baltic Fleet would pay a high price on the Juminda barrage when they were forced to evacuate these bases later in 1941 (see below). Many of these losses were due to the fact that the barrages forced shipping into narrow channels where they could be easily located and attacked, as well as the mines themselves.

In early August 1941, the 18th Army's 26th Infantry Corps laid siege to the port city of Tallinn (capital of Estonia). By mid-August the 42nd Infantry Corps (initially in OKH reserves and then 9th Army) had arrived with three infantry divisions, while 26th Corps headed eastwards towards Narva. By this time the Soviet 10th Rifle Corps was defending Tallinn with three rifle divisions reinforced with several naval infantry brigades and other units (around 50,000) personnel). In addition, a large portion of the Soviet Red Banner Baltic Fleet had remained in Tallinn to provide additional heavy artillery support to the defending Red Army troops. The main German offensive to capture the city commenced on 19th August. The fighting was fierce and it took the Germans four days to overcome the first defensive line, but by 24th August the German infantry had got to within six miles of the city. From 25th-26th August there was fighting in the city streets, and the Soviets decided to evacuate the defending force by sea.

The evacuation commenced on 27th August 1941 with around 30,000 Soviet troops being evacuated in two great convoys of 84 and then 78 ships.[546] The covering naval force dwarfed the German naval forces in the Northern Baltic Sea and included the cruiser Kirov, 18 destroyers (of all types), 6 torpedo-boats, 28 minesweepers, 83 small patrol boats and 6 submarines.[547] However the continuing German pressure forced around 11,400 Red Army soldiers to remain behind (as a rear guard to defend the port), and these were captured when the city fell on the 28th August. In the meantime the evacuation force had to fight its way through the narrow channels in the Juminda barrage: coming under attack from S-boats and especially heavy attack from Luftwaffe aircraft. Unfortunately, by this time *Luftflotte* 1 had established air-superiority over the western part of the Gulf of Finland, and *Fliegerführer Ostsee* was at last given some priority for aircraft to support the *Kriegsmarine* forces in the Baltic. In the end the Soviets lost 5 destroyers, 11 other warships and 25 transports evacuating Tallinn (as well as damage to the cruiser Kirov and many others), and, even worse, around half of the evacuated personnel were lost.[548] Of the 50,000 odd Red Army troops left to defend Tallinn, only around 15,000 ever made it back to the Soviet lines.

***

---

[544] Refer Volume IIIB 6. 2) b. – 'Soviet Naval Forces: June to December 1941 - The Red Banner Baltic Fleet - A Summary of Soviet Naval Operations and Naval Losses in the Baltic: June to December 1941'.

[545] H. Boog, et al., German Research Institute for Military History at Potsdam, Germany and the Second World War, Volume IV: The Attack on the Soviet Union, Clarendon Press (Oxford University Press), New York, 1996, p. 657.

[546] Barbarossa, Army Group North 1941, GMT, Hanford CA, 2000, Scenario outcomes, p. 18.

[547] H. Boog, et al., German Research Institute for Military History at Potsdam, Germany and the Second World War, Volume IV: The Attack on the Soviet Union, Clarendon Press (Oxford University Press), New York, 1996, p. 657.

[548] Ibid. Also, Barbarossa, Army Group North 1941, GMT, Hanford CA, 2000, Scenario outcomes, p. 18.

With the capture of Tallinn and the forced withdrawal of most Soviet naval vessels to the bay of Kronshtadt, the Germans were in a position to capture the main Baltic islands of Osel (Saaremaa) and Dago (Hiiumaa). Osel controls the entrances to the Gulf of Riga while Dago is strategically positioned in the southern part of the entrance to the Gulf of Finland. By early September 1941 the islands were garrisoned by 23,700 men of the Red Army's 3rd Rifle Brigade along with various support units (the garrison was originally assigned to the Soviet 27th Army). Both islands had also been heavily fortified, with the strongest forces and defences being deployed on Osel.[549] The code name for the German amphibious operation to capture these islands was Operation Beowulf, and it is noteworthy in that it was one of the few times that all branches of the Wehrmacht (army, navy and air force) were placed under a single army command at the operational level.[550]

The absence of suitable German transport ships and landing craft meant that the least risky option (for the Germans) was to invade from the nearby Estonian coast. The 61st Infantry Division, reinforced with assault pionier troops and additional artillery, was earmarked for the attack. The seaborne transport of this force was to be undertaken using around 100 barges and ferries, along with about 180 small assault boats, which had been assembled for this task.[551] For the first time since the start of Operation Barbarossa, significant German surface warships in the Southern Baltic (i.e. larger than S-boats and minelayers) were also put on standby to provide direct (artillery) support for the army and to cover the invasion against any enemy attempted breakout from the Gulf of Finland. The latter became of increasing concern to the OKH and OKM as September wore on (see below).

As a first step the small island of Vormsi, to the east of Dago, was seized on 9th September 1941. On 14th September the main attack on Osel was launched against the eastern coast of Muhu, a small island to the east of Osel and attached by a causeway. Initial resistance was fierce but by 16th September Muhu was secured, and by the 17th German infantry had established a bridgehead on Osel across the causeway. In the meantime the *Kriegsmarine* and the Finnish Navy mounted a series of diversionary operations aimed at distracting the defenders. This involved a series of feints which simulated landing preparations with a comparatively large number of torpedo-boats, S-boats and covering vessels. These units also fired at various shore installations, and on the whole were successful in confusing and distracting the defenders. However, on 13th September the Finnish coast defence ship Ilmarinen (a 3,900t vessel with 10 inch guns, which was very suitable for shore bombardment work) was moving to support these operations when it struck a mine off Hanko and was lost.

By 21st September 1941 all the elements of the 61st Infantry Division were on Osel and by the 23rd the division had pushed the Soviet defenders across the island to the heavily fortified Sorve (Svorbe) Peninsula in the southwest corner of the island. The Germans were then forced to assault the extensive bunker system on the peninsula using assault pionier troops and flamethrowers. The defence was so strong that the light cruisers Emden and Leipzig (from the covering force) were ordered to move up and shell the defenders with their 6 inch guns. On 5th October the last positions were overrun and the last surviving defenders capitulated.

On 12th October the assault began on the island of Dago (Hiiumaa) with a feint to the south of the island, and the actual landings on the west coast of the island using assault craft. In this instance the navy again assisted with diversionary manoeuvres in which the light cruiser Koln, along with several torpedo-boats and minesweepers, bombarded hostile batteries. The Osel defenders were gradually forced back to the Tahkuna Peninsula, on the north of the island, where the last of them surrendered on 21st October 1941. While a handful of Soviet patrol boats did attempt escape (without success), there was no chance of escape for the Soviet Osel-Dago garrison. Soviet losses amounted to approximately 19,000 captured and 4,700 killed (the entire garrison), while German killed, wounded and missing amounted to 2,850.[552]

***

---

[549] The Soviets had constructed deeply echeloned trench systems along the coast, centred mainly on their coastal gun batteries. Some of these batteries contained very heavy artillery. New coast batteries were positioned in July and August 1941 to cover the growing threat from the landward side of the islands (as 18th Army advanced), while the Sorve Peninsula was heavily fortified. All these fortifications were organised for all-round defence. Barbarossa, Army Group North 1941, GMT, Hanford CA, 2000, Scenario outcomes, p. 18.

[550] From the beginning (of planning), Operation Beowulf was viewed as an 'army operation' with the navy limited to providing assistance.

[551] Most of the barges and 'ferries' were provided by the *Erprobungsverband der Ostsee* (Trial Formation Baltic) and did not come from the Navy.

[552] Barbarossa, Army Group North 1941, GMT, Hanford CA, 2000, Scenario outcomes, p. 19.

While the invasion of the Baltic island was still ongoing, the OKM had become increasingly worried that the still powerful Soviet Red Banner Baltic Fleet might attempt some sort of last ditch breakout attempt from the Gulf of Finland, and possibly even out of the Baltic itself. It was felt that the fleet might attempt this when its last refuge, Kronshtadt and Leningrad, was threatened with land invasion. This view was reinforced by an intelligence report received around 15th September. Agents in Sofia had recorded an exchange of signals between the commander of the Soviet Baltic Fleet and the commander of the Soviet Black Sea Fleet. This exchange of signals included a reference to a request to the Swedish government, via the British, to permit the Soviet Baltic Fleet to enter a Swedish port. The request had not been granted, but the report indicated a new attempt was to be made.

Although Raeder and his naval staff were sceptical of any major breakout attempt (based on reports of the Baltic Fleet's overall readiness), on 20th September Hitler ordered the OKM to immediately prepare for this eventuality. Therefore on 21st September a powerful temporary naval detachment called the *Baltenflotte* (Baltic Fleet) was formed, and the Flag Officer Battleships (Admiral Otto Ciliax) was flown in from Brest to command it. The *Baltenflotte* consisted of two groups. The northern group consisted of the Tirpitz, Admiral Scheer, Nurnberg, Koln, destroyers Z 25, Z 26 and Z 27, and a flotilla of five S-boats. The southern group consisted of the Leipzig, Emden and another flotilla of S-boats. In addition all available Ju 88s in *Fliegerführer Ostsee* were placed on standby. The *Baltenflotte* left Schwinemunde on 23rd September, and later elements of this force (the Emden, Leipzig and Koln) were used to support the invasions of Osel and Dago as described above.

From 21st to 23rd September 1941, *Sturzkampfgeschwader* 2 (StG 2 with Ju 87s) carried out a series of successful attacks on the Soviet Baltic Fleet anchored in Kronshtadt and Leningrad. Both Soviet battleships were put out of action and other elements of the fleet were also heavily damaged. The battleship Oktyabrskaya Revoluciya (October Revolution) was unable to proceed under her own power and was towed to Leningrad for repairs, while the battleship Marat was all but sunk: the forward part of the hull as far back as the fore funnel was submerged and she was only prevented from sinking completely by the floor of Kronshtadt harbour. When it became obvious that what was left of the Soviet Baltic Fleet had no realistic prospect of breaking out, the heavy surface units in the *Baltenflotte* were ordered home. The Tirpitz and Admiral Scheer arrived in Gotenhafen (Gdynia) on 29th September, while the Nurnberg (with the three destroyers) followed a few days later. The Tirpitz remained in the southern Baltic Sea vicinity until 13-14th January 1942, when she left for Norwegian waters. The Admiral Scheer remained in the southern Baltic Sea vicinity until February 1942, at which time she also headed for Norway.

***

After the 1939-40 Winter War, the harsh (for the Finns) Moscow peace treaty of March 1940 included the 'leasing' to the USSR of the strategic naval facilities on the Hanko Peninsula. The Soviets promptly fortified this whole area and placed a large garrison force there. By 22nd June 1941 this garrison numbered some 25,300 men, and included the reinforced 8th Rifle Brigade and 99th Border Guard Regiment, along with numerous anti-tank, anti-aircraft, artillery, naval and naval-air units.[553] With the occupation of Dago, this gave the Soviets control of the entrance to the Gulf of Finland as well as bases from which to attack any shipping in the central Baltic. However with the loss of the Baltic Islands in September-October 1941, the Soviet positions on the Hanko Peninsula became untenable. After long deliberations the decision to evacuate the Hanko garrison (now numbering around 27,000 men) was taken by the Soviets on 23rd October 1941. From 27th October to the end of November, the Soviet Baltic Fleet managed to evacuate the majority of the personnel on Hanko in what was their most successful naval operation during 1941. In all, around 7,000 men of the original garrison were killed or missing (mainly due to the mine-barrages) and never made it back to Soviet lines. But around 20,000 men were successfully evacuated and they were used to stiffen the hard pressed Leningrad Front before the end of the year. For more details on the Soviet Baltic Fleet's evacuation of Hanko, refer to Volume IIIB.[554]

Around the end of November 1941 the formation of ice in the Gulf of Finland increasingly paralysed shipping movements. When it became clear that Leningrad was going to be besieged and not assaulted, the German and Finnish navies were forced to prepare for a continuation of the war in the Baltic into 1942. To obtain more favourable starting positions for 1942, Finnish commandos occupied the island of Suursaari on 14th December and at the beginning of January 1942 German troops occupied the island of Tyttarsaari. Neither island could be held during the winter of 1941-42, and they were both temporarily abandoned.

***

---

[553] Refer Volume IIIA 6. 2) d. - 'The Actual Strength of all Soviet Land Combat Units in a Deployed (D) State on 22nd June 1941 - Leningrad Military District (Northern Front from 24th June 1941) - The Hanko Peninsula Garrison' for details.
[554] Refer Volume IIIB 6. 2) b. – 'Soviet Naval Forces: June to December 1941 - The Red Banner Baltic Fleet - A Summary of Soviet Naval Operations and Naval Losses in the Baltic: June to December 1941'.

As mentioned previously, the second principal task of the *Kriegsmarine* in the Baltic was the protection of seaborne traffic to: Finland (mainly troop and supply convoys), Sweden (mainly resources shipments) and the eastern Baltic ports (mainly supplies for Army Group North). The most serious threat from the Soviet Red Banner Baltic Fleet was seen to be its submarines, of which 65 were available on 21st June 1941. So far we have examined what were essentially offensive operations by the Kriegsmarine in the Baltic during 1941, and while all these were occurring the comparatively routine business of German shipments across the Baltic continued.

The great volume of shipping to and from Sweden, Finland, Norway, Denmark and Germany had resulted in a wide variety of convoy and escort tasks for the German Navy. In the month of September alone, transports for Finland required 59 ships for 20,000 men, 4,278 horses, 2,454 vehicles and 56,935 tons of equipment. In the same month 16,834 tons of supplies were shipped to other Baltic ports from Konigsberg and Danzig, and 5,609 tons of captured material was brought back to Germany.[555]

These German shipping movements were hardly hindered by the Soviet Navy: from 22nd June to 31st December 1941 only one German registered vessel was torpedoed and sunk by Soviet submarines from the Red Banner Baltic Fleet.[556] Soviet submarines did manage to sink five Swedish merchant ships, forcing the Swedes to introduce escorted convoys. In return their losses were extremely heavy for little gain: the Soviets admitted to losing 36 submarines in 1941 with the majority being lost in the Baltic.[557] Overall, the 65 submarines in the Red Banner Baltic Fleet only managed to sink half as many merchant ships as the number lost through accidents on German mine-barrages during 1941.[558] This means that (on paper at least) the *Kriegsmarine's* 'defensive' operations proved to be the most successful German naval operations in the Baltic during 1941.

***

Finally it is worth looking at the outcome of U-boat operations in the Baltic during 1941. As mentioned earlier, only five small Type II D coastal submarines from the 22nd U-boat Training Flotilla conducted active patrols in the northern Baltic Sea area during the second half of 1941. As far as is known, none of these U-boats ventured past the island of Dago (Hiiumaa) and into the Gulf of Finland itself: they were only used for defensive patrols in the northern Baltic Sea area. These U-boats did not manage to sink any Soviet ships during 1941 due to the fact that the latter rarely ventured into the U-boat's patrol area, but they did contribute to the heavy toll paid by Soviet submarines operating in the Baltic, as follows.[559]

- U-140 unsuccessfully attacked a Soviet submarine west of Memel on 24th June 1941. On 21st July 1941 U-140 torpedoed and sank the Soviet submarine M-94 off Dago (Hiiumaa) Island.

- U-142 unsuccessfully attacked a Soviet submarine north of Gotland on 6th August 1941.

- U-144 torpedoed and sank the Soviet submarine M-78 west of Windau, Latvia, on 23rd June 1941.

- U-145 had an unsuccessful engagement with a Soviet submarine north of Gotland on 3rd July 1941.

- U-149 torpedoed and sank the Soviet submarine M-99 west of the entrance to the Gulf of Finland on 26th June 1941.

One U-boat was lost on operations against the Soviet Red Banner Baltic Fleet during 1941: U-144 was sunk by the Soviet submarine SHCH-307 north of Dago (Hiiumaa) Island on 9th August 1941. The four remaining U boats had all returned to training duties under the 22nd U boat Training Flotilla by September 1941.

***

---

[555] H. Boog, et al., German Research Institute for Military History at Potsdam, Germany and the Second World War, Volume IV: The Attack on the Soviet Union, Clarendon Press (Oxford University Press), New York, 1996, p. 661.
[556] The Oxford Companion to WWII, Oxford University Press, New York, 2001, p. 85. In 1942 they managed to sink 23 German and Finnish ships in the Baltic.
[557] The exact number lost and where they were lost is unknown. G.F. Krivosheev, et al, Soviet Casualties and Combat Losses in the Twentieth Century, ed. Colonel General G.F. Krivosheev, Greenhill Books, London, 1997. table 95 V, p. 256.
[558] At least 10 German, Swedish or Finnish merchant ships and 2 minesweepers were lost on the German mine-barrages during 1941. H. Boog, et al., German Research Institute for Military History at Potsdam, Germany and the Second World War, Volume IV: The Attack on the Soviet Union, Clarendon Press (Oxford University Press), New York, 1996, p. 654.
[559] K. Wynn, U-Boat Operations of the Second World War: Volume 1, Caxton Editions, Caxton Publishing Group, 2003, pp. 113-116.

8. Wehrmacht and Waffen SS Casualties from June 1941 to February 1942

No work of this nature on Operation Barbarossa would be complete without a review of the casualties suffered by the Wehrmacht and Waffen during 1941. In regards to the German FILARM model, accurate casualty and strength figures are important because these figures are also used to establish the overall number of Replacements (R) sent to the East Front during 1941.[560] In addition, the Wehrmacht and Red Army casualty and strength figures (each month) are an essential starting point for establishing the Relative Overall Combat Proficiencies (ROCPs) of the respective forces during 1941.[561]

Fortunately the key German archival records relating to Wehrmacht casualties from 1939 to around January 1945 are reasonably complete and consistent.[562] Surprisingly, the existing German casualty records for WWII are usually more consistent and complete than comparable records for the Western Allies.[563] Unsurprisingly, the Soviet and (today) Russian accounts of military and civilian casualties during the chaotic and desperate days of for 1941 are very disparate, and different Russian scholars and institutions have come up with widely varying figures for 1941.[564] To a far less extent, this is also the case in the subsequent years.[565]

For the East Front in 1941-42, the German casualty figure discrepancies between sources are relatively minor, and can largely be explained by one of several variables. These are that different sources include or exclude the following:

- Waffen SS casualties.

- The relatively small German force in Finland and the Northern tip of Norway, which should be considered part of the East Front.

- Army (*Heer*), *Luftwaffe* and/or *Kriegsmarine* branches, which were all part of the Wehrmacht.

- The recorded number of lightly wounded and unfit for service. As in most armies, personnel who were relatively lightly wounded and 'unfit for service' were often returned to service within a short period. This sometimes confuses the picture of 'total casualties' when considered over a period of several months.

Probably the most complete record of German casualties during Operation Barbarossa, and during the winter of 1941-42, is detailed in the accompanying tables: Weh Killed June 41-Feb. 42, Weh Wounded June 41-Feb. 42, and Weh MIA-POW June 41-Feb. 42 (pages 334-336).[566] These tables include killed, wounded, missing and POWs for all branches of the Wehrmacht on all fronts from 22nd June 1941 to the end of February 1942. The tables exclude approximately 43,000 Waffen SS casualties and 'unfit' personnel.

Tables Casualties East A and Casualties East B (pages 337-338) then extract the relevant data from these tables (above) and show the killed, wounded, missing and POWs for all branches of the Wehrmacht on the East Front from 22nd June 1941 to the end of February 1942, and from 22nd June to 31st December 1941. Note, both tables include the casualties suffered in Finland and Northern Norway (i.e. on the East Front), but exclude Waffen SS casualties and those personnel classified as 'sick and /or unfit' for service.

---

[560] After taking into account strength changes resulting from reinforcements, i.e. new units arriving at the front. Refer Volume IIB 4. 7 c. i. - 'The Resource Replacements (R) Available to the German Army, Waffen SS, Luftwaffe ground Forces and Naval Coastal Artillery, from 22nd June to 31st December 1941 - Replacements (R) Actually Issued to the German Ground Forces on the East Front During 1941 - German Personnel Losses and Replacements'.

[561] The relative ROCPs are is examined in detail in Volume V – 'The Relative Overall Combat Proficiency (ROCP) of Soviet and Axis Forces during WWII'.

[562] German records after January 1945 are not as consistent, and progressively deteriorate towards war's end. This appears to be because the Wehrmacht's record and administrative functions finally began to collapse as Germany itself was invaded. The desperate measures employed included very large numbers of *Volkssturm* 'troops' (roughly, people's militia). The *Volkssturm* was set up by the Nazi Party (not directly by the German Army) in October 1944, and included conscripted males between the ages of 13 to 60 years who were not already serving in auxiliary 'military' organisations. Most of these 'troops' were barely trained, poorly equipped and inadequately recorded (or any records were lost). They are often excluded from German Army casualty figures but are included in other German records for the overall Wehrmacht strength. Many *Volkssturm* are included in Allied and Soviet records of German casualties in 1945 as they often wore German Army style uniforms (they contributed very significantly to the large numbers of recorded German POWs from March to May 1945).

[563] For many of the campaigns conducted by the US and Commonwealth forces during WWII, it is impossible to find comprehensive accounts of the casualties. At best, high level figures are provided (often from unproven sources), and detailed centrally recorded information on killed, wounded, missing, POW and unfit often remains as just wishful thinking.

[564] Refer to Volume IIIB and Volume V for a detailed review of Soviet casualties in 1941, and a brief look at the casualties from 1942 to 1945. It includes a wide range of inconsistent figures from various Russian scholars and institutions.

[565] On balance, however, Russian WWII records after 1941-42 appear to be, in general, at least as 'accurate' as those from West (if the latter exist at all).

[566] Bundesarchiv-Militararchiv Freiburg (BA-MA RW) 6/v.543. OKW/Allgemeines Wehrmachtamt (Wehrmacht general office).

Table Weh Killed June 41-Feb. 42

Wehrmacht Personnel Killed from 22nd June 1941 to 28th February 1942.

	22nd June - 30th June	July	Aug.	Sept.	Oct.	Nov.	Dec.*	Jan. 42	Feb. 42	Total, 22nd June - 28th Feb. 42
Army; Total	**8,934**	**37,599**	**41,173**	**29,680**	**24,253**	**17,897**	**15,156**	**18,708**	**18,934**	**212,334**
(Officers only)	**524**	**1,922**	**1,565**	**931**	**975**	**802**	**445**	**623**	**652**	**8,439**
Eastern Front.	8,886	37,584	41,019	29,422	24,056	17,806	14,949	18,074	18,776	**210,572**
	524	1,919	1,563	920	968	802	424	563	638	**8,321**
Norway and Lapland (incl. in East Front figs).	3	1,440	1,692	1,930	252	861	197	184	165	**6,724**
	0	54	69	62	8	22	7	5	2	**229**
North Africa.	48	15	116	153	20	34	174	626	87	**1,273**
	0	3	2	5	2	0	19	60	8	**99**
Other Fronts & Territories.	0	0	38	105	177	57	33	8	71	**489**
	0	0	0	6	5	0	2	0	6	**19**
Kriegsmarine; Total	**113**	**201**	**95**	**363**	**174**	**180**	**128**	**33**	**1**	**1,288**
(Officers only)	**7**	**13**	**8**	**13**	**19**	**6**	**12**	**0**	**1**	**79**
Naval Operations East.	65	81	15	150	32	67	48	0	0	**458**
	3	7	0	5	4	2	1	0	0	**22**
Naval Operations West.	48	120	80	213	142	113	80	33	1	**830**
	4	6	8	8	15	4	11	0	1	**57**
Luftwaffe; Total	**697**	**1,391**	**842**	**888**	**1,235**	**747**	**627**	**564**	**304**	**7,295**
(Officers only)	**101**	**180**	**104**	**95**	**90**	**57**	**69**	**55**	**51**	**802**
Air Unit Personnel at Fronts.	312	441	261	221	161	94	128	114	100	**1,832**
	76	119	66	50	35	23	28	24	29	**450**
Air Unit Personnel: the Home Front.	38	112	43	104	114	82	142	90	63	**788**
	7	18	6	20	16	14	22	13	8	**124**
Personnel Training and other Causes.	37	123	118	134	133	84	60	53	101	**843**
	1	7	13	10	9	5	7	5	11	**68**
Ground Personnel at Fronts.	85	158	85	81	93	50	43	127	13	**735**
	8	5	3	1	1	1	1	1	2	**23**
Flak, Para, Airlanding Troops at Fronts.	225	557	335	348	734	437	254	180	27	**3,097**
	9	31	16	14	29	14	11	12	1	**137**
Eastern Front.	552	1,004	558	517	899	454	288	365	86	**4,723**
	72	126	64	53	49	24	21	24	23	**456**
Med. - Nth Africa Front.	2	18	32	29	10	95	87	27	19	**319**
	2	2	4	2		10	12	8	4	**44**
Western Front.	68	134	91	104	79	32	50	29	35	**622**
	19	27	17	10	16	4	7	5	5	**110**
Home Front.	75	235	161	238	247	166	202	143	164	**1,631**
	8	25	19	30	25	19	29	18	19	**192**
Wehrmacht; Total	**9,744**	**39,191**	**42,110**	**30,931**	**25,662**	**18,824**	**15,911**	**19,305**	**19,239**	**220,917**
(Officers only)	**632**	**2,115**	**1,677**	**1,039**	**1,084**	**865**	**526**	**678**	**704**	**9,320**

* From this data: the total Wehrmacht personnel killed on all fronts from 22nd June 1941 to 31st Dec. 1941 was 182,373 (7,938).

The Wehrmacht personnel killed on the East Front from 22nd June 1941 to 28th Feb. 1942 was 215,753 (8,799); 97.7% of the total.

The Wehrmacht personnel killed on the East Front from 22nd June 1941 to 31st Dec. 1941 was 178,452 (7,551); 97.9% of the total.

Compiled from *Bundesarchiv-Militararchiv* Freiburg, BA-MA RW 6/v.543. OKW/*Allgemeines Wehrmachtamt.*　　© Nigel Askey, 2018

***

Table Weh Wounded June 41-Feb. 42

Wehrmacht Personnel Wounded from 22nd June 1941 to 28th February 1942.

	22nd June - 30th June	July	Aug.	Sept.	Oct.	Nov.	Dec.	Jan. 42	Feb. 42	Total, 22nd June - 28th Feb. 42
Army; Total	**29,530**	**125,615**	**147,988**	**107,161**	**87,614**	**66,359**	**58,695**	**65,163**	**64,968**	**753,093**
(Officers only)	**1,056**	**4,410**	**4,620**	**2,814**	**2,599**	**2,347**	**1,234**	**1,625**	**1,605**	**22,310**
Eastern Front.	29,494	125,579	147,748	106,826	87,224	66,211	58,226	61,933	64,520	**747,761**
	1,056	4,408	4,616	2,806	2,577	2,340	1,213	1,522	1,581	**22,119**
Norway and Lapland	20	5,170	4,941	7,191	828	2,095	479	652	420	**21,796**
(incl. in East Front figs).	0	147	150	166	24	54	5	10	5	**561**
North Africa.	36	36	234	201	54	44	404	3,219	266	**4,494**
	0	2	4	2	11	0	18	102	20	**159**
Other Fronts &	0	0	6	134	336	104	65	11	182	**838**
Territories.	0	0	0	6	11	7	3	1	4	**32**
Kriegsmarine; Total	**32**	**256**	**126**	**186**	**118**	**76**	**71**	**21**	**1**	**887**
(Officers only)	**3**	**8**	**6**	**14**	**5**	**4**	**0**	**0**	**0**	**40**
Naval Operations East.	21	139	17	49	11	10	2	0	0	**249**
	2	5	0	10	0	2	0	0	0	**19**
Naval Operations West.	11	117	109	137	107	66	69	21	1	**638**
	1	3	6	4	5	2	0	0	0	**21**
Luftwaffe; Total	**1,079**	**2,801**	**1,793**	**1,854**	**2,705**	**1,820**	**1,433**	**863**	**332**	**14,680**
(Officers only)	**101**	**242**	**145**	**123**	**140**	**92**	**89**	**68**	**43**	**1,043**
Air Unit Personnel	329	412	260	211	242	175	121	121	125	**1,996**
at Fronts.	57	111	80	57	48	37	24	29	24	**467**
Air Unit Personnel:	32	74	55	57	55	55	52	47	54	**481**
the Home Front.	8	13	11	17	8	7	11	7	12	**94**
Personnel Training	31	97	99	73	84	57	67	45	54	**607**
and other Causes.	1	10	6	2	8	2	8	4	5	**46**
Ground Personnel	85	302	133	153	84	58	94	127	26	**1,062**
at Fronts.	3	6	4	3	5	2	9	0	0	**32**
Flak, Para, Airlanding	602	1,916	1,246	1,360	2,240	1,475	1,099	523	73	**10,534**
Troops at Fronts.	32	102	44	44	71	44	37	28	2	**404**
Eastern Front.	967	2,532	1,533	1,610	2,453	1,472	1,055	704	178	**12,504**
	85	200	114	92	113	62	47	53	20	**786**
Med. - Nth Africa Front.	5	17	27	24	31	217	209	32	20	**582**
	0	1	0	3	4	18	13	2	3	**44**
Western Front.	44	81	79	90	82	19	50	35	26	**506**
	7	18	14	9	7	3	10	2	3	**73**
Home Front.	63	171	154	130	139	112	119	92	108	**1,088**
	9	23	17	19	16	9	19	11	17	**140**
Wehrmacht; Total	**30,641**	**128,672**	**149,907**	**109,201**	**90,437**	**68,255**	**60,199**	**66,047**	**65,301**	**768,660**
(Officers only)	**1,160**	**4,660**	**4,771**	**2,951**	**2,744**	**2,443**	**1,323**	**1,693**	**1,648**	**23,393**

* From this data: the total Wehrmacht personnel wounded on all fronts from 22nd June 1941 to 31st Dec. 1941 was 637,312 (20,052).

The Wehrmacht personnel wounded on the East Front from 22nd June 1941 to 28th Feb. 1942 was 760,514 (22,924); 98.9% of total.

The Wehrmacht personnel wounded on the East Front from 22nd June 1941 to 31st Dec. 1941 was 633,179 (19,748); 99.4% of total.

Compiled from *Bundesarchiv-Militararchiv* Freiburg, BA-MA RW 6/v.543. OKW/*Allgemeines Wehrmachtamt.* © Nigel Askey, 2018

***

Table Weh MIA-POW June 41-Feb. 42

Wehrmacht Personnel Missing and POW from 22nd June 1941 to 28th February 1942.

	22nd June - 30th June	July	Aug.	Sept.	Oct.	Nov.	Dec.	Jan. 42	Feb. 42	Total, 22nd June - 28th Feb. 42
Army; Total	**2,708**	**9,053**	**7,896**	**4,977**	**3,804**	**3,150**	**5,355**	**10,519**	**4,729**	**52,191**
(Officers only)	**50**	**169**	**153**	**52**	**62**	**45**	**117**	**172**	**89**	**909**
Eastern Front.	2,707	9,051	7,830	4,896	3,585	3,122	4,682	7,075	4,355	47,303
	50	169	152	52	61	45	90	95	78	792
Norway and Lapland	0	616	151	336	23	132	88	64	29	1,439
(incl. in East Front figs).	0	21	8	6	0	4	3	2	2	46
North Africa.	1	2	66	73	7	27	620	3,444	333	4,573
	0	0	1	0	1	0	27	77	8	114
Other Fronts &	0	0	0	8	212	1	53	0	41	315
Territories.	0	0	0	0	0	0	0	0	3	3
Kriegsmarine; Total	**4**	**30**	**54**	**221**	**56**	**174**	**249**	**96**	**13**	**897**
(Officers only)	**2**	**0**	**3**	**1**	**0**	**3**	**37**	**9**	**4**	**59**
Naval Operations East.	4	16	24	41	15	6	4	0	0	110
	2	0	0	0	0	0	0	0	0	2
Naval Operations West.	0	14	30	180	41	168	245	96	13	787
	0	0	3	1	0	3	37	9	4	57
Luftwaffe; Total	**360**	**725**	**393**	**334**	**459**	**487**	**563**	**879**	**437**	**4,637**
(Officers only)	**68**	**134**	**86**	**72**	**75**	**60**	**71**	**82**	**68**	**716**
Air Unit Personnel	338	660	375	301	392	323	349	352	379	3,469
at Fronts.	65	130	83	70	74	55	65	67	66	675
Air Unit Personnel:	1	1	2	13	0	8	23	8	4	60
the Home Front.	0	1	1	2	0	2	3	2	0	11
Personnel Training	0	2	6	1	2	0	6	0	4	21
and other Causes.	0	0	2	0	0	0	1	0	1	4
Ground Personnel	8	4	1	3	3	19	59	29	20	146
at Fronts.	1	0	0	0	0	0	1	3	1	6
Flak, Para, Airlanding	13	58	9	16	62	137	126	490	30	941
Troops at Fronts.	2	3	0	0	1	3	1	10	0	20
Eastern Front.	284	552	275	240	374	253	196	282	233	2,689
	58	100	68	51	58	34	27	48	40	484
Med. - Nth Africa Front.	10	10	36	24	19	157	196	522	68	1,042
	0	0	4	5	6	11	22	21	13	82
Western Front.	65	160	74	56	64	69	142	67	128	825
	10	33	11	14	11	13	18	11	14	135
Home Front.	1	3	8	14	2	8	29	8	8	81
	0	1	3	2	0	2	4	2	1	15
Wehrmacht; Total	**3,072**	**9,808**	**8,343**	**5,532**	**4,319**	**3,811**	**6,167**	**11,494**	**5,179**	**57,725**
(Officers only)	**120**	**303**	**242**	**125**	**137**	**108**	**225**	**263**	**161**	**1,684**

* From this data: the total Wehrmacht personnel MIA & POW on all fronts from 22nd June 1941 to 31st Dec. 1941 was 41,052 (1,260). The Wehrmacht personnel MIA & POW on the East Front from 22nd June 1941 to 28th Feb. 1942 was 50,102 (1,278); 86.8% of total. The Wehrmacht personnel MIA & POW on the East Front from 22nd June 1941 to 31st Dec. 1941 was 38,157 (1,017); 92.9% of total.

Compiled from *Bundesarchiv-Militararchiv* Freiburg, BA-MA RW 6/v.543. OKW/*Allgemeines Wehrmachtamt.* © Nigel Askey, 2018

***

Table Casualties East A									
Wehrmacht Personnel Killed, Wounded, Missing and POW on the East Front from 22nd June 1941 to 28th Feb. 1942.									
	22nd - 30th June	July	Aug.	Sept.	Oct.	Nov.	Dec.	Jan. 42	Feb. 42	Total, 22nd June - 28th Feb. 42
Army										
Killed	8,886	37,584	41,019	29,422	24,056	17,806	14,949	18,074	18,776	**210,572**
(Officers only)	524	1,919	1,563	920	968	802	424	563	638	**8,321**
Wounded	29,494	125,579	147,748	106,826	87,224	66,211	58,226	61,933	64,520	**747,761**
	1,056	4,408	4,616	2,806	2,577	2,340	1,213	1,522	1,581	**22,119**
MIA & POW	2,707	9,051	7,830	4,896	3,585	3,122	4,682	7,075	4,355	**47,303**
	50	169	152	52	61	45	90	95	78	**792**
								Total	**All**	**1,005,636**
									Officers	**31,232**
Kriegsmarine										
Killed	65	81	15	150	32	67	48	0	0	**458**
(Officers only)	3	7	0	5	4	2	1	0	0	**22**
Wounded	21	139	17	49	11	10	2	0	0	**249**
	2	5	0	10	0	2	0	0	0	**19**
MIA & POW	4	16	24	41	15	6	4	0	0	**110**
	2	0	0	0	0	0	0	0	0	**2**
								Total	**All**	**817**
									Officers	**43**
Luftwaffe										
Killed;	552	1,004	558	517	899	454	288	365	86	**4,723**
(Officers only)	72	126	64	53	49	24	21	24	23	**456**
Wounded	967	2,532	1,533	1,610	2,453	1,472	1,055	704	178	**12,504**
	85	200	114	92	113	62	47	53	20	**786**
MIA & POW	284	552	275	240	374	253	196	282	233	**2,689**
	58	100	68	51	58	34	27	48	40	**484**
								Total	**All**	**19,916**
									Officers	**1,726**
Wehrmacht Total	**42,980**	**176,538**	**199,019**	**143,751**	**118,649**	**89,401**	**79,450**	**88,433**	**88,148**	**1,026,369**
(Officers only)	**1,852**	**6,934**	**6,577**	**3,989**	**3,830**	**3,311**	**1,823**	**2,305**	**2,380**	**33,001**
% of Total	**4%**	**17%**	**19%**	**14%**	**12%**	**9%**	**8%**	**9%**	**9%**	**100%**

The total casualties from 22nd June to 31st October 1941 (132 days) was 680,937; 66% of the total.

The total casualties from 1st November 1941 to 28th February 1942 (120 days) was 345,432; 34% of the total.

Compiled from *Bundesarchiv-Militararchiv* Freiburg, BA-MA RW 6/v.543. OKW/*Allgemeines Wehrmachtamt.*

© Nigel Askey, 2018

***

Table Casualties East B

Wehrmacht Personnel Killed, Wounded, Missing and POW on the East Front from 22nd June to 31st Dec. 1941.

	22nd - 30th June	July	Aug.	Sept.	Oct.	Nov.	Dec.	Total, 22nd June - 31st Dec. 41
Army								
Killed	8,886	37,584	41,019	29,422	24,056	17,806	14,949	**173,722**
(Officers only)	524	1,919	1,563	920	968	802	424	**7,120**
Wounded	29,494	125,579	147,748	106,826	87,224	66,211	58,226	**621,308**
	1,056	4,408	4,616	2,806	2,577	2,340	1,213	**19,016**
MIA & POW	2,707	9,051	7,830	4,896	3,585	3,122	4,682	**35,873**
	50	169	152	52	61	45	90	**619**
						Total	**All Officers**	**830,903** **26,755**
Kriegsmarine								
Killed	65	81	15	150	32	67	48	**458**
(Officers only)	3	7	0	5	4	2	1	**22**
Wounded	21	139	17	49	11	10	2	**249**
	2	5	0	10	0	2	0	**19**
MIA & POW	4	16	24	41	15	6	4	**110**
	2	0	0	0	0	0	0	**2**
						Total	**All Officers**	**817** **43**
Luftwaffe								
Killed	552	1,004	558	517	899	454	288	**4,272**
(Officers only)	72	126	64	53	49	24	21	**409**
Wounded	967	2,532	1,533	1,610	2,453	1,472	1,055	**11,622**
	85	200	114	92	113	62	47	**713**
MIA & POW	284	552	275	240	374	253	196	**2,174**
	58	100	68	51	58	34	27	**396**
						Total	**All Officers**	**18,068** **1,518**
Wehrmacht								
Killed	9,503	38,669	41,592	30,089	24,987	18,327	15,285	**178,452**
(Officers only)	599	2,052	1,627	978	1,021	828	446	**7,551**
Wounded	30,482	128,250	149,298	108,485	89,688	67,693	59,283	**633,179**
	1,143	4,613	4,730	2,908	2,690	2,404	1,260	**19,748**
MIA & POW	2,995	9,619	8,129	5,177	3,974	3,381	4,882	**38,157**
	110	269	220	103	119	79	117	**1,017**
Wehrmacht Total	**42,980**	**176,538**	**199,019**	**143,751**	**118,649**	**89,401**	**79,450**	**849,788**
(Officers only)	**1,852**	**6,934**	**6,577**	**3,989**	**3,830**	**3,311**	**1,823**	**28,316**
% of Total	**5%**	**21%**	**23%**	**17%**	**14%**	**11%**	**9%**	**100%**

The total casualties from 22nd June to 30th September 1941 (101 days) was 562,288; 66% of the total.

The total casualties from 1st October to 31st December 1941 (92 days) was 287,500; 34% of the total.

Compiled from *Bundesarchiv-Militararchiv* Freiburg, BA-MA RW 6/v.543. OKW/*Allgemeines Wehrmachtamt* (Wehrmacht general office)

© Nigel Askey, 2018

The figures in table <u>Casualties East B</u> concur very closely with another reputable source, which shows the German Army casualties on the East front in 1941 as 831,050. [567] Note, these tables exclude personnel classified as 'sick and /or unfit' for service (which we look at later). Despite this missing data there are several interesting (and rather enlightening) observations which can be made from these tables, which include the following.

- During the **(6 month) 1941 campaign on the East Front, the Wehrmacht suffered around 66% of its total losses in the first three months** (i.e. from 22nd June to the end of September 1941).

- From 22nd June 1941 to 28th February 1942 **(8 months), the Wehrmacht suffered around 66% of its total losses on the East front in the first four months of the campaign (i.e. from 22nd June to the end of October 1941).**

- Between June 1941 and February 1942, inclusive, the highest Wehrmacht casualty rates on the East Front occurred in August, July and September of 1941, respectively.

- During November and December 1941, and January and February 1942, the Wehrmacht casualty rates on the East Front remained surprisingly steady: around half the casualty rate suffered in July and August 1941.

- Between June 1941 and February 1942, inclusive, 98% of all Wehrmacht personnel killed, wounded, missing or POW, occurred on the East Front.

***

This is interesting because when one reads high level accounts of Operation Barbarossa (or watches the many documentaries on this subject), one gains the distinct impression that the Germans suffered a much heavier casualty rate during the Soviet's 1941-42 winter offensive than they did when the Wehrmacht was 'winning' and had the strategic/operational initiative in the summer and autumn of 1941. By all accounts, in the winter of 1941-42 the German Army was 'holding on by its fingernails', was suffering crippling supply shortages in all categories (most famously, winter clothing) and was forced to retreat large distance in the most critical front sectors. The figures above do omit 'sick and unfit' casualties, which includes frostbite and related conditions (discussed later in this chapter). Nevertheless, one would have expected all the German combat-related casualties to have increased when the Red Army was 'winning' (and had the operational initiative), and given the overall situation described in the 1941-42 Russian winter.

We would have definitely expected the number of missing and POW to increase dramatically as German units became more isolated (or sometimes cut off completely). After all, a very large proportion of the Red Army's casualties from June to October 1941 were missing personnel and POWs from the huge 'pockets' of Red Army troops created during this period. However we can see that the figures do not support the premise that this occurred to German units (to any significant extent) in the winter of 1941-42: apart from a slight increase in missing personnel and POWs in January 1942, the highest number of German POWs still occurred in July and August 1941!

In fact, it is obvious that the Wehrmacht suffered its highest casualty rates in the pitch battles during the summer and autumn 1941 period. These massive battles included: the Border Battles in the south (which included the largest tank battle in the world up to that time), the Battle of Minsk, the Battle of Smolensk, the fight to reach and take Leningrad, the Uman Pocket, the Battle of Kiev and the first phase of Operation Typhoon (the massive Vyazma and Bryansk pockets). This was also when the Wehrmacht and Red Army both suffered their highest tank and equipment losses, and when most of the Red Army units that existed in the Western USSR on 22nd June 1941 were all but wiped out. The sheer scale, intensity and ferocity of these battles is hard to comprehend. It is clear from the figures that, from the German perspective at least, the battles in the East from June to October 1941 were even more important, intense and costly than the battles during the winter of 1941-42.

It is also interesting to briefly compare these findings with the Red Army casualty-rate chronology. According to Russian sources, the USSR suffered 4,473,820 military casualties fighting the Wehrmacht in 1941, and a total of 6,328,592 military casualties fighting up to 31st March 1942. [568] A breakdown of these figures into dead, missing/POWs, wounded and unfit is shown in table <u>Soviet Casualties 1941</u>.

---

[567] Bundesarchiv-Militararchiv Freiburg (BA-MA RW) 6/v.552 and 6/v. 553. A difference of only 147 Army personnel.
[568] Compiled from: G.F. Krivosheev, et al (from the Russian General Staff), Soviet Casualties and Combat Losses in the Twentieth Century, ed. Colonel General G.F. Krivosheev, *Kandidat* of Military Science, Greenhill Books, London, 1997, table 69, pp. 96-97. This work is the English translation of the original 1993 work by the Russian General Staff. It effectively remains the official Russian version of Soviet military casualties during the 20th century. Although it has several rather glaring errors (particularly in relation to 1941), it remains the definitive work on this subject and is highly recommended for all students of the East Front and WWII. As far as this author knows, nothing as comprehensive on their WWII military casualties ever been published (or possibly even sponsored) by the US or British governments.

Table Soviet Casualties 1941					
Red Army and Navy Personnel Dead, Missing, POW, Wounded and Unfit on the East Front from 22nd June to 31st March 1942.					
	Dead*	Missing POW	Wounded	Unfit^	Total
22nd June - 30 Sep. 41	430,578	1,699,099	665,961	21,665	**2,817,303**
% of Total	15%	60%	24%	1%	
1st Oct - 31st Dec. 41	371,613	636,383	590,460	58,061	**1,656,517**
% of Total	22%	38%	36%	4%	
1st Jan. 42 - 31st Mar. 42	493,660	181,655	1,011,040	168,417	**1,854,772**
% of Total	27%	10%	55%	9%	

* Includes personnel who died of wounds and other causes in military hospitals.
^ Includes unfit due to frostbite.   © Nigel Askey, 2018

As we can see from this data, 63% of the total 1941 casualties occurred in the third quarter, which actually correlates well with the German casualty-rate chronology above (i.e. 66%). On the face of it we would expect this, i.e. this was when the biggest and most costly battles were fought.

However, digging deeper we find several things which are more enlightening. Firstly, there is very strong evidence that the Soviet military casualties amounted to approximately 5,550,000 personnel in 1941, at least 1.24 times greater than the official figure.[569] Secondly, the majority of Soviet casualties in the June-September period were POWs (60%) and only 15% died. However, after this period the proportion of POWs progressively dropped to only 10% while the number who died increased to a whopping 27%. In fact the number of Red Army and Navy personnel killed in combat in the main three months of the Soviet 1941-42 winter offensive was considerably greater than the number killed in combat during the disasters that befell the Red Army in the summer of 1941. The wounded figures essentially follow this trend; going from only 24% in the summer months to 55% in the 1941-42 winter.

The Soviet 'combat related' casualty figure percentages **do not** correlate with similar Wehrmacht figures. The Wehrmacht data from table Casualties East A shows the following.[570]

Table Summary Casualties East A				
Wehrmacht Personnel Dead, Missing, POW and Wounded on the East Front from 22nd June to 28th February 1942.				
	Dead	Missing POW	Wounded	Total
22nd June - 30 Sep. 41	119,853	25,920	416,515	**562,288**
% of Total	21%	5%	74%	
1st Oct - 31st Dec. 41	58,599	12,237	216,664	**287,500**
% of Total	20%	4%	75%	
1st Jan. 42 - 28th Feb. 1942	37,301	11,945	127,335	**176,581**
% of Total	21%	7%	72%	

© Nigel Askey, 2018

[569] This discussion is outside the brief of this volume (Volume IIB), but a review of Soviet casualties in 1941 is presented in Volume IIIB, and it includes some results of research work by Russian scholars.
[570] The Wehrmacht figures exclude 'unfit' (which we will consider later), and obviously the third quarter only contains two months of casualties compared to three in the Soviet data. However, these do not significantly alter the '% of Total' ratios, or have much significance in regards to the overall conclusions. Also, by March 1942 the Soviet winter offensive was starting to diminish (mostly due to losses and sheer exhaustion), and the Wehrmacht's casualty rate declined accordingly.

We can see that the proportion of Wehrmacht dead, missing/POW and wounded remained fairly steady from quarter to quarter. Even though the overall strategic and operational situation changed from June 1941 to February 1942, the German Army did not significantly alter its basic modus operandi. It is also clear that significant numbers of German soldiers never surrendered during the 1941-42 winter, despite many units being isolated or/and cut off for extended periods of time. The proportion of POWs never altered significantly from the summer months. In fact, given the bitterness of the fighting during the Soviet winter offensive (from December 1941 to early March 1942), and the apparent superiority of the Red Army in snow and winter conditions in general, these figures are very startling. From January to March 1942 (inclusive), which was the height of the Soviet 1941-42 winter offensive, not only did the Wehrmacht inflict a kill-loss casualty ratio of almost 7.2 to 1, but the ratio of combat-related deaths was approximately 10 to 1.[571]

The sheer numbers of the Soviet killed and wounded, and the almost unbelievable kill-loss ratios above, forces one to reconsider the competence of the Red Army and Soviet high command during the winter conditions of 1941-42. For the Red Army to suffer almost half a million dead soldiers in the first three months of 1942, they must have repeatedly launched massive attacks using unsupported infantry. Consider that this figure is considerably greater than the total number of US service personnel killed in the entire war!

It also begs the question; how bad was the average German soldier at the tactical level in the Russian snow? After all, it was the German Army that suffered most in the Russian winter of 1941; wasn't it? These questions will be examined in more detail with more comprehensive Soviet casualty figures, and the appropriate mathematical treatment.[572] One thing is clear, however, and that is that the Red Army and Soviet people paid a staggeringly high price in killed (and wounded) for their successful winter offensive to drive the Germans back from Moscow.

∗∗∗

Continuing with our examination in this chapter of German casualties in 1941, table Casualties East C shows the German Army casualties from an alternative source.[573] This table includes the German Army casualties suffered in Finland and Northern Norway (i.e. on the East Front), but excludes Waffen SS casualties and those personnel classified as 'sick and /or unfit' for service.

For the casualties in 1941, this source indicates the same or very similar numbers of wounded and POWs as the Army casualties shown in table Casualties East B. However, table Casualties East C indicates the Army suffered an additional 8,886 deaths during the whole 1941 campaign. It is possible this was from personnel dying from their wounds at a later date, as this figure represents around 1.4% of the 1941 wounded figure. Otherwise the data is very similar, and importantly, the overall casualty-rate chronology is almost identical. In this case the Army's casualties from 22nd June to 30th September 1941 (101 days) numbered 559,994 personnel, which represented 67% of the 1941 total. This compares to 562,288 Wehrmacht casualties, or 66% of the total, shown in table Casualties East B.

∗∗∗

---

[571] The German figures are corrected to include March 1942, by multiplying their 1942 losses by 1.33 (which is on the high side). Also all the Soviet 'unfit' are removed and assumed to **not** be combat-related casualties. Therefore we have 1,686,355 (Soviet total combat-related casualties) against 234,853 (Wehrmacht total combat related casualties), and 493,660 (Soviet dead) against 49,610 (Wehrmacht dead). The Wehrmacht 'unfit' casualties, including those due to frostbite, are considered later in this chapter (and are considered non-combat related casualties in the above). Note, however, that the German 'dead' includes those who died from exposure and frostbite, and these are included in the above.

Also, note, the Red Army's 'unfit' in table Soviet Casualties in 1941 represent only 4-9% of their total casualties in the winter of 1941-42, which seems an extremely low number considering the overall situation. It is very likely many Soviet 'unfit' casualties were not reported due to the overall administration state of the Red Army at this time and the lack of army medical facilities. This was even more likely if these personnel were returned to service after a reasonably short time: the Red Army wasn't in the habit of allowing soldiers with 'minor' health problems to avoid doing their duty at the front.

[572] Refer Volume IIIB 7. - 'The Soviet Armed Forces, Mobilisations and War Economy from June to December 1941 - Red Army and Navy Casualties from June 1941 to March 1942'. Also refer Volume V - 'Relative Overall Combat Proficiency (ROCP): the ROCP of Soviet and Axis Forces on the East Front during WWII'.

[573] Compiled from: P. E. Schramm (Hrsg) (ed.), *Kriegstagebuch des Oberkommandos der Wehrmacht* 1940-41 (II), Bernard and Graefe Verlag, Frankfurt am Main, 1982, pp. 1120-21. Also, P. E. Schramm (Hrsg) (ed.), *Kriegstagebuch des Oberkommandos der Wehrmacht* 1942 (I), Bernard and Graefe Verlag, Frankfurt am Main, 1982, pp. 298 and 306.

Table Casualties East C

German Army Casualties (Killed, Wounded, Missing and POW) in the East, 22nd June 1941 to 28th February 1942 (including *Befehlsstelle Finnland* forces on the East Front).

	Killed	Wounded	Missing & POW	Total
June *	8,886	29,494	2,707	**41,087**
(Officers only)	524	966	50	**1,540**
July	46,470	125,579	9,051	**181,100**
	2,443	4,498	169	**7,110**
August	41,019	147,748	7,896	**196,663**
	1,563	4,616	153	**6,332**
September	29,422	106,826	4,896	**141,144**
	920	2,806	52	**3,778**
October	24,056	87,224	3,585	**114,865**
	968	2,577	61	**3,606**
November	17,806	66,211	3,122	**87,139**
	802	2,340	45	**3,187**
December	14,949	58,226	4,682	**77,857**
	424	1,213	90	**1,727**
Totals, June - Dec. 41	**182,608**	**621,308**	**35,939**	**839,855**
(Officers only)	**7,644**	**19,016**	**620**	**27,280**
January 1942	17,544	59,928	7,875	**85,347**
	656	2,114	110	**2,880**
Feb-42	19,319	49,398	4,229	**72,946**
	584	1,421	76	**2,081**
Totals, June 41 - Jan.42	**219,471**	**730,634**	**48,043**	**998,148**
(Officers only)	**8,884**	**22,551**	**806**	**32,241**

* From 22nd to 30th June 1941.

The total casualties from 22nd June to 30th September 1941 (101 days) was 559,994; 67% of the 1941 total.
The total casualties from 1st October to 31st December 1941 (92 days) was 279,861; 33% of the 1941 total.

Compiled from: *Kriegstagebuch des* OKW (OKW War Diary) 1940-41 (II) and 1942 (I). © Nigel Askey, 2018

***

Another source indicates that the German Army suffered the casualties shown in table Casualties East D.[574] This table includes the German Army casualties suffered in Finland and Northern Norway (i.e. on the East Front), but excludes Waffen SS casualties and those personnel classified as 'sick and /or unfit' for service.[575]

In general, this source indicates a slightly lower overall number of Army casualties during 1941 than shown in table Casualties East B. Most of the difference stems from the additional 5,384 wounded shown in table Casualties East B. It is possible that some of these wounded were lightly wounded who were quickly returned to service and did not appear on the '10 day medical reports'. The figures for killed and missing are very similar (within a few hundred).

[574] Compiled from: H. Shustereit, *Vabanque: Hitlers Angriff auf die Sowjetunion 1941 als Versuch, durch den Sieg im Osten den Westen zu bezwingen*, Verlag E. S. Mittler & Sohn, Herford and Bonn, 1988. Ref: BA-MA III W 805/5-7. This BA-MA reference relates to reports on the '10 day troop sickness certificates (army)'.
[575] There is some confusion about whether these figures include the Waffen SS and forces in Finland. However, there is no reason the BA-MA III W 805/5-7 should treat German Army forces in Finland as a special case. In addition the Waffen SS reporting and administration infrastructure was not integrated into that of the Army in 1941, so there is little reason why they would include Waffen SS casualties. Furthermore, the German casualties in Lapland during 1941 amounted to 28 445 personnel in 1941, while Waffen SS casualties amounted to some 43,000. Adding or subtracting these figures (after separating them into killed, wounded, missing and unfit), would cause these figures to significantly deviate from almost all other reputable sources on German Army casualties in 1941.

Importantly, the overall casualty-rate chronology is almost identical. In this case the Army's casualties from 22nd June to 30th September 1941 (101 days) numbered 544,688, which represented 66% of the 1941 total. This compares to 562,288 Wehrmacht casualties, or 66% of the total, shown in table <u>Casualties East B.</u>

Table Casualties East D								
Army (*Heer*) Casualties (Killed, Wounded and Missing) on the East Front, 22nd June to 31st December 1941.								
	Killed		**Wounded**		**Missing**		**Total Casualties**	
	All*	**Officers**	**All***	**Officers**	**All***	**Officers**	**All***	**Officers**
22nd June - 30th June	8,886	524	29,494	966	2,707	50	41,087	1,540
1st July - 10th July	7,790	380	25,529	1,067	2,907	36	36,226	1,483
11th July - 20th July	11,544	472	38,320	1,147	3,042	74	52,906	1,693
21st July - 31st July	17,470	1,037	57,586	2,178	2,630	38	77,686	3,253
June - July Totals	**45,690**	**2,413**	**150,929**	**5,358**	**11,286**	**198**	**207,905**	**7,969**
1st Aug. - 10th Aug.	15,845	644	55,671	1,924	3,871	70	75,387	2,638
11th Aug. - 20th Aug.	14,009	475	49,540	1,429	2,834	53	66,383	1,957
21st Aug. - 31st Aug.	11,165	444	41,532	1,263	1,258	29	53,955	1,736
August Totals	**41,019**	**1,563**	**146,743**	**4,616**	**7,963**	**152**	**195,725**	**6,331**
1st Sept. - 10th Sept.	10,532	390	37,017	1,045	1,964	16	49,513	1,451
11th Sept. - 20th Sept.	9,617	310	37,334	999	1,048	15	47,999	1,324
21st Sept. - 30th Sept.	9,287	237	32,475	762	1,784	21	43,546	1,020
September Totals	**29,436**	**937**	**106,826**	**2,806**	**4,796**	**52**	**141,058**	**3,795**
1st Oct. - 10th Oct.	10,193	420	38,717	1,051	1,746	22	50,656	1,493
11th Oct. - 20th Oct.	6,595	230	20,557	597	707	11	27,859	838
21st Oct. - 31st Oct.	7,268	318	27,960	929	1,130	28	36,358	1,275
October Totals	**24,056**	**968**	**87,234**	**2,577**	**3,583**	**61**	**114,873**	**3,606**
1st Nov. - 10th Nov.	4,214	123	15,205	456	782	12	20,201	591
11th Nov. - 20th Nov.	7,477	429	26,784	1,238	1,361	22	35,622	1,689
21st Nov. - 30th Nov.	6,174	309	23,977	401	1,066	98	31,217	808
November Totals	**17,865**	**861**	**65,966**	**2,095**	**3,209**	**132**	**87,040**	**3,088**
1st Dec. - 10th Dec.	4,026	131	16,713	417	1,293	33	22,032	581
11th Dec. - 20th Dec.	4,358	130	17,096	351	1,035	41	22,489	522
21st Dec. - 31st Dec.	6,565	163	24,417	445	2,354	6	33,336	614
December Totals	**14,949**	**424**	**58,226**	**1,213**	**4,682**	**80**	**77,857**	**1,717**
Total	**173,015**	**7,166**	**615,924**	**18,665**	**35,519**	**675**	**824,458**	**26,506**

* Includes enlisted men and officer ranks.

The total casualties from 22nd June to 30th September 1941 (101 days) was 544,688; 66% of the 1941 total.

The total casualties from 1st October to 31st December 1941 (92 days) was 279,770; 34% of the 1941 total.

Source; BA-MA III W 805/5-7, 10 day troop sickness certificates (army).   © Nigel Askey, 2018

***

So far in our review of Wehrmacht casualties in 1941-42, we have looked at killed, wounded, missing and POWs. These categories are generally the norm when discussing military casualties, but there is another dimension we need to consider which is the 'sick and/or unfit'. These personnel are usually classified as 'non-combat related casualties' or sometimes 'operational losses'. They include personnel losses due to mental or physical health problems, accidents and losses due to exposure and frostbite. Although classified as 'non-combat related casualties', this is something of a misnomer because many of these casualties were caused by the overall operational and strategic situation, which was in turn often a direct result of combat.

In general the reporting and historical record of 'sick and/or unfit' casualties in WWII is less thorough than the other categories. This was due to several factors including: the state and (reporting) organisation of the overall medical facilities available, what level of sick or/and unfit warranted a report (most medical services had higher priorities), whether the treatment occurred within the front-line unit or at a rear-area hospital, and the transitory nature of sick and/or unfit casualties. The latter is probably the most difficult because most of the sick and/or unfit casualties eventually returned to military service: sometimes within in a few days and sometimes within a year. A very significant proportion of wounded also returned to military service, often within the time frame of the campaign being considered.

On 1st October 1941 the OKW formed a Statistical Section within the Wehrmacht Casualty Department of the OKW to study the nature of the heavy casualties then being experienced on the East Front.[576] The extensive survey and analysis that followed was based on 1,544,161 medical records sent to the Central Archive for Military Medicine from 1st September 1941 to 31st August 1942, along with the additional medical records of casualties from WWI.[577]

They found that in the First World War, for every thousand casualties caused by enemy action, 226 soldiers had been killed. During the French campaign of 1940 this total fell slightly to 219 soldiers (per 1,000 casualties) and on the East front in July 1941 it rose to 236 (per 1,000 casualties). In January 1942 (during the Soviet winter offensive) the ratio rose even further to around 244 killed per 1,000 casualties, but lulls in the fighting meant that the average figure for the first year of war on the East Front was 229 killed per 1,000 casualties. Therefore, when considered over a year, the death rate per 1,000 casualties was not much higher than during the French campaign. Similar analyses were carried out for other categories, including the proportion returned to service. The overall results of this survey are shown in table Cas Ratio-Ret to Service (below).[578]

In regards to casualties sustained during the first year of war in the East, the medical conclusions that were drawn from this analysis (that are relevant here) are as follows:

- Around 66% of the wounded remained in the Wehrmacht or Waffen SS, and approximately 56% returned to active duty (i.e. were capable of front-line duty) later in the war.

- Around 60% of 1941 wounded returned to active service within six months.[579]

- On average it took 98 days for a 'wound' casualty to return to active service.

- Around 98% of the 'unfit' personnel remained in the Wehrmacht or Waffen SS, and approximately 93% returned to active duty (i.e. were capable of front-line duty) later in the war.

- Around 49% of the 'unfit' personnel were fit again after one month, 23% were fit again after two months, and around 85% were fit for active service after twelve months.[580]

- On average it took 27 days for a casualty initially classified as 'unfit' to return to active service.

***

[576] This department was comparable to the OKW's Central Statistics Department.

[577] Germany and the Second World War; Volume I, Organisation and Mobilisation of the German Sphere of Power, Part 1, Wartime Administration, Economy and Manpower Resources 1939-1941, Kroener, B. R., et al, (German Research Institute for Military History at Potsdam), Clarendon Press (Oxford University Press Inc), New York, 2000, p. 726.

[578] Germany and the Second World War; Volume I, Organisation and Mobilisation of the German Sphere of Power, Part 1, Wartime Administration, Economy and Manpower Resources 1939-1941, Kroener, B. R., et al, (German Research Institute for Military History at Potsdam), Clarendon Press (Oxford University Press Inc), New York, 2000, Diagram III.V.1. Ref: Ref: *Sanitasbericht uber das Deutsche Heer imWeltkriege* 1914/18, vol. iii, *Der Heeressanitätsinspekteur* No. 1249/44 geh. (wiG Ib), 30 Jan. 1944: *Dr Hosemann, Die Wiedereinsatzfahigkeit nach Verwundungen, Erkrankungen (Sanitätsakademie der Bundswehr, Munchen, Sign.* 4320).

[579] Ibid, pp.726-727.

[580] Ibid, pp.727-729.

Table Cas Ratio-Ret to Service
Ratio of Casualties Due to Enemy Weapons vs. those made Unfit*, and Their Return to Fitness for Active Service.

	Average in WWI (1914-1918 all fronts)		French Campaign 1940, 10th May to 25th June.		East Front - July 1941		East Front - Jan. 1942		East Front, Average Frm. June 1941 to June 1942	
	Casualties due to wpns.	Sickness/ Unfit*	Casualties due to wpns.	Sickness/ Unfit*	Casualties due to wpns.	Sickness/ Unfit*	Casualties due to wpns.	Sickness/ Unfit*	Casualties due to wpns.	Sickness/ Unfit*
For every 1000 casualties caused by enemy weapons:	1,000	2,580	1,000	1,750	1,000	1,750	1,000	2,350	1,000	1,890
% ratio of casualties due to weapons/ unfit	258%		175%		175%		235%		189%	
Killed in action.	22.62%		21.90%		23.62%		24.43%		22.90%	
Died of wounds or sickness.	5.16%	0.44%	6.22%	0.60%	8.07%	0.60%	9.26%	0.84%	8.60%	0.67%
Wounded and unfit, not suitable for military service.	6.48%	1.71%	3.83%	1.00%	2.22%	1.00%	2.82%	0.92%	2.45%	0.98%
Wounded and unfit, fit for garrison and labour duties.	1.48%	1.48%	6.82%	4.60%	8.96%	4.60%	11.96%	6.64%	10.17%	5.19%
Wounded and unfit, restored to fitness for active duty.	64.26%	96.37%	61.23%	93.80%	57.13%	93.80%	51.53%	91.60%	55.88%	93.16%
Average number of days lost for ret to active service.	n/a	n/a	98	n/a	98	21	98	40	98	27
Overall % returned to service	**65.7%**	**97.9%**	**68.1%**	**98.4%**	**66.1%**	**98.4%**	**63.5%**	**98.2%**	**66.1%**	**98.4%**

* Includes personnel made unfit due to sickness, disease, accidents, exposure and frostbite (i.e., losses not directly attributable to enemy action).

Ref: *Sanitasbericht uber das Deutsche Heer imWeltkriege* 1914/18, vol. iii, *Der Heeressanitatsinspekteur* No. 1249/44 geh. (wiG Ib), 30 Jan. 1944: Dr Hosemann, *Die Wiedereinsatzfahigkeit nach Verwundungen, Erkrankungen (Sanitatsakademie der Bundswehr, Munchen, Sign . 4320).*

© Nigel Askey, 2018

The best available information showing the German Army's 'unfit and/or sick' and recuperated casualties in the East, from June 1941 to March 1942, is displayed in table Casualties East and Recuperated (below).[581] These records are mainly based on the '10 day troop sickness certificates' and associated medical reports by the army's medical services for OKH and OKW. As far as is known these figures no not include the casualty figures for the Waffen SS.[582]

In general, the casualty figures in this table for killed, missing/POW and wounded are slightly lower than some other sources. If we compare the 1941 casualties to the Army casualties in table Casualties East B (page 338), we find that the table below shows 28,481 fewer casualties. This is comprised of 6,368 killed, 1,359 missing/POW and 20,724 wounded. There is no reason to assume the Army's medical reports were less accurate than other reports, and the numbers above are almost identical to the casualties suffered by the Army in Norway and Lapland.[583] It is therefore most probable that the figures in table Casualties East and Recuperated do not include the German forces under *Befehlsstelle Finnland* (i.e. the German forces on the East Front in Norway and Finland).

The 'unfit and/or sick' casualties include personnel made unfit due to sickness, disease, accidents, exposure and frostbite (i.e., losses not directly attributable to enemy action). However, it excludes unfit personnel which were not transported out of the Army Group sectors for treatment. These personnel were usually treated by local divisional and army medical facilities, and were returned to duty after relatively short periods. There are few records of these unfit or lightly wounded casualties, but one source indicates that 1,630,000 German soldiers were treated in their units between 1st September 1941 and 31st August 1942 (one year, including the winter of 1941-42), and of these, 1,211,000 had required treatment at a military hospital.[584]

Even for unfit personnel who were transported out of the Army Group sectors, the return to duty rate was high. As we have seen from the above medical records, around 93% of these personnel remained in the Wehrmacht or Waffen SS and returned to active duty at a front later in the war. Around 49% were fit again after one month, 23% were fit again after two months, and around 85% were fit for active service after twelve months. On average it took 27 days for a casualty initially classified as unfit to return to active service. The recuperated casualties (originally classified as unfit and wounded) in table Casualties East and Recuperated only includes those who returned to active duty before the end of 1941. It excludes recuperated personnel that remained in the Wehrmacht and who returned to active duty later in the war.

It is interesting to note that in this table that the total casualties (including unfit) from 22nd June to 30th September 1941 (101 days) represented 58% of the total suffered in 1941. This compares to the value of 66% when unfit casualties are not included (table Casualties East B). This is because the unfit casualties steadily grew to a peak as the winter came on, unlike the other casualty types, so that by December 1941 it had grown to some 91,000. The sudden onset of winter led to a considerable increase of frostbite cases among the troops, who were inadequately equipped against the cold. The unfit casualties in December amounted to no less than 54% of the total German casualties, and probably around two thirds of these were directly attributable to frostbite and exposure. Soldiers with frostbite returned to fitness only a little more quickly than the wounded: as a rule, 70% of them were back with their units six months later, compared with 60% of the wounded.[585] On the other hand, mortality rates among frostbite cases were very low at only 1.5%. Overall, the 10-day troop sickness certificates and medical reports indicate that there were 228,000 (reported) cases of frostbite and/or exposure during the winter of 1941-42.[586]

***

---

[581] Germany and the Second World War; Volume I, Organisation and Mobilisation of the German Sphere of Power, Part 1, Wartime Administration, Economy and Manpower Resources 1939-1941, Kroener, B. R., et al, (German Research Institute for Military History at Potsdam), Clarendon Press (Oxford University Press Inc), New York, 2000, Diagram III.V.3. Ref: BA-MA III W 805/5-7, 10 day troop sickness certificates (army). For Jan -Mar. 1942: BA-MA RH 2/v. 2542; Halder, War Diaries, 1398.

[582] This makes sense because the Waffen SS recruitment and personnel administration (including payroll, medical, etc) was separate to that of the Army (*Heer*) in 1941, although the Waffen SS came under Army control operationally (as did the Luftwaffe ground forces).

[583] During 1941, the Wehrmacht casualties in Norway and Lapland amounted to 6 375 killed, 1 346 missing/POW and 20 724 wounded. Refer tables Weh Killed June 41-Feb. 42, Weh Wounded June 41-Feb. 42 and Weh MIA-POW June 41-Feb. 42.

[584] Germany and the Second World War; Volume I, Organisation and Mobilisation of the German Sphere of Power, Part 1, Wartime Administration, Economy and Manpower Resources 1939-1941, Kroener, B. R., et al, (German Research Institute for Military History at Potsdam), Clarendon Press (Oxford University Press Inc), New York, 2000, p. 727.

[585] Ibid. p.729.

[586] Ibid.

Table Casualties East and Recuperated

Army (*Heer*) Casualties (Killed, Missing, Wounded and Unfit) in the East, and Army (*Heer*) Recuperated Casualties in the East; 22nd June 1941-31 March 1942 (excluding *Befehlsstelle Finnland*; German forces on the East Front in Norway and Finland).

	June	July	Aug.	Sept.	Oct.	Nov.	Dec.	Jan. 1942	Feb. 1942	Mar. 1942	Total June - Dec. 41
Killed	8,883	36,144	39,334	27,492	23,804	16,945	14,752	←	←	←	167,354
Missing/POW	2,701	8,435	7,672	4,560	3,562	2,990	4,594	87,182	88,014	105,042	34,514
Wounded*	29,474	120,409	142,807	99,635	86,396	64,116	57,747	→	→	→	600,584
Unfit^	54,000	17,000	c 31,000	56,800	c 62,000	73,092	90,907	127,718	85,086	62,858	384,799
Total Casualties	95,058	181,988	220,813	188,487	175,762	157,143	168,000	214,900	173,100	167,900	1,187,251
Recuperated**	n/a	65,000	110,000	102,000	78,000	55,000	99,000	43,800	124,100	137,700	509,000

* Around 66% of the wounded remained in the Wehrmacht or Waffen SS, and approx. 56% returned to active duty at a Front later in the war. Refer table <u>Cas Ratio-Ret to Service</u>. Medical records ind. approx. 60% of 1941 wounded returned to active service within 6 months, & on average it took 98 days for a 'wound' casualty to return to active service.

^ Includes personnel made unfit due to sickness, disease, accidents and frostbite (i.e., losses not directly attributable to enemy action). Excludes 'unfit' personnel which were not transported out of the Army Group sectors for treatment. These personnel were usually treated by local divisional and army medical facilities, and were returned to duty after relatively short periods. Around 98% of the 'unfit' personnel listed above remained in the Wehrmacht or Waffen SS, and returned to active duty at a Front later in the war. Medical records indicate that around 49% were fit again after one month, 23% were fit again after two months, and around 85% were fit for active service after twelve months. On average it took 27 days for a casualty initially classified as 'unfit' to return to active service. Refer table <u>Cas Ratio-Ret to Service</u>.

** Comprises recuperated personnel who returned to duty on the East Front in 1941. Excludes recuperated personnel that remained in the Wehrmacht, and who returned to active duty (in the Field Army or the Replacement Army) later in the war (refer text).

The total casualties (including unfit) from 22nd June to 30th September 1941 (101 days) was 686,346, which was 58% of the total.
The total casualties (including unfit) from 1st October to 31st December 1941 (92 days) was 500,905; 42% of the total.

Source: BA-MA III W 805/5-7, 10 day troop sickness certificates (army). For Jan -Mar. 1942: BA-MA RH 2/v. 2542; Halder, War Diaries, 1398.

© Nigel Askey, 2018

Of special note here is an error presented in Kroener, B. R., et al, on the number of recuperated and replacements.[587] The stated figure for the period 22nd June to 31st December 1941 is 509,000. But we know for certain that the Wehrmacht had at least 561,600 ready replacement troops for the Army, and another 108,000 ready replacement troops for the Luftwaffe and Kriegsmarine, already in the Replacement Army in June 1941.[588] We have also established that at least 545,000 of these personnel were sent east as Replacements (R) for the Army in 1941. This figure, alone, is considerably greater than Kroener, B. R., et al's figure of recuperated and replacements. It appears the figure of 509,000 is actually **replacements coming from recuperated casualties**, which then matches what we would expect from the medical data shown in table <u>Cas Ratio-Ret to Service</u> and the total number of German wounded and unfit casualties suffered from June to December 1941.[589]

***

So far we have not included Waffen SS casualties, and accurate figures for Waffen SS casualties by month during 1941 are difficult (if not impossible) to come by. However the generally accepted figure for the period June to December 1941 is around 43,000 casualties.[590] This comprised around 8,000 killed, 22,000 wounded, 2,000 missing/POW and 11,000 unfit and or sick. All the large Waffen SS units in existence in June 1941 fought on the East Front, as well as several small units formed from foreign volunteers.[591] Overall the Waffen SS's pro rata casualties were only slightly higher than the Army's, with around 27% of their June 1941 strength becoming casualties.[592] This compares to around 23% for the Army.[593]

It is often stated that the Waffen SS suffered disproportionally higher casualties than the Army, and that this was almost entirely due to the fanatical nature of their soldiers and their apparent willingness to die if necessary. However, in research for this work I have found no significant quantitative-based evidence for this, and Operation Barbarossa is no exception. When one examines the individual combat histories of the Waffen SS units during 1941, it is evident that all the large units fought almost continuously from June to December 1941.[594] Furthermore, the Waffen SS motorised divisions and the LSSAH motorised brigade were often used as spearhead units within the motorised (panzer) corps; often fighting alongside the more heavily armed panzer divisions. They were equally often called upon as defend critical sectors, and their mobility (amongst other things) meant they were also used as highly mobile units against strong enemy attacks. The fact that their pro rata casualty rate for 1941 was only 4% higher than that for the Army (many units of which didn't serve in the East in 1941 at all) is, in fact, quite remarkable.

***

---

[587] Germany and the Second World War; Volume I, Organisation and Mobilisation of the German Sphere of Power, Part 1, Wartime Administration, Economy and Manpower Resources 1939-1941, Kroener, B. R., et al, (German Research Institute for Military History at Potsdam), Clarendon Press (Oxford University Press Inc), New York, 2000, Diagram III.V.3.

[588] Refer Volume IIB 4. 7) b. -'Replacements (R) available to the Wehrmacht from June to December 1941'.

[589] Also, there is no reason why the army's medical reports on casualties would incorporate information on fresh Replacements (R) being sent to the front. They would, however, have details on 'replacements' coming from recuperated casualties.

[590] N. Milton, The Waffen SS in the East 1941-1943, Coda Books Ltd, Henley in Arden, UK, 2011. T. Goldsworthy, Valhalla's Warriors: A History of the Waffen SS on the Eastern Front 1941-1945, Dog Ear Publishing, Indianapolis, 2007.

[591] C. Bishop, Hitler's Foreign Divisions: Foreign Volunteers in the Waffen-SS 1940-1945, Spellmount Ltd, Staplehurst, Kent, 2005.

[592] 43,000 casualties out of a June 1941 strength of 160,000.

[593] 1,215,702 casualties (830,903 killed, wounded and missing/POW, and 384,799 unfit) out of a June 1941 strength of 5,200,000.

[594] Refer Volume IIA 3. 9) - 'Waffen SS Combat Units' for more detail on all the Waffen SS units fielded in 1941, along with short unit histories for that period.

If we take the more accurate information regarding killed, wounded and missing/POW from table Casualties East B (page 338) which includes the casualties from North Norway and Lapland, utilize the information on 'unfit and/or sick' from table Casualties East and Recuperated, and add the Waffen SS casualties, we arrive at our best estimate of total Wehrmacht and Waffen SS casualties on the East Front in 1941. The results of this process are shown below.

Table Total Casualties East Front 1941

Wehrmacht and Waffen SS* Personnel Killed, Wounded, Missing, POW and Unfit^ on the East Front from 22nd June to 31st Dec. 1941 (including *Befehlsstelle Finnland* forces on the East Front).

	22nd Jun 30th June	July	Aug.	Sept.	Oct.	Nov.	Dec.	Total, 22nd June - 31st Dec. 41*
Killed	9,503	38,669	41,592	30,089	24,987	18,327	15,285	**186,452**
Wounded	30,482	128,250	149,298	108,485	89,688	67,693	59,283	**655,179**
MIA & POW	2,995	9,619	8,129	5,177	3,974	3,381	4,882	**40,157**
Unfit^	54,000	17,000	31,000	56,800	62,000	73,092	90,907	**395,799**
Tot., Armed Services	**96,980**	**193,538**	**230,019**	**200,551**	**180,649**	**162,493**	**170,357**	**1,277,587**

* To the Total is added 43,000 Waffen SS casualties; made up of 8,000 killed, 22,000 wounded, 2,000 missing & POW and 11,000 unfit. These casualties represented 27% of the Waffen SS strength in June 1941 (compared to 23% for the Army (*Heer*)).

^ Includes personnel made unfit due to sickness, disease, accidents and frostbite (i.e., losses not directly attributable to enemy action). Excludes 'unfit' personnel which were not transported out of the Army Group sectors for treatment.

© Nigel Askey, 2018

In many publications regarding Operation Barbarossa it is stated that the casualties suffered by the Wehrmacht during 1941 resulted in a critical weakening of the Field Army, and that this ultimately led to the failure of OKW to achieve its strategic objectives in 1941. This then led to the prolonged war of attrition on the East Front and ultimate defeat. The argument usually goes along the lines that the casualties sustained were inevitable when faced with such a huge adversary as the Red Army with its (apparently) 'inexhaustible' supplies of replacement manpower (the Soviet Union).

At first glance, and when viewed in isolation, the above table might support this argument: after all, how could the Wehrmacht possibly sustain close to 1,300,000 casualties in around six months and have any chance of defeating the USSR in 1941-42? In fact, one of the ways to demonstrate this is by using figures such as those above, and then implying (or stating outright) that the German Army on the East Front was therefore around a million men understrength by December 1941. Hence, defeat was inevitable because the casualties were inevitable, and any chance Germany had of winning World War II was doomed as soon as Germany invaded the USSR.

The basic problem with this argument is that it is, at best, much too simplistic. At worst, it is using very selected statistics to mislead the reader (and is therefore a spurious argument). The above argument takes no account of several critical factors that came into play. These were as follows (the footnotes indicate the main section in this volume where this item, or items, are discussed):

1. The numbers of ready Replacement (R) that Germany already had in its large Replacement Army, and the number actually sent east in 1941.[595]

2. The manpower newly mobilised via conscription during the second half of 1941, and the numbers of Replacements (R) that could have been sent east in 1941. [596]

---

[595] Refer Volume IIB 4. 7) b. and c. -'Replacements (R) available to the Wehrmacht from June to December 1941' and 'Replacements (R) Actually issued to the German Ground Forces on the East Front During 1941'.
[596] Refer Volume IIB 4. 4) b. vii. - 'Newly Conscripted Wehrmacht and Waffen SS Personnel) and Ibid.

3. The proportion of casualties that were classified as wounded or unfit, and the numbers and timing of recuperated casualties returning to the front (within the 1941 timeframe).

4. The combat units that existed in June 1941 and that arrived as reinforcements on the East Front after June 1941, and the units that remained in the West that could have been sent as reinforcements.[597]

5. The combat units that were newly mobilised from June to December 1941 and sent to the East.[598]

6. The fact that the Soviet armed forces in turn suffered between 4,500,000 and 5,550,000 military casualties in 1941 (depending on sources used).

All the above items are not simply 'what if' questions: they all existed as fact or as policy, and they were all implemented historically. The only question is how well they were implemented as part of a larger overall strategy. In the event, items 1. 3. and 6. (above) were well or very well implemented, while items 2. 4. and 5. were very poorly implemented. Other factors commonly stated as dooming Operation Barbarossa from the start are logistics (supply) and shortages of AFVs. As with the casualties discourse, these statements are usually too simplistic, not quantitatively based and/or use only selected statistics.[599]

***

In order to gain a more realistic perspective on German casualties in 1941, we should add at least some of the factors mentioned above to table <u>Total Casualties East Front 1941</u> (above). Firstly, we need to add some recuperated casualty data, and for the Army (*Heer*) this information is shown in table <u>Casualties East and Recuperated</u>.

Secondly, we need to add information relating to the Replacements (R) that were sent east from June to December 1941. We know for certain that the Wehrmacht had at least 561,600 ready replacement troops for the Army, and another 108,000 ready replacement troops for the Luftwaffe and Kriegsmarine, already in the Replacement Army in June 1941. We have also established that at least 545,000 of these personnel were sent east as Replacements (R) for the Army in 1941, with the bulk being dispatched from July to September 1941.[600] Obviously, personnel that arrived as part of reinforcing units are not included as Replacements (R). For example, the 2nd and 5th Panzer Divisions arrived on the East Front in September 1941: these are classified as 'reinforcements' and the personnel in these units are not considered to be Replacements (R).

This information has been added to table <u>Total Casualties East Front 1941</u> and is displayed in table <u>Casualties East 41, Recup and Rep</u> (below). With the additional information the reader is now better able to compare the numbers of personnel effectively leaving the front-lines (i.e. all types of casualties) against the numbers of personnel effectively arriving at the front-lines (i.e. new Replacements (R) and recuperated casualties). This is shown as the 'Net change' in strength. Note, this table does not include *Luftwaffe* and *Kriegsmarine* Replacements (R) sent east in 1941.[601]

To the 'debit' side should be added the Wehrmacht and Waffen SS forces withdrawn from the East during 1941. This includes around a third of the Luftwaffe air-combat units committed in June 1941, and can be estimated at around 350,000 men (including a proportion sent home on leave). To the 'credit' side should be added the new Army and Waffen SS units that arrived as reinforcements, and these amounted to approximately 500,000 men.[602] Therefore the net reduction in overall Wehrmacht and Waffen SS strength on the East Front from June to December 1941 was actually only around 74,000 men.

***

---

[597] Refer Volume IIB 2. - 'German Land Combat Unit Reinforcements on the East Front from 5th July to 31st December 1941'.

[598] Refer Volume IIB 4. 2) - 'German Land Combat Units Mobilised from 22nd June 1941 to 31st December 1941'.

[599] These items are addressed at length in Volume IIB 7) c. ii. - 'German Tank and Assault Gun Losses and Replacements", and Volume IIB 6. - 'The Supply Distribution Efficiency (SDE) for the Wehrmacht on the East Front from 22nd June to 31st December 1941'.

[600] For more information on German Replacements (R) sent to the East front in 1941, refer to Volume IIB 4. 7) - 'The Resource Replacements (R) Available to the German Army Waffen SS, Luftwaffe Ground Forces and Naval Coastal Artillery, from 22nd June to 31st December 1941'. In particular, section c. - 'Replacements (R) Actually Issued to the German Ground Forces on the East Front During 1941'.

[601] As mentioned, there were 108,000 Luftwaffe and Kriegsmarine replacements already in the Replacement Army in June 1941.

[602] Refer Volume IIB 2. A total of 24 divisions arrived as reinforcements from 4th July to the end of December 1941. This included 19 infantry divisions, the 2nd and 5th Panzer Divisions, the 60th Motorised Division, the 6th Mountain Division and the 7th Flieger Division. Of these divisions, only the 250th Infantry Division (the Spanish Blue Division) was mobilised after 4th July 1941 and quickly sent to the East Front. Most of the divisions arrived in July (nine divisions including one motorised division) and September (six divisions including two panzer divisions). There were also many separate regimental and battalions sized support units (and security forces) which arrived as reinforcements.

Table Casualties East 41, Recup and Rep

Wehrmacht and Waffen SS Casualties (Killed, Missing, Wounded and Unfit) in the East, and Army (Heer) Recuperated and Replacements in the East; 22nd June 1941-31 December 1941 (including *Befehlsstelle Finnland*; German forces on the East Front in Norway and Finland).

	June	July	Aug.	Sept.	Oct.	Nov.	Dec.	Total (plus Waffen SS)^^ June - Dec. 41
Killed	9,503	38,669	41,592	30,089	24,987	18,327	15,285	186,452
Missing/POW	2,995	9,619	8,129	5,177	3,974	3,381	4,882	40,157
Wounded*	30,482	128,250	149,298	108,485	89,688	67,693	59,283	655,179
Unfit^	54,000	17,000	c 31,000	56,800	c 62,000	73,092	90,907	395,799
Total Casualties	96,980	193,538	230,019	200,551	180,649	162,493	170,357	1,277,587
Recuperated**	n/a	65,000	110,000	102,000	78,000	55,000	99,000	509,000
New Replacements*^	40,000	110,000	124,000	90,000	70,000	45,000	66,000	545,000
Net Change	-56,980	-18,538	3,981	-8,551	-32,649	-62,493	-5,357	-223,587

* Around 66% of the wounded remained in the Wehrmacht or Waffen SS, and approximately 56% returned to active duty at a Front later in the war. Refer table Cas Ratio-Ret to Service. Medical records indicate around 60% of 1941 wounded returned to active service within six months, and on average it took 98 days for a 'wound' casualty to return to active service.

^ Includes personnel made unfit due to sickness, disease, accidents and frostbite (i.e., losses not directly attributable to enemy action). Excludes 'unfit' personnel which were not transported out of the Army Group sectors for treatment. These personnel were usually treated by local divisional and army medical facilities, and were returned to duty after relatively short periods. Around 98% of the 'unfit' personnel listed above remained in the Wehrmacht or Waffen SS, and returned to active duty at a Front later in the war. Refer table Cas Ratio-Ret to Service. Medical records indicate that around 49% were fit again after one month, 23% were fit again after two months, and around 85% were fit for active service after twelve months. On average it took 27 days for a casualty initially classified as 'unfit' to return to active service.

** Comprises recuperated personnel who returned to duty on the East Front in 1941. Excludes recuperated personnel that remained in the Wehrmacht, and who returned to active duty (in the Field Army or the Replacement Army) later in the war (refer text).

*^ 90,000 Replacements (R) were released in June 1941. These were already in the divisional Field Replacement Battalions on the East Front (part of the Replacement Army). The Replacements distribution is based on the number of Army troop replacements available in June 1941 (from the Replacement Army), and their movements East in 1941. Excludes *Luftwaffe & Kriegsmarine* Replacements. There were 108,000 additional replacement troops, for the Luftwaffe and Kriegsmarine, in the Replacement Army in June.

^^ To the Total is added 43,000 Waffen SS casualties; made up of 8,000 killed, 22,000 wounded, 2,000 missing & POW and 11,000 unfit. These casualties represented 27% of the Waffen SS strength in June 1941 (compared to 23% for the Army (Heer)).

© Nigel Askey, 2018

The total casualties (including unfit) from 22nd June to 30th Sep. 1941 (101 days) was 742,600, which was 58% of the total. (assumes half the 1941 Waffen SS casualties).
The total casualties (including unfit) from 1st Oct. to 31st Dec. 1941 (92 days) was 535,000; 42% of the total (assumes half of the 1941 Waffen SS casualties)

There is no doubt that by late December 1941 the German Army was not as strong as it had been in June, and many important units were exhausted and severely below their TOE strength (especially the panzer and motorised divisions). In addition, the replacements were not (yet) as experienced or as well trained as the men lost during the 1941 campaign. Nevertheless, the forces on the East Front in late December 1941 were definitely nowhere near a million men below the strength of the invading force in June 1941. In addition many of the German infantry divisions had not seen particularly heavy combat (compared to the panzer, motorised and Waffen SS divisions) and were still close to their TOE strength. This also goes some way to explaining why the Soviet 1941-42 winter offensive was not successful in literally annihilating the 'frozen' German Army Group Centre, and why the Red Army paid such a high price in killed and wounded.

When viewed across the Reich as a whole, the Wehrmacht and Waffen SS strength actually increased during Operation Barbarossa from 7,309,000 to 7,640,000 personnel (some 331,000 persons). This is illustrated in the table below.[603]

Overall Wehrmacht and Waffen SS Strength Change from June to December 1941	
Army, Luftwaffe, Navy and Waffen SS Strength, 22nd June 1941.	**7,309,000**
Army, Luftwaffe, Navy and Waffen SS Strength, 31st Dec 1941.*	**7,640,000**
Total casualties on the East Front.	**1,277,587**
Casualties who remained in the Wehrmacht and Waffen SS.	**822,540**
Irrecoverable losses on the East Front.	**455,047**
Total casualties on other Fronts.^	**15,900**
Casualties who remained in the Wehrmacht and Waffen SS.	**10,200**
Irrecoverable losses on other Fronts.	**5,700**
Newly Mobilised Recruits	**792,000**
* Estimated, based on the strength 4 days later, i.e. the strength on 4th Jan. 1942 was 7,648,000 personnel.	
^ Based on precise figures for killed, wounded, missing and POW; and an analogous estimate of unfit. © Nigel Askey, 2018	

A significant proportion of the new personnel went into Luftwaffe Flak forces and the Kriegsmarine, but most went into the Field Army and Replacement Army. If the OKW opted to deploy the bulk of this force (around 4,400,000 persons) on fronts other than the East Front in November-December 1941, then this was a strategic decision and was not inevitably due to heavy 'casualties'. To put it another way; the Red Army and VVS suffered four to five times as many casualties during 1941, and by late 1941 most of their existing armed forces were now far less well trained than the average Wehrmacht unit. Despite this, in December 1941 over 85% of the entire Soviet armed forces were deployed against the invaders and they were planning to attack. This situation was (again) not inevitable due to the size of the Red Army, but was due to a series of strategic decisions by the Stavka.

If there is one conclusion to be learned from the German FILARM model (detailed in Volume IIA and IIB) and Soviet FILARM model (detailed in Volume IIIA and IIIB), then it is that there was nothing pre-ordained about the Axis invasion of the USSR in June 1941. The Germans were not doomed to defeat in WWII due to the heavy casualties they were inevitably going to sustain in Operation Barbarossa during 1941. Neither were they doomed to defeat in 1941 for solely logistical (supply) reasons, or because of inadequate tank production.

At the same time the USSR was never destined to ultimately win the campaign in the East simply because of its great manpower and war-economy, or the huge expanses of land it could 'retreat' into. The Red Army that existed in June 1941 was all but destroyed in that year, and the USSR did not have inexhaustible reserves of available manpower and (especially) equipment in 1941. By the end of 1941 most of the Red Army troops in the field had barely adequate training and equipment, and the Soviet infrastructure was struggling to keep them adequately supplied to almost the same degree as the Germans. The Soviet people suffered almost unbelievable casualties in 1941, the Soviet economy was severely damaged and could easily have been a lot more damaged, and the USSR as an entity came much closer to defeat than commonly realised.

---

[603] Refer Volume IIB 4. 4) b. vii. - 'Newly Conscripted Wehrmacht and Waffen SS Personnel).

The outcome of Operation Barbarossa in 1941 was not pre-ordained because of macroscopic economic, social, demographic or geographic factors (unlike many of the military campaigns during WWII). The outcome was in fact quite finely balanced, especially during the critical period from July to October 1941; and it was determined by the tactical, operational and strategic decisions made by the various commands. Ultimately the final outcome lay with the key military and short-term policy decisions made by the highest commands; namely the OKW and the Stavka. Perhaps Operation Barbarossa is most fascinating because of this fact, and the drastic implications for the outcome of WWII. Hitler is quoted as saying "the world will hold its breath and fall silent when Barbarossa is mounted", and perhaps in this regard he was right.

**

Appendix A

Overall Status of Selected Weapons within the Army on 1st April 1941

Appendix A, Table I		
Overall Status of Selected Weapons within the Army (*Heer*) on 1st April 1941		
Weapons and Equipment	**No. Available**	**Appropriate Ammunition Types (No. Avail.)**
Small Arms		
Pistols	716,300	302,800,000
SMGs	144,460	
Type K 98 rifles (only)	4,198,800	9,552,000,000
MGs	192,600	
AT Rifle 38/39	18,101	2,043,700
2cm Flak	1,933	32,778,000
2cm *Flakvierling*	69	
2cm Tank Gun	2,711	14,300,900
3.7cm Tank Gun	1,459	2,778,600
5cm Tank Gun	1,138	663,800
7.5cm Tank & Ass-Gun Gun	1,151	2,219,400
2.8cm sPzb 41 AT Gun	130	188,500
3.7cm Pak 36 AT Gun	14,838	18,680,800
5cm Pak 38 AT Gun	719	713,100
5cm leGrW 36 Light Mortars	14,913	31,982,200
8cm GrW 34 Medium Mortars	10,549	12,436,000
10cm *Nebelwerfer* 35 and 40	459	1,523,000
15cm *Nebelwerfer* 41	411	199,500
7.5cm leIG 18 Light Infantry Guns	3,951	7,953,600
15cm sIG 33 Heavy Infantry Guns	797	1,153,300
7.5cm GebG 36 Mountain Guns	96	858,400
7.5cm leFK 18 Light Field Guns	106	151,500
10.5cm leFH 18/18M Light Field Howitzers	6,854	25,051,000
s 10cm K 18 Heavy Field Guns	730	2,323,600
15cm sFH 18 Heavy Field Howitzers	2,750	5,540,700
21cm Mrs 18 Heavy Howitzer (Mortar)	346	433,100
Teller (T) Mines		1,258,600
Boog, H., et al., Germany and the Second World War, Volume IV: The Attack on the Soviet Union, (German Research Institute for Military History at Potsdam), Clarendon Press (Oxford University Press), New York, 1996, Table I. III.3, p. 218. Ref: Report OKW WiRuAmt, 10 July 1941; supplemented from; Uberblick Munition, Apr. 1941, BA-MA RH 8/v. 1071b. © Nigel Askey, 2018		

***

Manufacture of Small Arms and Selected Artillery Types for the Wehrmacht during 1941

Appendix A, Table II												
Manufacture of Small-Arms and Selected Artillery Types for the Wehrmacht during 1941												
	Jan.	Feb.	Mar.	Apr.	May	Jun.	Jul.	Aug.	Sep.	Oct.	Nov.	Dec.
Small Arms												
Pistols	24,397	31,490	34,861	37,347	39,575	32,466	41,935	33,879	42,211	43,649	45,813	50,253
Rifles	121,543	125,773	121,006	118,907	124,963	123,959	105,063	101,479	106,647	78,884	66,514	76,565
SMGs	18,350	22,751	20,490	23,050	19,000	17,250	20,050	19,600	18,500	19,000	19,000	19,000
MGs	7,587	9,074	6,766	10,167	7,374	6,620	6,377	6,304	5,733	5,853	3,933	3,424
AT- Rifles	2,710	2,610	3,076	3,625	3,811	2,780	2,967	3,010	2,510	2,133	0	58
Anti-Tank Guns												
3.7cm Pak 36	122	192	178	195	109	183	114	135	95	39	3	0
4.7cm Pak (t)	33	30	22	9	31	26	11	14	8	28	28	44
5cm Pak 38	142	117	113	154	177	163	173	250	152	241	212	178
7.5cm KL/24 (StG)	31	45	40	41	37	35	51	49	61	43	60	55
Anti-Aircraft Guns												
2cm Flak	226	543	538	551	511	414	399	559	548	455	634	681
2cm *Flakvierling*	221	237	155	236	280	268	45	49	107	52	149	66
3.7cm Flak	59	42	63	47	70	39	50	63	36	54	45	54
5cm Flak	0	4	3	3	2	2	5	7	0	3	6	0
8.8cm Flak	90	81	107	165	164	168	179	197	151	192	192	175
10.5cm Flak	22	18	16	14	18	16	16	19	10	15	22	18
Tank Guns												
2cm Tank Gun	95	75	124	115	146	140	118	206	206	141	124	148
3.7cm Tank Gun	97	11	65	61	31	104	101	87	50	12	73	68
5cm Tank Gun	171	149	198	183	215	275	295	256	325	335	192	234
7.5cm Tank Gun	57	52	66	69	74	26	88	46	65	75	55	79
Light & Med Art.												
Mortars	1,111	1,233	1,340	1,221	1,205	1,073	1,136	967	413	260	205	207
Nebelwerfers	108	150	96	136	127	76	48	99	70	180	135	120
Infantry Guns	103	163	155	159	170	163	198	148	89	102	86	72
7.5cm GebG 36	14	10	8	0	10	9	0	1	0	25	1	0
Light Artillery Pieces	4	48	22	0	30	24	0	0	0	0	0	0
10.5cm leFH 18/18M	147	102	127	140	132	89	101	130	79	45	45	21
Hvy & Sup Hvy Art.												
s 10cm K 18	5	17	23	10	10	5	15	9	5	0	9	1
15cm sFH 18	63	57	64	46	53	38	41	45	32	39	10	10
15cm K18/39	3	6	7	10	9	7	7	10	8	1	3	4
17-42cm Hvy Art.	25	32	25	27	25	24	25	21	26	17	18	21

Kroener, B. R., et al, Germany and the Second World War; Volume I, Organisation and Mobilisation of the German Sphere of Power, Part 1, Wartime Administration, Economy and Manpower Resources 1939-1941, Clarendon Press (Oxford University Press), Oxford, 2000, Table II.VII.3. Ref: Reports on overall state of armaments, BA-MA RH 8/v. IO35ff.   © Nigel Askey, 2018

***

Approximate Overall Status for Selected Weapons within the Wehrmacht: 1st October 1939 to 1st January 1942

Appendix A, Table III				
Approximate Overall Status for Selected Weapons within the Wehrmacht: 1st October 1939 to 1st January 1942.				
	1st Oct. 1939	1st May 1940	1st June 1941	1st Jan. 1942
Army (*Heer*)				
Pistols: Types P 08 and P 38	630,000	528,800	769,500	889,550
Rifles: Type K 98	2,569,300	3,228,500	4,372,800	4,717,500
SMGs: Types MP 38 and MP 40	5,711	27,800	166,700	205,450
MGs	103,300	150,400	203,250	206,500
AT Rifles: Types PzB 38, 39 and 41	62	1,353	25,481	36,270
Light Mortars: 5cm leGrW 36	5,062	9,957	16,129	15,579
Medium Mortars: 8cm GrW 34	3,959	7,091	11,767	11,719
Light Infantry Guns: 7.5cm leIG 18	2,931	3,365	4,176	4,022
Heavy Infantry Guns: 15cm sIG 33	367	491	867	864
Light AA Guns: 2cm Flak 30 and Flak 38	895	1,487	2,153	2,690
Light AA Guns: 3.7cm Flak 18	63	na	na	na
Heavy AA Guns: 8.8cm Flak 18/36	na	na	na	104
Light Anti-Tank Guns: 3.7cm Pak 36	10,560	14,257	15,522	13,341
Light Anti-Tank Guns: 4.7cm Pak 36(t)		36	785	494
Medium Anti-Tank Guns: 5cm Pak 38			1,047	1,921
Nebelwerfers: 10cm NbW 40 and 15cm NbW 41	179	288	1,112	953
Hvy Rck Launching Equip: 28-32cm Rocket Systems.	na	na	6,791	2,249
Mountain Guns: 7.5cm GebG 36 and 7.5cm GebK 15	213	354	108	151
Light Field Guns: 7.5cm leFK 18	20	44	104	104
Light Field Howitzers: 10.5cm leFH 18/18M and 16	4,919	5,538	7,076	6,772
Heavy Field Howitzers: 15cm sFH 18	2,434	2,383	2,867	2,744
Heavy Field Guns: s 10cm K 18	400	709	760	732
Heavy Field Guns: 15cm K 18 and K 39	25	177	68	92
Super Heavy Artillery: Calibre 21-42cm *	47	163	442	541
Infantry Ammunition	6,665,459,000	8,459,496,000	9,774,200,000	7,175,853,000
Artillery Ammunition	29,363,000	57,180,000	90,464,000	63,630,000
Tanks and Anti-Tank Ammunition	35,793,000	77,102,000	78,631,000	69,403,000
Pz Kpfw I (Excludes kl Pz Bef Wg Command Tanks)	1,305	1,266	966	817
4.7cm Pak(t) Self-Propelled Guns ^		40	361	221
Pz Kpfw II (Includes Pz Kpfw II *Flamm* Tanks)	991	1,110	1,159	994
Pz Kpfw III (Excludes gr Pz Bef Wg Command Tanks)	151	785	1,440	1,864
Pz Kpfw IV	143	290	572	512
Sturmgeschütz (StuG) III		na	377	591
Pz Kpfw 35(t) (Includes Command Tanks)	125	143	187	192
Pz Kpfw 38(t) (Includes Command Tanks)	122	238	754	434
Armoured Reconnaissance and Command Vehicles	1,076	1,710	1,776	1,752
Armoured Personnel Carriers (APCs) and Half-Tracks	5,200	7,997	15,642	19,129

* Excludes rail guns, and includes 21cm Mrs 18, 21cm K 39, 24cm H 39, s 24cm K(t), 24cm K L/46, 24cm K 3, 30.5cm Mrs (t), and 35.5cm H M1.

© Nigel Askey, 2018

^ Includes 4.7cm Pak(t) (Sf) *auf Panzerkampfwagen* I *Ausf* B, and 4.7cm Pak(t) *auf Panzerkampfwagen* 35R(f) *ohne Turm*.

***

Appendix A, Table III (cont.)

Approximate Overall Status for Selected Weapons within the Wehrmacht: 1st October 1939 to 1st January 1942.

	1st Oct. 1939	1st May 1940	1st June 1941	1st Jan. 1942
Luftwaffe				
Small Arms (K 98 Rifles, Pistols and SMGs)	728,349	1,063,700	1,255,200	1,646,000
Light AA Guns (2cm to 3.7cm Calibre)	7,300	9,602	13,049	16,918
Heavy AA Guns (8.8cm to 10.5cm Calibre)	2,528	3,011	4,409	5,172
Reconnaissance Aircraft	642	664	823	691
Fighters, Night-Fighters and Fighter-Bombers	907	1,418	2,017	1,853
Twin Engine Fighters and Fighter-Bombers	438	372	232	94
Bombers	1,230	1,758	2,141	1,752
Dive Bombers	354	417	501	490
Transport Aircraft	706	800	719	991
Communication Aircraft	225	225	133	110
Aircraft belonging to C in C Navy	254	241	286	277
Tot. Aircraft (excl. Training + Similar Sup Aircraft)	**4,756**	**5,895**	**6,852**	**6,258**
Bombs, Aerial Mines and Torpedos	16,203,300	17,075,775	5,541,068	4,113,700
Navy (Kriegsmarine)				
Battleships			1	1
Battlecruisers	2	2	2	2
Battleships (old / obsolete)	2	2	2	2
Heavy Cruisers	5	3	4	4
Light Cruisers	6	4	4	4
Destroyers	22	10	15	18
Torpedo Boats	11	17	21	28
E-Boats	18	24	48	60
U-Boats	56	48	137	247
Mine-Detectors	32	35	37	54
Minesweepers	39	43	85	118
Training Vessels/Special Craft	75	na	na	na
Fleet Auxiliaries	437	na	na	na
Torpedoes	3,337	2,985	5,898	na
Mines, Booms	15,953	12,663	43,347	na

Kroener, B. R., et al, Germany and the Second World War; Volume I, Organisation and Mobilisation of the German Sphere of Power, Part 1, Wartime Administration, Economy and Manpower Resources 1939-1941, Clarendon Press (Oxford University Press), Oxford, 2000, Table II.V.7. Ref: Services' reports end Sept. 1939, BA-MA Wi/IF 5.844.

Survey army's armaments status, BA-MA RH 8/v. IO52a, IO88a, IO90a, IO91, IIIOa +b.

OKW ten-day surveys, BA-MA RW 19/1939, RL 2 III/713, 717.

© Nigel Askey, 2018

Lohmann and Hilderbrand Kriegsmarine. Also, Conway's All the World's Fighting Ships 1922-1946, 1980, p.225-232.

***

German Tank and Assault Gun Losses, Production, Rebuilt and Inventory: June to December 1941

Appendix A, Table IV

German Tank and Assault Gun Losses, Production, Rebuilt and Inventory: June-December 1941

German Tank and Assault Gun Losses, June-December 1941 ^^

	June	July	Aug.	Sept.	Oct.	Nov.	Dec.	Total
Pz I *	34	146	171	7	18	33	19	**428**
Pz II ^	16	117	106	32	65	30	92	**458**
Pz 35(t) **	26	26	26	26	26	26	6	**162**
Pz 38(t)	33	182	183	62	85	149	102	**796**
Pz III (37mm)	23	59	25	16	11	13	29	**176**
Pz III (50mm)	27	164	78	104	79	116	208	**776**
StuG III	3	11	26	12	23	10	19	**104**
Pz IV	16	111	70	23	55	38	65	**378**
Pz Bef *^	1	18	12	17	14	6	28	**96**
	179	**834**	**697**	**299**	**376**	**421**	**568**	**3,374**

* Includes Pz I *pionier* vehicles and ammunition carriers (i.e. all types).   ^ Excludes Pz II Flame Tanks (Sd Kfz 122).

** Comprises 157xPz 35(t) and 5xPZ35(t) Bef, all in the 6th Pz. Division. Average taken for losses each month.

*^ *Panzerbefehlswagen* (command tanks). Incls. Pz I *Kleine* Pz Bef (Sd Kfz 265) & Pz III Gross Pz Bef
   (Sd Kfz 266 - 268).

^^ Includes 240 plus tank losses in North Africa (mainly Pz II, III and IV).

Newly Manufactured German Tanks and Assault Guns Ready for Issue, June-December 1941

	June	July	Aug.	Sept.	Oct.	Nov.	Dec.	Total
Pz I	No longer produced							
Pz II	5	27	9	26	23	50	41	**181**
Pz 35(t)	No longer produced							
Pz 38(t) *	29	80	64	63	66	50	49	**401**
Pz III (37mm)	No longer produced							
Pz III (50mm)	88	176	185	182	174	198	198	**1,201**
StuG III	56	47	50	38	71	46	40	**348**
Pz IV	29	55	43	49	40	58	56	**330**
Pz Bef III		14	5	2			12	**33**
	207	**399**	**356**	**360**	**374**	**402**	**396**	**2,494**

* Includes all tanks used as command tanks.

© Nigel Askey, 2018

***

Appendix A, Table IV (cont.)

German Tank and Assault Gun Losses, Production, Rebuilt and Inventory: June-December 1941

Factory Rebuilt German Tanks and Assault Guns Ready for Issue, June-December 1941

	June	July	Aug.	Sept.	Oct.	Nov.	Dec.	**Total**
Pz I *		74	42	46	54	44	14	**274** *
Pz II ^	4	8	12	2	5	2	7	**40**
Pz 35(t)	2		2			1	5	**10**
Pz 38(t)	13	74	1	3		5		**96**
Pz III (37mm)	Rebuilt with 50mm guns (inc in Pz III (50mm) figures)							
Pz III (50mm)	23	25	10	13	13	13	22	**119**
StuG III **	◄------------------------------- 13 -------------------------------►							**13**
Pz IV	1	13	9	3	1	6	11	**44**
Pz Bef *^	2	4	11	8	1	9	5	**40**
	45	**198**	**87**	**88**	**74**	**80**	**64**	**636**

* Includes Pz I *pionier* vehicles and ammunition carriers (i.e. all types).   ^ Excludes Pz II Flame Tanks (Sd Kfz 122).

** Unknown, but estimated at 12-13% of losses (as per the Pz III and IV).

*^ Includes Pz I *Kleine* Pz Bef (Sd Kfz 265), but mostly Pz III Gross Pz Bef (Sd Kfz 266 - 268).

German Tank and Assault Gun Inventories, June-December 1941

	1st June	1st July	1st Aug.	1st Sept.	1st Oct.	1st Nov.	1st Dec.	**Six Month Change**
Pz I *	877	843	771	642	681	717	728	**-149**
Pz II ^	1,074	1,067	985	900	896	859	881	**-193**
Pz 35(t) **	170						19	**-151**
Pz 38(t)	746	755	727	609	613	594	500	**-246**
Pz III (37mm)	350	327	268	243	227	216	203	**-147**
Pz III (50mm)	1,090	1,174	1,211	1,328	1,419	1,527	1,622	**532**
StuG III	377						634	**257**
Pz IV	517	531	488	470	499	485	511	**-6**
Pz Bef *^	330	331	331	335	328	315	318	**-12**
Net change in the German tank and ass-gun inventory from 1st June 1941 to 1st Dec 1941								**-115**

* Includes Pz I *pionier* vehicles and ammunition carriers (i.e. all types except command tanks).

^ Excludes Pz II Flame Tanks (Sd Kfz 122), of which 90 were available on 1st June 1941.

** December inventory is for 11th December.

*^ Comprised of 160 Pz I *Kleine* Pz Bef (Sd Kfz 265) and 170 Pz III *Gross* Pz Bef (Sd Kfz 266 - 268).

Compiled from: Jentz, T.L., Panzer Truppen: Volume 1, The Complete Guide To The Creation and Combat Deployment of Germany's Tank Force 1933-1942, Schiffer Military History, Atglen, PA, 1996, pp. 254 - 271.

Boog, H., et al., Germany and the Second World War, Volume IV: The Attack on the Soviet Union, (German Research Institute for Military History at Potsdam), Clarendon Press (Oxford University Press), New York, 1996, Table I.III.4, p. 219, Table II.VI.I, pp. 1120-1122, and Diagram II. VI.2, p. 1129.

Ref: Ten Day Reports of OKH/GenQu, BA-MA III W 805/5 ff. *Uberblick uber den Rustungsstand des Heeres* (*Waffen und Gerat*) *Juni* 1941-*Januar* 1942, BA-MA RH 8/v. 1090, 1091.   © Nigel Askey, 2018

***

Production of Military Standard Motor Vehicles for the Army and Luftwaffe, August 1939 to December 1941

Appendix A, Table V

Production of Military-Standard Motor Vehicles for the Army and Luftwaffe, August 1939 to December 1941.

1939	Jan.	Feb.	Mar.	Apr.	May	June	July	Aug.	Sept.	Oct.	Nov.	Dec.
Motor Cycles								na	na	na	na	na
Light Staff Car								na	na	na	na	na
Medium Staff Car								na	na	na	na	na
Heavy Staff Car								na	na	na	na	na
Light Truck								1,173	823	781	708	618
Medium Truck								873	843	1,273	1,303	1,361
Heavy Truck								121	77	45	28	83
Sd Kfz 10 (1t) Half-Track								147	144	219	110	114
Sd Kfz 11 (3t) half-Track								54	65	70	45	41
Sd Kfz 6 (5t) Half-Track								23	20	40	15	15
Sd Kfz 7 (8t) Half-Track								35	20	85	60	28
Sd Kfz 8 (12t) Half-Track								15	5	2	1	0
Sd Kfz 9 (18t) Half-Track								14	13	9	12	2
Oth. Specialised Vehicles*								na	na	na	na	na
Total								**2,455**	**2,010**	**2,524**	**2,282**	**2,262**

1940	Jan.	Feb.	Mar.	Apr.	May	June	July	Aug.	Sept.	Oct.	Nov.	Dec.
Motor Cycles	na	na	na	na	na	na	na	5,209	3,905	4,098	4,652	4,211
Light Staff Car												
Medium Staff Car	c 2,670	c 2,670	c 2,670	c 2,670	c 2,670	c 2,670	c 2,670	2,503	2,236	2,194	2,236	2,217
Heavy Staff Car												
Light Truck	448		792	731	830	592	795	104	257	201	116	820
Medium Truck	1,299	3,467	2,691	2,931	3,033	3,274	3,604	2,356	2,305	2,911	2,128	2,327
Heavy Truck	95		190	247	322	210	256	167	880	347	357	420
Sd Kfz 10 (1t) Half-Track	114	235	25	323	232	195	206	268	285	301	302	235
Sd Kfz 11 (3t) half-Track	0	14	120	92	107	98	132	125	98	68	111	114
Sd Kfz 6 (5t) Half-Track	15	20	5	40	22	34	21	34	35	40	35	45
Sd Kfz 7 (8t) Half-Track	57	58	84	75	61	99	86	90	110	103	95	78
Sd Kfz 8 (12t) Half-Track	5	12	17	35	35	45	57	58	57	66	71	55
Sd Kfz 9 (18t) Half-Track	12	14	15	20	19	21	26	27	27	25	25	9
Oth. Specialised Vehicles*	na	na	na	na	na	na	na	1,266	2,100	1,799	1,995	2,006
Total	**4,715**	**6,490**	**6,609**	**7,164**	**7,331**	**7,238**	**7,853**	**12,207**	**12,295**	**12,153**	**12,123**	**12,537**

1941	Jan.	Feb.	Mar.	Apr.	May	June	July	Aug.	Sept.	Oct.	Nov.	Dec.
Motor Cycles	4,881	5,080	4,278	3,547	3,821	3,208	3,858	2,765	3,360	2,471	2,450	2,513
Light Staff Car	1,230	1,070	798	988	1,336	1,015	1,272	1,117	1,231	1,271	1,103	1,208
Medium Staff Car	633	829	910	845	931	863	1,067	925	804	605	650	712
Heavy Staff Car	476	437	138	342	137	184	312	320	306	190	258	359
Light Truck	926	929	822	636	650	634	531	728	709	1,001	612	907
Medium Truck	3,441	3,004	4,096	2,965	2,480	2,322	2,813	2,040	1,861	2,328	2,625	1,513
Heavy Truck	256	234	369	432	536	523	600	406	335	412	528	483
Sd Kfz 10 (1t) Half-Track	259	225	243	194	225	201	181	165	336	228	227	214
Sd Kfz 11 (3t) half-Track	160	150	105	152	81	135	133	96	190	114	135	106
Sd Kfz 6 (5t) Half-Track	35	40	34	37	25	20	25	25	25	30	40	34
Sd Kfz 7 (8t) Half-Track	60	160	118	117	117	120	67	83	118	117	136	111
Sd Kfz 8 (12t) Half-Track	68	76	77	67	72	59	54	67	82	53	71	74
Sd Kfz 9 (18t) Half-Track	26	19	28	28	22	14	19	30	22	28	31	27
Oth. Specialised Vehicles*	677	875	911	1,390	1,044	619	672	1,279	619	1,395	516	743
Total		**13,128**	**13,128**	**12,927**	**11,740**	**11,477**	**9,917**	**11,604**	**10,046**	**9,998**	**10,243**	**9,382**	**9,004**

* Mainly truck based vehicles, e.g. radio trucks, ambulances, AA weapon mounts, Breakdown trucks with cranes and or winches, etc
na - information not available. Ref: Reports on overall state of armaments, BA-MA RH 8/v. IO35ff.

Appendix B

Table of Contents, Volume I Part I: The Concepts and General Structure of the Integrated Land and Air Resource Model

Introduction

1. **Studying Military History Using Operational – Strategic Simulations**
   1) The Evolution of Military Simulations and War Gaming
   2) The Power of Military Simulations in the Study of Military History
   3) The Difference between Qualitative and Quantitative Analyses
   4) Tactical, Tactical-Operational, Operational and Strategic Military Simulations
      a. Tactical Level Simulations
      b. Tactical-Operational Level Simulations
      c. Operational Level Simulations
      d. Strategic Level Simulations

2. **The Integrated Land and Air Resource Model**
   1) What is an Integrated Land and Air Resource Model (ILARM)?
      a. The Underlying Principles
      b. The Fully Integrated Land and Air Resource Model (FILARM)
      c. The Partially Integrated Land and Air Resource Model (PILARM)
      d. Naval Forces Involved in Operation Barbarossa
   2) The Objectives of the Integrated Land and Air Resource Model
      a. The Strategic Context of the Military Campaign: Bottlenecks in the Mobilisation Process
      b. The Actual Personnel and Equipment Present
      c. Combat Unit Mobility
      d. Efficiency of Supporting Infrastructures
      e. Replacements
      f. New Equipment
      g. Operational Freedom of Action

3. **The Structure of the Fully Integrated Land and Air Resource Model (FILARM)**
   1) Resource Sources, Destinations and Paths outside the FILARM Model
   2) Resource Reallocation Paths within the FILARM Model
   3) Resource Allocation States inside the FILARM Model
      a. Combat Units: D, MD and MND
         i. Deployed (D)
         ii. Mobilised and Deployed (MD)
         iii. Mobilised and Not Deployed (MND)
      b. Supply and Support Infrastructure
      c. Reserves and Replacements (R)
         i. Replacements (R)
         ii. Campaign Start Reserves
         iii. Campaign Reserves
   4) Combat Unit Processes inside the FILARM Model
      a. Checking the TOE Authorisation of a Deployed (D) Combat Unit
      b. Check the TOE Authorisation of a MD or MND Combat Unit
      c. The Combat Process
         i. Key Terms and Concepts used in the Combat Process
         ii. Outcomes of the Combat Process
      d. The Attrition Process
         i. Outcomes of the Attrition Process

e.   The Disband and Shatter process
   i.   Combat Unit Shattering
   ii.   Combat Unit Disbandment

4.   The Structure of the Partially Integrated Land and Air Resource Model (PILARM)

1)   Resource Sources, Destinations and Paths outside the PILARM Model
2)   Resource Allocation States inside the PILARM Model
   a.   Combat Units: D and Reinforcement Units
     i.   Deployed (D)
     ii.   Reinforcement Units
   b.   Reserves and Replacements (R)
     i.   Replacements (R)
     ii.   Front Campaign Reserves
3)   Combat Unit Processes inside the PILARM Model
   a.   Check the TOE Authorisation of a Reinforcement Combat Unit

5.   The Order of Battle (OOB): the Force Deployment Matrices

6.   Tables of Organisation and Equipment (TOE)

1)   TOE Representation in a Table Format

7.   The Heterogeneous vs. the Homogeneous Model

1)   The Heterogeneous Model
2)   The Homogeneous Model and the use of Checksums

8.   Supply Distribution Efficiency (SDE)

1)   Supply Lift
2)   Supply Demand

9.   A Divisional Sized or Division Equivalent Combat Unit in WWII

1)   What was a Divisional Sized Combat Unit in 1941?
2)   Measuring Whether a Combat Unit can Reasonably be Called a Divisional Sized Combat Unit

Table of Contents, Volume I Part II: The Methodology Used for Analysing Weapon System Effectiveness, and the Structure of the 1941 Soviet and Axis Resource Database

1.   The Database Resolution Level

1)   Database Unit Resources in the Integrated Land and Air Resource Model

2.   Methodology for Calculating a Weapon System's or Database Unit's Overall Combat Power Coefficient (OCPC)

1)   Calculating Individual Weapon Combat Power Coefficients (WCPCs)
   a.   Rate of Fire (RF)
   b.   Number of Potential Targets per Strike (PTS)
   c.   Relative Incapacitating Effect (RIE)
   d.   Range Factors (RN)
   e.   Accuracy (A)
   f.   Reliability (RL)
   g.   Self-Propelled Artillery Factor (SPA
   h.   Aircraft Mounted Weapon Effect (AE)
   i.   Multi Barrelled Effect (MBE)
   j.   Typical Target Dispersion Factor (TDi)

2) Calculating a Non-Mobile Weapon System's or Squad's Overall Combat Power Coefficient (OCPC)
   a. Tactical Responsiveness Factor (TRF)
   b. Fire Control Effect (FCE)
   c. Concealment and Protection Factor (CPF)
   d. Defensive Dispersion Factor (DDF)
3) Calculating a Land Based, Motorised Mobile Fighting Machine's (MFM's) Overall Combat Power Coefficient (OCPC)
   a. MFM Weapons and Multi Barrelled Effect rules
   b. Battlefield Mobility Factor (MOF)
   c. Range of Action (RA)
   d. Protection Factor (PR)
   e. Shape and Size Factor (SSF)
      i. SSF Modifications due to Sloped Armour
      ii. SSF Modifications due to Size, Height and Shot Traps
   f. Open Top Factor (OTF)
   g. Rapidity of Fire Effect (RFE)
   h. Fire Control Effect (FCE)
      i. Turret Crew Efficiency (TCE)
      ii. Main gun Optics Quality (OPQ)
      iii. Turret Basket Effect (TBE)
      iv. Turret Drive Reliability (TDR)
      v. Target observation and Indicator Devices (TID)
   i. Ammunition Supply Effect (ASE)
   j. Half Track-Wheeled Effect (WHT)
4) Calculating an Aircraft's Overall Combat Power Coefficient (OCPC)
   a. Aircraft Mounted Weapons and Multi Barrel Effect Rules
   b. Aircraft Launched Weapons
   c. Battlefield Mobility Factor (MOF)
   d. Radius of Action (RA)
   e. Durability Factor (DUR)
   f. Aircraft Shape and Size Factor (SSF)
   g. Maximum speed and Manoeuvrability Factor (SpMvr)
   h. Ceiling Effect Factor (CL)

3. **Methodology for Calculating a Weapon System's or Database Unit's Specific Combat Attributes**

1) Relative Overall Attack Factor (ATT) and Relative Overall Defence Factor (DEF)
2) Effective Combat Ranges (R) and Aircraft Combat Radius (R)
3) Relative Anti-Personnel Value (APer)
4) Relative Anti-Armour Value (AT)
   a. Relative Anti-Armour Value (AT) for Land Based Weapon Systems and Squads
   b. Relative Anti-Armour Value (AT) for Aircraft
5) Relative Anti-Aircraft Value (AA)
   a. Relative Anti-Aircraft Value (AA) for Land Based Weapon Systems and Squads
   b. Relative Anti-Aircraft Value (AA) for Aircraft
6) Relative Fortification Destruction Effect (FDE)
7) Relative Armour Defence Strength (ARM)
8) Relative Assault Defence Strength (ADS) and Relative Assault Attack Strength (AAS)
   a. Relative Assault Defence Strength (ADS)
   b. Relative Assault Attack Strength (AAS)
9) Relative Overall Mobility (MOB)

10) Supply Demand Factor (SDF)
  a.   SDF Values for Land Based Weapon Systems and Squads
  b.   SDF Values for Aircraft

4. Resource Database Comments and Conclusions

Appendix A

Armour Penetration Figures: Historical Test Results vs. Calculated Values

Appendix B

Combat Aircraft versus Armour during WWII: Factors to Consider in Calculating Aircraft Relative Anti-Armour Values (AT)

***

Appendix C

Table of Contents, Volume IIA: The German Armed Forces (Wehrmacht), Mobilisation and War Economy from June to December 1941

Introduction

1. **Overview of the Structure and Terms Used in the German Fully Integrated Land and Air Resource Model (FILARM)**

    1) Chapter IIA - 2: The German Personnel and Equipment Resource Database

    2) Chapter IIA - 3: The Tables of Organisation and Equipment (TOE) for German Land Combat Units from 22nd June to 31st December 1941, and the Unit's Actual Organisation and Equipment in 1941

    3) Chapter IIB - 1: The Order of Battle (OOB) of German Land Combat Units from 22nd June to 4th July 1941

    4) Chapter IIB - 2: German Land Combat Unit Reinforcements on the East Front from 5th July to 31st December 1941

    5) Chapter IIB - 3: The Total Personnel and Equipment in a Deployed (D) State in the Reich from 22nd June to 4th July 1941

        a. Section IIB - 3 - 1): The Total Personnel and Equipment Allocated to Combat Units and in a Deployed (D) state in the German Army, Waffen SS, Luftwaffe Ground Forces and Naval Coastal Artillery from 22nd June to 4th July 1941

        b. Section IIB - 3 - 2): The Total Available Personnel and Equipment in the Reich on 1st June 1941

        c. Section IIB - 3 - 3): The Proportion of Total Available Resources which were in a Deployed (D) State in the Reich from 22nd June to 4th July 1941

    6) Chapter IIB - 4: German Mobilisation after 22nd June 1941: the Actual Strength of German Land Combat Units Mobilised from 22nd June to 31st December 1941

        a. Section IIB - 4 - 3): The Total Resources Allocated to Newly Mobilised Combat Units from 22nd June to 31st December 1941

        b. Section IIB - 4 - 4): The Total Resources in the Reich that were Available for Use by Newly Mobilised Units from 22nd June to 31st December 1941

        c. Section IIB - 4 - 5): Resources Unallocated to any Deployed (D), MD or MND Units in 1941

        d. Section IIB - 4 - 6): The Proportion of Total Available Resources Allocated to Deployed (D) and Newly Mobilised Units in 1941

        e. Section IIB - 4 - 7): The Resource Replacements (R) Available to the German Army, Waffen SS, Luftwaffe Ground Forces and Naval Coastal Artillery, from 22nd June to 31st December 1941

    7) Chapter IIB - 5: The Luftwaffe in 1941

        a. Section IIB - 5 - 1): The Structure of the Luftwaffe: June to December 1941

        b. Section IIB - 5 - 2): The Order of Battle and Actual Strength of all Luftwaffe Air Combat Units in a Deployed (D) State on 21st June 1941

        c. Section IIB - 5 - 3): Luftwaffe Strengths on 21st June 1941

        d. Section IIB - 5 - 4): Luftwaffe Air Combat Unit Reinforcements: June to December 1941

        e. Section IIB - 5 - 5): Overall Luftwaffe Combat Aircraft Usage, Production and Replacements (R): 22nd June to 31st December 1941

    8) Chapter IIB - 6: The Supply Distribution Efficiency (SDE) for the Wehrmacht on the East Front from 22nd June to 31st December 1941

    9) Chapter IIB - 7: German Naval Forces on the East Front: June to December 1941

    10) Chapter IIB - 8: Whermacht and Waffen SS Casualties from June 1941 to February 1942

2. **The German Personnel and Equipment Resource Database**

    1) German Light Infantry Weapons

    a.   Machine Guns

    b.   Small Arms

        i.   Rifles

        ii.   Sub Machine Guns

        iii.   Side Arms

        iv.   Hand Grenades

        v.   Rifle Grenades

2) German Squads Equipped with Light Infantry Weapons

    a.   Motorised Infantry Squads (*Schützen*)

    b.   Combat Engineer Squads (*Pionier*)

        i.   The Use and Availability of Mines in German *Pionier* Units in 1941

3) Heavy Infantry Weapons

    a.   Anti-Tank Rifles

    b.   Anti-Tank Guns (AT Guns)

        i.   3.7cm *Panzerabwehrkanone* 36 (PaK 36)

        ii.   5cm Panzerabwehrkanone 38 (PaK 38)

        iii.   4.7cm Panzerabwehrkanone (f) (Pak(f))

        iv.   2.8cm *schwere Panzerbüchse* 41 (s.Pzb 41)

    c.   Mortars

        i.   Granatwerfer 36 (GrW 36)

        ii.   Granatwerfer 34 (GrW 34)

    d.   Infantry Guns

        i.   7.5cm leichtes Infanteriegeschütz 18 (le IG 18)

        ii.   15cm schweres Infanteriegeschütz 33 (sIG 33)

4) Artillery Weapons

    a.   Light Divisional Artillery (75-105mm Guns, Howitzers, Gun-Howitzers)

        i.   75mm Field Guns

        ii.   75mm Mountain Guns

        iii.   105mm Howitzers

        iv.   Recoilless (RCL) Guns

    b.   Medium to Heavy Divisional Artillery (122-155mm Howitzers)

    c.   Heavy Corps Artillery (100-152mm Guns-Cannons)

    d.   Super Heavy Corps Artillery (200mm Plus; Guns, Howitzers and Mortars)

    e.   Railway Artillery

    f.   Coastal Artillery (East Front)

    g.   Rocket Artillery

5) Anti-Aircraft Weapons

    a.   Light to Medium AA guns (20-40mm)

    b.   Heavy AA guns (75-105mm)

6) Tanks

    a.   Panzerkampfwagen I

    b.   Panzerkampfwagen II

    c.   Panzerkampfwagen III

    d.   Panzerkampfwagen IV

    e.   Panzerkampfwagen 35(t)

    f.   Panzerkampfwagen 38(t)

    g.   Panzerkampfwagen 35-S 739(f)

    h.   Panzerkampfwagen 38-H 735(f)

    i.   Panzerkampfwagen B-2 740(f)

7) Command Tanks

    a.   Kleine Panzerbefehlswagen

    b.   Grosse Panzerbefehlswagen

    c.   Panzerkampfwagen 35-R 731(f)

8) Assault Guns
    a.   Sturmgeschütz III
9) Self-Propelled Artillery, Anti-Aircraft and Anti-Tank Guns (Tank Destroyers)
    a.   15cm sIG33(Sf) auf Panzerkampfwagen I Ausf B
    b.   2cm FlaK auf Fahrgestell Zugkraftwagen 1t (Sd Kfz 10/4)
    c.   Truck with Rear Mounted 2cm Flak 38 (Kfz 81)
    d.   3.7cm FlaK36 auf Fahrgestell Zugkraftwagen 5t (Sd Kfz 6/2)
    e.   2cm Flakvierling 38 auf Fahrgestell Zugkraftwagen 8t (Sd Kfz 7/1)
    f.   8.8cm FlaK 18(Sfl) auf Zugkraftwagen 12t (Sd Kfz 8) and auf Zugkraftwagen 18t (Sd Kfz 9)
    g.   10.5cm K18 auf Panzer Selbstfahrlafette IVa
    h.   4.7cm PaK(t) (Sf) auf Panzerkampfwagen I Ausf B
    i.   4.7cm PaK(t) auf Panzerkampfwagen 35R(f) ohne Turm
10) Flame-Thrower Tanks
    a.   Panzerkampfwagen II Flamm (Sd Kfz 122)
    b.   Flammwagen auf Panzerkampfwagen B-2(f)
11) Reconnaissance, Signal and Observation AFVs
    a.   Leichte Panzerspähwagen (MG) (Sd Kfz 221)
    b.   Leichte Panzerspähwagen (2cm) (Sd Kfz 222)
    c.   Schwere Panzerspähwagen (Sd Kfz 231/232) 8-Rad
    d.   Panzerspähwagen Panhard 178-P204(f)
    e.   Leichte Panzerspähwagen (Fu) (Sd Kfz 223)
    f.   Kleine Panzerfunkwagen (Sd Kfz 260/261)
    g.   Panzerfunkwagen (Sd Kfz 263) 8-Rad
    h.   Leichte Gepanzerte Beobachtungskraftwagen (Sd Kfz 253)
    i.   Mittlere Gepanzerte Beobachtungskraftwagen (Sd Kfz 254)
    j.   Schwere geländegängige gepanzerte Personenkraftwagen (Sd Kfz 247)
12) Armoured Personnel Carriers (APCs)
    a.   Mittlere Schützenpanzerwagen (Sd Kfz 251)
    b.   Leichte Schützenpanzerwagen (Sd Kfz 250)
13) Armoured Ammunition Carriers
    a.   Leichte Gepanzerte Munitionskraftwagen (Sd Kfz 252)
14) Miscellaneous AFVs and Armoured Trains
    a.   Minenräumwagen (Sd Kfz 300)
    b.   Brückenleger IV
    c.   Munitionsschlepper für Karlgerät
    d.   Armoured Trains (Eisenbahn Panzerzuge)
15) Transport and Prime Movers
    a.   Horse Teams
    b.   Motor Vehicle Nomenclature and Development History
        i.   The Einheits Vehicle Program
        ii.   The Schell Vehicle Program
    c.   Light Transports
    d.   Trucks
    e.   Motorcycles
    f.   Light Half-Tracks
        i.   Leichter Zugkraftwagen 1-ton (Sd Kfz 10)
        ii.   Leichter Zugkraftwagen 3-ton (Sd Kfz 11)
    g.   Medium Half-Tracks
        i.   Mittlerer Zugkraftwagen 5-ton (Sd Kfz 6)
        ii.   Mittlerer Zugkraftwagen 8-ton (Sd Kfz 7)
    h.   Heavy Half-Tracks
        i.   Schwerer Zugkraftwagen 12-ton (Sd Kfz 8)

      ii.   Schwerer Zugkraftwagen 18-ton (Sd Kfz 9)

16) German Aircraft

17) Fighter Aircraft

    a.   Messerschmitt Bf 109

18) Fighter Bomber Aircraft

    a.   Messerschmitt Bf 110

19) Ground Attack and Close Support Aircraft

    a.   Junkers Ju 87

    b.   Henschel Hs 123

20) Bomber Aircraft

    a.   Junkers Ju 88

    b.   Heinkel He 111

    c.   Dornier Do 17

21) Short Range Reconnaissance, Army Cooperation and Support Aircraft

    a.   Henschel Hs 126

    b.   Focke-Wulf Fw 189

22) Long Range Reconnaissance Aircraft

    a.   Junkers Ju 86P

23) Transport Aircraft

    a.   Junkers Ju 52

    b.   Fieseler Fi 156

    c.   DFS 230

    d.   Messerschmitt Me 321

24) Coastal Aviation, Patrol and Anti-Ship Aircraft

    a.   Heinkel He 59

    b.   Heinkel He 60

    c.   Heinkel He 114

    d.   Heinkel He115

    e.   Arado Ar 196

    f.   Blohm und Voss Bv 138

    g.   Dornier Do 18

    h.   Dornier Do 24

3. The Tables of Organisation and Equipment (TOE) for German Land Combat Units from 22nd June to 31st December 1941, and the Unit's Actual Organisation and Equipment in 1941

1)   Tables of Organisation - *Kriegsstärkenachweisungen* (KStN)

2)   German Army Infantry Units

    a.   Infantry Division Waves (*Welle*)

    b.   Ist Wave Infantry Divisions

        i.   The German Division's Organisation and Equipment: Enhanced Combat Efficiency

        ii.   Ist Wave Infantry Division Variations: Actual Organisation and Equipment

    c.   2nd Wave Infantry Divisions

        i.   2nd Wave Infantry Division Variations: Actual Organisation and Equipment

    d.   3rd Wave Infantry Divisions

        i.   3rd Wave Infantry Division Variations: Actual Organisation and Equipment

    e.   4th Wave Infantry Divisions

        i.   4th Wave Infantry Division Variations: Actual Organisation and Equipment

    f.   5th Wave Infantry Divisions

        i.   5th Wave Infantry Division Variations: Actual Organisation and Equipment

    g.   6th Wave Infantry Divisions

        i.   6th Wave Infantry Division Variations: Actual Organisation and Equipment

 h. 7th Wave Infantry Divisions
  i. 7th Wave Infantry Division Variations: Actual Organisation and Equipment
 i. 8th Wave Infantry Divisions
  i. 8th Wave Infantry Division Variations: Actual Organisation and Equipment
 j. 11th Wave Infantry Divisions
  i. 11th Wave Infantry Division Variations: Actual Organisation and Equipment
 k. 12th Wave Infantry Divisions
  i. 12th Wave Infantry Division Variations: Actual Organisation and Equipment
 l. 12th Wave Light (*Jäger*) Infantry Divisions
  i. 12th Wave Light Infantry Division Variations: Actual Organisation and Equipment
 m. 13th Wave Static Infantry Divisions
  i. 13th Wave Static Infantry Division Variations: Actual Organisation and Equipment
 n. 14th Wave Static Infantry Divisions
  i. 14th Wave Static Infantry Division Variations: Actual Organisation and Equipment
 o. 15th Wave Occupation (Static) Infantry Divisions
  i. 15th Wave Occupation Infantry Division Variations: Actual Organisation and Equipment
 p. An Overview of the Distribution of Equipment in German 1st -15th Wave Infantry Divisions on 22nd June 1941
  i. Anti-Tank Gun Distribution by Type
  ii. Field Artillery Distribution by Type
  iii. Motor Vehicle Distribution by Nationality
 q. 17th Wave Infantry Divisions
  i. 17th Wave Infantry Division Variations: Actual Organisation and Equipment
 r. The 250th Infantry Division (the Spanish Blue Division)
 s. Separate Infantry Regiments
 t. Separate Infantry Battalions
3) German Army Armoured and Mechanised Units
 a. Panzer Divisions
  i. 1940 Panzer Divisions vs 1941 Panzer Divisions
  ii. German Panzer Division TOE vs Soviet Tank Division TOE, June 1941
  iii. Equipment Shortages and Variations in Panzer Divisions, June 1941
  iv. 1st Panzer Division: Actual Organisation and Equipment
  v. 2nd Panzer Division: Actual Organisation and Equipment
  vi. 3rd Panzer Division: Actual Organisation and Equipment
  vii. 4th Panzer Division: Actual Organisation and Equipment
  viii. 5th Panzer Division: Actual Organisation and Equipment
  ix. 6th Panzer Division: Actual Organisation and Equipment
  x. 7th Panzer Division: Actual Organisation and Equipment
  xi. 8th Panzer Division: Actual Organisation and Equipment
  xii. 9th Panzer Division: Actual Organisation and Equipment
  xiii. 10th Panzer Division: Actual Organisation and Equipment
  xiv. 11th Panzer Division: Actual Organisation and Equipment
  xv. 12th Panzer Division: Actual Organisation and Equipment
  xvi. 13th Panzer Division: Actual Organisation and Equipment
  xvii. 14th Panzer Division: Actual Organisation and Equipment
  xviii. 15th Panzer Division: Actual Organisation and Equipment
  xix. 16th Panzer Division: Actual Organisation and Equipment
  xx. 17th Panzer Division: Actual Organisation and Equipment
  xxi. 18th Panzer Division: Actual Organisation and Equipment
  xxii. 19th Panzer Division: Actual Organisation and Equipment
  xxiii. 20th Panzer Division: Actual Organisation and Equipment
  xxiv. 5th Light Division (21st Panzer Division): Actual Organisation and Equipment
  xxv. 22nd Panzer Division, September 1941
  xxvi. 23rd Panzer Division, September 1941
  xxvii. 24th Panzer Division, December 1941
 b. Separate Panzer Brigades
  i. 100th Independent Panzer Brigade

      ii.   101st Independent Panzer Brigade
   c.   Separate Panzer Regiments
      i.   203rd Panzer Regiment
   d.   Separate Panzer Battalions and Panzer Companies
      i.   40th Special Panzer Battalion (zbV)
      ii.   211th Panzer Battalion
      iii. Panzer-Kompanie Paris
      iv. 5th Company/Panzer Regiment 31
      v.   212th Panzer Battalion
      vi. 213th Panzer Battalion
      vii. Panzer Kompanie FG z.b.V.12
   e.   Flame-Panzer Battalions
      i.   100th and 101st Flame-Panzer Battalions
      ii.   102nd Flame-Panzer Battalion
   f.   Assault Gun Battalions
   g.   Self-Propelled Panzerjäger Battalions (Armoured)

4)   German Army Motorised Units
   a.   Motorised Divisions
      i.   Motorised Division Variations: Actual Organisation and Equipment
   b.   Separate Motorised Infantry Brigades
      i.   900th Motorised Demonstration Brigade (*Lehr-Brigade* 900)
   c.   Separate Motorised Infantry Regiments
      i.   Gross-Deutschland Motorised Infantry Regiment
      ii.   Lehr Regiment Brandenburg (800 zbV)
   d.   Separate Motorised Infantry Battalions
      i.   Führer Escort Battalion *(Führer-Begleit-Bataillon* – FBB)
      ii.   100th Special Motorised Infantry Battalion (for Special Purpose - zbV)
      iii. 300th Special Motorised Infantry Battalion (for Special Purpose - zbV)

5)   German Army Cavalry Units
   a.   1st Cavalry Division

6)   German Army Mountain Units
   a.   Mountain Divisions
      i.   Mountain Division Variations: Actual Organisation and Equipment
   b.   Separate Mountain Units

7)   Luftwaffe Airborne Units
   a.   7th Fleiger Division
   b.   Separate Airborne Units
      i.   1st Luftlande Sturm Regiment

8)   German Army, Military-Police and Police, Security, Guard and Militia Units
   a.   Security Divisions
      i.   Security Division Variations: Actual Organisation and Equipment
   b.   Separate Security Brigades
      i.   16th Wave Replacement (*Ersatz*) Brigades
   c.   Separate Security Regiments
   d.   Separate Guard Battalions (*Wachbataillon*)
   e.   The Landesschützen Force and Militia Battalions (Landesschützen-Bataillon)
   f.   Military Police Units
      i.   Motorised Military Police Battalions
      ii.   Motorised Traffic Control Battalions
   g.   Ordnungspolizei Forces
      i.   HQ Motorised Police Regiment (*Polizei-Regiment (motorisiert)*)
      ii.   Police Rifle Battalions (*Polizei-Bataillon*)
   h.   Naval Security Battalions

9)   Waffen SS Combat Units

a. Waffen SS Motorised Divisions
   i. SS Das Reich Motorised Division
   ii. SS Totenkopf Motorised Division
   iii. SS Wiking Motorised Division

b. Waffen SS Motorised Brigades
   i. Leibstandarte SS Adolf Hitler (LSSAH) Motorised Brigade
   ii. SS Kampfgruppe Nord (Brigade-Nord)
   iii. 1st SS Brigade Reichsführer
   iv. 2nd (mot) Brigade Reichsführer SS

c. Waffen SS Cavalry Units
   i. SS *Kavallerie* Regiment 1 and SS *Kavallerie* Regiment 2

d. *Polizei* Division (SS)

e. Separate Waffen SS *Freiwilligen* (Volunteer) Infantry Regiments and Battalions
   i. SS Freiwilligen Legion Niederlande
   ii. SS Freiwilligen Legion Flandern
   iii. Finnisches Freiwilligen Bataillon der Waffen SS
   iv. SS Freiwilligen Verband Danemark / Freikorps Danmark
   v. SS Freiwilligen Legion Norwegen

10) **German Army Corps, Army and Army Group Level Units**

a. Higher Headquarter (HQ) Units
   i. Army Group HQs
   ii. Army HQs
   iii. Panzer Group HQs
   iv. Army Corps HQs
   v. Special Corps Command HQs (*Hohere Kommando* z.b.V.)
   vi. Motorised (Panzer) Corps HQs
   vii. Commander of the Army Group Rear Area (RHG) HQ

b. Higher Headquarters Signal Units
   i. Army Group / Army Signal Regiments
   ii. Army Group / Army Signal Battalions
   iii. Panzer Group Signal Regiments

c. Artillery Units
   i. Artillery Headquarter Units (*Harko, Arko* and *z.b.V.* HQs)
   ii. Motorised Artillery Observation Battalions
   iii. Motorised Heavy 150mm Field Howitzer Battalions
   iv. Motorised Heavy 105mm Gun Battalions
   v. Motorised Mixed Artillery Battalions
   vi. Motorised Heavy 150mm Gun Battalions
   vii. Motorised Heavy 210mm Howitzer Battalions (Type 1 and 2)
   viii. Motorised Heavy 210mm Gun Battalions
   ix. Motorised Heavy 240mm Howitzer Battalions
   x. Motorised Heavy 240mm Gun Battalions
   xi. Motorised Super Heavy Howitzer Battalions
   xii. German Railroad Artillery Battalions and Batteries
   xiii. Coastal Artillery Battalions and Batteries
   xiv. Horse-Drawn Corps and Miscellaneous Artillery Units

d. Rocket Artillery (*Nebelwerfer*) Units
   i. Motorised Special Rocket Launcher Regiment HQs
   ii. Motorised Rocket Launcher Regiments
   iii. Motorised Rocket Launcher Battalions
   iv. Motorised Decontamination Battalions

e. Anti-Tank Units
   i. Motorised Anti-Tank Battalions
   ii. Self-Propelled Heavy Anti-Tank Companies

f. Army Anti-Aircraft (Flak) Units
   i. Motorised Army Anti-Aircraft Battalions
   ii. Mechanised Army Light Anti-Aircraft Companies
   iii. Mechanised Army Light Anti-Aircraft Battalions

g.   Machine Gun Battalions

h.   Combat Engineer (*Pionier)* and Engineer Units

    i.   Motorised Special Engineer Regiment HQs

    ii.   Motorised Combat Engineer (*Pionier)* Battalions

    iii.   Combat Engineer (*Pionier*) Battalions

    iv.   Motorised Engineer Bridge Construction Battalions

    v.   Engineer Bridge Construction Battalions

    vi.   Motorised Assault Boat Companies

    vii.   Motorised Type B Bridge Columns

    viii.   Separate Bridge Columns: Type (A-T)

    ix.   Armoured Mine Clearing Battalion

i.   Army Construction Units

    i.   Army Construction HQs

    ii.   Construction Battalions

    iii.   Road Construction Battalions

    iv.   Motorised Snow Clearing Sections

j.   Armoured Trains

k.   Railroad Engineer (*Eisenbahn Pionier*) and Construction Units

    i.   Railroad Engineering Regiment HQs

    ii.   Railroad Engineering Battalion HQs

    iii.   Railroad Pionier Companies

    iv.   Railroad Switching Companies

    v.   Railroad Engineer Construction Companies and Battalions

11) Luftwaffe Anti-Aircraft (Flak) Units

a.   Luftwaffe Flak HQs

b.   Luftwaffe Mixed Flak Battalions

c.   Luftwaffe Light Flak Battalions

12) Review of the Authorised Sizes of German Divisions and Brigades, from 22nd June to 31st December 1941

13) The Principal Regiments and Battalions, Assigned to German Army and SS Divisions and Brigades in 1941

***

Appendix D

Table of Contents, Volume IIIA: The Soviet Armed Forces, Mobilisation and War Economy from June to December 1941

The following is the Table of Contents for Volume IIIA. It is subject to change, although any changes will comprise additional content.

***

Introduction

1. Overview of the Structure and Terms Used in the Soviet Fully Integrated Land and Air Resource Model (FILARM)

2. The Soviet Personnel and Equipment Resource Database

1) Soviet Light Infantry Weapons
   a. Machine Guns
   b. Small Arms
2) Soviet Squads Equipped with Light Infantry Weapons
3) Heavy Infantry Weapons
   a. Anti-Tank Rifles
   b. Anti-Tank Guns (AT Guns)
   c. Mortars
   d. Infantry Guns
4) Artillery Weapons
   a. Light Divisional Artillery (75-105mm Guns, Howitzers, Gun-Howitzers)
   b. Medium to Heavy Divisional Artillery (122-155mm Howitzers)
   c. Heavy Corps Artillery (100-152mm Guns-Cannons)
   d. Super Heavy Corps Artillery (200-305mm Guns, Howitzers and Mortars)
   e. Railway and Coastal Artillery
   f. Rocket Artillery
5) Anti-Aircraft Weapons
   a. Anti-Aircraft Machine Guns (AAMGs)
   b. Light to Medium AA guns (20-40mm)
   c. Heavy AA guns (75-105mm)
6) Tanks
   a. T-27 Tankette
   b. T-37 Amphibious Tankette
   c. T-38 Amphibious Tankette
   d. T-40 Amphibious Tankette
   e. T-26 Light Tank
      i. The T-26 and Fire Control Efficiency
   f. T-50 Light Tank
   g. T-60 Light Tank
   h. BT-2 and BT-5 Fast Tanks
   i. BT-7 Fast Tank
   j. T-28 Medium Tank
   k. T-34 Medium Tank
      i. The T-34 in WWII: the Legend vs. the Performance
   l. T-35 Heavy Tank
   m. KV-1 Heavy Tank
      i. KV-1 Shortcomings during 1941-42
   n. KV-2 Heavy Tank
7) Armoured Cars
   a. Light and Medium Armoured Cars
      i. BA-27 and BA-27M Medium Armoured Car
      ii. D-8 and D-12 Light Armoured Cars
      iii. D-13 Medium Armoured Car
      iv. FAI and FAI-M Light Armoured Car
      v. BA-20 and BA-20M Light Armoured Cars

    b.   Heavy Armoured Cars
       i.   BAI Heavy Armoured Car
       ii.   BA-3 Heavy Armoured Car
       iii. BA-6 and BA-6M Heavy Armoured Cars
       iv.   BA-10 and BA-10M Heavy Armoured Cars
    c.   The Dearth of Soviet Wheeled and Semi-Tracked AFVs, and its Effect on the Success of 'Deep Battle'
8) Armoured Trains
9) Transport and Prime Movers
    a.   Horse Teams
    b.   Trucks
       i.   *Gorkovsky Avtomobilny Zavod* (GAZ)
       ii.   *Zavod Imeni Stalina* (ZIS)
       iii. *Yaroslavskiy Auto Zavod* (YaAZ)
       iv.   Soviet Motor Vehicle production from 1941 to 1945, and the Effects of Lend Lease
       v.   Trucks in the Soviet FILARM Model
    c.   Light Transports
       i.   GAZ-A
       ii.   GAZ-M1 and GAZ-415
       iii. GAZ-11
       iv.   GAZ-61
       v.   GAZ-64
       vi.   ZIS-101 and ZIS-101A
       vii. KIM-10
       viii. Light Transports in the Soviet FILARM Model
    d.   Motorcycles
       i.   The Izhevsk Machine Building Plant (IZh)
       ii.   The Leningrad Motorcycle Factory (L, LMZ)
       iii. The Kharkov Motorcycle Factory (KhMZ)
       iv.   The Taganrog Machine Tool Works (TIZ)
       v.   The Podolsk Mechanical Factory (PMZ)
       vi.   The Moscow Motorcycle Factory (MMZ)
    e.   Tractors (Prime Movers)
       i.   T-27 Tankette, Light Tractor
       ii.   T-20 Komsomolets, Light Armoured Tractor
       iii. *Chelyabinskiy Traktornyy Zavod* (ChTZ)
       iv.   ChTZ S-60 Medium-Heavy Tractor Stalinets
       v.   ChTZ S-65 Heavy Tractor Stalinets
       vi.   S-2 High Speed Heavy Tractor Stalinets
       vii. *Stalingradskiy Traktornyy Zavod* (STZ)
       viii. *Kharkovskiy Traktornyy Zavod* (KhTZ)
       ix.   STZ-3 Medium Tractor
       x.   STZ-5 High Speed Medium Tractor
       xi.   *Kharkovskiy Parovoznyi Zavod* (KhPZ)
       xii. *Kommunar* Medium Tractor
       xiii. *Komintern* Medium-Heavy Tractor
       xiv. *Voroshilovets* Heavy Tractor
       xv.   Soviet Halftrack Vehicles
       xvi. ZIS-22 and ZIS-22M Halftracks
       xvii. GAZ-60 Halftrack
       xviii. ZIS-33 Halftrack
       xix. Tractors in the Soviet FILARM Model
10) Fighter Aircraft
    a.   Polikarpov I-16
    b.   Curtiss P-40
11) Fighter Bomber Aircraft
    a.   Polikarpov I-153, I-15bis and I-15
    b.   Yakovlev Yak-1
    c.   Lavochkin LaGG-3
    d.   Mikoyan-Gurevich MiG-1 and MiG-3
    e.   Petlyakov Pe-3bis
    f.   Hawker Hurricane IIB
12) Ground Attack and Close Support Aircraft
    a.   Ilyushin Il-2

      b.   Sukhoi SU-2
      c.   Arkangelski Ar-2
  13) Bomber Aircraft
      a.   Tupolev SB-2
      b.   Ilyushin DB-3/Il-4
      c.   Petlyakov Pe-2
      d.   Tupolev TB-3
      e.   Petlyakov Pe-8/TB-7
      f.   Yakovlev Yak-2/Yak-4
  14) Short Range Reconnaissance, Army Cooperation and Support Aircraft
      a.   Polikarpov R-5
      b.   Polikarpov R-Z
      c.   Nyeman R-10
      d.   Polikarpov U-2/Po-2
  15) Coastal Aviation, Patrol and Anti-Ship Aircraft
      a.   Beriev MBR-2/Be-2
      b.   Beriev KOR-1 (Beriev-2)
      c.   Beriev KOR-2 (Beriev-4)
      d.   Chyetverikov MDR-6 (Chye-2)
      e.   Tupolev MR-6 (R-6)
      f.   Heinkel HD-55 (KR-1)
      g.   Consolidated PBY (GST)

3. The Tables of Organisation and Equipment (TOE) for Soviet Land Combat Units from 22nd June to 31st December 1941

  1) Red Army Rifle Units
      a.   Rifle Divisions, 5th April 1941
      b.   Rifle Divisions, 29th July 1941
      c.   Rifle Divisions, 6th December 1941
      d.   Rifle Brigades, 22nd June 1941
      e.   Rifle Brigades, 15th October 1941
      f.   Ski Battalions, 1941
  2) Red Army Armoured, Mechanised and Motorised Units
      a.   A Brief History of Soviet Pre-War Mechanised Forces
      b.   Tank Divisions, 22nd June 1941
        i.   Soviet Tank Division TOE vs German Panzer Division TOE, June 1941
        ii.   The Soviet 1941 Tank Division and its failure in 'Deep Battle'
      c.   Tank Divisions, 10th July 1941
      d.   Tank Brigades, 1941
      e.   Mechanised Divisions, 22nd June 1941
      f.   Motorised Divisions, 22nd June 1941
      g.   Motorcycle Regiments, June 1941
  3) Red Army Cavalry Units
      a.   A Brief History of Soviet Pre-War Cavalry Forces
      b.   Cavalry Divisions 22nd June 1941
      c.   Mountain Cavalry Divisions, 22nd June 1941
      d.   Cavalry Divisions, 6th July 1941
  4) Red Army Mountain Units
      a.   A Brief History of Soviet Pre-War Mountain Forces
      b.   Mountain Rifle Divisions, 22nd June 1941
  5) Red Army Airborne Units
      a.   A Brief History of Soviet Pre-War Airborne Forces
      b.   Soviet Airborne Brigades, April 1941
      c.   Soviet Airborne Brigades, September 1941
  6) Soviet Naval Ground Combat Units
      a.   Soviet Naval Infantry Brigades, 22nd June 1941
      b.   Soviet Naval Rifle Brigades, 18th October 1941
  7) NKVD, the Overall Organisation and Combat Capable NKVD Units

    a.   NKVD Border Guard Forces
       i.   NKVD Border District HQs, June 1941
      ii.   NKVD Border Guard Detachments (Units), June 1941
     iii.   NKVD Border Regiments, post 22nd June 1941
     iv.   NKVD Remount Cavalry Regiments, June 1941
    b.   NKVD Rail Security Forces
       i.   NKVD Rail Security Division and Brigade HQs, June 1941
      ii.   NKVD Rail Security Battalions and Regiments, June 1941
     iii.   NKVD Armoured Security Trains, 1941
    c.   NKVD Industry Guard and Special Installation Security Forces
       i.   NKVD Industry Guard and Special Installation Security Division and Brigade HQs, June 1941
      ii.   NKVD Industry Guard and Special Installation Security Battalions and Regiments, June 1941
    d.   NKVD Convoy Escort Forces
       i.   NKVD Convoy Escort Division and Brigade HQs, June 1941
      ii.   NKVD Convoy Escort Battalions and Regiments, June 1941
    e.   NKVD Operational (Mobile) Forces
       i.   NKVD Motorised Rifle Division for Special Purpose, June 1941
      ii.   NKVD Separate Motorised Rifle Battalions and Regiments, June 1941
     iii.   NKVD Motorised Rifle Divisions, post 22nd June 1941
     iv.   NKVD Separate Cavalry Regiments, June 1941
      v.   NKVD Rifle Divisions, post 22nd June 1941
    f.   NKVD Kremlin Garrison, Separate Motorised Rifle Regiment
    g.   Political Officers (*Commissar*, *Politruk*, *Pompolit*, *Zampolit*)
8) Soviet Militia Units
    a.   Militia Rifle Divisions, 1941
    b.   Moscow Militia Rifle Divisions, 1941
    c.   Militia Fighter Battalions
9) Red Army Corps, Army and Front Level Units
    a.   Red Army Corps and Army Level Artillery Units
       i.   Corps Artillery Regiments
      ii.   RVGK Cannon and Howitzer Regiments
     iii.   RVGK Super Heavy Howitzer Regiments, (BM)
     iv.   RVGK High Power Artillery Battalions, (OM)
      v.   RVGK Mortar Battalions
     vi.   RVGK (Army) Artillery Regiments, September 1941
     vii.   RVGK Rocket Artillery Regiments and Battalions
    b.   Red Army Corps and Army Level Anti-Tank Units
       i.   RVGK Anti-Tank Brigades, April 1941
      ii.   Anti-Tank Regiments, July-November 1941
    c.   Red Army Corps and Army Level Anti-Aircraft Units
       i.   Army Anti-Aircraft Battalions
    d.   Red Army Corps and Army Level Engineer Units
       i.   Engineering Regiments and Battalions, June 1941
      ii.   Pontoon Bridge Regiments and Battalions, June 1941
     iii.   Army Construction Battalions
    e.   Soviet Headquarter (HQ) Units
       i.   Rifle Corps HQs
      ii.   Mechanised Corps HQs
     iii.   Cavalry Corps HQs
     iv.   Airborne Corps HQs
      v.   Army HQs
     vi.   Front HQs
     vii.   PVO Air Defence Corps HQs
10) Soviet Strategic Defence Ground Forces
    a.   PVO-strany, National Air Defence Ground Units
    b.   Fortified Sectors or Regions
    c.   Coastal Artillery
11) Railroad Artillery and Armoured Trains
    a.   Railroad Artillery
    b.   Armoured Trains

12) Review of the Authorised Sizes of Soviet Divisions and Brigades, from 22nd June to 31st December 1941
    a.   Pre-war Divisions and Brigades
    b.   Post-June 1941 divisions and brigades

13) The Principal Regiments and Battalions, Assigned to Red Army and NKVD Divisions and Brigades on 22nd June 1941

4. The Order of Battle (OOB) of Soviet Land Combat Units on 22nd June 1941

5. The Transfer Schedule of Soviet Land Combat Units, which were a Deployed (D) State, to the USSR's Western Fronts from 23rd June to 31st December 1941

1) The Siberian Divisions

6. The Actual Strength of all Soviet Land Combat Units in a Deployed (D) State on 22nd June 1941

1) Review of the Overall Strengths of Selected Red Army Units and PVO forces on 22nd June 1941
    a.   The Rifle Divisions
    b.   The Mechanised Corps
    c.   The AT Brigades
    d.   The Fortified Sectors
    e.   The PVO Ground Forces

2) The Leningrad Military District (Northern Front from 24th June 1941)
    a.   Rifle Divisions
    b.   1st Mechanised Corps
    c.   10th Mechanised Corps
    d.   The Hanko Peninsula Garrison
    e.   Leningrad Military District, Front, Army and Corps Support Units
    f.   Total Manpower and Equipment in the Leningrad Military District, 22nd June 1941

3) The Baltic Special Military District (Northwestern Front from 22nd June 1941)
    a.   Rifle Divisions
    b.   NKVD Rifle Divisions
    c.   5th Airborne Corps
    d.   3rd Mechanised Corps
    e.   12th Mechanised Corps
    f.   Garrisons on the Islands of Oesel (Saaremaa) and Dago (Hiiumaa)
    g.   Baltic Special Military District, Front, Army and Corps Support Units
    h.   Total Manpower and Equipment in the Baltic Special Military District, 22nd June 1941

4) The Western Special Military District (Western Front from 22nd June 1941)
    a.   Rifle Divisions
    b.   4th Airborne Corps
    c.   6th Cavalry Corps
    d.   6th Mechanised Corps
    e.   11th Mechanised Corps
    f.   13th Mechanised Corps
    g.   14th Mechanised Corps
    h.   17th Mechanised Corps
    i.   20th Mechanised Corps
    j.   Western Special Military District, Front, Army and Corps Support Units
    k.   Total Manpower and Equipment in the Western Special Military District, 22nd June 1941

5) The Kiev Special Military District (Southwestern Front from 22nd June 1941)
    a.   Rifle Divisions
    b.   Mountain Rifle Divisions
    c.   1st Airborne Corps
    d.   5th Cavalry Corps
    e.   4th Mechanised Corps
    f.   8th Mechanised Corps
    g.   9th Mechanised Corps
    h.   15th Mechanised Corps
    i.   16th Mechanised Corps

j.   19th Mechanised Corps

k.   22nd Mechanised Corps

l.   24th Mechanised Corps

m.   Kiev Special Military District, Front, Army and Corps Support Units

n.   Total Manpower and Equipment in the Kiev Special Military District, 22nd June 1941

6)   The Odessa Military District (Including the 9th Separate Army)

a.   Rifle Divisions

b.   Mountain Rifle Divisions

c.   3rd Airborne Corps

d.   Cavalry Divisions

e.   2nd Mechanised Corps

f.   18th Mechanised Corps

g.   Odessa Military District, Front, Army and Corps Support Units

h.   Total Manpower and Equipment in the Odessa Military District, 22nd June 1941

***

Appendix E

Table of Contents, Volume IIIB: The Soviet Armed Forces, Mobilisation and War Economy from June to December 1941

The following is the preliminary Table of Contents for Volume IIIB. It is subject to change, although any changes will comprise additional content.

***

Introduction

1. The Actual Strength of all Soviet Land Combat Units in a Deployed (D) State on 22nd June 1941

1) Reserves of the Stavka GK (Headquarters of the Main Command)
   a. The 16th Army
     i. Rifle Divisions
     ii. 5th Mechanised Corps and the Lepel Offensive Operation
     iii. Total Manpower and Equipment in the 16th Army, 22nd June 1941
   b. The 19th Army
     i. Rifle Divisions
     ii. 26th Mechanised Corps
     iii. Total Manpower and Equipment in the 19th Army, 22nd June 1941
   c. The 20th Army
     i. Rifle Divisions
     ii. 7th Mechanised Corps
     iii. Total Manpower and Equipment in the 20th Army, 22nd June 1941
   d. The 21st Army
     i. Rifle Divisions
     ii. 25th Mechanised Corps
     iii. Total Manpower and Equipment in the 21st Army, 22nd June 1941
   e. The 22nd Army
     i. Rifle Divisions
     ii. Total Manpower and Equipment in the 22nd Army, 22nd June 1941
   f. The 24th Army
     i. Rifle Divisions
     ii. Total Manpower and Equipment in the 24th Army, 22nd June 1941
   g. Separate Stavka Reserves
     i. Rifle Divisions
     ii. 21st Mechanised Corps
     iii. Total Manpower and Equipment in the Separate Stavka Reserves, 22nd June 1941
   h. Total Manpower and Equipment in the Reserves of the STAVKA GK, 22nd June 1941
2) Internal Military Districts and Non-Active Fronts
3) The Moscow Military District
   a. Rifle Divisions
   b. Moscow Military District, Front, Army and Corps Support Units
   c. Total Manpower and Equipment in the Moscow Military District, 22nd June 1941
4) The Orel Military District
   a. Rifle Divisions
   b. 23rd Mechanised Corps
   c. Orel Military District, Front, Army and Corps Support Units
   d. Total Manpower and Equipment in the Orel Military District, 22nd June 1941
5) The Kharkov Military District
   a. Rifle Divisions
   b. 2nd Airborne Corps
   c. Kharkov Military District, Front, Army and Corps Support Units
   d. Total Manpower and Equipment in the Kharkov Military District, 22nd June 1941
6) The Volga Military District
   a. Volga Military District, Front, Army and Corps Support Units
   b. Total Manpower and Equipment in the Volga Military District, 22nd June 1941
7) The North Caucasus Military District

- a. Rifle Divisions
- b. Mountain Rifle Divisions
- c. North Caucasus Military District, Front, Army and Corps Support Units
- d. Total Manpower and Equipment in the North Caucasus Military District, 22nd June 1941

8) The Transcaucasus Military District
- a. Rifle Divisions
- b. Mountain Rifle Divisions
- c. Cavalry and Mountain Cavalry Divisions
- d. 28th Mechanised Corps
- e. Transcaucasus Military District, Front, Army and Corps Support Units
- f. Total Manpower and Equipment in the Transcaucasus Military District, 22nd June 1941

9) The Archangel'sk Military District
- a. Rifle Divisions
- b. Archangel'sk Military District, Front, Army and Corps Support Units
- c. Total Manpower and Equipment in the Archangel'sk Military District, 22nd June 1941

10) The Ural Military District
- a. The Ural Military District, Front, Army and Corps Support Units
- b. Total Manpower and Equipment in the Ural Military District, 22nd June 1941

11) The Siberia Mlitary District
- a. The Siberia Military District, Front, Army and Corps Support Units
- b. Total Manpower and Equipment in the Siberia Military District, 22nd June 1941

12) The Central Asia Military District
- a. Rifle Divisions
- b. Mountain Rifle Divisions
- c. 4th Cavalry Corps
- d. 27th Mechanised Corps
- e. The Central Asia Military District, Front, Army and Corps Support Units
- f. Total Manpower and Equipment in the Central Asia Military District, 22nd June 1941

13) The Transbaikal Military District
- a. Motorised Rifle Divisions
- b. Separate Tank and Mechanised Divisions
- c. The Transbaikal Military District, Front, Army and Corps Support Units
- d. Total Manpower and Equipment in the Transbaikal Military District, 22nd June 1941

14) The Far Eastern Front
- a. Rifle Divisions
- b. Mountain Rifle Divisions
- c. Cavalry Divisions
- d. Rifle Brigades
- e. Airborne Brigades
- f. 30th Mechanised Corps
- g. Separate Tank and Mechanised Divisions
- h. The Far Eastern Front, Front, Army and Corps Support Units
- i. Total Manpower and Equipment in the Far Eastern Front, 22nd June 1941

15) The Soviet Tank Deployment Matrix
- a. The Deployment and Composition of Red Army and NKVD Armoured Forces on 22nd June 1941
- b. The Importance of Soviet Tank Deployment in June 1941
- c. A Comparison of the Numbers of Available Soviet and Wehrmacht AFVs during June - July 1941
- d. Soviet Tank Deployment and the Possible Intent of Stalin in 1941-1942
  - i. Evidence for the First Hypothesis: Invasion of Rumania and Hungary
  - ii. Evidence for the Second Hypothesis: Western Military District Screen Defence
  - iii. Evidence for the Third Hypothesis: Echeloned Defences and Counter-Attack
  - iv. Some Observations on the 'Lutsk-Rovno-Dubno-Lvov' Border Battle
  - v. Conclusion regarding the Possible Intent of Stalin in 1941-1942

16) Total Personnel and Equipment in the Soviet Army, NKVD, Air Force, PVO and Navy on 22nd June 1941
- a. Review of the Total Personnel and Equipment in the Armed Forces of the USSR on 22nd June 1941
  - i. Overall Review of Available Equipment, Other than Tanks and Aircraft
  - ii. Review of Available Motor Vehicles and Other Transport Types
  - iii. Review of Available Artillery Pieces and Mortars
  - iv. Review of Available Total Personnel

17) Total Personnel and Equipment Allocated to Combat Units and in a Deployed (D) state in the Soviet Army, NKVD, Air Force Ground Units, PVO Ground Units and Naval Ground Units on 22nd June 1941

    a.   Rear Area Transport Available for Supply Distribution on 22nd June 1941

18) The Proportion of Total Available Resources which were in a Deployed (D) State in the USSR on 22nd June 1941

2. Soviet Mobilisation After 22nd June 1941: the Actual Strength of all Soviet Land Combat Units Mobilised from 22nd June to 31st December 1941

1) The use of the Homogeneous Model to Study Soviet Ground Force Mobilisation after 22nd June 1941

2) Definition of Deployed (D), Mobilised and Deployed (MD), and Mobilised and Not Deployed (MND) in the Soviet FILARM Model

3) The MD and MND Matrices

    a.   The Structure of the MD and MND Matrices

        i.   FILARM Classification

        ii.   Combat Unit Designation

        iii.   Start Formation Date

        iv.   Formation Region

        v.   Primary Source of Personnel and Equipment

        vi.   Amount of Reserves Used

        vii.   Start Strength when Deployed (D)

        viii.   Completed Formation Date

        ix.   Deployment (D) Date

        x.   Where Deployed (D)

        xi.   Comments

        xii.   The Total Number of Combat Units Mobilised and Deployed (MD), and the Total Amount of Reserves Used by MD Units

        xiii.   The Total Number of Combat Units Mobilised and Not Deployed (MND), and the Total Amount of Reserves Used by MND Units

        xiv.   The Total Number of Combat Units Mobilised and the Total Amount of Reserves Used by All Mobilised Combat Units

        xv.   The Total Number of Combat Units Mobilised With a Specific TOE, and the Total Amount of Reserves Used by Mobilised Units which Used this TOE

    b.   Resources Used by Mobilised Combat Units with a Specific TOE

        i.   Reserve Personnel Allocated to MD Combat Units by Month

        ii.   Reserve Personnel Allocated to MD Combat Units by Month, Excluding Forces Remaining in the Transcaucasus in 1941

4) Red Army and Soviet Militia Rifle Units Mobilised from 22nd June to 31st December 1941

    a.   Rifle Divisions Mobilised from 22nd June to 31st December 1941

    b.   Militia Rifle Divisions Mobilised from 22nd June to 31st December 1941

    c.   Rifle Brigades Mobilised from 22nd June to 31st December 1941

    d.   Ski Units Mobilised from 22nd June to 31st December 1941

    e.   Militia Fighter Battalions Mobilised from 22nd June to 31st December 1941

5) Soviet Armoured, Mechanised and Motorised Units Mobilised from 22nd June to 31st December 1941

    a.   Tank Divisions Mobilised from 22nd June to 31st December 1941

    b.   Tank Brigades Mobilised from 22nd June to 31st December 1941

    c.   Mechanised Divisions Mobilised from 22nd June to 31st December 1941

6) Red Army Cavalry Units Mobilised from 22nd June to 31st December 1941

    a.   Cavalry Divisions Mobilised from 22nd June to 31st December 1941

    b.   Mountain Cavalry Divisions Mobilised from 22nd June to 31st December 1941

    c.   Cavalry Corps HQs Mobilised from 22nd June to 31st December 1941

7) Red Army Mountain Units Mobilised from 22nd June to 31st December 1941

    a.   Mountain Divisions Mobilised from 22nd June to 31st December 1941

8) Red Army Airborne Units Mobilised from 22nd June to 31st December 1941

    a.   Airborne Brigades Mobilised from 22nd June to 31st December 1941

    b.   Airborne Corps HQs Mobilised from 22nd June to 31st December 1941

9) Soviet Naval Ground Units Mobilised from 22nd June to 31st December 1941

    a.   Naval Infantry Brigades Mobilised from 22nd June to 31st December 1941

    b.   Naval Rifle Brigades Mobilised from 22nd June to 31st December 1941

10) NKVD Combat Units Mobilised from 22nd June to 31st December 1941
   a.   NKVD Motorised divisions Mobilised from 22nd June to 31st December 1941
   b.   NKVD Rifle Divisions Mobilised from 22nd June to 31st December 1941
   c.   NKVD Border Regiments Mobilised from 22nd June to 31st December 1941
   d.   NKVD Security or Rifle Brigades Mobilised from 22nd June to 31st December 1941

11) Red Army Corps and Army Level Units Mobilised from 22nd June to 31st December 1941
   a.   RVGK (Army) Artillery Regiments Mobilised from 22nd June to 31st December 1941
   b.   RVGK Mortar Battalions Mobilised from 22nd June to 31st December 1941
   c.   RVGK Rocket Artillery Regiments and Battalions Mobilised from 22nd June to 31st December 1941
   d.   Anti-Tank (AT) Regiments Mobilised from 22nd June to 31st December 1941
   e.   Anti-Aircraft (AA) Battalions Mobilised from 22nd June to 31st December 1941
   f.   RVGK Engineer and Construction Battalions Mobilised from 22nd June to 31st December 1941
   g.   Armoured Trains Mobilised from 22nd June to 31st December 1941
   h.   Soviet Army and Front HQs Mobilised from 22nd June to 31st December 1941
      i.   Army HQs Mobilised from 22nd June to 31st December 1941
      ii.   Front HQs Mobilised from 22nd June to 31st December 1941

12) Soviet Ground Forces Mobilised in the Far East from 22nd June to 31st December 1941
13) The Soviet Tank MD and MND Matrix
14) The Total Resources Allocated to Newly Mobilised Units from 22nd June to 31st December 1941
   a.   Rear Area Transport Available for Supply Distribution from 22nd June to 31st December 1941
15) The Total Resources in the USSR that were Available for Use by Newly Mobilised Units from 22nd June to 31st December 1941
   a.   Total Available Resources in the USSR Unallocated to Deployed (D) Units on 22nd June 1941
   b.   New Resources Produced and Received in the USSR from 22nd June to 31st December 1941
16) Resources Unallocated to any Deployed (D), MD or MND Units in 1941
17) The Proportion of Total Available Resources Allocated to Deployed (D) and Newly Mobilised Units in 1941
   a.   Conclusions in Regard to the Weaknesses, Bottlenecks and Constraints on the Soviet Mobilisation Process in 1941
      i.   Rear Area Support Unit
      ii.   Transport
      iii.   Machine Guns (MGs)
      iv.   Mortars
      v.   Anti-Tank (AT) and Divisional Field Guns
      vi.   Medium to Heavy artillery
      vii.   Tanks
      viii. Anti-Aircraft (AA) Weapons
18) The Resource Replacements (R) Available to the Red Army, NKVD, PVO and Soviet Militia from 22nd June to 31st December 1941
   a.   Small Arms Used by all Ground Combat Units in the USSR in 1941, including Replacements (R)
   b.   Personnel Used by all Types of Replacements (R)
   c.   The Timing of Replacements (R) in the Period June to December 1941

3.   The Soviet Air Forces in 1941

1)   The structure of the Soviet Air Forces (VVS): June to December 1941
   a.   The VVS Overall Command Structure
   b.   The Structure of the VVS KA Aviation Divisions: June 1941
   c.   The Structure of the VVS VMF Aviation Brigades: June 1941
   d.   The Structure of the VVS Aviation Divisions: July to December 1941
2)   The Order of Battle and Actual Strength of all Soviet Air Combat Units in a Deployed (D) State on 1st June 1941
   a.   Aircraft Serviceability and Numbers of Operational Aircraft
   b.   VVS-Leningrad Military District (Northern Front from 24th June 1941)
   c.   VVS-Baltic Special Military District (Northwestern Front from 22nd June 1941)
   d.   VVS-Western Special Military District (Western Front from 22nd June 1941)
   e.   VVS-Kiev Special Military District (Southwestern Front from 22nd June 1941)
   f.   VVS-Odessa Military District, Including 9th Separate Army (Southern Front)
   g.   VVS-Long Range Bomber Aviation (DBA)
   h.   VVS Forces in the Internal Military Districts
   i.   VVS-Far Eastern Front

3) The Soviet Aircraft Deployment Matrix
   a. The Composition of the Soviet VVS KA, VVS VMF and PVO Air Forces on 1st June 1941
   b. Numbers and Deployment of Modern Aircraft in the VVS on 1st June 1941, and comparison to the Luftwaffe's invasion forces
      i. Fighters
      ii. Ground Support-Ground Attack Aircraft
      iii. Bombers
   c. Soviet Aircraft Deployment and the Possible Intent of Stalin in 1941-1942
      i. Evidence for the First Hypothesis: Invasion of Rumania and Hungary
      ii. Evidence for the Second Hypothesis: Western Military District Screen Defence
      iii. Evidence for the Third Hypothesis: Echeloned Defences and Counter-Attack
4) Soviet Air Combat Unit Reinforcements: June 1941 to January 1942
   a. The Transfer of Deployed (D) Air Combat Units to the USSR's Western Fronts: June to December 1941
   b. Newly Mobilised VVS KA, VVS VMF and PVO Air Combat Units: June 1941 to January 1942
5) Overall Soviet Combat Aircraft Usage, Production and Replacements (R): 22nd June to 31st December 1941
   a. Review of the VVS Aircraft Losses in 1941

4. The Relative Supply Distribution Efficiency (SDE) for the Soviet Armed Forces from 22nd June to 31st December 1941

1) SDE for all Deployed (D) Land Combat Units on 22nd June 1941
2) SDE for all Deployed (D) Land Combat Units in the Western Military Districts on 22nd June 1941
3) SDE for all MD and MND Land Combat Units from 22nd June to 31st December 1941
4) SDE for all Deployed (D), MD and MND Land Combat Units from 22nd June to 31st December 1941
5) Inclusion of the Soviet Air Force's (VVS) Air Combat Units in the SDE Calculation
6) Parameters Relating Specifically to the Calculation of the Soviet Relative SDE in 1941
   a. Specific Weapon System or Squad Supply Demand Factors (SDFs)
   b. The Soviet Soldiers' Apparent Ability to 'Live Off the Land'
   c. Proportion of Available Rear Area Trucks, Tractors and Light Transports Allocated to Rear Area SDE functions
      i. Proportion Available on the 22nd June 1941
      ii. Proportion Available from the 22nd June to 31st December 1941
   d. Average Lift Capacity of Soviet Motorised Vehicles and Horse Teams: Measured in Metric Ton Kilometres per Day
      i. Average Transport Load Capacity (L)
      ii. Average Distance Moved Per Day (D)
      iii. Comparison of Average Soviet and German Lift Capacity (L*D)
7) Parameters Relating to the Calculation of Soviet and Axis Absolute Supply Levels During 1941
   a. Definition of Attack, General, Defensive and Minimal Supply
      i. Accumulation of Supplies over Time
      ii. Supply Levels and the Effect on Combat Operations at the Operational and Tactical Level
   b. Supply Level Attenuation with Distance from a Railhead or Supply Stockpile
   c. An Examination of the Soviet and German Rail Networks Available to Support Combat Operations on the East Front during 1941 and into 1942
8) Conclusions Relating to the Soviet Armed Force's SDE in 1941

5. Soviet Naval Forces: June to December 1941

1) VMF High Level Commands: June 1941
2) The Red Banner Baltic Fleet
   a. The Actual Strength of Soviet Naval Units in the Baltic: June 1941
   b. A Summary of Soviet Naval Operations and Naval Losses in the Baltic: June to December 1941
3) The Black Sea Fleet
   a. The Actual Strength of Soviet Naval Units in the Black Sea: June 1941
   b. A Summary of Soviet Naval Operations and Naval Losses in the Black Sea: June to December 1941
4) The Northern Fleet
   a. The Actual Strength of Soviet Naval Units in the Arctic Region: June 1941
   b. A Summary of Soviet Naval Operations and Naval Losses in the Arctic Region: June to December 1941

5) The Pacific Fleet
   a. The Actual Strength of Soviet Naval Units in the Pacific: June 1941
   b. A Summary of Soviet Naval Operations and Naval Losses in the Pacific: June to December 1941
6) Separate Inland Waterway Flotillas
7) Soviet Naval Vessel Reinforcements: July to December 1941

6. A Review of the Numbers and Strengths of Soviet Land Combat Units Mobilised from June to December 1941

1) The Number of Soviet Land Combat Units Mobilised and Deployed (MD) in 1941
2) The Authorised Strength (TOE) of Soviet Land Combat Units Mobilised in 1941
3) The Actual Strength of Soviet Land Combat Units Mobilised in 1941
4) The Number of Soviet Land Combat Units Mobilised in 1941, Including Divisional Equivalents Resulting from Replacements (R)
5) Soviet Combat Units Mobilised in the Moscow-Tula-Kalinin-Gorki Area in 1941
6) Soviet Losses in 1941, Measured in Terms of Divisional Equivalents
7) Comments and Conclusions Regarding the Soviet Mobilisation and War Philosophy

7. Soviet Armed Forces Casualties from June 1941 to March 1942

1) The Official Russian Figures, as of 2017
2) The Ongoing Discourse and Supplementary Figures Relating to Soviet 1941-42 Casualties

***

Selected Bibliography

As a complete work with six distinct volumes, *Operation Barbarossa: Complete Organisational and Statistical Analysis, and Military Simulation* uses hundreds of published and unpublished sources and references. Therefore the bibliography (below) only pertains to those sources referenced in Volumes I, IIA and IIB. A significant proportion of the works listed below are English translations of the original German work, and, where available, these have been listed. In other cases the original German version is shown.

Unpublished Sources

Bundesarchiv-Militararchiv, Freiburg, (Federal German Military Archives, Freiburg).

BA-MA III W 805/5 to 8. OKW/Wehrwirtschafts-und Rustungsamt (WiRuAmt) (OKW War Economy and Armaments Department).

BA-MA o.S. 234, Wall chart of the Ob.d.L as of 20th June 1941.

BA-MA RH 2/435D, Oberkommando des Heeres/Generalstab des Heeres (Army High Command/General Staff).

BA-MA RH 2/436, Oberkommando des Heeres/Generalstab des Heeres (Army High Command/General Staff).

BA-MA RH 2/v. 1343, Oberkommando des Heeres/Generalstab des Heeres (Army High Command/General Staff).

BA-MA RH 2/v. 2542, Oberkommando des Heeres/Generalstab des Heeres (Army High Command/General Staff).

BA-MA RH 8/v: IO35ff, IO52a, IO71b, IO88a, IO90, IO90a, IO91, IIIOa +b, OKH/Heereswaffenamt (mit Geschaftsbereich) (Army Ordnance Office (with range of authority)).

BA-MA RH II III/32, OKH/GenStdH/Operations-Abteilung (Op Abt) (OKH/Army General Staff/Operations Department).

BA-MA RL 2 III/700 to 734, R.d.L. u. OB.d.L./Generalstab d. Lw/Generalquartiermeister (Luftwaffe General staff/ Quartermaster-General).

BA-MA RL 2 III/736, R.d.L. u. OB.d.L./Generalstab d. Lw/Generalquartiermeister (Luftwaffe General staff/ Quartermaster-General).

BA-MA RM 7/1206, OKM/Seekriegsleitung/Operationsabteilung (Naval War Staff/Operations Department).

BA-MA RM 7/395, OKM/Seekriegsleitung/Operationsabteilung (Naval War Staff/Operations Department).

BA-MA RM 7/808, OKM/Seekriegsleitung/Operationsabteilung (Naval War Staff/Operations Department).

BA-MA RW 19/1379ff, OKW/Wehrwirtschafts-und Rustungsamt (WiRuAmt) (War Economy and Armaments Department).

BA-MA RW 19/1939, OKW/Wehrwirtschafts-und Rustungsamt (WiRuAmt) (War Economy and Armaments Department).

BA-MA RW 6/v. 180, OKW/Allgemeines Wehrmachtamt (Wehrmacht general office).

BA-MA RW 6/v. 543. OKW/Allgemeines Wehrmachtamt (Wehrmacht general office).

BA-MA RW 6/v. 552, OKW/Allgemeines Wehrmachtamt (Wehrmacht general office).

BA-MA RW 6/v. 553, OKW/Allgemeines Wehrmachtamt (Wehrmacht general office).

BA-MA Wi/I F 5.844. OKW/Wehrwirtschafts-und Rustungsamt (WiRuAmt) (OKW War Economy and Armaments Department).

Bundesarchiv-Militararchiv, RHD - Drucksachen (Printed matters, other).

BA-MA RHD 2/2; BA-MA RHD 4/272; BA-MA RHD 11/1 to 11/53, 11/1a and 11/1b; BA-MA RHD 18/22, 18/24, 18/25, 18/25a, 18/27, 18/28, 18/29, 18/46, 18/52, 18/55, 18/56-I, 18/57-I and II, 18/71, 18/75, 18/76, 18/77.

National Archives and Records Administration, Washington DC.

T311/R51, Records of the 16th Army (Kriegsgliederung des AOK 16).

T312/R1387, Records of the 6th Army (Kriegsgliederung des AOK 6).

T312/R1531, Records of the 7th Army (Kriegsgliederung des AOK 7).

T312/R265, Records of the 4th Army (Kriegsgliederung des AOK 4 (4. Armee und 2. Panzergruppe)).

T312/R276, Records of the 9th Army (Kriegsgliederung des AOK 9).

T312/R368, Records of the 11th Army (Kriegsgliederung des AOK 11).

T312/R668, Records of the 17th Army (Kriegsgliederung des AOK 17).

T312/R777, Records of the 18th Army (Kriegsgliederung des AOK 18).

T312/R994, Records of the Norway Army (Kriegsgliederung des AOK Norwegen).

T313/R18, Records of the 1st Panzer Army (Kriegsgliederung des Panzer AOK 1 (1. Panzergruppe).

T313/R226, Records of the 3rd Panzer Army (Kriegsgliederung des Panzer AOK 3 (3. Panzergruppe).

T313/R331, Records of the 4th Panzer Army (Kriegsgliederung des Panzer AOK 4 (4. Panzergruppe).

T501/R7, Records of the Higher SS and Associated Police Commands, and the Chief of the Order-Police.

T-78/R404, R867 and R871, OKH, Army general office (Organisation and Structure of the Army), (OKH Allgemeines Heeresamt (Organisation und Gliederung des Heeres).

Other Sources

Glantz, D.M. , research paper 'Forgotten Battles of the German-Soviet War (1941-1945)' Vol. I (unpublished), David. M. Glantz, 1999.

The Public Records Office in the UK, AIR40/1207, The German Air Force: first line strength at three monthly intervals during the European War 1939-1945.

USAF Historical Research Agency, Alabama, HRA 137.306-14 on microfilm A1128.

***

Published Sources

Ailsby, C., Images of Barbarossa, Ian Allan Publishing, Shepperton, Surrey, 2001.

Allen, T. B., War Games, Heinemann-Mandarin, London, 1989.

Atlas of World War II, Jordan, D., Wiest, A., Amber Books Ltd, London, 2008.

Australian Design Group, World in Flames Rules Book, Final Edition, 1996.

Badsey, S., Normandy 1944, Osprey Military Campaign Series, Reed International Books Ltd, London, 1990.

Barbarossa: The Axis and the Allies, Erickson, J. (ed.), Dilks, D. (ed.), Edinburgh University Press, Edinburgh, 1994

Bean, T., Fowler, W., Russian Tanks of WWII: Stalin's Armoured Might, Ian Allan Publishing, London, 2002.

Beiersdorf, H., Bridgebuilding Equipment of the Wehrmacht 1939-1945, Schiffer Publishing Ltd, Atglen, 1998.

Beiersdorf, H., KFZ-Anhanger der Wehrmacht 1935-1945, Podzun-Pallas Verlag, Friedberg, 2001.

Bellamy, C., Absolute War, Pan Books, London, 2008.

Bergstrom, C., Mikhailov, A., Black Cross Red Star: Air War Over the Eastern Front Volume I, Pacifica Military History, Pacifica, California, 2000.

Bishop, C., Hitler's Foreign Divisions: Foreign Volunteers in the Waffen-SS 1940-1945, Spellmount Ltd, Staplehurst, Kent, 2005.

Bishop, C., Luftwaffe Squadrons 1939-45, Amber Books Ltd, London, 2006.

Borries, V.B., Curtis, T., Barbarossa: Army Group North 1941, GMT Games, Hanford CA, 2000.

Braithwaite, R., Moscow 1941, Profile Books Ltd, London, 2007.

Buckner, A., The German Infantry Handbook: 1939-1945, Schiffer Publishing Ltd, Atglen, PA, 1991.

Bull, S., Stormtrooper: Elite German Assault Soldiers, Publishing News Ltd, London, 1999.

Chamberlain, P., Doyle, H., Jentz, T.L., Encyclopedia of German Tanks of WWII, Arms and Armour Press, London, 1994.

Chant, C., Artillery of World War II, Brown Partworks Ltd, London, 2001.

Chant, C., Artillery, Amber Books (Summertime Publishing Ltd), London, 2005.

Chant, C., Tanks, Silverdale Books, Leicester, UK, 2004

Chazette, A., L'Administration Allemande en France par Militarbefehlshaber in Frankreich, 39-45 Magazine No. 152-February 1999, Heimdal Editions, Bayeux.

Clark., A., Barbarossa: The Russian-German Conflict 1941-45, Weidenfeld & Nicolson (Orion House), London, 1995.

Conway's All the World's Fighting Ships 1922-1946, Chesneau, R. (ed), et al, Conway Maritime Press, London, 1980.

Crofoot , C., The Order Of Battle of the Soviet Armed Forces: The Sleeping Bear, Volume 1: 22nd June 1941, Part One, The Nafziger Collection Inc, West Chester, OH, 2001.

Crosby, F., The Complete Guide to Fighters and Bombers of the World, Anness Publishing Ltd-Hermes House, London, 2006.

Culver, B., Laurier, J., Sdkfz 251 Half-Track 1939-1941, Osprey Military, New Vanguard, Oxford, 1998.

Davies, N., Europe at War 1939-1945, Pan Books (Pan Macmillan Ltd), London, 2007.

De Wever, B. et al, Local Government in Occupied Europe, Academia Press, Ghent, 2006.

de Zeng IV, H. L., Stankey, D. G., Creek, E. J., Bomber Units of the Luftwaffe 1933-1945: A reference Source Volume 1, Ian Allan Publishing, Hinckley, UK, 2007.

de Zeng IV, H. L., Stankey, D. G., Creek, E. J., Bomber Units of the Luftwaffe 1933-1945: A reference Source Volume 2, Ian Allan Publishing, Hersham, Surrey, 2008.

de Zeng IV, H. L., Stankey, D. G., Dive Bomber and Ground-Attack Units of the Luftwaffe 1933-1945, Volume 1, Ian Allan Publishing, Hersham, Surrey, 2009.

de Zeng IV, H. L., Stankey, D. G., Dive Bomber and Ground-Attack Units of the Luftwaffe 1933-1945, Volume 2, Ian Allan Publishing, Hersham, Surrey, 2013.

Deighton, L., Blitzkrieg, Jonathan Cape Ltd, London, 1979.

Delaney, J., The Blitzkrieg Campaigns: Germany's Lightning War Strategy in Action, Caxton Editions, London, 2000.

Department of the Army, US Army Command and General Staff College (USACGSC), The Evolution of Modern Warfare: Book of Readings, C610, Fort Leavenworth, April 1991.

Donald, D., Bombers of WWII, Grange Books, Rochester, UK, 1998.

Doyle, H,. Jentz, T., Sarson, P., StuG III Assault Gun 1940-1942, Osprey Military, London, 1996.

Dunn, W. S. Jnr., The Soviet Economy and the Red Army 1930-1945, Praeger Publishers, Westport, CT, 1995.

Dunnigan, J., The Complete War Games Handbook, William Morrow and Company, New York, 1992.

Dunnigan, J.F., Nofi, A.A., The Pacific War Encyclopedia, Checkmark Books-Facts on File Inc, New York, 1998.

Dupuy, Colonel T.N. Numbers, Predictions and War, Hero Books, Fairfax Virginia, 1985.

Dupuy, Colonel T.N. Understanding Defeat, NOVA Publications, McLean, VA, 1995.

Dupuy, Colonel T.N. Understanding War: History and Theory of Combat, Paragon House Publishers, NY, 1987.

Edwards, R., Panzer: A Revolution in Warfare 1939-1945, Arms and Armour Press, London, 1993.

Edwards, R., Scouts Out: A History of German Armored Reconnaissance Units in WWII, Stackpole Books, Mechanicsberg, PA, 2013.

Ellis, C., Chamberlain, P., The 88; The Flak/Pak 8.8cm, Parkgate Books Ltd, London, 1998.

Ellis, C., Verier, M., Elite Attack Forces: Airborne at War, Chartwell Books Inc, Edison, New Jersey, 2007.

Ellis, J., Brute Force: Allied Strategy and Tactics in the Second World War, Andre' Deutsch Ltd, London, 1990.

Ellis, J., World War II: A Statistical Survey, Facts on File Inc, New York, 1993.

Engelmann, J., German Artillery in WWII 1939-1945, Schiffer Publishing Ltd, Atglen, PA, 1995.

Engelmann, J., German Light Field Artillery 1935-1945, Schiffer Publishing Ltd, Atglen, PA, 1995.

Erickson, J., The Road to Stalingrad, Stalin's War with Germany: Volume I, Phoenix-Orion Books Ltd, London, 1998.

Fey, W., Armor Battles of the Waffen SS 1943-45, J.J. Fedorowicz Publishing, Winnipeg, Manitoba, 1990.

Fleischer, W., German Heavy 24cm Cannon Development and Operations 1916-1945, Schiffer Publishing Ltd, Atglen, 1998.

Fleischer, W., German Light and Heavy Infantry Artillery 1914-1945, Schiffer Publishing Ltd, Atglen, 1995.

Ford, R., The World's Great Machine Guns, Silverdale Books, Wigston, Leicester, UK, 2005.

Forty, G., German Tanks of World War Two, Arms and Armour Press, London, 1988.

Forty, G., Land Warfare, Arms and Armour Press, London, 1997.

Forty, G., Livesey, J., The Complete Guide to Tanks and AFVs, Hermes House, London, 2006.

Frank, R., German Heavy Half-Tracked Prime Movers 1934-1945, Schiffer Publishing Ltd, Atglen, PA, 1996.

Frank, R., German Light Half-Tracked Prime Movers 1934-1945, Schiffer Publishing Ltd, Atglen, PA, 1997.

Frank, R., German Medium Half-Tracked Prime Movers 1934-1945, Schiffer Publishing Ltd, Atglen, PA, 1997.

Frank, R., Lastkraftwagen der Wehrmacht, Podzun Pallas, Friedberg/H, 1992.

Franks, N., Aircraft versus Aircraft, Grub Street, London, 1998.

Fugate, B. I., Operation Barbarossa, Presidio Press, Novato, CA, 1984.

Gander, T. J., Field Rocket Equipment of the German Army, Almark Publishing Company, London, 1972.

Gander, T., Chamberlain. P., Weapons of the Third Reich; an Encyclopedic Survey of all Small Arms, Artillery and Special Weapons of the German Land Forces 1939-1945, Doubleday and Company Inc, New York, 1979.

Gander, T., Heavy Artillery of WWII, Airlife Publishing Ltd, Rambsbury, UK, 2004

Germany and the Second World War, Volume IV: The Attack on the Soviet Union, Boog, H., et al. (German Research Institute for Military History at Potsdam), Oxford University Press, New York, 1996.

Germany and the Second World War; Volume I, Organisation and Mobilisation of the German Sphere of Power, Part 1, Wartime Administration, Economy and Manpower Resources 1939-1941, Kroener, B. R., et al, (German Research Institute for Military History at Potsdam), Clarendon Press (Oxford University Press Inc), New York, 2000.

Glantz, D. M., Barbarossa Derailed: The Battle for Smolensk 10 July - 10 September 1941 Volume 1, Helion & Company Ltd, Solihull, UK, 2012.

Glantz, D. M., Barbarossa, Hitler's Invasion of Russia 1941, Tempus Publishing, Stroud, Gloucestershire, 2001.

Glantz, D. M., House, J.M., The Battle of Kursk, Ian Allan Publishing Ltd, Shepperton, Surrey, UK, 1999.

Glantz, D.M. , research paper 'Red Army Ground Forces in June 1941' (unpublished), David. M. Glantz, 1997.

Glantz, D.M., Stumbling Colossus, University Press of Kansas, Lawrence, Kansas, 1998.

Goldsworthy, T., Valhalla's Warriors: A History of the Waffen SS on the Eastern Front 1941-1945, Dog Ear Publishing, Indianapolis, 2007.

Gooderson, I., Allied Fighter-Bombers Versus German Armour in North-West Europe 1944-1945: Myths and Realities, Journal of Strategic Studies, Volume 14, Issue 2, June 1991.

Goss, C., Sea Eagles Volume One: Luftwaffe Anti-Shipping Units 1939-41, Classic-Ian Allan Publishing, Hersham, Surrey, UK, 2005.

Green, M., Tiger Tanks, Motorbooks International, Osceola WI, USA, 1995.

Green, W., Aircraft of the Third Reich, Volume One, Aerospace MasterBooks, Aerospace Publishing Ltd, London, 2010.

Green, W., Swanborough, G. Soviet Air Force Fighters Part 2, WW2 Aircraft Fact Files, Pilot Press Ltd, London, 1978.

Green, W., Swanborough, G. The Complete Book of Fighters, Greenwich Editions, London, 2004.

Guderian, H., Achtung Panzer!, Cassel Military, London, 1992, (first published 1937).

Guderian, H., Panzer Leader, Futura Publications, London, 1974, (first published 1952).

Gunston, B., Aircraft of WWII, Octopus Books Ltd, London, 1980.

Hahn, F., Waffen und Geheimwaffen des deutschen Heeres 1933-45, Bernard & Graefe Verlag GMBH & Co KG, Monch, 1998.

Harrison, G. A., Cross-Channel Attack, BDD Special Editions, New York, (The Center of Military History, Washington, 1951).

Harrison, M., Accounting for war, Cambridge University Press, Cambridge, 2002.

Harrison, M., The Economics of World War II, Cambridge University Press, Cambridge, 2000.

Hart, L., History of the First World War, Papermac-Macmillan Publishers Ltd, London, 1997.

Haupt, W., A History of the Panzer Troops, Schiffer Publishing Ltd, Atglen, PA, 1990.

Healy, M., Kursk 1943, Osprey Military Campaign Series, Reed International Books Ltd, London, 1993.

Hitler's Army: The Evolution and Structure of German Forces 1933-1945, Command Magazine (ed.), Combined Books Inc, Conshohocken, PA, 1996.

Hogg, I., Sarson, P., Bryan, T., Artillery in Colour 1920-1963, Blandford Press, Poole-Dorset, UK, 1980.

Hogg, I.V., German Artillery of WWII, Greenhill Books, London, 1997.

Hogg, I.V., Infantry Weapons of WWII, Saturn Books Ltd, London, 1997.

Hogg, I.V., The Illustrated Encyclopedia of Artillery, Quantum Publishing Ltd, London, 2003.

Hogg, I.V., Weeks, J., The Illustrated Encyclopedia of Military Vehicles, Quantum Publishing Ltd, London, 2003.

Hughes, Dr M., Mann, Dr C., Fighting Techniques of a PanzerGrenadier 1941-1945, MBI Publishing Company, Osceola, WI, 2000.

Jane's Fighting Aircraft of WWII, The Random House Group Ltd, London, 2001.

Jentz, T. L., Germany's Tiger Tanks: Tiger I & II Combat Tactics, Schiffer Publishing Ltd, Atglen, PA, 1997.

Jentz, T., Doyle, H., Sarson, P., Flammpanzer German Flamethrowers 1941-1945, Osprey, London, 1995.

Jentz, T.L., Germany's Panther Tank: The Quest For Combat Supremacy, Schiffer Publishing Ltd, Atglen, PA, 1995.

Jentz, T.L., Panzer Truppen: Volume 1, The Complete Guide To The Creation And Combat Deployment of Germany's Tank Force 1933-1942, Schiffer Military History, Atglen, PA, 1996.

Jentz, T.L., Panzer Truppen: Volume 2, The Complete Guide To The Creation And Combat Deployment of Germany's Tank Force 1943-1945, Schiffer Military History, Atglen, PA, 1996.

Jentz, T.L., Tank Combat in North Africa; the Opening Rounds, Schiffer Military History, Atglen, PA, 1998.

Jerchel, M., Trojca, W., The Panzerkampfwagen III at War, Concord Publications Co, Hong Kong, 1997.

Johnson, C., Modern Military Series: Artillery, Octopus Books Ltd, London, 1975.

Journal of Slavic Military Studies, Tank Forces in Defence of the Kursk Bridgehead, Frank Cass, London, Volume 7, No 1, March 1994.

Kaltenegger, R., Weapons and Equipment of the German Mountain Troops in WWII, Schiffer Publishing Ltd, Atglen, 1995.

Kamenir, V. J., The Bloody Triangle: The Defeat of Soviet Armor in the Ukraine, June 1941, Zenith Press, Minneapolis, MN, 2008.

Kampe, H. G., Personenkraftwagen der Wehrmacht, Podzun-Pallas Verlag, Friedberg/H., 1993.

Keilig, W., Das Deutsche Heer 1939-1945, Podzun Verlag, Bad Nauheim, 1956.

Kershaw, R., War Without Garlands: Operation Barbarossa 1941/42, Ian Allan Publishing, Shepperton, UK, 2000.

Ketley, B., Fledgling Eagles: Luftwaffe Training Aircraft 1933-1945, Classic-Ian Allan Publishing, Hersham, Surrey, UK, 2009.

Kliment, C.K., Nakladal, B., Germany's First Ally: Armed Forces of the Slovak State 1939-1945, Schiffer Publishing ltd, Atglen, 1997.

Koch, H.A., Flak; Die Geschichte der Deutschen Flakartillerie 1935-1945, Podzun, Bad Nauheim, 1954.

Kurowski, F., Panzer Aces, Stackpole Books, Mechanicsburg, PA, 2004.

Lefevre, E., Brandenburg Division: Commandos Of The Reich, Histoire and Collections, Paris, 2000.

Lefevre, E., Panzers in Normandy Then and Now, Battle of Britain Prints International Ltd, London, 1990.

Lohmann, W., Hilderbrand, H. H., Die Deutsche Kriegsmarine 1939-1945; Gliederung, Einsatz, Stellenbesetzung, Band I & II, Podzun, Bad Nauheim, 1956-1964.

Lucas, J., Battlegroup!: German Kampfgruppen Action of World War Two, Arms and Armour Press. London, 1993.

McNab, C., Order of Battle German Kriegsmarine in WWII, Amber Books Ltd, London, 2009.

McNab, C., Order of Battle German Luftwaffe in WWII, Amber Books Ltd, London, 2009.

Mehner, K., Die Deutsche Wehrmacht 1939-1945; Fuhrung und Truppen, Militair Verlag Patzwall, Norderstedt, 1993.

Melvin, M., Manstein; Hitler's Greatest General, Phoenix (Orion Books Ltd), London, 2010.

Messenger, C., World War Two Chronological Atlas, Bloomsbury Publishing, London, 1989.

Michulec, R., 4.Panzer Division on the Eastern Front (1) 1941-1943, Concord Publications Co, Hong Kong, 1999.

Michulec, R., Panzertruppen at War, Concord Publications Co, Hong Kong, 1998.

Michulec, R., Wehrmacht Support Vehicles, Concord Publications Co, Hong Kong, 1999.

Milsom, J., German Military Transport of World War II, Arms and Armour Press, London, 1975.

Milsom, J., Russian Tanks 1900-1970, Galahad books, New York, 1970.

Milton, N., The Waffen SS in the East 1941-1943, Coda Books Ltd, Henley in Arden, UK, 2011.

Mitcham, S.W. Jr., German Order of Battle Volume One: 1st-290th Infantry Divisions in WWII, Stackpole Books, Mechanicsburg, PA, 2007.

Mitcham, S.W. Jr., German Order of Battle Volume Three: Panzer, Panzer Grenadier and Waffen SS Divisions in WWII, Stackpole Books, Mechanicsburg, PA, 2007.

Mitcham, S.W. Jr., German Order of Battle Volume Two: 291st-999th Infantry Divisions, Named Infantry Divisions, and Special Divisions in WWII, Stackpole Books, Mechanicsburg, PA, 2007.

Mitcham, S.W. Jr., The Panzer Legions, Stackpole Books, Mechanicsburg, PA, 2007.

Mollo, A., The Armed Forces of World War II: Uniforms, Insignia and Organisation, Orbis Publishing, London, 1981.

Mombeek, E., Bergstrom, C., Pegg, M., Jagdwaffe: Barbarossa The Invasion of Russia June-December 1941, Ian Allen Publishing Ltd, Hersham, Surrey, 2003.

Moore, P., Operation Goodwood: July 1944 A Corridor of Death, Helion & Company Ltd, Solihull, UK, 2007.

Mueller-Hillebrand, B., Das Heer 1933-1945, Band II: Die Blitzfeldzüge 1939-1941, Frankfurt am Mein, 1956.

Mueller-Hillebrand, B., Das Heer 1933-1945, Band III: Der Zweifrontenkrieg, Darmstadt & Frankfurt am Mein, 1969.

Muller, R., D., Ueberschar, G., R., Hitler's War in the East: A Critical Assessment, Berghahn Books, New York, 2002.

Munoz, A. J., Forgotten Legions: Obscure Combat Formations of the Waffen SS, Paladin Press, Boulder, Colorado, 1991.

Munson, K., Fighters and Bombers of WWII, Peerage Books (Blandfors Press Ltd), London, 1969.

Nafziger, G.F., The German Order of Battle: Infantry in WWII, Greenhill Books, London, 2000.

Nafziger, G.F., The German Order of Battle: Panzers and Artillery in World War II, Greenhill Books, London, 1999.

Nafziger, G.F., The German Order of Battle: Waffen SS and Other Units in World War II, Combined Publishing, Conshohocken, PA, 2001.

Nehring, W. K. (General), Die Geschichte der Deutschen Panzerwaffe 1916-1945, Motorbuch Verlag, Stuttgart, 1974.

Nelkon, M., Parker, P., Advanced Level Physics, New Cartesian Third Edition, Heinemann Educational Books Ltd, London, 1974.

Newton, S. H., German Battle Tactics on the Russian Front 1941-1945, Schiffer Publishing Ltd, Atglen, PA, 1994.

Niehorster, L. W. G., German World War II Organisational Series, Volume 1/II-1: 1st and 2nd Welle Army Infantry Divisions (1st September 1939), The Military Press, Milton Keynes, UK, 2006.

Niehorster, L. W. G., German World War II Organisational Series, Volume 1/II-2: 3rd and 4th Welle Army Infantry Divisions (1st September 1939), The Military Press, Milton Keynes, UK, 2007.

Niehorster, L. W. G., German World War II Organisational Series, Volume 3/I: Mechanized Army Divisions (22nd June 41) (2nd Revised Edition), The Military Press, Milton Keynes, UK, 2004.

Niehorster, L. W. G., German World War II Organisational Series, Volume 3/I: Mechanized Army Divisions (22nd June 41), Dr. L. W. G. Niehorster, Hannover, 1990.

Niehorster, L. W. G., German World War II Organisational Series, Volume 3/II: Higher Headquarters - Mechanized GHQ Units (22nd June 41) (2nd Revised Edition), The Military Press, Milton Keynes, UK, 2005.

Niehorster, L. W. G., German World War II Organisational Series, Volume 3/II: Mechanized GHQ Units and Waffen SS Formations (22nd June 41), Dr. L. W. G. Niehorster, Hannover, 1992.

Niehorster, L. W. G., German World War II Organisational Series, Volume 3/III: Waffen-SS Mechanized Formations and GHQ Service Units (22nd June 41), The Military Press, Milton Keynes, UK, 2008.

Niehorster, L. W. G., German World War II Organisational Series, Volume 3/V: Military Government, Security, and Provost Marshal Forces; Prisoner-of-War Administration (22nd June 41), The Military Press, Milton Keynes, UK, 2010.

Norris, J., Fuller, M., 88mm FlaK 18/36/37/41 & PaK 43 1936-45, New Vanguard, Osprey Publishing Ltd, Oxford, 2002.

Oswald, W., Kraftfahrzeuge und Panzer der Reichswehr, Wehrmacht und Bundeswehr. Katalog der Deutschen Militarfahrzeuge von 1900 bis heute, Motorbuch Verlag, Stuttgart, 1982.

Otto, R., Wehrmacht, Gestapo und sowjetische Kriegsgefangene im deutschen Reichsgebiet 1941-1942, Schriftenreihe der Vierteljahrshefte fur Zeitgeschichte; Band 77, Oldenbourg Verlag, Munchen, 1998.

Pavelec, S. M., WWII Data Book; The Luftwaffe 1933-1945, Amber Books Ltd, London, 2010.

Pegg, M., Transporter Volume One: Luftwaffe Transport Units 1939-1943, Classic-Ian Allan Publishing, Hersham, Surrey, UK, 2006.

Perret, B., Chappel, M., Badrocke, M., Sturmartillerie and Panzerjager 1939-1945, Osprey Publishing Ltd, Oxford, 1999.

Perrett, B., Culver, B., Laurier, J., German Armoured Cars and Reconnaissance Half-Tracks 1939-45, Osprey Publishing Ltd, Oxford, 1999.

Perrett, B., Knights of the Black Cross, Grafton Books, London, 1990.

Perrett, B., Laurier, J., Panzerkampfwagen IV Medium Tank 1936-1945, Osprey Publishing Ltd, Oxford, 1999.

Perrett, B., Sarson , P., Hadler, T., German Light Panzers 1932-1942, Osprey Publishing Ltd, Oxford, 1998.

Petter, D. P., Pioniere - Entwicklung einer deutschen Waffengattung, Wehr & Wissen Verlag, Darmstadt, 1963.

Piekalkiewicz, J., The German 88 Gun in Combat, Schiffer Military History, West Chester, PA, 1992.

Price, A., Great Aircraft of WWII: Messerschmitt 109, Abbeydale Press, Wigston, UK, 2007.

Prien, J., Stemmer, G., Jagdgeschwader 3 'Udet' in World War II, Schiffer Military History, Atglen, USA, 2002.

Purnell's Illustrated Encyclopedia of Modern Weapons and Warfare: Phoebus Publishing, London, 1971-80.

Richter, K. C., Die bespannten Truppen der Wehrmacht, Motorbuch Verlag, Stuttgart, 1997.

Rosado, J., Bishop, C., Wehrmacht Panzer Divisions 1939-45, Amber Books Ltd, London, 2005.

Rosch, B., Luftwaffe Support Units: Units, Aircraft, Emblems and Markings 1933-1945, Classic-Ian Allan Publishing, Hersham, Surrey, UK, 2009.

Rottman, G., Volstad, R., German Combat Equipments 1939-45, Osprey (Reed International), Men-at-Arms Series, London, 1991.

Sawodny, W., German Armoured Trains in World War II, Schiffer Publishing Ltd, Atglen, PA, 1989.

Sawodny, W., German Armoured Trains on the Russian Front 1941-1944, Schiffer Publishing Ltd, Atglen, PA, 2003.

Schneider, W., Tigers in Combat I, JJ Fedorowicz Publishing Inc, Winnipeg, Canada, 1994.

Schneider, W., Tigers in Combat II, JJ Fedorowicz Publishing Inc, Winnipeg, Canada, 1998.

Schramm, P.E. (Hrsg) (ed.), Kriegstagebuch des Oberkommandos der Wehrmacht 1940-41 (II), Bernard and Graefe Verlag, Frankfurt am Main, 1982.

Schramm, P.E. (Hrsg) (ed.), Kriegstagebuch des Oberkommandos der Wehrmacht 1942 (I), Bernard and Graefe Verlag, Frankfurt am Main, 1982.

Seaton, A., The Russo-German War 1941-45, Presidio Press, Novato, CA, 1993.

Sharp, C, C., Soviet Artillery Corps, Divisions and Brigades 1941-1945, Soviet Order of Battle World War II: Volume VI, George F. Nafziger, West Chester, OH, 1995,

Sharp, C, C., Soviet Cavalry Corps, Divisions and Brigades 1941-1945, Soviet Order of Battle World War II: Volume V, George F. Nafziger, West Chester, OH, 1995.

Sharp, C, C., Soviet Guards Rifle and Airborne Units 1941-1945, Soviet Order of Battle World War II: Volume IV, George F. Nafziger, West Chester, OH, 1995.

Sharp, C.C., Soviet Mechanised Corps and Guards Armoured Units 1942-1945: Soviet Order of Battle WWII: Volume III, George. F. Nafziger, West Chester, OH, 1995.

Sharp, C.C., Soviet Militia Units, Rifle and Ski Brigades 1941-1945, Soviet Order of Battle WWII: Volume XI, George F. Nafziger, West Chester, OH, 1996.

Sharp, C.C., Soviet Mountain, Naval, NKVD, and Allied Divisions and Brigades, 1941 to 1945, Soviet Order of Battle WWII: Volume VII, George F. Nafziger, West Chester, OH, 1995

Sharp, C.C., Soviet Rifle Divisions Formed Before June 1941, Soviet Order of Battle WWII: Volume VIII, George F. Nafziger, West Chester, OH, 1996.

Sharp, C.C., Soviet Rifle Divisions Formed From June to December 1941, Soviet Order of Battle World War II: Volume IX, George F. Nafziger, West Chester, OH, 1996,

Sharp, C.C., Soviet Tank, Mechanised, Motorised Divisions and Tank Brigades of 1940-1942, Soviet Order of Battle WWII: Volume I, George F. Nafziger, West Chester, OH, 1995.

Sharpe, M., Scutts, J., March, D., Aircraft of WWII; a Visual Encyclopedia, PRC Publishing Ltd, London, 2000.

Shepperd, A., France 1940; Blitzkreig in the West, Osprey (Reed International), Campaign Series, London, 1990.

Shustereit, H., Vabanque: Hitlers Angriff auf die Sowjetunion 1941 als Versuch durch den Sieg im Osten den Westen zu bezwingen, Verlag E. S. Mittler & Sohn, Herford and Bonn, 1988.

Smirnov, A., Surkov, A., *1941: Boi v Belorussii, Frontovaya Illyustratia* (Frontline Illustration), Moscow, 2003.

Smith, J. R., Creek, E. J., Kampfflieger Volume Two: Bombers of the Luftwaffe July 1940-December 1941, Ian Allen Publishing Ltd, Hersham, Surrey, 2004.

Smith, P. C., Stuka Volume One: Luftwaffe Ju 87 Dive-Bomber Units 1939-1941, Ian Allen Publishing Ltd, Hersham, Surrey, 2006.

Soviet Casualties and Combat Losses in the Twentieth Century, Krivosheev G.F. (ed.), et al, Greenhill Books, London, 1997.

Stahel, D., Operation Barbarossa and Germany's Defeat in the East, Cambridge University Press, New York, 2011.

Stolfi, R.H.S., German Panzers on the Offensive, Russian Front-North Africa 1941-1942, Schiffer Publishing Ltd, Atglen, PA, 2003.

Stolfi, R.H.S., Hitler's Panzers East, University of Oklahoma Press, Norman and London, 1991.

Surmondt, J., Tanks & Armoured Vehicles of WWII, TAJ Books Ltd, Cobham, Surrey, UK, 2004.

Taylor, B., Barbarossa to Berlin: Volume One, Spellmount, Staplehurst, Kent, 2003.

Tessin, G., Verbande und Truppen der deutschen Wehrmacht und Waffen-SS im Zweiten Weltkrieg 1939-1945; Band 2-5, Mittler & Sohn, Frankfurt-Main, 1965.

Tessin, G., Verbande und Truppen der deutschen Wehrmacht und Waffen-SS im Zweiten Weltkrieg 1939-1945; Band 6-15, Biblio Verlag, Osnabruck, 1972-1988.

Tessin, G., Verbande und Truppen der deutschen Wehrmacht und Waffen-SS im Zweiten Weltkrieg 1939-1945; Band-1, Biblio Verlag, Osnabruck, 1977.

Tessin, G., Waffen-SS und Ordnungspolizei im Kriegsensatz 1939-1945, Biblio Verlag, Osnabruck, 2000.

The Aviation Factfile; Aircraft of WWII, Winchester, J. (ed.), Grange Books, Rochester, Kent, 2007.

The Cassell Atlas of the Second World War, Young, Brig P. (ed.), Cassell, London, 1999.

The Encyclopedia of Aircraft of WWII, Eden, P. (ed.), Amber Books Ltd, London, 2008.

The German Army 1933-1945: An order of Battle Volume V, Cole, L. (ed.), Military Press International, Milton Keynes, 1999.

The German Army 1939-1945: An order of Battle Volume III, Panzer Armies, Panzer Groups, Mountain, Parachute, and SS Armies, Corps I-XXXVIII, Westwood, D. (ed.), Military Press International, Milton Keynes, 1998.

The German Army 1939-1945: An order of Battle Volume IV, The Infantry Corps XXXX-CI, Motorised Corps, Armoured Corps, Mountain Corps, Cole, L. (ed.), Military Press International, Milton Keynes, 1999.

The German Army Order of Battle 1939-1945: Ground Troops of the Army, Navy, Luftwaffe, Waffen SS and Police. Volume VI: Divisions - (Part I), Cole, L. (ed.), Terry, N. (ed.), Military Press International, Milton Keynes, 2001.

The German Army Order of Battle 1939-1945: Ground Troops of the Army, Navy, Luftwaffe, Waffen SS and Police. Volume VII: Divisions - (Part 2), Cole, L. (ed.), Terry, N. (ed.), Military Press International, Milton Keynes, 2001.

The Illustrated Book of Guns, Miller, D. (ed.), Salamander Books Ltd, London, 2004.

The Initial Period of War on the Eastern Front: 22nd June-August 1941, Proceedings of the Fourth Art of War Symposium, Garmisch, October 1987, Glantz, D.M. (ed.), Frank Cass & Co Ltd, London, 1997.

The Journal of Slavic Military Studies: Volume 9 December 1996 Number 4, Glantz, D.M. (ed.), Frank Cass, London, 1996.

The Journal of Slavic Military Studies: Volume 9 June 1996 Number 2, Glantz, D.M. (ed.), Frank Cass, London, 1996.

The Journal of Slavic Military Studies: Volume 9 March 1996 Number 1, Glantz, D.M. (ed.), Frank Cass, London, 1996.

The Operational Art of War, Century of Warfare User Manual, Tallonsoft, 1998.

The Oxford Companion to WWII, Dear, I. C. B., et al. (ed.), Oxford University Press, New York, 2001.

The Times Atlas of the Second World War, Keegan, J. (ed.), Times Books Ltd, London, 1989.

The War Against Hitler: Military Strategy in the West, Nofi, A. (ed.),Combined Books Inc, Conshohocken, PA, 1995.

Thomas, N., Andrew, S., The German Army 1939-45 (3) Eastern Front 1941-43, Osprey Publishing Ltd, Oxford, 1999.

U.S. War Department, Handbook On German Military Forces, Louisiana State University Press, Baton Rouge, 1990.

U.S.A.F. German Aircraft and Armament: Informational Intelligence, Summary No. 44–32, October 1944 (Informational Intelligence Summary), New York: Brassey's Inc., 2000 (first edition 1944). Strategic Bombing Survey, Aircraft Division Industry Report. Exhibit I – German Airplane Programs vs Actual Production.

Umbreit, H., Der Militarbefehlshaber im Frankreich 1940-1944, Militargeschichtliches Forschungsamt, Harald Boldt Verlag, Boppard-Rein, 1968.

Vajda F. A., Dancey P., German Aircraft Industry and Production 1933-1945; Illustrated Edition, Society of Automotive Engineers Inc, Warrendale, PA, 1998.

Vajda, F. A., Dancey, P., German Aircraft Industry and Production, 1933-1945, Society of Automotive Engineers Inc; illustrated edition, Warrendale, PA, 1998.

von Mellenthin, F. W., Panzer Battles, Ballantine Books, New York, 1971, (first published 1956).

von Senger und Etterlin, Dr. F. M., German Tanks of WWII, Galahad Books, New York, 1969.

von Senger und Etterlin, F. M., Die Panzergrenadiere Geschichte und Gestalt der mechanisierten Infanterie 1930-1960, J.F. Lehmans, Munchen, 1961.

Wadmann, D., Aufklarer Volume One; Luftwaffe Reconnaissance Aircraft and Units 1934-1941, Midland (Ian Allan Publishing), Hersham, 2007.

Wadmann, D., Pegg, M., Jagdwaffe: Holding the West 1941-1943, Ian Allan Publishing (Classic), Surrey, 2003.

Waffen SS in Action, Combat Troops Number 3, Squadron/Signal Publications Inc, Carrollton, Texas, 1973.

Warplanes of the Luftwaffe, Ed. Donald, D., Aerospace Publishing Ltd, London, 1994.

Weal, J., Jagdgeschwader 2 'Richthofen', Aviation Elite Units, Osprey Publishing Ltd, Oxford, 2000.

Weal, J., Jagdgeschwader 27 'Afrika', Aviation Elite Units, Osprey Publishing Ltd, Oxford, 2003.

Weal, J., Jagdgeschwader 51 'Molders', Aviation Elite Units, Osprey Publishing Ltd, Oxford, 2006.

Weal, J., Jagdgeschwader 52 'The Experten', Aviation Elite Units, Osprey Publishing Ltd, Oxford, 2004

Weal, J., Jagdgeschwader 53 'Pik-As', Aviation Elite Units, Osprey Publishing Ltd, Oxford, 2007.

Weal, J., Jagdgeschwader 54 'Grunherz', Aviation Elite Units 6, Osprey Publishing Ltd, Oxford, 2001.

Weller, J., Weapons and Tactics; Hastings to Berlin, Nicholas Vane, London, 1966.

West Point Atlas for the Second World War: Europe and the Mediterranean, Griess, T. E. (ed.), Square One Publishers, New York, 2002.

Westermann, E., B., FLAK; German Anti-Aircraft Defences, 1914-1945, University Press of Kansas, Lawrence, 2001.

Wheeled Vehicles of the Wehrmacht, Ellis, C. (ed.), Kristall Productions Ltd and Avocet Books, Surbiton, Surrey, 1988.

White, B.,T., Tanks and Other Armoured Fighting Vehicles of World War II, Blandford Press, London, 1975.

Wilbeck, C.W., Sledgehammers: Strength and Flaws of Tiger Tank Battalions in WWII, The Aberjona Press, Bedford, Pennsylvania, 2004.

Williamson, G., Aces of the Reich, Arms and Armour Press, London, 1989.

Williamson, G., Volstad, R., German Military Police Units 1939-45, Osprey Publishing, Oxford, 1989.

Wilson, S., Aircraft of WWII, Aerospace Publications Pty ltd, Fyshwick, ACT, Australia, 1998.

Wolfgang, F., Eiermann, R., Die motorisierten Schutzen und Panzergrenadiere des deutschen Heeres 1935 - 1945, Wolfersheim Berstadt, Podzun Pallas, 1999.

Wood, T., Gunston, B., Hitler's Luftwaffe, Salamander Books Ltd, London, 1997.

WWII History Magazine, March 2002 Edition, Sovereign Media, Reston, VA, 2002.

Wynn, K., U-Boat Operations of the Second World War Volume 1: Career Histories, U1-U510, Caxton Editions (Caxton Publishing Group), Chatham, 1997.

Zaloga, S. J., Ness, L .S., Red Army Handbook 1939-1945, Sutton Publishing Ltd, Stroud, Gloucestershire, UK, 1998.

Zaloga, S., Bagration 1944, Osprey Military Campaign Series, Reed International Books Ltd, London, 1996.

Zaloga, S., Kinnear, J., Sarson, P., T-34-85 Medium Tank 1944-1994, Osprey Military (Reed International Books Ltd), London, 1996.

Zaloga, S., Sarson, P., Sherman Medium Tank 1942-1945, Osprey Military, Osprey Publishing Ltd, London, 1993.

Zaloga, S., Sarson, P., T36/76 Medium Tank 1941-1945, Osprey Military (Reed International Books Ltd), London, 1994.

Zaloga, S.J., Kinnear, J., Sarson, P., KV1 and 2 Heavy Tanks 1941-1945, Osprey Military (Reed International Books Ltd), London, 1995.

Zaloga, S.J., Laurier, J., M18 Hellcat Tank Destroyer 1943-97, Osprey Publishing Ltd, Oxford, 2004.

Zetterling, N., Normandy 1944, J.J. Fedorowicz Publishing Inc, Winnipeg, Canada, 2000.

***

Lightning Source UK Ltd.
Milton Keynes UK
UKHW050748290322
400764UK00002B/51